Davenport/Leibold/Voelpel   Strategic Management
in the Innovation Economy

Strategic Management in the Innovation Economy

Strategy Approaches and Tools
for Dynamic Innovation Capabilities

By
Thomas H. Davenport,
Marius Leibold
and Sven Voelpel

Bibliographic information published by Die Deutsche Bibliothek
Die Deutsche Bibliothek lists this publication in the Deutsche Nationalbibliografie;
detailed bibliographic data is available in the Internet at http://dnb.ddb.de.

www.publicis-erlangen.de/books
www.wiley-vch.de

ISBN 3-89578-263-7

A joint publication of Publicis Corporate Publishing and Wiley-VCH Verlag GmbH & Co KGaA

Printed in Germany

Foreword

Many companies know today that the key for survival is in out-innovating the competition by 'leapfrogging' competitors with value innovation, and not with direct competitive strategies. At Siemens we have realized this perhaps earlier than many other companies, especially those in less technology-intensive industries, and we have taken purposeful steps to create and share knowledge inside our company and with our stakeholders for increased levels of innovation. Not surprisingly, we see many companies battling for survival due to mindsets and approaches that are rooted in traditional ways of competing, or attempting to replicate past successes.

While we have seen many scholarly books and articles emerging on innovation management or strategic innovation, we have noticed a dearth of managerial guides concerning appropriate approaches and tools for strategic management focused on the innovation economy. Most textbooks in use at universities and other places of business learning are still primarily based on the primacy of competitive strategies in the industrial economy. I have been gratified to see this book emerging as one of the first to specifically address strategic management mindsets, approaches and tools relevant to the challenges of the innovation economy.

In our globally networked world, characterized by integrated supply and demand chains, outsourcing (even of innovation), innovative new business ecosystems, and the search for value innovation, it is essential that firms keep rejuvenating themselves through the development of new, experimental business models. The challenge of managing both traditional, sustaining business models and innovative, disruptive business models certainly requires particular strategic management mindsets and capabilities. There is no alternative, however, to adopting these for surviving in a turbulent but exciting world of new creative opportunities and challenges.

This book provides a new platform for strategic management approaches and tools, and I trust it will find a particular place in the field of strategic management for innovation, both in business practice and education.

Heinrich von Pierer
Chairman of the Supervisory Board
Siemens AG

Preface

The Challenge to Traditional Concepts of Strategy and Business

Business strategy and strategic management have long been viewed as the concept and process that link an organization and its competitive environment. The turbulence and significant shifts in the environment towards a knowledge-networked society since especially the mid-1990s, and increasing evidence of company failures due to traditional business models and strategy approaches, imply that traditional ways of articulating strategy and practicing strategic management have to be seriously reconsidered.

Since the 1950s, various approaches to strategic management have been popularized, and these were appropriate for the industrial economy and its competitive features. With a significant new era of what some call 'revolutionary' change – the era of the knowledge-networked innovation economy – now being experienced, it is becoming evident that the traditional approaches to strategic management are showing serious deficiencies in dealing with the discontinuous links between an enterprise and its environment. The very nature of the business enterprise of the 21st century is being transformed, as well as the key notions of innovation and its effects on value creation, value capture and value sustainability.

A number of significant new driving forces in the business environment have created substantial uncertainty in the competitive landscape, and are bringing about fundamental changes in the traditional boundaries of nations, industries and companies. And such changes continue to challenge the traditional rules of competition. The driving forces of the innovation economy have removed the certainty and stability in the economic environment from almost every industry.

The competitive landscape has consequently been undergoing a fundamental change to produce a variety of new industries and combination of old industries, e.g. financial services industry, life sciences industry, 'edutainment' (education and entertainment) industry, the ICT industry (information and communications technology), and the 'individual living environment' industry (previously the home furnishings industry). These are not just new names for old diversifying industries, but new industries based on enterprise business models linked to intellectual capital and organizational rejuvenation, in contrast to business models linked to physical capital (land, buildings, machinery, etc.). Numerous examples are highlighted in this book of fundamental changes in the 'way of doing business' of enterprises in various industries, based on new value innovation concepts that have gained rapid customer acceptance.

New Ways of Value Innovation

The shift to new value innovation, i.e. innovative customer value propositions (products and services), and/or how they are innovatively newly created and provided, breaks decisively with the old industrial economy, in which information scarcity encouraged value capture through knowledge hoarding and physical assets. Successful companies today are those that transform purposefully-shared and networked-knowledge into new value-creating innovations, and aggressively use this to capture new opportunities and additional profit. Furthermore, value innovation is no longer achieved by finding and protecting a defensible position in a single, traditional industry. Rather, it is gained by innovating value in a business ecosystem, i.e. a company network spanning a number of potentially synergistic industries and value chains, that is quicker and better at using knowledge, and reinventing or adapting the system as the firm co-evolves with other organizations and individuals. The impact on strategic management, both in strategic thinking (mindset, approaches, formulating), and strategy implementation (implementation processes, methods, tools and practices) is profound.

The drive to innovate is even more important in the knowledge-networked innovation economy of the early 21st century, where the rapid sharing of knowledge forces players to reinvent and adapt constantly. In addition, ruptures in traditional boundaries in value chains are requiring companies to rethink how they go to market, what they need to own, and how they deal with suppliers and customers. The result is industry value chains today undergoing almost continuous innovation. The innovation value chain – one might call its new form a value web, an extended enterprise, a business ecosystem, or a value constellation – challenges firms that thrived with an integrated, self-contained approach.

It is becoming evident that the best value-capturing mechanisms now operate outside the individual firm's boundaries. Yet, the value created by a firm's own initiatives may be essential to the viability of its entire business ecosystem. The nature and definition of the firm are also undergoing profound changes, thanks to the ubiquity of information and leveraging of knowledge. The firm is shifting from a self-contained value-creation and -capture apparatus into one part of an interdependent community whose members continually negotiate responsibility for value creation and the right to value capture.

Focus on a Traditional Business Model only is Inadequate for a Firm's Survival

In the more stable industrial economy, enterprises were used to operate a single business model in a particular industry. In the fast-changing innovation economy, mainly driven by advanced technology, knowledge-networking and globalization, the resulting socio-techno-economic environment is one that challenges the essence of relatively stable traditional business models that firms used to achieve their particular goals.

No matter how successful and superior a company's current business model has been, it will be easily imitated, diluted and commoditized by others and challenged by new business models in the innovation economy. Moreover, major and unpredictable changes in the business environment, the increasing importance placed on innovation and knowledge as value-creating attributes, and the accelerating pace of the business environment create major challenges in sustaining the efficacy of existing business models.

Towards a New Strategic Management Approach for the Innovation Economy

This book proposes a new strategic management approach for the innovation economy – the *poised strategy* approach. The innovation economy requires substantially different ways in which corporations are led, businesses are managed, and organizational capabilities and structures are developed and utilized. Managing multiple business models, with different approaches for sustaining and disruptive business models, and shifting the focus to business ecosystem collaboration and not just company and industry value chain effectiveness, renews organizational energies and rejuvenates company life. This raises a number of challenges concerning ambidextrous leadership and managerial capabilities, and innovation-enabling organizational structures, as addressed in this book.

Organizational energy, in the sense of positive and continuous dynamics (or impetus) to be able to rejuvenate organizational value, is the result of managing a portfolio of business models for desired value-innovation activities in business ecosystems. This is achieved through dynamic innovation capabilities, with focus on a relevant range of 'speed-to-market' value-innovation configurations.

The Key Message of This Book

This book provides understanding of the dramatic shifts in the innovation economy and the resulting significant implications for traditional strategic management theory and applications. It furthermore helps the reader to learn and discover pre-eminent writings as well as methods and tools for strategic management in the innovation society. Strategic management in the innovation economy requires a new mindset, rooted in a systemic (networked, interactive) view and not a traditional (mechanistic) value-chain, industry-bound, or an existing (physical, internal) resource capability orientation. Companies can no longer focus only on efficient *intra*-organizational knowledge creation and sharing, but should also include the *inter*-organizational realm, as well as other relevant stakeholders in its business ecosystem.

The *key message is that the new knowledge-networked innovation economy requires a totally different strategic management mindset, approach and toolbox.* The traditional approaches are not completely obsolete, but used on their own they are deficient for sustainable organizational performance and survival in today's knowledge-networked innovation economy.

Step by step, each chapter leads the reader towards a better understanding of the knowledge-networked environment, the need for a new managerial mindset, new strategic management approach, and appropriate tools to assist in the processes of strategic management in the innovation economy. Per chapter the authors furthermore offer a brief introduction and theoretical overview, followed by selected research papers and viewpoints, which are concluded by clearly related and embedded case examples.

Who Should Read this Book and How Should It Be Used?

The book is aimed primarily for use at MBA-level and business executive courses, as well as for capstone undergraduate courses in strategic management. In addition, strategists and top managers will find it an effective aid in understanding the shifts and impacts of the knowledge-networked society on strategic management in the innovation economy, as well as the need for new tools and methods. The book originated from a realization that students and business leaders cannot be educated/oriented in strategy by simply reviewing extant strategic management theory and applications. Our approach is not to teach theory or cases, but to understand the evolution of strategic management thought, related to historical timeframes and contexts, and the difficulties of extant strategic management approaches and tools in dealing with major shifts and 'discontinuities' in the environment. Additionally, we provide integrated substantiation for a new approach by corporate leaders and strategists to strategic management in the innovation economy – *poised strategic management*.

The contents and style of the book are significantly different from the usual strategic management textbooks. The content is a unique combination of theory, published articles, and case examples, all designed to make key points and bring across messages that substantiate the proposals for new and complementary strategic management approaches and applications. The style of the book is easily readable by advanced students and business executives alike. Case vignettes are provided to amplify key points, and a list of questions are provided at the end of each chapter to stimulate further review, comparison and debate.

The overall learning objective is to provide a strong basis (aptly argued and substantiated) for the acceptance of a new strategic management approach and tools to be used complementary to extant strategy approaches and tools. The purpose is not to make a case that extant approaches and tools are obsolescent or invalid in the innovation economy, but that they are inadequate if used on their own.

The major points of uniqueness of the book are:

- The concept of *poised strategic management*, in contrast to the traditional concept of analytical, mechanistic strategic management approaches and processes.
- The analogy of poised strategy with Einstein's theorem of $E = MC^2$, with *purposeful energetic rejuvenation* – to counter the inexorable process of entropy of an enterprise – through management of multiple business models, both sustaining and disruptive in nature.
- The strong differentiation between, and the linkages necessary, between the concepts of *business model* and *strategy*.
- The total departure from the traditional mechanistic process of analysis-formulation-implementation-change to strategic management (as still evidenced in most strategic management textbooks), to a *holistic, interactive process* that enables the

breaking of the mold of the traditional business model thinking for appropriate disruptive innovation.

- The presentation of a *range of appropriate tools to enable strategy innovation* as part of the poised strategy approach.

- A *framework for appropriate leadership and management requirements* for poised strategic management, with *practical guidelines* and examples for implementation.

- The concept of *poised scorecard (PSC)* in contrast to the traditional balanced scorecard (BSC). The latter focuses on single enterprise strategy dynamics, while the PSC emphasizes innovative stakeholder systems dynamics and their measurement, for innovation performance across enterprise value chains and business ecosystems.

The Writing of This Book

This book became reality due to stimulating personal meetings and an intensive virtual knowledge exchange between the authors. The common systems-oriented background, dynamic teaching and practical experiences, and exposure to learning-based corporate case examples allowed the authors to make it happen. But many other people's contributions have made this book possible. First of all, we are indebted to Gerhard Seitfudem for his incisive and excellent professional editorial assistance. Many thanks are due to Michael Beer, Quinn Mills, Charles Baden-Fuller, Alan Mac-Cormack, Dorothy Leonard, Richard Whittington and other colleagues in personal and group (e.g. conference) interactions. Our discussions with them, their ideas, queries and comments helped us greatly in shaping our thoughts, for which we are of course solely responsible. Special thanks to Ms Hanneke du Preez for the word processing of the chapter texts, and to our research assistants Mr Solomon Habtay and Ms Eden Tekie at Stellenbosch University, and Mr Chris Streb and Ms Alexandra Wisniewski at International University Bremen, for reading and editing ably on the early draft chapters. Walter Claassen, vice-rector (research) at Stellenbosch University, provided strong support by his continuous interest, positive comments, and enabling seminal research funding, and we thank him for that. And last but not least, we thank our postgraduate students as well as the managers and executives who have been exposed to our concepts and ideas, and co-refined these with us over the past two years through critical debate and practical applications.

Thomas Davenport, Boston, USA
Marius Leibold, Stellenbosch, South Africa
Sven Voelpel, Bremen, Germany

Contents

IV Strategy, Business Models and Organizational Energy

V New Strategic Management Processes and Tools

VI Strategy Leadership and Management in the Innovation Economy

I The Innovation Economy and Strategy

Synopsis

The chapter motivates that there has been a fundamental change from the industrial economy to the innovation economy, and that this has particular implications for strategic management and its traditional dimensions. It includes the initial outline of a new 'formula' for business dynamics, i.e. $E = MC^2$ (Einstein's well-known formula, applied and expanded in later chapters), and three key requirements of management in the innovation economy. Major 'box' examples are of a country (Germany) and an industry (global wine industry), with implications for firms. The case example concerns India and its innovative businesses, and one relevant article is included.

Chapter 1
The Global Innovation Economy and Strategic Management

Nature of the Global Innovation Economy

Historians of the late 20th and early 21st century are already recording the significant shift in the features of the global economy between 1980 and 2005. The proportion of economic value now attributable to the innovative capacity of intangible capital in business has dramatically shifted to 80% of market values as reflected in the Dow Jones Industrial Average (DJIA) in 2005. By contrast, in 1980 the same index reflected market values due to intangible assets at nearly zero. In other words, the value of the DJIA in 1980 – only 25 years ago – was largely confined to traditional book values, or hard assets. Since then, the value of the innovative capacity of intellectual assets as a component of total market values has increased exponentially.

As a consequence, the foundations of traditional economic and business thinking, and strategic management, have been shaking. The nature of economic value and wealth creation, not only for enterprises but also for countries, regions, and industries, has become fundamentally different, requiring not only new mindsets but also new management approaches and tools. It is not surprising to hear the reaction of some observers, rooted in traditional practices that resulted in past successes, that nothing has really changed, that the old economy is "alive and well," or to contend that traditional economic and business activities are 'just more information and knowledge-based' than in the past. The fundamental criterion, however, is how value is created, captured, and sustained in an economy, and if this is fundamentally different from the past, new strategic management approaches have to be adopted.[1]

The speed of technological change has had great impact on the three-phase sequence from value creation to value capture to value sustainability. Innovations such as greater microprocessing power, Internet protocol networking, hyper-storage, and genomics are transforming value chains in almost every industry. In the past, many of these value chains, and the very structure of industry in the old economy, were knitted together by closely-held, protected information in vertically integrated companies. Today, however, these technology innovations are rendering information abundant, ubiquitous, fast, and free, enabling innovative value creation, capture, and sustainability for firms and industries.

The ubiquitous availability of information and knowledge is perhaps the single most significant contributor to corporate innovation and change. As Nobel laureate economist

Ronald Coase concluded almost 70 years ago, the boundaries of the firm are defined by its transaction costs. Hard to acquire and imperfect information contributed to high transaction costs, which in turn led firms in many industries to vertically integrate. For instance, it cost General Motors (GM) far less to source its own parts internally than to search the globe for suppliers. Similarly, by keeping information inside its boundaries, an integrated company could create value in one division (e.g., drug discovery) and capture it in another (e.g., drug sales and marketing). Today, as the costs of sharing and using information fall, companies and their industries have an impetus to "de-integrate," as is consistent with the Coase theory. Think of GM's spin-off of its parts division, now the Delphi Automotive Systems Corporation. The trend of de-integration is accelerating as the Internet and other services give companies access to even more information. Companies can now work with suppliers of both goods and services from virtually any place in the world. The impact: The threshold of cost set by the availability of information can no longer define the firm's or the industry's boundaries.

The drive to innovate is even more important in the new 'innovation economy', where the rapid sharing of knowledge forces players to reinvent and adapt constantly. In addition, ruptures in traditional boundaries in value chains are requiring companies to rethink how they go to market, what they need to own, and how they deal with suppliers and customers. The result is industry value chains of today undergoing almost continuous innovation in products, services, processes, business models, and management approaches. The innovation value chain – one might call its new form a value web, an extended enterprise, a business ecosystem, or a value constellation – challenges firms that thrived with an integrated, self-contained approach.

The best value-capturing mechanisms now operate outside the individual firm's boundaries. Yet, the value created by a firm may be essential to the viability of the entire business ecosystem. The nature and definition of the firm are also undergoing profound changes, thanks to the ubiquity of information. The firm is shifting from a self-contained value-creation and -capture apparatus into one part of an interdependent community whose members continually negotiate responsibility for value creation and the right to value capture (see Box: Getting Innovative at 3M).[2]

The shift to new value innovation breaks decisively with the old economy, in which information scarcity encouraged value capture through knowledge hoarding. Information asymmetries still exist, of course; a company can create a superior competitive position, with advantaged pricing and customer information, for example. But in an information-suffused environment, asymmetries alone are more fleeting and less reliable sources of value capture than they previously were. Companies that close off their knowledge to the outside world may also be closing themselves off from externally-sourced innovations. Successful companies will be those that transform information into value-creating knowledge, and aggressively use this knowledge to innovate and capture additional profit. Knowledge asymmetries may be the best innovation resource in the 'innovation economy', and when used to create further new asymmetries, also the most enduring in terms of their innovative capabilities.

The above line of reasoning suggests that value capture is no longer achieved by finding and protecting a defensible position in a single, traditional industry. Rather, it is gained by innovating value in a business ecosystem that is quicker and better at

Getting Innovative at 3M

Few companies in the world are more famous for their exceptional product ideas and innovations than 3M. Founded in 1902, the company first focused on sandpaper products. In the 1920s, the company invented the world's first waterproof sandpaper, which reduced airborne dusts in automobile manufacturing. The next major breakthrough occurred in 1925 when a young lab assistant came up with the idea for masking tape. This soon led to more diversification of the product and became the first of a variety of Scotch Tapes. During the next decades, the company's history was marked by milestones of innovation in various industries such as pharmaceuticals, radiology, and energy control. Today everybody knows and uses Post-it, one of the company's most simple, but best-known products.

For this company it is an everyday challenge to come up with new innovative ideas and to turn them into a commercial success. In today's economy, growth and innovative breakthroughs often determine the survival of the company itself. In the 1990s, 3M realized that product developers did not know how to make big, profitable innovations and breakthroughs part of their daily routine. There was no system that they could utilize to become innovative, therefore breakthroughs were a matter of coincidence. This was dangerous for a company whose reputation and survival largely depended on successful innovations. Management 'managed' the product developers, who were largely working independently, by keeping out of their way. The developers, on the other hand, worked according to the aphorism: 'It's better to seek forgiveness than ask for permission'.

3M became aware that too much of the company's growth was the result of incremental changes to existing products. In fact, new innovations were few and far between. This was not what the top managers at 3M expected of their company, so they came up with a very challenging objective: in future, 30% of sales would have to come from products that had not existed four years earlier.

This had an effect on the way many employees, especially the product developers and scientists, perceived their role in innovation. The answer to that challenge: They introduced the 'lead user process' to become more innovative and make big breakthroughs. Research and experience have found that many breakthroughs were initially not made by manufacturers, but by lead users. These can be companies, organizations, or individuals in more than one industry, with needs advanced beyond those of the average user and beyond the scope of ordinary product solutions – needs that often lead them to search for solutions themselves. Using this insight, the lead user process within a business ecosystem refines those ideas into commercially useful and marketable innovations and products, of both incremental and disruptive nature.

In the 2000 decade, with a new CEO from General Electric, 3M began to focus not just on product innovations, but on new business processes and management approaches. The company adopted the Six Sigma approach to process improvement and employed it across the enterprise. There was also a new focus on individual productivity and the use of knowledge worker technology. With both innovative new products and effective ways of doing business, 3M's profits and market value rose substantially.

using knowledge, and reinventing or adapting the system as the industry evolves. The impact on strategic management, both in strategic thinking (mindset, approaches, formulating), and strategy implementation (implementation processes, methods, tools, and practices) is profound.

Drivers of the Innovation Economy

We believe that the global economy has passed a 'tipping point'[3] in the transition from an industrial, goods-centered to an innovation, service-centered logic. Dominant logic and innovative technologies, methods and concepts evolve in a particular way to form something new. This is not an abrupt emergence, since the underlying elements change gradually. Instead, there is a tipping point that signals and validates a radical shift. A two-question stress test can be applied to the proposition that we are now in an innovation economy: First, what are the underlying enablers or drivers for this transition? If the enablers have endurance, the new dominant logic will likely be sustained and advanced. Second, will it change the view of how resources and capabilities are converted into new value and competitive advantage? If an innovation economy logic prevails, this logic should fundamentally change the mindsets, approaches, and mental models of the managers and researchers who determine how value and competitive advantage are conceptualized, and how resources are leveraged and allocated. Eight drivers of the transition to an innovation economy are listed below.[4]

Eight Drivers of the Innovation Economy

1. *New Global Infrastructure for Wealth Creation.* Networks, enabled by the Internet and mobile communications, are becoming the basis of economic activity and progress. This is not unlike how railroads, roads, power grids, and the telephone supported the vertically integrated enterprise in the industrial economy.

2. *New Sources of Value.* In the innovation economy, value is mainly created by knowledge and intellectual capital, not physical assets. These resources provide increasing returns and not decreasing returns, if rightly applied. Innovations in services, processes, business models, and management approaches become as important as innovations in physical products.

3. *New Ownership of Wealth.* In the industrial economy, wealth was owned by powerful individuals (tycoons) and groups. Today stock ownership is more dispersed, and growth in wealth comes especially from new entrepreneurs.

4. *New Educational Models and Institutions.* The model of pedagogy and knowledge-enabling is changing to interactive, dispersed, self-paced learning. Physical location is less important than nodes of learning communication networks. Knowledge and learning are not separate activities, but are embedded into the work process as needed.

---

5. *New Business Models.* The possibilities of significant disintermediation of traditional vertically integrated enterprises and their value chains have enabled a plethora of new business models (new configurations of the business concept of value creation, value capture, and value sustainability) to arise. The value engineering focus has shifted to value innovation.

6. *Empowered Customers.* Knowledge-empowered customers are driving innovations in many industries and enterprises. Customers co-create value along with the companies that serve them. Customer knowledge management (CKM) is a rich source of new value creation (beyond CRM).

7. *Leveraging of Global Supply and Demand Chains.* Globalization of the world economy, and network-integration of supply and demand chains enable innovative value configurations. Value innovation shifts from the supply chain to the demand chain, with focus on brand equity development.

8. *New Governance Structures.* Industrial-age bureaucracies are transforming into network-driven governance structures, with performance measures shifting to network scorecards for knowledge, innovation, and sustainable value creation and capture.

A common denominator of the drivers of the innovation economy is that each draws on information and communications technology (ICT) advances that enable universal access to knowledge that previously was dispersed and difficult to reach. This connected knowledge system, based on accepted compatibility standards, enables the real-time coordination of dispersed organizational activities and groups, the management of cross-functional processes, and the synchronization of the myriad points of customer contact that are integral to the new dominant economic logic. However, even with advanced ICT, coordination and integration are still difficult. Some industries and businesses are still in the early stages of transition to the new innovation-centered dominant logic, and the tipping point argument is based on the fact that all industries and enterprises are now affected by the new economic realities and their impacts.

What is a Business Model?

A business model is simply the 'way of doing business' that a firm has chosen: its entire system for creating and providing consistent value to customers and earning a profit from that activity, as well as benefit for its broader stakeholders. It refers to the core architecture or configuration of the firm, specifically how it deploys all relevant resources (not just those within its corporate boundaries), to create differentiated value for customers at a profit, with responsibility to the physical environment and society at large (profit, planet, and people).

(See also Chapter 4 for elaboration of the concept of a business model.)

The innovation economy does not mean that the business fundamentals of profitability, competitive customer value propositions, efficient and effective business processes (and their reengineering), and learning and growth objectives have changed. What has changed dramatically, however, is the way in which these are achieved. Historically, strategists were not particularly concerned with business models (see box), because each industry had a standard model, and strategists assumed the model in that industry; today, with the disintermediation of traditional vertically integrated enterprises and their value chains, a myriad of new business models have emerged that are different from the industrial-age template, often making old business models obsolete.

The following two diagrams illustrate the major differences in features between the industrial economy and the innovation economy (Figure 1.1), with illustration of how the latter is underpinned by new (empowered) customer needs (Figure 1.2).

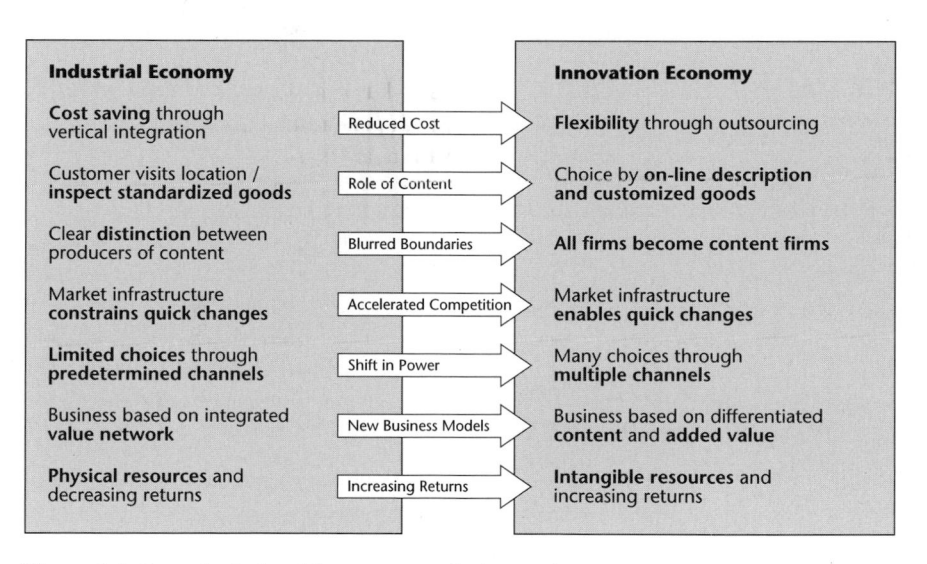

Figure 1.1 From the industrial economy to the innovation economy

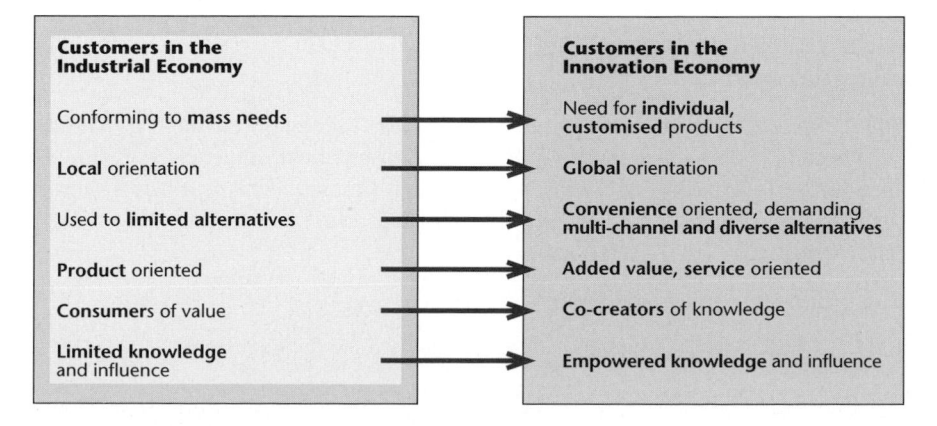

Figure 1.2 Underpinned by new customer needs

Implications of the Innovation Economy for Business Enterprises and Public Institutions

The era of the innovation economy is already transforming the leading companies in each industry worldwide, and forcing them to compete in entirely new ways that take advantage of this vast array of changes. Simultaneously, it is causing innovative entrepreneurial firms to arise, and together this is causing major disruptions in all traditional industries as we knew them in the 20th century.

Although ICT is often cited as spearheading this change in especially two ways, i.e. an exponential increase in processing power (Moore's law[5]) and an exponential increase in connectivity (Metcalfe's law[6]), the causes of fundamental change in enterprises and industries are much wider – residing in managerial mindsets, management principles and practices, and organizational cultures. Moore's law (the power of information and computer technology grows exponentially as its cost diminishes) now applies to industries and enterprise conditions as much as to technology. Metcalfe's law (the value of a network increases by n^2, with n = the number of players in the network) is leveraging human, financial, and brand capital on a worldwide basis, often disruptively in comparison to traditional industry practices and business models.

The core principles that underpin the modern enterprise are all being challenged – replication, specialization, hierarchy, extrinsic rewards, restructuring, business process reengineering, enterprise resource planning, supply chain synchronization, customer relationship management – if not in their fundamental nature, then in their application. While most traditional business management principles of the industrial economy are still valid in a limited sense (for existing, proven business models that are still successful in some environments), they are totally inadequate in coping with disruptive change, either in an adaptive or creative way.

Competition in the innovation economy is now increasingly characterized by the rapid emergence of brand-owning companies that devote their energies to organizational and strategic fitness[7] to create and meet customer need experiences, and to drive value innovation in business processes across supply and demand chains and within their particular links. Effective supply and demand chains support deeper levels of customer 'success' (beyond customer satisfaction and relationships), as well as leverage and utilize customer knowledge (CKM),[8] and value chain partner knowledge for appropriate innovation.

The innovation economy requires a new formula for successful business dynamics, akin to Einstein's classic equation for the relationship between energy and mass (energy equals mass multiplied by the speed of light squared). This is a highly useful metaphor[9] in understanding the new dynamics of successful business enterprises in the innovation economy:

$E = MC^2$ (Einstein's classic equation)

$E_b = MI^2$ (Applied in 21st century business context – see the next line)

or $\text{Energy}_{business} = \text{Management} \times (\text{Innovation} \times \text{Speed})$

This means that the energy of a business model (be it the business model of a company, non-profit organization, industry, country, or region) equates to the required nature of management particularly oriented towards innovation and speed-rate of continuous value innovation, relevant to particular market needs, and speed-to-market with consistency and reliability in a business ecosystem. The equation is based on the previously outlined innovation economy characteristics and drivers, and subsequent elaboration in this book.

The resulting key requirements of management in the innovation economy are:

- *Foresight and insight* into global changes at all levels of society, and the imagination and instinct for innovation to enable them to design and test entirely new approaches to business based on these principles.

- A *co-creating mentality* to enable changes in the business ecosystem environment, processes, and practices, jointly with business and governmental 'partners' (i.e., not only an 'adaptive' mentality, but also actively 'co-creative', requiring high levels of courage and risk acceptance). This implies also the targeted co-sharing of capabilities with selected outside organizations, and the sourcing of innovation from any possible provider.

- *Broad innovation* in all aspects of a business – not just in products or the Research & Development (R&D) organization.

- *Ability to effect cultural change and unleash energy in organizations* for high levels of paradox: a climate for continuous and speedy disruptive innovations, with simultaneous focus on effectiveness and efficiency of proven business models.

These key managerial requirements apply not only to corporate and business management, but also to the management of public institutions and even countries. Strategic political and public leadership based on foresight, insight, courage to co-creatively effect fundamental change with associated risks, and ability to change stakeholder (e.g., community) mindsets and practices are essential to lead public institutions and countries wisely in the global innovation economy (see Box with example of Germany).[10]

As in the relativity equation, time accelerates (C^2) and shortens the period for reaching higher capital market valuations and earnings multiples for companies because of greater innovation leverage in human, financial, and brand capital. Because of the ubiquity, anonymity, and accessibility of network technology and its potential for co-creating new, innovative value through leveraging intangible capital through multitudes of stakeholder connectivities, it is creating a new meritocracy in which capable managers from all corners of the globe compete with far less restrictions than ever before. It provides the greatest new opportunities in memory for developing countries, where the fear of the 'digital divide' is strongest. We are now poised for a managerial mindset to move from 'competition for survival' to 'competition for the earned privilege of defining future innovative value' that includes new business models, economic models, and socio-cultural models.[11]

The Challenge Facing Germany in the Global Innovation Economy

In many ways, Germany could not be a better launching pad for new companies or technologies. It is a rich country, offering young people an excellent practical and academic education, and its central position in the increasingly integrated European market provides easy access to suppliers and customers, thanks mainly to a highly efficient infrastructure and a modern communications network. Yet Germany has one big weakness in building high-tech industries: a decades-old entrepreneurial gap. Compared with Silicon Valley, where 73 percent of all companies that have annual sales of more than $50 million were established after 1985, the share of such companies in Munich and Stuttgart is only 17 percent and 20 percent, respectively. Except for the software powerhouse SAP, no company founded in Germany since the early 1970s has become a global leader in a new technology. This deficit is all the more unfortunate because technology companies are the most likely to grow at above-average rates and – in contrast to most established businesses – to raise employment levels.

The source of the problem is not a shortage of financial capital available for new enterprises, as many people assume, but rather a shortage of adequate human capital. Germany has a number of skilled fund managers but still lacks a broad base of experienced venture capitalists and first-generation entrepreneurs who – mostly after selling their businesses – can pass on their know-how to the next generation of high-tech enterprises. To mitigate this shortage, the private and public sectors in Germany have launched imaginative initiatives that help people with good ideas enter business and help big, established companies develop and finance innovations.

Spurring Innovation in Big Companies

Young people already know how greatly stock markets value innovation. But big German companies also need to see and act on the link between growth through innovation and higher share values. Market capitalization focuses much more strongly on growth expectations in the long term (upward of five years) than on short-term profit forecasts. At many established German companies, attempts to create a broadly innovative climate are still in their infancy. Such companies must try to inject the mechanisms of a start-up into the culture of an existing corporation – a process described as the creation of a "virtual start-up." This requires a great deal of sensitivity on management's part. People who run established companies are finding that entrenched faith in their core businesses counts for little in fast-moving, innovative industries. Increasingly, success or failure depends on how quickly a company's virtual start-up can transform ideas into attractive products and services and innovate to meet sophisticated customer requirements.

It is important for innovative companies not only to generate internal ventures but also to get firsthand experience of the way venture capital can successfully spur innovations, for such investment plays a crucial role in weaving start-ups into established corporations. Germany's industry has awakened to the strategic importance of venture capital: BASF, DaimlerChrysler, Deutsche Telekom, SAP, Siemens, and other companies have set up corporate venture capital funds. But many of them must still develop clearer value propositions, both for themselves and for their start-ups, and gain the confidence of the top managers of young firms, who often fear getting sucked into big corporations or developing a big-company mentality. Germany still has a long way to go before it matches the United States, where more than 25 percent of venture capital invested in new companies comes from existing companies in established industries.

Implications for Strategic Management: Challenges to Traditional Orthodoxy

The purpose of this book (see also Foreword) is to propose strategic management frameworks, approaches, tools, and their underlying managerial-cultural mentalities, appropriate for the necessary levels of enterprise value creation, value capture, and value sustainability in the innovation economy. This section provides an overview of these challenges and their key dimensions, with elaboration in the subsequent chapters of the book.

What are the implications of the innovation economy (and its drivers) for strategic management? Do these shifts in the economic features and business practices of the early 21st century change any of the well-established paradigms of strategic management, or should there be a need for change? Especially in the past fifteen years, many strategic management thinkers have been drawn into the search for new approaches to make sense of the increasingly turbulent environment, and to develop tools to identify new sources of value and sustainable exploitation of that value. The major themes of the previous decade – shareholder value maximization, resource-based theory, and dynamic organizational capabilities – continue to influence strategic management theory and research. Whereas the 1980s were dominated by aggressive competitive strategic thinking that was reflected in market share gains, economies of experience, competitive positioning, and business portfolio optimization, the 1990s were characterized by a focus on efficiencies as a principal source of increased profitability: restructuring, refocusing, cost cutting, unbundling, downsizing, outsourcing, and reengineering.

The critical strategic management challenge in the first decade of the 21st century now becomes how organizations can continually adapt, shape, change, innovate, create, and network to survive and prosper in global market environments that are quickly becoming more unpredictable, with organizations that have become more virtual, mobile, and porous, with technologies that are becoming revolutionary and integrative, and with people that are more independent, knowledgeable, assertive, and mobile. A new overall organizational purpose, or strategic thrust, seems to emerge: unlocking the mystery of organizational self-renewal and innovation resulting from knowledge-centered creativity and energy leveraged inside and outside the organization and beyond the confines of a single traditional industry.

This task is daunting, as the fundamental shifts in environmental forces seem to challenge deeply held strategic management ideas, beliefs, orientations, approaches, and tools. Table 1.1 indicates these challenges to strategic management orthodoxy.

In the more turbulent world of the innovation economy, traditional approaches and structured processes to strategic management can no longer cope with the complexity of new value opportunities and demands. New problems are being confronted, requiring new solutions that involve fundamental transformation of strategic management thinking and practices.

When organizations fail to make this leap into new strategic management thinking, they quickly find themselves supplanted by new entrepreneurs who are not encum-

Table 1.1 Challenges to strategic management orthodoxy

	From	To
Ideas & values	• Classical/neo-classical strategy (orthodox) • Organization as systematic machine	• Multiple changing paradoxes • Organization as systemic organism
Strategic orientation	• Strategic planning and "fit" • Rational strategy and single business model • Resources & competencies	• Strategic 'shaping' and partial 'misfit' in traditional boundaries • 'Fuzzy' strategy and multiple business models • Capabilities & innovation
Market environment	• Local/national/regional • Traditional industry and value chain	• Global, transnational, metanational, glocal • Reinvented industry; business ecosystem
Organization & control	• Bureaucratic • Direction, control • Value chain; single (and internal) organization	• Meritocratic • Guiding, cohering, focusing, measuring • Value system; multiple (internal & external) organizations
Performance measures	• Shareholder value • Financial performance	• Stakeholder value • Non-financial performance (in addition to financial)
Objectives	• Profit/growth/control • Single organization objectives	• Self-renewal/sustainability/innovation • Multiple org. objectives
Role of the managerial team	• Optimization of quality and productivity • Application of raw energy • Repetitive day-to-day operations • Processing of resources & information • Separation and specialization of work and organization	• Quality = productivity = adaptability and response • Application of ideas • Quest for innovation • Processing of knowledge & capabilities • Holistic approach and integration to work and organization
Process perspective	• Parts interact in sequence of steps • End-to-end efficiency; standardization the answer • Hierarchical, linear information flows	• Whole emerges from interacting parts • Micro- to macro-integrity key; feedback and customization the answer • Multiple, boundary-less, non-linear knowledge networking

bered by the technology, structures, and assumptions of traditional players. This has indeed been happening in computer software, telecommunications, airlines, beverages, financial services, life sciences, and almost all other industries.

Each one of the above challenges is addressed and illustrated in practical business context throughout this book, including examples of how firms are now complementing traditional strategic management approaches with innovative approaches for renewal and sustainability. The implications of these challenges for strategy dimensions of context, content, and process are outlined below.

Implications for Strategy Dimensions: Context, Content, and Process

Three dimensions of strategy, and thus strategic management, are usually identified: *context, content,* and *process.* The implications of the major shifts due to the global innovation economy on these strategic management dimensions are subsequently reviewed.

a) Strategy Context: Global, Multiple Business Models, Customization, and Collaboration

Strategy researchers, writers, and practitioners largely agree that every strategy context is unique and amenable to analysis in terms of boundaries, borders, structures, systems, and policies. With increasing globalization, emergence of virtual corporations, and breakdown of traditional industry boundaries, the traditional ways of approaching strategy context are being challenged. Analytical approaches alone are unable to capture the multidimensionality and heterogeneity of the global environment, as one views four major contexts for strategy-making today:

- *Globalization*: The world market for capital and human capital has few barriers at the moment, and manufacturing capacity is also becoming increasingly mobile. More enterprises are entering global markets as multinational, transnational, and metanational organizations. Traditional classifications according to country, industry, and organizational type are consequently becoming increasingly irrelevant. The major reason for this is that knowledge and innovation move quickly and easily across traditional boundaries and industries.

- *Multiple business models*: Due to the fast rate of change and innovation today, organizations have to develop and manage multiple business models simultaneously, both traditional ones for efficiency and new ones for experimentation, incubation, and learning. While overall corporate strategy now requires multiple business models, each business model requires a different strategy – and this is not the same as traditional business entity strategy. Yet in one recent research study, many executives were not even able to identify the primary business model used in their companies.[12]

- *Customization*: This refers to the new focus on customers as the real "drivers" of organizations, even co-creators of value, rather than something external and ancillary to the organization. Knowledge-driven technologies enable this occurrence.

- *Collaboration*: Integrated global demand and supply chains require a significantly different degree of collaboration among stakeholders. In many parts of supply and demand chains, collaboration is now replacing competition, as witnessed especially in supply chains of automobiles, computers, and telecommunications. Furthermore, many traditional internal value chain functions are now moving to outside the company, such as R&D, production, and raw material sourcing, in collaboration with former competitors (e.g., 'open-source' innovation).[13]

b) Strategy Content: Functional, Business, Corporate, and Network Levels

The product of a strategy process is referred to as the strategy content – what is, and what should be, the strategy for the enterprise and each of its constituent units. Most often, this is encapsulated in documented 'plans' on four levels of the organization, viz., functional, business, corporate, and network levels.

- *Functional Level*: This involves strategies for different activities within an organization linked to specialization skills, such as marketing strategy, financial strategy, operations strategy, etc. This traditional categorization often results in internal organizational barriers, 'silos' of knowledge, and resistance to change. In a turbulent environment, such functional strategy content results in the inability to respond rapidly and innovatively in a coherent, integrated way.

- *Business Level*: Strategy at business level requires the grouping of functional level strategies for a distinct set of products and/or services, intended for a specific group of customers. Often termed strategic business units (SBUs), these organizations focus narrowly on their own industry and market share, and consequently suffer from a lack of agility and adaptability, not to mention a lack of pro-active innovation of their core businesses.

- *Corporate Level*: Many enterprises are in two or more distinctly differentiated types of businesses, i.e. multi-businesses (several SBUs) or multi-industry activities, requiring corporate level strategy. A well-known technique is to consider a corporation as a "portfolio" of discrete businesses, each in a separate industry, but logically synergizing in terms of technologies, processes, or markets.

  The challenge of turbulent, knowledge-enhanced environments is that traditional synergy measurement tools (such as core competencies) and traditional opportunity evaluation tools (such as market opportunity analysis) are unable to cope with the dynamic nature of knowledge-networked environments. Corporate portfolio tools and measures to 'fit' into traditional competitive environments have often been devised for relatively static industry and market conditions.

- *Network Level*: Most multi-company organizations consist of a few parties, such as strategic alliances, joint ventures, and consortia. When a strategy is developed for a group of such firms, which may number from a few to hundreds, it is called a network level strategy. Such multi-company strategies are rare, and should be pursued more frequently. Yet even they are insufficient for today's business environment. The difficulty with this approach is that today network strategies are not only on multi-company levels, but also on functional, process, business, and corporate levels of organizations. Vertical and horizontal knowledge networking is proliferating on a formal and informal basis (e.g., 'communities of practice'), and traditional strategy content approaches are unable to capture the dynamics of these networking for sustainable value innovation. Traditionally, innovation has been seen as the domain of R&D, marketing (e.g., product development), and processes/technology. Today, entire new industries are being created due to rapid and widespread innovations in customer value propositions and value system configurations (disintermediation, reintermediation, convergence, etc.) that "leapfrog" traditional industries, which is in turn fueled by the knowledge economy.

c) Strategy Process: Analysis, Formulation, Implementation, and Change

Traditionally, most strategic management textbooks have portrayed the strategy process as a basically linear progression through several distinct steps. A differentiation is usually made between *strategy analysis, strategy formulation, strategy implementation, and strategy change*.

In the *analysis* stage, a SWOT-analysis (strengths-weaknesses-opportunities-threats analysis) of the organization is usually made. Next, in the *formulation* stage, strategists determine which strategic options are available to them, evaluate each of the so-called "generic" or "grand" strategy options, and choose one or more of them. Subsequently, in the *implementation* stage, the selected strategic option(s) is translated into a number of concrete activities/programs that are then started. Finally, in the strategy *change* stage, the documented strategy (or strategic plan) is periodically reviewed, results are compared, and changed if required.

This view of the strategy process is now being seriously challenged due to the realities of the global innovation economy and its major forces. Four significant deficiencies can be highlighted:

- *The emphasis on rationality and analysis*:
  The true nature of strategic thinking is now emerging as more emergent, holistic, intuitive and creative rather than as analytical and rational.[14] Strategizing is about envisioning opportunities and threats, perceiving strengths and weaknesses, and creating or shaping the future, for which sense-making, imagination, and judgment are more important than analysis and logic. This constitutes a fundamental shift in the view of cognitive processes of the strategist.

- *The presumption of linearity of processes*:
  The division of the strategy process into a number of sequential steps is fallacious, because, in reality, the strategy process is fuzzier, with analysis, formulation, and implementation activities on-going and intertwined. Strategies are usually formed incrementally through various forms of interaction inside and outside organizations, including inter-related processes, as managers continually think and act, letting strategies emerge as they progress. At the same time, rigorous thinking is still necessary in strategy, with conclusions tied to evidence and analysis whenever possible.

- *The assumption of comprehensiveness of the strategy process*:
  The assumption of the traditional strategy process is that strategy is made for the entire organization and everything can be radically changed all at once. Yet, it is almost impossible to get the various aspects of an organization lined up to go through change at the same time. The rate and direction of any change are seriously limited by the cultural, political, and cognitive history of the firm, and strategic change has often not been revolutionary. In the innovation economy, organizations are able to experiment with radical new business models alongside gradually changing existing business model(s). Experimenting is now often necessitated by radical changes in the environment. Every organization should have a variety of experiments underway at any time.[15]

- *The homogenization of organization culture*:
  Diversity and sharing, not conformity and protection, are the acknowledged basis for creativity and innovation. Open-sourcing and other forms of cross-boundary collaboration in ideas and processes unleash innovation potential. Traditional organization culture mitigates against strategy processes leveraged across boundaries.

Is the Old (Industrial) Economy Still Alive and Well?

When we observe the global economic landscape of today, we certainly still see agricultural commodities, mines, factories, buildings, storage depots, retail stores, assembly lines, stocks, and physical infrastructures such as harbors, energy plants, and telecommunications towers. From this perspective, it seems that the old economy of physical assets is alive and the most important feature of our value landscape. That is a myopic view, as it does not portray the real important value – and its tremendous growth – that is now residing in knowledge and innovation: the innovation in brands, products, services, customer benefits, and customer solutions, due to the shift in power and value from physical assets to innovative energy in networked knowledge assets. The physical resources of an economy are certainly still important as enablers of final products, but the real value-added in society is due to innovation drivers focusing on demand chains. Even companies providing the most traditional products can make this shift. Cemex, for example, the Mexico-based cement firm, is notable not for its cement, but for its innovative processes, use of information and knowledge, and customer relationships.

The shift in power and value creation in the global economy from supply chains to demand chains in the past ten years – i.e. towards customers, designers, retailers, demand chain influencers, and marketers – is primarily a result of companies now basing their core value-added on intellectual assets and not physical assets. Supply chain management is of course still critically important, but it can largely be standardized, optimized, outsourced, duplicated, and controlled (also through increasing knowledge). Certainly, some key technological and other innovations arise in supply chains, but the real dynamic innovative power has shifted to demand chains. This is not only in high-technology areas, but also in all types of economic activity including very traditional industrial and producing sectors of the economy. The wine industry is

How the Global Wine Industry is being Changed by the Innovation Economy

Up to the early 1990s, the global wine industry was dominated by large wine producing companies, often vertically integrated with extensive wine farms (or farming members), large wine producing facilities, bottling and labeling plants, distribution facilities, and extensive marketing (including branding) activities. This situation was more prevalent in the 'New World' wine countries such as Australia, USA, Chile, and South Africa. But also in the 'Old World' wine countries such as France, Spain, Italy, and Germany, the focus was similarly on cultivation, production and quality, and geographic controls. The most important economic value was regarded as control of farm (grape) production, wine production capabilities and quality controls, and protection of origin-specific 'terroir' image.

In the mid-1990s a new type of wine industry entrepreneur emerged, the so-called 'negociant', a Francophile word for 'merchant', but actually having a larger and more innovative content. These companies do not own any wine farms, do not own or operate any wine production activities, do not package wine, do not design wine labels or bottle any wine, and also do not own or operate any distribution facilities. However, what they do own are innovative and market-relevant brands, and their related sustaining capabilities. In the space of just ten years, some of these companies are selling more of their own wine brands than the leading traditional large wine producing companies. They are still regarded as 'upstarts' and a temporary phenomenon by some, but others have realized that in the global wine industry value (and income) has shifted irrevocably from the production side to the demand side. Consider two leading negociants in the South African wine industry, Vinfruco and Western Wines, who started in the mid-1990s. In the space of ten years their leading brands, viz. Arniston Bay and Kumala respectively, have become the top-selling South African brands in the United Kingdom, the world's largest wine importing market, outperforming the leading brands of traditional large South African wine companies such as Distell and KWV. An innovative new business model has now transcended the existing (traditional) business models in the wine industry.

Why and how did this happen? During interviews executives at Vinfruco (now Omnia Wines, resulting from a recent merger) and Western Wines, revealed their focus on especially three core capabilities: Knowledge of customer needs and required benefits; innovative capability to co-design brands with key retailers in the market; and ensuring integrated and reliable supply and demand chains to deliver consistent customer value as promised in their brands. In essence, they focus on superior knowledge and brand innovation, realizing that this is where value now resides, and not in ownership of physical resources – the traditional economy view. Of course, this requires knowledge of customer trends, needs, and behavior, knowledge of wine farming (where, what, and how to source the right grapes, and ensuring supply), knowledge of wine production and quality levels, design of wine styles that are right for certain markets, co-design of wine labels, knowledge of wine packaging, knowledge of wine distribution and logistics, and knowledge of wine retailing and merchandising. But these capabilities (and value) reside in knowledge and innovation, not in physical resources. Even the traditional large grape-growing firms such as Gallo are placing increased emphasis on detailed, quantitative analysis of customer preferences and sales patterns. In the innovation economy, characterized by the predominant value of intangible resources, companies stuck in the traditional industry value parameters are likely to increasingly suffer if they do not adapt or extend their traditional business models.

In the global wine industry, the struggle for 'ownership' of prominent brands and their markets are evidenced by the increasing mergers and takeovers in 2003-2005, for example, Constellation Brands (BRL Hardy, Mondavi, Nobilo), Foster's (Wolf Blass, Beringer Blass), Gallo (Gallo, Ecco Domani), and Southcorp (Lindemans, Rosemount, Penfolds). Buying brands is one strategy, but the important issue is to energize and manage innovative capabilities for survival.

a good example of how knowledge and innovation have shifted the power in global value systems and changed the key success factors in the industry (see box).

To answer the question about the old economy's existence and relevance, the answer is a qualified yes, it still exists and is still relevant. However, its relative importance has declined to such an extent that we can state with confidence that we are now in the era of the innovation economy, characterized by the creative energy of knowledge-networked new or reinvented business models.

Conclusion

The innovation economy is a reality, as expressed in the fundamental changes in 21st century economy features and its eight key drivers. The major new requirements for management are environmental foresight and insight, a co-creating mentality, and ability to effect cultural change to unleash energy (expressed as $E_b = MI^2$) for rapid innovation in organizations. This applies to businesses, public institutions, industries, and countries alike. The challenges to strategic management orthodoxy were highlighted, especially concerning strategic management paradigms, strategy orientation, organization and control, and role of the management team.

Finally, the deficiencies in the traditional application of strategy dimensions of content and process in coping with the challenges of the innovation economy were indicated. The next chapter (Chapter 2) reviews the changing concepts of business and innovation, and the relevance of traditional approaches to strategic management, in appropriate detail.

Innovating Our Way to the Next Industrial Revolution*

By Peter M. Senge and Goran Carstedt

What's so new about the New Economy? Our real future lies in building sustainable enterprises and an economic reality that connects industry, society and the environment.

Much of what is being said about the New Economy is not all that new. Waves of discontinuous technological change have occurred before in the industrial age, sparked by innovations such as the steam engine in the 18th century; railroads, steel, electrification and telecommunications in the 19th century; and auto and air transport, synthetic fibers and television in the first half of the 20th century. Each of those technologies led to what economist Joseph Schumpeter called "creative destruction", in which old industries died and new ones were born. Far from signaling the end of the industrial era, these waves of disruptive technologies accelerated and extended it.

What would constitute the beginnings of a truly postindustrial age? Only fundamental shifts in how the economic system affects the larger systems within which it resides – namely, society and nature. In many ways, the industrial age has been an era of harvesting natural and social capital in order to create financial and productive capital. So far there is little evidence that the New Economy is changing that.

The industrial-age assault on natural capital continues. Vague hopes about "bits for atoms" and "demassification" are naive at best, echoes of talk about "paperless offices" 20 years ago. The rate of losing species has not slowed.

Most New Economy products end up where Old Economy products do: in increasingly scarce landfills. Globalization is destroying the last remnants of stewardship for natural resources in industries such as forest products: Today, buy-and-sell decisions are executed by faceless agents living on the other side of the world from the people and ecosystems whose futures they decide. Moreover, New Economy growth stimulates related growth in Old Economy industries – along with the familiar pattern of suburban sprawl, pollution, loss of habitat and competition for natural resources.

The New Economy's effects on social capital are more complex but no less disturbing.[1] Industrial progress has tended to destroy cultural as well as biological diversity,

---

* Taken with permission from *MIT Sloan Managament Review* Vol. 42 No. 2, Winter 2001, pp. 24-38

despite the protests of marginalized groups like the Provençal farmers who oppose the globalization of food production. Likewise, although changes in traditional family and community structures have brought greater freedom for women and many ethnic groups, the past decade also has brought worldwide increases in divorce rates, single-parent families and "street" children. Global markets, capital flows and e-commerce open up new opportunities for emerging economics, but they also create new generations of technological haves and have-nots. According to the World Bank, the poorest quartile of humankind has seen its share of global income fall from 2.5% to 1.25% over the past 25 years. More immediately, eroding social capital manifests in the isolation, violence and frenzy of modern living.

The challenge today is to develop sustainable businesses that are compatible with the current economic reality. Innovative business models and products must work financially, or it won't matter how good they are ecologically and socially.

Individuals and small circles of friends carve out increasingly private lives amidst increasingly distrustful strangers, preferring to "bowl alone". We almost take for granted road rage, deaths of spectators at sporting matches and kids, shooting kids at school.[2] The "24-7" job has become the norm in many industries, the latest step in subjugating our lives to the clock, a process begun with the mechanization of work at the outset of the industrial era.

Judged by its impact on natural and social capital, so far the New Economy looks more like the next wave of the industrial era than a truly postindustrial era. Why should we care? Because the basic development patterns of the industrial era are not sustainable. At U.S. National Academy of Sciences home secretary Peter Raven says, quoting the Wildlife Conservation Society's George Schaller, "We cannot afford another century like the last one." Plus, there are other possibilities.

Corporate Heretics

"Is genuine progress still possible? Is development sustainable? Or is one strand of progress – industrialization – now doing such damage to the environment that the next generation won't have a world worth living in?"[3]

Those are not the words of the Sierra Club or Greenpeace, but of BP chairman John Browne. In 1997, Browne broke rank with the oil industry to declare, "There is now an effective consensus among the world's leading scientists and serious and well-informed people outside the scientific community that there is a discernible human influence on the climate." Moreover, he argued that "the time to consider the policy dimensions of climate change is not when the link between greenhouse gases and climate change is conclusively proven, but when the possibility cannot be discounted."[4]

Equally important, BP looks at the situation as a business opportunity. "There are good commercial reasons for being ahead of the pack when it comes to issues to do with the environment," says Bromme. Since 1997, the company has become active in public forums on global climate, has begun to reduce emissions in exploration and production, has started to market cleaner fuels and has invested significantly in alternative sources of energy (such as photovoltaic power and hydrogen). All the while, Browne has led an effort to build a more performance-oriented culture, and company profits have been at an all-time high.

The Dimensions of Sustainability

Rationalism, the belief in reason, has dominated society throughout modern times. It remains the dominant perspective in business and education. Yet it has limits. It cannot explain the passion that motivates entrepreneurs committed to a new product idea nor the imagination of scientists testing an intuition. Nor does it explain why a quiet walk on a beach or a hike into the mountains may inspire both. These can only be understood by seeing how naturalism, humanism and rationalism infuse one another. Naturalism arises from our innate sense of being part of nature. Humanism arises from, the rich interior life that connects reason, emotion and awareness – and ultimately allows us to connect with one another. Epochs in human history that have nurtured all three have stood out as golden ages.

Rationalism

Naturalism   Humanism

Three Worldviews Required
for Building Sustainable Enterprises

BP is but one example of the shift in thinking that is becoming evident in many companies and industries. Appliance maker Electrolux uses water- and powder-based paints (rather than hazardous solvent-based paints), prioritizes the use of recycled materials, and has introduced the world's first family of refrigerators and freezers free of the chlorofluorocarbons that contribute to ozone depletion. In 1999, Toyota and Honda began selling hybrid cars that combine internal combustion and electric propulsion, perform comparably to competitors – and can achieve up to 70 miles per gallon today, with prospects for two to three times that mileage in a few years.[5] In 1998, Xerox introduced its first fully digitized copier, the Document Centre 265, which is more than 90% remanufacturable and 97% recyclable. The product has only about 200 parts, an order of magnitude less than its predecessor. Its sales have exceeded forecasts. According to Fortune, remanufacturing and waste reduction saved Xerox $250 million in 1998. Some firms, such as Interface Inc., a $1.3 billion manufacturer of commercial carpet tiles, which saved about $140 million in sustainable waste reductions from 1995 to 1999, are even rethinking their basic business model. Interface's goal is to stop selling product altogether. Instead, it will provide floor-covering services, leasing products and later taking them back for 100% recycling. Assessing the environmental impact of the carpeting industry, chairman Ray Anderson says bluntly, "In the future, people like me will go to jail."[6]

These examples are all just initial steps, as each of these companies would readily admit. Ultimately, sustainability is a challenge to society as a whole. Nonetheless, business can play a legitimate leadership role as a catalyst for larger changes. We believe that a new environmentalism is emerging, driven by innovation, not regulation – radical new technologies, products, processes *and* business models. More and more businesses are recognizing the opportunities this creates. "Sustainability not only helps improve the world, but also energizes the company," says ABB's GEO Goran Lindahl.

The good news is that change through market-driven innovation is the type of change our society understands best. The problem is that much in today's business climate appears to run in the opposite direction. Short-term financial pressures, the free-agent work force, dramatic opportunities to start new companies and get rich quickly, often cynical mass media, and industrializing countries aspiring to catch up to the industrialized world's consumption standards – these hardly seem like the conditions for increasing stewardship of the earth.

The challenge today is to develop sustainable businesses that are compatible with the current economic reality. Innovative business models and products must work financially, or it won't matter how good they are ecologically and socially. To explore how to achieve this, the SoL Sustainability Consortium was formed to bring together like-minded corporate executives experienced in organizational learning who also see sustainability becoming a cornerstone of their business strategy.[7] Together, we are asking: Can organizations committed to sustainability work with the forces propelling most of the New Economy in the opposite direction? And, can organizational-learning principles and tools help in realizing the changes that this will require?

Between Two Stories

The first reality confronting businesses that are serious about sustainability is ambiguity, starting with the question: What do we mean by *sustainability*? The ambiguity inherent in sustainability has deep cultural roots.

"We are in trouble just now because we do not have a good story," says cultural historian Thomas Berry. "We are in between stories. The old story, the account of how the world came to be and how we fit into it ... sustained us for a long period of time. It shaped our emotional attitudes, provided us with life purposes and energized our actions. It consecrated our suffering and integrated our knowledge. We awoke in the morning and knew where we were. We could answer the questions of our children.[8] In a sense, sustainability requires letting go of the story of the supremacy of the human in nature, the story that the natural world exists as mere "resources" to serve human "progress". But most of us grew up with this story, and it is still shared by the vast

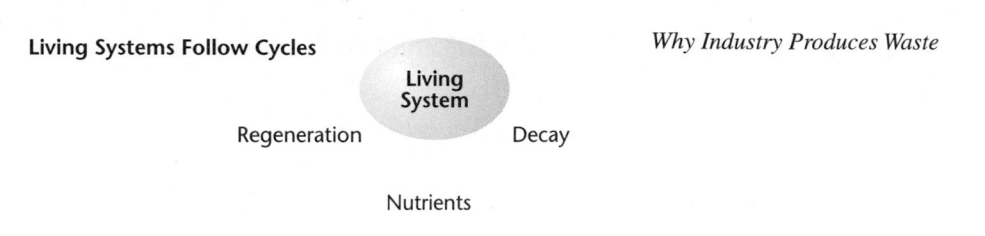

Living Systems Follow Cycles

Why Industry Produces Waste

Industrial-Age Systems Do Not

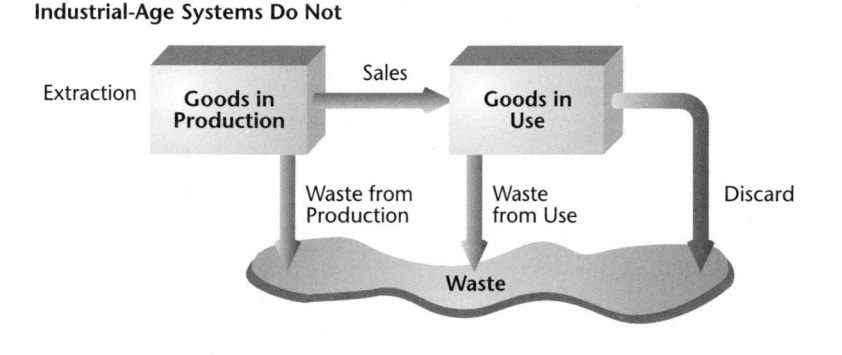

majority of modern society. It is not easy to let it go, especially when we are uncertain about what the new story will be. Businesses seeking sustainability can easily feel like a trapeze artist suspended in the air. They have let go of a secure worldview without knowing what they can hang on to.

Yet the dim outlines of a new story are emerging. At its root are two elements: a new picture of the universe and a new sense of human possibility. "We are just beginning to explore what it means to be part of a universe that is alive ... not just cosmos but cosmogenesis," in the words of Barry and physicist Brian Swimme. Moreover, the new universe story "carries with it a psychic-spiritual dimension as well as a physical-materialistic dimension. Otherwise, human consciousness emerges out of nowhere ... an addendum [with] no real place in the story of the universe."[9] Echoing Barry, Roger Saillant, former Ford executive and now Visteon vice president, says, "The new story will have to do with personal accountability... new communities in business and elsewhere based on knowing that there is no parent to take care of us and that we have a stewardship responsibility for future generations." Saillant adds that gradually "a larger intelligence will emerge. Those special moments when we glimpse that our actions are informed by a larger whole will become more frequent." Interface marketing vice president Joyce LaValle foresees a similar shift: I think this will actually get easier as we proceed. But first we must go through a kind of eye of the needle."

According to John Ehrenfeld, president of the International Society for Industrial Ecology, the challenge arises because sustainability "is a radical concept that stretches our current ideas about rationality. It has often been framed as environmentalists against business. But this generates polarization and misses the three very different worldviews needed to move forward: rationalism, naturalism and humanism." Only by embracing all three can we begin to understand what sustainability actually means. (See "The Dimensions of Sustainability.")

Naturalism: Biomimicry and the Logic of Natural Systems

The diverse innovations that created the first Industrial Revolution sprang from the same guiding image that inspired the preceding scientific revolution – the image of the machine. "My aim", wrote 17th-century scientist Johannes Kepler, "is to show that the celestial machine is to be likened not to a divine organism but rather to a clock-work."[10] The assembly line became the prototypical organization – with managers as controllers and workers operating in rigid routines, all coordinated by bells, whistles and production schedules. The assembly line was so successful it became the model for other types of organizations, including the 19th-century urban school system. Although the machine-age organization achieved previously unimaginable productivity, it also created a mechanized organizational environment that dehumanized and fragmented how people worked together.

If the machine inspired the industrial age, the image of the living system may inspire a genuine postindustrial age. This is what life sciences writer Janine Benyus calls "biomimicry", innovation inspired by understanding how living systems work. "What is consistent with life is sustainable," says Benyus. For example, in nature there is no waste. All byproducts of one natural system are nutrients for another. Why should industrial systems be different? We would not ask engineers to build bridges that defy the laws of gravity nor chip designers to violate laws of physics. Why should we expect businesses to violate the law of zero waste?

All living systems follow cycles: produce, recycle, regenerate.

Focusing on ecoefficiency may distract companies from pursuing radically different products and business models – changes that require shifts in mental models. This is unlikely to occur without mastering the human dimensions of learning and change.

By contrast, industrial-age systems follow a linear flow of extract, produce, sell, use, discard – what "Ecology of Commerce" author Paul Hawken calls "take-make-waste".

Indeed, the primary output of today's production processes is waste. Across all industries, less than 10% of everything extracted from the earth (by weight) becomes usable products. The remaining 90% to 95% becomes waste from production.[11] Moreover, what is sold creates still more waste – from discard and from use (for example, from auto exhaust). So, while businesses obsess over labor and financial capital efficiency, we have created possibly the most inefficient system of production in human history.

What would industrial systems that conform to natural principles look like? First, they would be circular rather than linear, with significant reductions in all waste flows. (See "How Industry Can Reduce Waste.") This implies three specific waste-reduction strategies: resource productivity, clean products, and remanufacturing, recycling and composting.[12]

Strategy 1. Resource productivity reduces waste from production through ecoefficient production technologies and the design of production processes in which wastes from one process become nutrients for another.

Strategy 2. Clean products (say, hybrid cars) reduce waste from goods in use through nonpolluting product technologies.

Strategy 3. Remanufacturing and recycling (creating "technical nutrients") and designing more products that are biodegradable (creating "natural nutrients") reduce waste from discard.

Architect William McDonough and chemist Michael Braungart summarize the three strategies with the simple dictum: "Waste equals food".

Second, companies would invest in nature's regenerative processes. They would do fewer things that compromise regeneration, such as paying over wetlands, and would invest some surpluses in restoring natural capital – for example, companies like Interface plant trees to match business miles traveled because increasing forest cover reduces greenhouse gases.

Third, following Buckminster Fuller's dictum, companies would "learn how to live on our energy income [solar, wind, hydrogen] rather than off our principal [oil and gas]." Living on our income would not only reduce resource extraction, but also eliminate the side effects of using minerals, like auto emissions.

Thinking in more systemic terms may appear simple, but it raises important questions about current corporate environmentalism. For example, ecoefficiency has become a goal for companies worldwide, with many realizing significant cost savings from eliminating waste from production. That is good in some ways, but troubling in others. Thinking about the larger system shows that ecoefficiency innovations alone could actually worsen environmental stresses in the future.

Ecoefficiency innovations reduce waste from production, but this does not alter the number of products produced nor the waste generated from their use and discard. Indeed, most companies investing in cost-reducing ecoefficiency improvements are doing so with the aim of increased profits and growth. Moreover, there is no guarantee that increased economic growth from ecoefficiency will come in similarly ecoefficient ways. In today's global capital markets, greater profits show up as investment capital that could easily be reinvested in old-style eco-inefficient industries.

To put it another way, nature does not care about the industrial system's efficiency. Nature cares about its impact in *absolute terms.* If a vastly more ecoefficient industrial system grows much larger, it conceivably could generate more total waste and destroy more habitat and species than a smaller, less ecoefficient economy.

The answer is not necessarily zero growth. The implications of naturalism are more subtle: We can sustain growth only by reducing total material throughput and total accumulated waste. Ecoefficiency gains are laudable but dangerously incomplete, as is any strategy that fails to consider the industrial-natural system as a whole. A systemic approach would reduce all sources of waste: from production, use and discard.

Managers' faith in ecoefficiency also illustrates the power of mental models. Industrial-age managerial practice has always been about increasing efficiency. Increased natural-resource productivity that translates directly into lower costs offers a compelling business case, one that does not challenge established thinking deeply. However,

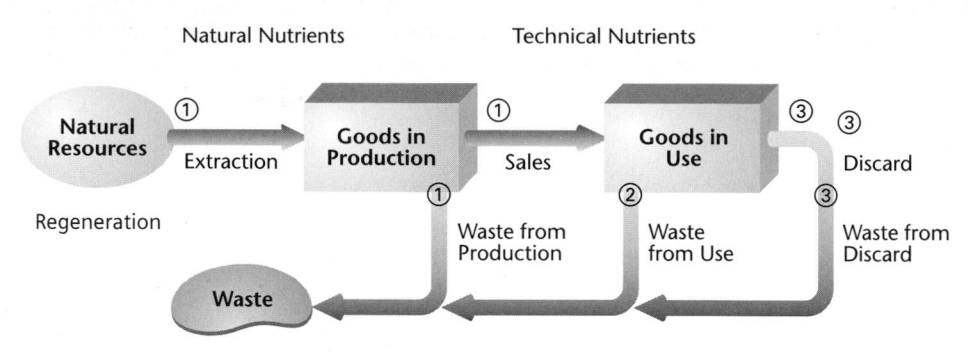

① Resource Productivity
② Clean Products
③ Remanufacture, Recycle, Compost

How Industry Can Reduce Waste: A Cyclic Industrial System That Mimics Nature

focusing on ecoefficiency may distract companies from pursuing radically different products and business models – changes that require shifts in mental models, not just shifting attention within existing mental models.

This is unlikely to happen without mastering the human dimensions of learning and change.

Humanism: The Logic of Learning

"The prevailing system of management has destroyed our people," said total-quality pioneer W. Edwards Deming. "People are born with intrinsic motivation, self-esteem, dignity, curiosity to learn, joy in learning." Echoing Deming, anthropologist Edward Hall declares, "Humans are learning organisms *par excellence*. The drive to learn is as strong as the sexual drive – it begins earlier and lasts longer." The premise of work on learning organizations has been that thriving in today's knowledge-based market-places means reversing the destructiveness that Deming speaks about and cultivating people's drive to learn.

In fall 1999 the sustainability consortium was hosted by the Xerox "Lakes" team that had developed the Document Centre 265 copier. Already aware of the team's innovations in design for remanufacture (more than 500 patents came from the Lakes project) and the product's success in the marketplace, we learned about how the team's Zero waste vision translated into a manufacturing facility with virtually no waste and eventually became embraced by many of the team's suppliers. But it still wasn't clear *how* the team had achieved those accomplishments.

Late in the day, Rhonda Staudt, a young engineer who was one of the lead designers, was talking about the team's innovations when she was interrupted by David Berdish, veteran of many organizational-learning projects at Ford. "Rhonda," Berdish said,

"I understand what a great opportunity this was for you and how exciting it was. I work with engineers, and I know the excitement of pushing the technological envelope. But what I really want to know is why you did this. What I mean is: 'What was the stand you took and who were you taking that stand for?'"

Rhonda looked at David for a long time in silence and then, in front of many peers and a few superiors, began to cry. "I am a mom," she answered. We had all heard the Lakes motto, "Zero to landfill, for the sake of our children." But now we were in its presence. Roger Saillant of Visteon turned to Peter and whispered, "Seamlessness". Peter knew exactly what he meant: when what we do becomes inseparable from who we are.

We have all spent much of our lives in institutions that force us to be someone we are not. We commit ourselves to the company's agenda. We act professionally. After a while, we have lived so long in the house of mirrors that we mistake the image we are projecting for who we really are. The poet David Whyte quotes an AF&T manager who wrote, "Ten years ago, I turned my face for a moment … and it became my life."

Over the past decade, many companies have attempted to build learning organizations with little grasp of the depth of the changes required. They want to increase imagination and creativity without unleashing the passion that comes from personal vision. They seek to challenge established mental models without building real trust and openness. They espouse systems thinking, without realizing how threatening that can be to established "quick fix" management cultures. There is a difference between building more-sustainable enterprises because there is profit in it and because it is one's life's work. The journey ahead will require both.

If understanding natural systems establishes the guiding ideas for sustainability innovations, then learning provides the means to translate ideas into accomplishments. But, just as the logic of natural systems conflicts with take-make-waste industrial systems, so too does the logic of a learning culture conflict with traditional, control-oriented organizational cultures. To a controlling culture, a learning culture based on passion, curiosity and trust appears to be out of control. But, in fact, it is based on a different type of control. "We are not trying to eliminate control and discipline in our organizations," says retired CEO William O'Brien, formerly with Hanover Insurance Co. "We are trying to substitute top-down discipline based on fear with self-discipline. This does not make life easier for people in organizations. It makes it more demanding – but also more exciting."

These two tensions – between natural systems and industrial systems on the one hand and between learning and controlling on the other – may appear to make sustainable enterprises impossible. However, deeper currents in the New Economy could also cause those tensions to become immutable forces transforming traditional industrial-age management.

A New Business Logic

Kevin Kelly, editor at large of Wired, observes that the "emerging new economic order … has three distinguishing characteristics. It is global. It favors intangibles – ideas, information and relationships. And it is intensely interlinked." Kelly sees electronic networks generating new patterns of "organic behavior in a technological matrix". But he suggests that the real changes are not ultimately about technology but communication. According to Kelly, in the world that is emerging, "Communication is the economy".[13]

Today, perhaps the earth as a living system is communicating to us through increasingly turbulent weather patterns. Perhaps our frayed social structures are communicating to us through increasing acts of child violence. Are we listening? If the New Economy is revolutionizing communication, can it enable deeper listening. If so, we may discern a new business logic emerging, one that starts with rethinking how firms create value and continues by redefining "customers", "employees", "suppliers" – and ultimately the company itself.

From Things to the Value provided by Things

"Production is increasingly not where value is created," says Ting Ho, vice president of strategy for global-logistics Internet startup Zoho. "The traditional company produced something that it then had to sell. Today, we must understand a customer and serve a genuine need."

At the heart of the industrial-age growth machine was a kind of mass hypnosis – convincing consumers that happiness meant owning a new thing. A new washing machine. A new computer. A new car. However, people do not want a hunk of steel in the driveway. They want the benefits it provides – whether they are tangible benefits like transport or intangible benefits like freedom or fun.

What does it mean to create new business models on the basis of that understanding? For Interface, it means shifting from selling carpets to providing floor-covering services, automatically taking back worn carpet tiles or replacing entire sections if a customer wants a different color. For Dow Chemical, it means leasing "dissolving services," then reusing the solvents. For Carrier, the world's leading manufacturer of air-conditioning equipment, it means renting cooling services rather than selling air conditioners. For IKEA, according to its published mission statement, it means providing services to help people "make a house or apartment into a home" rather than selling furniture. All these firms believe that "higher profits will come from providing better solutions rather than selling more equipment", in the words of "Natural Capitalism" authors Amory and Hunter Lovins and Paul Hawken.

Providing services rather than just selling products creates a potential new alignment between what is sound economically and what is sound environmentally.

From the standpoint of sustainability, providing services rather than just selling products creates a potential new alignment between what is sound economically and what

Organizational Learning's Ten-Year March

To attain sustainability, executives should ponder Senge's earlier writings and the experiences of those who have attempted to build learning organizations.

By Patrick L. Porter

Ten years ago Ford Motor Company executive Nick Zeniuk inherited the unenviable task of turning around the company's storied Lincoln Continental franchise. Zeniuk, the business and launch leader for the Continental line, was asked to redesign the product, while cutting costs, improving quality and speeding time to market. Plagued by political infighting and disagreements among 1,000 engineers and managers, the billion-dollar project was four months behind schedule and falling on every measure.

Zeniuk's transformation efforts might have ended then had he not learned about Peter Senge's work on organizational learning. Zeniuk read Senge's then new book, "The Fifth Discipline", as well as a paper Senge had published at about the same time in MIT Sloan Management Review, "The leader's New Work: Building Learning Organizations" (fall 1990, pp. 7-23; reprint 3211). "I had an epiphany," recalls Zeniuk. "Everything I needed was there."

A year-long effort ensued in which Zeniuk, program manager Fred Simon and the leadership team practiced the now familiar techniques that foster organizational learning – systems thinking, personal mastery, surfacing and testing mental models. and building shared vision. Slowly, the ideas gained credence among rank-and-file engineers who began to use the learning tools in their work groups. "At first they thought it was a boondoggle." says Zeniuk. "But then they noticed that we were beginning to behave differently. We had started asking them questions. We would stop and actually listen to them. We began to encourage them to do things in a different way."

It took nearly three years, but Zeniuk and his colleagues completely transformed the troubled project. "We saved a couple of hundred million dollars in expenditures, including 560 million of a $92 million launch budget for the 1995 Lincoln," says Zeniuk, who today travels the world teaching others about organizational learning. "We launched the car two weeks ahead of schedule. And we were the first Ford program to produce a prototype that was almost product-ready. Many of the learning practices carried over to the highly successful 1998 Continental."

Stories like Zeniuk's abound. Since Senge's 1990 writings on organizational learning, scores of companies, nonprofits, government agencies – even entire school districts – have used his learning tools to move away from industrial-age, command-and-control work environments to ones founded on individual commitment.

Senge is the first to admit that his work on organizational learning has many antecedents, including Jay Forrester's groundbreaking work on systems dynamics, W. Edwards Deming's half-century evocation of quality management, and the work of Chris Argyris on the impact of mental models on shared work. But it was Senge who pulled these and other threads together and connected them to organizational learning in a way that captured the imagination of business and government leaders.

What have we learned during the past decade about the value of Organizational learning? Richard Teerlink, the recently retired chairman and CEO of Harley-Davidson, believes that it is the only way to build a lasting company that can adjust to changing times. "As Eric Hoffer, the longshoreman philosopher said, 'in times of change it is the learners who will inherit the earth, while the dullards are beautifully equipped for a world that no longer exists.'" says Teerlink. "If you believe as I do that people are the only sustainable competitive advantage, then leaders have to view their responsibility differently. They must create an environment in which groups of people voluntarily come together around a shared vision and work toward shared goals. And that's what Peter Senge's learning tools enable you to do." Dave Meador, treasurer of DTE Energy in Detroit, Michigan, is using Senge's learning tools to help the utility company profit from deregulation. "We're going through a lot of change as the industry transforms," says Meador. "These tools help us avoid getting stuck in an old mind-set. They help us stay open-minded to a changing marketplace, which enables us to build the internal capacity to learn and adapt."

Meador first learned of Senge's work a decade ago at Chrysler Corp., where he used organizational learning to engage line managers in activity-based costing. "We shifted from an environment of compliance to one of commitment, in which people acted because they really believed it would help them accomplish their business objectives," says Meador. "And I went from extreme frustration and fear of failure to really making a contribution and adding value to the enterprise."

Today, Meador cannot imagine working for a company that fails to embrace organizational learning. "At DTE, we're creating an environment in which people can raise questions and recommend alternative ideas, and do that in the spirit of learning and trying to grow the business. But we can engage many more people in solving complex issues, which avoids putting the burden of decision making on a handful of senior executives."

If you were to take the time, you could find hundreds of stories like Dave Meador's. Zeniuk says he knows dozens of teams that have transformed themselves with these methods. "But there aren't a lot of stories about a whole company transforming itself into a learning organization," he adds. "The immune system in big companies tends to resist this work. And the resistance is not necessarily conscious. It's simply the inertia that's naturally there. Ford continues to use these methods. Visteon does so too at very high levels. Shell is building a learning organization. And even the U.S. government is starting to use them. But I can't tell you that a whole company has transformed itself using these tools."

Perhaps someday a large company will institutionalize organizational learning to the point that it becomes part of the companywide cultural fabric. But many obstacles stand in the way, says Senge. Some groups master organizational learning only to backslide, ending up where they began when learning champions retire or move on. At other companies, short-term thinking makes managers and employees unwilling to tackle fundamental change.

Says Senge, "The number one impediment in this work is that it takes time, patience, perseverance and dedication. Most people in most organizations are not geared for that. Most management groups want things to happen quickly, because they're planning to be in the job for only a short time and they tend to think that they'd better reap the benefits on their watch. This has been and continues to be the main reason that Deming's work didn't get applied and that our organizational-learning work still struggles."

Patrick L. Porter is a contributing editor to MIT Sloan Management Review

is sound environmentally. A company's business model no longer requires designed-in obsolescence to push customers into buying new products. Instead, producers have an incentive to design for longevity, efficient servicing, improved functioning, and product take-back. Such design allows for maintaining relationships with customers by continually ensuring that products are providing the services that people desire – at the lowest cost to the provider.

The shift from "the value is in the stuff" to "the value is in the service the stuff provides" also may lead to a radical shift in the concept of ownership. Swiss industry analyst Walter Stahel and chemist Braungart have proposed that, in the future, producers will own what they produce forever and therefore will have strong incentives to design products to be disassembled and remanufactured or recycled, whichever is more economical. Owning products forever would represent a powerfull step toward changing companies' attitudes about product discard.

Such ideas signal a radical shift in business models, one that will not come easily. It starts with how a company thinks of itself in relation to its customers: as a producer of things people buy or a provider of services through products made and remade? Marketing strategist Sandra Vandermerwe argues that such a view is essential to true customer focus, providing value *for* customers as well as obtaining value from customers.[14] It also shifts producers' time horizons. As Volvo discovered years ago, when a company is only selling cars, its relationship with the customer ends with the purchase. When it is providing customer satisfaction, it just begins.

From Producers and Consumers to Cocreators of Value

Focusing on the services provided by products also shifts the very meaning of "customer". Customers are no longer passive; they are cocreators of value. Thirty years ago, futurist Alvin Toffler coined the term "prosumer", people who actively participate in generating the value they derive from any product.[15] "Today, prosumers are everywhere," says Kelly, "from restaurants where you assemble your own dinner to medical self-care arenas, where you serve as doctor and patient." As Kelly says, the essence of prosumerism today is that "customers have a hand in the creation of the product."[16]

Prosumerism is infiltrating diverse marketplaces, especially those where internet technology is strong. One of Amazon.com's most popular Web-site features is customer reviews of books, CDs and other products. The five-year-old magazine Fast Company now rivals Business Week, Fortune and Forbes, partly because of its "Company of Friends", a Web-site feature that allows subscribers to get together to discuss common concerns, form support networks for projects, or tell the magazine their interests. "I can go to our Web site and determine which are the 10 most frequently forwarded articles," says editor Alan Webber. "Our readers are no longer just an audience but cocreators of product."

How does that shift to prosumers relate to sustainability? It starts with activist customers who think for themselves. And activist customers are organizing themselves. "Thanks largely to the Internet," say C. K. Prahalad and V. Ramaswamy, "consumers have increasingly been engaging themselves in an active and explicit dialogue with manufacturers of products and services."[17] They add, "The market has become a forum." Or, as the popular "Cluetrain Manifesto" puts it, the market is becoming "a community of discourse."[18] With the inmates running the asylum, will they start to change the rules? What if people start talking to one another? What if they talk about the state of the world and how different types of products affect the quality of people's lives?

Leading Web-based companies, because they relate to their customers differently, also gain a different sense of what truly concerns customers. "Without a doubt, sustainability of our current lifestyle – personally and environmentally – matters to a lot of our readers," says Webber. "These were among the concerns that motivated us to start the magazine, and we've seen nothing to persuade us otherwise".

At this stage, it is speculation whether self-organizing networks of customers will unearth the deeper values essential to building sustainable societies. But it is no speculation that shifts in consumer behavior will be essential in creating such societies. One of the most significant concentrations of power in the industrial era has been the growth of a massive advertising industry applying psychological savvy to manipulate consumer preferences. "Soap operas" acquired their name because they were devised by Procter & Gambler and other consumer-goods companies to market soap. Could this be another form of centralized control that becomes history, the victim of the freer flow of information and interaction that allows people to know more and learn faster?

Homo sapiens has been around longer than *Homo consumer*. People still care deeply about the world their children will live in. Building sustainable enterprises will require tapping and harnessing that caring.

Many market-oriented companies sense just such a shift emerging in consumer preferences. For example, Nike has a host of recycled and recyclable products coming to market. For a company that sells the image of fitness, it is not surprising that Darcy Winslow, general manager of sustainable products and services, says: "Corporations in the 21st century cannot be fit if we don't prioritize and neutralize our impact on the environment."

From Compliant Employment to Committed Members of Social Networks

There are few companies today that do not struggle with the implications of the free-agent work force. The traditional employment contract based on good pay and benefits in exchange for loyalty is vanishing in many industries. Entrepreneurial opportunities are enticing, especially to young people. Most companies respond by trying to rework the old contract. They increase salary and benefits. They offer stock. They invent creative new perks. But in so doing, they miss entirely the change that might make the greatest difference: a mission worthy of people's commitment.

In 1991, IKEA faced the daunting challenge of extending its European business success to North America, the "graveyard of European retailers". It was clear from the outset that IKEA managers could not say "Here's how we do it in Sweden", and expect much enthusiasm. Achieving strong returns for a distant corporate office was not enough. Being part of a proud and widely imitated European firm had limited meaning. It became clear that IKEA's North American management team had to find ways to truly engage people.

It turned out that North Americans, like Europeans, were concerned about the environment. Eventually, some 20,000 IKEA employees in North America and Europe participated voluntarily in a two-day training session on "The Natural Step", an intuitive introduction to the system conditions that must be met by a sustainable society. Not only did that engage people in selling the company's environmentally oriented products and creating related product and service ideas, it engaged them in working for IKEA. From 1990 through 1994, North American sales increased 300%.

Most companies respond by trying to rework the old contract. They increase salary and benefits. They offer stock. They invent creative new perks. But in so doing they miss entirely the change that might make the greatest difference: a mission worthy of people's commitment.

The free-agent image connotes to many employers lack of commitment, people seeking a purely transactional relationship with a company. Perhaps the opposite is true. It may be a unique opportunity for organizations that truly value commitment. If we actually thought of people as free, we would have to approach them with respect, knowing that they can choose where to work. "It is amazing the commitment that people feel toward our focus on sustainability and the environment," says Vivienne Cox, BP vice president for marketing. "In a very tough business environment, it really matters to people who have many options in their lives".

Most industrial-age companies wanted what *they* regarded as committed employees. Today, the definition of commitment is changing, and paternalism is giving way to more-adult relationships. "People stay with a firm, in many instances, because they see an alignment between their personal values and those they perceive the firm to be committed to," says Ged Davis, who is Shell's vice president for global business environment. If enterprises are not committed to anything beyond making money, why should managers be surprised that workers make transactional commitments?

Kelly also notes that in the competitive labor markets found in fast-growing industries, people change companies but maintain their loyalty "to advancing technology or to the region".[19] And to trusted colleagues. One key person may take groups of people from employer to employer like the Pied Piper.[20] Project teams form, un-form and then re-form like the teams of writers, actors and technical specialists that make movies. Yet larger social networks remain intact. Increasingly, such networks are the keepers of values and commitments and the subtle know-how that makes winners and losers. Longer-term relationships embedded in fluid but enduring social networks are a new phenomenon that most companies have not yet understood.

"Companies have felt that workers needed them more than they needed workers," says Peter Drucker. "This is changing in ways that most companies still do not seem to grasp."[21]

From Separate Businesses to Ecological Communities

"The great benefits reaped by the New Economy in the coming decades," says Kelly, "will be due in large part to exploring and exploiting the power of decentralized and autonomous networks," which in many ways now resemble "an ecology of organisms, interlinked and coevolving, constantly in flux, deeply entangled, ever expanding at its edges."

"In traditional businesses, everything was piecework," says Zoho's Ho. "Now we are all part of larger system and our success depends on understanding those systems." For example, the traditional relationship between producer and supplier was neat and tidy. Producers wanted reliable supply at the lowest possible cost. Today, cost maybe only one of several criteria that shape successful producer-supplier relationships. "Both as a supplier and with our suppliers, we are continually codesigning and co-innovating," says Ho. "There is no other way to keep pace with rapid changes and expanding knowledge."

Paradoxically, the realization that all enterprises are part of complex, evolving systems imparts new meaning to relationships and trust. As Webber has said, "The New Economy starts with technology and ends with trust."[22] People who are co-innovating must know each other and trust each other – in ways unnecessary in traditional relationships between providers and customers. That leads to the question: Can partners in complex supply networks co-innovate more-sustainable practices?

For example, Nike has programs in place with six of its material suppliers to collect 100% of their scrap and recycle it into the next round of products. The goal is to scale this up to all material suppliers. Similarly, all the big steps in design for remanufacture require intense cooperation up and down supply chains. "If you don't have suppliers hooked in, the whole thing will fail," says former Lakes chief engineer John Elter. The Xerox team hosted "supplier symposiums" where "we taught suppliers what remanufacturing means and gave them the basic tools for remanufacture," says Elter. Even more important, they assured suppliers that they would share in the cost savings – because used parts would go back to the suppliers for remanufacture. "The key is that suppliers participate in the economic benefit of remanufacturing because they don't have to make everything new. "This is a big deal. Plus, they are developing new expertise they can apply with other customers."

Can organizations committed to sustainability work with the forces propelling most of the New Economy in the opposite direction?

Building the necessary alignment for product take-back among networks of wholesalers, retailers and customers is equally daunting. "Without doubt, one of the biggest challenges with our 'Evergreen Service Contract' [Interface's model for selling floor-covering services rather than carpeting]," says chairman Ray Anderson, "is transforming mental models built up over generations" – such as those of purchasing departments in big companies whose incentives are based purely on cost of purchase, rather than on lifetime costs and aesthetic benefits.

Intense cooperative learning will never occur unless companies view their fates as linked. That is why the shift from seeing a world of suppliers and customers to one in which "we are all part of larger systems" is essential. Companies that do not recognize their interdependence with suppliers, distributors and customers will never build the trust needed to shift established mental models.

"Tennyson had it only half right when he said nature was 'red in tooth and claw,'" writes Janine Benyus. "In mature ecosystems, cooperation seems as important as competition. [Species cooperate] in order to diversify and … to fully use the habitat." Companies that see one another only as competitors may likewise find their habitat disappearing as the world around them changes.

From Closed Doors to Transparency

The world in which key corporate decisions could be made behind closed doors is disappearing. In 1995, Shell encountered a dramatic and unexpected reaction to its plans to sink in the North Sea its Brent Spar oil platform, which was approaching the end of its productive lifetime. Despite the fact that the company had gone through a three-year process to identify the best environmental option and had the concurrence of the U.K. government, the situation became a public-relations nightmare when other governments objected to the plan. Shell had failed to realize that its private decision had become a public one, a harsh lesson learned by many other companies, from Nike to Ford to Microsoft in recent years.

There is an old saying in the field of ecology: "There is no 'away.'" The old world of corporate inner sanctums isolated managers from many of their decisions' social and environmental consequences, distant in time and space from those who made the decisions. As transparency increases, these feedback loops are closing, and consequences must be faced. In this sense, transparency is a powerful ally to naturalism and may drive many of the changes needed to implement more-naturalistic, circular business processes and models.

The world in which key corporate decisions could be made behind closed doors is disappearing

Growing transparency already has led to the inclusion of voices traditionally outside the inner circle. Several years ago, Greenpeace objected to the chlorides IKEA used in the printing of catalogs. Few in the industry thought there was any cost-effective alternative. But working together, Greenpeace and IKEA found a Finnish printing company that could produce catalogs without chlorides. IKEA presented its chloride-free catalog at an environmental conference in Washington and set a new industry standard. This experience showed that Greenpeace and IKEA could work together productively by focusing on tangible problems and by believing that breakthroughs were possible. Such trust can only be built over time.

Growing transparency is also leading to new accounting and performance-management practices. Shell and others are moving toward "triple-bottom-line" accounting – assessing economic, environmental and social performance in a balanced way. The Global Reporting Initiative provides practical guidelines for such changes. "Adopting GRI guidelines and triple-bottom-line practices is an enormously difficult step," says

New Competencies

The challenges of building sustainable enterprises describe a strange new world few firms are equipped to understand, let alone navigate. The members of the SoL Sustainability Consortium came together, believing that their preceding work with organizational-learning principles and tools might make a difference in meeting these challenges.

Today, Consortium members are engaged in projects on sustainability frameworks (from which the ideas on naturalism and humanism came), new energy sources, implementing new business models, and nurturing new leadership networks embodying competencies that build upon the leadership skills for learning organizations (published in the MIT Sloan Management Review 10 years ago[1]):

- building shared vision,
- surfacing and testing mental models, and
- systems thinking.

Research on mental models and dialogue[2] needs to be scaled up to allow strategic conversations that involve hundreds and even thousands of people. As Juanita Brown, founder of Whole Systems Associates, says, "The questions we are facing will require members of organizations to learn together at an unprecedented rate, often on a global scale." Starting in 1999, Brown's colleagues Bo Gyllenpalm and David Isaacs helped several large Swedish organizations convene conversations on "Infocom (information and communications services) and the Environment." Convening

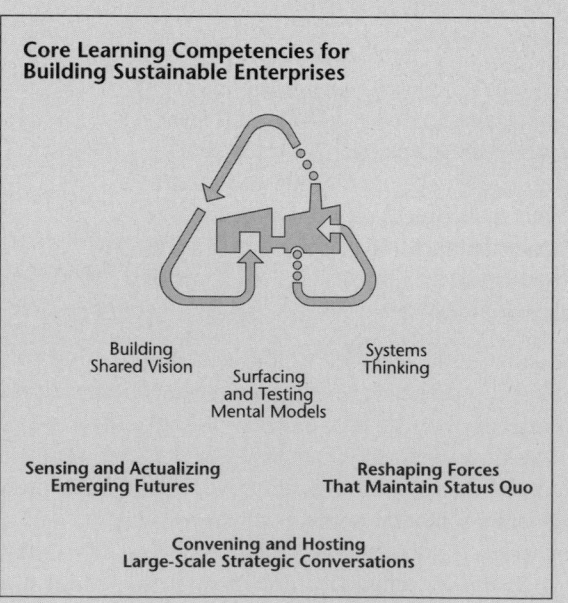

Core Learning Competencies for Building Sustainable Enterprises

Building Shared Vision

Surfacing and Testing Mental Models

Systems Thinking

Sensing and Actualizing Emerging Futures

Reshaping Forces That Maintain Status Quo

Convening and Hosting Large-Scale Strategic Conversations

and hosting such large-scale conversations require particular methodologies. But Brown believes that the key lies in "questions that challenge current experiences and assumptions, while evoking new possibilities for collective discovery." For example, "How can infocom technology and services support the evolution of a sustainable and renewable environment?"

Most attempts at large-scale change fail because otherwise competent leaders do not understand the complex forces maintaining the status quo. Getting a CEO to support sustainability is not enough. Bottom-up environmental innovations also often fail. Leaders at all levels must understand the multiple "balancing processes" that on the one hand, make any complex organization viable, but on the other, consistently defeat large-scale change. Leadership strategies must address these balancing forces. For example: relevance (people asking, "What does sustainability have to do with my job?"), believers vs. nonbelievers (the Polarization that passionate advocates for social and environmental causes can create), the tyranny of established metrics (most current metrics reflect take-make-waste mental models, and new metrics aimed at life-cycle costs are useless without changes in mental models), and purpose (if the company's core purpose is perceived as making money, people's commitment may be below the threshold required to lead significant change).[3] All meaningful work on shared vision rests on distinguishing "creating" from "problem solving". Problem solving seeks to make things we don't like go away. Creating seeks to make things we care about come into being. This is a vital distinction for innovation. When problem solving dominates an organizational culture, life is about survival rather than about bringing into reality things that people care about. Recent research on leadership among entrepreneurs and scientists reveals a particular creative capacity – sensing and actualizing emerging futures. Successful leaders see the world as "open, dynamic, interconnected and full of possibilities."[4] They are both committed and "in a state of surrender" as cognitive scientist Francisco Varcia expresses it. Economist W. Brian Arthur adds that "cognizing" in business today follows three stages:

- "Observe, observe, observe: become one with the world."
- "Reflect and retreat: listen from the inner place where knowing comes to the surface."
- "Act in an instant: incubate and bring forth the new into reality."

[1] P.M. Senge, "The Leader's New Work: Building Learning Organizations", MIT Sloan Management Review 32 (fall 1990): p. 7-23.

[2] W. Isaacs, "Dialogue: The Art of Thinking Together" (New York: Doubleday/Currency, 1999).

[3] These are four of 10 basic challenges to sustaining deep change addressed in P. Senge et al., The Dance of Change: The Challenges to Sustaining Learning Organizations' (New York: Doubleday/Currency, 1999).

[4] J. Jaworski and 0. Scharmer, "Leadership in the New Economy: Sensing and Actualizing Emerging Future", SoL working paper, www.SoLonline.org/Resources/working_papers.html

consultant John Elkington. "But companies like Shell, Ford and many others feel they must do this if they want to lead, rather than just react to change."

But the path toward broader accountability is fraught with perils. Last spring, Ford's first "Corporate Citizenship Report", based loosely on GRI guidelines, was greeted with as much cynicism as appreciation. The New York Times ignored most of the report (which included lengthy sections on reducing emissions and radical redesign of manufacturing processes) to announce that "Ford Is Conceding SUV Drawbacks."[23] The article focused on a three-page section of the 98-page report that discussed the dilemma of having a profitable product line that had environmental and safety problems. The Wall Street Journal was more personal, suggesting that chairman William Clay Ford was a hypocrite for both making and criticizing SUVs, a "guilt-ridden rich kid" who should either embrace his customers' preferences or leave the business to those who do.[24]

Ultimately, transparency is about awareness. With increasing awareness will come pressures for greater accountability for social and natural capital as well as financial capital. Gradually, this will lead to innovations in the larger social context as well.

It is impossible to predict the range of social innovations that growing transparency will ultimately foster. Perhaps new collaborative action-research networks will create the right climate of objectivity and compassion, tough standards and fair reporting combined with a spirit of learning together. Perhaps more-participative media, building on successful experiments such as those of Fast Company, will enable new levels of collaborative innovation. It may even be time to question the traditional limited-liability status of corporations, which uniquely favors owners of financial capital. Today's world of abundant financial capital and limited natural and social capital differs profoundly from the world of a century ago, when there was a need to protect individual investors. "In a world where learning and knowledge generation are the basis for corporate survival and wealth creation, managers must see a company as a living being, a human community," says writer and former Shell executive Arie de Geus. "Yet, today's managers inherit a very different worldview, focused on the optimism of financial capital. Is it not inconsistent to emphasize knowledge creation, on the one hand, and then treat a company as a machine for producing money, which is owned by its financial investors on the other?"

Perhaps when we are able to rediscover "company" (from the Latin *com-panis,* sharing of bread), as "living community", we will also rediscover its place within the larger community of living systems where it rightfully resides.

The Logic of Revolutions

The New Economy is both not new and new. It continues industrial-age patterns, yet it also may hold the seeds for a truly postindustrial world. As such, it brings us to a crossroads. We can either continue moving ever more rapidly in a direction that cannot be sustained, or we can change. Perhaps, no time in history has afforded greater possibilities for a collective change in direction.

"Creative engineers understand the role of constraints," says Elter of his Lakes experience. "Design engineers always deal with constraints: time, weight, operability. These are all real. The extraordinary creativity of [our] team had its source in recognizing a different constraint – the constraint of nature, to produce no waste. Zero to landfill is an uplifting constraint. It's worth going after. It's not manmade." Constraint and creativity are always connected. No artist paints on an infinite canvas. The artist understands that rather than just being limits, constraints can be freeing, especially when those constraints that have genuine meaning are recognized. What if product and business designers everywhere recognized that their constraints came from living systems? What if they adhered to the simple dictums: waste equals food; support natures regenerative processes; live off energy income, not principal, and, borrowing from Elter's team, do it for the children. As occurred with the Lakes engineers, might this tint free everyone's creativity in previously unimaginable ways?

Such rethinking will not happen all at once. It will not arise from any central authority. It will come from everywhere and nowhere in particular. The first Industrial Revolution, according to author Daniel Quinn, was "the product of a million small beginnings. [It] didn't proceed according to any theoretical design [and] was not a utopian undertaking."[25] Likewise, the next Industrial Revolution, if it is to happen, will have no grand plan and no one in charge. It will advance, in Quinn's words, on the basis of "an outpouring of human creativity", innovations not just in the technological but in the human landscape as well – the only way a new story can arise.

Case Example
From Outsourced Subcontractors to Strategic Innovation Partners[*]

There are still people, it seems, who think India's outsourcing industry is just a bunch of poorly paid clerks with PhDs doing mind-numbing drudge work. Until recently, one of them was the senior US insurance executive who visited the business processing arm of Wipro, India's third-largest software and services company.

He was soon disabused (re-oriented) by his hosts. What they showed him was a virtual back office staffed by insurance specialists equipped to handle a full range of tasks, from receiving claims to adjudicating them up to a value of £500 000. "We understand everything!" Raman Roy, head of the division, told his visitor. He immediately clinched a contract.

Another myth is shattered by a stroll around the modern campus-style head-quarters in Bangalore of companies such as Wipro and Infosys, where corporate customers' global information networks are managed round the clock from space-age control rooms. If these are sweatshops, the Ritz hotel is a dosshouse.

Even judged by the blistering speed of information technology industry change, India's achievement is astonishing. In barely a decade, it has created a range of businesses with more than 800 000 employees and annual sales close to $20bn, almost all exports. The corporate names on the welcome boards at Bangalore reception desks read like the Fortune 500. And that, industry leaders say, is only the start. Roy foresees annual growth of 50% or more and a trebling of business-processing jobs to 1.2-million by 2008.

The larger companies are plotting their next leap: to evolve from subcontractors into strategic partners, sharing risks with customers. Many are busy hiring consultants with experience in target industries including banking, health care and telecommunications. The goal, says Roy, is to "suck out knowledge" from customers, to serve them better.

India's ambitions seem to know no bounds. But these companies still face hurdles. One is building customer trust. They must also manage increasing complexity and scale, while keeping footloose employees loyal. Intensifying competition for skilled labor makes that harder. The industry recognizes all those challenges and is seeking to meet them.

---

[*] Adapted from: "India Rides the Wave", *Business Day*, March 30, 2005, 16

But one potential hazard lies beyond its control: a backlash against outsourcing in the US, by far its biggest market. Although the threat has receded as US job creation has recovered, an economic downturn could revive it, along with hysteria about industrial "hollowing out".

Pressure for protectionist measures could quickly follow (although such legislation would be difficult to enforce on multinational firms). If that happened, all the earnest arguments heard in Bangalore these days about outsourcing being a "win-win" game, and trade a two-way street, would be unlikely to cut much political ice in the west.

India's information technology industry knows that. But it also senses a powerful counter-trend running in its favor. Fiercer global competition, bigger commercial risks, faster innovation, shorter product cycles and shortages of key staff are all transforming its western customers' methods of doing business.

And the most sophisticated Indian firms, such as Wipro and Infosys, are establishing consulting and systems integration capabilities in the U.S. and other client markets, so that they cannot accurately be called foreign outsourcers.

Even the outsourcers are outsourcing. Wipro chairman Azim Premji says the company is defining its technological "crown jewels" ever more narrowly and entrusting work performed in-house to partners. That is an imperative of its commercial survival. The belief that it will continue and grow even stronger is the industry's biggest bet on the future.

Questions

1. Why are incremental (or gradual) innovations not enough for a company such as 3M?

2. Some observers would disagree with the view that there is an "innovation economy" or even a "new economy". Analyze these views and their counterparts, and provide your own opinion, in view of the various 'drivers' of the innovation economy.

3. "The core principles that underpin the modern enterprise are all being challenged". Provide a logical review of this statement, with a concise contrast of the 'industrial economy enterprise' with the 'innovation economy' enterprise.

4. Why are some highly-developed countries (such as Germany) facing major challenges in the innovation economy? Are there more examples of such countries, and what are the challenges for developing countries such as China and India?

5. Select any enterprise known to you and provide a logical review of why the traditional (analytical) strategy dimensions of context, content and process are inadequate to cope with the challenges of the innovation economy.

6. To what extent is a major wine producing company such as Gallo, renowned for its 'terroir', marketing and production knowledge capabilities, affected by the challenges of the innovation economy?

7. To what extent is there a relative shift in power and value creation activity – from supply chains to demand chains – in the innovation economy?

8. Provide an insightful review of the concepts of creativity, innovation and energy, and the relationships among them.

9. Select 2-3 industries, and review how the 'driving' forces in the innovation economy are affecting their traditional characteristics and dynamics (e.g. the steel, pharmaceuticals, banking, entertainment and education industries).

References

Chapter 1: The Global Innovation Economy and Strategic Management

[1] Various authors have recently emphasized the differences in economic activity due to ways in which value is created since about 1990. One insightful analysis is by Germany, R. and Muralidharan, R. (2001), "The Three Phases of Value Capture: Finding Competitive Advantage in the Information Age," *Strategy & Business*, Issue 22, First Quarter, 1-10.

[2] See Von Hippel, E., Thomke, S. and Sonnak, M. (1999), "Creating Breakthroughs at 3M," *Harvard Business Review*, Vol. 43, Issue 4, 47-57

[3] The concept of a 'tipping point' has been extensively explained by Malcolm Gladwell. See Gladwell, M. (2000), *The Tipping Point: How Little Things can Make a Big Difference*, London: Abacus, Little, Brown and Company.

[4] Various authors have been analyzing the drivers towards an innovation economy. A prominent view is provided by Tapscott, D. (2001), "Rethinking Strategy in a Networked World," *Strategy & Business*, Issue 24, Third Quarter, 2-8.

[5] Gordon Moore is the retired co-founder of Intel Corporation. Moore, G.E. (1965), "Cramming More Components onto Integrated Circuits," *Electronics*, Vol. 38, No. 8, 114-117.

[6] Robert Metcalfe founded 3Com Corporation and designed the Ethernet protocol for computer networks.

[7] The concept of 'organizational fitness' and 'strategic fitness' has been extensively researched and elaborated by Michael Beer of Harvard, and associates. See Beer, M. and Eisenstat, R. (2004), "How to Hold an Honest Conversation About your Strategy," *Harvard Business Review*, Vol 82, Issue 2, 82-89; and Beer, M., Voelpel, S., Leibold, M., and Tekie, E. (2005): "Strategic Management as Organizational Learning: Developing Fit and Alignment Through a Disciplined Process", *Long Range Planning*, Vol. 38, Issue 3, (in print).

[8] See Gibbert, M., Leibold, M. and Probst, G. (2002), "Five Styles of Customer Knowledge Management, and How Smart Companies Use Them to Create Value," *European Management Journal*, Issue 20, 459-469.

[9] This metaphor was first postulated in a different context (business-to-business e-business) in Means, G. and Schneider, D. (2000), *Meta-Capitalism*, New York: John Wiley & Sons, Inc., xviii.

[10] Adapted from Kluge, J., Meffert, J. and Stein, L. (2000), "The German Road to Innovation," *The McKinsey Quarterly*, Special Edition: Europe in Transition, Issue 2, 98-105.

[11] See Means, G. and Schneider, D. (2000), op.cit., xxi.

[12] Jane C. Linder and Susan Cantrell, "What Makes a Good Business Model, Anyway?" Accenture Institute for Strategic Change Working Paper, 2001, online at http://www.accenture.com/xd/xd.asp?it=enweb&xd=ideas%5Coutlook%5Cpov%5Cpov_busmod.xml.

[13] See Chesbrough, H.W. (2003), "The Era of Open Innovation', *MIT Sloan Management Review*, Issue 44, Vol. 3, 35-41.

[14] Mintzberg, H. (1994), *The Rise and Fall of Strategic Planning*. New York: Free Press.

[15] Thomke, S. (2003), *Experimentation Matters*, Boston: Harvard Business School Press.

Innovating Our Way to the Next Industrial Revolution

[1] Social capital refers to "connections among individuals – social networks and the norms of reciprocity and trustworthiness that arise with them". See: F.D. Putnam, "Bowling Alone" (New York: Simon & Schuster, 2000). p. 19. It is also the necessary context for developing human capital. – skills and knowledge embedded in people. See: J.S. Coleman, "Social Capital and the Creation of Human Capital", *American Journal of Sociology* 94 (1988): pp. 95-120.

[2] "Why Is Everyone So Short-Tempered?" *USA Today*, July 18, 2000, sec. A, p. 1.

[3] J. Browne. "Respect for the Earth!" a 2000 BBC Reith Lecture, available from BP, London.

[4] J. Browne, "Rethinking Corporate Responsibility", *Reflections* 1.4 (summer 2000): pp. 48-53.

[5] See www.rmi.org/sitepages/pid175.asp for Rocky Mountain Institute publications about the hypercar.

[6] E.P. Gunn, "The Green CEO", *Fortune*, May 24, 1999, pp. 190-200.

[7] The SoL (Society for Organizational Learning) Sustainability Consortium was established by BP and Interface and now includes established SoL members Royal Dutch/Shell, Ford, Xerox. Harley-Davidson, Detroit-Edison, Visteon and the World Bank, along with new members Nike and Northeast Utilities. The group's current projects – on product development, innovation across complex supply networks, new energy sources, and leadership and cultural change – are described at www.SoLonline.org and are being studied through a National Science Foundation grant.

[8] T. Berry, "The Dream of the Earth" (San Francisco: Sierra Club Books, 1990), pp. 123.

[9] Ibid., pp. 131-132.

[10] D. Boorstin, "The Discoverers: A History of Man's Search To Know His World and Himself" (New York. Random House, 1985), pp. 108-109.

[11] See P. Hawken, A.B. Lovins and L.H. Lovins, "Natural Capitalism" (New York: Little Brown and Co., 1999), p. 14; R.U. Ayers, "Industrial Metabolism", in J.S. Ausubel and H.E. Sladovich, eds., "Technology and Environment" (Washington, D.C.: National Academy Press, 1989); and A.B. Lovins, L.H. Lovins and P. Hawken, "A Road Map for Natural Capitalism", *Harvard Business Review* 77 (May-June 1999): pp. 145-158.

[12] These three strategies, in concert with ideas below, relate closely to the four strategies of "natural capitalism", three of the four "system conditions' of "the natural step" described in J. Holmberg and K.-H. Robert, "Backcasting From Nonoverlapping Sustainability Principles – A Framework for Strategic Planning", *International Journal of Sustainable Development and World Ecology* 7 (2000): 1-18; and William McDonough, "Hannover Principles: Design for Sustainability" (New York: William McDonough Architects, 1992). Available through McDonough Braungart Design Chemistry, Charlottesville, Virginia (info@mbdc.com) or downloadable from www.mcdonough.com/principles.pdf.

[13] K. Kelly, "New Rules for the New Economy" (New York: Penguin Books, 1999), pp. 2, 5, 31.

[14] S. Vandermerwe, "How Increasing Value to Customers Improves Business Results", *MIT Sloan Management Review* 42 (fall 2000): p. 28.

[15] A. Toffler, "The Third Wave" (New York: William Morrow, 1980).

[16] Kelly, "New Rules", pp. 121-122.

[17] C.K. Prahalad and V. Ramaswamy, "Co-opting Customer Competence", *Harvard Business Review* 78 (January-February 2000): pp. 79-87.

[18] R. Levine, C. Locke, D. Seads and D. Weinberger, "The Cluetrain Manifesto: The End of Business as Usual" (Cambridge, Massachusetts: Perseus Press, 2000), xiv.

[19] Kelly, "New Rules", p. 28.

[20] B. Wysocki Jr., "Yet Another Hazard of the New Economy: The Pied Piper Effect", *Wall Street Journal*, March 30, 2000, sec. A, p. 1.

[21] P.F. Drucker and P. Senge, "Becoming a Change Leader", video conversations, Peter E. Drucker Foundation for Nonprofit Management, New York, and SoL (the Society for Organizational Learning), Cambridge, Massachusetts, forthcoming.

[22] A. Webber, "What's So New About the New Economy?" *Harvard Business Review* 71 (January-February 1993): pp. 24-42.

[23] K. Bradsher, "Ford Is Conceding SUV Drawbacks", *New York Times*, May 12. 2000, sec. A, p. 1.

[24] B. Yates, "On the Road: Pecksniffs Can't Stop SUV", *Wall Street Journal Europe*, May 19, 2000, sec. A, p. 26.

[25] D. Quinn, "My Ishmael" (New York: Bantam Books, 1997), pp. 200-201.

II The Changing Nature of Business and Challenges to Traditional Strategic Management

Synopsis

The chapter analyzes and motivates the deficiencies in traditional strategic management approaches in view of the changing nature of business in the innovation economy. It also traces the changing views regarding the concepts of business and innovation, including a changing model of the enterprise. Four key challenges to conventional strategic management wisdom are highlighted. The major 'box' example is the global automobile industry, and the case examples concern demand-supply chain innovation by P&G, Wal-Mart and McGraw-Hill.

Chapter 2
The Relevance of Traditional Approaches to Strategic Management in the Innovation Economy

The Changing Concepts of Business and Innovation

The previous chapter indicated that while the fundamentals of business survival still remain the same (profitability, resulting from a loyal customer support base due to particular competitively-differentiated products – or 'value proposals'), the core paradigms and principles of how to sustainably achieve that in the innovation economy are all being seriously challenged. The very nature of the business enterprise of the 21st century is being transformed, as well as the key notions of innovation and its effects on value creation, value capture, and value sustainability.

Business strategy and strategic management have long been viewed as the concept and process that link an organization and its environment. The current turbulence and significant shifts in the environment imply that traditional ways of articulating strategy and practicing strategic management have to be seriously reconsidered. Since the 1950s, various approaches to strategic management have been popularized, and some have served very well in their particular eras. With a significant new era of massive, revolutionary change – the era of the innovation economy – now being entered since the late 1990s, it is becoming evident that all of the traditional approaches to strategic management are showing serious deficiencies in dealing with the discontinuous links between an enterprise and the environment.

This chapter illustrates the changing concept of the business enterprise (as depicted by the transformation of traditional business models), describes the changing views of the nature of innovation, and then reviews the evolution of traditional approaches to strategic management and their relevance today. The difficulties (or deficiencies) of these approaches in dealing with the new environmental realities are highlighted and discussed, with indication of practical business examples.

The Changing Model of the Business Enterprise

Figure 2.1 represents the prevailing model for business enterprises of the past 100 years and more.[1]

Companies have traditionally had a large base of physical capital. The asset types have varied as widely as business itself: manufacturing sites, distribution centers,

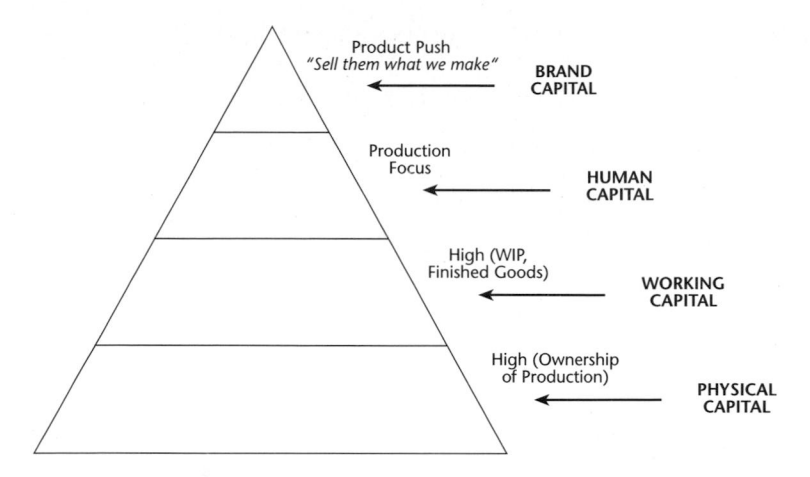

Figure 2.1 Traditional business model

branches of financial institutions, hospitals or health care facilities, retail outlets, telecommunications infrastructure, entertainment production centers, and so on. Managing these assets effectively in the past 20 years has called for tremendous focus on building or integrating domestic and global operations, streamlining supply chains, integrating with supplier bases and distribution networks, standardizing and improving business processes, installing related technology, and generally improving operating performance and efficiency.

In parallel, financial managers have focused on improving return on capital, return on investment, EBITDA, asset returns, and other measures of effective management of broad capital bases. Industry consolidation has, among other things, involved the consolidation of domestic and global physical capital to achieve scale economies and align physical capital with markets served.

Companies in the 1990s also focused intently on more efficient use of working capital (ingredients, raw materials, parts inventory, work-in-process, finished goods) with the objective of increasing inventory turns, lowering the carrying cost of inventory, and improving the efficiency of fulfillment systems to decrease product obsolescence and increase customer responsiveness. Key performance indicators have tended to focus on throughput, inventory turnovers, capital efficiency, and working capital as a reflection of the growing efficiency and responsiveness of supply chains.

To a large degree, the tremendous focus on the more efficient use of working capital in the 1990s was a result of the major economic shift in the 1980s. Prior to the 1980s the real cost of capital tended to be negative or zero for several decades. In essence, the real interest rate on capital (nominal interest rate minus inflation) tended to be zero or negative because of the high levels of inflation. Under these conditions, with the exception of some amount of product spoilage, obsolescence, storage cost, etc., working capital was virtually free; the carrying charges on raw materials, inventory, work-in-process, and finished goods were essentially zero or negative. Among managers there was, accordingly, little emphasis on productivity improvement or better management of working capital through reducing inventory, improving transportation and distribution, reducing warehousing for finished goods, or any other major initiative of the type launched in the 1990s to better manage and reduce working capital.

The sudden onset of real interest rates in the 1980s and 1990s changed all of this. Companies now faced real costs to their operations, and this abruptly generated awareness that owning and managing all of the factors of production, with their attendant working capital demands, might no longer be the preferred business model. They then embarked upon initiatives to reengineer processes, improve productivity, and optimize supply chains.

Company employees – human capital – in the 1990s tended to concentrate on the factors of production. Process models looked carefully at all elements of the supply chain: sourcing, manufacturing, distribution, supply chain-related financial accounting, new product development and product introduction through company supply chains, marketing and promotional alignment with the supply chain, and integration of selling with the supply chain. Although in recent years there has been a growing emphasis on customer requirements and customer responsiveness – in effect, on brand capital – the predominant focus of most major companies has continued to be product development, manufacturing, and sales "push" to customers rather than customer ownership and customer "pull".

In short, the financial, operating, and business process model for most companies has been based – intuitively or explicitly – on a concept of the enterprise as a physical asset-based pyramid organized to produce and sell products. Recent investments in technology (e.g., Enterprise Resource Planning (ERP) and Customer Relationship Management (CRM) systems) have been designed to facilitate this business and process model and to provide tools for understanding and managing it better. As yet there is still no alternative technological approach for the large enterprise, although more flexible alternatives such as web services are being investigated by many firms.

During the late 1980s and 1990s, initiatives to improve and synchronize the supply chain assumed that there was great advantage in having many of the factors in the supply chain under company control, often within its "four walls." Companies worked somewhat independently to identify and design the best supply chain and process models and were most comfortable when they controlled them end-to-end. The ERP wave changed this view somewhat by applying a consistent process model to companies in specific industries. During this wave of effort, many major companies achieved a best practice model for internal processes, and some degree of process standardization appeared in many industries.[2] Toward the end of the 1990s, most companies were still working hard to organize and control their supply chains and install ERP and CRM systems to better manage their processes. Simultaneously, at the end of the 1990s pressures were building up for a rapid and dramatic revolution, as Figure 2.2 illustrates. CEOs now feel compelled to transform their companies from the conventional business model to the less capital-intense business model illustrated on the right hand side of the figure. In order to better leverage their capital and focus on core competencies, brand-owning companies are determining how to rely less and less on an internal base of physical capital. Instead, they adopt the strategy of outsourcing

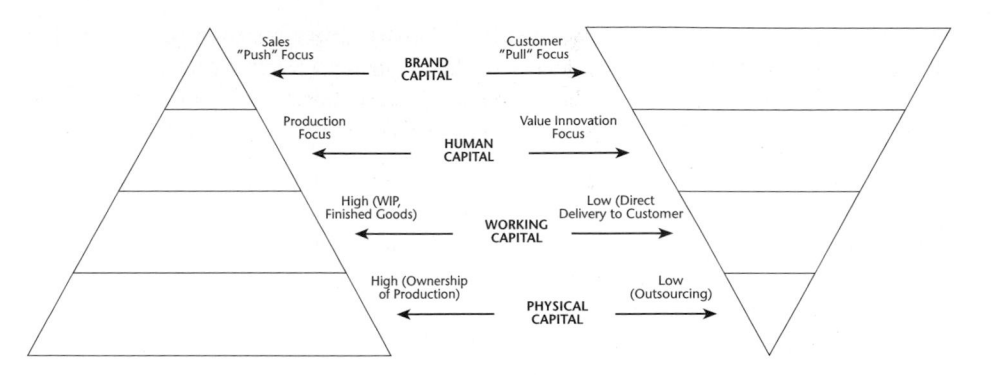

Figure 2.2 The transformation of the traditional to the 21st century business model

non-core physical capital activities across the supply and demand chains as well as outsourcing support functions.

The 21st century business model tends to split companies into relatively low-capital brand-owning companies on the one hand, and companies clustered around these brand-owning companies in external or outsourced networks on the other hand. The networks provide the supply chain, demand chain, and support services – such as financial processing, accounting, technology, human resources – for brand-owning companies.

A low-capital, brand owning company operating in close cooperation with an out-sourced network is a relatively new business phenomenon, which can be termed as particular value-adding communities operating purposefully in the larger entities of business ecosystems. The athletic shoe companies Nike and Reebok are examples of this approach – they outsource manufacturing, consumer sales, and distribution while focusing on product design and marketing.

Accompanying the dramatic effort to lower the base of physical capital and to out-source, is an equally dramatic effort to lower working capital. As brand owners out-source parts manufacture, physical product systems, and large chunks of final assem-bly for their proprietary designs and branded products, they keep little if any manufac-turing inventory in-house. To the degree that they do manufacture, they may focus on highly specialized subassemblies or focus on simply doing kit assembly of a few large systems and sub-assemblies supplied by their outsourced network. In short, large manufacturers become systems integrators of larger, separately assembled subassem-blies. In many cases, they may move to manufacturing nothing at all and have finished products shipped by their outsourced network to their fulfillment centers or directly to consumers.

Clearly, spinning off manufacturing and related operating processes, generally to an outsourced network, frees up enormous amounts of capital that can be focused on brand development, customer ownership, supply network management, and other industry leadership processes. These trends have been evident for some time. In recent decades, for example, the issue of whether to own, lease, or rent has become familiar in organizations of nearly every size. Make versus buy versus rent has become a common decision point. Much physical capital that was historically owned by corporations is now leased; in high tech and dot.com companies, much is rented. Microsoft, often depicted as "the most valuable corporation in the world," has but a few million dollars in fixed assets. What, then, does a corporation need to own?

The trends have been evident for some time, but they are now changing the rules across a broad front. Standard accounting and financial measurements no longer tell the whole story. The application of capital internally to manufacturing, service delivery, or infrastructure upgrades may be a grave strategic error. Conventional performance metrics related to throughput or inventory and asset turns within the four walls are less relevant. Human capital is focused more on customers and leveraged more effectively to drive growth. Outsourced and offshored processes require not only transformation of business models, but transformation of the labor force in high-cost economies to make it more adaptable, flexible, and knowledge-based. This realization is only beginning to take place in the United States and Western Europe.[3]

Similarly, brand capital is developed more effectively to retain customers and derive far greater revenue from new channels to customers. For example, electronic business-to-business disintermediates many non-value-added processes and allows customers to better access and leverage the supply chain. E-business-to-business companies can take advantage of this by offering superior access and responsiveness to these customers and creating stronger ties – all of which adds to brand capital.

Business processes today have less of a pure operational character and answer instead to definitions such as "rapid alliance development," "outsourcing," business "ecosystems management," and "demand and supply chain management." Investments tend to focus on customer ownership, customer management, brand ownership, and related market-centric requirements. And the market tends to reward with high price-earnings multiples those companies that have the flexibility and discipline to master these skills.

It is no exaggeration to say that for the 21st century company, an entirely new business model is required with entirely new definitions of strategy and business processes. (See box for an example in the auto industry).

The automobile industry example reflects events in every other industry in the global economy. This is dramatically changing our assumptions about economic growth, value creation, and strategic management of organizations. In the innovation economy, the network will be the value innovation engine, with the traditional focus on optimization of an individual business model in an established industry being replaced by a focus on optimization of multiple business models in a collaborative network context (as indicated in Chapter 1). What does all of this hold for traditional strategic management approaches and practices? The next section reviews and comments on this question, while Chapter 3 outlines a new strategic management mindset for the innovation economy.

The Changing Automobile Enterprise Business Model

An example of the dramatic transformation in business models is in the global auto industry. For the past several years, the industry has concentrated on improving its supply chains, reducing time-to-market for new models, and increasingly integrating global operations. The auto industry has also experienced tremendous consolidation as the major companies have begun to merge and the number of original equipment manufacturing (OEM) brands has been reduced to a shorter list of nameplates. At the same time, the industry has become more detached from its dealer networks, and this has given rise to the growing phenomenon of megadealers who offer products and brands from many different automotive manufacturers.

Further dramatic shifts are occurring, as suggested in Figure 2.3. The OEM model, represented on the left of the diagram, is rapidly transforming into a vehicle brand owner (VBO) model. Major manufacturers (such as Ford, General Motors, and Daimler-Chrysler) are moving to outsource much of the manufacture of the parts and subassemblies of their vehicles. Some firms, such as Porsche, even subcontract final assembly of vehicles. At the same time, there has been a growing interest in investing downstream in distribution and dealer networks.

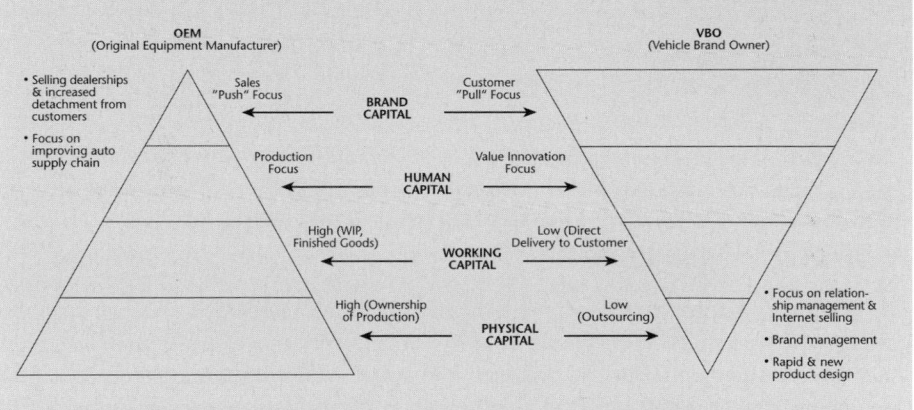

Figure 2.3 Auto industry business model in the innovation economy

These shifts reflect the reality of the auto industry, in which very little profit has been made in recent decades on the cars themselves (the most profitable product has been light trucks). Servicing and repair, the aftermarket, and related businesses such as auto finance have been the principal moneymakers. Thus, it has increasingly made sense to transition major companies to the role of VBOs. As such, the companies may outsource manufacturing, create new alliances and supply chain networks, manage outsourced relationships, and focus on customer responsiveness, vehicle design, distribution, service and repair, and the aftermarket. At the same time, auto manufacturers are learning to use the Internet as a major consumer communications and sales tool. The financial markets are increasingly recognizing these transformations – and beginning to reward them accordingly.

The evidence for this fundamental change is the creation of automotive value chains and their wider business ecosystems. There are at least two broad approaches:

a) Some automotive companies are using technology to create a captive network of suppliers for parts and sub-assemblies, as well as other products and services. The network is, by definition, closely tied to the company (particularly for Japanese auto manufacturers). It can use Internet-based tools to cooperate on product design and specifications. It can also bid on additional work – for example, to produce products and services for downstream elements of the supply chain, to supply the brand-owning nameplate manufacturer, or to deliver original equipment or aftermarket services directly to the consumer. The network is knit together by various supply and purchasing technology tools that exchange information, conduct bidding processes, and integrate the supply chain for manufacturing and delivery.

b) Automotive companies that use similar technology but do not require a fully captive supply base represent an alternative approach. In this model, design and subassembly specifications are provided through a more open communications and network approach to a broader set of potential players. This open architecture model allows a vast array of manufacturing and service providers to participate in bidding and to compete furiously with each other on the basis of traditional measures such as reliability, quality, and price, as well as new performance measures such as the ability to interface with metamarket technology, fit quickly and easily into the virtual supply chain, and create and dissolve business alliances efficiently. As these concepts are currently evolving, some automakers have joined together to form multi-company supply networks with common standards.

Source: Adapted from Means, G., and Schneider, D., op.cit.

The Relevance of the Traditional Approaches to Strategic Management

The traditional approaches to strategic management are predicated upon an emphasis on analysis, reason, and periods of stability. This is very much in keeping with Newton's mechanistic model of the universe and Fayol's view of the management function. There is a presumption that a combination of analysis, experience, and insight can lead to reliable predictions regarding the future – an environment "out there" which has to be adapted to. Furthermore, the analytical mindset typical of most of the 20th century presumes that any organization, industry, or market can be understood through reductionism – reducing the whole to its constituent parts for scrutiny and future direction. In today's dynamic networked world, it is increasingly being accepted that the whole is more than the sum of the parts, and holistic thinking and approaches should complement reductionist ones.

Table 2.1 illustrates the various eras in strategic management approaches in the 20th century, with each era depicting the respective major focus of strategic management.

The above table is of necessity a generalization, i.e. in reality the eras are not strictly limited to a particular decade (or number of decades). Furthermore, many prominent authors such as Grant, Mintzberg, and Collis and Montgomery depict these eras in more elaborate or different ways.[4] Nevertheless, there seems to be general consensus

Table 2.1 The focus of strategic management in various eras of time in the 20th century

Period / Issue	1950s – 1960's	1970s	1980s	1990s
Dominant focus	*Planning*: Business and Budgetary planning	*Balancing*: Optimizing corporate entities and functions	*Positioning*: Industries, markets, and firms "adapting" and achieving unique "fit"	*Resources & Capabilities*: Resource-based view for competitive advantage
Main concerns	• Planning growth • Capital and operational budgeting • Financial control	• Balancing a portfolio of SBU's/firms/products • Synergy of resources and functions	• Choosing industries and markets, and positioning within them • Adapting and fitting to the environment	• Sources of competitive advantage within the firm • Responding to hyper-competition
Principal concepts and tools	• Investment planning • Financial budgeting • Economic forecasting • Linear programming	• Portfolio planning matrices (e.g. BCG, GE, Shell directional policy) • SWOT analyses	• Industry analysis (e.g. "5 Forces"-model) • Competitor analyses • Value chain analyses • PIMS-analyses	• Resource analyses • Core competency analyses • Capability analyses • BPR (Business Process Reengineering) • BSC (Balanced Scorecard) • TQM (Total Quality Management)
Organizational & implementation issues	• Formal structures and procedures • Financial management predominant	• Multidivisional structures • Diversification • Quest for market share growth	• Industry restructuring • Value chain configuration • Positioning evaluations	• Restructuring around key resource competences • Focus on building core competencies • Outsourcing • Alliances

regarding the dominant focus of these eras, evolving from business and budgetary planning in the 1950s/60s to a focus on firm resources and capabilities in the 1990s.

The evolution of strategic management has been driven more by the practical needs of business than by the development of theory. The emergence of the planning approach was associated with the problems faced by managers in the 1950s and 1960s in coordinating decisions and maintaining control in increasingly large and complex enterprises. The emphasis on longer-term planning during the 1960s reflected concern with achieving coordination and consistency in investment planning during a period of stability and expansion. The typical format was a five-year business planning document that set goals, objectives, forecast key economic trends, established priorities in each business area, and allocated capital expenditure. Ansoff, widely regarded as one of the founding figures of the discipline of corporate strategy, defined strategy as follows:[5]

"Strategic decisions are primarily concerned with external rather than internal problems of the firm, and specifically with the selection of the product-mix that the firm will produce and the markets to which it will sell".

During the 1970s, attention shifted towards strategic management as a quest for performance based on a balancing of sources of profitability. This was a result of the oil industry 'shocks' of 1973/4 and 1979, that ushered in a new era of macro-economic instability. Businesses simply could not forecast five years ahead any more with the resultant shift from planning to balancing market opportunities and threats with various business strengths and weaknesses (the so-called SWOT-analysis). At the Boston Consulting Group (BCG), the focus of investigation was on the determinants of profitability differences within industries – i.e., studies pointing to the critical role of market share and economies of experience.[6] Various types of portfolio planning matrices, such as those from BCG, GE (General Electric), and SDP (Shell Directional Policy matrix) became popular.

During the 1980s, the focus shifted towards competitive positioning of the firm through analysis of industry structure and competition. Michael Porter of Harvard Business School pioneered the application of industrial organization economics for analyzing the determinants of firm profitability.[7] The emphasis on strategic management was a quest for optimal positioning (or 'fit') – companies needed to locate within the most attractive industries or markets where they should seek to become market leaders. Porter made the point that "competitive strategy is about being different – it means deliberately choosing a different set of activities to deliver a unique mix of value".[8] The principal concepts and tools of the positioning era become industry analysis (the so-called "5-forces" model), competitor analysis, market analysis, value chain analysis, and PIMS (profit impact of market strategy) analysis.

In the late 1980s and early 1990's, the intensifying competition to achieve market share leadership led to a shift in strategic management focus towards internal firm resources and capabilities – the difference between companies' resources and the need to develop core competencies for establishment of unique positions of competitive advantage. Various authors, such as Grant pointed to the firm's resources and capabilities, and their unique leveraging, as a primary source of profitability and the basis for formulating longer-term strategy.[9] Resource analysis, core competency analysis, capability analysis, and business process reengineering (BPR) became popularly known as the RBV (resource-based view), and organizational emphasis on restructuring, reengineering, outsourcing, and allying to build unique capabilities was evidenced.

In the middle to late 1990s, the dimension of dynamic capabilities was added to the RBV due to high-velocity industry and market changes. Hyper-competition and high-velocity strategies contend that one firm will outperform another if it is more adept at rapidly and repeatedly disrupting the current situation by creating unprecedented and unconventional dynamic capabilities, i.e. repeatedly forming new, albeit temporary, competitive advantages based on different resource combinations than the existing pattern. Authors such as D'Aveni, Chakravarthy, Eisenhardt and Brown, and Eisenhardt and Martin identified various principles of hyper-competition and dynamic capabilities, and proposed that corporate strategy should center on managing strategy processes rather than strategic positioning.[10]

For purposes of discussing the current deficiencies of the abovementioned traditional approaches to strategic management, they can be grouped into two broad categories, viz. 'outward-in' vs. 'inward-out' approaches and 'prediction' vs. 'learning' approaches.

'Outward-in' vs. 'Inward-out' Approaches

The planning, balancing and positioning approaches to strategic management can be grouped as 'outward-in' approaches, i.e. first analyzing the external (macro, industry, market, etc.) environment and then analyzing and competitively gearing the internal (firm) environment. It is based on implicit assumptions of periodic relatively stable (or static) environmental conditions, relevance of forecasting and prediction, and achievement of particular industry positioning objectives over an extended period of time.

In the innovation economy – with its high rate of environmental discontinuities due to the disruptive impact of networking technologies, speed of globalization, and fast rate of product, business and industry innovation – accurate environmental forecasting and prediction are impossible in many, if not most, industries. Companies that continue to focus on 'the competition', on leveraging and extending current capabilities to retain or extend their positions in the 'existing industry', and striving for periodic optimum 'fit with their environment', are faced with major dilemmas. A focus on matching and beating the competition leads to reactive, incremental, and often imitative strategic actions – not what is required in the fast-changing innovation economy. Even in relatively stable or slow-changing industries (which are increasingly difficult to find) the concepts and tools of the 'outward-in' approaches are becoming deficient when used on their own.

The resources and capabilities approach to strategic management can be termed an 'inward-out' approach, i.e. first focusing on the firm's internal resources and capabilities and their leveraging possibilities, and then incorporating the 'realities' of the external environment. An inwardly-driven focus on resources and capabilities within a company, however, significantly limits a company's opportunity horizon and introduces resistance to change if the market is evolving away from a company's traditional forte. It also leads to an emphasis on existing customers – the conventional focus on retaining and better satisfying existing customers tends to promote hesitancy to challenge the competency status quo for fear of losing or dissatisfying existing customers. Some authors, such as Leonard-Barton, have pointed to the possibility of core competencies turning into 'core rigidities', emphasizing the potential of an inwardly driven focus on capabilities leading to resistance to change.[11]

'Prediction' vs. 'Learning' Approaches

The planning, balancing, positioning and resource-based approaches can also be termed 'predictive' approaches, as they all attempt to predict a particular environment and probable position or fit of a company within that environment through its strategic thrusts. With the increasing inability to predict the future, the focus of strategic management has to change fundamentally. Plans have now come to be seen not as descriptions of future performance, but as a basis for initiating flexible and speedy responses to a changing present. GE's Jack Welch shifted his attention in the 1990s from sophisticated strategic plans to the pressing current strategic issues that his company faced. Some Japanese companies, such as Matsushita, have explicitly adopted a philosophy that views strategic management not as a grand plan based on forecasts and insights about the future, but as a 'design of experiments' to provide a basis for learning and adaptation.[12]

Mintzberg is well-known for his criticism of 'predictive' approaches, which he terms the 'fallacy of prediction', and that strategy-making cannot be organized, formalized, or detached from operational issues.[13] He also distinguishes between strategy formation as either 'deliberate' or 'emergent', i.e. either a process of prediction, planning, and formalization, or as an on-going 'emergent' process resulting from various (ongoing) external impacts and internal decisions. 'Emergent' strategies are the result of a learning approach to strategic management, as reflected in the dynamic capabilities view that arose especially in the latter part of the 1990s (see Table 2.1).

The 'learning' approach to strategic management changes the character of the concepts and techniques commonly utilized in the 'prediction' approach. The task of strategic management is now one of managing adaptation, with the proposition that the only sustainable competitive advantage for an organization is the ability to learn faster than its competition. The 'learning' approach seems to have emanated from the seminal work of Peter Senge on organizational learning, which enjoyed considerable popularity during the 1990s.[14] The learning approach has proved its value to many organizations and intuitively makes sense in the innovation economy. Kaplan and Norton have incorporated this approach in a model of strategic management termed the 'balanced scorecard' (BSC), which indicates the dynamics and managerial requirements between learning, organizational processes, customer value, and profitability.[15]

The 'organizational learning' approach of the 1990s, however, has a serious deficiency, which renders it inadequate to cope with major discontinuities of the innovation economy. The learning approach (as conventionally formulated and applied) works well in evolutionary periods, and when focused on a single organization. When revolutions occur, with a blurring of boundaries between industries and firms, and various new forms of knowledge networking arise or exist, the learning approach is ineffective. When major discontinuity impacts, fundamental strategic remodeling (or new business models), and not strategic repositioning is necessary. Organizations are only recently becoming aware of the notion of how disruptive change occurs in living, organic, and open systems, and biologists and economists, among others, expect periods of equilibrium to be interrupted by major disruptions – so-called 'punctuated equilibrium'. Since the middle 1990s, the organizational learning approach has been extended by knowledge management (KM), and traditional strategic management practices have adopted KM with vigor, viewing it as a concept to improve organizational learning and thus competitive capabilities. However, even KM is inadequate as a basis for strategic management in the innovation economy, as innovation requires different corporate culture, focus, objectives, processes, systems, and performance measures to KM and organizational learning, as illustrated in Table 2.2.[16]

When evolution is replaced by revolution, or the potential for revolution, both the predictive and learning paradigms are ineffective. The existing strategic management system – including defined purpose (vision, mission, objectives, etc.), organizational structure, planning processes, measurement practices, core competency focus, human resource management, culture norms, and evaluation and reward systems – is more a source of organizational inertia than a proactive force for dynamic change. Prior experiences, business process improvement, balancing and "mapping" strategic processes, and historic "formulas" for success become more of impediments to innovative strategic management that is required for dealing with the turbulent innovation economy. Large incumbent firms in an industry, and those very successful in the past, are especially susceptible to becoming victims of traditional strategic management approaches.

Four Challenges to the Conventional Strategic Management Wisdom

Four significant challenges to the conventional strategic management wisdom can be identified, viz.:

- The dramatic shift from visible assets and invisible customers to invisible assets and visible customers.
- The reality that vertical and horizontal organizations are being displaced by networks of intrafirm, extrafirm, and interfirm relationships.
- Displacement of the focus on analytical deconstruction of competition (and competitive 'outperformance') and markets, to a focus on holistic construction and collaboration (and 'unique performance' and sustainability) for innovative value.
- Descriptive and reactive traditional strategic management mindsets being forced to shift to creative and proactive strategic mindsets.

Each of these four challenges is subsequently discussed.

Table 2.2 Differences between organizational learning, knowledge management, and innovation requirements in conceptual basis, focus, objective, culture, and other key dimensions

	Information systems infrastructure (ISI)	Intellectual property (IP)	Individual learning (IL)	Organizational learning (OL)	Knowledge management (KM)	Innovation (I)
Conceptual Basis	The worth of information for improved management	Codified knowledge as a capital asset	Both formal and informal training are required for learning	Enhancing the organization's ability to respond to change	Professional expertise can be leveraged through sharing	Creativity can be enhanced through purposeful diversity
Focus	Data and information	Tangible intellectual assets; patents, copy-rights, brands, trademarks, and other explicit knowledge	Creating more valuable human capital	Creating social capital; developing general competencies and capacities such as teamwork; anticipating change, and continuous improvement	Mission-specific professional expertise that is primarily tacit in nature	Creating new products, processes, and problem solutions
Objective	Provide decision support, control, and organizational performance data and information to organizational participants	Maximize return from intellectual property	To enhance the value of human capital through education and training	Facilitate group learning and group capacities for dealing with change	Acquire, explicate, and communicate professional expertise	Create potential for maximum return from new ideas and experiments
Processes	Acquisition, storage, dissemination, and application of data and information; systems development processes	Licensing; use of brokers to sell licensing rights	Formal training programs as well as apprenticeships, on-the-job training, etc.	Organizational development, teamwork, empowerment, case management, development-focused career paths, and quality programs	Benchmarking, best practices, expert networks, self-organizing groups, and communities of practice	Establishing revenue goals related to new products, brainstorming, making funding available for innovation projects, idea fairs, incubators
Systems	Computer and communications systems and applications; systems for planning, control, and decision support	Topical keyword search systems; databases of client needs	Computer-based training; career planning	Environmental scanning and competitive intelligence; CSCW, emergent systems, performance measurement systems, executive information systems, and "digital nervous" systems	Knowledge repositories and directories; expert systems, shared electronic workspaces, group support systems for problem solving	Group support systems for idea generation, online application and approval for funding of collaborative innovation projects in integrated demand & supply chains
Performance Measures	Efficiency and effectiveness of acquisition, storage, dissemination, and application of information; user satisfaction	Incremental ROI from new revenue streams; quantification of the value of intellectual property	Number of programs successfully completed; advancements of those trained	Cycle times and costs; productivity; customer satisfaction; quality; balanced score-cards (BSC)	Quality and timeliness of decisions; knowledge-sharing behavior; reuse of knowledge; maintaining pace of market leaders; balanced scorecards (BSC)	ROI from new products and processes, patents applied for and awarded, projects funded; systemic scorecards
Culture	Efficient operations; effective support of business functions; utilization of cutting-edge computer technology	Financial-based leveraging of existing property	"University" culture	"Change-friendly" culture	Knowledge-sharing culture	"Creativity-friendly" culture

The Dramatic Shift from Visible Assets and Invisible Customers to Invisible Assets and Visible Customers

As indicated in the previous part of this chapter, until recently the most important assets in the production of new societal value (products, services) have been land and capital in the form of machinery, raw materials, and cash. The financial statements of most companies are still mirroring the value of these visible, tangible assets. In the field of strategic management, the focus has been on managing these visible assets in such a way that shareholder value, i.e. return on shareholders' funds, is maximized. In the global knowledge economy of today, it is intangible capital which is becoming preeminent for improved performance and organizational fitness in a turbulent environment.

By having superior intellectual resources, an organization can exploit and develop its traditional visible resources better and differently than competitors, even if some or all of those traditional resources are not unique. Therefore, knowledge (for innovation) can be considered the most important (invisible) strategic resource of any company today, and the ability to identify, acquire, integrate, store, share, apply, and protect it, among other objectives, has significant implications for strategic management. The nature of invisible assets, and their sources and performance measurements, are radically different from those of visible assets, and require completely different strategic management approaches and tools.

Concomitant with the abovementioned shift, there is also a dramatic shift from invisible, group-segmented customers to visible, individualized customers. Developments, for example in technology and knowledge diffusion, are empowering both customers and organizations with individual customer profiles, interactions, and customized satisfaction now possible – even in industries with large numbers of consumers. Customers are increasingly being treated as individuals, not as objects belonging to a constructed segment or class of customer, which leads to closer connections and a richer diversity of innovative customer value propositions through formal arrangements, informal co-option techniques, monitoring techniques, and individualization/customization of products and services.

The change from customers as markets to customers as individuals represents a dramatic change from mass production to mass customization in an increasing number of industries. This shift means that conventional strategic management approaches and tools are significantly challenged – customers, industries, and competitors are not just "out there" or given, and not fully amenable to quantitative analysis based on the ideal of objectivity. Turning to individualization and co-evolution calls for changing the philosophy, approaches, and tools of strategic management.

The Reality that Vertical and Horizontal Organizations are Being Displaced by Networks of Intrafirm, Extrafirm, and Interfirm Relationships

Vertical and horizontal organizational structures are based on traditional thinking on how organizations allocate resources to achieve superiority and success. They display mechanistic, often one-directional "funnels" or "chains" of value-adding activities and relationships. A view of organizations as latent processes influenced and activated by empowered customers, on request, and empowered human resources inside and outside the organization, fundamentally change the strategic management perspective. As a consequence, we see that markets, functions, and hierarchies are being supplanted by network structures of multi-dimensional nature – i.e., not only vertical and horizontal, but on multi-dimensional levels.

Increasingly diverse networks of intrafirm relationships (inside organizations), extrafirm relationships (inside the firm's value system of suppliers, distributors, etc.), and interfirm relationships (with all relevant stakeholders in its ecosystem) are necessary. For example, customized production starts and ends with the customer, and the organization has to activate appropriate processes (inside and outside) rapidly in order to fulfill individual customer needs. The stable organizing element is not found in the structure of the organization, but in the structure of the evoked processes, and the traditional strategy-structure continuum becomes a meaningless relation as a dimension for determining the fit between an organization and the environment.

In effect, the tremendous shift to networking in demand and supply chains, wider business ecosystems, and the nurturing of relationships in the innovation economy points firstly to the necessity of a new strategic management mindset in which organizational structure is a variable, rather than a given or stable element. Every task that an organization must perform should be evaluated in terms of whether it should be done by the organization itself, or by some external supplier. Traditional strategic management approaches are unable to cope with the need for flexible organizational designs and redesigns, to not only respond to but also to inevitably stimulate changes. Secondly, assets are becoming parts of the environment, being no longer under company control or 'ownership'. In many industries today, companies can access the same assets, machinery, engineers, marketers, knowledge, and capital, and it is becoming very difficult to develop unique assets as a competitive 'weapon'. Instead, there is an increased focus on the human capital of an organization as a network-specific resource base, and not firm-specific only. The difference between organizations cannot be effected any more by strategies controlled by an ideal type of hierarchical machine, but rather in the uniqueness of how they organize and integrate networks of customers and human capital, and how they are continuously improving these relationships.

Displacement of the Focus on Competition through Analytical Deconstruction, to a Focus on Holistic Construction of Value through Collaboration

Competitive advantage, as displayed by all traditional strategic management approaches, reflects the underlying rationale of attempting to achieve an edge over rivals. A resource-based logic asserts that competitive advantage is the root of value creation, is sustainable, and can be achieved by exceptional scarce, valuable, inimitable, and non-substitutable assets. More recently, the dynamic capabilities approach contends that sustained competitive advantage is impossible in situations of hyper-competition and high-velocity environmental changes – according to this theory, firms should be enabled to repeatedly form new, albeit temporary, competitive advantages based on different asset combinations than the existing pattern. Such environments have been called "blue ocean" strategies by Kim and Maubourgne, because they involve innovative and wide-open competitive environments.[17]

The purpose displayed with the traditional approach is to be faster, better, cheaper, or more special than the competition. In the global innovation economy, the concept of competitive advantage is now being seen differently as: the firm's potential relative to the overall processes and resources in business ecosystems and organizational networks, with a balancing of competitive advantage with collaborative co-evolution. A sustained competitive advantage is regarded as a misplaced objective, even a possible self-defeating one, in a dynamic, nonlinear systems context. Thus, a firm's real 'competitive advantage' is both its contributions to the ecosystem and systemic enterprise, and acting as an essential 'attractor' shaping and influencing ecosystem patterns of behavior. The traditional focus on competition has the inherent dangers of a myopic view of the existing 'industry', 'market', and 'competitors'. This has been called a "red ocean" strategy by Kim and Maubourgne, because of its bloody, highly contested nature. Analytical deconstruction of these entities tends to lock mindsets in traditional boundaries and practices, while holistic construction through particular network collaboration unleashes innovative energy and new market value.

In many industries, the shift to both competitive and collaborative activity is evident, especially in collaborative enterprise resource management (ERM) and supply chains. The automobile industry has been highlighted as one prominent example, with collaboration at the one end of the automobile industry's 'value chain', and intense competition at the other end (the customer end). In global context, a focus towards collaboration in geographical industry clusters, such as a country's wine industry, is becoming prominent – for example, the Australian wine industry competes with the Californian wine industry through increasing internal collaboration, as well as external value system collaboration. Even the fiercest of competitors often find themselves acting in consortia to create new opportunities – witness Kodak and Fuji in jointly developing the advanced photo system, and GM and Toyota in the context of the NUMMI plant in automobile manufacturing in California.

Descriptive and Reactive Mindsets Being Forced to Shift to Innovative, Proactive Strategic Mindsets

Traditional strategic management approaches reflect a mindset to mirror the world in a descriptive sense – a complex and turbulent world 'out there'. This indicates a strategic imagination that identifies the patterns in the environment, labels the regularities that associates images necessary to cut through and perceive the mass of data generated by analysis, and utilize judgment and action based on experience. Roos and Victor indicate that a descriptive imagination manifests itself in the perceived need to 'see' five industry forces during a strategy-making process, and a range of diagnostic and forecasting techniques whereby the world is programmed, "mapped" and profiled[18] – value chains, '2-by-2' matrices, portfolio matrices, competitive 'diamonds', and internal scorecards all belong to this mindset.

The major fallacy of the descriptive strategic mindset is a continuously expanding range of new descriptions, such as different industry analyses, different SWOT analyses, different competence analyses, different portfolio analyses, different scenario analyses, different value chain and scorecard mapping, etc. All of these attempts are aimed at searching for a "perfect" strategy based on ever-increasing complex analyses, descriptions, and alternative reaction scenarios. The level of complexity of these models may exceed the ability of human strategists to attend to all of them.[19] Both the prediction and learning approaches to strategic management focus on analytical activities and gathering of experience, which, like data and information, are arguably essential resources for strategy making. Both Hamel, as well as Roos and Victor call for a new theory of strategy management that would enable the field to develop creative, proactive strategic mindsets.[20]

Are Traditional Strategic Management Approaches Irrelevant?

In closing, it should be emphasized that traditional strategic management approaches and tools are not entirely irrelevant or obsolete. There are situations in which prediction or learning approaches can be appropriate, but the key issue is that these approaches used on their own are likely to be ineffective in a turbulent, networked innovation economy. New forms of strategic management approaches are necessary, which are proactive, collaborative, and systemic, to constructively bridge the disruptions and discontinuities in the environment of the early 21st century. Acquiring a new strategic mindset, as a basis for understanding the nature and application of new strategic management approaches, is the theme of the next chapter.

Sparking Strategic Imagination[*]

By Johan Roos

Over the course of the past two decades, it has become increasingly, abundantly clear that companies must find ways to be more innovative, more flexible and better prepared.

Yet despite a steady supply of new jargon, models and techniques, the practices by which most companies create strategy have by and large not helped firms become more prepared for the unexpected. They remain mired in the mind-set of a very different and less complex competitive era. Strategy has been reduced to calculation and analysis, nearly devoid of the imaginative spark that could bring it to life. For the development *Truly innovative strategy must emanate from more than objective analysis.* and communication of strategy to become the inspired and inspiring process it must be, it is up to company leaders to alter their strategizing practices in three crucial, perhaps counterintuitive, ways.

Be More Subjective and Less Generic

Strategy theory and practice have always prized rational analysis and increasingly given it precedence over the wisdom born of experience. Consequently, strategy jargon, tools and practices have become homogenized, and strategies often represent generic constructs rather than the unique stance of a company's leadership. To create vibrant strategy, leaders have to create a culture that recognizes the valuable contribution, beyond purely objective thinking, that every strategist can make. Necessary analysis and assessments of facts should not be an excuse to avoid taking personal stances on critical matters. Facts should not be used to obscure or negate people's practical wisdom. If strategies are to be deeply insightful and keenly motivational, they must have an intuitive, subjective and imaginative component.

Explore New Ways to Stimulate Insights and Communication

Ever since the 1960s, strategists have been relying on abstract bubbles, grids and arrows to convey the essence of their businesses. The tradition of presenting strategies

---

[*] Taken with permission from *MIT Sloan Managament Review* Vol. 46 No. 1, Fall 2004, p.96

in textual and visual formats such as slide presentations and reports must be complemented with media more attuned to how people make sense of the world. Because knowledge stems from all our senses, not just from a "disembodied mind," kinesthetic processes often can access deeper insights than can verbal or written communication. When we use our hands, millions of neurons fire to help us describe, create and challenge what we are touching. Over the past few years, my colleagues and I have drawn upon established learning psychology to help many managers to "craft sense" of a variety of business challenges: The act of assembling objects in a carefully guided process – such as a three-dimensional model of the firm in its competitive landscape – can stimulate strategists to see the familiar in new ways and even create entirely new understandings of what needs to be done. Leaders who encourage experimentation with such practices can dramatically improve how strategies are developed, visualized and communicated, as well as understood.

Recognize that Context Matters

Onsite or offsite, strategizing is primarily confined to meeting rooms with laptops, PC projectors, video links, flipcharts and strong coffee. But a familiar meeting room at headquarters or a conference center is not necessarily the best place to stimulate and access people's imaginations, personal insights or their ability to make sense of a situation. In all endeavors, even the serious work of creating strategy, people are inspired – perhaps to breakthrough thinking – by their surroundings. Imagination is intertwined with our senses: Visions, goals and priorities look, sound, feel and smell very differently in the repair shop, call center or the reception area of a major client or supplier. Leaders should encourage strategists to break the old conventions of the strategizing milieu, thereby enabling them to make new connections between themselves, the task and the team. Corporate fascination with tedious analyses, spreadsheets and endless slideshows should be losing its luster, as it has often led to nothing but flawed and uninspired strategy. It is up to dissatisfied leaders to question the conventional formula and reinvent the components of strategy creation by engaging more of what makes people human – our imagination.

What Makes a Strategy Brilliant[*]

By Brian Huffman

"The art of war is simple; everything is a matter of execution."
Napoleon Bonaparte

"If you're so smart, why aren't you rich?"
Anonymous

Is strategy a joke? Does Napoleon's observation apply to business as well as war? Is business only a matter of "execution"? And if it is more than that, and if clever strategies really do win the day, then – seriously – why aren't all smart people rich?

"In many organizations," notes Hamel (1996), "corporate planning (strategy) departments are being disbanded ... [C]onsulting firms are doing less and less 'strategy' work and more and more 'implementation' work." Porter (1996), himself an ardent proponent of strategy, states that business has lost its faith in strategy, preferring to spend its time on "concrete" and "actionable" concerns such as operational effectiveness. Tom Peters has never had to pay the $100 he offered to the first manager who could demonstrate that a successful strategy had resulted from a planning process.

There are two possible explanations for the business world's disappointment with strategy. First, the science of strategy has not lived up to the expectation that it should provide us with strategy-making methods – a reasonable expectation since the very existence of strategy case courses presupposes those people who believe that such methods exist and can be taught. Still, there is little empirical evidence to suggest that strategies can be produced by teachable formal methods. In fact, brilliant strategies come from "beyond the box" thinking – beyond the box of tried and true methods, beyond the box of our current strategic paradigm.

Great works of art are produced without methods; so too are brilliant strategies. The secret lies in learning to recognize them and working hard to achieve them.

The second explanation is that business people know how often strategy can be overwhelmed by tactics. They are in a better position than ivory tower denizens to see the truth of Napoleon's words, to see that execution is critical. Wheeler (2000) describes two examples of strategies that were soundly defeated by tactics: Civil War General Joseph Hooker's "perfect plan" that

---

[*] Taken with permission from *Business Horizons*, July-August 2001, pp. 13-20

failed at Fredericksburg because of tactical actions on both sides; and a brilliant strategy at ABC that failed because of Ted Turner's bold tactical responses.

Although tactical actions generally flow from strategy, unexpected exigencies often call for tactics that radically depart from the strategic plan. A newly minted MBA does not generally expect the necessity of these departures nor appreciate the hard tactical work needed to make a strategy succeed.

Two points are to be made here. First, there are no methods for creating brilliant strategies; nonetheless, brilliant strategies can be produced in the absence of methods, and managers can at least learn to recognize them. Such an ability is important because true brilliance may come from organizational members who lack the political power to sell and implement it. Second, tactics are as important as strategy, and this importance needs to be emphasized.

Certain criteria can be used to help managers recognize brilliant strategy. Students should be taught to use these criteria in strategy-evaluating history courses (as opposed to the existing strategy-generating case courses). They must also be taught to appreciate the importance of tactics by the history course approach.

What's Wrong with Strategy?

A popular book on strategic management does not define the word *strategy* until page 127, the fourth page of the fourth chapter. It could be that students are not ready to understand that definition, which is fairly complex, until they have read the first 126 pages. But it could also be that the definition is overly complex. Strategy in business can be defined simply as the general statement of how a firm intends to win. Strategy is not specific; it is not a step-by-step plan. It is about the more distant future, whereas tactics are about the nearer future. Although strategy should be in place before the game begins, it may be modified, or even completely rewritten, by tactical actions as the game progresses.

Tactics can be defined simply as the competitive actions taken either to implement a strategy or to respond to a competitor's actions. Tactics are "strategy-in-process". If we have the initiative, our tactics are generally slave to our strategy; if the enemy has the initiative, our tactics are generally slave to his strategy.

Strategies do work. The success of the U.S. and allied forces in Operation Desert Storm was due in no small part to a clever end-run strategy. And strategies can be essential. In chess, states Gulko (1997), "everything hinges on the formulation of a long-term strategy."

Business strategy critics do not criticize strategy per se. No one would seriously maintain that companies would be better off running on instinct. However, there is still much to criticize. First there is serious doubt as to whether strategy-making can be taught at all. If one can strategize according to some method, then strategy-making can be taught; but if there is no method, then it cannot. Criticism can be classified according to the position the critic takes on the existence of a method. Critics maintain that the current strategic paradigm as outlined in the Figure 1:

1. is well suited as a method for generating strategies, if only it is applied correctly; or

2. can be used as a method for generating strategies after a recommended fix is made; or

3. cannot be used as a method for generating strategies no matter what changes are made and no matter how useful the paradigm may be for other purposes, such as evaluating strategy-because strategy-making methods cannot exist.

Three criticisms fall into the first category. Porter asserts that the strategic paradigm can be used to generate strategies, but that businesses have misused it and have become sidetracked into focusing on operational effectiveness rather than on strategy formulation. He believes that strategy is about "positioning", which requires trade-offs, and that most managers misunderstand the concept of trade-offs, incorrectly believing that they are unnecessary. Henderson (1989) accepts the strategic paradigm as a strategy generator, but states that more effort needs to be expended in understanding competitive behavior in the market. Brandenburger and Nalebuff (1995) also accept the paradigm as a strategy generator, but feel that Porter's Five Forces deserve more emphasis.

The criticisms of Courtney, Kirkland, and Viguerie (1997) and Hamel (1996) fit into the second category. Courtney et al. maintain that the current paradigm is useful only for generating strategies for businesses facing low levels of uncertainty, and offer an alternative approach for businesses facing higher levels of uncertainty. Hamel believes strategy must be revolutionary and points out that the current paradigm is about planning, not strategizing. He is especially critical of two of the key players in the current paradigm: top management and planning specialists (technocrats). Top management, he maintains, is often too vested in maintaining the status quo to allow the necessary revolution to take place. And asking planning technocrats to deliver a creative strategy, he says, is "like asking a bricklayer to create Michelangelo's Pieta." Nevertheless, Hamel's criticism belongs in the second category because he does not entirely give up the hope that a process does exist for generating strategy. In fact, he recommends a process in which strategy development is supposed to be "bottom-up" (or democratic) to achieve diversity of perspective and at the same time be "top-down" (or management-directed) to achieve unity of purpose. He does not, however, clarify how a process is supposed to begin at both ends of the organizational spectrum simultaneously.

Hamel and Prahalad (1989) fall somewhere between the second and third categories. They imply that no paradigm would be very useful for making strategy, and are "not comforted" by the thought that the current one "can be reduced to eight rules for excellence, seven S's, five competitive forces, four product life cycle stages, three generic strategies, and innumerable two-by-two matrices." They point out that even "reasonable strategic concepts" like the product life cycle often have "toxic side effects", such as creating a preference for selling businesses rather than defending

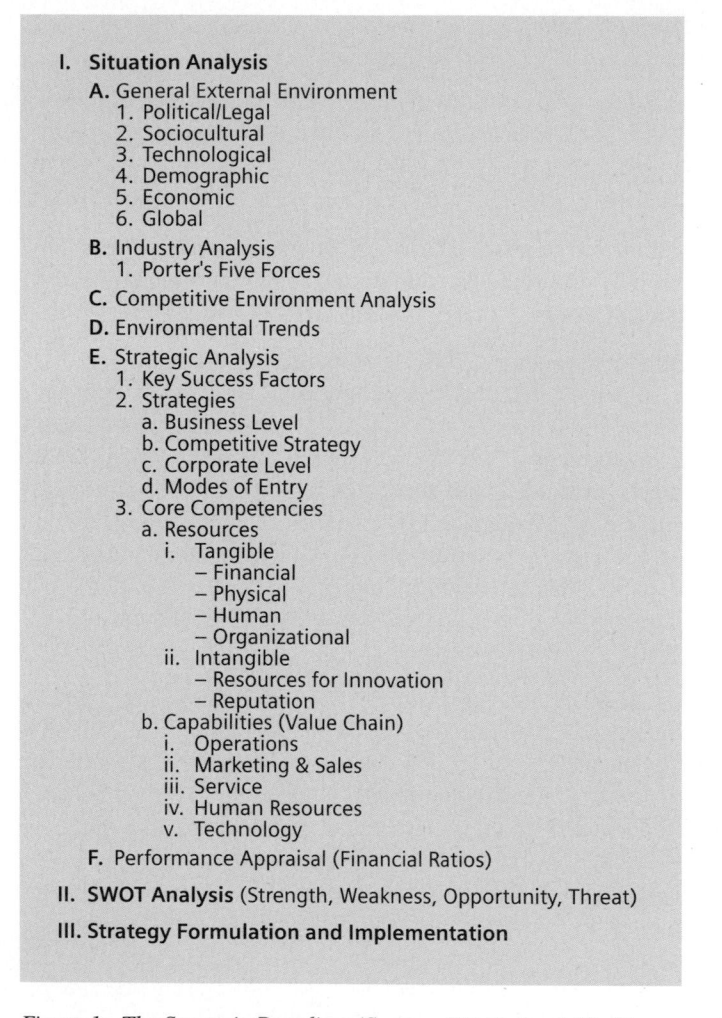

I. **Situation Analysis**

   A. General External Environment
      1. Political/Legal
      2. Sociocultural
      3. Technological
      4. Demographic
      5. Economic
      6. Global

   B. Industry Analysis
      1. Porter's Five Forces

   C. Competitive Environment Analysis

   D. Environmental Trends

   E. Strategic Analysis
      1. Key Success Factors
      2. Strategies
         a. Business Level
         b. Competitive Strategy
         c. Corporate Level
         d. Modes of Entry
      3. Core Competencies
         a. Resources
            i. Tangible
               – Financial
               – Physical
               – Human
               – Organizational
            ii. Intangible
               – Resources for Innovation
               – Reputation
         b. Capabilities (Value Chain)
            i. Operations
            ii. Marketing & Sales
            iii. Service
            iv. Human Resources
            v. Technology

   F. Performance Appraisal (Financial Ratios)

II. **SWOT Analysis** (Strength, Weakness, Opportunity, Threat)

III. **Strategy Formulation and Implementation**

Figure 1: The Strategic Paradigm (Source: Hitt, Ireland, Hoskisson, and Nixon 1997)

them. And they argue that using the current paradigm as a strategy generator results in predictable strategies that can easily be decoded by rivals.

Mintzberg's (1994) criticism fits into the third category. He points out that methods for generating strategies rest on three fallacies: that prediction is possible, that strategy can be developed by staff specialists who are not involved in the day-to-day operations of the business, and above all, that strategy-making can be formalized. He says that innovation, a necessary characteristic of a good strategy, has never been institutionalized "and likely never will be."

Mintzberg, as well as Campbell and Alexander (1997) and Freedman (1992), all reject the possibility of a methodology or formalized process for developing strategy, insisting that strategies can only come from experienced managers who intuitively understand key interrelationships that influence behavior in their businesses. In such a view, strategic planning specialists cannot hope to understand a business system the way managers do, so only experienced managers are capable of making the important big-picture observations necessary to formulate brilliant strategy. Mintzberg calls this capability "synthesis", Campbell and Alexander call it "insight", and Freedman calls it "systems thinking" or "seeing wholes" (terms he credits to Peter Senge).

In considering the question of what method companies should use to develop the insights they need to strategize, Campbell and Alexander admit, "The answer is, we don't know. Rival camps sell different solutions, but none has been able to demonstrate that its solutions are clearly the best. In fact, since strategy is about insights, almost by definition there is no best way."

Ohmae (1982) also rejects the notion that teachable methods exist for making brilliant strategy. He believes that strategies come from a particular state of mind rather than from rigorous analysis or some rote process. He also shows, an awareness of the political power issue, noting that in Japan "chief executives are typically over 60 – well past the age when they are likely to be able to generate dynamic strategic ideas."

Can Strategy Be Made by a Method?

If, as many believe, there are no methods for generating strategies, must we then give up the search? If the present strategic paradigm does not work as a method for developing strategies, does that mean a method cannot be found? Is it reasonable to expect that strategy-generating methods exist?

Strategy-making Methods and "Newness"

"Normal science ..., often suppresses fundamental novelties because they are necessarily subversive of its basic commitments ... No part of the aim of normal science is to call forth new sorts of phenomena; indeed, those that will not fit the box are often not seen at all. Nor do scientists normally aim to invent new theories, and they are often intolerant of those invented by others. Instead, normal-scientific research is directed to the articulation of those phenomena and theories that the paradigm already supplies."
    Kuhn (1996)

Kuhn's words apply to any normal science, including the social science of business strategy. Therefore, the science of business strategy does not involve a search for new phenomena any more than the normal science of classical physics involved a search for modern physics. The unpleasant and inescapable truth for all those involved in strategy research is this: If making strategy is essentially about making something "new" (and many argue that this is the case), then strategy-making is beyond normal science.

In the late 1970s and early 1980s, the Japanese taught American manufacturers a new strategic paradigm in the school of hard knocks. The Japanese strategy of manufacturing products that were simultaneously high in quality and low in cost was well beyond the box of the existing Western strategic paradigm (according to which those goals should have been mutually exclusive). Nothing about the normal practice of business strategy at that time would have led an American company to develop a strategy that could have protected itself against the Japanese attack, since that sort of attack was considered impossible.

Serious errors in the strategic paradigm of the 1970s became more and more obvious, and by the late 1980s strategy writers clearly had begun to smell a rat. As Hamel and Prahalad observed, "As 'strategy' has blossomed, the competitiveness of Western companies has withered. This may be a coincidence, but we think not."

But didn't the Japanese produce their strategy using a paradigm? Hardly. As Womack, Jones, and Roos demonstrated in their 1990 The Machine That Changed the World, the Japanese strategy of simultaneously pursuing high quality and low cost was not the result of strategic thinking on their part, but rather an evolutionary adaptation to the poverty they experienced after World War II. Whatever their implicit paradigm may have been, it was not written down and was not being taught as a method for creating strategy. Mintzberg and Lampel (1999) note that there are even strategy researchers who believe the Japanese have no strategic paradigm.

"Strategies may be the result of evolution or learning, rather than planning, more often than business leaders would like to admit."

Evolution (as opposed to any strategic paradigm) as the source of successful strategy has been recognized in the literature. Laudon and Laudon (1998), for example, note, "Studies of successful strategic systems have found that they are rarely planned but instead evolve slowly over a long time." Indeed, so many authors believe in evolution as a source of strategy that Mintzberg and Lampel have identified the "learning school" as one of the ten dominant schools of thought in business strategy.

Strategies may be the result of evolution or learning, rather than planning, more often than business leaders would like to admit. H. Edward Wrapp (1984), himself a business executive, saw evolution as the dominant process. He observed that corporate strategy is not the result of a planning process, but the outgrowth of day-to-day operating decisions by top-level managers who get involved in low-level decisions both to stay informed and to push the company in the direction they want it to move. Wrapp's work shows that, like Napoleon, top managers concentrate on tactics rather than on making sweeping policy decisions – which they seem to believe could straitjacket the organization.

"Newness", then, is not to be found in strategic paradigms. Normal science does not seek new phenomena, and the strategic paradigm is normal science. Therefore, if newness is a requisite of successful strategy (and authors such as Prahalad insist on this), then successful strategies cannot be generated by strategic paradigms.

Strategy-making Methods and Predictability

Despite what Prahalad and others say, maybe "newness" is not absolutely required for strategic success. There are not many truly new moves in chess, but chess matches are still won by using standard moves unpredictably. It is, after all, fairly rare that one faces an opponent like the Japanese, who have been spawned in an entirely different competitive ocean and who therefore play by a completely new set of rules. Even if a teachable strategic paradigm cannot be used to generate truly new strategies, might it not at least be capable of generating strategies that are unexpected and therefore successful?

"Rommel, you magnificent bastard, I read your book!"
   George C. Scott as General Patton in the motion picture Patton, when he was pummeling
   Rommel's forces after having studied Rommel's book and anticipated his strategy

"It should be noted that Japan has never preceded hostile action by a
declaration of war. We have concluded that it is a possibility a fast-
raiding Japanese carrier force might arrive in Hawaiian waters with no
prior warning from our intelligence services. The most favorable time to
the enemy would be dawn. He would probably employ a maximum of six
carriers and strike on a weekend."
   U.S. Army/Navy Report accurately predicting Japanese attack on Pearl Harbor, 1941

"We're glad to find a competitor managing by the portfolio concept –
we can almost predict how much share we'll have to take away to put
the business on the CEO's sell list."
   Anonymous senior executive (Hamel and Prahalad 1989)

The above three quotes are witness to the fact that strategy-generating methods yield predictable strategies. Predictable strategies do not necessarily lose; the Japanese did very well with their "predictable" attack on Pearl Harbor. In fact, strategies often succeed precisely because they do conform to the common sense embedded in the prevailing paradigm. Nevertheless, they are expected by the enemy and will hardly catch him completely flatfooted. In spectacular upsets and stunning victories, one usually sees the unpredictable, the "revolution", such as in the Japanese business strategy of high quality and low cost.

Keegan (1973) states that between the first and second world wars, the highest echelons of the German military "formed the opinion that the tank could be discounted as a weapon of war ... and not, as the British tank pioneers were beginning to perceive, of strategic, perhaps even war-winning significance." Fortunately for them, lower-ranking officers such as Heinz Guderian did not buy in to that. German victories in France at the beginning of WWII depended on the unpredictably swift advance of their army, which would not have been possible had Germany stuck to its outdated paradigm.

General Robert E. Lee also fought in an unpredictable manner by often running absolutely contrary to the accepted military strategic paradigm of his day, dividing his forces in the face of vastly larger enemy forces. He achieved his many victories not in spite of having divided his forces, but *because* he divided them.

Young and Bradley (1995) and Alexander (1993) both describe how a bad strategy (according to the existing paradigm) became a good one in the Inchon landing during the Korean War. General Douglas MacArthur proposed landing there knowing it was such a "terrible idea" that the North Koreans would never expect it.

The successes of MacArthur, Guderian, and Lee are not unique in history; winning strategies have often involved doing something completely unpredictable in that it is contrary to the existing strategic paradigm. This observation actually goes back to the very origins of Western strategic thought, to Heraclitus of Ephesus (ca. 500 BC), who delineated a concept known as "the coincidence of opposites." According to this concept, it is sometimes smart to avoid better ways of attacking because that is just what the enemy expects. Thus, "bad strategy" (that contrary to the paradigm) is good strategy because it is unpredictable.

So once again the strategic paradigm fails. Strategies generated by strategic paradigms are predictable, and predictable strategies are bad. But although we may never find methods to generate brilliant business strategies, all is not lost. Brilliance will still pop up. It will come about as it always has, either as part of an evolutionary process or as the product of an unknown anti apparently unknowable process inside the head of the experienced manager. Making brilliant strategy is not the problem; the problem is being able to recognize it when we see it. This is especially important because, again, the most creative strategies may come from those with the least power to promote them successfully.

Recognizing Brilliant Strategy

There are two problems with the way strategy is taught in universities vis-a-vis the way it is used in industry. The first is that the focus has been on developing strategies rather than on evaluating them. The second is that the importance of tactics has been badly understated. Here we focus on the first problem by suggesting a number of useful criteria to be used in recognizing brilliant strategy. It should be clear that even if a strategy is judged on the basis of the following criteria to be brilliant, it could nonetheless subsequently fail (although brilliant strategies should generally outperform the lesser ones).

"The successes of MacArthur, Guderian, and Lee are not unique in history; winning strategies have often involved doing something completely unpredictable in that it is contrary to the existing strategic paradigm."

Evaluation Criteria from the Science of Business Strategy

The strategic paradigm outlined in Figure 1 is an obvious first place to look for criteria to evaluate business strategy. It may seem inconsistent to reject that paradigm for the purpose of making strategy while accepting it for the purpose of evaluation. But the tasks of making and evaluating are not the same. According to the paradigm, a business strategy should be judged good or bad based on the following:

1. How well does it fit the general external environment? Does it consider the political/legal, sociocultural, technological, economic, demographic, and global aspects of the outside world?
2. How well does it fit the industry in question (Porter's Five Forces)?
3. Does it consider environmental trends?
4. How well does it identify key success factors and deal with their ramifications?
5. How well does it take advantage of the firm's current core competencies, or call for acquiring core competencies necessary for the strategy to succeed?

Evaluation Criteria from Military Science

Although articles on business strategy often refer to or derive from military strategy, it is often argued that the business and military worlds are too different for cross-fertilization. For one thing, much is usually made of the difference between their respective goals. In particular, business writers like Brandenburger note that business is not necessarily a zero-sum game. But neither is war. Neo-Clausewitzians, says Anatol Rapoport in his 1968 introduction to Clausewitz's *On War,* have "gone to great lengths to explain the limitations of the zero-sum game as a paradigm of conflict, and to point out that even enemies have some common interests."

Conversely, business, like most wars, can result in zero-sum. Strategy textbooks have begun to reflect the warlike, competitive nature of business by including chapters on competitive response, rather than leaving students with the naive assumption that our competitors will sit back and do nothing while we eat their lunch. Ohmae also stresses the more aggressive nature of business, stating that "without competition there would be no need for strategy."

If the military and business worlds are not that different, then criteria used to judge military strategy may be useful in judging business strategy as well. The U.S. Army uses two sets of criteria to evaluate strategy: the "Tenets of Army Operations" and the "Principles of War." The former is for an ex post analysis, whereas the latter is for evaluating a strategy a priori – the time orientation we want to take in evaluating business strategy. Thus, a military or business strategy is judged brilliant if it is in accordance with the nine principles of war: it has a clear objective; it has an offensive orientation; it masses resources at one decisive place and time; it uses forces economically; it calls for maneuvers that give our forces the situational advantage; it institutes unity of command; it considers the security of our forces; it will surprise the enemy; and it is simple.

Evaluation Criteria from Art Criticism

Strategic thinking is an art, and thus a particular strategy is a work of art. So we should be able to judge a strategy the way we judge art. There are three basic questions in art criticism: What was the artist trying to do? Given that, how well was it done? And was it worth doing?

The film *Raiders of the Lost Ark* may not seem like great art, but it is nonetheless judged as great because it scored well on those three questions. The director tried to recreate the feeling of the old Saturday morning movie serials, that feeling was achieved (it was well done), and the result was a very entertaining film (it was worth doing).

The art criticism questions could easily be adapted for evaluating business strategy. A strategist should know what he is trying to do, so the first question is easily answered. Whether or not the strategy was worth doing will depend on the value the critic assigns to the task the strategist set for himself (for example, a strategy that is expected to increase the bottom line by 20 percent is certainly worth doing). The question of how well the strategy is done will depend on the critic's subjective judgment (which may be disconcerting to the strategist, but agreement among strategy critics may be fairly strong, as is often the case in art criticism).

Evaluation Criteria from Game Theory

Modern game theory was developed to help explain the complex web of natural competition. As in business, players in games of strategy have a choice of action, and their actions are interdependent. Surprisingly, the optimal strategy in game theory is based on the pessimistic assumption that one's opponent already knows one's strategy. A player with this degree of pessimism will only launch a strategy so good that it does not need secrecy to be successful. In games in which there is imperfect information (such as in poker as opposed to chess), the optimal strategy also requires players to distribute their bluffs irregularly on a controlled probability basis. Players who do not bluff telegraph perfect information to their opponents (forfeiting the benefit of imperfect information).

Two criteria for business strategy evaluation can be inferred here. First, business strategies that do not depend on secrecy can be judged superior to those that do. Second, strategies that effectively employ disinformation (bluffing) can be judged superior to those that either do not use disinformation or use it poorly.

Evaluation Criteria from Artificial Intelligence and Chess

The chess world was shocked when IBM's Deep Blue computer bested world chess champion Garry Kasparov 3 $\frac{1}{2}$ to 2 $\frac{1}{2}$. Krol (1999) even speculated that the world may have seen the first demonstration of a computer passing the Turing test – the acid test for demonstrating that artificial intelligence has been achieved. And in a *Time* article two weeks after his defeat in May 1997, Kasparov said that in Game 2 "we saw something that went well beyond our wildest expectations of how well a computer would be able to foresee the long-term positional consequences of its decisions." Kasparov even described Deep Blue in nearly human terms as "psychologically stable, undisturbed, and unconcerned."

On the other hand, Gulko (1997) maintains that Deep Blue was not playing according to any strategy, that "even after Kasparov found himself in a truly horrendous bind, the computer made an entirely pointless move", and that Deep Blue demonstrated many times that it was playing with no sort of discernible plan. "Deep Blue made senseless if typically computer-like moves," he says, "and was thus far from passing the Turing test for artificial intelligence." Moreover, Gulko notes, far from being "human-like", Deep Blue's play lacked creativity, imagination, intuition, and planning.

Two criteria for business strategy evaluation can be derived from these observations. First, good strategies need to be creative. Second, they must reflect a purpose. A strategy can be judged creative if, for example, it is a surprise to the evaluator. It can be judged as reflecting a purpose if it projects far into the future, anticipating several rounds of competitive moves, responses, and countermoves.

The Strategy Classroom

Anyone who has ever learned to play a game of strategy knows that the key to winning is experience. It would certainly be silly to expect someone who has just learned the rules of chess to play his first game with any measure of strategic creativity.

A Little League coach once attempted to teach baseball strategy to a group of fourth-graders. It was not a pretty picture. The players lay in a semicircle around the coach watching the clouds roll along while he engaged in an animated (but completely ignored) soliloquy about what a player should do when, say, there was one out and a runner on third. Even if the kids had had the temperament to listen, they would still have been unable even to understand, much less appreciate, the advice being given.

Coaches and college professors may like to talk about strategy, but unless they are talking to experienced players their message will be over the listeners' heads. Strategy-making is learned by playing, not by listening.

It may seem that solving cases in a case course is playing the game, and that the students should learn how to make strategies as they work through more and more cases. The problem with that argument, however, is that each business situation is so unique that each case is really a completely different game. The business student, in effect, plays only one game of baseball, one game of hockey, and so on.

Moreover, the strategy case study is a safe and "dumbed-down" version of the real game-safe because the situation is not real, dumbed down because it gives the student all the information necessary (presumably) to produce a winning strategy. This pre-packaging of salient information may lead students to assume that only information that is readily obtainable is relevant, or to become overconfident in their ability to recognize salient factors in the real world where they must actually hunt for them. Students may inadvertently be taught to believe that industry experience is not necessary – one need only breeze in, look at the facts, and put together a guaranteed winning strategy.

Finally, case studies are not always completely honest. They often direct students toward desirable conclusions. It is difficult to see how students could learn to produce truly "out of the box" solutions when cases are designed to push them into a box.

How else might business strategy courses be taught? They could be taught as history courses – the same approach the military uses in teaching strategy. Students could be told what strategy an unidentified business intended to pursue in a situation disguised so that they would not know whether or not the strategy was ultimately successful, and could therefore evaluate it without the benefit of 20/20 hindsight. Such histories would sometimes involve strategies that had been winners and sometimes those that had been losers. The goal would be to teach students to apply the evaluation criteria and recognize the winners.

Students could also evaluate subsequent tactical moves (again without the benefit of knowing whether or not those tactics succeeded). The goal would be to instill a respect for the hard work involved in making strategies succeed, then to create the awareness that strategies are not cast in stone – deviations sometimes must be made.

The military has found that generals, such as George Patton, who have a firm grasp of military history are the ones best able to recognize brilliant strategies. They are also the ones most capable of eventually learning what cannot be taught: how to create brilliant ones themselves.

It is unfortunate that neither the present approach to strategy education nor this new approach will produce students who can immediately create brilliant strategies. This recommended approach, however, at least recognizes that fact and focuses efforts on what can be done.

Max Planck, the father of quantum theory and therefore the father of modern physics, once said that his discoveries were so incredible he had a hard time believing them himself. Just as it was especially difficult for a physicist to see that classical physics was seriously flawed, it will be especially difficult for business strategists to see that business strategy is likewise flawed. Nevertheless, a change in the focus of strategy is needed.

The present focus on formalized processes for creating strategies needs to give way to a focus on criteria for evaluating them and an emphasis on the importance of tactics in making or breaking them. Strategy case courses need to be recast as strategy history courses, with an emphasis on evaluating strategies and being able to recognize brilliant ones when we see them. Universities and business trainers would not be producing strategists – but they aren't producing them now. They would, however, be producing students who may save good strategies from being overlooked and who have a healthy respect for both industry experience and the power of tactics.

Strategic Sourcing – from Periphery to the Core[*]

By Mark Gottfredson, Rudy Puryear, and Stephen Phillips

Outsourcing has become strategic – yet many executives remain unprepared. A new era of capability sourcing will trigger organizational redesign and require a new set of managerial skills.

For years, "sourcing" has been just another word for procurement – a financially material, but strategically peripheral, corporate function. Now, globalization, aided by rapid technology innovation, is changing the basis of competition. It's no longer a company's *ownership* of capabilities that matters but rather its ability to *control and make the most of critical capabilities*, whether or not they reside on the company's balance sheet. Outsourcing is becoming so sophisticated that even core functions like engineering, R&D, manufacturing, and marketing can – and often should be moved outside. And that, in turn, is changing the way firms think about their organizations, their value chains, and their competitive positions.

Forward-thinking companies are making their value chains more elastic and their organizations more flexible. And with the decline of the vertically integrated business model, sourcing is evolving into a strategic process for organizing and fine-tuning the value chain. The question is no longer whether to outsource a capability or activity but rather *how* to source every single activity in the value chain. This is the new discipline of "capability sourcing."

Perhaps the best window on the new sourcing landscape is a handful of vanguard companies that are transforming what used to be purely internal corporate functions into entirely new industries. Firms like United Parcel Service in logistics management, Solectron in contract manufacturing, and Hewitt Associates in human resource management have created new business models by concentrating scale and skill within a single function. As these and other function-based companies grow, so does the potential value of outsourcing to all companies.

It's not always obvious which functions have the most potential for developing scale and skill. Virgin, for instance, has successfully extended its brand management capabilities from planes and trains to music, mobile phones, personal finance, and even

---

[*] Taken with permission from *Harvard Business Review*, Vol. 83, No. 2, Febuary 2005, pp. 132-139

bridal wear. And you might still think of Nike as a sneaker and sportswear company. But as it lends its brand and merchandising expertise to an increasing array of products – from golf instruction centers to MP3 players to eyewear – it's evolving into a focused provider of marketing services to other companies.

Migrating from a vertically integrated company to a specialized provider of a single function is not a winning strategy for everyone. But all companies need to rigorously assess each of their functions to determine in which they have sufficient scale and differentiated skills and in which they don't. Greater focus on capability sourcing can improve a company's strategic position by reducing costs, streamlining the organization, and improving quality. Finding more-qualified partners to provide critical functions usually allows companies to enhance the core capabilities that drive competitive advantage in their industries.

Yet despite the enormous opportunities available through capability sourcing, our research indicates that many executives remain unprepared for this transformation. A recent Bain survey of large and medium-sized companies reports that 82% of large firms in Europe, Asia, and North America have outsourcing arrangements of some kind, and 51% use offshore outsourcers. But almost half say their outsourcing programs fall short of expectations, only 10% are highly satisfied with the costs they're saving, and a mere 6% are highly satisfied with their offshore outsourcing overall.

The reason these efforts often fail to measure up to expectations, even purely in terms of cost savings, is that most companies continue to make sourcing decisions on a piecemeal basis. They have not put hard numbers against the potential value of capability sourcing, and they've been slow to develop a comprehensive sourcing strategy that will keep them competitive in a global economy. To realize the full potential of sourcing, companies must forget the old peripheral and tactical view and make it a core strategic function.

In this article, we'll describe how and why the role of sourcing is changing in the twenty-first-century economy and lay out a practical strategic framework to guide companies through the transition.

The Changing Basis of Competitive Advantage

For over a century, companies competed on the basis of the assets they owned. AT&T, with its direct control of the American telephone network; Bethlehem Steel, with its large-scale manufacturing plants; and Exxon, with its vast oil reserves, each dominated its respective industry. But in the 1980s, the basis of competition began to shift from hard assets to intangible capabilities. Microsoft, for example, became the de facto standard in the computing industry through its skill in writing and marketing software. Wal-Mart transformed retailing through its proprietary approach to supply chain management and its information-rich relationships with customers and suppliers.

A similar shift occurred in the worldwide auto industry. When U.S. automakers began losing market share to Japanese companies, they were forced to confront a growing gap in both cost and quality. Recognizing that upstream component quality was critical to their end product and seeing the success of the Japanese *keiretsu* model of networked suppliers, the Big Three began to move design, engineering, and manufacturing work to specialized partners. They hammered out strategic sourcing relationships for complex subassemblies such as seats, steering columns, and braking systems. To win a significant share of their business, chosen suppliers had to meet tough cost and quality specifications. More important to ensure the long-term success of a partnership, both parties had to open their books, sharing detailed information that became the basis for continual quality and cost improvements over many years. Both parties shared in the savings generated from improved efficiency, which provided ongoing incentives to identify and remove unnecessary costs.

This new approach to sourcing had profound effects on the automakers' operations and management. For example, Chrysler established what it called "value managed relationships," in which it consolidated component purchases with the few suppliers it believed could sustain competitive costs, high quality, and efficient delivery. The carmaker and its key suppliers set a common goal of achieving the lowest total systems cost. Before it could reach this goal, however, Chrysler had to refocus its entire procurement function so that it could manage the new, highly collaborative sourcing relationships. That required the company to train and promote a different kind of manager who was capable of understanding system economics, not just one who knew how to nickel-and-dime the supplier base.

The same dynamics were also at work in the credit card industry, which restructured in response to a dramatic change in the basis of competition fueled by technological innovation. In the 1970s, most banks that issued credit cards also processed their own transactions in a very labor-intensive manner. But as computers automated transaction processing, the economies of scale grew significantly, and individual issuers started to pool their transactions to drive down costs. The industry began to separate into those companies that issued cards and managed customers, on the one hand, and those that processed transactions, on the other, as transaction-processing underwent rapid commoditization.

It's no Longer Ownership of Capabilities that Matters but Rather a Company's Ability to Control and Make the Most of Critical Capabilities.

For example, despite having enviable scale in its own transaction-processing operations, American Express, in a prescient strategic move, spun off its transaction-processing business in 1992. Then the company negotiated a long-term service contract with the newly independent entity, First Data. Although Amex executives considered transaction processing a strategic capability – without reliable and efficient processing, it was very difficult to make money in the credit card business – they also saw that commoditization was eliminating any proprietary advantage. As a spin-off, First Data could aggregate Amex's volume with that of other companies (issuing banks would have been reluctant to outsource processing to Amex as a competitor), in that way, American Express could gain additional scale advantages while ensuring long-term cost effectiveness. Going forward, Amex was able to focus on the issuing side of the credit card business and enhance its core capabilities in marketing and risk management.

The decisions Chrysler and American Express made required them to challenge one of the basic tenets of business strategy: that you should always keep strategic capabilities within your walls. As globalization and technology transform more industries, all companies will eventually have to let go of that comfortable but simplistic guideline. A series of geopolitical, macroeconomic, and technological trends has opened the world's markets, made business capabilities much more portable, and produced a level of discontinuity that has no precedent in modern economic history. These events include the fall of the Berlin wall, China's embrace of capitalism, the advent of worldwide tariff reduction agreements, and the spread of cheap, accessible telecommunications infrastructure. In the new era of capability sourcing, companies' value chain decisions will increasingly shape their organizations and determine the kinds of managerial skills they need to acquire and develop in order to survive amid increasingly fluid industry boundaries.

Capability Sourcing at 7-Eleven

To illustrate the power of capability sourcing, let's take a detailed look at one dramatically successful practitioner, which began as a most traditional, vertically integrated company.

Back in 1991, when 7-Eleven's current CEO Jim Keyes was named vice president of planning and chairman of the executive committee, the retailer was losing both money and market share. As the major oil companies added minimarts to more and more of their gas stations, the convenience store industry was becoming crowded and cut-throat, putting both revenue and margins under intense pressure. To attract more customers, 7-Eleven needed to cut its operating costs substantially, expand the range of its products and services, and increase the freshness of food items.

Keyes launched a business review aimed at tightening operations, rebuilding competitive advantage, and perhaps divesting a few noncore businesses. The deeper he and his team got, however, the more apparent it became that 7-Eleven was trying to do too many things and was not good enough at any of them. The core of the business, Keyes believed, was merchandising skill – the pricing, positioning, and promotion of gasoline, ready-to-eat food, and sundries for consumers driving cars. But 7-Eleven had always been vertically integrated, controlling most of the activities in its value chain. The company operated its own distribution network, delivered its own gasoline, made its own candy and ice. It even owned the cows that produced the milk it sold. Managers were required to do lots of things other than merchandising – store maintenance, credit card processing, payroll, and IT systems management. Keyes found it hard to believe that the company could be best-in-class in every one of those functions.

As part of his initial assessment, Keyes studied the company's highly successful Japanese unit, whose keiretsu model of tight partnerships with suppliers was unique within 7-Eleven. By relying on an extensive and carefully managed web of suppliers to carry out many day-to-day functions, the Japanese stores were able to reduce their costs and enhance the quality of their operations, spurring rapid growth and strong profits. After considering many options, Keyes concluded that the best way to save the U.S. company was to adopt the Japanese model. The goal he set was to "outsource everything not mission critical." This marked an abrupt and deliberate break with the company's vertically integrated past.

All activities were on the table. Keyes's team even evaluated strategic functions such as product distribution, advertising, and procurement, attempting to identify outside partners with greater expertise and scale. Simply put, if a partner could provide a capability more effectively than 7-Eleven could itself, then that capability became a candidate for outsourcing. Over time, the company relinquished direct ownership of many parts of its business, including HR, finance, IT management, logistics, distribution, product development, and packaging. Yet despite moving at a rapid pace, Keyes remained cautious about losing control and avoided the temptation to take a one-size-fits-all approach to outsourcing.

The way 7-Eleven has structured each partnership depends on how important each function is to the company's competitive distinctiveness. For routine capabilities like benefits administration and accounts payable, 7-Eleven picks providers that can consistently fulfill cost and quality requirements. More strategic capabilities require more complex arrangements. Gasoline retailing, for example, represents an important source of revenue to many 7-Elevens, as gas is often the reason customers come to the stores. So while the firm outsources gasoline distribution to Citgo, it maintains proprietary control over gas pricing and promotion – activities that could differentiate its stores if done well.

The company has paid similarly close attention to its relationship with Frito-Lay, since snack foods are one of the most important product lines for convenience stores. By allowing Frito-Lay to distribute its products directly to the stores, 7-Eleven has been able to take advantage of the chip maker's vast warehousing and transport system. But unlike other convenience store companies, 7-Eleven doesn't allow Frito-Lay to make critical decisions about order quantities or shelf placement. Instead, the retailer mines its extensive data on local customer purchasing patterns to make those decisions on a store-by-store basis.

The choice 7-Eleven has made to maintain control over product selection and stocking illustrates a critical issue in strategic sourcing partnerships: when to keep vital data confidential and when to share them with a partner. Similarly key was 7-Eleven's decision to rely on an outside vendor, IRI, to maintain and format detailed customer purchasing behavior data while keeping the data themselves proprietary. This gives 7-Eleven a picture of the mix of products its customers want in different locations without relying on outside decision makers like Frito-Lay for such information. In this way, 7-Eleven is able to structure its supplier relationships to gain a capability without relinquishing control over decisions that could make or break its business.

The Endgame: Dynamic Sourcing

Given the rapidly shifting contours of the global economy, companies need to be able to anticipate changes in the economics and geography of outsourcing. It wasn't long ago, for example, that most big companies had to own their own warehouses and operate their own distribution systems. Third party logistics specialists had neither the skill nor the scale to handle those functions. But today, suppliers like UPS and FedEx are competing fiercely to offer full-service logistics networks, and even the largest companies can now outsource warehousing, distribution, and related activities. Such trends will only accelerate in the future, and those companies that have recognized and prepared for them will be the first to capitalize on them.

So, to ensure that it doesn't quickly become obsolete, a sourcing strategy needs to consider not only present circumstances but also future alternative scenarios. What trends will influence the sourcing options available for each key capability? Is the supplier base growing rapidly, and are innovative new outsourcers emerging? Are different regions of the world investing heavily in particular capabilities – like contract manufacturing or customer service – and will they offer greater cost or quality advantages in the future? The answers to such questions may encourage a company to pursue certain sourcing opportunities that might not be highly attractive based on current numbers but could offer dramatic benefits in the coming months and years. Or they may lead a company to negotiate short-term sourcing contracts to keep options open, rather than enter into long-term relationships. Ultimately, a company's skill in quickly remolding its sourcing arrangements in response to market conditions and rivals' moves may be its strongest competitive advantage.

For a few targeted product segments, 7-Eleven has identified opportunities that call for an even deeper level of collaboration. Company executives figured out that their traditional, do-it-yourself approach to creating branded products was cutting the company off from the superior scale, resources, and creativity of major food suppliers. So they began sharing information with a select group of manufacturers, allowing them to create custom products for 7-Eleven stores. For example, 7-Eleven worked with Hershey to develop an edible straw based on the candy maker's popular Twizzler treat. In return, Hershey gave 7-Eleven the exclusive right to sell the straw for its first 90 days on the market. To further promote the unique product, 7-Eleven joined with its syrup supplier, Coca-Cola, to come up with a Twizzler flavored version of its proprietary Slurpee drink. Such exclusive arrangements reduce the strategic risk of sharing customer information while greatly expanding the set of unique products 7-Eleven can offer.

Likewise, when the data on beer sales showed that certain packaging options were more successful than others, 7-Eleven forged a tight partnership with Anheuser-Busch to build sales in those categories. Anheuser-Busch helped 7-Eleven develop a product assortment and establish merchandising standards for a new display. The beer giant also agreed to give 7-Eleven first-look opportunities at new products. In return, 7-Eleven shares its customer information so together the two companies can develop innovative marketing programs, such as a cobranded NASCAR promotion targeting 7-Eleven's core customers and a Major League Baseball promotion campaign.

Anheuser-Busch is also using 7-Eleven store data, provided daily by IRI, to test a new order forecasting system that would link the retailer's orders more tightly with deliveries from the brewer's wholesalers.

In addition to restructuring and enhancing existing activities, 7-Eleven has used creative sourcing partnerships to pioneer entirely new capabilities. It realized, for example, that by being a onestop source for a broad range of products and services, it could gain a leg up on more narrowly focused competitors. So it has set up a consortium to provide multipurpose kiosks in its stores. American Express supplies ATM functions. Western Union handles money wires, and CashWorks furnishes check-cashing capabilities, while EDS integrates the technical functions of the kiosks. Here, too, 7-Eleven maintains control over the data – in this case, information on how customers use the kiosks – which it views as critical to its competitive edge.

Some of 7-Eleven's outsourcing relationships tie suppliers' financial interests to its own. The company took an equity stake in Affiliated Computer Services, for instance, one of its major IT outsourcers. 7-Eleven also agreed to share productivity gains from a services agreement with Hewlett-Packard. In an even deeper collaboration, the company created a joint venture with prepared foods distributor E.A. Sween: Combined Distribution Centers (CDC) is a directstore delivery operation that supplies 7-Elevens with sandwiches and other fresh goods. By drawing on the skills and scale of a specialist, 7-Eleven was able to cut its distribution costs from more than 15% of revenues to 10% and eventually hopes to cut that figure in half again. But cost reduction is only a secondary benefit. The real gains have come in service. When it

The Measure of Success

For 7-Eleven, strategic sourcing has translated into industry dominance. In the past two years, the mini-mart retailer has led all major rivals in same-store merchandise growth, inventory turn rate, and revenue per employee.

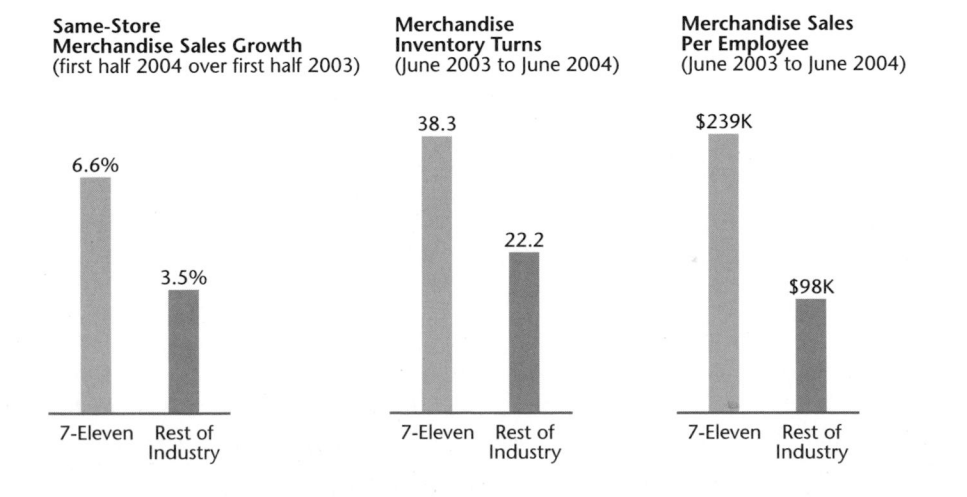

Same-Store Merchandise Sales Growth (first half 2004 over first half 2003)

6.6% — 7-Eleven
3.5% — Rest of Industry

Merchandise Inventory Turns (June 2003 to June 2004)

38.3 — 7-Eleven
22.2 — Rest of Industry

Merchandise Sales Per Employee (June 2003 to June 2004)

$239K — 7-Eleven
$98K — Rest of Industry

owned its own distribution network, 7-Eleven delivered fresh goods to its stores only a couple of times a week. CDC now makes deliveries to stores once, and soon twice, a day. More frequent deliveries mean fresher products, which draw more customers into the stores. By almost any measure, 7-Eleven's sourcing strategy has transformed the company. In narrowing its focus to a small, strategically vital set of capabilities – in-store merchandising, pricing, ordering, and customer data analysis – the company has reduced its capital assets and overhead while streamlining its organization. It reduced head count 28% from 43,000 in 1991 to 31,000 in 2003 and flattened its organizational structure, cutting managerial levels in half from 12 to six. Today, 7-Eleven consistently outperforms competitors. Same-store sales have grown in four out of the last five years. In the past two years, it has dominated the industry's vital statistics, with same-store merchandise growth at almost twice the industry average, revenue per employee at just about two-and-a-half times higher, and inventory turns at 72% more than the industry average. (See the exhibit "The Measure of Success.") Furthermore, after its acquisition of two regional U.S. chains (Christy's Markets in the Northeast and Red D Mart in the Midwest), the firm's new business model helped grow sales by more than 30% and increase gross profit margins by 2%. 7-Eleven's stock appreciation over the past five years has outpaced all major competitors, including Casey's General Stores, the Pantry, and Uni-Mart.

Should you always keep strategic capabilities within your walls? As globalization and technology transform more industries, all companies will eventually have to let go of that comfortable but simplistic guideline.

A Framework for Capability Sourcing

As companies like Chrysler, American Express, and 7-Eleven have discovered, a strategic approach to sourcing can dramatically improve your company's competitive position. So how do you make something that's always been tactical more strategic? You need to stop focusing on incremental cost improvement targets, step back, and reevaluate your strategy and your capabilities. In working through this process with clients, we've found that three steps can ensure that decisions are made objectively and are based on facts.

The first step is to identify the components of your business that represent the *core of the core*. These are the activities that your company does better and cheaper than its rivals. For 7-Eleven, the core of the core is in-store merchandising and product ordering. For drug maker Pfizer, it's developing and marketing pharmaceutical compounds. For American Express, it's identifying customer segments and creating card offerings tailored to them. Everything else exists to support the core of the core.

In deciding what to outsource and what to keep inside, 7-Eleven considered two factors: whether a capability was proprietary and whether it was common enough that outside suppliers could achieve scale or other advantages by supplying it to multiple companies. To determine proprietary value, executives asked themselves two ques-

What Should You Outsource?

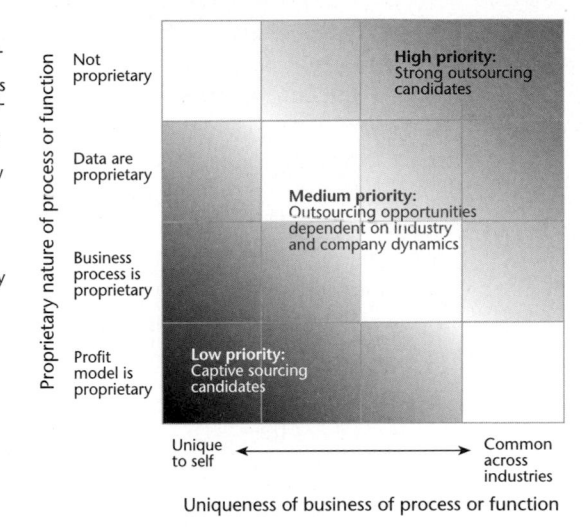

Using this sourcing opportunities map, you can determine which functions have the highest outsourcing potential and which should remain under your company's control. The vertical axis measures how proprietary a capability is for your company. The horizontal axis plots how common the capability is within or outside your industry. The less proprietary and the more common a function is, the stronger a candidate it is for outsourcing.

Proprietary nature of process or function

- Not proprietary
- Data are proprietary
- Business process is proprietary
- Profit model is proprietary

High priority: Strong outsourcing candidates

Medium priority: Outsourcing opportunities dependent on industry and company dynamics

Low priority: Captive sourcing candidates

Unique to self ⟷ Common across industries

Uniqueness of business of process or function

How Strong Are Your Capabilities?

Once you've determined which capabilities offer the highest potential value from outsourcing, you need to see how well, and how efficiently, your company currently performs each one of them. This exercise may surprise you: If your cost per transaction is low enough and your quality high enough, you should be thinking of selling that function as a new business in itself.

Company's ability to perform function

- Better than it needs to be
- Sufficient
- Not good enough

Source to reduce cost; sacrifice capability if necessary

Consider creating a new business (If adjacent to core business)

Source to reduce cost

Source to increase capability at lower cost

Source to increase capability even at higher cost *if necessary*

Above industry median | At industry median | Below industry median

Cost per transaction

tions: Did 7-Eleven carry out the capability in a way that generated measurably more value than its competitors could deliver? And would the company suffer a high degree of strategic damage if rivals could imitate that capability? To determine commonality, they had to look outside their company – even outside their industry. They tried to identify capabilities in which outside suppliers were building scale across their industry, or across several industries, because these common business processes or capabilities could pose an immediate or future threat to 7-Eleven's cost position.

By plotting each of your required capabilities on a sourcing opportunities map like the one in the exhibit "What Should You Outsource?" you can judge the relative merits of your company's outsourcing possibilities. The vertical axis of the map measures how proprietary a process or function is; the horizontal dimension assesses the degree of commonality, both within and outside your industry. Capabilities that fall in the upper right portion of the map are strong candidates for outsourcing. Those that appear in the lower left section are potential prospects for captive sourcing. Such capabilities may even be candidates for "insourcing" – that is, if you determine that your company is really the best at a given function, you may have an opportunity to perform this function for other companies. One example of successful insourcing is FedEx, which plans and manages inbound transportation for more than 1,500 product suppliers into 26 General Motors power train facilities. This capability puts FedEx at the leading edge of the $225 billion logistics-outsourcing industry.

Opportunities that fall in the middle of the sourcing opportunities map generally require more detailed analysis of both your company and your industry. You will need to consider such factors as regulation, standards, and alternative products to figure out what will happen to those capabilities in the future. To provide a quick sense of the relative financial stakes involved, and highlight the biggest opportunities, the sourcing opportunities map should be populated with bubbles scaled to represent the cost dollars at stake for each capability.

Once you've discovered which capabilities promise high potential for alternative sourcing, the next question is: How should you source them? You need to figure out how your capabilities stack up to what's required. Do you meet, exceed, or fall short of cost and quality requirements? A *capability assessment map* like the one in the exhibit "How Strong Are Your Capabilities?" plots each capability according to its cost and quality relative to top-performing competitors or suppliers. This map will help you determine which key capability gaps your company needs to fill. Perhaps equally important, it will identify any current activities that you could perform with less rigor without incurring any strategic penalty.

Where capabilities fall on this grid establishes appropriate goals for an outsourcing relationship. Functions that fall, for instance, in the upper left (relatively high-cost functions whose quality levels exceed requirements) should be outsourced to low-cost providers – even if it means a reduction in quality. Capabilities that fall in the lower left (high cost functions performed relatively poorly) require outsourcing partners that can both reduce costs and improve quality.

7-Eleven had always been a vertically integrated company, delivering its own gasoline, making its own candy and ice. It even owned the cows that produced the milk it sold.

The capability assessment map also gives you another way to identify insourcing opportunities. Capabilities that fall in the upper right (low-cost, high-quality functions) could become the basis for attractive new businesses.

Following the first two steps of our framework can help you determine what type of control you need over each of your capabilities. The third step is a kind of reality check in which you determine whether a capability that is a strong candidate for strategic sourcing can be carried out at a distance without any loss of quality.

The issue of physical proximity may not seem very strategic, but globalization and advances in technology ensure that it's a constantly moving target. For many functions, including transaction processing, design, engineering, and customer service, the Internet and an increasingly sophisticated telephone infrastructure have made physical proximity much less relevant, at least from a cost perspective. The necessary information and outputs can be transferred electronically at high speed and low cost. For tangible products that must be shipped, however, proximity plays a large role in both cost and timeliness considerations; it may not be feasible to manage the movement of such products from afar. There may also be customer service constraints. Certain product development, sales, and service tasks, for example, may require local interactions. Capabilities that do not require physical proximity are good candidates for offshoring, whether through a traditional outsourcing arrangement or, for proprietary capabilities, through a captive operation.

If you go through this three-step analysis, your company should have the outline of a comprehensive capability sourcing strategy. You will know which capabilities you need to own and protect, which can be best performed by what kind of partners, and how to structure a productive relationship. Formulating the strategy is, of course, only the first stage of a sourcing effort: Partners then have to be chosen, contracts negotiated, and management structures established and monitored. As 7-Eleven found, the success of the strategy often hinges on the creativity with which partnerships are organized and managed. But only by first taking a broad, strategic view of capability sourcing can your company make the most of its sourcing choices.

Case Example
How the Innovation Economy is Shifting the Focus of Value Creation*

Shifting (Relatively) From Product Innovation to Supply Chain Innovation: Procter & Gamble and Wal-Mart

Toward the middle of the twentieth century, most (demand) markets had developed to the point where their submarkets, or segments, were large enough to support efficient-scale production and market development. These segments were defined by demographics and psychographics (e.g., children's aspirin, jogging shoes). In response, mass marketing companies adapted or differentiated their products to fit these markets in a sort of "theme and variations" strategy. The rise of mass markets created huge benefits for society, and also formed the dominant paradigm of how companies are managed today.

Today, the locus of value creation is shifting from product innovation to supply chain innovation. This shift is gradual but accelerating quickly. Most companies today live partly in both worlds, and their managers are struggling with this transition. This is equally true for product companies and service companies.

General Foods in its heyday characterized the mass market paradigm. The company turned product innovation into a science, and distributed its goods to broad, homogeneous markets, and market segments, in a largely standard way. Dell represents the emerging new era of "precision" markets. This company carefully selects its customers, and individualizes every transaction to "sell what it has", often changing its product features and pricing literally minute by minute.

A watershed event in this market shift was the new relationship that P&G (Procter & Gamble) and Wal-Mart developed about ten years ago. Before this, P&G was a classic mass marketer like General Foods. With Wal-Mart, however, P&G changed its strategy. Instead of serving Wal-Mart in a standard, arm's-length way, P&G focused on creating inter-company supply chain processes like vendor-managed inventory that radically increased Wal-Mart's profitability on P&G products. This increased profitability drove P&G's sales to Wal-Mart and its own profitability through the ceiling. As one key P&G Vice President put it, "Wal-Mart's CFO became our prime customer".

---

* Adapted from Byrnes, J. (2005), "The Age of Precision Markets," *Harvard Business School Working Knowledge*, April 4

At the same time, P&G withdrew from distributing directly to many smaller accounts, choosing instead to set up master distributors. No longer did "one size fit all".

The "offensive terminal point" is a key concept in military strategy. It reflects the principle that the narrower your front, the deeper you can penetrate the battlefield. By analogy, in its days as a mass marketer, P&G's customer engagement "front" was very broad, and therefore its offensive terminal point (inter-company supply chain) was very shallow. As a precision marketer in this new era, however, P&G carefully manages its customer relationships to develop a very deep offensive terminal point with a few customers like Wal-Mart, while choosing a much more standard, arm's-length relationship with others, and sometimes withdrawing completely from a direct relationship with still other customers. This enables both P&G and Wal-Mart to innovate faster and symbiotically, through sharing knowledge of "precision" markets and shifting focus relatively from product innovation to supply chain innovation.

Shifting Value Creation Closer to the Customer: McGraw-Hill and College Textbooks[*]

Manipulating the demand-supply chain does more than improve customers' performance and benefits to suppliers – suppliers can also use this approach to discover completely new value propositions for customers. Suppliers can thus extract new value from current accounts by escaping the commodity trap (and also, in some cases, find new customers). Consider a real-life example based on the changing textbook publishing industry.

A typical university bookstore decides which books to sell (assortment planning), estimates how many of them it needs (inventory management), and then places its

Exhibit 1
The conventional demand-supply chain: College textbooks

Bookstore's demand chain

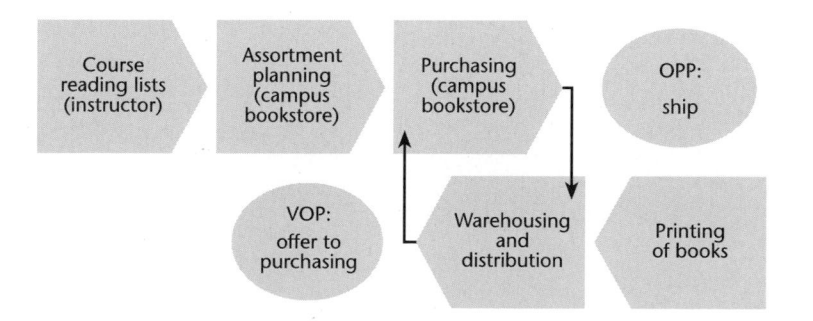

---

[*] Adapted from: Holström, J., et. al., "The Other Side of the Supply Chain", *The McKinsey Quarterly*, Vol. 1, 2000, 62-71

orders with publishers. Each publisher's VOP (value ordering point) is thus a straightforward offer to purchasing, and the ship-to-order OPP (order purchasing point) is the publisher's warehouse or distribution center (see Exhibit 1).

This system may seem to work nicely for bookstores, but for students it works less well: books are expensive; some of the cost is unnecessary, since teachers often assign only parts of books; and if the bookstore underestimates demand, some students must wait for the publisher to make extra shipments. What should a publisher do to help its customers (the bookstores) help their customers (the students)?

The publisher can start by examining the whole demand-supply chain. Although the retailer's assortment-planning process appears to respond to student demand, it is really shaped by instructors, who choose the reading lists for courses. One publisher, McGraw-Hill, therefore moved its VOP back to instructors, offering to tailor collections of reading materials for each of them. How? By moving the OPP out of the warehouse and forward to the retailer. McGraw-Hill's Primis electronic-publishing system allows instructors to choose standard McGraw-Hill textbook chapters from a database and to add complementary materials (such as course objectives, instructions, old test questions, and teaching cases) from a variety of sources (see Exhibit 2). All of the readings are then combined into a single package that is printed and bound in the bookstore.

This assemble-on-demand system benefits bookstores, students, and publishers in several ways. Even if a bookstore has the syllabus for a course in hand well before the first day of classes, the manager cannot know precisely how many students will enroll in the course that year. The new model largely eliminates this problem, and the bookstore also saves display and storage space. As for students, most tailored textbooks are cheaper than their standard mass-produced counterpart because they include only the text and readings instructors actually require. Furthermore, on-campus print technology makes the publisher's unit costs independent of batch sizes, so print runs do not have to reach a certain minimum, and the publisher can avoid the crushing cost of returns, which can amount to 30 percent of sales. McGraw-Hill has used this new value offering to win over teachers on more than 1,000 US college campuses, and several competitors are now following suit.

Exhibit 2
The new demand-supply chain: College textbooks

Bookstore's demand chain

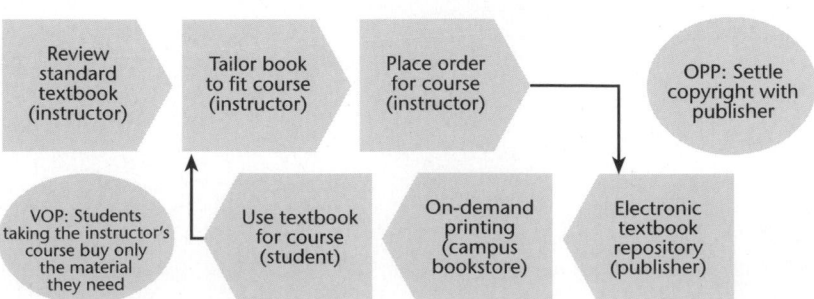

Questions

1. Some prominent strategic management authors contend that traditional (20th century) strategic management approaches are adequate in any environment, and do not require any significant changes, renewal or complementation. Review the various viewpoints in this 'debate', and make your own (motivated) conclusions.

2. Why has the decade of the 1990's witnessed an emphasis on BPR (business process reengineering), TQM (total quality management), outsourcing, downsizing and 'core competencies' in strategic management? Are these techniques and emphases still relevant in the innovation economy of today?

3. Review the major analytical approaches to understand the external environment of an enterprise, and provide your view on the need for additional/new environmental 'sense-making' approaches and tools.

4. Some observers contend that an organization should not strive for a continuous "fit" with its environment, but a discontinuous or punctuated "misfit". Provide a logical review of the various viewpoints on this topic, and give your own opinion.

5. The traditional strategic management approaches are often contrasted as dichotomies of 'prediction' vs. 'learning', or 'deliberate' vs. 'emergent', or 'outward-in' vs. 'inward-out', or 'design/configuration' vs. 'incremental'. Review the similarities and differences among these various dichotomies in strategic management approaches.

6. "In the innovation economy, the network will be the value innovation engine". Provide an insightful review of the meaning of this statement.

7. The 21st century business model has emerged from a number of trends, and "they are now changing the rules on a broad front". What 'rules' are being changed (or reshaped) and why?

8. What new (or different) organizational capabilities are required for the 21st century business enterprise? Are these really 'new', or just a shift in emphasis (or approach) to organizational capabilities in internal and external business value chains?

9. "What's wrong with strategy?". This question is increasingly posed by prominent authors, and some contend that strategy cannot be created by a methodological approach. Provide an insightful review of the viewpoints in this regard.

10. Provide an insightful comparison (e.g. similarities, differences), between the concepts of organizational learning, knowledge management, and innovation.

References

Chapter 2: The Relevance of Traditional Approaches to Strategic Management in the Innovation Economy

[1] This figure and the subsequent elaborations are largely based on Means, G. and Schneider, D. *op.cit.*, 2-18, and various other observers.

[2] Davenport, T.H., "The Coming Commoditization of Processes," *Harvard Business Review*, June 2005.

[3] See, for example, Friedman, T.L. (2005), *The World Is Flat*, New York: Farrar, Straus, and Giroux; also Pink, D.H. (2005), *A Whole New Mind*, New York: Riverhead.

[4] Grant, R.M. (2002), *Contemporary Strategy Analysis*, Fourth Edition, Oxford: Blackwell Publishers; Mintzberg, H. (1994), "The Rise and Fall of Strategic Planning", *Harvard Business Review*, 72(1), 107-114; Collis, D.J. and Montgomery, C.A. (1995), "Competing on Resources: Strategy in the 1990s", *Harvard Business Review*, 73(4), 118-128.

[5] Ansoff, H.I. (1965), *Corporate Strategy*, New York: McGraw-Hill Inc.

[6] Boston Consulting Group (1978), *Perspectives on Experience*, Boston: Boston Consulting Group.

[7] Porter, M.E. (1980), *Competitive Strategy*, New York: The Free Press.

[8] Porter, M.E. (1996), "What is Strategy?", *Harvard Business Review*, 74(6), 61-78.

[9] See e.g., Grant, R.M, (1991), "The Resource Based Theory of Competitive Advantage: Implications for Strategy Formulation", *California Management Review*, 33(3), 114-135.

[10] D'Aveni, R.A. (1974), *Hypercompetition: Managing the Dynamics of Strategic Maneuvering*, New York: Free Press; Chakravarthy, B. (1997), "A New Strategy Framework of Coping with Turbulence", *Sloan Management Review*, 38(2), 69-82; Eisenhardt, K.M. and Martin, J.A. (2000), "Dynamic Capabilities: What Are They?", *Strategic Management Journal*, 21, 1105-1121; Eisenhardt, K.M. and Brown, S.L. (1999), "Patching: Restitching Business Portfolios in Dynamic Markets", *Harvard Business Review*, 77(3), 72-82.

[11] Leonard-Barton, D. A. "Core Capabilities and Core Rigidities: A Paradox in Managing New Product Development." *Strategic Management Journal* 13 (1992): 111-125.

[12] Camillus, J. (1997), "Shifting the Strategic Management Paradigm", *European Management Journal*, 15(1), 1-7.

[13] Mintzberg, H. (1994), *op.cit.*

[14] Senge, P. (1990). *The Fifth Discipline*, London: Century.

[15] Kaplan, R.S. and Norton D.P. (1996), *The Balanced Scorecard*, Boston: Harvard Business School Press.

[16] Adapted from: King, W.R. (2001), "Strategies for Creating a Learning Organization", *Information Systems Management*, 18(1), 13.

[17] Kim, W.C. and Mauborgne, R., *Blue Ocean Strategy*, Boston: Harvard Business School Press, 2005.

[18] Roos, J. and Victor, B. (1999), "Towards a New Model of Strategy-Making as Serious Play", *European Management Journal*, 17(4), 348-355.

[19] Davenport, T.H. and Beck, J.C., *The Attention Economy*, Boston: Harvard Business School Press, 2001.

[20] Hamel, G. (1998), "Strategy Innovation and the Quest for Value", *Sloan Management Review*, 39(2): 7-14; Roos, J. and Victor, B. (1999), *op.cit.*

What Makes a Strategy Brilliant

Bevin Alexander, *How Great Generals Win* (New York: Norton, 1993).

Adam Brandenburger and Barry J. Nalebuff, "The Right Game: Use Game Theory to Shape Strategy", *Harvard Business Review*, July-August 1995, pp. 57-71.

Andrew Campbell and Marcus Alexander, "What's Wrong with Strategy?" *Harvard Business Review*, November-December 1997, pp. 42-51.

Carl von Clausewitz, *On War*, ed. and intro. by Anatol Rapoport (Baltimore: Penguin Books, 1968).

Hugh Courtney, Jane Kirkland, and Patrick Viguerie, "Strategy Under Uncertainty", *Harvard Business Review*, November-December 1997, pp. 67-79.

David H. Freedman, "Is Management Still a Science?" *Harvard Business Review*, November-December 1992, pp. 26-38.

Russell W. Glenn, "No More Principles of War?" *Parameters: U.S. Army War College Quarterly*, Spring 1998, pp. 48-66.

Boris Gulko, "Is Chess Finished?" *Commentary*, July 1997, pp. 45-47.

G. Hamel, "Strategy as Revolution", *Harvard Business Review*, July-August 1996, pp. 69-82.

G. Hamel and C.K. Prahalad, "Strategic Intent", *Harvard Business Review*, May-June 1989, pp. 63-76.

Headquarters, Department of the Army, *FM 100-5: Operations* (Washington, 1993).

Bruce D. Henderson, "The Origin of Strategy", *Harvard Business Review*, November-December 1989, pp. 139-143.

Michael A. Hitt, R. Duane Ireland, Robert Hoskisson, and Robert D. Nixon, *Strategic Management: Competitiveness and Globalization,* 2nd ed. (Minneapolis/St. Paul: West Publishing, 1997).

Garry Kasparov, "IBM Owes Mankind a Rematch", *Time,* May 26, 1997, pp. 66-67.

John Keegan, *Guderian* (New York: Ballantine, 1973).

Marina Krol, "Have We Witnessed a Real-Life Turing Test?" *Computer,* March 1999, pp. 27-30.

Thomas S. Kuhn, *The Structure of Scientific Revolutions,* 3rd ed. (Chicago: University of Chicago Press, 1996).

Kenneth C. Laudon and Jane P. Laudon, *Management Information Systems,* 5th ed. (Upper Saddle River, NJ: Prentice-Hall, 1998).

John McDonald, *Strategy in Poker, Business and War* (New York: Norton, 1989).

Henry Mintzberg, "The Fall and Rise of Strategic Planning", *Harvard Business Review,* January-February 1994, pp. 107-114.

Henry Mintzberg and Joseph Lampel, "Reflecting on the Strategy Process", *Sloan Management Review,* Spring 1999, pp. 21-30.

Kenichi Ohmae, *The Mind of the Strategist: The Art of Japanese Business* (New York: McGraw-Hill, 1982).

Michael E. Porter, "What Is Strategy?" *Harvard Business Review,* November-December 1996, pp. 61-78.

Tom Wheeler, *Leadership Lessons from the Civil War* (New York: Currency Doubleday, 2000).

James P. Womack, Daniel T. Jones, and Daniel Roos, *The Machine That Changed the World* (New York: Rawson Associates, 1990).

H. Edward Wrapp, "Good Managers Don't Make Policy Decisions", *Harvard Business Review,* July-August 1984, pp. 8-21.

Peter Young and Omar Nelson Bradley, *Great Battles of the Modern World* (New York: Barnes & Noble Books; London: Bison Books, 1995).

III A New Strategy Mindset for the Innovation Economy

Synopsis

The chapter motivates the necessity of a new strategic mindset for value innovation, and its major requirements in e.g. mental space, while also providing definitions and taxonomies of innovation (including the contrasting of sustaining and disruptive innovation, and open and closed innovation). Major 'box' examples are Siemens, Virgin Atlantic, J&J; the case example is IBM, and two relevant articles are included.

Chapter 3
The New Strategy Mindset: Co-Shaping Value Innovation

Evolving Strategy Mindsets in the Past Century

In the previous chapter, the extant approaches to strategic management were reviewed in the context of traditional and changing concepts of the business enterprise – i.e., how the dominant logic and major practices of strategic management changed from

Twentieth Century	Thought leaders in management continually move away from tangible output with embedded value in which the focus was on activities directed at discrete or static transactions. In turn, they move toward dynamic value creation and exchange relationships that involve performing processes and exchanging skills and/or services in which value is co-created with the consumer. The mindset changes from a focus on resources on which an operation or act is performed (operand resources) to resources that produce effects (operant resources).	Twenty-first Century
Goods-Centered Model of Exchange		Service-Centered Model of Exchange
Concepts:		Concepts:
• tangibles		• intangibles,
• statics		• innovation
• discrete transactions		• dynamics
• operand resources		• co-creative processes
		• relationships
		• operant resources

Classical and Neoclassical Economics (1800-1920)

  'Formative' Management Thought (Descriptive: 1900-1950)

    'Professional' Management School of Thought (1950-2000)
- Customer orientation and marketing concept
- Value determined in marketplace
- Manage managerial functions to achieve optimal output
- Management science emerges and emphasizes use of optimization techniques

      Management as a 'Social and Economic Process' (1980-2000)
- Market orientation processes
- Services marketing processes
- Relationship marketing processes
- Quality management processes
- Supply chain management processes
- Resource management and competitive processes

        Management as a 'Co-Shaping Value-Innovation Process' (2000 +)
- Reinventing customer value
- Co-opting customer and supplier knowledge
- Network management processes
- Ambidextrous management: efficiency and disruption

Figure 3.1 Towards a new dominant mindset for strategic management

the 1950s to the last decade of the 20th century. Enterprises, as living systems that operate and strive to survive and succeed in a competitive environment, have certain beliefs, views, understanding, and principles of how they regard themselves and their environment – often referred to as mindsets or mental models/space.[1]

This chapter outlines and motivates the need for new managerial mindset(s) concerning the nature of value, innovation, business sustainability, and especially strategy. Such managerial mindset is essential as an underlying basis for the new strategic management approach for the early 21st century, which is presented and illustrated in Chapter 4. In the innovation economy, the core truths of business and strategy still apply – businesses must create value for customers and capture some of that value (adequate for survival) for shareholders. But a fundamental shift has taken place in how competitive value creation and provision to customers are now effected, in comparison to the industrial economy, and managers must thoroughly grasp this to adopt the appropriate underlying mindset for strategic management in the innovation economy.

Although there were significant shifts in managerial mindsets during the 20th century, as reflected in Figure 3.1, the great shock in the late 20th and early 21st century is that systems cannot be fully understood by analysis.[2] The properties of the parts are not intrinsic properties, but can be understood only within the context of the larger whole. Thus, when we speak of management as a co-evolutionary process, we do not mean systematic processes that can be analytically reduced, mechanistically planned, or fully controlled, but rather systemic processes that can be holistically understood, influenced, guided, cultivated, and broadly measured. These concepts are further explained below.

The Nature of Managerial Mindsets for Business Innovation

Business in the 21st century will never again be the same as it was in the 20th century – the rules of the innovation economy have made a – seemingly sudden – transition from a state of continuity to a state of discontinuity. Some companies have made the mental "jump" successfully: under Jack Welch, General Electric has reframed its business and has seen performance benefits as a result; IBM has transformed from a mainframe computer company to a computing and business process services company; others such as Johnson & Johnson, L'Oreal, General Motors, Shell, Proctor & Gamble and Corning are shedding their traditional business identities and business models and emerging to new ones.

Old, rigid mindsets create "cultural lock-in" – the inability to change (see box).[3] The heart of the problem of cultural lock-in is the existence of a hidden set of rules, or mindsets, that govern the enterprise.[4] Mental models are the core concepts of the corporation, the beliefs and assumptions, the cause-and-effect relationships, the guidelines for interpreting language and signals, the stories repeated within the corporate walls. Mental models are invisible in the corporation – they are neither explicit nor examined, but they are pervasive. When well crafted, mental models allow manage-

Cultural Lock-in

For half a century, until Johnson & Johnson introduced Tylenol, Bayer Aspirin drove the growth of Sterling Drug. Out of fear of cannibalizing its Bayer Aspirin leadership, Sterling Drug refused to introduce its leading European non-aspirin pain reliever (Panadol) to the United States. Instead, it tried to expand its Bayer line overseas but failed. This failure ultimately led to its acquisition by Eastman Kodak. Sterling Drug had become immobilized, unable to change its half-century-old behavior due to cultural rigidities. Its strong culture – its rules of thumb for decision making, its control processes, the information it used for decision making – blocked its progress and ultimately sealed its fate. It had locked itself into an ineffective approach to the market place despite clear signs that it needed to act in a new way.

ment to anticipate the future and solve problems. But once constructed, mental models tend to become self-reinforcing, self-sustaining, self-limiting, and rigid.

Mental models manifest themselves in corporate-control systems. These systems are designed to ensure the predictable achievement of goals, whether cost control, the control of capital expenditures, or the control of the deployment of key personnel. Unfortunately, control systems can also create "defensive routines" in organizations, including the failure to challenge the status quo, the failure to encourage a diversity of opinions, the failure to disagree with superiors (thereby displeasing them), communicating in ambiguous and inconsistent ways, and making these failures, even when known, "undiscussable." Change becomes impossible if traditional mindsets are impervious to renewal.

Corporate-control systems also undermine the ability of the organization to innovate at the pace and scale of the market. Under the assumption of continuity, for example, the arguments for building a new business can be reversed, since its probable success cannot be proved in advance. Under these circumstances, it is more likely that ideas based on the incremental growth of current capabilities and value propositions will be encouraged. Corporate-control systems limit creativity through their dependence on convergent thinking. Convergent thinking focuses on clear problems and provides well-known solutions quickly. It thrives on focus – order, simplicity, routine, clear responsibilities, unambiguous measurement systems, and predictability are the bedrock of convergent thinking. Convergent thinking is tailor-made for the assumption of continuity. While convergent thinking can be effective at handling small, incremental changes and differences, transformational changes completely disrupt the existing system.

Discontinuity, on the other hand, thrives on a different kind of thinking, i.e. divergent thinking. Divergent thinking focuses on broadening – diverging – the context of decision making. It is initially more concerned with questions than with getting to the answers in the fastest possible way. Divergent thinking places enormous value on getting the questions right and then relinquishes control to conventional convergent-thinking processes.

Redesigning the corporation to evolve quickly rather than to operate well requires more than simple adjustments; the fundamental concepts of operational excellence are insufficient for a corporation seeking to evolve at the pace and scale of the markets. Only as long as the enterprise is redesigned to evolve at the pace and scale of new networked business ecosystem realities, will long-term performance improve. Companies have to be redesigned from top to bottom, on the assumption of discontinuity. Management must stimulate the rate of creative destruction through the generation or acquisition of new business models, without losing control of existing traditional operations. If the enterprise is robust through its dynamic business models, the rate of creative destruction within the corporation will determine the continued long-term competitiveness and performance of the company.

From a Conventional Competitive-Goods Mindset to a Collaborative-Value Innovation Mindset

For the past 50 years, competition has dominated the mindset of strategic thinking, planning, and implementation. With strategic thinking embedded in the building of competitive advantage, companies often achieve no more than incremental improvement – imitation and incremental innovation, and not core value (or disruptive) innovation.[5] Companies need to escape from the conventional competitive-goods mindset and adopt a collaborative value-innovation mindset, as illustrated in Table 3.1.[6]

Before elaborating further on each of the above contrasting mindsets and their key elements, two important points need to be realized:

a) The contrasting mindsets are not mutually exclusive, i.e. even open, shared systems have to be targeted, cohered, and influenced. The contrasts are depicted as opposites or absolutes for purpose of exposition, but in reality a (flexible) range of possibilities (and practices) exists.

b) Most companies operate, or should operate, multiple business models, some requiring elements of a conventional mindset to make traditional business models more effective, while simultaneously requiring a value-innovation mindset for new and experimental business models. Some observers refer to this as 'ambidextrous' or 'paradoxical' management,[7] requiring managerial qualities that allow for handling different mindsets and practices at the same time. This might mean, for example, combining convergent and divergent thinking within the same organization (though not necessarily within the same person's brain!) It is clear, however, that having a conventional mindset with traditional business model focus only would result in eventual disaster for an enterprise in the dynamic innovation economy.

The following box illustrates how Siemens focuses on changing the strategy mindsets of its managers.[8]

Table 3.1 Contrasting a conventional mindset with a value innovation mindset

Key elements of strategy mindsets	Conventional mindset (goods-centered dominant logic)		Value innovation mindset (value/service-centered dominant logic)
Industry assumptions	Industry's conditions are given	→	Industry's conditions can be shaped
Goods	People exchange for goods, i.e. effects from operand resources	→	People exchange for value/service, i.e. effects from operant resources
Customers	Recipients of goods; market segments and group needs	→	Co-producers of value/service; individual profiles and custom needs
Value	Embedded in the operand resources; determined by the producer	→	Resulting from operant resources; determined by the customer
Capabilities	Leveraging current capabilities of a company	→	Leveraging current and potential capabilities of networks
Competition	Outperform/beat the competition	→	Reinvent value to shift the competitive base
Boundaries	Fixed, static company and market boundaries; closed systems	→	Flexible, dynamic company, market and network connections; open systems
Innovation	Incremental (product, processes, company, etc.)	→	Disruptive (value, business model, processes, etc.)
Systems & functions (internal & external)	Closed, protected; Focus on internal value chain	→	Open, shared; focus on external & internal value systems

Changing Managerial Mindsets at Siemens

In recent research at Siemens, a practice of challenging existing strategy imaginations (mindsets) was revealed by the company's focus on transcending, rather than beating, competitors. In transcending competitors, a recurring theme was to ruthlessly adopt the perspective of the customer in order to discover whether a new product would actually be superior to the old one, and would consequently provide superior value.

An interesting example of adopting the customer's perspective in transcending competitors was emphasized in an interview with the Top Plus Program manager at Siemens Medical Solutions:

"... we looked at existing products from the customer perspective. While this may sound trivial, it is not. Usually, in medical solutions, you look at it from the technological perspective... What we did was ask our customers: 'what would you want from us if you knew what is technologically doable.' The result of this was sophisticated magnetic resonance systems that did not use the traditional tunnel-technology, but instead used an 'open' design. The result: patients did not feel as claustrophobic, and our direct customers, the medical doctors, were happy".

The central question in the approach of challenging imagination at Siemens was: are the current businesses an adequate reflection of the market needs, buyer preferences, and technological requirements? In other words, is the current definition of the industry or industries in which Siemens competes an accurate reflection of reality? The research evidence demonstrated that often customers, and in particular corporate customers, would not pay heed to the definition of industry boundaries, but would instead demand highly integrated solutions that often cut across several of the industries served by Siemens.

Given the blurring of industry boundaries, Siemens' managers considered it expedient to re-define industry boundaries. To cite a colorful evocation of this point by the assistant to the CEO of the Information and Communications business unit: "If we only think in terms of telephony networks, and nothing but the network, we have a problem. No question: it's good to think about the developments of networks, how existing networks can be improved, and can be made more efficient and customer-friendly. But if we do this, we fail to realize forces that impact the network as such. That's the 'frog's perspective.' I see the net and nothing but the net. What I see is the number of data bits that gets transported, I wonder how more data can get transported and that kind of thing ... I don't grab the steer by its horns, all I do is perhaps get hold of its tail".

Siemens interviewees emphasized the importance of 'defying old paradigms.' The company exhibited a variety of approaches by which old paradigms were defied, old ways of 'doing things around here' were challenged and path-dependent behavioral patterns were questioned. Importantly, the need to defy old paradigms was seen as a function of the past successes achieved by using a specific paradigm, such as the telex technology. Put differently, the more successful Siemens became In exploiting a specific technology such as telexes, the more important was the need to defy this very paradigm at the time when it was most successful. Indeed, it was discovered that past successes could lead to: "systematic biases against innovation ... Particularly if a new technology competes with an old one, reactions and biases against the new technology can kill its commercial potential immediately. The fax machine is a good example. Siemens actually invented the fax machine, but since the telex technology provided excellent profits that could be cannibalized by the fax technology, we sold the fax to the Japanese. The rest is history".

Given the deeply ingrained nature of 'ways of doing things around here,' often radical approaches to defying old paradigms were necessary. In the Top Plus Program, Siemens made use of defying old paradigms as a 'shock therapy.' This was particularly evident in the new approach to portfolio management, which no longer supported cross-subsidies between the individual business units. It was repeatedly emphasized, that "no one should feel safe or comfortable in such divisions simply because the group as a whole is doing well. Let me emphasize once again, we will not support cross-subsidies" (von Pierer, speech, June 21, 2001).

Importantly, while 'shock therapies' to defying old paradigms were being encouraged, a prudent approach to defying old paradigms was simultaneously being advocated, because it was realized that sudden defiance of old paradigms, particularly where they referred to capabilities and skills that were considered core competencies, could lead to demotivation and frustration.

The above-mentioned approach of Siemens is in many ways the antithesis of extant strategy-making approaches of the 20th century. Since especially 1994, some prominent researchers have been questioning the traditional strategic management approach and practices. In the following table (Table 3.2) depicting the major questioning themes of some prominent authors, Mintzberg traced the 'fall and rise of strategic planning,' concluding that strategy makers should act as catalysts who support strategy-making by breaking, rather than extending the existing mindset.[9] Likewise, Brown and Eisenhardt have alerted their readers to approaches to unleash collective intuition, accelerate constructive conflict, and maintain decision pacing, rather than

Table 3.2 Recent emphases on new strategy mindsets in the literature: some prominent views

Concepts	Underlying rationale
Emergent thinking (Mintzberg, 1994)	Breaking the traditional frame of strategic 'planning'.
Changing the rules of the game (Hamel, 1998)	Shift in thinking about innovation from the traditional product-centric view to that of systemic view of businesses model innovation.
Concept of "Ba" (Nonaka & Konno, 1998)	"Ba" as a shared space (physical, virtual, or mental space) for emerging relationships that serves as a foundation for knowledge creation and sharing.
Dynamic capabilities (Brown & Eisenhardt, 1998)	Capabilities that are essential building blocks required to develop a dynamic strategy when competing at the "edge of chaos."
Dynamic thinking (Markides, 1999)	A dynamic process of continuously searching for new strategic positions while competing in current position, managing both positions simultaneously.
New value curves (Kim & Mauborgne, 1999)	Configure offerings to customers by looking across traditional boundaries of competition, thereby creating new market space.
Strategic inflection points (Grove, 2000)	A point where industry dynamics fundamentally transform due to discontinuous changes, consequently prompting changes in how business is done.
Conceptual road-mapping (Govindarajan & Gupta, 2001)	Create new customer value proposition by proactively and constantly creating new and superior business models.
Organizational sense-making (Weick, 2001)	Realize the limitations of conventional strategies and managerial approaches and focus on making sense of the complex and discontinuous changes in the environment.
Second curve leaps (Pietersen, 2002)	The time to make critical change is when organizations are still successful and not when they are on the brink of failing (in this case, a series of continuous reinventing change).
Open innovation (Chesbrough, 2003)	Making the boundary between the firm and the environment more porous, becoming "open" to the easy flow of ideas, innovation and knowledge both from inside and outside the organization.

adhering rigorously to a strategy-making approach over time. Hamel empirically confirmed the importance of discontinuous strategy that nurtures a culture of 'corporate rebels' in detailed analyses across 20 industries. Weick has emphasized new bases for organizational 'sense-making', and Chesbrough has been advocating a mindset shift towards dynamic, open and shared boundaries between firms, functions, and systems.

Elaborating on Key Elements of a Strategy Mindset

The key elements of a strategy mindset can also be described as a set of mental spaces occupying individuals' minds at any particular period of time. Fauconnier[10] describes mental space as providing a medium in which cognitive activities can take place, i.e. the partial cognitive structures that emerge when we think and talk. And it is in these mental spaces that domains are defined, reasoned, changed, and merged for purposes of understanding and action. Furthermore, mental spaces are inter-connected and can be modified as thought and discourse unfold.

As reflected in Table 3.3, there are a number of (interrelated) key types of mental space, including market space (views of customers' needs, goods/products and exchange), industry space (industry assumptions, views of competition, and views of industry systems and practices), geographic space (geographic and virtual boundaries), and capability space (views of resources, competencies and innovation dynamics).

Market Space

Market space consists of customers and products. Customers are fundamentally changing the dynamics of the marketplace where they are playing an active role in creating and competing for value, becoming part of the enhanced network of the organization that includes suppliers, partners, and competitors. Due to technological advances, customers can access the same information as that of producers/manufacturers, shifting the balance of power from that of makers/sellers of products and services to that of buyers/users. This level of "transparency" is changing the nature of the relationship between buyers and sellers, doctors and patients, politicians and citizens, teacher and students, and all the relationships between corporations and their stakeholders.[11] Furthermore, customers are no longer interested in simply buying a product, but also the experience and convenience that goes along with it, such as in the case of electronic banking and online transactions, automobiles, mobile telephones, wine, and property.

The role of goods/products and primary unit of exchange are also changing: While the goods-centered dominant logic views people as acting to exchange for goods, the value-innovation logic views people as acting to acquire the benefits of services. Goods and customers were traditionally seen as operand resources (enterprises 'do things' to these resources); in the value-innovation view, goods and customers are transmitters of operant resources (embedded co-producers, mutually shaping benefits/value, only functioning occasionally as an operand resource).

Industry Space

Industry space has typically been viewed as comprising competitors, the demand and supply chain, and various impacting 'forces'. While traditionally competitors were considered to be those that are in the same line of business, trends such as globalization, deregulation, and information technology have brought about discontinuities that have resulted in the convergence of industries and the breaking down of traditional boundaries, thereby reshaping the business landscape and the sources of competitive advantage. As a result, competitors previously deemed irrelevant and unrelated to established business have become either direct or indirect competitors. Furthermore, suppliers have shifted from being distinct and separate entities providing products and services to becoming collaborators and partners in creating and offering value to customers. Similarly, as discussed in the previous section, the industry value chain has evolved from an industry system to one that crosses a variety of industries, co-evolving cooperatively and collaboratively with others in a business ecosystem. Therefore, focus has shifted from "outperforming" the competition to that of co-evolving (both in collaboration and competition) with customers, partners, competitors, suppliers, etc., in creating customer value and focusing on "unique performance".

Geographic Space

Even in the global and internetworked economy, geography still matters. Geographic space includes clusters, regions, and global space. Companies in clusters – geographically proximate collections of related businesses – have progressed from being isolated businesses into linked networks collaborating and competing to attract innovation and investment, as well as enabling technology and knowledge transfer. Regions have historically been inward-looking with regard to their concentrations of investment, resources, and capital. However, in the era of the innovation economy, they must become open to the external environment in order to take advantage of opportunities that might arise and link themselves with various entities in the business ecosystem to exploit these opportunities.

Globalization has been intensifying due to advancements in information technology and deregulation, and has focused on the "homogenizing" of customer needs. However, the confined perspective of catering for a "standardized" global market has transformed to that of "local customizations" in response to cultural and business variations in different parts of the world.

Capability Space

Capability space includes resources, competencies, and particular skills dynamics. Due to the shift from an industrial-based to a knowledge- and information-based economy and in order to gain competitive advantage, organizations are relying more on intellectual (intangible) assets (e.g. knowledge, ideas, skills) and less on the physical (tangible) assets. The building of competencies does not merely consist of training employees and accumulating relevant information, but rather instilling commitment to learning, knowledge creation and its sharing, to enhance individual and organizational skills and expertise. The dynamics of capability have also shifted from organizations simply becoming adaptive to the changing environment to that of being proactive, creative, and emergent in shaping the external environment. Innovation dynamics form part of capability space, and because of its importance, it is elaborated in the subsequent section.

Table 3.3 summarizes the above-mentioned types of mental space, i.e. elements of strategy mindsets, also indicating managerial levers to cultivate new mental space.

Table 3.3 Elements of strategy mindsets

Contrasting traditional with new mental space			Levers to cultivate new mental space		
Types of mental space	Traditional perception	New perception	Types of new mental space	Levers/ techniques	Business examples
Market Space *Customers*	Invisible	Visible	*New Customer/ Market Space*	Redefine buyer	Philips
				Apply new data mining techniques	Starbucks, eBay
				Prosumerism	IKEA, Quicken
Products	Physical	Non-physical	*New Product & Services Space*	Experimentation with new technologies and processes	Virgin Atlantic
				Communities of Practice (CoP)	Microsoft, Holcim
				Networked Incubation	Ford's Consumer Connect
Industry Space *Competitors*	Similar	Dissimilar	*New Value Chain Space*	Deconstruct the traditional value chain	Dell
Supply chain	Linear, competitive	Non-linear, collaborative			
Value chain	Industry system	Business ecosystem		Reconfiguration/ reintermediation techniques	Amazon
Geographic Space *Clusters*	Internal	External			
Regions	Inward, supportive	Open, linked		Systemic scorecards (including BSC)	BRL Hardy, Wal-Mart
Global	Standardized	Local, meta-national			
Capability Space *Resources*	Visible	Invisible	*New Capability Space*	Reconstitute core competencies	Disney
Competencies	Training, information	Learning, knowledge		Disturb existing processes and resources	Shell
Dynamics	Adaptive	Creative, emergent		Knowledge creation techniques ("Ba")	Skandia

The latter are elaborated in Chapter 5 – new strategic management tools in the innovation economy.

The following box illustrates how Virgin Atlantic has been challenging its industry's conventional mental space, thereby becoming a consistent value innovator.[12]

Virgin Atlantic: Flying in the Face of Conventional Logic

When Virgin Atlantic Airways challenged its industry's conventional logic by eliminating first-class service in 1984, the airline was simply following the logic of value innovation. Most of the industry's profitable revenue came from business class, not first class. And first class was a big cost generator. Virgin spotted an opportunity. The airline decided to channel the cost it would save by cutting first class service into value innovation for business-class passengers.

First, Virgin introduced large, reclining sleeper seats, raising seat comfort in business class well above the industry's standard. Second, Virgin offered free transportation to and from the airport – initially in chauffeured limousines and later in specially designed motorcycles called LimoBikes – to speed business-class passengers through snarled city traffic.

With those innovations, which were on the product and service platforms, Virgin attracted not only a large share of the industry's business-class customers but also some full economy fare and first-class passengers of other airlines. Virgin's value innovation separated the company from the pack for many years, but the competition did not stand still. As the value curves of some other airlines began converging with Virgin's value curve, the company went for another leap in value, this time from the service platform.

Virgin observed that most business-class passengers want to use their time productively before and between flights and that, after long-haul flights, they want to freshen up and change their wrinkled clothes before going to meetings. The airline designed lounges where passengers can take showers, have their clothes pressed, enjoy massages, and use state-of-the-art office equipment. The service allows busy executives to make good use of their time and go directly to meetings without first stopping at their hotels – a tremendous value for customers that generates high volume for Virgin. The airline has one of the highest sales per employee in the industry, and its costs per passenger mile are among the lowest. The economics of value innovation create a positive and reinforcing cycle.

When Virgin first challenged the industry's assumptions, its ideas were met with a great deal of skepticism. After all, conventional wisdom says that in order to grow, a company must embrace more, not fewer, market segments. But Virgin deliberately walked away from the revenue generated by first-class passengers. And it further rejected conventional wisdom by conceiving of business in terms of customer solutions, even if that took the company well beyond an airline's traditional offerings. Virgin has applied the logic of value innovation not just to the airline industry but also to insurance, music, and entertainment retailing. The company has always done more than leverage its existing assets and capabilities. It has been a consistent value innovator.

The Changing Mindset Concerning Business Innovation

Views of Innovation

A wide (and often confusing) range of views about innovation, its types, and classifications exist. Many are still rooted in the mechanical, logical progressions of the industrial economy. In today's complex and fast-changing environment, businesses and markets are constantly modifying each other and co-evolving in many ways. In the dynamic networked environment of the innovation economy, where 'balance', 'positioning', and single-enterprise efforts are inadequate, the identification must be with non-linearity, disequilibrium, and value-generating relationships across enterprise boundaries.

The following box displays various views of innovation, illustrating its multidimensionality and variety of viewpoints.

Some Views of Innovation

- Innovation: the act or process of innovating; something newly introduced, new method, custom, device, etc.; change in the way of doing things; renew, alter. – *Webster's New World Dictionary* (1982), Second College Edition.

- "The literature on organizational innovation is rich in lessons ... describes processes that are also prevalent in the natural universe. Innovation is fostered by information gathered from new connections; from insights gained by journeys into other disciplines or places; from active, collegial networks and fluid, open boundaries. Innovation arises from ongoing circles of exchange, where information is not just accumulated or stored, but created. Knowledge is generated from new connections that weren't there before." – Margaret J. Wheatley (1992), *Leadership and the New Science*, San Francisco: Bern Publishers, 113.

- "To explain innovation, we need a new theory of organizational knowledge creation... The cornerstone of our epistemology is the distinction between tacit and explicit knowledge... the key to knowledge creation lies in the mobilization and conversion of tacit knowledge." – Ikujiro Nonaka and Hirotaka Takeuchi (1995), *The Knowledge-Creating Company,* New York: Oxford University Press, 56.

- 'Industrial innovation includes the technical design, manufacturing, management and commercial activities involved in the marketing of a new (or improved) product or the first commercial use of a new (or improved) process or equipment' – Chris Freeman (1982), *The Economics of Industrial Innovation*, (2nd ed.), London: Frances Pinter.

- '... innovation does not necessarily imply the commercialization of only a major advance in the technology state of the art (a radical innovation), but it

---

includes also the utilization of even small-scale changes in technological know-how (an improvement or incremental innovation)...' – Roy Rothwell and Paul Gardiner (1985), 'Invention, innovation, re-innovation and the role of the user', *Technovation*, 3, 168.

- 'Innovation is the specific tool of entrepreneurs, the means by which they exploit change as an opportunity for a different business or service. It is capable of being presented as a discipline, capable of being learned, capable of being practiced' – Peter Drucker (1985), *Innovation and Entrepreneurship: Practice and Principles,* New York: Harper and Row, 19.

- 'Companies achieve competitive advantage through acts of innovation. They approach innovation in its broadest sense, including both new technologies and new ways of doing things' – Michael Porter (1990), *The Competitive Advantage of Nations*, London: MacMillan.

- 'Successful exploitation of new ideas' – DTI Innovation Unit definition (1994), London: Department of Trade and Industry.

The golden thread weaving through all definitions of innovation is that of *change*. When analyzing the concept of change, it reveals essentially two dimensions:[13]

- *Change in the value* (benefits/services/products) which an enterprise offers, and *processes* (ways, methods) in which they are created and delivered. Traditionally these are termed 'product' and 'process' innovation, although these terms can sometimes be confusing. For example, a new design of a car, a new insurance package for accident-prone babies and a new home entertainment system would all be examples of product innovation. Change in the manufacturing methods and equipment used to produce the car or the home entertainment system, or in the office procedures and sequencing in the insurance case would be examples of process innovation.

  Sometimes the dividing line is blurred – for example, a new jet-powered sea ferry is both a product and a process innovation. Services represent a particular case of this where the product and process aspects often merge – for example, is a new holiday package a product or process change?

- *The degree of novelty involved.* Evidently, updating the styling on a car is not the same as coming up with a completely new concept of a car which has an electric engine and is made of new composite materials as opposed to steel and glass. Similarly, increasing the speed and accuracy of a lathe is not the same thing as replacing it with a computer-controlled laser-forming process. There are degrees of novelty in these, running from minor, incremental improvements right through to disruptive changes which transform the way we think about and use them. Sometimes these changes are common to a particular sector or activity, but sometimes they are so radical and far-reaching that they change the basis of society – for example, the role played by steam power in the Industrial Revolution or the ubiquitous changes resulting from today's communications and computing technologies.

The ways in which we view, i.e. our mindsets, concerning these different degrees of novelty, are important. The ways in which we approach incremental, day-to-day change will differ from those used occasionally to handle a radical step-change in product or process. But it should also be remembered that it is the perceived degree of novelty which matters: novelty is very much in the eye of the beholder. For example, in a giant, technologically advanced organization like Shell or IBM, advanced networked information systems are commonplace, but for a small car dealership or food processor, even the use of a simple PC may still represent a major challenge.

Taxonomies of Innovation

Some observers provide a wide array of taxonomies of innovation, while others attempt to simplify into dichotomies and major categorizations. Geoffrey Moore[14] offers an extensive taxonomy, as illustrated in the box below.

A Broad Taxonomy of Innovation

- *Disruptive Innovation*. Gathers much attention, particularly in the press, because markets appear as if from nowhere, creating massive new sources of wealth. It tends to have its roots in technological discontinuities, such as the one that enabled Motorola's rise to prominence with the first generation of cell phones, or in fast-spreading fads like the collector card game Pokémon.

- *Application Innovation*. Takes existing technologies into new markets to serve new purposes, as when Tandem applied its fault-tolerant computers to the banking market to create ATMs and when OnStar took Global Positioning Systems into the automobile market for roadside assistance.

- *Product Innovation*. Takes established offers in established markets to the next level, as when Intel releases a new processor or Toyota a new car. The focus can be on performance increase (Fitleist Pro V1 golf balls), cost reduction (HP inkjet printers), usability improvement (Palm handhelds), or any other product enhancement.

- *Process Innovation*. Makes processes for established offers in established markets more effective or efficient. Examples include Dell's streamlining of its PC supply chain and order fulfillment system, Charles Schwab's migration to online trading, and Wal-Mart's refinement of vendor-managed inventory processes.

- *Experiential Innovation*. Makes surface modifications that improve customers' experience of established products or processes. These can take the form of delighters ("You've got mail!"), satisfiers (superior line management at Disneyland), or reassurers (package tracking from FedEx).

- *Marketing Innovation*. Improves customer-touching processes, be they marketing communications (use of the Web and trailers for viral marketing of The Lord of the Rings movie trilogy) or consumer transactions (Amazon's e-commerce mechanisms and eBay's online auctions).

- *Business Model Innovation*. Reframes an established customer need base, reinvents value proposition(s) to the customer, redefines a company's established role in the value system, or combinations of these. Examples include Gillette's move from razors to razor blades, IBM's shift to on-demand computing services, and Apple's expansion into consumer retailing.

- *Structural Innovation*. Capitalizes on disruption to restructure industry relationships. Innovators like Fidelity and Citigroup, for example, have used the deregulation of financial services to offer broader arrays of products and service to consumers under one umbrella. Nearly overnight, those companies became sophisticated competitors to traditional banks and insurance companies.

We might add to this list the concept of "managerial innovation" – applying new management ideas for better performance.[15] Admittedly, the breadth of and overlap among the above types of innovation can be problematic. Which types of innovations should a company pursue, and why? In practice, most companies address only product innovation in any organized or official fashion.[16] But this means that many other potential types of innovation are not seriously addressed.

There was a time when the notion of core competences was invoked to solve this problem: selecting the things you are best at and focus your innovative resources accordingly. But identifying what competencies are truly core is both difficult and risky. Companies have discovered that being the best at something does not guarantee a competitive advantage or survival if the basis of the industry is fundamentally shifting. A distinctive competence is valuable only if it drives purchase preferences in evolving markets.

Clayton Christensen and Michael Raynor[17] offer a more simple and powerful taxonomy of innovation, i.e. the distinction between sustaining and disruptive innovation:

- A *sustaining innovation* targets demanding, high-end customers with better performance than what was previously available. Some sustaining innovations are the incremental year-by-year improvements that all good companies grind out. Other sustaining innovations are breakthrough, leapfrog-beyond-the-competition products. It does not matter how technologically difficult the innovation is, as the established competitors almost always win the battles of sustaining technology. Because this approach involves making a better product that they can sell for higher profit margins to their best customers, the established competitors have powerful motivations to fight sustaining battles, and they often have the resources to win.

- *Disruptive innovations*, in contrast, do not attempt to bring better products to established customers in existing markets. Rather, they disrupt and redefine that trajectory by introducing products and services that are not as good as currently available products. But disruptive technologies offer other benefits – typically, they are simpler, more convenient, and less expensive products that appeal to new or less-demanding customers.

Once the disruptive product gains a foothold in new or low-end markets, the improvement cycle begins. And because the pace of technological progress out-strips customers' abilities to use it, the previously not-good-enough technology eventually improves enough to intersect with the needs of more demanding customers. When that happens, the disruptors are on a path that tends to ultimately crush the incumbents. This distinction is important for innovators seeking to create new-growth businesses. Whereas the current leaders of the industry almost always triumph in battles of sustaining innovation, successful disruptions have been launched most often by entrant companies. Disruption tends to have a paralyzing effect on industry leaders. With resource allocation processes designed and per-fected to support sustaining innovations, they are constitutionally unable to respond. They are always motivated to go up-market, and almost never motivated to defend the new or low-end markets that the disruptors find attractive. Christensen and Raynor call this phenomenon asymmetric motivation – the core of the 'innovator's dilemma', and the beginning of the 'innovator's solution'.[18]

This effective taxonomy of innovation can be illustrated in a simple matrix, as indicated in Figure 3.2.

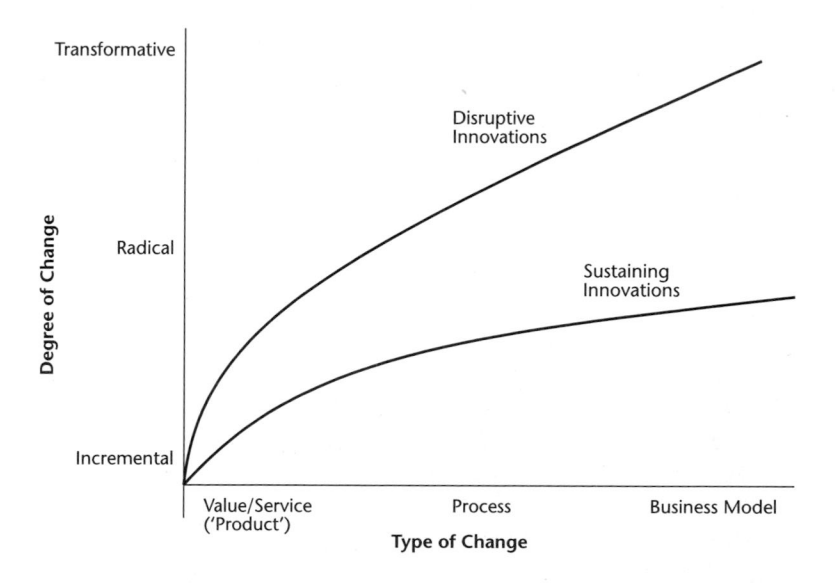

Figure 3.2 Dimensions of innovation space

In the figure, it is evident that sustaining innovation based on incremental change in value/service and processes is probably the most well-known and 'easiest' type of innovation, rooted in a goods-competitive mindset. On the other hand, disruptive innovation based on transformative change in business models is the most complex and risky, but essential in the innovation economy based on a disruptive value-innovation mindset.

Evolving Innovation Process Mindsets

Mindsets about innovation processes have evolved over time, and have shaped the ways in which we attempt to manage it. Early models saw it as a linear sequence of functional activities. Either new opportunities arising out of research gave rise to applications and refinements which eventually found their way to the market-place ('technology push'), or else the market signaled needs for something new which then drew through new solutions to the problem ('need pull', where necessity becomes the mother of invention).

The limitations of such early models and extant approaches to the innovation process are clear; in practice, innovation is a coupling and matching process where interaction is the critical element. Sometimes the 'push' will dominate, sometimes the 'pull', but successful innovation requires interaction between the two.

Rothwell[19] provides a useful historical perspective on this, suggesting that our appreciation of the nature of the innovation process has been evolving from simple linear models (characteristic of the 1960s) through to increasingly complex interactive models (Table 3.4). His 'fifth-generation innovation' concept sees innovation as a multi-factor process which requires high levels of integration at both intra- and inter-firm levels and which is increasingly facilitated by IT-based networking. Although such fifth-generation models appear complex, they still involve the same basic process framework.

Failure to understand fully the changing processes of innovation in the innovation economy leads to application of a partial or outdated practice. Table 3.5 provides an overview of the difficulties that arise if an outdated or partial view of innovation is taken.[20]

As indicated in Tables 3.4 and 3.5, there is a fundamental shift in how companies generate new ideas and value, and bring them to market. For most of the 20th century, the 'closed innovation' model worked well – internal R&D focus, product innovation orientation, self-reliance, tight control and generation of own ideas to develop, manufacture, market, distribute, and service new products.

Toward the end of the 20th century, though, a number of factors combined to erode the underpinnings of closed innovation.[21] Chief among these factors was the dramatic rise in the number and mobility of knowledge workers, making it increasingly difficult for companies to control their proprietary ideas and expertise. Another important factor was the growing availability of private venture capital, which has helped to finance new firms and their efforts to commercialize ideas that have spilled outside the 'silos' of corporate research labs.

Table 3.4 Five generations of innovation process mindsets/models

Generation		Key features
First/second:	1960's +	Simple linear models – need pull, technology push
Third:	1970's +	Coupling model, recognizing interaction between different elements and feedback loops between them
Fourth:	1990's +	Parallel model, integration within the firm, upstream with key suppliers and downstream with demanding and active customers, emphasis on linkages and alliances
Fifth:	2000 +	Systems integration and extensive networking, flexible and customized response, continuous experimentation and testing

Table 3.5 Problems with outdated or partial views of innovation

Partial view of innovation	Typical result
Strong R&D capability	Technology which fails to meet user needs and may not be accepted
The province of specialists in white coats in the R&D laboratory	Lack of involvement of others, and a lack of key knowledge and experience input from other perspectives
Meeting customer needs	Lack of technical progression, leading to inability to gain competitive edge by anticipating future needs
Technology advances	Producing products which the market does not want or designing processes which do not meet the needs of the user or which are opposed
The province only of large firms	Weak small firms with too high dependence on a few large customers
Only about 'breakthrough' changes	Neglect of the potential of incremental innovation. Also an inability to secure and reinforce the gains from radical change because the incremental performance ratchet is not working well
Associated only with key individuals	Failure to utilize the creativity of the remainder of employees, and to secure their inputs and perspectives to improve innovation
Only internally generated	The 'not invented here' effect, where good ideas from outside are resisted or rejected
Only externally generated	Innovation becomes simply a matter of filling a shopping list of needs from outside and there is little internal learning or development of technological competence
Only about products	Neglect of potential for innovation in services, processes, business models, management approaches, and other forms

Table 3.6 Contrasting principles/views of closed and open innovation

Closed innovation principles/views	Open innovation principles/views
The smart people in our field work for us.	Not all of the smart people work for us so we must find and tap into the knowledge and expertise of bright individuals outside our company.
To profit from R&D, we must discover, develop, and ship it ourselves.	External R&D can create significant value; internal R&D is needed to claim some portion of that value.
If we discover it ourselves, we will get it to market first.	We don't have to originate the research in order to profit from it.
If we are the first to commercialize an innovation, we will win.	Building a better business model is better than getting to market first.
If we create the most and best ideas in the industry, we will win.	If we make the best use of internal and external ideas, we will win.
We should control our intellectual property (IP) so that our competitors don't profit from our ideas.	We should profit from others' use of our IP, and we should buy others' IP whenever it advances our own business model.

Such factors have wreaked havoc with the virtuous cycle that sustained closed innovation. Now, when breakthroughs occur, the scientists and engineers who made them have outside options that they previously lacked.

In this new model of open innovation, firms commercialize external (as well as internal) ideas by deploying outside (as well as in-house) pathways to the market. Specifically, companies can commercialize internal ideas through channels outside of their current businesses in order to generate value for the organization. Some ways for accomplishing this include startup companies (which might be financed and staffed with some of the company's own personnel) and licensing agreements. In addition, ideas can also originate outside the firm's own labs and be brought inside for commercialization. The pharmaceutical firm Eli Lilly, for example, at any given time has about 150 innovation projects underway at small biotechnology firms it works with as partners. It also created a startup organization, InnoCentive, in order to tap the innovations of scientists all around the world who could solve important biology and chemistry problems on Lilly's (and later other firms') behalf. In environments such as Lilly's, the boundary between a firm and its surrounding environment is more porous, enabling innovation to move easily between the two.

Table 3.6 indicates the contrasting views of closed and open innovation.[22]

The locus of innovation in many industries is migrating today beyond the confines of the central R&D departments, and is now situated among various startups, universities, research consortia, incubators, and other outside organizations. This phenomenon goes well beyond high technology industries and firms – other industries such as automotive, health care, financial services, and consumer packaged goods are all adopting open innovation views and principles. Specifically, in the fifth generation innovation mindset, the role of R&D is extending far beyond the traditional boundaries of the firm. In a knowledge-networked world, the co-leveraging of new ideas, expertise and insight to co-shape value innovation in a broader and faster context becomes paramount.

Conclusion

In the innovation economy, mindsets of the enterprise, strategy, and innovation have experienced fundamental change. Figure 3.3 indicates the shift in strategy mindsets from the 1980s to the early 2000s, with corresponding shift in strategic management orientation and practices.[23]

To survive and thrive in an increasingly turbulent landscape, it has become necessary to create new relationships and new mental space with diverse members in the socio-cultural business system that includes employees, partners, suppliers, competitors, and most importantly, customers. The open and easy flow of knowledge, ideas, skills, and expertise among such members increases the sources of competitive advantage whereby organizations can create new value propositions that enable them to capture unique strategic positions.

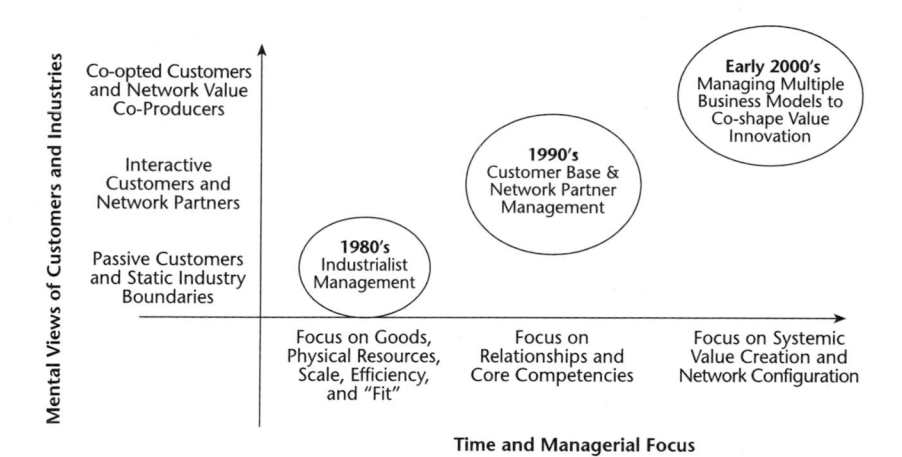

Figure 3.3 Shifting strategy mindsets and managerial focus

The Era of Open Innovation[*]

By Henry W. Chesbrough

Companies are increasingly rethinking the fundamental ways in which they generate ideas and bring them to market – harnessing external ideas while leveraging their in-house R&D outside their current operations.

In the past, internal R&D was a valuable strategic asset, even a formidable barrier to entry by competitors in many markets. Only large corporations like DuPont, IBM and AT&T could compete by doing the most R&D in their respective industries (and subsequently reaping most of the profits as well). Rivals who sought to unseat those powerhouses had to ante up considerable resources to create their own labs, if they were to have any chance of succeeding. These days, however, the leading industrial enterprises of the past have been encountering remarkably strong competition from many upstarts. Surprisingly, these newcomers conduct little or no basic research on their own, but instead get new ideas to market through a different process.

Consider Lucent Technologies, which inherited the lion's share of Bell Laboratories after the breakup of AT&T. In the 20th century, Bell Labs was perhaps the premier industrial research organization and this should have been a decisive strategic weapon for Lucent in the telecommunications equipment market. However, things didn't quite work out that way. Cisco Systems, which lacks anything resembling the deep internal R&D capabilities of Bell Labs, somehow has consistently managed to stay abreast of Lucent, even occasionally beating the company to market. What happened?

Although Lucent and Cisco competed directly in the same industry, the two companies were not innovating in the same manner. Lucent devoted enormous resources to exploring the world of new materials and state-of-the-art components and systems, seeking fundamental discoveries that could fuel future generations of products and services. Cisco, on the other hand, deployed a very different strategy in its battle for innovation leadership. Whatever technology the company needed, it acquired from the outside, usually by partnering or investing in promising startups (some, ironically, founded by ex-Lucent veterans). In this way, Cisco kept up with the R&D output of perhaps the world's finest industrial R&D organization, all without conducting much research of its own.

---

[*] Taken with permission from *MIT Sloan Managament Review* Vol. 44 No. 3, Spring 2003, pp. 35-41

The story of Lucent and Cisco is hardly an isolated instance. IBM's research prowess in computing provided little protection against Intel and Microsoft in the personal computer hardware and software businesses. Similarly, Motorola, Siemens and other industrial titans watched helplessly as Nokia catapulted itself to the forefront of wireless telephony in just 20 years, building on its industrial experience from earlier decades in the low-tech industries of wood pulp and rubber boots. Pharmaceutical giants like Merck and Pfizer have also watched as a number of upstarts, including Genentech, Amgen and Genzyme, has parlayed the research discoveries of others to become major players in the biotechnology industry.

From Closed to Open

Is innovation dead? Hardly, as punctuated by the recent advances in the life sciences, including revolutionary breakthroughs in genomics and cloning. Then why is internal R&D no longer the strategic asset it once was? The answer lies in a fundamental shift in how companies generate new ideas and bring them to market. In the old model of closed innovation, firms adhered to the following philosophy: Successful innovation requires control. In other words, companies must generate their own ideas that they would then develop, manufacture, market, distribute and service themselves (see "The Closed Innovation Model"). This approach calls for self-reliance: If you want something done right, you've got to do it yourself.

For years, the logic of closed innovation was tacitly held to be self-evident as the "right way" to bring new ideas to market and successful companies all played by certain implicit rules. They invested more heavily in internal R&D than their competitors and they hired the best and the brightest (to reap the rewards of the industry's smartest people). Thanks to such investments, they were able to discover the best and greatest number of ideas, which allowed them to get to market first. This, in turn, enabled them to reap most of the profits, which they protected by aggressively controlling their intellectual property (IP) to prevent competitors from exploiting it. They could then reinvest the profits in conducting more R&D, which then led to additional breakthrough discoveries, creating a virtuous cycle of innovation.

For most of the 20th century, the model worked – and it worked well. Thanks to it, Thomas Edison was able to invent a number of landmark devices, including the phonograph and the electric light bulb, which paved the way for the establishment of General Electric's famed Global Research Center in Niskayuna, New York. In the chemical industry, companies like DuPont established central research labs to identify and commercialize a stunning variety of new products, such as the synthetic fibers Nylon, Kevlar and Lycra. Bell Labs researchers discovered amazing physical phenomena and harnessed those discoveries to create a host of revolutionary products, including transistors and lasers.

Toward the end of the 20th century, though, a number of factors combined to erode the underpinnings of closed innovation in the United States. Perhaps chief among these factors was the dramatic rise in the number and mobility of knowledge workers, making it increasingly difficult for companies to control their proprietary ideas and expertise. Another important factor was the growing availability of private venture capital, which has helped to finance new firms and their efforts to commercialize ideas that have spilled outside the silos of corporate research labs.

Such factors have wreaked havoc with the virtuous cycle that sustained closed innovation. Now, when breakthroughs occur, the scientists and engineers who made them have an outside option that they previously lacked. If a company that funded a discovery doesn't pursue it in a timely fashion, the people involved could pursue it on their own – in a startup financed by venture capital. If that fledgling firm were to become successful, it could gain additional financing through a stock offering or it could be acquired at an attractive price. In either case, the successful startup would generally *not* reinvest in new fundamental discoveries, but instead, like Cisco, it would look outside for another technology to commercialize. Thus, the virtuous cycle of innovation was shattered: The company that originally funded a breakthrough did not profit from the investment, and the firm that *did* reap the benefits did not reinvest its proceeds to finance the next generation of discoveries.

In this new model of *open innovation*, firms commercialize external (as well as internal) ideas by deploying outside (as well as in-house) pathways to the market. Specifically, companies can commercialize internal ideas through channels outside of their current businesses in order to generate value for the organization. Some vehicles for accomplishing this include startup companies (which might be financed and staffed with some of the company's own personnel) and licensing agreements. In addition, ideas can also originate outside the firm's own labs and be brought inside for commercialization. In other words, the boundary between a firm and its surrounding environment is more porous, enabling innovation to move easily between the two (see "The Open Innovation Model").

The Closed Innovation Model

In closed innovation, a company generates, develops and commercializes its own ideas. This philosophy of self-reliance dominated the R&D operations of many leading industrial corporations for most of the 20th century.

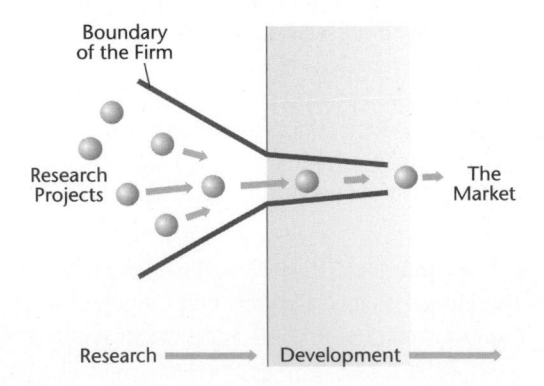

Boundary of the Firm

Research Projects

The Market

Research ➡ Development ➡

Contrasting Principles of Closed and Open Innovation

Closed Innovation Principles	Open Innovation Principles
The smart people in our field work for us.	Not all of the smart people work for us* so we must find and tap into the knowledge and expertise of bright individuals outside our company.
To profit form R&D, we must discover, develop and ship it ourselves.	External R&D can create significant value; internal R&D is needed to claim some portion of that value.
If we discover it ourselves, we will get it to market first.	We don't have to originate the research in order to profit from it.
If we are the first to commercialize an innovation, we will win.	Building a better business model is better than getting to market first.
If we create the most and best ideas in the industry, we will win.	If we make the best use of internal *and external* ideas, we will win.
We should control our intellectual property (IP) so that our competitors don't profit from our ideas.	We should profit from others' use of our IP, and we should buy others' IP whenever it advances our own business model.

* This maxim first came to my attention in a talk by Bill Joy of Sun Microsystems over a decade ago. See, for example, A. Lash, "The Joy of Sun," The Standard, June 21, 1999

At its root, open innovation is based on a landscape of abundant knowledge, which must be used readily if it is to provide value for the company that created it. However, an organization should not restrict the knowledge that it uncovers in its research to its internal market pathways, nor should those internal pathways necessarily be constrained to bringing only the company's internal knowledge to market. This perspective suggests some very different rules (see "Contrasting Principles of Closed and Open Innovation"). For example, no longer should a company lock up its IP, but instead it should find ways to profit from others' use of that technology through licensing agreements, joint ventures and other arrangements.

One major difference between closed and open innovation lies in how companies screen their ideas. In any R&D process, researchers and their managers must separate the bad proposals from the good ones so that they can discard the former while pursuing and commercializing the latter. Both the closed and open models are adept at weeding out "false positives" (that is, bad ideas that initially look promising), but open innovation also incorporates the ability to rescue "false negatives" (projects that initially seem to lack promise but turn out to be surprisingly valuable). A company that is focused too internally – that is, a firm with a closed innovation approach – is prone to miss a number of those opportunities because many will fall outside the organization's current businesses or will need to be combined with external technologies to unlock their potential. This can be especially painful for corporations that have made substantial long-term investments in research, only to discover later that some of the projects they abandoned had tremendous commercial value.

The classic example is Xerox and its Palo Alto Research Center (PARC). Researchers there developed numerous computer hardware and software technologies – Ethernet and the graphical user interface (GUI) are two such examples. However, these inventions were not viewed as promising businesses for Xerox, which was focused on high-speed copiers and printers. In other words, the technologies were false negatives[1] and they languished inside Xerox, only to be commercialized by other companies that, in the process, reaped tremendous benefits. Apple Computer, for instance, exploited the GUI in its Macintosh operating system while Microsoft did the same in its Windows operating system.

How Prevalent Is Open Innovation?

This is not to argue that all industries have been (or will be) migrating to open innovation. At this point, different businesses can be located on a continuum, from essentially closed to completely open. An example of the former is the nuclear-reactor industry, which depends mainly on internal ideas and has low labor mobility, little venture capital, few (and weak) startups and relatively little research being conducted at universities. Whether this industry will ever migrate towards open innovation is questionable.

At the other extreme, some industries have been open innovators for some time now. Consider Hollywood, which for decades has innovated through a network of partnerships and alliances between production studios, directors, talent agencies, actors, scriptwriters, independent producers and specialized subcontractors (such as the suppliers of special effects). The mobility of this workforce is legendary: Every waitress is a budding actress; every parking attendant has a screenplay he is working on.

Many industries – including copiers, computers, disk drives, semiconductors, telecommunications equipment, pharmaceuticals, biotechnology and even military weapons and communications systems – are currently transitioning from closed to open innovation. For such businesses, a number of critically important innovations have emerged from seemingly unlikely sources. Indeed, the locus of innovation in these industries has migrated beyond the confines of the central R&D laboratories of the largest companies and is now situated among various startups, universities, research consortia and other outside organizations. This trend goes well beyond high technology – other industries such as automotive, health care, banking, insurance and consumer packaged goods have also been leaning toward open innovation.

The Open Innovation Model

In the new model of open innovation, a company commercializes both its own ideas as well as innovations from other firms and seeks ways to bring its in-house ideas to market by deploying pathways outside its current businesses. Note that the boundary between the company and its surrounding environment is porous (represented by a dashed line), enabling innovations to move more easily between the two.

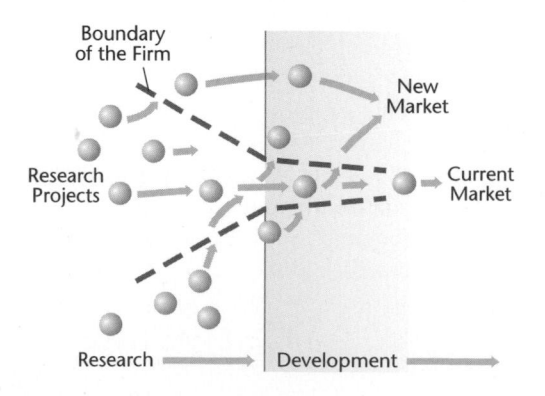

Consider Procter & Gamble, the consumer-product giant with a long and proud tradition of in-house science behind its many leading brands. P&G has recently changed its approach to innovation, extending its internal R&D to the outside world through the slogan "Connect & Develop." [2] The company has created the position of director of external innovation and has set a goal of sourcing 50% of its innovations from outside the company in five years, up from an estimated 10% this year.[3] This approach is a long way from the "not invented here," or NIH, syndrome that afflicts many large, successful industrial organizations. Recently, P&G scored a huge success with Spin-Brush, an electric toothbrush that runs on batteries and sells for $5. The idea for the product, which has quickly become the best-selling toothbrush in the United States, came not from P&G's labs but from four entrepreneurs in Cleveland.

P&G also tries to move its own innovations outside. Recently, the company instituted a policy stating that any idea that originates in its labs will be offered to outside firms, even direct competitors, if an internal business does not use the idea within three years.[4] The goal is to prevent promising projects from losing momentum and becoming stuck inside the organization.

The Different Modes of Innovation

Indeed, many companies have been defining new strategies for exploiting the principles of open innovation, exploring ways in which external technologies can fill gaps in their current businesses and looking at how their internal technologies can spawn the seeds of new businesses outside the current organization. In doing so, many firms have focused their activities into one of three primary areas: *funding, generating* or *commercializing innovation.*

Funding Innovation

Two types of organizations – *innovation investors* and *benefactors* – are focused primarily on supplying fuel for the innovation fire. The original *innovation investor* was the corporate R&D budget but now a wide range of other types has emerged, including venture capital (VC) firms, angel investors, corporate VC entities, private equity investors and the Small Business Investment Companies (SBICs), which provide VC to small, independent businesses and are licensed and regulated by the U.S. Small Business Administration. Their capital helps move ideas out of corporations and universities and into the market, typically through the creation of startups. In addition to financing, innovation investors can supply valuable advice for helping startups avoid the common growing pains that afflict many fledgling firms.

With the recent economic downturn and the implosion of numerous dot-com firms, innovation investors have understandably turned somewhat gun-shy. However, though it seems these players are down, they are hardly out. VCs currently have about $250 billion in capital under management, of which $90 billion is idle.[5] When the economy rebounds, innovation investors will likely spot and fund new developments in areas like genomics and nanotechnology, which will likely spur the next economic wave of innovation.

Innovation benefactors provide new sources of research funding. Unlike investors, benefactors focus on the early stages of research discovery. The classic example here is the National Science Foundation (NSF), an independent agency of the U.S. government. Through its awards and grants programs, the NSF provides about 20% of federal support for academic institutions to conduct basic research. The Defense Advanced Research Projects Agency (DARPA) has also been a key benefactor, particularly for the early work in much of the computer industry.

Some companies are devoting a portion of their resources to playing the role of benefactor. By funding promising early-stage work, they get a first look at the ideas and can selectively fund those that seem favorable for their industry. An interesting development with innovation benefactors is the possible rise in philanthropy from private foundations, especially those backed by wealthy individuals. For example, the billionaire Larry Ellison, chairman and CEO of software giant Oracle, has founded an organization that provides about $50 million annually for basic research in cancer, Parkinson's and Alzheimer's diseases as well as other disorders. Interestingly, the foundation was set up specifically for early exploration – research so embryonic that scientists aren't able to obtain funds through traditional grants, such as those awarded by the NSF.

Generating Innovation

There are four types of organizations that primarily generate innovation: *innovation explorers, merchants, architects* and *missionaries*. Innovation explorers specialize in performing the discovery research function that previously took place primarily within corporate R&D laboratories. Interestingly, a number of explorers evolved as spinoffs of laboratories that used to be a part of a larger organization. Just a year ago, for example, PARC became a separate, independent entity from Xerox. Similarly, Telcordia Technologies was formed from the divestiture of the Bell System and is now home to about 400 researchers with a broad range of expertise, from software engineering to optical networking.

An interesting development with explorers has been taking place with the major government labs, such as Sandia National Laboratories, Lawrence Livermore National Laboratory and the MIT Lincoln Laboratory. In the aftermath of the end of the Cold War, these organizations have been seeking new missions for their work and much of their basic research is finding applications in commercial markets. Consider Lincoln Laboratory, which has conducted radar and other defense research since the 1950s. Technology developed there for missile detection has recently been adapted to cancer treatment, enabling microwave energy to be focused more effectively at tumors.

Innovation merchants must also explore, but their activities are focused on a narrow set of technologies that are then codified into intellectual property and aggressively sold to (and brought to market by) others. In other words, innovation merchants will innovate but only with specific commercial goals in mind, whereas explorers tend to innovate for innovation's sake. For the merchants, royalties from their IP enable them to do more research in their areas of focus. Indeed, such companies rise and fall with the strength of their IP portfolios.

One example of an innovation merchant is Qualcomm, which conducts extensive internal research on telecommunications, including code division multiple access (CDMA), a standard for wireless technology. Originally, Qualcomm manufactured cellular phones and software products such as the Eudora e-mail program, but today it focuses on licensing its CDMA technology and producing the associated chipsets for use by other cell-phone manufacturers. Qualcomm currently boasts more than 100 licensees, including Motorola, Nokia and Kyocera.

Innovation architects provide a valuable service in complicated technology worlds. In order to create value for their customers, they develop architectures that partition this complexity, enabling numerous other companies to provide pieces of the system, all while ensuring that those parts fit together in a coherent way. Boeing, for example, will engineer the overall design of an aircraft like the 747, after which companies like GE can then develop and manufacture the jet engines and other constituent parts. Innovation architects work in areas that are complex and fast-moving, which disfavors the "do-it-yourself" approach. To be successful, innovation architects must establish their systems solution, communicate it, persuade others to support it and develop it in the future. They must also devise a way to capture some portion of the value they create, otherwise they will find it impossible to sustain and advance their architecture.

For example, the dramatic rise of Nokia in wireless communications has been due, in part, to the strong lead it took in establishing the global system for mobile communication (GSM) technology as a standard for cellular phones. Accomplishing that required working closely with a number of other companies, as well as the governments of many European countries. Specifically, Nokia research helped define the now-accepted standards for moving GSM from a narrow- to broad-bandwidth spectrum and the company pushed hard to establish that technology: It willingly licensed the research to others and partnered with companies (including competitors) to develop the chipsets necessary for implementing the standard.[6] Those efforts have helped Nokia to become the world's dominant supplier of wireless-phone handsets, controlling nearly 40% of the global market.

Innovation missionaries consist of people and organizations that create and advance technologies to serve a cause. Unlike the innovation merchants and architects, they do not seek financial profits from their work. Instead, the mission is what motivates them. This is characteristic of many community-based nonprofits and religious groups but also occurs in the software industry. Here, user groups help define how a particular software program will evolve. These organizations, which include professional programmers as well as hobbyists, not only identify bugs (and possible ways to fix them), but additionally might even create a "wish list" of potential features that the next generation of a software product might include.

The evolution of the computer operating system Linux exemplifies this approach. Originally developed by Linus Torvalds, Linux has advanced over the years thanks to the arduous efforts of an informal network of programmers around the world. The software is freely available to anyone, and it has become a viable alternative to commercial offerings such as Microsoft Windows NT.

Commercializing Innovation

Lastly, two types of organization are focused on bringing innovations to market: innovation marketers and one-stop centers. Innovation marketers often perform at least some of the functions of the other types of organization, but their defining attribute is their keen ability to profitably market ideas, both their own as well as others'. To do so, marketers focus on developing a deep understanding of the current and potential needs in the market and this helps them to identify which outside ideas to bring in-house. Most of the drugs that are currently in Pfizer's pipeline, for instance, originated outside the company.

Another example of an innovation marketer is Intuit, which sells personal financial software products such as the popular Quicken program. For a number of years, Intuit has been able to keep Microsoft at bay – one of the very few companies that can make that claim – by maintaining close and disciplined interactions with its customers to gain in-depth knowledge about their needs. In keeping with the innovation marketer's role, Intuit has become adept at identifying and adapting outside technologies to satisfy those needs. In this way, the company has consistently been able to profit from innovations it did not discover. For example, it acquired two of its popular products – TurboTax (a tax-preparation program) and QuickBooks (small-business accounting software) – from the outside and enhanced both programs to meet its customers' needs.

Innovation one-stop centers provide comprehensive products and services. They take the best ideas (from whatever source) and deliver those offerings to their customers at competitive prices. Like innovation marketers, they thrive by selling others' ideas, but are different in that they typically form unshakable connections to the end users, increasingly managing a customer's resources to his or her specifications. For example, the Web site for Yahoo! enables people to shop, send e-mail, manage their personal finances, hunt for jobs and keep up-to-date on current events.

While Yahoo! targets consumers, other one-stop centers are focused on business-to-business interactions. IBM's Global Services division, for instance, sells IT solutions to other companies, and interestingly, will install and service hardware and software from any vendor, including IBM's competitors. In other words, it will provide the best solution to its customers, regardless of the origin of those products.

Although many companies are focusing on just funding, generating or commercializing innovation, some are continuing to do all three. As mentioned earlier, industrial powerhouses like GE, DuPont and AT&T (with Bell Labs) were the exemplars of this approach in the United States during the 20th century, and the success of those corporations has cast the mold for most central R&D organizations. To this day, a number of companies, called *fully integrated innovators*, continue to espouse the closed innovation credo of "innovation through total control."

IBM in the mainframe computer market is one such example. Thanks to the company's T.J. Watson Research Center and its other internal R&D labs, virtually all of the value-added components inside an IBM mainframe computer come from IBM itself. This includes the semiconductor circuits that power the main processing unit, the disk storage, the high-speed circuitry that routes signals, the tape backup storage, the operating system and the different application programs. To accomplish that, IBM must manage technology advances in both hardware and software within different internal divisions, coordinating future releases of software and new versions of hardware to assure its customers of continued improvements in price and performance.

IBM's mainframe business raises an important point: A corporation can deploy different modes of innovation in different markets. Specifically, IBM is a one-stop center for consulting services and a fully integrated innovator with respect to mainframes. Another important point is that competing modes can coexist in the same industry. In pharmaceuticals, for example, Merck has remained a fully integrated innovator while Pfizer is becoming an innovation marketer. It remains to be seen which of those modes (or perhaps another) will dominate.

All of the different modes will evolve in an open innovation environment, and future ones will probably emerge as well. One possible development is the rise of specialized intermediaries that function as brokers or middlemen to create markets for IP.[7] More than likely, there won't be one "best way" to innovate, although some modes will face greater challenges than others.

Fully integrated innovators, for instance, have become an endangered species in many industries. As ideas spill out of the central R&D labs of large corporations, the other modes of innovation are in a position to profit from them. In fact, these other modes have risen in prominence in response to the perceived limitations of fully integrated innovators. Much of IBM's innovation, for instance, has been migrating from the fully integrated mode toward the one-stop center approach.

The explorer mode depends on external sources of funding because of the considerable resources and uncertainty of conducting long-term research. Outside of the life sciences, this support has dwindled substantially in the past decade, making a number of explorers vulnerable. Recent societal concerns, such as for "homeland security" in the United States, may supply a new impetus for government funding, and already many explorers are making the transition. Sandia National Labs, for instance, is currently developing robots for disabling bombs. It is questionable, however, whether new security research missions will fit with the strengths and abilities of the current explorers or whether a new cadre of them will arise instead.

Innovation merchants also face significant challenges. Although the concept of supplying innovation to a "marketplace for ideas" is attractive in theory, it is devilishly tricky to accomplish. For one thing, merchants must determine how best to gain access to the complementary assets that might be needed to commercialize an innovation. Another issue is that the laws for IP protection are ill-defined at best, making it risky for merchants to limit their revenue stream solely to the marketing of their IP.

Innovation architects encounter a different set of challenges in their roles of organizing and coordinating complex technologies. Although ideas are plentiful, that very abundance can make it extremely difficult to create useful systems. Furthermore, innovation architects, through the harnessing of a broad network of companies, must balance the creation of value with the need to capture a portion of that value. Boeing, for instance, is able to do so by acting as the systems assembler for its aircraft. With other technologies, however, the means by which innovation architects can benefit from their roles is not so straightforward.

Several of the modes of innovation rely on a continued supply of useful ideas and technologies from the outside. Although university research is now more abundant and of higher quality than in the past, the flow of that knowledge into the commercial sector faces several obstacles. Such research is necessarily filtered through the silos of academic departments and that process tends to discourage cross-discipline break-throughs. In addition, universities are now allowed to patent their discoveries, and although the change has benefited professors (who are able to form their own com-mercial ventures), it has also taxed the efforts of companies, particularly small firms, to profit from that source of innovation.

Long Live Open Innovation

Today, in many industries, the logic that supports an internally oriented, centralized approach to R&D has become obsolete. Useful knowledge has become widespread and ideas must be used with alacrity. If not, they will be lost. Such factors create a new logic of open innovation that embraces external ideas and knowledge in conjunc-tion with internal R&D. This change offers novel ways to create value – along with new opportunities to claim portions of that value.

However, companies must still perform the difficult and arduous work necessary to convert promising research results into products and services that satisfy customers' needs. Specifically, the role of R&D needs to extend far beyond the boundaries of the firm. Innovators must integrate their ideas, expertise and skills with those of others outside the organization to deliver the result to the marketplace, using the most effec-tive means possible. In short, firms that can harness outside ideas to advance their own businesses while leveraging their internal ideas outside their current operations will likely thrive in this new era of open innovation.

Strategic Innovation and the Science of Learning[*]

By Vijay Govindarajan and Chris Trimble

Theory-focused planning helps executives pursue ventures so cutting-edge that no road maps exist. The key is learning from strategic experiments.

Entrepreneurship is a competence in only the rarest corporation. Pity, as its absence has led to the death of many revered companies. In an economic environment characterized by dramatic change, the ability to explore emerging opportunities by launching and learning from *strategic experiments* is more critical to survival than ever.

A strategic experiment is a risky new venture within an established corporation. It is a multiyear bet within a poorly defined industry that has no clear formula for making a profit. Potential customers are mere possibilities. Value propositions are guesses. And activities that lead to profitable outcomes are unclear.

Most executives who have been involved in strategic experiments agree that the key to success is learning quickly. In a race to define an emerging industry, the competitor that learns first generally wins. Unfortunately, habits embedded in the conventional planning process disable learning. A better approach, *theory-focused planning*, differs from traditional planning on six counts.

The Need for Strategic Innovation

In the late 1990s, Corning Inc. began to explore a possibility far beyond its existing lines of business. The strategic experiment, Corning Microarray Technologies (CMT), sought to usher in a new era in genomics research. (See "About the Research.") DNA microarrays, glass slides with thousands of tiny DNA samples printed on their surfaces, were a key piece of experimental apparatus for measuring DNA interactions in large sample sizes. Seeking to disrupt a status quo that offered researchers a devil's choice between time-consuming self-printing and the purchase of an expensive closed-standard system, CMT sought to introduce reliable, inexpensive microarrays as part of a new open-standard system.

---

[*] Taken with permission from *MIT Sloan Management Review* Vol. 45 No. 2, Winter 2004, pp. 67-75

With the anticipated explosion in genomics research that followed the completion of the mapping of the human genome, CMT expected a robust market. Still, the unknowns were daunting. Would a standard compatible with CMT's product be widely adopted? Would Corning's expertise in adhering tiny quantities of fluid to glass be readily transferred to microarrays? Could CMT lower costs to a point that compelled laboratories to invest in entirely new systems for genomics experimentation?

During recent years of economic malaise, many corporations have decided against such strategic experiments. Only a few have taken significant risks, recognizing that cycles of boom and bust mask a fundamental truth: The world is always changing. The pace of change does not mirror the manic financial markets; it is steadier and surer. Globalization brings new markets, nontraditional competitors and new sources of uncertainty, such as armed conflict in the Middle East and the entry of China into the World Trade Organization. More subtle changes are also important, including the aging of the population in developed economies and the rise of a new middle class in emerging ones. This dynamic environment affects industries new and old, high tech and low tech, in manufacturing and services. Unanticipated opportunities emerge just as imitators neutralize existing competitive advantages.

The life of any business is finite.[1] For companies to endure, the drive for efficiency must be combined with excellence in entrepreneurship. Through the process of strategic innovation, new businesses must emerge before old ones decay. As Ray Stata, chairman of Analog Devices Inc. (ADI), observes, "Everything has a life, and you always have to be looking beyond that life. The primary job of the CEO is to sense and respond ... with the benefit of inputs from the organization ... and to be an encouraging sponsor for those who see the future."

Despite some commonalities, strategic innovation differs from technological or product innovation. New technologies do not always yield successful products, nor are new products always strategically significant. Furthermore, some companies, such as Southwest Airlines Co., succeed through innovative strategies alone – without much innovation in either the underlying technologies or the products and services sold to customers.

A strategic innovation breaks with past practice at least in one of the three areas: value-chain design, conceptualization of customer value and identification of potential customers.

A strategic innovation is a creative and significant departure from historical practice in at least one of three areas.[2] Those areas are design of the end-to-end value-chain architecture (for example, Dell Inc.'s direct-sales model); conceptualization of delivered customer value (IBM Corp.'s shift from selling hardware and software to selling complete solutions); and identification of potential customers (Canon Inc.'s pioneering focus on developing photocopiers for small offices rather than large corporations).

Strategic innovation involves exploring the unknown to create new knowledge and new possibilities. It proceeds with strategic experiments to test the viability of new business ideas.

The Learning Imperative

In hindsight, executives involved with strategic experiments would no doubt agree on this: If there is one thing you can expect, it is that your initial expectations are wrong.[3] For example, when AT&T consulted McKinsey & Co. in the mid-1980s for advice on the cellular-telephone market, the company concluded that the worldwide potential was 900,000 units. Today, 900,000 new subscribers become mobile-phone users every three days.[4] When information is scarce and the future unknowable, intelligent people may make poor judgments. The error magnitudes for market-potential estimates are often measured in multiples rather than percentages. Establishing an expenditure level that is even in the right ballpark is nearly impossible on the first go-round.

To improve initial expectations and resolve the many unknowns associated with any new business, management teams must learn.[5] That learning must come through trial and error. The alternative – sufficient research, study and analysis to generate the perfect plan – is not practical for strategic experiments.

How does one learn by trial and error? Scientists have given us the scientific method: Design an experiment, predict outcomes on the basis of a hypothesis, measure outcomes, compare outcomes to predictions, and draw conclusions about the hypothesis based on the comparison. The last step is at the heart of the learning process.

In the ideal, scientific experiments meet five criteria: (1) results are available quickly, (2) results are unambiguous, (3) experiments can be isolated from outside influences, (4) experiments are inexpensive, and (5) they are repeatable. But strategic experiments are hardly ideal. They meet none of those criteria. Feedback may not be available for years, results are ambiguous, key variables cannot be isolated, and the experiments are too expensive to repeat.

This does not mean there is a better framework for ensuring timely learning, only that learning as strategic experiments proceed is difficult. Hence, many executives cultivate an experiment-and-learn attitude in themselves and among colleagues.

Still, lessons are not magically revealed, even to those with open minds. Learning requires conscious effort. It is an active pursuit, and the planning cycle provides the natural context for it. Alas, conventional planning approaches create barriers to learning.

The Conventional Planning Mind-Set

Understandably, executives view a rigorous financial-planning process as a crucial asset and are loath to alter it. A performance-oriented culture, one that holds people accountable for the numbers in the plans, is frequently touted as a hallmark of successful companies.[6] Even corporations that give leaders of strategic experiments freedom to create entirely different organizations – with different leadership styles, hiring practices, values and operating assumptions – often insist that budgeting and performance reviews fall under the established planning system.

Although conventional planning systems do not create barriers to learning for all types of innovation, planning approaches can and should be altered within strategic experiments.[7] The bedrock assumptions underlying conventional planning approaches do not apply. Historically, planning and control systems were designed to *implement a proven strategy* by ensuring *accountability* under the presumption of *reliable predictability*.[8] Planning systems for strategic experiments, by contrast, should be designed to *explore future strategies* by supporting *learning*, given the unpleasant reality of *reliable unpredictability*.

The difference between those opposing mind-sets becomes clear in the evaluation of outcomes. The first step in evaluating an outcome is to compare it to the prediction made in the plan. Any disparity can be explained in one of two ways: either the strategy was improperly implemented or the prediction was wrong. If the former holds true, someone must be held accountable. But if the prediction was wrong, future expectations must be adjusted given the new information. An accountability mind-set is so ingrained in many corporations that disparities between predictions and outcomes are almost always attributed to management performance. The performance expectation (the prediction) is sacred.

In a mature business, that is reasonable. But a presumption of reliable predictability is not an appropriate premise for planning within strategic experiments. When the future is unknowable, the foremost planning objective must be *learning*, not *accountability*. Certainly, managers must be accountable, but on a more subjective basis. How quickly are they learning? How quickly are they responding to new information?

Despite reliable unpredictability, predictions must be made. Learning follows from the diligent analysis of disparities between predictions and outcomes, with specific attention to the *stories, models* or *theories* upon which the predictions are based. Theory-focused planning provides the needed structure for such analysis. It leads to improved theories and improved predictions – proof that learning is happening. Better predictions, in turn, lead to better choices about strategy and funding levels.

A conventional planning mind-set, however, can derail a strategic experiment. For example, Corning Microarray Technologies encountered several unexpected barriers to getting to market. No supplier could make DNA shipments in the necessary quantities with sufficient quality and reliability. In early trials, processes for manufacturing microarrays failed to meet quality and reliability standards generally accepted for Corning products.

That should have resulted in reconsideration of early choices about the manufacturing process and reevaluation of expectations. However, operating under the presumption of reliable predictability and within a culture that emphasized numbers, the general manager felt pressure to turn around a business he saw as underperforming. No time for reevaluation; only an urgency to work harder. Tensions escalated as the team failed to catch up. Finally, senior management stepped in, replaced several managers, reset expectations (of financial results, time to market and quality) and revisited basic questions about the approach to manufacturing microarrays.

Six Changes Make Theory-Focused Planning Work

Theory-focused planning requires six alterations to the conventional planning process. The first three changes relate to *building* a theory to make predictions (the forward-looking part of planning).

Change No. 1: Level of Detail. Instead of demanding a lot of detail, limit focus to a small number of critical unknowns.

In planning for an established business, incorporating details such as revenue breakdowns by product line or by region is useful. Fine-grained comparisons between predictions and outcomes can help isolate and resolve problems. But such detail is unrealistic for a strategic experiment. The unknowns are too great. Further, the lessons are not in the details but in a handful of *critical unknowns* that can make or break a business.

Critical unknowns generally fall into three categories: market, technology and cost unknowns. For example, there were many unknowns for ADI when, in the early 1990s, it pursued the commercialization of a new semiconductor technology, micro-electromechanical machines (MEMS) – chips with tiny moving parts. However, three unknowns were clearly the most crucial:

- *Most critical market unknown:* The most promising early application for MEMS was in new systems for launching automotive air bags. But would automakers risk a new approach?

- *Most critical technology unknown:* Could MEMS be manufactured at levels of reliability sufficient for an automotive-safety application?

- *Most critical cost unknown:* Could manufacturing yields be improved to levels consistent with other semiconductor manufacturing processes?

No amount of a priori analysis could resolve those unknowns, only experimenting and learning.

ADI's conventional planning did not emphasize a small number of critical unknowns. Like most corporations' planning, it focused on detailed projections of revenues, margins and profitability; planning discussions revolved around evaluations of those metrics. In spite of that, the critical unknowns were eventually resolved favorably, and today MEMS is profitable. Still, with a planning system that supported learning, the major uncertainties could have been resolved sooner, with fewer crises.

Change No. 2: Communication of Expectations. Instead of focusing on the predictions themselves, focus on the theory used to generate the predictions and the theory's underlying assumptions.

Traditionally, predictions are recorded as numbers – usually precise ones. (More sophisticated plans for new ventures may include a range or perhaps a best-case, expected-case and worst-case scenario.) But in planning for a strategic experiment, the focus should be on the assumptions underlying the predictions, not on the predictions themselves. The most clearly communicated and detailed item in any plan for a strategic experiment should be a thorough description of the theory used to generate the predictions. Without a shared story about how a strategic experiment is expected to work, a management team cannot learn. Managers will not come to the same conclusions as new information is revealed.

Currently, the theory and its underlying assumptions are lost between the time when predictions are made and the time when those predictions are compared with outcomes, usually months later. The culprit is the ubiquitous spreadsheet. When you open a spreadsheet, you immediately see numbers – that is, the predictions themselves. To understand the logic behind those numbers, you would have to dig deep into the underlying equations. And after a few weeks, even the person who built the spreadsheet would find that difficult.

One approach to telling a story about how a business is expected to work is the *influence* or *bubble-and-arrow* diagram, which shows how multiple variables influence outcomes. (See graphic, "Drawing Influence Diagrams.") The influence diagram should convey how each major category of spending – such as research, product development, manufacturing, marketing and sales – ultimately affects revenues. The most important spending categories to include are those directly related to the critical unknowns. If possible, each bubble on the diagram should represent something measurable. Thus, a framework is established for gathering evidence that confirms or contradicts each cause-and-effect relationship.

Drawing Influence Diagrams

Learning from strategic experiments requires building and then testing a theory. For a management team to learn together, the theory must be recorded, shared and later revisited. A good communication technique for capturing the essence of a theory – cause-and-effect relationships – is the influence diagram.*

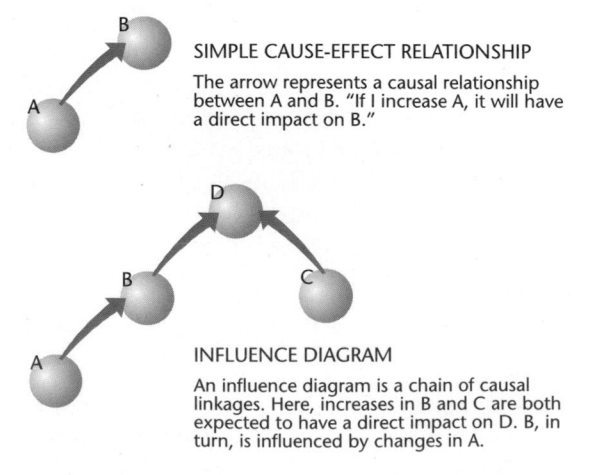

SIMPLE CAUSE-EFFECT RELATIONSHIP

The arrow represents a causal relationship between A and B. "If I increase A, it will have a direct impact on B."

INFLUENCE DIAGRAM

An influence diagram is a chain of causal linkages. Here, increases in B and C are both expected to have a direct impact on D. B, in turn, is influenced by changes in A.

* The influence diagrams in each exhibit were created with *think* software from High Performance Systems, Inc., Lebanon, New Hampshire.

In 2001, Thomson Corp.'s Thomson Learning launched its own strategic experiment – Universitas 21 Global (U21G). Pursued in partnership with a worldwide consortium of universities, U21G ushered in a new era in higher education. U21G was conceived as a university with no campus and no classrooms. All operations were to be conducted completely online. When it opened in May 2003, U21G offered only an MBA degree and recruited from a few major Asian cities. But its leaders expect to add new programs and expand across the continent within a few years.

For U21G, faculty salaries will be a significant expense, and the effect of student-to-faculty ratio on student satisfaction in the online environment is a critical unknown. Theoretically, online learning offers the opportunity for a single faculty member to reach a wider audience. However, students may be more demanding of faculty than at a traditional university, seeking personal responses to e-mail on issues such as career advice or clarification of course concepts. What assumption can one make about adding extra faculty?

The relationship between the two factors is unknowable in advance. It cannot be extrapolated from experience at traditional institutions: It must be discovered. As the U21G provost commented, "We have a lot of experimentation to do ... to offer online instruction in ways that allow us to have a higher student-to-faculty ratio without sacrificing quality. I cannot say what the student-to-faculty ratio will be. I can only speculate." More is unknown than simply the appropriate student-to-faculty ratio to achieve high student satisfaction. The very nature of the relationship is unknown.[9]

An influence diagram can capture a basic hypothesis about the relationship, as well as a theory of how student satisfaction ultimately affects revenues. The theory can be stated as follows: Adding faculty reduces the student-to-faculty ratio, which increases student satisfaction, which enhances the perceived attractiveness of U21G in the market, which leads to higher enrollments and higher revenues. The diagram also can show how increases in other major budget categories related to critical unknowns might have an impact on revenues – for instance, how an increase in sales and marketing spending might increase perceived product attractiveness and therefore enrollments. (See graphic, "Predicting an Uncertain Future.")

Change No. 3: Nature of Predictions. Instead of making specific numerical predictions for specific dates, predict the trends.

In a typical planning cycle, managers are asked to agree to a top-line number and a bottom-line number for the following year. For a strategic experiment, there is a better approach. Because any single-point prediction is certain to be wrong, and because new ventures are dynamic, it makes more sense to focus on trends. The rate and direction of change of a performance measure is usually a more important piece of information than its current value.

An easy way to incorporate the prediction of trends into plans is to supplement influence diagrams with trend graphs. Because such graphs represent many predictions over small intervals of time, they may appear to ask a great deal of planners. But the predictions do not require nearly the same level of accuracy as plans for a mature business. The *shape* of the curve is what is important. Simply choosing whether weeks, months or quarters is the right label for the x-axis (time) and estimating the

Predicting an Uncertain Future

Influence diagrams capture cause and effect, but a set of predictions is also needed to drive learning because analysis of disparities between predictions and outcomes is the critical learning step. Strategic experiments are highly uncertain. As a result, predictions can be made in the form of trend graphs, rather than numbers for specific dates.

INFLUENCE DIAGRAMS IDENTIFY BASIC HYPOTHESES ABOUT ACTIONS AND OUTCOMES.

TREND GRAPHS ENHANCE STORIES. THEY MAKE HYPOTHESES ABOUT EXPECTED OUTCOMES EXPLICIT FOR LATER TESTING.

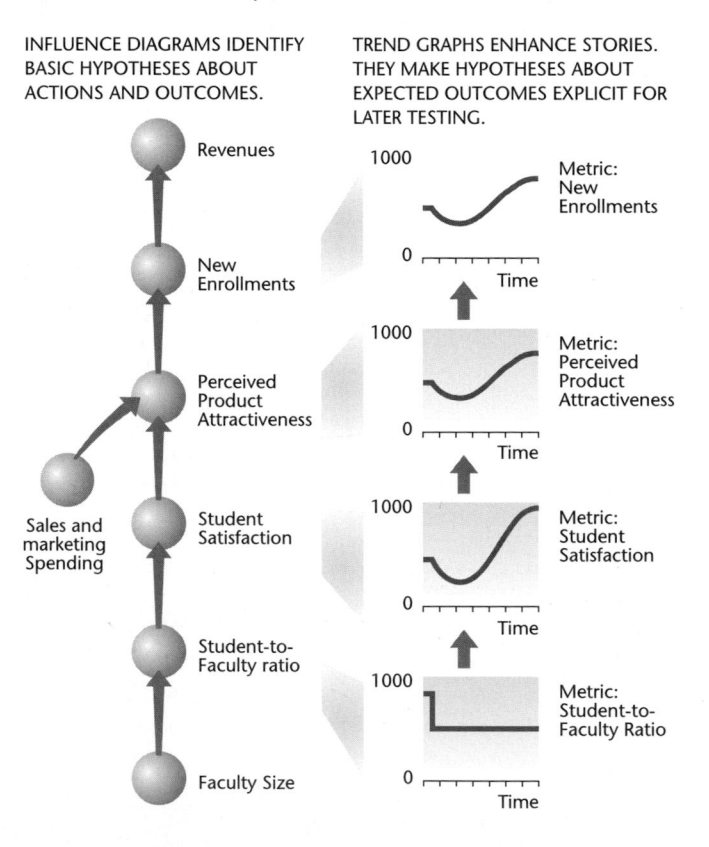

magnitude of expected change (is a 10% change expected, a doubling, an increase by a factor of 10?) for the y-axis (the performance measure) is good enough. The purpose of graphing expected trends is to provide a quick warning if the actual trend is significantly different. If it is, say, a different direction or much faster or slower than expected, a change in strategy may be necessary.

To understand how combining influence diagrams with trend predictions results in a more complete theory, consider how U21G might have predicted the performance trends that could follow an increase in faculty. Clearly, an increase will immediately decrease student-to-faculty ratio. Beyond that, the supposition is that it will initially *decrease* student satisfaction – if new faculty struggle in the online environment for a while. It is the shape of the plot of actual outcomes over time, rather than any single student-satisfaction score, that will demonstrate if this worse-before-better hypothesis is correct. To evaluate the long-term impact of increased faculty, U21G would have to wait for the trend to play out. The remaining trend graphs, for perceived product attractiveness and enrollments, indicate a theory that the market reaction is not instantaneous – information about student satisfaction may be absorbed slowly by the market.

The second set of changes to traditional planning relate to *testing* the theory by comparing the predictions with actual outcomes (the evaluative part of planning).

Change No. 4: Frequency of Strategic Reviews. Instead of reviewing outcomes annually to reevaluate fundamental business assumptions, do so monthly – or more frequently as necessitated by new information.

In mature businesses, outcomes may be reviewed as often as weekly. However, such reviews are generally quick status checks to identify any variances that require immediate attention for getting back on plan. For most corporations, it is only during the major annual planning cycle that the strategy of the business is reconsidered. Between planning periods, management teams focus on execution.

If learning as quickly as possible is a primary goal in managing a new venture, the strategy itself – in particular, the critical unknowns highlighted on the influence diagram – must be reevaluated at least monthly. Leaders must be prepared to make major course changes at each review. To many, a monthly strategic review will seem onerous. But the time required for each review is much less than for the typical annual-planning exercise because it addresses only the critical unknowns.

More frequent strategic reviews would have been particularly helpful to a multinational corporation we will call Capston-White, which launched a venture to commercialize services for managing printing, imaging and copying assets within large organizations. After about two years, the management team decided that to be credible, the company needed a wide range of offerings, from maintenance to complex consulting services. Outside advisers confirmed the validity of the one-stop-shop strategy, and additional resources were committed.

Tremendous hiring followed, plus construction of a sophisticated IT system to support the expected growth. However, the most critical assumption – whether the market was really ready for expanded service – was not quickly tested. IT executives – the potential customers – *claimed* they were interested in managing their printing and imaging assets more sensibly, but in reality they had more pressing concerns. One executive associated with the venture explained: "If you asked CIOs in the late 1990s, they were concerned with two big things, the Y2K

When higher-level executives turned to the strategic experiment and made the necessary changes, the cost was much higher than it would have been with more frequent reviews.

bug and the euro. Plus they were worried about getting a hot new Internet infrastructure up and running." So the new service offerings did not attract customers as expected.

Nonetheless, driven by a culture of accountability to the plan and by an assumption of reliable predictability, the venture's general manager kept investing heavily, expecting imminent growth despite all evidence to the contrary. The annual planning rhythm and the small size of the venture relative to the corporation caused the disappointing revenues to escape bold action from senior management for nearly two years. When executives finally made dramatic budget cuts and changes in leadership, the cost was much higher than it would have been with more frequent reviews.

Change No. 5: Perspective in Time. Instead of reviewing only current-period outcomes, consider the history of the strategic experiment in its entirety and look at trends over time.

If the format for predicting is a trend graph, then the same format for reporting outcomes must be used. But in many corporations, little previous history is considered during planning reviews. Often only the results from the most recent period are reported, along with year-to-date figures. If historical data are used at all, they go into a regression analysis to forecast revenues.

But lessons are embedded in history. Each performance measure identified on the influence diagram should be plotted over time. Updated plots should be regularly compared with predicted trends. In that way, rates of change are readily visible, and the shape of each plotted curve enhances intuition as predictions are updated. Companies can avoid the dangerous mind-set that one finance executive described: "With new ventures, you have to have a short memory, because you know you are going to fail a lot."

Change No. 6: Nature of Measures. Instead of relying on a mix of financials and nonfinancials to measure outcomes, focus on leading indicators.

Traditional plans emphasize financial outcomes. But financial outcomes are highly ambiguous in new ventures – profitability, for example, is many years away, and precision about the magnitude of early losses is difficult. To learn as quickly as possible, plans for strategic experiments should emphasize leading indicators, which provide the first clues to whether the assumptions in the plan are realistic. (See graphic, "From Verbal Theory to Diagrams.")

With an influence diagram, it is easy to identify the leading indicators: they are the measures closest to the bottom and closest to the bubbles for key budget categories. For example, the influence diagram for U21G indicates that student-to-faculty ratio and student satisfaction are leading indicators.

For New York Times Digital (NYTD), the online subsidiary of the New York Times Co., a critical unknown was the extent to which online readership would cannibalize subscriptions to the paper's print version. Naturally, the possibility created tension between NYTD and the newspaper. To resolve the issue, NYTD conducted substantial research and discovered the unexpected. As one NYTD executive explained: "The Web opened up a whole new audience for discovery and sampling. Nobody comes on the Web and reads the whole paper in one sitting. It is a different kind of experience. So we were able to use the Web site as a vehicle to generate subscriptions to the newspaper."

NYTD closely monitored a leading indicator of its contribution to the corporation's overall performance: subscription gains and losses attributable to NYTD. Soon it was clear that gains outweighed losses. New readers from outside the New York metropolitan area were subscribing to the newspaper after sampling it online. Soon the Web site became the newspaper's second most important source of new subscriptions.

From Verbal Theory to Diagrams

For many, trying to draw an influence diagram immediately is challenging. Instead, a written narrative of how a business is expected to work can be created, then studied for cause-and-effect statements that can be readily translated into a diagram. For example, Corning might have described its theory about how the Microarray Technologies venture was expected to work as follows:

"We must combine our own expertise in precision glass manufacturing and the control of tiny quantities of fluid with outside knowledge of biotechnology. If we can do this effectively, we should be able to develop an outstanding process for manufacturing microarrays. Product reliability will be high, and costs will be low enough that we can offer significant value to potential customers, who otherwise must create their own microarrays or purchase expensive closed systems for experimentation. Provided that we can encourage the adoption of open standards that are consistent with our product design, the market should find our product highly attractive, and we should achieve rapid revenue growth."

The corresponding influence diagram (bottom) is not a complete description of the business. Instead, it focuses on the critical unknowns described above.

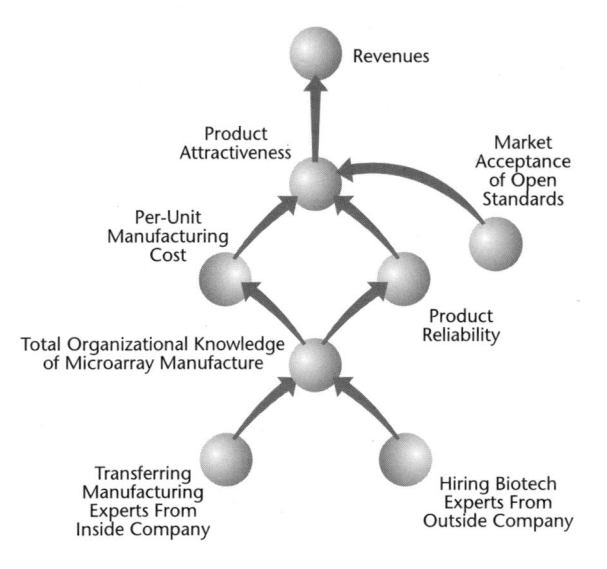

Sailing Over the Edge of the Known World

Theory-focused planning is appropriate when more is unknown than known – when an industry is just emerging, no business model is established, and the uncertainties are so large that not even the basic nature of the relationships between activities and outcomes is clear. In this context, planning must support the objective of *testing* a strategy through experimentation. Reliable predictions are not possible.

Theory-focused planning represents a significant departure from conventional planning practices, starting with the idea that planning within strategic experiments must emphasize learning, not accountability. Unfortunately, corporations often become disciplined followers of planning protocols that do the opposite – they emphasize accountability over learning.

To establish a context for learning, theories that generate predictions must be explicitly shared, recorded and later revisited. Influence diagrams and performance-over-time graphs are two excellent tools that support the process. Additionally, learning is most likely to occur when the planning process focuses on critical unknowns, demands monthly strategic-change reviews, includes history going back to the venture's inception, and emphasizes leading indicators.

About the Research

Beginning in 2000, we investigated innovative efforts at 10 corporations. Some efforts were strategic experiments. Others were narrower process or product innovations, and those served as a comparison group. A conclusion from our research is that conventional planning systems disrupted learning within the strategic experiments but did not do so within the comparison group. The strategic experiments in our sample include

The New York Times Co. Formed New York Times Digital to build The New York Times on the Web and Boston.com and created a profitable online news division.

Corning Inc. Created Corning Microarray Technologies to mass-produce DNA microarrays for use in genomics research.

Analog Devices Inc. Commercialized microelectromechanical systems (MEMS), a new semiconductor technology that adds tiny moving parts to standard chips.

The Thomson Corp. In partnership with a global consortium of universities, launched Universitas 21 Global, an online university offering an MBA degree in Asia.

Capston-White. Sought to commercialize a new line of services for managing fleets of printing and imaging devices within corporations.

Eastman Kodak Co. Had its subsidiary in India introduce products and services related to digital photography.

The innovative efforts we studied that did not constitute strategic experiments include

Cisco Systems Inc. Implemented e-business practices ranging from online sales and service to online coordination of supply networks and online management of employee services.

Unilever. Introduced (through its subsidiary, Hindustan Lever) a branded salt to rural India, incorporating revolutionary distribution techniques and new formulations to encapsulate iodine.

Nucor Corp. Introduced minimill technology and thin-slab casting technology to the steel industry.

Stora Enso North America. Launched initiatives to improve the efficiency of interactions within the paper supply chain with platforms for business-to-business commerce.

We conducted semistructured interviews lasting 60 to 90 minutes with as many as 12 executives at each company. Each interview was recorded, transcribed and coded. In addition, archived planning documents were gathered and studied. An in-depth case study was written about each company.

Some important interview questions were: What expectations were set for the strategic experiment? By what process were these expectations formed? How and by what process did expectations change? How did perceptions of performance form? What were the primary measures of performance? How and why did perceptions of performance change? When were major strategic changes made? What was the accepted rationale for these changes?

The case studies demonstrate the many ways that conventional planning approaches hinder learning within strategic experiments. The most prevalent pattern in the data was that, within performance-oriented, disciplined-planning cultures, leaders of strategic experiments frequently felt compelled to defend the performance of their fledgling businesses. The criterion was the ability either to meet original expectations or to surpass benchmarks for certain measures commonly accepted in other parts of the organization. The structure of the planning process reinforced such discussion by emphasizing simple comparisons between expectations and outcomes. This internal struggle over performance perceptions overwhelmed the type of debate needed – about underlying theory and whether actual outcomes supported that theory. Among other prevalent patterns: (a) interviewees rarely mentioned key assumptions underlying expectations; (b) historical data, needed to unravel lessons learned, were rarely discussed; and (c) major changes were made only in the context of the annual review.

At Cisco, Unilever, Nucor and Stora Enso North America, there were uncertainties, but the uncertainties were limited, more easily identified and discussed, and more quickly resolved. In one case (Unilever), the uncertainties amounted to nothing more than the values of certain operational parameters within a well-understood business model. The parameters were identified in advance, agreed upon by all executives involved and tested in a straightforward manner. In another case (Cisco), the data necessary to resolve uncertainties were more technical and available in much shorter time frames. Such substantive differences allowed learning to occur despite conventional planning practices.

We also tested and refined our recommendations by asking small teams of executives to use them in a computer-simulated strategic experiment. Several hundred executives from numerous organizations participated. We evaluated the effectiveness of the planning process we advocate by running the simulation twice – before and after introducing our recommendations. Performance was much better in the second run, as measured both by the profitability of the simulated businesses and the quality of the intrateam and classroom discussion during and after the simulation.

Case Example
IBM's Radical New Mindset: Innovating Customers' Businesses, and Itself*

IBM's Chief Executive Samual J. Palmisano is out to transform the very nature and image of Big Blue, a nickname derived a half-century ago from the company's muscular blue mainframe computers. His goal is to carry IBM beyond that 20th century legacy, beyond computing and, yes, beyond 'Blue' – while making IBM as indispensable to clients today as it was during the heyday of mainframes.

The change at IBM is palpable. The number of employees focused on business rather than pure technology has leaped from 3,500 in mid-2002 to more than 50,000 today – out of a total of 330,000. And that's growing at more than 10,000 a year. Meanwhile, in a painful process, other employees are exiting by the thousands – those in administration and computer repair, for instance, and from shuttered offices in Germany and Scandinavia.

It was over a lunch in Cincinnati two years ago that Palmisano got his first inkling of Big Blue's next act. Palmisano was talking business with A.G. Lafley, CEO of Procter & Gamble Co. (P&G), one of IBM's big customers. At one point, Lafley asked Palmisano to estimate how many of P&G's 100,000 employees it truly needed to keep on its payroll. When Palmisano didn't venture a guess, Lafley stunned him by saying that P&G might be able to get by with only a quarter of its workforce. Specialized service companies might be able to handle everything else, from human resources to customer care.

For IBM's new CEO, Lafley's idea delivered a strong jolt of the future. "We saw it as an industry shift," he recalls. Palmisano was already an expert in technology services, such as running data centers and managing companies' computing operations. Working under former CEO Louis V. Gerstner Jr., he had helped rescue a struggling IBM in the '90s by building its then-modest services division into a $40 billion behemoth. But what Lafley was suggesting was far bigger. It stretched beyond revamping computer systems and stitching together new networks. If other CEOs were entertaining similar thoughts, a vast new market could emerge.

Over the past two years, Palmisano has built these concepts into a strategy that would be laughable – if it weren't so serious. His goal is to free IBM from the confines of the $1.2 trillion computer industry, which is growing at just 6% a year. Instead of merely

---

* Adapted from Hamm, S. (2005), "Beyond Blue," *Business Week*, April 18, 36-42

selling and servicing technology, IBM is putting to use the immense resources it has in-house, from its software programmers to its 3,300 research scientists, to help companies like P&G rethink, remake, and even run their businesses – everything from accounting and customer service to human resources and procurement. "We're giving our clients a transformational lift," says Palmisano.

While Palmisano looks out at the world through thick glasses, he's not short on vision. He expects that within 10 years IBM could build an annual revenue stream of as much as $50 billion in business consulting and outsourcing services. If so, Palmisano will have created a second services miracle and hitched IBM to a crucial growth market. And in the process, his company will be fixing – or running – big chunks of the world's business.

Why has Palmisano embarked on such a risky adventure? In truth, he has little choice. The world of computing that IBM long ruled is increasingly becoming a commodity business. Ruthlessly efficient Dell, fresh from its conquest of the PC market, is climbing up in servers and even tech services. Dell's services, which focus on setting up computer systems, are still small compared with IBM's $46 billion services business, but they are growing at more than 30% annually and are expected to hit $4 billion this year. "The big question is: Will services go the same way hardware has? We think it will," says Steve Meyer, a vice-president in Dell's services unit.

IBM, with its legions of PhDs and closets full of patents, is not built to duke it out with the likes of Dell. Palmisano's strategy promises a neat escape. Instead of battling in cutthroat markets, he takes advantage of all the low-cost technology by packaging it, augmenting it with sophisticate hardware and software, and selling it to customers in a slew of what he calls business transformation services. That way IBM rides atop the commodity wave – and avoids drowning in it.

The danger? Simple. An IBM stumble would spell slower growth and smaller profits, undermining its research-driven business model and its position atop the corporate tech world. Palmisano has only to reflect on IBM's sorry state in the early 1990s to taste the consequences of falling short now. The initial challenge is to make a grand vision that can sound threatening or full of hype into a must-have. McDonald's, for instance, last year decided not to hand over its accounting and finance operations after IBM promoted the idea, opting to keep everything in-house instead.

To win over lukewarm customers, IBM might be tempted to offer overly favorable terms for unpredictable long-term contracts. This poses another risk. Time and again, tech companies have misjudged the actual costs of running companies' ever-changing computing operations. As a result, they lose money on the deals for years. That's what happened with IBM's contract to run computing for JPMorgan Chase & Co., which the bank dissolved late last year when it took back control. That was a technology deal, not operations outsourcing, but the same uncertainties apply.

IBM faces strong competition as it forges into alien territory. The most potent rival is Accenture. The $15.6 billion services giant has been dipping a big toe into business process outsourcing. While Accenture cannot match IBM's tech skills or research staff, it outguns IBM in business expertise. "IBM is genetically a technology company," says Joel P. Friedman, president of Accenture's BPO unit. "I think our history of solving business problems and our industry knowledge gives us an enormous advantage." Accenture notched $2.2 billion in BPO revenues last year, up 50%, while IBM's business outsourcing and related revenues hit $3 billion, a 45% gain.

Challenging both IBM and Accenture are aggressive Indian outsourcers, including Wipro and Tata Consultancy Services Ltd. Wipro's BPO business is going gangbusters and hiring about 1,400 employees per month. They offer customers lower costs but without the operational makeover IBM promises – which they view as risky. "We believe making changes at the customer end will be very hard," says T.K. Kurien, head of Wipro's BPO business. "Nine times out of 10 you will fail."

Glimpses of Greatness

Still, if Palmisano and his crew fend off rivals and prove the skeptics wrong, the opportunities are enormous. Market researcher IDC estimates that in IBM's target markets, nearly half a trillion dollars are already flowing to outsourcers in everything from HR to industrial design. It expects the field to grow by 8% to 11% per year. Merrill Lynch's Milunovich figures that this new business could heat up annual growth in IBM Global Services from less than 5% a year over the next few years to as much as 9%, excluding currency effects. Business services promise to pretty up profits, too. Analysts haven't made estimates yet, but IBM's senior vice-president for strategy, J. Bruce Harreld, says the company will be able to achieve 20% operating-profit margins – double the margins in traditional tech services.

In its pursuit of vital industry experience, IBM – much like an eager college intern – is sometimes willing to work for free. IBM's unpaid partnership with the Mayo Clinic dates back to a cocktail party in 2000 in Mayo's hometown of Rochester, Minn., where IBM has a computer factory. A Mayo employee and an IBMer realized that scientists at both companies were working on genomics research. This soon led to joint projects on gene profiling of leukemia cells, and a published paper in a scientific journal in 2003. This is not the kind of connection that Dell, Accenture, or Wipro is likely to make.

IBM and Mayo quickly moved on to a more ambitious project: changing the way medical research is done. They set out to gather data on 4.5 million patients and to make it easily searchable by researchers – but without compromising patients' privacy. A research task that used to take five people a year can now be done by one person in 15 seconds. Eventually, Mayo and IBM believe, physicians will tap into a vast storehouse of data, real-time, when they're diagnosing patients. "This is the way to transform the way we practice medicine," says Dr. Nina M. Schwenk, chairperson of Mayo's Information Technology Committee. And for IBM, it's a foot in the door of the $1.4 trillion health-care business.

While IBM had plenty of skilled engineers in Rochester, they practically needed brain transplants if they were to do breakthrough work for Mayo. So the company sent some of its brightest engineers back to school. Working with the University of Minnesota, the company arranged in 2003 for a series of three-day crash courses in everything from molecular biology to protein sequence analysis. So far, 50 people have taken the classes. Nothing illustrates more starkly the gyrations at IBM: engineers who once worked on a fading family of mainframe-style computers are now helping to chart the future of medicine. "Part of your job is to be a visionary," says Jeffrey Tenner, one of the engineers. Now IBM is directing part of its Rochester staff toward bioinformatics, privacy, and regulation compliance – all skills learned through the Mayo alliance.

Leveraging Success

While IBM has forged cozy ties with Mayo, the business payoff is still unclear. IBM's goal with this alliance and others is to take lessons and turn them into products and services to sell within the industry. The Mayo work has led to a new software product for medical research. Other health-care products are on the way. And IBM is hoping one day to manage patient databases or networks of health-care organizations.

The Mayo alliance is now a model for forging research and development linkups with clients. Late last year, in quick succession, it struck up R&D alliances with Honeywell International and Boeing. The 10-year Boeing deal teams Boeing's military command systems expertise with IBM's facility with databases and collaboration. "This alliance with IBM is unique in the industry," says Roger F. Roberts, head of Boeing's Space & Intelligence Systems business. "We share our strategies, we share our R&D, and we offer joint solutions for customers."

IBM doesn't wait around for clients to come to it with R&D projects. Engineers are encouraged to dream up products and peddle them to potential customers. IBM engineer and cycling enthusiast Bryan Streimer, for example, rigged up a wireless heart-rate system to alert family members if a cyclist has a heart attack on the road. IBM channeled Streimer's invention into an electric pill dispenser, which it's developing for Danish electronic device maker Bang & Olufsen. If patients forget to take a pill on schedule, the device calls their cell phone. Now IBM is helping a British mobile-phone carrier build a new business offering wireless medical alert systems.

With those victories under its belt, IBM is scrounging for new markets. In addition to its four original businesses – accounting, HR, customer service, and procurement – it is now plowing into six others. They include after-sales service for consumer electronics, insurance-claims processing, and supply-chain optimization. The old IBM would have studied for many months before deciding whether to enter these new businesses. This time, it has set up small SWAT teams to work with a handful of initial clients and launch businesses. This is in some cases a tough sell. "These are markets we're making. A client may not have thought of doing this before," says Ginni Rometty, managing partner of IBM Business Consulting Services.

Plenty of pitfalls lie ahead. But for companies like IBM that bank on innovation, there's little choice but to create new markets and exploit them. "In the past, IBM defended the mainframe against client-server computing and PC," Palmisano says. "We're not defending the past anymore." No, IBM is off and running into a new world of business, beyond computers. So long, Big Blue.

Questions

1. "Mental models (in organizations) manifest themselves in corporate control systems". Provide a concise discussion of this statement.

2. The conventional organizational mindset (goods-centered dominant logic) is not seen as mutually exclusive from the value-innovation mindset (value/service-centered dominant logic). What are the underlying reasons for this view?

3. In its 'Top Plus Program', Siemens makes use of radical approaches to defy old paradigms. Discuss these, and indicate your opinion if these are also relevant for other organizations (in different industries).

4. Virgin Atlantic challenged the traditional assumptions in the international passenger airlines industry. Can any organization use similar approaches to challenge traditional industry assumptions?

5. Various taxonomies (or views) of innovation exist. What are the reasons for this, and what should be the dominant taxonomy (or taxonomies) for purpose of strategic management?

6. Views concerning the process of innovation have evolved from simple linear models to open systems innovation. Provide a concise review of the reasons for this evolvement.

7. Why is the locus of innovation today often migrating beyond the confines of centralized R&D departments?

8. With IBM's new focus (and mindset) of innovating customers' businesses, what new organizational capability challenges are posed for IBM to be successful?

References

Chapter 3: The New Strategy Mindset: Co-Shaping Value Innovation

[1] See Leibold, M., Voelpel, S.C., and Tekie, E.B. (2004), Managerial Levers in Cultivating New Mental Space for Business Innovation, *South African Journal of Business Management*, 35(4), 61-71.

[2] Adapted from Vargo, S.L. and Lusch, R.F. (2004), Evolving to a New Dominant Logic for Marketing, *Journal of Marketing*, 68(1), 1-17.

[3] Foster, R.N. and Kaplan, S. (2001), *Creative Destruction: Why Companies That are Built to Last Underperform the Market – And How to Successfully Transform Them.* New York: Currency/Doubleday.

[4] Foster, R.N. and Kaplan, S. (2001), *op.cit.* This subsection is based on their seminal work.

[5] Kim, W.C. and Mauborgne, R. (1999), "Strategy, Value Innovation, and the Knowledge Economy", *Sloan Management Review*, 40(3), 41-54.

[6] Adapted from Kim, W.C. and Mauborgne, R. (2004), "Value Innovation: the Strategic Logic of High Growth", *Harvard Business Review*, 82(7/8), 172-180; and Vargo, S.L. and Lusch, R.F. (2004), *op.cit.*

[7] Tushman, M.L. and O'Reilly III, C.A. (1996), Ambidextrous Organization: Managing Evolutionary and Revolutionary Change, *California Management Review*, 38(4), 8-30.

[8] Gibbert, M. (2004), Crafting Strategy Imaginatively: Lessons Learnt from Siemens, *European Management Journal*, 22(6), 669-684.

[9] Mintzberg, H. (1994), *The Rise and Fall of Strategic Planning: Reconceiving Roles for Planning, Plans, Planners*, New York: Free Press; Hamel, G. (1998), The Challenge Today: Changing the Rules of the Game, *Business Strategy Review*, 9(2), 19-26; Nonaka, I. and Konno, N. (1998), The Concept of "Ba": Building a Foundation for Knowledge Creation, *California Management Review*, 40(3), 40-54; Brown, S.L. and Eisenhardt, K.M. (1998), *Competing on the Edge: Strategy as Structured Chaos*, Boston: Harvard Business School Press; Markides, C.C. (1999), A Dynamic View of Strategy, *MIT Sloan Management Review*, 40(3), 55-63; Kim, W.C. and Mauborgne, R. (1999), Creating New Market Space, *Harvard Business Review*, 77(1), 83-93; Grove, A. (1996). *Only the Paranoid Survive*, New York: Doubleday; Weick, K.E. (2001), *Making Sense of the Organization*, Oxford: Blackwell; Pietersen, W. (2002), *Reinventing Strategy: Using Strategy Learning to Create and Sustain Breakthrough Performance*, New York: Wiley; and Chesbrough, H.W. (2003), The Era of Open Innovation, *MIT Sloan Management Review*, 44(3), 35-41.

[10] Fauconnier, G. (1994), *Mental Spaces*, Cambridge: Cambridge University Press.

[11] Tapscott, D. and Ticoll, D. *The Naked Corporation: How the Age of Transparency will Revolutionize Business,* New York: Free Press, 2003.

[12] Kim, W.C. and Mauborgne, R. (2004), *op.cit.*, 178.

[13] Tidd, J., Bessant, J. and Pavitt, K. (1997), *Managing Innovation*, Chichester. John Wiley & Sons, 6.

[14] Moore, G.A. (2004), Innovating Within Established Enterprises, *Harvard Business Review*, 82(7/8), 87-92.

[15] Davenport, T.H., and Prusak, L., *What's the Big Idea: Creating and Capitalizing on the Best Management Thinking*, Boston: Harvard Business School Press, 2003.

[16] Linder, J.C., Jarvenpaa, S., and Davenport, T.H. "Toward an Innovation Sourcing Strategy," *MIT Sloan Management Review*, Summer 2003, 43-49.

[17] Christensen, C.M. and Raynor, M.E. (2003), *The Innovator's Solution: Creating and Sustaining Successful Growth*, Boston: Harvard Business School Press, 34.

[18] Christensen, C.M. and Raynor, M.E. (2003), *op.cit.*, 35.

[19] Rothwell, R. (1992), Successful Industrial Innovation: Critical Success Factors for the 1990's, *R&D Management*, 22(3), 221-239.

[20] Tidd, J., Bessant, J. and Pavitt, K. (1997), *op.cit*, 31.

[21] Adapted from Chesbrough, H.W. (2003), *op.cit*, p.36.

[22] Adapted from Chesbrough, H.W. (2003), *op.cit*, p.38.

[23] Leibold, M., Voelpel, S.C., and Tekie, E.B. (2004), *op.cit.*, p.4.

The Era of Open Innovation

[1] The early work on PARC comes from D.K. Smith and R.C. Alexander, "Fumbling the Future: How Xerox Invented, Then Ignored, the First Personal Computer" (New York: William Morrow & Co., 1988). The story was revisited in M. Hiltzik, "Dealers of Lightning" (New York: HarperBusiness, 1999). An alternative perspective – that Xerox managers did not "fumble" these technologies but consciously ushered them out the door – can be found in H. Chesbrough, "Graceful Exits and Foregone Opportunities: Xerox's Management of Its Technology Spinoff Companies," Business History Review 76 (winter 2002): 803-838.

[2] N. Sakkab, P&G's senior vice president for R&D for Global Fabric and Home Care, described P&G's new innovation strategy in an address to the Industrial Research Institute. See N. Sakkab, "Connect & Develop Complements Research & Develop at P&G," Research Technology Management 45 (March-April 2002): 38-45.

[3] H. Chesbrough, interview with Larry Huston, August 5, 2002. Huston, director of external innovation at Procter & Gamble, noted as well that the "Connect & Develop" initiative had strong support from P&G's board of directors and that there has been a board subcommittee working on the issue.

[4] Sakkab, "Connect & Develop," 38-45.

[5] "Too Much Ventured Nothing Gained: VCs Are a Hurting Bunch. New Companies Feel Their Pain," Fortune, November 25, 2002.

[6] For an account of Nokia's R&D approach to GSM, see M. Häikiö, "Nokia: The Inside Story" (London: Financial Times Prentice Hall, 2002), 120-121 (in particular).

[7] M. Sawhney, E. Prandelli and G. Verona, "The Power of Innomediation," MIT Sloan Management Review 44 (winter 2003): 77-82; and J.D. Wolpert, "Breaking Out of the Innovation Box," Harvard Business Review 80 (August 2002): 76-83.

Strategic Innovation and the Science of Learning

[1] The need to reinvent strategies during times of discontinuous change has been noted in C.K. Prahalad and G. Hamel, "Competing for the Future" (Boston: Harvard Business School Press, 1994); G. Hamel, "Strategy as Revolution," Harvard Business Review 74 (July-August 1996): 69-82; W.C. Kim and R.A. Mauborgne, "Value Innovation: The Strategic Logic of High Growth," Harvard Business Review 75 (January-February 1997): 103-112; and C.C. Markides, "All the Right Moves: A Guide To Crafting Breakthrough Strategy" (Boston: Harvard Business School Press, 1999).

[2] This definition of strategic innovation is consistent with the perspective advanced by V. Govindarajan and A.K. Gupta, "Globalization in the Digital Age," chap. 9 in "The Quest for Global Dominance: Transforming Global Presence Into Global Competitive Advantage" (San Francisco: Jossey-Bass, 2001); and C.K. Prahalad and G. Hamel, "Competing for the Future," Harvard Business Review 72 (July-August 1994): 122-128.

[3] This observation has been made by other researchers. For example, see C.M. Christensen, "Discovering New and Emerging Markets," chap. 7 in "The Innovator's Dilemma: When New Technologies Cause Great Firms To Fail" (New York: Harper Business, 1997); and Z. Block and I.C. MacMillan, "Developing the Business Plan," chap. 7 in "Corporate Venturing: Creating New Businesses Within the Firm" (Boston: Harvard Business School Press, 1993).

[4] See A. Wooldridge, "A Survey of Telecommunications," Economist, Saturday, Oct. 9, 1999, p. 1; and "Cellphone Ownership Soars," USA Today, Friday, Aug. 2, 2002, sec. A, 1A.

[5] The study of whether and how individuals or organizations can learn from experience has a long tradition in the organizational-learning literature. See, for example, D.A. Levinthal and J.G. March, "The Myopia of Learning," Strategic Management Journal 14 (winter 1993): 95-112; B. Levitt and J.G. March, "Organizational Learning," Annual Review of Sociology 14 (1988): 319-340; J.E. Russo and P.J.H. Shoemaker, "The Personal Challenges of Learning," chap. 8, and "Learning in Organizations," chap. 9, in "Winning Decisions: Getting It Right the First Time" (New York: Doubleday, 2002). However, the subject of how control systems can be improved to support learning better has not received treatment in this literature.

[6] See K.A. Merchant, "Rewarding Results: Motivating Profit Center Managers" (Boston: Harvard Business School Press, 1989); and J.A. Maciariello and C.J. Kirby, "Management Control Systems: Using Adaptive Systems To Attain Control" (New York: Pearson Education, 1994).

[7] This notion has also been advanced by R.G. McGrath and I.C. MacMillan, "Discovery-Driven Planning," Harvard Business Review 73 (July-August 1995): 44-54. Theory-focused planning is based on the same premise – that conventional planning is inappropriate when more is unknown than known. However, it differs in most particulars. The discovery-driven planning approach is appropriate when the industry being entered is established, the business model well known, and the uncertainties for the venture can be reduced to identifiable operational parameters. Theory-focused planning is appropriate when the industry is emerging, the business model is experimental, and the uncertainties so great that the basic nature of the relationships between activities and outcomes is unknown.

[8] See, for example, R.N. Anthony and V. Govindarajan, "Management Control Systems," 11th ed. (New York: McGraw-Hill, 2004), which focuses on the use of planning and control systems to implement (as opposed to test) strategies. Within this context, there have been several important developments in the field of management planning and control. One example is the value in combining financial measures ("outcome measures") and nonfinancial measures ("performance drivers") in evaluating the performance of managers, a development

that goes as far back as the "measurement project" at General Electric Co. in the 1950s. See Anthony, "Management Control Systems," 557-564. The notion of blending financial and nonfinancial measures in the context of implementing strategies has been refined by others. See, for example, J.K. Shank and V. Govindarajan, "Strategic Cost Management: The New Tool for Competitive Advantage" (New York: Free Press, 1993) for a development of the concept of "key success factors," or R.S. Kaplan and D.P. Norton, "The Balanced Scorecard: Translating Strategy Into Action" (Boston: Harvard Business School Press, 1996). Our objective in this article is to redefine planning and control for a different purpose – testing a highly uncertain strategy through experimentation and learning, when a priori predictions of the future are not possible.

[9] Again, refer to McGrath and MacMillan's concept of discovery-driven planning (DDP). In this example, DDP would be appropriate if the question were whether the necessary student-to-faculty ratio is 10:1. But for Universitas 21 Global, the question is much more fundamental: To what extent does student-to-faculty ratio have an impact on student satisfaction? Theory-focused planning is designed to facilitate resolution of this type of unknown.

IV Strategy, Business Models and Organizational Energy

Synopsis

This chapter presents and motivates a new approach – poised strategic management – for the innovation economy. Its major elements are discussed, as well as its context, content and process dimensions. The formula $E_b^n = MI^2$ is expanded and applied, indicating the relationship between poised strategy and organizational rejuvenation (organizational re-energization, to avoid rapid organizational entropy). Furthermore, the concept of a business model (BM), need for a portfolio of BM's, concept and applications of a business ecosystem, and relationships between BM and strategy are discussed. Major 'box' examples are Encyclopedia Britannica (box), and various other firms, and the case example is Xerox (illustrating how Xerox manages various BM's, including the handling of successes and failures of new BM's).

The New Strategic Management Approach for the Innovation Economy: Poised Strategy

The New Strategic Management Approach and its Key Elements

Considering the deficiencies of the traditional strategic management approaches for the innovation economy (Chapter 2), and the requirements of a new strategy mindset to co-shape value-innovation (Chapter 3), this chapter outlines an (appropriate) new approach to strategic management in the innovation economy of the early 21st century. Each element of the new strategic management approach is subsequently described. The rest of the chapter compares the differences in context, content, and processes between the new approach and the extant strategic management approaches, illustrated by several business examples. The chapter concludes with particular prerequisites and cautions in using this approach.

The new strategic management approach for the innovation economy is described as follows:

> **Poised strategy to manage multiple business models for sustaining and disruptive value innovation in collaborative business networks.**

The key elements of this definition are:

- *Poised strategy*: the overall term to distinguish from strategy as planning, balancing, positioning (fit), and resource leveraging – the traditional approaches. The concept 'organizational poise' refers to a dynamic capability rooted in a specific mindset, range of diverse dexterities ('ambidextrous' capabilities)[1], and an ability to effectively rejuvenate (positively energize and change) itself. An 'unpoised' organization may suffer from limitations in managerial mindsets, narrow range of dexterities (e.g., unable to move into diverse or emerging business landscapes), and/or paralyzing inertia (lack of positive, creative energy for change).

- *Multiple business models*: managing several business models simultaneously. Managing only one successful business model that usually becomes quickly 'traditional', with future continued success not guaranteed, is inadequate in the innovation economy. Enterprises require a portfolio of business models, with new business models destined to eventually replace traditional ones (discussed later in this chapter).

- *Sustaining and disruptive value innovation*: enterprises require both sustaining (i.e., incremental) and disruptive (i.e., inflective, breakthrough) innovation capabilities for survival, as indicated in Chapter 3.
- *Collaborative business networks*: in an increasingly networked economy, knowledge and innovation for new value creation arise from collaboration in business networks, which include business ecosystems, traditional industry clusters, supply and demand chains, and internal company value chains. Astute leveraging of business networks for value innovation, with relevant internal company functions moving outside the enterprise (e.g., 'open' innovation), is becoming a key success factor for enterprises. We elaborate upon these dimensions in the following sections of the chapter.

Context, Content, and Process Dimensions of Poised Strategy

The following table (Table 4.1) illustrates the major differences between the poised strategy approach of the early 21st century and the traditional approaches previously outlined.

Table 4.1 Content, context, and process dimensions of the poised strategy approach in comparison to traditional approaches

	Context	Content	Process
Late 20th Century	• Analysis of industries, competition, markets, and value chains. • Company and product/service focus.	Strategic plans: network, corporate, business, functional levels (mechanistic and systematic).	Linear, reductionistic, 'closed' innovation; periodic and control directive.
Early 21st Century	• Insight and foresight of business ecosystems and business model reinvention. • Networked value innovation focus.	Strategic frameworks: business models; business ecosystems; value innovation options. (dynamic and systemic).	Non-linear, holistic, 'open'-innovation; continuous business model reinvention; and coherence-enabling mechanisms.

As a basis for the necessary further elaboration of the strategy dimensions and concepts indicated in Table 4.1, it is now possible to extend Table 2.1 (various eras of strategic management) to include the poised strategy approach of the early 21st century. This is indicated in Table 4.2, with subsequent elaboration.

Table 4.2

The focus of strategic management in various eras of time: 1950's to early 21st century

1950's-1960's	1970's	1980's	1990's	Early 21st Century
Planning: Business and budgetary planning	*Balancing*: Optimizing corporate entities and functions	*Positioning*: Industries, markets and firms "adapting" and achieving unique "fit"	*Resources & Capabilities*: Resource-based view for competitive advantage	*Organizational poise* Value innovation through multiple business models
• Planning growth • Capital and operational budgeting • Financial control	• Balancing a portfolio of SBU's/firms/products • Synergy of resources and functions	• Choosing industries and markets, and positioning within them • Adapting and fitting to the environment	• Sources of competitive advantage within the firm • Responding to hyper-competition	• New value innovations from collaborative business networks • Portfolio of traditional and new business models • Corporate rejuvenation
• Investment planning • Financial budgeting • Economic forecasting • Linear programming	• Portfolio planning matrices (e.g. BCG, GE, Shell directional policy) • SWOT (Strengths-Weaknesses-Opportunities-Threats) analyses	• Industry analysis (e.g. "5 Forces"-model) • Competitor analyses • Value Chain analyses • PIMS (Profit Impact of Market Strategies) analyses	• Resource analyses • Core competency analyses • Capability analyses • BPR (Business Process Reengineering) • BSC (Balanced Scorecard) • TQM (Total Quality Management)	• Business ecosystem sensing • Business model reinvention • Knowledge-networking inside and outside the firm • Leveraging various types of innovation, both sustaining and disruptive • Open innovation processes • SSC (Systemic Scorecard) • Sense-making tools
• Formal structures and procedures • Financial management predominant	• Multidivisional structures • Diversification • Quest for market share growth	• Industry restructuring • Value chain configuration • Positioning evaluations	• Restructuring around key resource competence • Focus on building core competencies • Outsourcing • Alliances	• Business network enablers • Self-organization drivers • Coherence enablers • Sense-making capabilities • Internal and external structures

Poised strategy for corporate rejuvenation

Poised strategy involves the capability of an enterprise to continually rejuvenate itself with value innovation from multiple business models. In Chapter 1, the well-known Einstein-formula of $E = MC^2$ was translated into 21st century business context as follows:

$$E_b = MI^2 \quad \text{or}$$

$$\text{Energy}_{business} = \text{Management (Innovation} \times \text{Speed)}$$

This formula can now be further refined as:

$$E_b^n = MI^2 \quad \text{or}$$

Organizational Energy (from Portfolio of Multiple Business Models)	=	Managing Value-Innovation Activities in Collaborative Business Networks (with Dynamic Capabilities and Increasing Speed-to-Market)

Thus, a poised strategic management approach provides essential rejuvenation (organizational energy) capabilities, emanating from the ambidextrous management of multiple business models that are co-shaped in collaborative business networks (also termed 'business ecosystems'). The following key concepts are henceforth discussed:

- The nature and key elements of a business model: there are various and often confusing views of the concept of a business model, and these are reviewed and clarified.

- Managing a portfolio of multiple business models for value innovation: The need for, and the managerial requirements of managing a portfolio of diverse (sustaining and disruptive) business models are discussed with business examples.

- Business ecosystems and co-shaping value innovation: the concept of a business ecosystem is further elaborated, with business examples of successful value innovations through application of business ecosystem thinking and implementation.

- The relationship between 'business model' and 'strategy': the range of salient relationships (differences, linkages and synergies) between the concepts of business model and strategy are outlined and illustrated.

- Poised strategy and organizational energy: all single, traditional business models are subject to a high degree of entropy, the loss of energy in relatively closed business systems. Poised strategy focuses on rejuvenating the enterprise through dynamic re-energizing activities based on multiple business models in various business ecosystems – Einstein's seminal concept of 'novelty by combination'. These concepts and relationships are elaborated in this subsection.

To complete the entire picture of further exposition, the particular processes and tools of the poised strategy approach (the 'how to') are the focus of Chapter 5, while the managerial and organizational requirements of poised strategy are the subject of Chapter 6.

The Nature and Key Elements of a Business Model

A business model was described in Chapter 1 as the 'way of doing business' or the 'business concept'[2] that a firm has chosen, i.e. its entire system for creating and providing consistent value to target customers and earning benefits for all its stakeholders, including adequate profitability for its shareholders. Because of divergent views of the key elements of a business model, it is useful to review a number of views and then extract an integrated (generic) approach:

- Timmers provides a definition of a business model as being:[3]
  - an architecture for the product, service, and information flows, including a description of the various business actors and their roles;
  - a description of the potential benefits for the various business actors; and
  - a description of the sources of revenues.
- Schmid *et al.* distinguish six generic elements of a business model:[4] mission, structure, processes, revenues, legal issues, and technology. When designing a business model and applying the framework, Schmid *et al.* emphasize that all six generic elements and the dynamics of the respective elements have to be considered.
- According to Viscio and Pasternack, a business model comprises of five elements:[5] global core (with five key missions: identity, strategic leadership, capabilities, control mission, and capital mission), business units, services, governance, and linkages. This model defines the elements individually as well as collectively, indicating that the model must generate a 'system' value in addition to the value from the individual parts. This system value establishes what should be inside and what should be outside the organization. It additionally assists in setting the standards for performance expectations from each of the elements.
- Hamel states that the elements of a 'business concept' and 'business model' are the same; a business model is simply a business concept that has been put into practice.[6] A business concept comprises four major components: core strategy, strategic resources, customer interface, and value network. Intermediating between the components are three elements – customer benefits, configuration of competencies, and company boundaries – that link and relate the major components.

As evident from the above descriptions, there are overlapping and common elements among the components and dimensions of business models suggested by various authors. Synthesizing these views, a generic definition of a business model and its core elements is as follows:

The particular business concept (or way of doing business) as reflected by the enterprise's core value proposition(s) for customers; its configured value network(s) to provide that value, consisting of own strategic capabilities as well as other (e.g., outsourced/allianced) value networks and capabilities; and its leadership and governance enabling capabilities to continually sustain and reinvent itself to satisfy the multiple objectives of its various stakeholders (including shareholders).

From this definition, the generic elements in business models are defined as:

- Particular customer base (specific need categories);
- Customer value proposition (which could also involve new customer base);
- Value network (re)configuration for that value creation and delivery; and
- Leadership capabilities that ensure the satisfaction of relevant stakeholders.

These generic elements of a business model are reflected in Figure 4.1.

A more simplistic way of depicting the key elements of a business model is indicated in Figure 4.2.

The non-linearity of the key elements of a business model is evident from the multiple linkages and interactions among the four generic elements, while the holistic nature of a business model derives from the ability to see all four elements as a 'whole', i.e. inseparably linked. In other words, when considering one element, the consideration of the other elements immediately comes into the 'mental picture'. This is the power

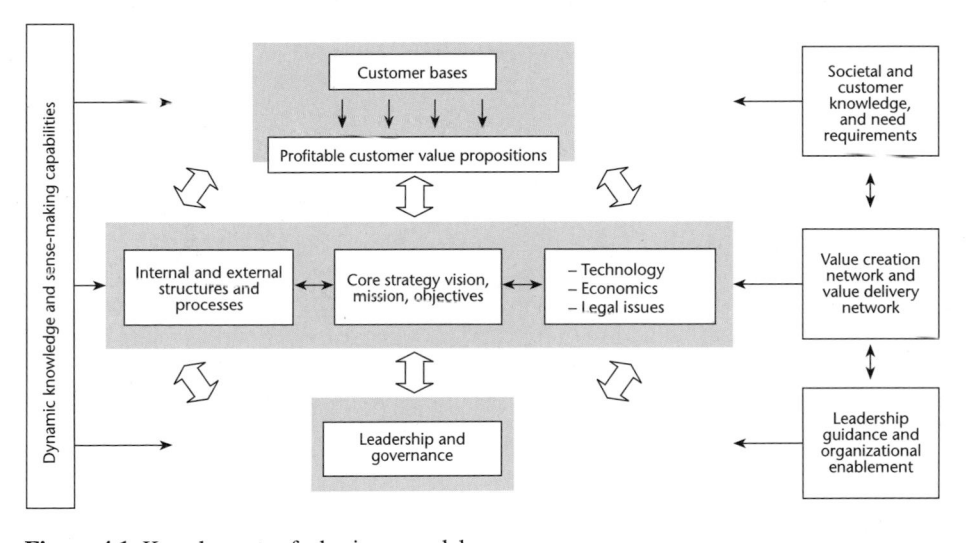

Figure 4.1 Key elements of a business model

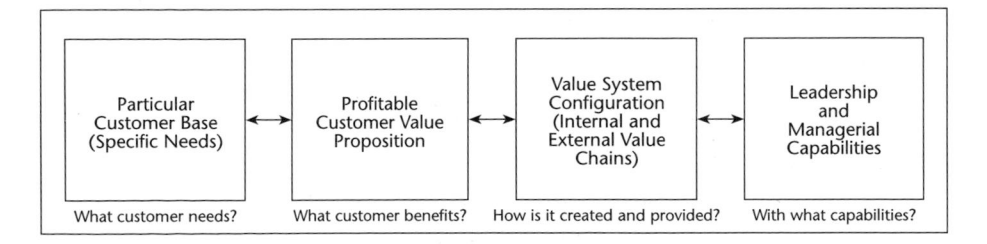

Figure 4.2 Generic (and non-linear) elements of a business model

of the concept of a business model: the ability for anyone to quickly grasp the 'way of doing business' of an enterprise (or separate business unit) – the four elements can be held easily and mutually-linked in anyone's mind.

The Need for a Portfolio of Business Models in an Enterprise

In the more stable industrial economy, enterprises used to operate a single business model in a particular industry. In the fast-changing innovation economy, mainly driven by advanced technology, knowledge-networking, and globalization, the resulting socio-techno-economic environment is one that challenges the essence of relatively stable business models that firms used to achieve their particular goals.

These driving forces have created substantial uncertainty in the competitive landscape by bringing about fundamental changes in the traditional boundaries of nations, industries, and companies. And such changes continue to challenge the traditional rules of competition (as depicted in Chapter 1). The driving forces of the innovation economy have removed the certainty and stability in the economic environment from almost every industry. And consequently, the competitive landscape has undergone a fundamental change to produce a variety of new industries and combination of old industries, e.g. financial services industry, life sciences industry, 'edutainment' (education and entertainment) industry, the ICT industry (information and communications technology), and the 'individual living environment' industry (previously the home furnishings industry). These are not just new names for old diversifying industries, but new industries based on new enterprise business models, due to fundamental changes in the 'way of doing business' in a particular industry and their acceptance by increasingly large customer bases.

No matter how successful and superior a company's current business model seems to be, it will be 'imitated, diluted and commoditized' by others and challenged by new business models.[7] Additionally, major and unpredictable changes in the business environment, the increasing importance placed on innovation and knowledge as value-creating attributes, and the accelerating pace of the business environment create major challenges in sustaining the efficacy of existing business models.[8]

An example of how discontinuity in the environment can lead a company (*Encyclopedia Britannica*) that was rooted in traditional business model thinking to its near downfall is portrayed in the box below.[9]

The significance of changing the 'rules of the game' in today's business landscape includes an orientation towards, and a capability of having a portfolio of (multiple, diverse) business models, rather than having a singular focused strategy based on one business model. This does not mean that a traditional business model should be closed down, especially not if it is still profitable (even if profitability is declining), but rather that both traditional and new/emerging/incubating/developing business models have to be managed simultaneously. This is not easy, as industry incumbents tend to resist disruptive change partly because the kind of change being required is radical and challenging. That is, what is needed is no longer a matter of incremental change, but

Encyclopedia Britannica's near demise by focusing on a single business model

Since 1768, *Encyclopedia Britannica* has evolved through 15 editions and to this day it is regarded as the world's most comprehensive and authoritative encyclopedia. In the 1970s, Britannica grew into a serious commercial enterprise. The content was revised every four or five years, and the company built one of the most aggressive and successful direct sales forces in the world. By 1990, sales of Britannica's multivolume sets had reached an all-time high of about US$650 million. Since 1990, however, its sales have collapsed by over 80 per cent. Britannica was under serious threat from a new competitor: the CD-ROM.

The CD-ROM came from 'nowhere' and destroyed the printed encyclopedia business. Whereas Britannica sells for US$1500-2000 per set, CD-ROM encyclopedias sell for US$50-70, with the vast majority of copies given away for free to promote the sale of computers. While the marginal manufacturing cost of Britannica is about US$250 for production plus about US$500-600 for salesperson's commission, the CD-ROM's marginal cost is US$1.50 per copy.

Britannica's executives initially seemed to have viewed the CD-ROM encyclopedia as an irrelevance, but as revenues plunged, it became obvious that regardless of the quality, CD-ROM encyclopedias were a serious competition. As sales continued to plummet, the company eventually put together its own CD-ROM version of the encyclopedia, and tried to graft it onto its traditional business model.

The CD-ROM version engendered yet another crisis: it could not possibly produce the US$500-600 sales commission its traditional counterpart produced. To avoid a revolt by the sales force, Britannica executives decided to bundle the printed product with its digital counterpart. The CD-ROM was given free to buyers of the multivolume set. Anyone who wanted to buy just the CD-ROM would have to pay US$1000. The decision appeased the sales force briefly, but did nothing to stem the continuing collapse of sales. In 1995, the company was put up for sale, and after 18 months it was sold for less than half of the book value. In less than five years, one of the greatest brand names in the English-speaking world, with a heritage of more than 200 years, was nearly destroyed by an inexpensive, plastic disk.

With the benefit of hindsight, it is evident that Britannica should have started to experiment with additional (new) business models when (and even before) new disruptive technologies emerged. Past successes blinded management to any possibility that a new competitive business model could emerge and become a serious challenge to their existing business model. Had they adopted the right mindset and innovative network capabilities, additional business models would have been experimented with and tested at an early stage, and some would have supplanted the traditional one. It would also have enabled management to realize that their industry has shifted into a *knowledge-accessing industry*, away from the limiting *printed encyclopedia industry*, due to new customer need satisfactions, new customer value propositions, new value system configuration requirements, and their new organizational capability demands.

It will be important to witness, and also to make strategic sense of, the implications of the rapidly growing Wikipedia Knowledge portal for traditional business models in this field. See www.wikipedia.org.

realizing a discontinuous transformation in both organization and industry. Some of the difficulties incumbents face arise when a successful business model encourages top management to focus organizational energies and resources on refining and extending that existing business model. Entrenched managerial routines and commitment to the existing business model often bring failure to the company when discontinuities occur in the business environment, which is characteristic of the innovation economy.[10]

Additionally, incumbents could easily become inept because of their reluctance to deconstruct their established business model (e.g., sales and distribution systems and long-term relationships with suppliers and customers), and this hesitation becomes one of the greatest competitive advantages for new competitors. For this reason, companies have to preemptively 'cannibalize' their own businesses to remain competitive. Allowing 'creative destruction' entails the paradox, and a challenge for managers, of perfecting (improving, making efficient) products and services only to destroy (cannibalize, reinvent) them when necessary, i.e. to be superseded by new business models. Nevertheless, it is important to realize that if organizations are to defend themselves against competitors, they should play the role of creator and destroyer of their own business models through managing a portfolio of multiple business models.

There are many examples of this cannibalization in virtually every industry. In consumer products, manufacturers make and sell branded products, while at the same time working with retailers on store brands. Software companies sell software packages, as well as offering "application service provider" capabilities over the Internet. Electric utility firms sell energy to consumers and businesses, while exploring the business model of selling Internet connections through electric power lines. Some of these business model portfolios are more successful than others, but they are necessary no matter what the competitive environment.

A significant challenge is to 'unlearn' past successes and their causes, which tend to lead to path dependency, i.e. the syndrome of 'it worked in the past so it must work in the future'. Corporate managers may have 'excess of rationality', or 'widely established principles of good management', that persuade them to disregard important new technologies and markets.[11] As a result, changes in organizations often do not occur unless they are on the verge of collapsing, or when facing major disruptions. For organizations to learn how to survive and compete in a fast-changing competitive landscape, they should significantly unlearn their traditional strategy mindset, ways of thinking and doing, and their fixation on existing business models.

In general, traditional strategic management approaches involve a competitive orientation with companies predominantly attempting to be more effective (or 'fitter') to achieve unique positions in the existing industry. This is rooted in mechanistic, boundary-oriented industry thinking with companies striving to continuously improve themselves ('running harder and harder'). In today's more turbulent environment, organizations should rather strive to systematically reinvent themselves ('run differently and smarter').

Sustaining and Disruptive Business Innovation in a Portfolio of Business Models

It was illustrated in Chapter 3 (see Figure 3.2) that disruptive business model capability, based on transformative value-innovation, is essential in today's innovation economy, in contrast to sustainable business model capability, based on incremental innovation and a goods-competitive mindset. Christensen and Raynor distinguish between two types of disruptive innovation and two types of sustainable innovation (see Table 4.3) and make a strong case that a disruptive business model is a valuable corporate asset.[12]

Table 4.3 Major types of sustaining and disruptive innovations

Sustaining innovations	Disruptive innovations
Nature: Targets demanding, high-end customers with better performance than what was previously available ('making a better mouse-trap')	**Nature:** Offering new benefits in value propositions targeted at new less-demanding customers. It does not attempt to bring better products to established customers in existing markets ('making a new mouse catching device')
1. *Incremental*, e.g. annual improvements	1. *Original-market disruptions*, e.g. low-end disruptions at the low end of the original value network
2. *Significantly differentiated*, e.g. breakthrough, 'leapfrog' product propositions (in same industry)	2. *New-market disruptions*, e.g. creation of an entirely new value network

It should be emphasized that the argument is not against aggressive pursuit of sustaining innovations of the existing business model of an enterprise; it is for simultaneous pursuit of sustaining and disruptive business models. The dilemma is that sustaining innovations are so attractive and 'logical' relative to disruptive ones that the very best sustaining companies systematically ignore disruptive threats until it is almost too late. Large industry incumbents especially face powerful and path-dependent forces that motivate them to continue with their existing business model instead of introducing counter-measures centered on disruptive value-innovation. Conversely, new entrants to an evolving industry often do not have success in competing on a sustaining innovation basis, but rather on a disruptive one, as illustrated in the following box.[13]

Sustaining Business Models are less Successful than Disruptive Business Models for New Entrants

For new entrants, it is advisable to define an opportunity that is disruptive relative to all the established players in the targeted market, or not to invest in the idea at all. If it is a sustaining innovation relative to the business model of a significant incumbent, one is picking a battle one is very unlikely to win.

The Internet is a good example: throughout the late 1990s, investors poured billions into Internet-based companies, convinced of their "disruptive" potential. An important reason why many of them failed was that the Internet was a sustaining innovation relative to the business models of a host of companies. Prior to the advent of the Internet, Dell Computer, for example, sold computers directly to customers by mail and over the telephone. This business was already a low-end disruptor, moving up its trajectory. Dell's banks of telephone salespeople had to be highly trained in order to walk their customers through the various configurations of components that were and were not feasible. They then manually entered the information into Dell's order fulfillment systems.

For Dell, the Internet was a sustaining technology. It made Dell's core business processes work better, and it helped Dell make more money in the way it was structured to make money. But the identical strategy of selling directly to customers over the Internet was very disruptive relative to Compaq's business model, because that company's cost structure and business processes were targeted at in-store retail distribution.

The theory of disruption would conclude that if Dell (and Gateway) had not existed, then start-up Internet-based computer retailers might have succeeded in disrupting competitors such as Compaq. But because the Internet was sustaining to powerful incumbents, entrant Internet computer retailers have not prospered.

The attempts that IBM and Kodak made in the 1970s and 1980s to beat Xerox in the high-speed photocopier business is another example. These companies were far bigger, and yet they failed to outmuscle Xerox in a sustaining-technology competition. The firm that beat Xerox was Canon – and that victory started with a disruptive tabletop copier strategy.

Similarly, corporate giants RCA, General Electric, and AT&T failed to outmuscle IBM on the sustaining-technology trajectory in mainframe computers. Despite the massive resources they threw at IBM, they could not make a dent in IBM's position. In the end, it was the disruptive personal computer makers, and not the major corporations who picked a direct, sustaining-innovation fight, who bested IBM in computers.

Airbus entered the commercial airframe industry head-on against Boeing, but doing so required massive subsidies from European governments. In the future, the most profitable growth in the airframe industry will probably come from firms with disruptive strategies, such as Embraer and Bombardier's Canadair, whose regional jets are aggressively stretching up-market from below, or 'light jet" manufacturers such as Eclipse and Avocet, who are taking an even lower position in the aviation market.

The above examples of different types of sustaining and disruptive business models illustrate the need to manage a portfolio of multiple business models, including both types, as part of poised strategic management. To understand how disruptive business models arise, it is important to grasp the concept of business ecosystems and co-shaping of value innovation inside and outside organizations, as discussed below.

Business Ecosystems and Co-Shaping of Value Innovation to Form New Business Models

How do new value innovations arise in the innovation economy? The poised strategy approach proposes that a company be viewed not as a member of a single industry, but as part of a business ecosystem that crosses a variety of industries, and that is open to multidimensional knowledge impacts and influences. From an ecosystem perspective, the boundaries of the firm and industry are regarded as variable, and shaped by many actors in the business community. The strategy focus of an individual firm is to co-shape and co-perform with the other players in the business community and to build co-opted capabilities (including with customers) in the ecosystem, often around new innovations. The critical dimension of an ecosystem is that it spans a variety of industries, stakeholders, organizations, markets, and customers, and not only those limited to an organization's traditional industry, customer base, and supply chain. This reflects current business reality, which displays a proliferation of new industries, "blurring" of traditional boundaries, deconstruction of "old" industries, and innovative new cross-industry linkages – such as, 'Bankassurance'. Other examples are 'Edutainment' (education and entertainment industry boundaries blurring) and 'Lifesciences' (pharmaceutical, agriculture, chemical, human wellness/fitness), as Novartis illustrates in its strategy approach.[14]

In a business ecosystem, companies and customers co-evolve knowledge and capabilities around a new value proposition (or 'product/service'): they work collaboratively and competitively to support development of new products, satisfy different customer needs, configure new value chains, and incorporate new rounds of innovations. The basic tension is between the parts and the whole – the emphasis on the parts has been called mechanistic, reductionistic, or atomistic; the emphasis on the whole is termed holistic, organismic, or ecological. In 21st century science, the holistic perspective has become known as systemic, as opposed to systematic. Each part can be seen as an organ that shapes the other parts, thus being both an organized and self-organized being. In contemporary theories of living systems, the concept of organization has been refined to that of self-organization, and understanding the patterns of self-organization is regarded as the key to understanding the essential nature of life.

Business ecosystems thinking requires a grasp of the integrated whole of business within its environment, whose essential properties arise from relationships among its parts. "Systemic thinking" is the basis of this mindset, i.e. understanding of a phenomenon within the context of a larger whole. The recent great shock to strategic management, as stated previously, has been that systems cannot be understood by analysis. The properties of the parts are not intrinsic properties, but can be understood only within the context of the larger whole. Accordingly, systems thinking does not concentrate on basic building blocks, but rather on basic principles of holistic organization – it is the whole that determines the behavior of the parts. The business ecosystem concept can now be defined as: a community of business and related organisms and their environment, interacting as an ecological unit, spanning various (interrelated) industries.

Examples of Business Ecosystems Thinking and its Increasing Innovation Opportunities

"Ecosystems that cater to interrelated customer requirements may be the next big thing in retailing. They could answer the consumer's desire for speed and efficiency and the retailer's need for growth – perhaps at the expense of other industries". – Jevin Eagle, Elizabeth Joseph and Elizabeth Lempres.[15]

"Think of the business environment as a series of ecosystems, with 'keystone' companies such as Microsoft and Wal-Mart providing for the health of all who do business with them. The challenge is to take explicit advantage of the opportunities provided by the ecosystem while avoiding the traps in such environments". – Marco Iansiti and Roy Levien.[16]

Successful businesses are those that co-evolve rapidly and effectively by bringing together resources, partners, suppliers, customers, and other agents to create cooperative networks and thereby new value innovations. This implies that in a 'business ecosystem', companies work cooperatively and competitively to generate new products/services, to satisfy customer needs, to incorporate needs, and to incorporate future innovations. Moore provides relevant examples of business ecosystem evolution in the automobile and retailing industries.[17] From an ecosystem perspective, therefore, the poised strategy focus of an individual firm should be to co-shape and co-perform with the other players in the business community and to build co-opted capabilities in the ecosystem. Figure 4.3 provides a systemic framework for understanding this co-shaping of the development of new business models.

Organizations, as ongoing concerns, have aspirations to attain a certain level of profit if they are to sustain themselves. Additionally, as previously discussed, a business model should have an economic feasibility to sustain the existing business model as well as to provide funds for experimenting with different models. Figure 4.3 indicates that a new business model arises not only from reconfiguring an organization's core business strategy and dynamic capabilities, but also from making sense of socio-cultural dynamics and opportunity gaps, reinventing of customer value proposition(s),

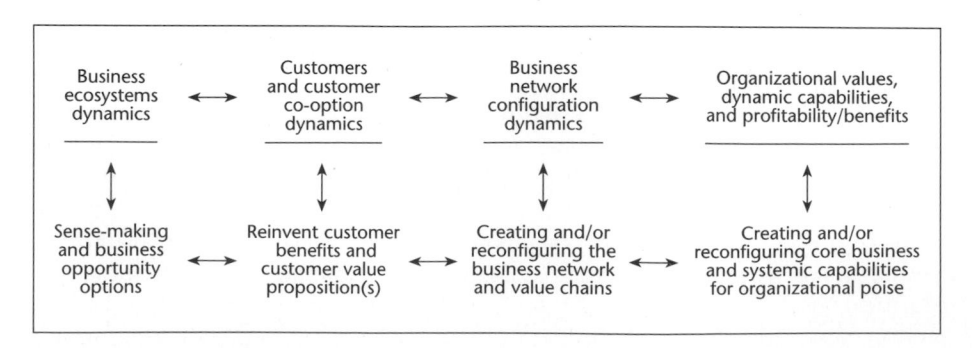

Figure 4.3 Co-shaping value innovation to form new business models

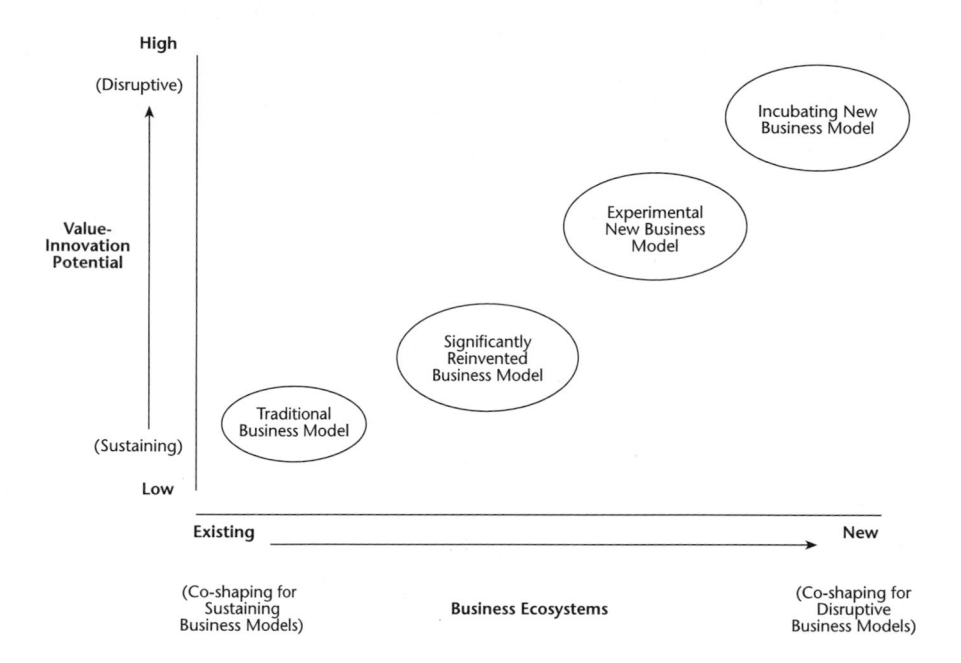

Figure 4.4 Hypothetical example of a portfolio of multiple business models

and reconfiguring the business network and its value chains. This improves and sharpens managerial sense-making of socio-cultural business system dynamics, for managers to guide, cultivate, and shape self-organizing creative activities in the organization for the creation and building of new business models. Such systemic thinking therefore provides the basis for continuous sustaining innovation, by responding (creatively and/or adaptively) to the changing environment through co-shaped customer value propositions.

Figure 4.4 illustrates a simplified conceptual view of a portfolio of multiple business models in business ecosystems, each of which should be present within an organization at the same time.

The figure illustrates that while managing an existing (traditional) business model efficiently while it is still profitable, an enterprise should simultaneously manage a family of incubating (being formed), experimental (being tested in the market place), and significantly reinvented (e.g., incrementally innovated) business models.

Business ecosystems thinking recognizes that traditional hierarchical strategic management structures and their logic should be complemented, if not replaced, with approaches such as self-organization that magnify rather than obscure individual differences, and should focus on business relationships, communities, patterns, and relative benefits. Strategic success now becomes a function of a firm's talent for thriving in dynamic nonlinear systems that rely on network feedback and emergent relationships. The particular processes and tools for such a poised strategic management approach, i.e. managing multiple business models for sustaining and disruptive value innovation in business ecosystems, are discussed in Chapter 5.

The Relationship between Business Model and Strategy

The concept of a business model differs from the concept of strategy in at least four ways, as can be deduced from the previous sections of this chapter. For purpose of clarity, these differences are listed below:

- First, a business model starts by seeking and creating value for the *customer*, and constructs the model around delivering that value consistently and reliably. Strategy is mainly concerned with *competition*, i.e. how to compete in a well-defined industry.

- Second, a business model forms the underlying *rationale* for being in business, i.e. a value-providing entity in society, while a strategy is the *plan* of how to put that business model (differentially) into action.

- A third difference lies in the creation of *value for the business*, versus creation of *value for the shareholder*. Oftentimes, the financial dimensions of a business are left out of the business model. The model is assumed to be financed out of internal corporate resources, so that financing issues do not figure prominently in the business model, or the model of a startup is to be financed through early stage venture capital. Clearly, though, the ability to translate value in the business into value for the shareholder requires the *incorporation of the financial domain* to the construct of a business model.

- Fourth, a business model construct consciously assumes that knowledge of customers and third parties is cognitively limited and biased by the earlier success of the firm. Strategy generally requires careful, analytical calculation and choice, which assumes that there is a great deal of reliable information available. It similarly assumes that any cognitive limitations on the part of the firm are of limited importance. In a business model construct, it is therefore important to *network*, share knowledge, and co-shape new value innovations with outside stakeholders, while in strategy development these activities were mainly *internalized*.

The two concepts of business model and strategy are clearly complementary, but they are not the same. Simultaneously, when someone develops a business model, he or she needs to develop a strategy to determine how to compete with that business model. In that respect, strategic reasoning may influence and inform business model design, and the business model itself could be the point of differentiation. Although the business model design has important implications for value capture, it is really more about value creation: how the firm creates value with partners, suppliers, and customers.

Constructing business models in environments characterized by high complexity and ambiguity has much in common with Weick's notion of sense-making: 'Sense-making is about contextual rationality. It is built out of vague questions, muddy answers, and negotiated agreements that attempt to reduce confusion'.[18] This process is closely related to Prahalad and Bettis's notion of a dominant logic, since that logic is intended to reduce ambiguity and make sense of complex choices faced by managers.[19] While this logic is useful and beneficial, it comes at a cost of possible and real failure of some new business models. The case example of Xerox (see end of this chapter) illustrates the failure of two spin-off business models, not because of shortcomings in the perceived value innovation opportunities, but because they failed to develop appropriate business models that were capable of realizing the value latent in the opportunities.

When looking at business corporations, it is important to realize the following salient relationships between business model and strategy:

a) A corporation is a diversified business enterprise consisting of a number of separate businesses, business units, or business divisions. Each of these businesses is often competing in a different industry.

b) For each industry its businesses compete in, the corporation should not have a single business model only, but multiple business models to enable both sustaining and disruptive value innovations to emerge and flourish. In effect, a corporation should have a poised strategy that involves multiple business models for each of its industries it is active in (with some new business models leading into new industries, or causing new industries to be established in due course).

c) Each business model, either traditional or new, should have a strategy, i.e. an implementation thrust for that business model that differentiates itself from existing or potential competitors.

Poised Strategy and Organizational Energy

As indicated earlier, poised strategy involves the capability of an enterprise to continually rejuvenate itself with value innovation from multiple business models, some of these being traditional business models, and some being new business models in various stages of development. Organizational energy is the driving force for creativity and rejuvenation, and results from the dynamic interactions between multiple business model activities. This in turn emanates from dynamic activity relationships of the enterprise in its business ecosystem, which includes demand and supply chains and internal value chains, and various other stakeholders.

The need for renewal of organizational energy through the dynamic interplay of diverse business models is best described by the concepts of 'entropy' and 'novelty by combination'.[20] The concept of entropy finds its origin in thermodynamics, but has been applied within the context of economic theory. It is borrowed to represent the erosion in the temporary competitive advantage that a particular business model represents, resulting from the loss occurring through the voluntary or involuntary sharing of information and knowledge – through memetic evolutionary pressure.[21] The concept of entropy suggests that this value will diffuse such that the ability of a particular business model to provide a competitive advantage is diminished. Healthy organizations and business ecosystems are those that continually rejuvenate themselves, while those that fail to do so will eventually decline as their competitive position is eroded. The concept of entropy suggests that the direction of entropic decay is fixed, but its timing is indeterminate, in part due to 'novelty by combination' which can provide new sources of energy or value.

Innovation is a result of creative thought that Einstein described as "combinatorial play". Renewal of a business model through innovation highlights the dualism of the two concepts of entropy and innovation. Entropy is particularly applicable when discussing innovation theory because it stresses the qualitative changes that are not readily predictable in nature. Innovation induces qualitative changes in enterprises, industries, and the economy in a manner that fosters a dynamism that is often unpredictable in nature. New economic theory also supports this dynamism: the concept of "increasing returns" explains economic developments based on the dynamic conditions arising from the increasingly knowledge-networked innovation economy.[22]

Entropy describes the degradation of energy to perform work. Energy is simply defined as the capacity to do work. The 'law of entropy', based on the Second Law of Thermodynamics, describes the increasing randomization of energy as part of the structure of the universe.[23] The energy dilemma does not involve the amount of energy that is available; it involves the form in which the energy is available. The universe is involved in a constant process of converting one form of energy into another form and in doing so, it inevitably must convert part of the original energy into more randomized, less usable, heat energy. Potential energy is organized energy whereas heat represents randomized, disorganized energy. All forms of energy are degraded incessantly and irreversibly to an inferior, lower-quality, more-randomized form of energy, i.e. heat. A very important characteristic of entropy is that it pertains only to a system that we refer to as a closed system: An entity that does not exchange energy, information, or mass with anything outside the system.

Even in the most complex energy transformations, there is a forward direction to the process because only an outside energy source can reverse a heat-process within a closed system. We know empirically that things do not organize themselves into artifacts that are more complex unless new energy is inserted from outside the system. This fact is obvious because a broken window will not repair itself. Without competent management, without the energy to organize and structure transactions, a business will fail, a victim of entropy. For example, in computer systems it is a well-known fact that without new software, without the infusion of new energy from outside the computer system, a computer will never acquire new capabilities, but its hard-drive will fill up with defects and clutter due to the degeneration of the data it holds.

The second Law of Thermodynamics is closely interwoven with the future of the universe and with all life on earth. The definition of life revolves around three prerequisites: The organism must be able to replicate itself, the organism must be capable of energy conversion, and the organism must be subject to evolution. The essence of evolution is an increase in complexity, as is obvious when we consider the evolution of living organisms over eons of time. An increase in complexity entails an increase in the orderliness of the organizational character of the organism: Life represents a decrease of entropy, a decrease of randomness. Such a decrease in randomization can only come about as a result of an infusion of energy from the outside of the closed system, from the outside of the organism. Therefore, the ability to utilize energy by converting to a usable format, is the essence of all things that we call alive or living. Business enterprises have long been viewed as living organisms that are born, grow, mature, and die, and thus the analogy is direct and strong.

In practical business and strategy terms, the above realities have the following implications: an enterprise with only a traditional business model, and strategic management based on traditional strategy-making approaches, suffers from a high degree of entropy, i.e. a degradation of energy due to its focus on making its traditional business model operate more efficiently within relatively closed systems. A poised strategy approach, conversely, focuses on openness to business ecosystems, co-evolution with outsiders across various industries, and an infusion of energy from experimental and other types of new business models. The 'serious play' that Roos and Victor refer to in their work (see Chapter 2), emanates from the 'combinatorial' play earlier mentioned, and such play is constituted by a combination of both internal and external role-players. In the innovation economy of today, it is essential that organizations rejuvenate themselves through the development and implementation of poised strategy, i.e. effectively managing multiple business models in business ecosystems through co-evolving activities.

In many cases, the form of energy that is consumed by poised strategy and a portfolio of business models is management attention. It takes more attention to monitor and make sense of multiple business models than it does for one, and it takes more attention to monitor and make sense of an ecosystem than an individual organization. Yet management attention is a scarce resource that is becoming scarcer all the time.[24] In order to succeed with poised strategy, organizations will have to become much more conscious of management attention, and will have to free up attention for the new strategic environment we have described.

Conclusion: The Challenges of Poised Strategic Management

The new strategic management approach for the innovation economy was earlier described as:

Poised strategy to manage multiple business models for sustaining and disruptive value innovation in collaborate business networks (also termed business ecosystems).

This approach requires ambidextrous capabilities of management. Managers securely employed in a large enterprise, itself with a strong culture – including its beliefs and dominant logic derived from a successful and well-established existing business model – may feel little incentive to search for alternatives outside that successful model. On the other hand, increasing evidence of corporate venturing with new business models abound, seeking to harness the forces of the innovation.

It is also important to realize that poised strategic management does not imply that a firm always has to be a 'prime mover' in its business ecosystem. Being a prime mover should not be confused with 'first mover', i.e. being first with a new value innovation. A prime mover is often a company that succeeds in perfecting a new industry standard through the appropriateness of its business model. Conversely, a company could successfully be a follower in a new industry created by a prime mover, as the range of innovative differentiations in the market is wide.

Whatever the range of business opportunities, it is evident that multiple business models arise through knowledge-networked co-shaping of value innovations in business ecosystems spanning a number of industries. The innovation economy necessitates a new strategic management approach to handle this, i.e. a poised strategy. The processes and tools to achieve this are the theme of Chapter 5.

The Ambidextrous Organization*

By Charles A. O'Reilly III and Michael L. Tushman

*Established companies can develop radical innovations –
and protect their traditional businesses. The secret?
Create organizationally distinct units that are tightly
integrated at the senior executive level.*

The Roman God Janus had two sets of eyes – one pair focusing on what lay behind, the other on what lay ahead. General managers and corporate executives should be able to relate. They, too, must constantly look backward, attending to the products and processes of the past, while also gazing forward, preparing for the innovations that will define the future.

This mental balancing act can be one of the toughest of all managerial challenges – it requires executives to explore new opportunities even as they work diligently to exploit existing capabilities – and it's no surprise that few companies do it well. Most successful enterprises are adept at refining their current offerings, but they falter when it comes to pioneering radically new products and services. Kodak and Boeing are just two of the more recent examples of once dominant companies that failed to adapt to market changes. Kodak excelled at analog photography but hasn't been able to make the leap to digital cameras. Boeing, a longtime leader in commercial aircraft, has experienced difficulties in its defense-contracting businesses and has recently stumbled in the face of competition from Airbus.

The failure to achieve breakthrough innovations while also making steady improvements to an existing business is so commonplace – and so fascinating – that it has become a battleground of management thought. For decades, scholars have spun theories to explain the puzzle and offered advice on how to solve it. Some have argued that there's no way out of the conundrum – that established companies simply lack the flexibility to explore new territory. Some have suggested that big companies adopt a venture capital model, funding exploratory expeditions but otherwise staying out of their way. Others have pointed to cross-functional teams as the key to creating breakthrough innovations. Still others have claimed that a company may be able to shift back and forth between different organizational models, focusing on exploitation for a period and then moving into exploration mode.

---

* Taken with permission from *Harvard Business Review* Vol. 82 No. 4, 2004, pp. 74-81

We recently decided to test these and other theories by taking a close look at the real world, examining how actual, contemporary businesses fare when they attempt to pursue innovations that lie beyond their current products or markets. Do they succeed in achieving breakthroughs? Do their existing businesses suffer? What organizational and managerial structures do they use? What works, and what doesn't?

We discovered that some companies have actually been quite successful at both exploiting the present and exploring the future, and as we looked more deeply at them we found that they share important characteristics. In particular, they separate their new, exploratory units from their traditional, exploitative ones, allowing for different processes, structures, and cultures; at the same time, they maintain tight links across units at the senior executive level. In other words, they manage organizational separation through a tightly integrated senior team. We call these kinds of companies "ambidextrous organizations," and we believe they provide a practical and proven model for forward-looking executives seeking to pioneer radical or disruptive innovations while pursuing incremental gains. A business does not have to escape its past, these cases show, to renew itself for the future.

Exploiting and Exploring

To flourish over the long run, most companies need to maintain a variety of innovation efforts. They must constantly pursue *incremental innovations*, small improvements in their existing products and operations that let them operate more efficiently and deliver ever greater value to customers. An automaker, for example, may frequently tweak a basic engine design to increase horsepower, enhance fuel efficiency, or improve reliability. Companies also have to make *architectural innovations*, applying technological or process advances to fundamentally change some component or element of their business. Capitalizing on the data communication capabilities of the Internet, for instance, a bank can perhaps shift its customer-service call center to a low-labor-cost country like India. Finally, businesses need to come up with *discontinuous innovations* – radical advances like digital photography that profoundly alter the basis for competition in an industry, often rendering old products or ways of working obsolete.

All these types of innovation can have different targets. Some may be aimed at a firm's current customers. Others may be delivered to an existing market that lies beyond a company's current customer base – a car insurer may create a new kind of policy for boat owners, for instance. Still others may be focused on serving an entirely new market that has yet to be clearly defined – people who download online music, for example. As shown in the exhibit "A Map of Innovation," the types of innovation and the targeted markets can be plotted in a matrix.

In our research with colleagues Wendy Smith, Robert Wood, and George Westerman, we studied how companies pursued innovations throughout this matrix. In particular, we looked for companies that attempted to simultaneously pursue modest, incremental innovations (toward the lower-left area of the matrix) and more dramatic, break-

A Map of Innovation

To compete, companies must continually pursue many types of innovation – incremental, architectural, and discontinuous – aimed at existing and new customers. Plotting your companies' innovation efforts in the matrix below will immediately reveal any areas you may have overlooked.

	Incremental innovations Small improvements in existing products and operations	**Architectural innovations** Technological or process advances to fundamentally change a component or element of a business	**Discontinuous innovations** Radical advances that may profoundly alter the basis of competition in an industry
New customers			
Existing customers			

through innovations (toward the upper-right area). We ended up focusing on 35 attempts to launch breakthrough innovations undertaken by 15 business units in nine different industries. We studied the structure and results of the breakthrough projects as well as their impact on the operations and performance of the traditional businesses.

Companies tended to structure their breakthrough projects in one of four basic ways. Seven were carried out within existing *functional designs*, completely integrated into the regular organizational and management structure. Nine were set up as *cross functional teams*, groups operating within the established organization but outside the existing management hierarchy. Four took the form of *unsupported teams*, independent units set up outside the established organization and management hierarchy. And 15 were pursued within *ambidextrous organizations*, where the breakthrough efforts were organized as structurally independent units, each having its own processes, structures, and cultures but integrated into the existing senior management hierarchy. The exhibit "Organizing to Innovate" provides an overview of these four structures.

We tracked the results of the 35 initiatives along two dimensions. First, we determined their success in creating the desired innovations, as measured by either the actual commercial results of a new product or the application of practical market or technical learning. Second, we looked at the performance of the existing business. Did results hold steady, improve, or decline as the firm worked on its breakthroughs? We found that the organizational design and management practices employed had a direct and significant impact on the performance of both the breakthrough initiative and the traditional business.

Organizing to Innovate

In our examination of 35 different attempts at breakthrough innovation, we discovered that businesses tend to apply one of four organizational designs to develop and deliver their innovations. More than 90% of those using the ambidextrous structure succeeded in their attempts, while none of the cross-functional or unsupported teams, and only 25% of those using functional designs, reached their goals.

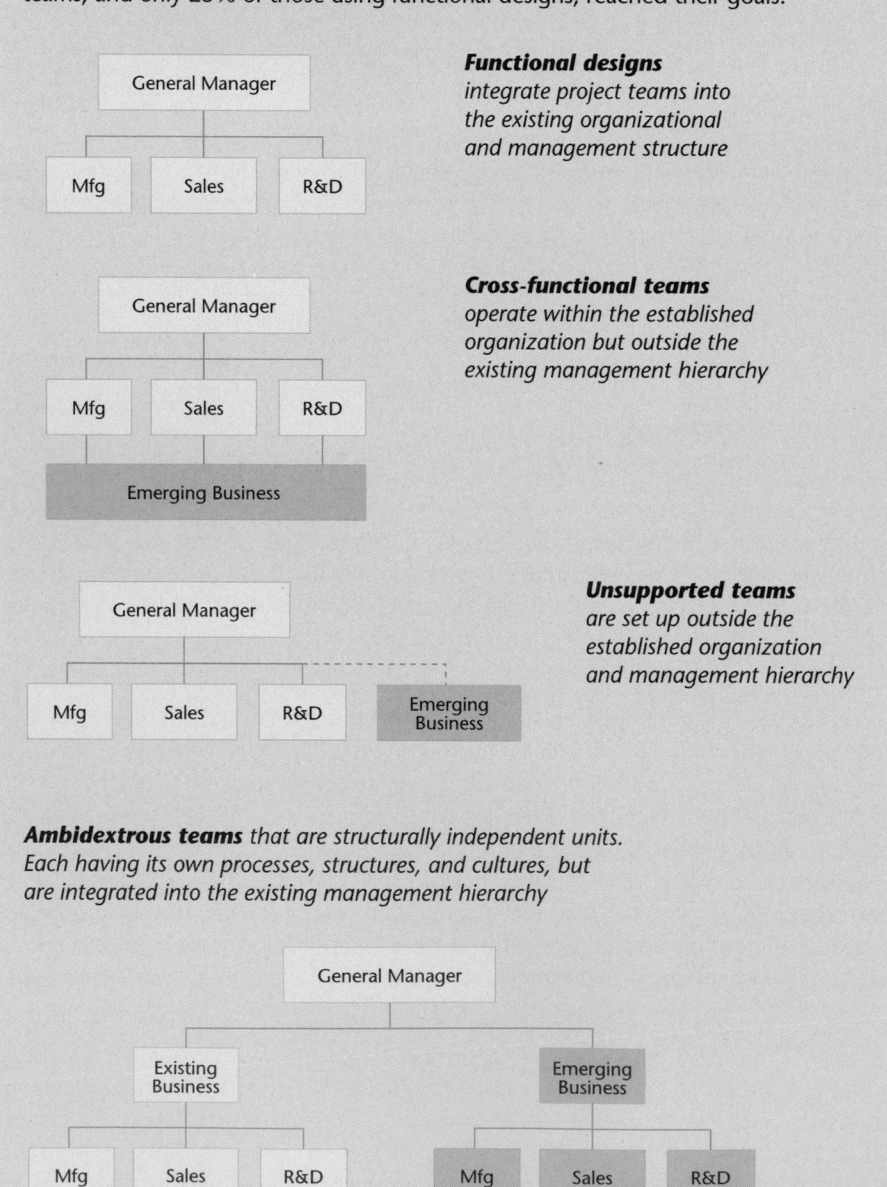

Functional designs *integrate project teams into the existing organizational and management structure*

Cross-functional teams *operate within the established organization but outside the existing management hierarchy*

Unsupported teams *are set up outside the established organization and management hierarchy*

Ambidextrous teams *that are structurally independent units. Each having its own processes, structures, and cultures, but are integrated into the existing management hierarchy*

When it came to launching breakthrough products or services, ambidextrous organizations were significantly more successful than the other three structures. While none of the cross-functional or unsupported teams and only a quarter of the functional designs produced real innovations, *more than 90% of the ambidextrous organizations achieved their goals.* (An exception was breakthrough innovations intended to directly substitute for existing products; in these instances, functional designs performed as well as ambidextrous designs.)

The superiority of ambidextrous designs became even more apparent when we examined eight cases in which a company originally organized its breakthrough initiative around functional designs, cross-functional teams, or unsupported teams and then shifted to an ambidextrous design. In seven of the eight cases, the initiative's performance increased substantially after the change. In contrast, three companies started from an ambidextrous design and then moved to one of the others; performance decreased substantially in two of these cases.

When we measured the effects of all 35 initiatives on their existing businesses, we found that ambidextrous organizations were again clearly superior. In almost every instance in which an ambidextrous structure was used, the competitive performance of the existing product either increased or held steady. By contrast, the results of the traditional operations frequently declined where functional designs, cross-functional teams, or unsupported teams were employed. At a theoretical level, it's easy to explain why ambidextrous organizations would outperform other organizational types. The structure of ambidextrous organizations allows cross-fertilization among units while preventing cross-contamination. The tight coordination at the managerial level enables the fledgling units to share important resources from the traditional units – cash, talent, expertise, customers, and so on – but the organizational separation ensures that the new units' distinctive processes, structures, and cultures are not overwhelmed by the forces of "business as usual." At the same time, the established units are shielded from the distractions of launching new businesses; they can continue to focus all their attention and energy on refining their operations, improving their products, and serving their customers.

But how *exactly* do ambidextrous organizations work? By looking more deeply into the experiences of two such organizations – *USA Today* and Ciba Vision – we can begin to identify the key managerial and organizational characteristics that underpin their ability to both exploit and explore.

A Newspaper Reinvents Itself

In the late 1990s, *USA Today* was a thriving business, but it faced an uncertain future. The national newspaper, a division of the Gannett Corporation, had come a long way since its founding in 1982, when its colorful brand of journalism was widely ridiculed by critics. After losing more than half a billion dollars during its first decade, the paper turned its first profit in 1992 and continued to expand rapidly, becoming the most widely read daily newspaper in the United States. With well-heeled business travelers making up the bulk of its subscriber base, it also became an attractive platform for national advertisers, bringing in a steady flow of revenue.

But as the 1990s progressed, storm clouds appeared on the horizon. Newspaper readership was falling steadily, particularly among young people. Competition was heating up, as customers increasingly looked to television and Internet media outlets for news. And newsprint costs were rising rapidly. Tom Curley, *USA Today*'s president and publisher, recognized that the company would have to expand beyond its traditional print business to maintain strong growth and profits; such expansion, he realized, would require dramatic innovations. The company would need to find ways to apply its existing news-gathering and editing capabilities to entirely new media.

Acting on his beliefs, Curley in 1995 chose Lorraine Cichowski, *USA Today*'s general manager of media projects and former editor of the paper's Money section, to launch an online news service called USAToday.com. He gave her free rein to operate independently from the print business, and she set up a kind of skunk-works operation, bringing in people from outside *USA Today* and housing them on a different floor from the newspaper. She built a fundamentally different kind of organization, with roles and incentives suited to the instantaneous delivery of news and to an entrepreneurial, highly collaborative culture. With Internet use exploding, the venture seemed primed for success.

But results were disappointing. Although USAToday.com was making a small profit by the end of the decade, its growth was sluggish and had little impact on the broader business's results. The problem, Curley saw, was that the new unit was so isolated from the print operation that it was failing to capitalize on the newspaper's vast resources. Although Cichowski was a member of Curley's executive team, she had little support from other members. Viewing her unit as a competitor with the print business, they had little incentive to help her succeed and made few efforts to share their considerable resources with her. Soon, USAToday.com found itself starved of cash, as the newspaper continued to consume most of the available capital, and the online unit began losing talented staff.

Cichowski pushed to have her business spun out entirely from the newspaper, as other companies were doing with their Internet ventures, but Curley had a very different view. He had come to believe that the new unit required not greater separation but greater integration. In 1999, he decided that *USA Today* should adopt a "network strategy," in which it would share news content across three platforms: the newspaper, USAToday.com, and Gannett's 21 local television stations. Curley described his vision: "We're no longer in the newspaper business – we're in the news information space, and we'd better learn to deliver content regardless of form."

To execute that strategy, Curley knew he had to create an ambidextrous organization that could sustain the print business yet also pursue innovations in broadcasting and online news. So in 2000, he replaced the leader of USAToday.com with another internal executive who was a strong supporter of the network strategy, and he brought in an outsider to create a television operation, USAToday Direct. Both the online and television organizations remained separate from the newspaper, maintaining distinctive processes, structures, and cultures, but Curley demanded that the senior leadership of all three businesses be tightly integrated. Together with Karen Jurgenson, the editor of *USA Today*, the heads of the online and television units instituted daily editorial meetings to review stories and assignments, share ideas, and identify other potential synergies. The unit heads quickly saw, for example, that gaining the cooperation of *USA Today*'s reporters would be crucial to the success of the strategy (print journalists are notorious for hoarding stories), and they jointly decided to train the print reporters in television and Web broadcasting and outfit them with video cameras so they could file stories simultaneously in the different media. The moves quickly paid off, as the reporters realized that their stories would reach a much broader audience – and that they would have the opportunity to appear on TV. A new position of "network editor" was also created in the newsroom to help reporters shape their stories for broadcast media.

At the same time, Curley made larger changes to the organization and its management. He let go of a number of senior executives who did not share his commitment to the network strategy, ensuring that his team would present a united front and deliver consistent messages to the staff. He also changed the incentive program for executives, replacing unit-specific goals with a common bonus program tied to growth targets across all three media. Human resource policies were changed to promote transfers between the different media units, and promotion and compensation decisions began to take into account people's willingness to share stories and other content. As part of that effort, a "Friends of the Network" recognition program was established to explicitly reward cross-unit accomplishments.

Yet even as sharing and synergy were being promoted, the organizational integrity of the three units was carefully maintained. The units remained physically separate, and they each pursued very different staffing models. The staff members of USAToday.com were, on average, significantly younger than the newspaper's reporters and remained far more collaborative and faster paced. Reporters continued to be fiercely independent and to focus on more in-depth coverage of stories than the television staff.

Because of its ambidextrous organization, *USA Today* has continued to compete aggressively in the mature business of daily print news while also developing a strong Internet franchise and providing Gannett television stations with coverage of breaking news. During the Internet collapse, when other papers' profits plunged, *USA Today* made $60 million, fueled in large part by the company's ability to continue to attract national advertisers and by revenues from its profitable USAToday.com operation.

A New Lens on Growth

Another company that has used an ambidextrous organization to spur growth through radical innovation is Ciba Vision. Established in the early 1980s as a unit of the Swiss pharmaceutical giant Ciba-Geigy (now Novartis), the Atlanta-based Ciba Vision sells contact lenses and related eye-care products to optometrists and consumers. Although the company produced some innovative new products in its early years, such as the

The Scope of the Ambidextrous Organization

Ambidextrous organizations encompass two profoundly different types of businesses – those focused on exploiting existing capabilities for profit and those focused on exploring new opportunities for growth. As this table indicates, the two require very different strategies, structures, processes, and cultures.

Alignment of:	Exploitative business	Exploratory business
Strategic intent	cost, profit	innovation, growth
Critical tasks	operations, efficiency, incremental innovation	adaptability, new products, breakthrough innovation
Competencies	operational	entrepreneurial
Structure	formal, mechanistic	adaptive, loose
Control, rewards	margins, productivity	milestones, growth
Culture	efficiency, low risk, quality, customers	risk taking, speed, flexibility, experimentation
Leadership role	authoritative, top down	visionary, involved

Ambidextrous Leadership

Different alignments held together through senior-team integration, common vision and values, and common senior-team rewards.

tions provide an overarching goal that permits exploitation and exploration to coexist. Curley's "network strategy" and Bradley's "Healthy Eyes for Life" were compelling visions that underscored the strategic necessity of ambidexterity and the benefits for all employees, both those in the traditional units and those in the breakthrough initiatives.

USA Today, well aware of the natural skepticism of newspaper reporters, took a particularly aggressive approach to communicating its new vision, strategy, and organization. Curley launched the effort by appearing at a company meeting dressed as a cyberpunk, complete with blue hair. The message, he recalled, was: "It's a new world, and we need to be ready to move into it." Jurgenson began sending daily e-mails to the entire news staff in which she highlighted the concrete accomplishments of the new approach – for example, explaining exactly how one reporter was able to take a story originally intended for the newspaper and get it onto the Web site and the television stations. In addition, all members of the company's management committee were expected to hold weekly communications meetings within their units as well as workshops focused on the changes employees had to make in their own jobs. As Curley now puts it, "When change is at a revolutionary level, you can't be aggressive enough in confronting the issues."

The forces of inertia in companies are strong. The legions of once successful firms that have fallen on hard times or gone out of business underscore how hard it is to break out of a rut, especially a comfortable, profitable rut. The findings of our research should therefore be heartening to executives. Not only can an established company renew itself through the creation of breakthrough products and processes, but it can do so without destroying or even hampering its traditional business. Building an ambidextrous organization is by no means easy, but the structure itself, combining organizational separation with senior team integration, is not difficult to understand. Given the executive will to make it happen, any company can become ambidextrous.

Competing with Dual Business Models: A Contingency Approach[*]

By Constantinos Markides and Constantinos D. Charitou

How can a company adopt two different business models in the same market? This question has become particularly pressing for an increasing number of established companies that have recently come under attack from "strategic innovators" – companies that attack the established players by using radically different business models. The success of these attackers in gaining market share has created a big dilemma for established companies. On the one hand, by embracing the new business models that the innovators have introduced in their markets, established companies can potentially take advantage of a great growth opportunity. On the other hand, because the new business models often conflict with the established ones, companies that try to compete by adopting both of them risk mismanaging both and destroying value.

How, then, can established companies embrace the new business models without diluting and destroying their existing models? Our research explores this question and offers a contingency solution to this problem. We show that the challenge for companies is to balance the benefits of keeping the two business models separate while at the same time integrating them enough so as to allow them to exploit synergies with one another. We describe four possible strategies that companies can use to achieve such a balance and identify what separates success from failure for each strategy.

Consider the following cases:

• In February 1989, Singapore Airlines established a low-cost subsidiary to compete in the low-end, point-to-point segment of the airline market. Originally named Tradewinds but renamed Silkair in 1992, the low-cost operator has thrived in the last ten years. Silkair currently has a fleet of 9 aircraft and operates 117 services a week to 26 regional destinations. Despite competing with a strategy (or business model) which is fundamentally different from the hub-and-spoke strategy of its parent and

---

[*] Taken with permission from *Academy of Management Executive* Vol. 18 No. 3, 2004, pp. 22-36

despite inherent conflicts between the activities of the two companies, Singapore Airlines has been successful in making Silkair a profitable and integral part of its network strategy. This success stands in stark contrast to the attempts of numerous other airline companies to do the same thing. For example, in the last decade, efforts by Continental Airlines (by setting up Continental Lite), British Airways (by setting up GO), and KLM (by setting up Buzz) to compete in the low-cost, point-to-point segment of the airline market have all ended in failure.

• In 1992, in an attempt to compete against lowcost PC clones, IBM launched Ambra – its own clone sold at low prices without overt IBM branding. Ambra was intended to mimic Dell's direct selling model without alienating resellers. At its launch, Ambra president David Middleton claimed that Ambra would capture at least 10 per cent of what was a $10 billion market. IBM management dismissed fears of sales cannibalization, arguing that Ambra personal computers would appeal to a different customer segment than the customers buying IBM-branded PCs. Yet, Ambra turned out to be a classic example of Porter's (1980) argument that a company trying to play a differentiation and a low-cost game at the same time will find itself stuck in the middle. Prompted by declining sales, a conflicting brand portfolio, and an overburdened cost structure, IBM closed Ambra in 1994. IBM's failure to play the differentiation and low-cost games simultaneously stands in stark contrast to the success of several other companies who have done exactly that. Companies such as Toyota (with its Lexus car), Mercedes (with its Mercedes A-class), VW (with is Skoda and SEAT brands), Intel (with its low-cost Celeron chip), the Gap (with its Old Navy brand), SMH (with its Swatch brand), and Nestle (with its Nespresso subsidiary) are all examples of organizations that have found ways to compete successfully through both differentiation and low-cost strategies.

• In early 1989, the small Danish bank Lan & Spar introduced a low-cost direct (phone or fax) arm to attract price-sensitive customers. The direct bank was set up to compete head to head with the bank's existing branch network by offering low-interest loans to those customers who interacted with the bank by phone. By 1997, Lan & Spar bank had evolved into the world's first online real time PC bank, serving its customers through its branch network, the Internet, and the phone. While operating three different concepts proved difficult, the bank succeeded in tripling its market share in ten years and is now one of the most profitable banks in Denmark. This success once again contrasts sharply with the failed attempts by several banks to develop an Internet banking service over the last ten years. Prominent banks such as NatWest in the UK and Bank One in the USA have found it difficult to operate their existing branch networks while serving their customers through the Internet as well.

What explains the different fortunes of these companies in competing with dual strategies? For example, why have most airline companies in the world found it next to impossible to compete in the low-cost, point-to-point segment of the airline market while Singapore Airlines has made this same challenge look so easy? Why have so many companies in the fast-moving consumer goods (FMCG) business (such as Unilever and P&G) found it so difficult to compete against low-cost private-label competitors while other companies (such as SMH, the Gap, and VW) have succeeded in competing with differentiation and low-cost strategies at the same time?

We aim to answer this question in this article. According to Michael Porter,[1] the challenge with attempting to manage two different business models in the same market is that the two models (and their underlying value chains) could conflict with one another. For example, by selling its tickets through the Internet just like its low-cost competitors, British Airways risks alienating its existing distributors (the travel agents). Similarly, if Unilever moves aggressively into private label, it risks damaging its existing brands and diluting the organization's strong culture for innovation and differentiation. The existence of such trade-offs and conflicts means that a company trying to compete in both positions simultaneously risks paying a huge straddling cost and degrading the value of its existing activities.

The challenge with attempting to manage two different business models in the same market is that the two models (and their underlying value chains) could conflict with one another.

The primary solution that has been offered on how to solve this problem is to keep the two business models (and their underlying value chains) physically separate in two distinct organizations. This is the "innovator's solution" that is primarily associated with Clayton Christensen's work on disruptive innovation,[2] but other academics have advocated it as well.[3] Even Michael Porter has come out in favor of this strategy. Despite arguing that most companies attempting to compete with dual strategies will likely fail, he has also proposed that: "companies seeking growth through broadening within their industry can best contain the risks to strategy by creating stand-alone units, each with its own brand name and tailored activities." [4]

The rationale for this solution is quite straightforward. The presence of conflicts means that the existing organization and its managers will often find that the new business model is growing at their expense. They will therefore have incentives to constrain it or even kill it. Therefore, by keeping the two business models separate, you prevent the company's existing processes and culture from suffocating the new business model. The new unit can develop its own culture, processes, and strategy without interference from the parent company. It can also manage its business as it sees fit without being suffocated by the managers of the established company who see cannibalization threats and channel conflicts at every turn.

As sensible as this argument might be, the separation solution is not without problems and risks. Perhaps the biggest cost of keeping the two businesses separate is failure to exploit synergies between the two. For example, a recent study by a group of McKinsey consultants found that "the simple injunction to cordon off new businesses is too narrow. Although ventures do need space to develop, strict separation can prevent them from obtaining invaluable resources and rob their parents of the vitality they can generate."[5] Similarly, a team of MIT researchers reported that "spinoffs often enable faster action early on, but they later have difficulty achieving true staying power in the market. Even worse, by launching a spinoff, a company often creates conditions that make future integration very difficult."[6] For these reasons, several academics have argued in favor of keeping the new business model integrated with the existing organization. To achieve such a difficult task, firms need to develop an "ambidextrous" organizational infrastructure.[7]

As these two perspectives demonstrate, there is no "right" answer to the problem. If the firm keeps the two business models separate, it gives the new model a fighting chance to survive without interference from the parent company, but it also denies the new model valuable assets, resources and knowledge that reside in the parent company. On the other hand, if the two business models are integrated, the new model benefits from the resources and knowledge of the parent but also risks inappropriate interference and mismanagement from the parent.

Four Strategies for Managing Dual Business Models

This discussion suggests to us that rather than adopting an either/or perspective, we may be better off approaching the issue from a contingency perspective.[8] Specifically, the existing literature suggests that two key variables influence how a firm should manage two business models simultaneously: (1) how serious the conflicts between the two businesses are – because this determines whether a separation strategy would be especially beneficial or not; and (2) how strategically similar the new market is perceived to be to the existing business – because this determines how important the exploitation of synergies between the two will be.[9] When we plot these two dimensions in a matrix (see figure), we end up with four possible strategies for competing with two different business models.[10]

Separation is the preferred strategy when the new market is not only strategically different from the existing business but also when the two markets face serious tradeoffs and conflicts. On the other hand, no separation is necessary when the new market is very similar to the existing business and presents few conflicts that need managing. In such a case, embracing the new business model through the firm's existing organizational infrastructure is the superior strategy.

An interesting scenario emerges when the new market is strategically similar to the existing business, but the two face serious conflicts. In such a case, it might be better to separate for a period of time and then slowly merge the two concepts so as to minimize the disruption from the conflicts.

Another interesting scenario arises when the new market is fundamentally different from the existing business, but the two are not conflicting in a serious way. In such a case, it might be better to first build the new business inside the organization so as to leverage the firm's existing assets and experience (and learn about the dynamics of the new market) before separating it into an independent unit.

Deciding when to separate and when to keep the new business inside is only part of the solution.

However, deciding when to separate and when to keep the new business inside is only part of the solution. We know of companies that separated the new business model and were successful (e.g., Singapore Airlines) but also of companies that did the same thing and were unsuccessful (e.g., Continental Airlines). Similarly, there are companies that integrated the new business model and were successful (e.g., SMH) but also

This finding is consistent with the work of Lawrence and Lorsch on how companies achieve integration and differentiation simultaneously.[11] In their seminal study, they found that compared to unsuccessful companies, successful ones were able to achieve high degrees of both integration and differentiation. They also found that the level of differentiation needed in each firm was a function of the external environment facing the firm (i.e., dynamic environments require more differentiation). This meant that firms operating in dynamic environments had to be highly differentiated, a condition that would make it more difficult to maintain the required state of integration. On the other hand, firms operating in stable environments could achieve the appropriate level of integration more easily. All this meant that successful firms used a different combination of devices for achieving integration: the firms in dynamic environments used more integrating devices (and more elaborate ones) than the firms in stable environments. But both sets of firms used integrating devices, no matter how small the need for integration was.

Simply separating the new business model from the parent is not enough to ensure success.

Determinants of Success

This is exactly what we found in our study as well. To highlight what we mean, consider the 42 sample firms that separated the new business model into an independent unit. Of these, 10 were classified as successful and 32 as not successful. Using this sample, we ran multiple regression analyses to identify the determinants of success. We found the following results:

- on average, the higher the degree of autonomy that corporate headquarters gave the new unit to make financial and operational decisions, the more effective was the firm in its response;

- on average, the more differentiated the budgetary and investment policies of the new unit relative to the parent, the more effective was the firm in its response. On the other hand, firms were (on average) less effective in competing in the two strategic positions when they adopted different evaluation and incentive systems in the new unit (compared to the established business);

- on average, firms that assigned an insider to be the CEO of the new unit were more effective in their response than firms that used outsiders;

- on average, firms that allowed the new unit to develop its own culture were more effective in their response than firms that didn't.

What these results suggest is that successful firms give much more operational and financial autonomy to their units than unsuccessful firms. They also allow the units to develop their own cultures and budgetary systems and to have their own CEOs. These are all policies consistent with the notion that the new units need freedom to operate as they see fit in their own environment. Note, however, that this autonomy did not come at the expense of synergies. The parent still kept close watch over the strategy of the unit, and cooperation between the unit and the parent was encouraged through common incentive and reward systems. In addition, the CEO of the units was transferred from inside the organization so as to facilitate closer cooperation and active exploitation of synergies.

The survey results found strong support in our field research. For example, a senior executive at a major U.S. office supplies firm commented as follows:

"I refused to have a P&L for the dot.com operation and a different P&L for the main business. This could only have created frictions and political infighting. All the VPs are measured on our consolidated sales, not the sales of the parent versus the unit. And no matter what method the customer uses to place an order [phone, Internet, store], the salesperson responsible for the region will get the credit for it."

Similarly, the strategy director of a major European airline company suggested the following:

"It makes absolutely no sense to create a separate low-cost subsidiary and not give it the freedom to decide what to do in its market. But it is equally silly to ignore that we have been in the airline business for more than half a century. Surely our subsidiary can learn something from us!"

All in all, our results explain why we argued above that separation is neither necessary nor sufficient to ensure success. Even if a firm decides to separate the new business model, it must still find ways to exploit its existing strengths (such as its brand name, financial resources, and industry experience) in the new unit. In this sense, the question that needs to be asked is not: "Should we separate or not?" but rather: "What activities in our value chain do we separate, and what activities do we keep integrated?"[12]

> *The question that needs to be asked is not: "Should we separate or not?" but rather: "What activities in our value chain do we separate, and what activities do we keep integrated?"*

The Integration Strategy

Often, the new business model presents few conflicts with the existing business model of a firm. For example, the Internet and online distribution of computers was certainly a challenge for Dell, but the new way of selling computers was not particularly disruptive to Dell's existing business model. In these cases, embracing the new model through the firm's existing organizational infrastructure may be the optimal strategy. This is especially the case when, in addition to the absence of conflicts, the two business models serve strategically similar businesses and so stand to gain from exploiting synergies among them.

Edward Jones

Consider for example Edward Jones, one of the leading brokerage firms in the US retail brokerage industry.[13] The firm decided right from the start that it would not respond to online trading by creating a separate unit. According to the current managing partner, Doug Hill, the reason was simple: "We have elected not to follow the crowd. We think online trading is for speculators and entertainment. We are not in the entertainment business. We are in the 'peace of mind' business."

How then is Edward Jones responding to the online threat? By purposely focusing on its established business model and using the Internet as an opportunity to improve its existing value proposition to its targeted customers. This means looking at the Internet as simply another distribution channel and using it to offer customers better service and more information. Jones's value proposition is face-to-face personal dealings with clients to offer them long-term, conservative investment advice. As a result, the Internet is used not for online trading but as a way of enhancing the relationship with the customer. As the ex-CEO John Bachmann reiterated in a recent article in *Fortune* magazine: "You will not buy securities over the Internet at Edward Jones. That's going to be true as far as I can see into the future. ... If you aren't interested in a relationship and you just want a transaction, then you could go to E-Trade if you want a good price. We just aren't in that business."[14]

Another Example: Merrill Lynch

Merrill Lynch is another company that responded to online trading with an integrated strategy. The company launched an online trading channel within the traditional business and adjusted its processes and incentives accordingly so that the online business could co-exist seamlessly with the existing business. The company developed two new products – Unlimited Advantage and Merrill Lynch Direct – both of which were integrated with the company's existing operations and IT infrastructure. The online products were integrated with the company's existing products so that customers – old or new – could choose from a menu of choices what level of advice they needed and what kind of trading they wanted to undertake. The company's compensation policy was also adjusted so that brokers are now compensated on the value of the total assets they manage, no matter how these assets were acquired (i.e., online or via the established network).

Opportunity Framing

But as with the separation strategy described above, we found that simply integrating the new way of competing into the existing infrastructure is not enough to ensure success. The most successful firms in our sample were those that not only integrated the new business model (thus leveraging the existing business's competences and knowledge) but also treated the new way of competing as a wonderful new opportunity to grow the business. As a result, they made sure that the strengths of the traditional business were leveraged but also took extreme care not to suffocate the new business with the firm's existing policies. A good example of this is Merrill Lynch's decision described above to change its incentive systems so that its brokers would have an incentive to support online trading.

The successful firms' decision to protect the new way of competing from the existing firms' policies and mindsets was based on their belief that the new way was more of an opportunity than a threat. This is important because, as categorization theory argues, framing an external development as an opportunity results in greater involvement in the process of resolving it as well as participation at lower levels of the organization and actions directed at changing the external environment.[15] Clark Gilbert and Joe Bower make a similar point.[16] They argue that when an organization first confronts a conflicting business model, it is better to look at it as a threat rather than as an opportunity. Framing it as a threat will generate serious commitment in the organization to respond to the threat aggressively. However, when the organization is ready to actually create a new business model to exploit the new market, it is better to look at it as an opportunity. This way, old models and assumptions will be set aside, and the new model will be evaluated on its own merits. According to Gilbert and Bower, recognizing the need to manage competing frames simultaneously is the key to effective response.

Viewing the new model as an opportunity influenced the firms' actions in two ways: (a) how they approached it; and (b) what they actually did to take advantage of it.

Consider, for example, the following two quotes from senior managers at two US firms. The first is VP at a major office supplies firm, whose company was rated as very *successful* in adopting Internet distribution:

"We got onto the Internet long before anybody else knew what the Internet was. In fact, our biggest problem for the first two years was persuading our *customers* to use it! But we persisted because I knew in my bones that the Internet was *it*. This new technology was going to be the future. It would be the medium that would allow us to do great new things."

The second quote is from the CEO of a major bookseller whose company was rated as *unsuccessful* in adopting online distribution of books:

"We were late in implementing it but not in evaluating it. And our evaluation was that this thing did not make sense. Yet, every time I tried to explain our reasons why we wouldn't do it to Wall Street, my share price went down! Even in 1997 when online distribution of books went from zero to 6%, superstores increased their share from 10% to 22% – yet our stock price dropped by 40%. So in the end, we decided we had to do something."

Why is the framing of the decision as an opportunity so important? The rationale given to us is that by looking at it as an opportunity, the firm approaches the task in a proactive, strategic manner rather than as a hasty knee-jerk reaction to a problem. The new market is evaluated in a reasoned and deliberate way, and necessary resources are allocated to exploit and grow the opportunity. More importantly, the most respected managers in the organization are assigned to the task, and the project receives high-level attention and care. Finally, looking at it as an opportunity encourages the firm to take a long-term view of the investment. This ensures resources and long-term commitment even when the initial results are not encouraging.

But the main reason why it was important to view the new way of competing as an opportunity was that it allowed managers to put old models and assumptions aside and approach the opportunity in a creative and entrepreneurial way. This in turn allowed them to put in place strategies that not only took advantage of the opportunity but also put on the defensive the very companies that introduced the new models in the industry. In a sense, the established companies found ways to attack their attackers.

The main reason why it was important to view the new way of competing as an opportunity was that it allowed managers to put old models and assumptions aside and approach the opportunity in a creative and entrepreneurial way.

To understand how they did this, it is important to remember that often the new business models create markets that have much lower margins than the traditional markets. This suggests that even in the best-case scenario when an established company is *successful* in embracing the new model, the end result will be cannibalization of existing sales and much lower margins! Consider, for example, the following comment from a VP at a major fast-moving consumer goods company:

"The issue is not whether we can respond to the private label threat successfully. I believe we can do it, either internally or through a separate unit. But what is the purpose of doing this if the end result is to destroy the industry? I don't want to play *their* game. What we need to do is to find a response that builds on our competences and restores the margins in this business."

The logic of this argument was echoed in another comment that an SMH executive made to us to explain the reasoning behind the development of the Swatch back in the early 1980s:

"We had to defend the low end of the market against cheap Japanese watches. But we did not want to simply compete on price… We had to find a way of producing something that was *cheap enough* [emphasis added] but was still Swiss quality."

Both of these comments point to what we believe is the key to the success of the companies that chose the integration strategy: embracing the new business model in a creative way that builds upon the competences of the established competitors *and* restores the margins in the business to a higher level than the attacking companies have. In the process of doing this, established companies counterattack their own attackers.

SMH and Swatch

Consider, for example, the SMH story again. In the early 1960s, the Swiss dominated the global watch industry. This dominance all but evaporated in the 1970s when companies such as Seiko (from Japan) and Timex (from the US) introduced cheap watches that used quartz technology and provided added functionality and features (such as the alarm function, date indication, etc). The Swiss share of global world production declined from 48 per cent in 1965 to 15 per cent by 1980. In response, the Swiss introduced the Swatch. Not only did the new watch introduce style as a competitive dimension, but more importantly, it was sold at a price that was on average three times higher than the average Seiko price. Since its launch in 1983, Swatch has become the world's most popular time piece with more than 100 million sold in over 30 countries.

The secret of this success lies in two areas. First, note that the established competitors (the Swiss) were selling their product on the basis of performance when they suddenly came under attack. The attack took the form of: "Our watches are good enough in performance and superior to the Swiss in price." What the Swiss did was to turn this rationale on its head. They sold their Swatch on the following premise: "Our watches are good enough in price and superior to the Japanese in performance (i.e., style)." This sounds easy but it requires a fundamental (dare we say revolutionary?) change in mindset! Instead of adopting the attackers' mindset that said: "Minimize price subject to a performance which is good enough," the new mindset needed is one that says: "Maximize performance subject to a price that is good enough."

Second, it is one thing to say this and another to do it. In effect, what the Swiss did was to produce something that delivered low cost *and* differentiation at the same time – managing two conflicting strategies simultaneously. They achieved this end by eliminating many product attributes that they thought were unnecessary (thus cutting costs) while enhancing certain other product features like style and design (thus building differentiation). They also found ways to cut other costs (in manufacturing and in materials used) and to build differentiation in other ways (for example, through the Swatch Club). The end result was a strategy that embraced the key features of the new business model in such a creative way that the original attackers had to find their own response to the Swiss counterattack!

Gillette

Another example of the same strategy is Gillette's response to the disposable razor threat in its business. Disposables entered the razor market on the premise that: "Our products are good enough in performance and superior to Gillette's in price." How did Gillette respond to this threat? By building upon the premise that: "Our disposables are good enough in price and superior to other disposables in performance."

Rather than debate whether to manufacture a cheaper disposable or not, Gillette chose to tackle the threat in a creative manner. By adopting the mindset: "We need to maximize performance subject to a price that is good enough," they developed a number of innovative disposable products that competed not on price but on performance. For example, in 1994 they introduced the Custom Plus line that was a disposable with a lubricating strip. In late 2002, they introduced a new line of disposable razors with proprietary technology. By successfully adopting the low-cost *and* differentiation strategies at the same time, Gillette has managed to maintain a 45 per cent market share in disposables.

The lesson from these success stories is simple: it *is* possible to manage two conflicting strategies without keeping them apart. But to do so requires creativity and a willingness to go beyond simply imitating a new business model. By focusing only on finding ways to accommodate a new model so as to minimize potential conflicts, established companies may be missing an opportunity to exploit the new model in ways that leverage their unique competences and restore their markets to higher levels of profitability.

It is important to stress here that it is one thing to say that companies such as Swatch and Gillette adopted a low cost and differentiation strategy and another to suggest that they were the *best* differentiator and the cost leader at the same time! The key thing to remember here is that both Swatch and Gillette stuck to their basis of competitive advantage (differentiation) but found a way to do it better (at a lower cost). They did *not* adopt a cost leader's strategy, which is based on skills in the manufacturing process, and, therefore, chose not to compete head on with their attackers (where they would no doubt lose). Instead, they built their new strategy on unique design and marketing skills, playing the game differently than their attackers.

The Phased Integration Strategy

Under certain circumstances, the most appropriate strategy is to either separate or integrate the new way of competing *but not right from the start.* For example, when the new business model serves a market that is strategically similar to the existing business but the two ways of competing face serious conflicts between them, the firm faces a difficult challenge: on the one hand, it stands to benefit if it integrates the two and exploits the synergies between them; on the other hand, integration might lead to serious internal problems because of all the conflicts. In such a case, it might be better to separate for a period of time and then slowly merge the two concepts so as to minimize the disruption from the conflicts. This is the *phased integration* strategy.

> *Under certain circumstances, the most appropriate strategy is to either separate or integrate the new way of competing but not right from the start.*

Lan & Spar Bank

The Danish bank Lan & Spar is a good example of a company that followed the phased integration strategy. When it decided to set up a Direct Bank alongside its branch network, it kept the two concepts separate for three years before merging them into one. CEO Peter Schou explained their strategy as follows:

"It was a difficult situation to have two concepts at the same time. We couldn't really afford to merge the two concepts from the very beginning because we would have suffered a huge cannibalization cost. Our interest margin at the branch was 10 per cent a year whereas at the Direct Bank it was only 3 per cent a year. If we had allowed all of our customers to switch overnight from traditional banking to direct banking, we would have lost a lot of money. We had to manage the transition carefully."

As with the separation strategy described above, the challenge that the firm faces in the phased integration strategy is to keep the new business model protected from the mindsets and policies of the existing business while at the same time trying to exploit synergies between the two businesses. But there is an added complication: The firm knows that the separation is only temporary and that the new unit will have to be integrated sooner or later with the existing organization. The challenge is to keep the new unit separate but also prepare it for the eventual marriage.

Companies can use a number of tactics to achieve this. For example, Lan & Spar separated the Direct Bank from the rest of the organization but made sure that the IT infrastructure that supported the telephone bank was compatible with the established bank's IT systems. Furthermore, the bank made sure that the employees developed common values and a common culture by insisting that employees from both parts of the organization meet regularly, attend the same company-wide events, and have similar experiences with the senior managers of the bank. Managers from the main bank were transferred into the Direct Bank, and the decisions on how to merge the two banks were taken in meetings between the managers of both units. The two concepts were finally merged three years after the creation of the Direct Bank, and all financial indicators suggest that the merger has been a great success.

Charles Schwab and e.Schwab

Another company that followed the phased integration strategy was Charles Schwab. It had originally set up e.Schwab, its online brokerage business, as a separate unit. But it prepared e.Schwab for eventual integration by having it report directly to co-CEO David Pottruck and by staffing it with senior managers from the existing retail organization. In addition, e.Schwab's technology platform was designed to integrate with Schwab's IT systems, and the new unit's product and pricing policies were designed to be compatible with the parent's policies. The eventual merger of the two concepts was again judged to be a great success.

The Phased Separation Strategy

When the two business models do not conflict with each other in any serious way but the markets they serve are fundamentally different, the firm faces another interesting challenge. On the one hand, given the lack of conflicts, it could integrate the new model with the existing organization without much difficulty. On the other hand, integration will not bring many benefits and might even constrain the development of the new way of competing into a viable business for the firm. In such a case, it might be better to first build the new business inside the organization so as to leverage the firm's existing assets and experience before separating it into an independent unit. This is the *phased separation* strategy.

Preparing a unit for marriage is the challenge facing companies that choose the phased integration strategy. By contrast, the challenge facing companies that choose the phased separation strategy is to prepare a unit for divorce.

Preparing a unit for marriage is the challenge facing companies that choose the phased integration strategy. By contrast, the challenge facing companies that choose the phased separation strategy is to prepare a unit for divorce.

Tesco and Tesco.com

This is exactly how Tesco, the UK's biggest and most successful supermarket chain, is approaching its online distribution arm, Tesco.com. The company's home delivery service was started in the mid-1990s under the name Tesco Direct. The first trials involved one store in west London sending small deliveries to pensioners who couldn't get to the store. The home shopping idea developed over the years, first with customers placing orders from a paper catalogue, then from a take-away CD-ROM, and eventually through the company's website. By 2000, Tesco's Internet arm was taking 10,000 orders a week, mostly in the greater London area. By 2003, orders were up to 110,000 per week, and the home delivery service covered all the main stores throughout the UK.

Over time, the online distribution business developed a life of its own. According to Nick Lansley, the Tesco IT technologies manager:

"We started by offering a narrow range of grocery items, but by the summer of 1996 we wondered why we shouldn't sell every item in a Tesco store online. Why not books and clothes and electronic items? We could either mess about by adding one product group to another or putting everything on there. We decided to sell everything. It was a huge leap, but we felt it was now or never. We weren't worried about competitors. Only Sainsbury was a possible rival, and they weren't doing anything that we knew about. But we wondered how to do this. Go to the Board and ask for millions of pounds to build dedicated depots and logistics systems? We looked at other models that we already had developed in-house at Tesco stores." By 2001, Tesco Direct was reorganized as a full subsidiary of Tesco and was renamed Tesco.com – the first step in the divorce proceedings. The online arm redefined its mission from online grocery distribution to online retailer of anything (books, CDs, other non-food items), and senior managers were hired to lead the new business in the future. In 2003, the Tesco board told Tesco.com management that if everything went well, they planned to spin off the unit as a limited company. The online arm was now such a different business that it made little sense to keep it under Tesco management. It had to be given the freedom and autonomy to develop as it saw fit.

According to an analyst who covers Tesco, the evolution of Tesco.com into a separate business was understandable:

Online is seen as a complement to and not a competitor of the traditional offline experience. The online business is allowing Tesco to expand into diversified goods such as CDs and books and is providing additional growth. This diversification is going on in an ad hoc manner. There are obviously teething problems with this development. Buying music or books online at Tesco.com is a very poor experience and is not integrated with the core grocery business. They seem to be experimenting in public view. Why are they doing this? Food online does not provide great margins so they want to expand into higher margin areas. What is critical for them is the behaviour of consumers – will they prefer to shop for these items in dedicated sites (e.g., Amazon) or one that provides integrated products and services (e.g., Tesco.com)? They are using third party suppliers for these products (which now include mobile phones and banking services) as a way to minimize inventory risk. They haven't ironed out their 'going to market' strategy. This is a big challenge for them. Customers want a seamless shopping experience.

As with the integration strategy described above, the challenge that firms face in the phased separation strategy is to get the two businesses to exploit any synergies between them while keeping the new business model protected from the existing business. But there is an added twist here: preparing the new unit for eventual separation. As the Tesco example shows, there is no set way of doing this. But the challenge remains: how to coexist with something that you will divorce eventually.

No Single Best Way

At least in the academic literature, there have been disagreements about whether and how a company could manage two different and conflicting business models at the same time. Some have argued that because of conflicts between the two business models, a company ought to keep them physically separate so as to protect the new model from interference by the managers of the established business. Others have proposed that such a solution deprives the two business models of the opportunity to exploit synergies between them. They have therefore argued in favor of an integrated strategy.

In this article we have proposed that under certain circumstances the separation strategy is preferable to the integrated strategy, but under certain other circumstances, the integrated strategy might be preferable to separation. Specifically, we have argued that separation is the preferred strategy when the new market is not only strategically different from the existing business but also when the two business models face serious tradeoffs and conflicts. On the other hand, no separation is necessary when the new market is very similar to the existing business and presents few conflicts that need managing. In such a case, embracing the new business model through the firm's existing organizational infrastructure is the superior strategy. We have also described the circumstances when a firm might prefer to separate (integrate) the new business model at first before integrating it with (separating it from) the existing business. We have therefore proposed that the best way to approach the issue is through a contingency perspective.

Furthermore, we have argued that simply separating or integrating the new business model is not enough to ensure success. If the preferred strategy is separation, the company must still find ways to exploit its existing strengths (such as its brand name, financial resources, and industry experience) in the new unit without constraining it. Similarly, if the preferred strategy is integration, the company must still strive to protect the new business model from excessive interference or mismanagement by the parent, all in the name of exploiting synergies. In this sense, the question that needs to be asked is not: "Should we separate (integrate) or not?" but rather: "What activities in our value chain do we separate, and what activities do we keep integrated?"

Thus, our study suggests that the decisionmaking process that executives must go through involves three steps. First, the question: "Should we adopt the new business model or not?" should be asked. The answer to this question depends on the specific circumstances of each firm. If the decision is made that the firm ought to adopt the new business model, the second question that must be asked is: "Should we separate or integrate the new business model, or should we follow one of the phased strategies?" The answer to this question will most likely depend on the two key variables that we identified above that define the axes of the figure. Finally, once the separation/integration decision is made, the question arises: "Given our choice, how can we manage the new unit successfully?"

Our article has focused on the last question and has identified several variables that can influence how well a second business model is managed in each of the four quadrants of the figure. For example, we have found that companies that adopt the *separation* strategy will do better if they:

- give operational and financial autonomy to their units but still maintain close watch over the strategy of the unit and encourage cooperation between the unit and the parent through common incentive and reward systems;
- allow the units to develop their own cultures and budgetary systems;
- allow each unit to have its own CEO who is transferred from inside the organization (rather than hiring an outsider).

Similarly, we have found that companies that adopt the *integration* strategy will do better if they:

- treat the new business model as a wonderful new opportunity to grow the business (rather than see it as a threat);
- leverage the strengths of the traditional business to find ways to differentiate themselves (rather than imitating the strategies of their attackers);
- approach the task in a proactive, strategic manner rather than as a hasty knee-jerk reaction to a problem;
- take extreme care not to suffocate the new business with the existing policies of the firm.

Notwithstanding the success stories described in this article, our large-sample regression results also show that simultaneously pursuing two business models that have inherent conflicts and market dissimilarities is extremely problematic and likely to fail. In this article we have focused on the outliers. Firms that are considering whether to adopt a second business model or not must keep in mind that the odds are still against them. But as our study of the outliers has shown, the rewards from a nuanced contingency approach to competing with dual business models can be great.

Appendix: Research Design and Sample

Our main research question was: "What differentiates the successful firms in *each quadrant* of the figure?" To answer this question, we had to carry out four basic tasks: (1) identify enough established firms that have adopted a second business model in their markets; (2) map each firm on our two-by-two matrix (according to the conflicts and synergies that each saw in their second business model); (3) identify the successful and unsuccessful firms in each quadrant; and (4) examine what differentiates the successful firms in each quadrant.

We first tried to identify a sample of established firms that have adopted a second business model. We decided to look for these firms in a number of European and US industries where we knew that new business models had made inroads in the last few years. Specifically, we examined the following industries: banking, general insurance, life & health insurance, brokerage, supermarkets, airlines, FMCGs, bookstores, office supplies, and electronic trading systems. The new business models introduced in these industries were: direct (telephone or Internet) banking; direct general insurance; direct life and health insurance; online brokerage trading; home ordering and delivery of groceries; low-cost, no-frills airline service; private label in FMCGs; online distribution of books; online distribution of office supplies; and screenbased electronic trading systems.

We then interviewed ten established companies in Europe and the US. The interviews were conducted in person (mainly at the company's head office) and usually lasted between two and four hours depending on the number of people interviewed in each company. Following the interviews, we prepared several short case studies describing the various insights that were generated. Using the ideas developed from the fieldwork and the relevant streams of literature, we then prepared a detailed questionnaire addressing our research questions. A thirteen-page questionnaire specific for each industry was sent to 740 established companies in the sample industries. We received 115 completed questionnaires from 98 different companies.

Our questionnaire attempted to quantify the reasons that prompted an established firm to respond to the introduction of a new business model in its market, the nature of the response, and the strategies used to manage two business models simultaneously. For the purposes of this article, we were particularly interested in three items from our questionnaire data: (1) the nature and magnitude of conflicts between the established company's existing business model and the newly introduced business model – so as to assess the degree to which a separation strategy between the two models might be beneficial; (2) how related the markets that the two business models were attempting to serve were – so as to assess whether exploitation of synergies between the two was necessary or beneficial; and (3) how successful the firm was in managing two business models at the same time.

The degree of conflicts between the two business models was estimated based on managerial perceptions of various risks that the established firm might face by competing simultaneously in both businesses. Table A lists the ten conflicts or risks that we measured.

Table A

Potential Conflicts Between Two Different Business Models
Risk of cannibalizing the existing customer base
Risk of destroying or undermining the value of the existing distribution network
Risk of compromising the quality of service offered to customers
Risk of undermining the company's image or reputation and the value associated with it
Risk of destroying the overall culture of the organization
Risk of adding activities that may confuse the employees and customers regarding the company's incentives and priorities
Risk of defocusing the organization by trying to do everything for everybody
Risk of shifting customers from high-value activities to lowmargin ones
Risk of legitimizing the new business, thus creating an incentive for other companies to also enter this market

Respondents were asked to assess the difficulty of trying to compete simultaneously in the two different strategic positions in their industry based on these underlying risks. A five-point (Likert) scale was used to measure the extent (or size) of each of the risks, ranging from "Not at all" (=1) to "Very much" (=5). The scores for the ten items were averaged to provide a mean value of the degree of conflicts for every established firm in the sample. The higher the value was, the higher the degree of conflicts between the firm's existing business and the new way of competing in the industry. Values ranged from 1 to 4.44, with an overall mean of 1.91 (Cronbach's alpha = 0.87).

To measure the strategic similarity between the two markets that the two business models were attempting to serve, we followed the logic and recommendations of several academic researchers who have argued that relatedness between two markets should be measured at the *strategic asset* level rather than the market level.[17] We operationalized strategic relatedness based on three broad categories of strategic assets: (1) customer assets (such as service reputation, customer loyalty, brand awareness, and good customer relationships); (2) channel assets (such as access to distribution channels and supply networks, and good distribution/network relationships); and (3) process assets (such as efficient supply chains for madetoorder or standardized products and services, human capital, and the overall skill level of the labor force).

Eight different indicators of these strategic assets were identified for each of the eleven industries in the sample. These indicators included:

- the extent to which the company offers *personal* service support to its customers;
- the extent to which the company offers *technical* service support to its customers;
- the degree to which the product or service offering must be customized or not;
- the extent to which the purchase was a major or minor one for the customer;
- media advertising;
- push marketing (i.e., the importance of maintaining a high level of marketing expenditures on distribution channels and the associated infrastructure);

- the overall skill level of the labor force (i.e., the importance of maintaining an employee base of high-skilled staff);
- the importance of having low-cost staff. Respondents were asked to rate the importance of these strategic-asset indicators in order to compete effectively in (a) the traditional business and (b) the new business. A five-point scale was used, ranging from "Not important at all" (=1) to "Very important" (=5).

To measure the degree of strategic relatedness between the two businesses (i.e., the extent to which the two businesses emphasize the same strategic assets), we created a variable counting the number of strategic-asset indicators considered by the responding executives to be "Important" or "Very important" for each of the two businesses (i.e., those indicators that were rated either '4' or '5' on the scale for both the traditional business and the newly created one). The variable was coded from 0 (which means that none of the eight indicators was considered important for both businesses) to 8 (which means that all eight indicators were considered important for the two businesses). The higher the value of this variable was, the higher the degree of strategic relatedness between the two businesses.[18] Values ranged from 0 to 8, and the mean was 3.8.

Having calculated these two variables for each firm, we were able to map the firms on our matrix. Since there is no theoretical rationale as to what the cutoff points are (between minor/serious conflicts and low/high relatedness), we decided to err on the conservative side. As reported above, the mean value for conflicts for the whole sample was 1.91 (on a scale of 1-to-5). We therefore classified any values above 3.5 as "serious" conflicts. Similarly, the mean value of strategic relatedness for the whole sample was 3.8 (on a scale of 0-to-8). We therefore classified any values above 5 as "high" strategic relatedness.

Our final task was to assess which firms were successful in competing with dual strategies and which were not. To determine "success" we used three complementary approaches.

We first asked all responding firms to assess their own effectiveness in adopting the new business model along nine performance criteria. Specifically, we asked them to assess whether by embracing the new model, they: (a) prevented the new business from expanding into the traditional business and hurting existing operations; (b) prevented existing customers from leaving the company; (c) attracted new customers; (d) increased revenues and improved profitability; (e) developed new skills and competencies; (f) improved the quality of products and services; (g) cut costs; (h) became more competitive overall in the industry; and (i) became part of the new, growing business. A sixpoint scale was used, ranging from "Very ineffective" (=1) to "Very effective" (=6). A mean score of the nine items was calculated as the measure for statistical analysis. The higher the score was, the higher the firm's effectiveness in adopting the new business model and competing in the two strategic positions simultaneously. Values ranged from 2.56 to 6, with an overall mean of 4.6 (Cronbach's alpha = 0.72).

Second, we asked the responding firms to give us an overall assessment (on a scale of 1 to 6) of how effectively they thought they had adopted the new business model. Although self-assessment measures such as the ones used here are prone to bias, they have also been shown to be reliable.[19] To reduce self-reporting bias, we also employed a third measure of success: sector (industry) analysts from seven fund management companies in London and on Wall Street were asked to rate each of our responding firms on an "overall effectiveness" scale. The analysts rated only companies in the industries that they covered, and they used the same 1-to-6 scale.[20]

Those companies that rated themselves as 6 on the "overall effectiveness" scale or 5 and above on the scale calculated as the mean of the nine performance criteria and also received a rating of 6 from the analysts were selected as successful responders. This screening procedure produced a total of 17 firms that were deemed to have responded successfully to the new business model. Seven of the successful firms were placed in quadrant A, three in quadrant B, 5 in quadrant C, and two in quadrant D. Five of these firms were already the subject of the field-based research undertaken before the survey questionnaire was sent out. Sixteen more firms from all four quadrants of our matrix were selected at this stage for further study through field research. Our goal in talking to managers in these firms was to understand what differentiated the successful firms in each quadrant. The insights presented in this article are based mainly on this field research and partly on our analysis of our questionnaire data.

Strategy as Ecology[*]

By Marco Iansiti and Roy Levien

Stand-alone strategies don't work when your company's success depends on the collective health of the organizations that influence the creation and delivery of your product. Knowing what to do requires understanding the ecosystem and your organization's role in it.

Wal-Mart's and Microsoft's dominance in modern business has been attributed to any number of factors, ranging from the vision and drive of their founders to the companies' aggressive competitive practices. But the performance of these two very different firms derives from something that is much larger than the companies themselves: the success of their respective business ecosystems. These loose networks of suppliers, distributors, outsourcing firms, makers of related products or services, technology providers, and a host of other organizations affect, and are affected by, the creation and delivery of a company's own offerings.

Like an individual species in a biological ecosystem, each member of a business ecosystem ultimately shares the fate of the network as a whole, regardless of that member's apparent strength. From their earliest days, Wal-Mart and Microsoft – unlike companies that focus primarily on their internal capabilities – have realized this and pursued strategies that not only aggressively further their own interests but also promote their ecosystems' overall health.

They have done this by creating "platforms" – services, tools, or technologies that other members of the ecosystem can use to enhance their own performance. Wal-Mart's procurement system offers its suppliers invaluable real-time information on customer demand and preferences, while providing the retailer with a significant cost advantage over its competitors. (For a breakdown of how Wal-Mart's network strategy contributes to this advantage, see the exhibit "The Ecosystem Edge".) Microsoft's tools and technologies allow software companies to easily create programs for the widespread Windows operating system-programs that, in turn, provide Microsoft with a steady stream of new Windows applications. In both cases, these symbiotic relationships ultimately have benefited consumers – Wal-Mart's got quality goods at lower prices, and Microsoft's got a wide array of new computing features – and gave the firms' ecosystems a collective advantage over competing networks.

---

[*] Taken with permission from *Harvard Business Review* Vol. 82 No. 3, 2004, pp. 68-78

The Ecosystem Edge

Benefits attributable to ecosystem management	Global procurement	0.5%
	Centralized buying	2%
	Optimized product mix	2%
	Distribution efficiencies	2%
	Other operating efficiencies	2%
	Information sharing	6%
	Lower shrinkage rates	0.5%
	Preferred real estate rental rates	2%
	Low labor costs	5%
Wal-Mart's total margin advantage in retail groceries		22%

More than half of Wal-Mart's cost advantage in the retail grocery business results from how the company manages its ecosystem of business partners. For example, by sharing information, Wal-Mart is better able to match supply and demand across the entire ecosystem, increasing productivity and responsiveness for itself – and for its partners. (Source: authors' analysis of company data.)

Over time, the companies in the ecosystems made investments to leverage their relationships and began to depend on Wal-Mart and Microsoft for their own success. For example, Procter & Gamble integrated its ERP system with Wal-Mart's, and AutoCad integrated Microsoft's programming components into its applications. Although Wal-Mart and Microsoft have been criticized for being tough on their business partners, the complex interdependencies among companies that these industry giants encouraged have made their business networks unusually productive and innovative – and allowed the two companies to enjoy sustained superior performance. Each of these ecosystems today numbers thousands of firms and millions of people, giving them a scale many orders of magnitude larger than the companies themselves and an advantage over smaller, competing ecosystems.

Although Wal-Mart and Microsoft have been astonishingly successful in organizing and orchestrating their vast business networks, their two ecosystems aren't anomalies. Most companies today inhabit ecosystems that extend beyond the boundaries of their own industries. The moves that a company makes will, to varying degrees, affect its business network's health, which in turn will ultimately affect the company's performance – for ill as well as for good. But despite being increasingly central to modern business, ecosystems are still poorly understood and even more poorly managed. We offer a framework here for assessing the health of your company's ecosystem, determining your place in it, and developing a strategy to match your role.

What Is a Business Ecosystem?

Consider the world around us. Dozens of organizations collaborate across industries to bring electricity into our homes. Hundreds of organizations join forces to manufacture and distribute a single personal computer. Thousands of companies coordinate to provide the rich foundation of applications necessary to make a software operating system successful.

Many of these organizations fall outside the traditional value chain of suppliers and distributors that directly contribute to the creation and delivery of a product or service. Your own business ecosystem includes, for example, companies to which you out-source business functions, institutions that provide you with financing, firms that provide the technology needed to carry on your business, and makers of complementary products that are used in conjunction with your own. It even includes competitors and customers, when their actions and feedback affect the development of your own products or processes. The ecosystem also comprises entities like regulatory agencies and media outlets that can have a less immediate, but just as powerful, effect on your business.

Drawing the precise boundaries of an ecosystem is an impossible and, in any case, academic exercise. Rather, you should try to systematically identify the organizations with which your future is most closely intertwined and determine the dependencies that are most critical to your business. If you look carefully, you will most likely find that you depend on hundreds, if not thousands, of other businesses. It is helpful to subdivide a complex ecosystem into a number of related groups of organizations, or business domains. These may in some cases represent something as well defined as a conventional industry segment. Each ecosystem typically encompasses several domains, which it may share with other ecosystems.

For an ecosystem to function effectively, each domain in it that is critical to the delivery of a product or service should be healthy; weakness in any domain can undermine the performance of the whole. In the case of Microsoft, the company's performance depends on the health of independent software vendors and systems integrators, among many others. (For a depiction of some of the crucial domains in Microsoft's software ecosystem, see the exhibit "Microsoft and Its Ecosystem.")

In the boom years of the Internet, there was an almost universal euphoria about the potential of business networks. Vast, connected communities of companies would enjoy unheard of efficiencies in operations and innovation. New technologies would disrupt traditional companies and create unprecedented opportunities for innovation, as well as for the growth of new companies. Network effects – the increasing value of a product or service as the number of people using it grows – would create enormous value and remove barriers to entry in businesses as different as B2B exchanges and grocery delivery. But things were not so simple, as the disastrous failures of companies like PetroCosm and Webvan made clear.

The implosion of the Internet bubble made it obvious that members of a network share a common fate, meaning that they could rise and fall together. Many had predicted the bubble could not last, of course, but the sharpness, suddenness, and violence of the

Microsoft and Its Ecosystem

Microsoft's success depends on the health of the numerous domains – some of which comprise thousands of organizations – that make up its software ecosystem. (Source: Company data)

Domain	Number of Firms
System integrators	7,752
Development services companies	5,747
Campus resellers	4,743
Independent software vendors	3,817
Trainers	2,717
Breadth value-added resellers	2,580
Small specialty firms	2,252
Top value-added resellers	2,156
Hosting service providers	1,379
Internet service providers	1,253
Business consultants	938
Software support companies	675
Outbound hardware firms	653
Consumer electronics companies	467
Unsegmented resellers	290
Media stores	238
Mass merchants	220
Outbound software firms	160
Computer superstores	51
Application service provider aggregators	50
E-tailers	46
Office superstores	13
General aggregators	7
Warehouse club stores	7
Niche specialty stores	6
Subdistributors	6
Applications integrators	5
Microsoft Direct resellers	2
Microsoft Direct outlets	1
Network equipment providers	1
Network service providers	1

fall surprised most people. The stunning reversal of the virtuous cycle, which had seemed to automatically drive endless exponential growth, left many questioning their faith in the power of business networks. Instead of abandoning their faith, business leaders should work to understand the phenomenon more deeply. The analogy between business networks and biological ecosystems can aid this understanding by vividly highlighting certain pivotal concepts. (For a discussion of similarities and differences between the two types of ecosystems, see the sidebar "How Useful an Analogy?", p. 230)

Assessing Your Ecosystem's Health

So what is a healthy business ecosystem? What are the indications that it will continue to create opportunities for each of its domains and for those who depend on it? There are three critical measures of health-for business as well as biological ecosystems.

Productivity. The most important measure of a biological ecosystem's health is its ability to effectively convert nonbiological inputs, such as sunlight and mineral nutrients, into living outputs – populations of organisms, or biomass. The business equivalent is a network's ability to consistently transform technology and other raw materials of innovation into lower costs and new products. There are a number of ways to measure this. A relatively simple one is return on invested capital.

When we analyzed companies' aggregate return on invested capital in three broadly defined industries – software, biotechnology, and Internet services – over the past decade, we discovered striking productivity differences among these three ecosystems. Software firms averaged better than a 10% return on invested capital, while biotechnology businesses had a negative return of roughly 5%, and, predictably, Internet companies had a negative return of nearly 40%.

Most interesting was the change in productivity over time. (See the exhibit "The Relative Health of Three Business Ecosystems." While the return on invested capital in the software and biotechnology ecosystems didn't vary much from year to year, it plummeted between 1996 and 1997 in the Internet services ecosystem, as companies like Yahoo and AOL began charging exorbitant fees to companies seeking traffic from their portals. The plunging figures precede by more than three years the actual collapse of the Internet sector in 2002. Clearly, an assessment of this ecosystem's health before the collapse might have helped companies – Cisco, for example, which supplied Internet services companies with essential technology – reduce their dependence on a precarious network in which they had such big stakes.

Robustness. To provide durable benefits to the species that depend on it, a biological ecosystem must persist in the face of environmental changes. Similarly, a business ecosystem should be capable of surviving disruptions such as unforeseen technological change. The benefits are obvious: *A company that is part of a robust ecosystem enjoys relative predictability, and the relationships among members of the ecosystem are buffered against external shocks.* Think, for example, of the relationship between Microsoft and its community of independent software vendors, which collectively survived the adoption of the World Wide Web.

The Relative Health of Three Business Ecosystems

Two measures of an ecosystem's health over time are its productivity and its robustness. The chart on the top shows differences in productivity – measured according to the average return on invested capital – among the software, biotechnology, and Internet services ecosystems. The chart on the bottom shows the robustness – measured according to the number of firms – in the same three ecosystems. (Source: authors' analysis of data from publicly traded companies identified by SIC code (software and biotechnology) or by initial public offering records (internet services).)

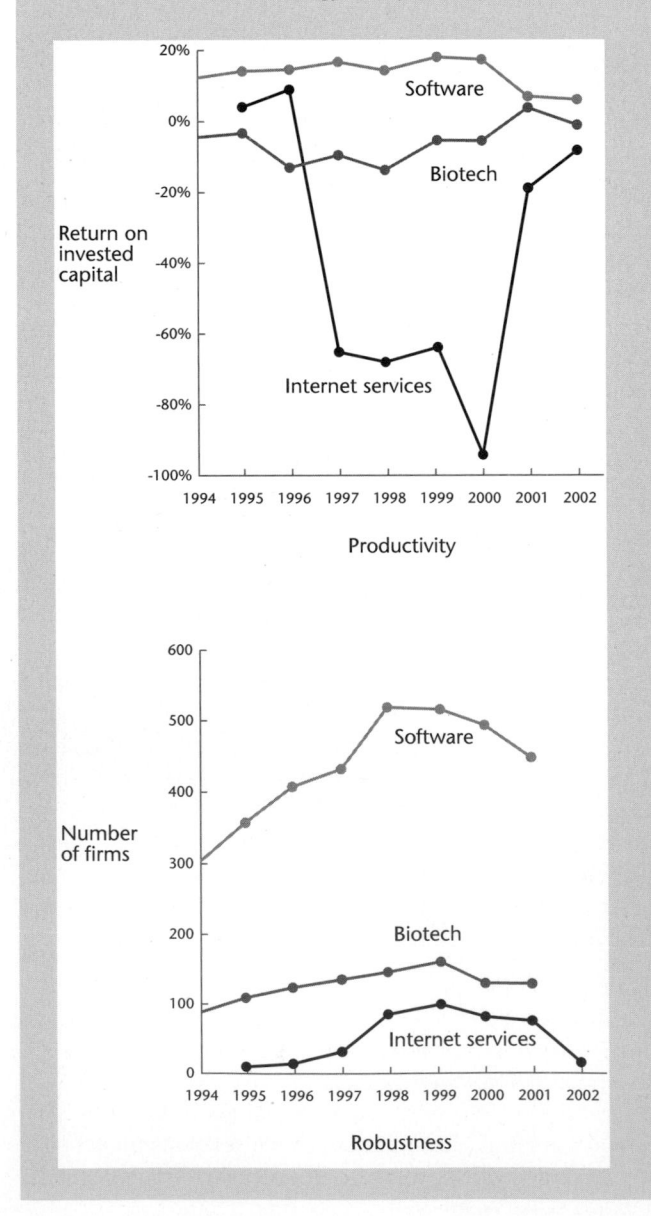

Perhaps the simplest, if crude, measure of robustness is the survival rates of ecosystem members, either over time or relative to comparable ecosystems. Again, it is instructive to apply this measure to the software, biotechnology, and Internet services communities. In software, we see strong growth over the decade, with some contraction around the technology recession of 2001, as the exhibit shows. The biotech community's population line is relatively flat, which masks a lot of industry churn-new startups replacing companies that went out of business. The Internet ecosystem's dramatic collapse in 2002 needs no elaboration, though, as we have noted, it seems to have been foreshadowed by the fall of one measure of ecosystem productivity, return on investment.

Niche Creation. Robustness and productivity do not completely capture the character of a healthy biological ecosystem. The ecological literature indicates that it is also important these systems exhibit variety, the ability to support a diversity of species. There is something about the idea of diversity, in business as well as in biology, that suggests an ability to absorb external shocks and the potential for productive innovation.

The best measure of this in a business context is the ecosystem's capacity to increase meaningful diversity through the creation of valuable new functions, or niches. One way to assess niche creation is to look at the extent to which emerging technologies are actually being applied in the form of a variety of new businesses and products. The computing and automobile industries exhibit very different profiles in this vein. While the computing industry's enthusiastic embrace of innovative technologies has led to the sustained creation of opportunities for entirely new classes of companies, the automobile industry has historically sought to prevent additional niches from emerging.

It is critically important to appreciate that although healthy ecosystems should create new niches, it does not follow that old niches must persist. In fact, decreased diversity in some areas of an ecosystem enable the creation of niches in others. The collapse of mainframe-related business niches gave rise to a plethora of new domains related to personal computing and client-server networks. In biological evolution, reduced diversity at one level can lead to the creation of a stable foundation that enables greater and more meaningful diversity at other, sometimes higher, levels. For example, the standardization of a simple DNA alphabet, as well as a few basic mechanisms of metabolism and several basic models for organisms, serves as the building blocks for the enormous variety of life on earth.

So how can you promote the health and stability of your own ecosystem, thereby helping to ensure your company's well-being? It depends on your role – current and potential – within the network. Are you one of the niche players that make up the bulk of most ecosystems? If you occupy one of the few hubs or nodes characteristic of networks, are you using that position to act as an indispensable keystone? Do you dominate your ecosystem? If not, do you harbor ambitions to dominate it – and are you aware of the risks that come with that role? The answers to these questions may be different for different parts of your business. They may also change as your ecosystem changes. (See the sidebar "Match Your Strategy to Your Environment.")

Match Your Strategy to Your Environment

A company's choice of ecosystem strategy – keystone, physical dominator, or niche – is governed primarily by the kind of company it is or aims to be. But the choice also can be affected by the business context in which it operates: the general level of turbulence and the complexity of its relationships with others in the ecosystem.

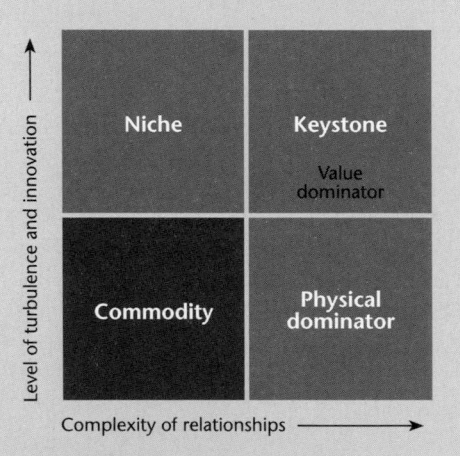

If your business faces rapid and constant change and, by leveraging the assets of other firms, can focus on a narrowly and clearly defined business segment, a niche strategy may be most appropriate. You can develop your own specialized expertise, which will differentiate you from competitors and, because of its simple focus, foster the unique capabilities and expertise you need to weather the turbulence of your environment.

If your business is at the center of a complex network of asset-sharing relationships and operates in a turbulent environment, a keystone strategy may be the most effective. By carefully managing the widely distributed assets your company relies on – in part by sharing with your business partners the wealth generated by those assets – you can capitalize on the entire ecosystem's ability to generate, because of its diversity, innovative responses to disruptions in the environment.

If your business relies on a complex network of external assets but operates in a mature industry, you may choose a physical dominator strategy. Because the environment is relatively stable and the innovation that comes with diversity isn't a high priority, you can move to directly control the assets your company needs, by acquiring your partners or otherwise taking over their functions. A physical dominator ultimately becomes its own ecosystem, absorbing the complex network of interdependencies that existed between distinct organizations, and is able to extract maximum short-term value from the assets it controls. When it reaches this end point, an ecosystem strategy is no longer relevant.

If, however, your business chooses to extract maximum value from a network of assets that you don't control – the value dominator strategy – you may end up starving and ultimately destroying the ecosystem of which you are a part. This makes the approach a fundamentally flawed strategy.

If you have a commodity business in a mature and stable environment and operate relatively independently of other organizations, an ecosystem strategy is irrelevant - although that may change sooner than you think.

The Keystone Advantage

Keystone organizations play a crucial role in business ecosystems. Fundamentally, they aim to improve the overall health of their ecosystems by providing a stable and predictable set of common assets – think of Wal-Mart's procurement system and Microsoft's Windows operating system and tools – that other organizations use to build their own offerings.

Keystones can increase ecosystem productivity by simplifying the complex task of connecting network participants to one another or by making the creation of new products by third parties more efficient. They can enhance ecosystem robustness by consistently incorporating technological innovations and by providing a reliable point of reference that helps participants respond to new and uncertain conditions. And they can encourage ecosystem niche creation by offering innovative technologies to a variety of third-party organizations. The keystone's importance to ecosystem health is such that, in many cases, its removal will lead to the catastrophic collapse of the entire system. For example, WorldCom's failure had negative repercussions for the entire ecosystem of suppliers of telecommunications equipment.

By continually trying to improve the ecosystem as a whole, keystones ensure their own survival and prosperity. They don't promote the health of others for altruistic reasons; they do it because it's a great strategy.

Keystones, in many ways, are in an advantageous position. As in biological ecosystems, keystones exercise a system-wide role despite being only a small part of their ecosystems' mass. Despite Microsoft's pervasive impact, for example, it remains only a small part of the computing ecosystem. Both its revenue and number of employees represent about 0.05% of the total figures for the ecosystem. Its market capitalization represents a larger portion of the ecosystem – typical for a keystone because of its powerful position – but it has never been higher than 0.4%. Even in the much smaller software ecosystem, in which the company plays an even more crucial role, Microsoft's market cap has typically ranged between 20% and 40% of the combined market cap of software providers. This is a fraction of the more than 80% of total market capitalization of the much larger ecosystem of computer software, components, systems, and services that IBM held during the 1960s.

Broadly speaking, an effective keystone strategy has two parts. The first is to create value within the ecosystem. Unless a keystone finds a way of doing this efficiently, it will fail to attract or retain members. The second part, as we have noted, is to share the value with other participants in the ecosystem. The keystone that fails to do this will find itself perhaps temporarily enriched but ultimately abandoned.

Keystones can create value for their ecosystems in numerous ways, but the first requirement usually involves the creation of a platform, an asset in the form of services, tools, or technologies that offers solutions to others in the ecosystem. The platform can be a physical asset, like the efficient manufacturing capabilities that Taiwan Semiconductor Manufacturing offers to those computer-chip design companies that don't have their own silicon-wafer foundries, or an intellectual asset, like the Windows software platform. Keystones leave the vast majority of value creation to others in the ecosystem, but what they do create is crucial to the community's survival.

The second requirement for keystones' success is that they share throughout the ecosystem much of the value they have created, balancing their generosity with the need to keep some of that value for themselves. Achieving this balance may not be as easy as it seems. Keystone organizations must make sure that the value of their platforms, divided by the cost of creating, maintaining, and sharing them, increases rapidly with the number of ecosystem members that use them. This allows keystone players to share the surplus with their communities. During the Internet boom, many businesses failed because, although the theoretical value of a keystone platform was increasing with the number of customers, the operating cost was rising, as well. Many B2B marketplaces, for example, continued to increase revenue despite decreasing and ultimately disappearing margins, which led to the collapse of their business models.

A good example of a keystone company that effectively creates and shares value with its ecosystem is eBay. It creates value in a number of ways. It has developed state-of-the-art tools that increase the productivity of network members and encourage potential members to join the ecosystem. These tools include eBay's Seller's Assistant, which helps new sellers prepare professional-looking online listings, and its Turbo Lister service, which tracks and manages thousands of bulk listings on home computers. The company has also established and maintained performance standards that enhance the stability of the system. Buyers and sellers rate one another, providing rankings that bolster users' confidence in the system. Sellers with consistently good evaluations attain PowerSeller status; those with bad evaluations are excluded from future transactions.

Additionally, eBay shares the value that it creates with members of its ecosystem. It charges users only a moderate fee to coordinate their trading activities. Incentives such as the PowerSeller label reinforce standards for sellers that benefit the entire ecosystem. These performance standards also delegate much of the control of the network to users, diminishing the need for eBay to maintain expensive centralized monitoring and feedback systems.

The company can charge commissions that are no higher than 7% of a given transaction – well below the typical 30% to 70% margins most retailers would charge. It is important to stress that eBay does this because it is good business. By sharing the value, it continues to expand its own healthy ecosystem – buyers and sellers now total more than 70 million – and thrive in a sustainable way.

The Dangers of Domination

Keystones exercise the power of their position within an ecosystem in a somewhat indirect manner. But ecosystem dominators wield their clout in a more traditional way, exploiting a critical position to either take over the network or, more insidiously, drain value from it.

The *physical dominator* aims to integrate vertically or horizontally to own and manage a large proportion of a network directly. Once the dominator becomes solely responsible for most of the value creation and capture, there is little opportunity for a meaningful ecosystem to emerge. Physical dominators, the ultimate aggressors, eventually control much of an ecosystem. But at least they are responsible for creating the value that they capture. During the heyday of mainframes, IBM dominated the computing ecosystem, providing most of the products and services its customers needed. The strategy was effective, allowing IBM to create and extract enormous value for long periods of time. But it failed when IBM encountered the PC ecosystem, which was much more open and distributed, supported by effective keystone strategies put forth by the likes of Microsoft and Apple (and, yes, even IBM itself), and which reached much higher levels of innovation and flexibility.

By contrast, a *value dominator* has little direct control over its ecosystem, occupying in some cases just a single hub. It creates little, if any, value for the ecosystem; a value dominator extracts as much as it can. By sucking from the network most of the value created by other members, it leaves too little to sustain the ecosystem, which ultimately collapses and brings the value dominator down with it.

One need only look to Enron for a sobering example. It is useful to contrast Enron's approach to its ecosystem with eBay's. The two companies faced similarly daunting challenges in the late 1990s: how to use the Internet to form numerous individual markets, in the process generating massive business networks of trading partners of which they would be the hub. Enron started by leveraging its established and unique position in the energy sector, and its aggressive, blue-chip managerial talent, to improve the efficiency of high-value but traditionally fragmented markets. eBay's beginnings were much more humble. It had few assets and focused initially on the narrow collectors' market.

In the years that followed, Enron and eBay moved to create and nourish hundreds of new markets. And this is where their paths drastically diverged. eBay took the keystone route, sharing the wealth it generated and, along the way, creating an enormous and healthy ecosystem of trading partners. Enron became a value dominator, extracting as much value as it could from the new markets it entered by using its strategic position to exploit asymmetries in information across the market. The aggressive behavior of Enron's traders impeded the type of trust that eBay was building in its communities.

The results are starkly instructive. The implosion of Enron's ecosystem ultimately led it to conceal in illegal partnerships its resulting market losses. Meanwhile, eBay boasted positive cash flow from the start and ended up generating huge profits. The company that shared the wealth ended up making the money.

How Useful an Analogy?

Haven't there been enough biological analogies in business literature? It's a fair question, but we feel strongly that the analogy between evolved biological systems and networks of business entities is too often misunderstood. A sophisticated examination of this analogy is essential to improving our understanding about how such networks operate.

There are certainly strong parallels between business networks and biological ecosystems. Both are characterized by a large number of loosely interconnected participants that depend on one another for their effectiveness and survival. If the ecosystem is healthy, individual participants will thrive; if the ecosystem is unhealthy, individual participants will suffer. In business, that's because the companies, products, and technologies of a business network are, like the species in a biological ecosystem, increasingly intertwined in mutually dependent relationships outside of which they have little meaning. Moreover, the consequences of these relationships often are beyond the control of any of the network participants. Rather, they result from the overall state of the system, which is subject to continuous change, including constant upheavals in membership.

Modern business networks and biological ecosystems also are characterized by the presence of crucial hubs that assume the keystone function of regulating ecosystem health. An example of a biological keystone is the sea otter, which helps regulate the coastal ecosystem of the Pacific Northwest by consuming large numbers of sea urchins. Left unchecked, sea urchins overgraze a variety of invertebrates and plants, including kelp, which in turn support a food web that is the engine of near-shore productivity.

The decline of the sea otter population in the nineteenth and twentieth centuries, when they were trapped for their fur, had a profoundly negative impact on a wide variety of coastal fish and other organisms.

Like keystones in business networks, sea otters represent only a small part of the biomass of their community but exert tremendous influence. Note, too, that, as in business ecosystems, some individual members of the community – the sea urchins that get eaten by the otters – suffer as a result of the keystone's behavior, but the community as a whole benefits.

The biological counterparts of the two other primary roles we have identified in business ecosystems – the dominator and the niche player – are more obvious. Many weeds, which supplant other species in their ecosystems, are classic dominators. And most species in nature, like most companies in the business world, are niche players, with a specialized function that contributes to the functioning of their ecosystems.

The analogy isn't perfect, of course. For example, inputs like sunlight and nutrients in biological systems can be fairly constant or at least follow predictable cycles. Inputs like technology in business ecosystems are constantly changing. But to be perfect, an analogy would have to be so simplistic that it would offer little real insight.

Note, too, that our use of the term 'ecosystem' is probably closer to the biological term 'community': We follow others in choosing ecosystem, rather than the generic-sounding community, because it clearly signals that we are discussing a complex system and that we are working with a biological analogy. Indeed, the familiar concept and vivid terminology of the biological ecosystem can help focus managerial attention on features of modern business networks that are often ignored by conventional theories about markets and industry structure but that underlie many drivers of business success and failure.

Leveraging a Niche

In business ecosystems, most firms follow niche strategies. A niche player aims to develop specialized capabilities that differentiate it from other companies in the network. By leveraging complementary resources from other niche players or from an ecosystem keystone, the niche player can focus all its energies on enhancing its narrow domain of expertise.

When they are allowed to thrive, niche players represent the bulk of the ecosystem and are responsible for most of the value creation and innovation. They typically operate in the shadow of a keystone, which offers its resources to niche players, or a dominator, which works to exploit or displace them.

Because a niche player is naturally dependent on other businesses, it needs to analyze its ecosystem and identify the characteristics of its keystones and dominators, current or potential. Do strong keystones exist? Are there multiple keystones competing to play the same role? How far removed are the dominators?

An example of a niche player is Nvidia, a designer of integrated circuits known as graphics accelerators, which are the foundation for video games and a host of other multimedia applications. Because it has no plants of its own, Nvidia leverages the manufacturing platforms of two keystone companies, Taiwan Semiconductor Manufacturing and IBM. It also leverages their intellectual assets (their component libraries and design tools), not to mention the assets of several other firms, including assembly and testing companies. This complex web of relationships enables Nvidia to avoid the significant costs and risks associated with owning and operating manufacturing, assembly, and test operations. The company can focus its resources on product design, quality assurance, marketing, and customer support. At the same time, its interdependencies mean the company must share the fate of the other participants in the ecosystem. Thus, Nvidia's performance is tied not only to that of Taiwan Semiconductor Manufacturing and IBM but also to that of library providers like Artisan Components and design tool providers like Synopsis.

Despite the best, highly specialized strategies, niche players usually find that they come into conflict with other niche players, keystones, and especially dominators. Innovation – at the core of their strategy of specialization and differentiation – is critical to their success in these battles. Niche players that do not or cannot actively advance and evolve their products toward the edges of the ecosystem may find that the frontier of a keystone's expanding platform will approach the niche they occupy – often forcing the niche player to let its product be incorporated into the platform. Indeed, a keystone's moves to improve an ecosystem's overall health sometimes come at the expense of a niche member, which gets swallowed up by the keystone. Still, differentiation provides a powerful defense, as Intuit has demonstrated by consistently protecting its position in financial management software against competitive offerings by Microsoft.

In fact, niche players can sometimes wield surprising power in the face of keystones. For example, the computer industry has witnessed the emergence of loosely coupled technology interfaces through which different computer systems, components, or applications interact with one another without following strict design rules. A good example is extensible markup language (XML). Such interfaces have loosened the bonds that typically tied a niche player to its keystone's platform. This has made it easier for niche players to end a relationship with a keystone that is extracting too much value from a system or whose platform doesn't offer sufficient value. Niche players can use this kind of leverage to keep keystones honest and prevent them from becoming dominators. Intuit, while it continues to leverage Microsoft tools and pro-

More Than Strategy

The implications of operating in an interdependent business ecosystem are not felt only in the corner office and at corporate strategy-setting sessions. They ripple through an entire organization and have some of their most immediate and concrete impact at the level of individual products and their design. It is no longer possible to design, or even conceive of, a product in isolation. Products exist in the context of other products. Think of how music players and snow-boarding jackets, GPS devices and calendars, cameras and computers have begun to merge functions.

This creates opportunities for innovation and product development. Because (at least in healthy product ecosystems) new products can leverage the capabilities provided by existing products, designers can exploit these capabilities as raw materials for the creation of new functionality.

But the connections that enable such opportunities also pose difficult design challenges. First of all, innovators need to learn to leverage the broad range of external capabilities available in the ecosystem. Additionally, it becomes increasingly important for developers to think of a product not just in terms of something that someone will use but as a platform that other products and services might be able to exploit. Moreover, the designers of almost all products can no longer assume that users care much about the identity or features of their products, only about how they fit in with and enhance the systems of which they are a part.

gramming components, has worked consistently to reduce the cost of switching to other platforms, thus obtaining greater control over its own future.

It is also important to remember that even though a niche player may have relatively little leverage in comparison to a keystone, there are typically hundreds if not thousands of niche players that will move away from a keystone if its behavior begins to stray into domination.

Roles in an ecosystem aren't static. A company may be a keystone in one domain and a dominator or a niche player in others. And niche players may eventually become the keystones for their own new ecosystems. For instance, Nvidia created a powerful graphics programming platform, which has spawned additional communities of graphics application developers.

Business Ecology

The ecosystem-based perspective we have described has a number of broad implications for managers. One is the central importance of interdependency in business: A company's performance is increasingly dependent on the firm influencing assets outside its direct control. This has wide-ranging implications for strategy, operations, and even policy and product design.

Related to this is the importance of integration. Because a company operating in today's networked setting can use resources that exist outside of its own organization, integration now represents a critical form of innovation. This fundamentally changes the capabilities needed and the structure of corporate functions in areas including business operations, R&D, strategy, and product architecture. (See the sidebar "More Than Strategy".)

The broad scattering of innovation across a healthy ecosystem and the diversity of organizations in it also change the nature of technological evolution. Rather than involving individual companies that are engaged in technology races, battles in the future will be waged between ecosystems or between ecosystem domains. Increasingly, the issue won't be simply "Microsoft versus IBM" but rather the overall health of the ecosystems that each fosters and depends on.

Finally, *a firm that takes an action without understanding the impact on its many neighboring business domains, or on the ecosystem as a whole, is ignoring the reality of the networked environment in which it operates.* Think again of the Internet boom. When AOL and Yahoo struck aggressive deals with their dot-com partners in those optimistic years, they financially weakened those companies. Their actions may have temporarily bolstered their individual performance and masked the inherent troubles of weaker Internet firms, but the collective effect on the system was destabilizing and ultimately catastrophic. Contrast this with Wal-Mart's partners, which, despite the retailer's tough demands, continue for the most part to thrive financially.

No one would argue that AOL or Yahoo was unaware of the fact that they were embedded in a network of interdependent firms. Both explicitly viewed themselves as

233

hubs in these networks. But without a framework for assessing network health, they proceeded with strategies that optimized short-term financial gains while undermining critical domains in their ecosystems – strategies from which they still are struggling to recover.

Case Example
Xerox[*]

The success of the original Xerox copier, the Model 914 – which generated more revenues when more copies were made – established the dominant logic for Xerox's copier business, imposing a certain cognitive bias in future years. This logic motivated Xerox to develop ever-faster machines that could handle very high copy volumes, with maximum machine uptime and availability, and, in turn, discouraged development of low-speed copiers. Meanwhile, Xerox's monopoly of plain-paper copying technology ended, as an action brought by the Federal Trade Commission forced the company to accept a consent decree requiring it to license its patents and to offer machines for sale, as well as on lease. Kodak and IBM entered the high end of the market. At the same time, a host of Japanese manufacturers entered the low end – where Xerox was weak – employing different product configurations, pricing strategies and distribution channels, in effect a different business model.

Xerox's business model as of the late 1970s is summarized in the first column in the table below, according to the attributes described above. It targeted its products and sales efforts to major corporate customers and government organizations. Its value proposition was 'high quality copies in high volume, at a low monthly lease rate'. Xerox organized its value chain to deliver completely configured copier systems sold through its own direct sales organization; and comprehensive maintenance services by its own technicians. It priced its products and services so that it made some money on its equipment, but made the bulk of its profits from sales of services and supplies (such as toner).

This business model did not require partnerships with third-party organizations, enabling Xerox to conduct its own research. It performed all of the required product development activities to launch and support new products. Xerox manufactured most of its products internally and it distributed all of its products through its own channels of distribution. It additionally provided its own financing to customers, and its own service and support. Xerox even made its own paper to ensure the proper handling characteristics when feeding paper into a copier, though here it has to support other companies' paper as well.

---

[*] Adapted from Chesbrough, H. and Rosenbloom, R.S. (2002), "The Role of the Business Model in Capturing Value from Innovation: Evidence from Xerox Corporation's Technology Spin-off Companies", *Industrial and Corporate Change*, 11(3), 529-555

Xerox – Selected Spin-off Business Models Compared on Key Attributes							
	Xerox	**3Com**	**Adobe**	**SynOptics**	**Metaphor**	**LiveWorks**	**Documen-tum**
Identified market segment	Corporate and government market	Corporate PC market	PC, Mac and laser-printer market	IBM-installed token ring segment	Knowledge workers in corporations	Work-groups in corporations	Project teams in corporations
Clear value proposition	High-quality copies at a low monthly lease rate	Establishes file and printer sharing between IBM PCs	Enables output of richer document types	Faster network speed on same lines	Enables non-technical queries of corporate databases	Facilitate remote group collaboration	Organize document management via previously installed equipment
Elements of value chain	Developed entire copier system, including supplies; sold through a direct sales force	Focused on Ethernet protocol, and add-on boards	Focused on supplying fonts to laserprinter mfrs, and software firms	Developed software and add-on boards for high-speed networking	Developing and sold entire systems, from hardware to software to distribution	Developed and sold entire systems, from hardware to software to distribution	Developed software compatible with installed customer equipment
Defined cost and profit	Modest profit on equipment, high profit on supplies, or per 'click'	High volume, low unit cost	Very high fixed cost	Very low variable cost	High fixed costs, low installation costs	High fixed costs, high margin, low unit volume	High costs, high margins, low volume
Positioned in value network	First mover in 'dry' copy process; did not require or pursue partners	Set the IEEE 802 standard; utilized PC distribution channel	Defined the PostScript standard for scalable fonts	Prolonged life and value of IBM token ring copper wire	No third parties or complementors utilized	No third parties or complementors utilized	Leveraged Xerox sales, customer's installed equipment
Formulated competitive strategy	Compete on technology, product quality, product capability	Compete on standard, new channels	Strong network externalities, high switching costs	Compete performance and time to market	Compete on superior technology and usability	Compete on superior technology	Add value to customer documents, lock in customer

In 1968, C. Peter McColough, who had led sales and marketing of the 914, was appointed Chief Executive of Xerox, with Joe Wilson remaining as Chairman until his untimely death in 1971. As the growth of copier revenues began to flatten at the end of the 1960's McColough set a new direction toward 'The Architecture of Information'. His first steps toward realizing this vision were to enter the computer business in 1969 through the billion dollar acquisition of Scientific Data Systems (SDS) and to establish the Xerox-PARC research facility in 1970 to lead the way technologically. Although SDS soon collapsed – shut down in 1975 – PARC outperformed all expectations, inventing many of the foundations for the future of desktop computing.

The Single Business Model: Path-dependent Commercialization of Xerox-PARC Technologies

The research community within Xerox flourished during the 1970s, with generous budgets and few restraints on freedom to explore new boundaries. The first commercial payoff from PARC technology emerged in 1977 as Xerox entered the electronic printing business with a high-speed laser printer. Xerox's high-speed copier business model worked beautifully with the new printer technology, creating a new, large, and profitable business. The same year, Xerox took the first steps toward building a major line of business intended to serve the 'Office of the Future'. An Office Products Division, newly established in Dallas, marketed a stand-alone electronic word processor, but resistance from corporate executives delayed efforts to launch products based on the more advanced network and workstation technologies developed at PARC. In 1979, the first 'office system' offering used Ethernet technology to link word processors and printers; in 1981, the 'Star' workstation was introduced as the centerpiece of an integrated system for office automation.

The latter move set a pattern for the business model to be used to exploit PARC's innovations in computing. Customers were offered an integrated system, comprising a set of proprietary technologies, with no option to use third-party equipment or software. Xerox initially offered the Star workstation for purchase at $16 995; the requisite network facilities and shared printer raised the cost of a three-user system to over $100 000. These systems then were sold primarily to Fortune 1000 companies through a direct sales force and supported by a field service organization. This revolutionary technology was taken to market by Xerox replicating many elements of the business model that had worked so well for its copiers.

Some of the PARC scientists, though, sensed that more could be done. They questioned the pace at which Xerox was pursuing commercialization of their inventions, or disagreed with the company's commitment to proprietary standards and 'systems only' marketing. In pursuit of what they regarded as underexploited latent value, they chose to leave Xerox to found new companies to exploit individual component technologies. This created a situation in which during the 1980s and 1990s a number of new PARC technologies were being exploited simultaneously by Xerox within its integrated systems, and by independent entrepreneurial spin-off companies as stand-alone innovations. This offers an opportunity to compare commercialization practices in a setting where the technologies and market environments were similar, while the business models employed were sharply different.

Exploring the Effects of Selected Spin-off Business Models

Of the six spin-offs indicated in the box, two (3Com and Adobe) borrowed extensively from Xerox's then-prevailing business model. The other four (SynOptics, Metaphor, LiveWorks, and Documentum) were based on significantly new (radically different) business models. Two are highlighted here, i.e. LiveWorks and Documentum, one being an eventual 'failure' and the other a success.

a) **LiveWorks**

LiveWorks is a relatively recent PARC spin-off, formed in 1992, that set up to commercialize an innovative electronic whiteboard. This whiteboard could capture comments on one board, and then transmit and display those comments on a separate whiteboard. This was useful for coordinating group work activities between remote sites – an exciting value proposition for any company with multiple work locations that had to coordinate the work of remote groups. The idea emerged from within PARC, which used the technology itself to link its West Coast developers with other Xerox personnel in other locations.

However, LiveWorks never developed a viable business model. Early sales were made to customers within Xerox; when the decision was taken to expand the business, a Xerox technologist was recruited to manage the spin-off. While the initial management identified a number of technical challenges to be fixed, the company was merely opportunistic in its sales. The company has a high-cost manufacturing strategy, so that the revenues it did generate did not yield a profit. It tried to use Xerox's own sales force to sell its products, but this was not effective. It never did connect with third parties to establish a larger value network. As Mark Myers, then the chief technical officer of Xerox, recalled, '… we thought we would work out the business concept someplace after we got to market … We knew there had to be [a market] out there … [but we] couldn't figure out how to make money'.

By the time that company executives realized that the initial approach would not succeed, a lot of money had been spent. Alternative business models, such as licensing the technology to other manufacturers, were not explored until the end of the company's life. The company was shut down in 1997, after losing tens of millions of dollars. People who saw the whiteboards in action found them to be an exciting technology. Arguably, the failure of LiveWorks was not due to technology with little inherent value. In our judgment, the failure was in the inability to unlock the potential value of that technology through the development and execution of a viable business model.

b) **Documentum**

Documentum, by contrast, illustrates what can happen when promising Xerox PARC technologies are commercialized through an effective business model. An opportunity was sensed to help Xerox's customers' teams manage documents more effectively. Xerox had earlier conducted an extensive analysis of its customer needs through a study called Express. Express demonstrated the problems faced by many large Xerox customers that had enormous document flows to coordinate, for activities such as reporting progress on clinical drug trials to the Food and Drug Administration (FDA). There was a strong potential value proposition for any company that could help companies manage this, since it would reduce costs and speed up the processes in the companies that were creating these document flows.

Xerox already had the component technologies for document management solutions in hand at PARC. What was lacking was a process to get these technologies out of the lab and into the market through an appropriate business model.

Six months were spent examining document workflow software products. Significant time was invested at customer locations to understand what document management problems customers were having. It was learned about the already installed hardware and software platforms that a document management solution would have to work with, in order to be incorporated into the customer's premises. This was a key insight missing at PARC, where the technologists were trying to implement solutions on top of proprietary hardware architectures that were incompatible with customers' installed equipment. Eventually, a product architecture that could provide real solutions to these customer needs was identified, and to do so in a way that was compatible with customers' installed equipment, so that every sale would not require an entirely new system to be installed.

This led to the formation of a business model that would create value for the customer and revenue for the document technology contained in the venture. Once customers adopted the Documentum approach, their subsequent use tended to lock them into the company's products. Documentum initially made extensive use of Xerox's sales channels, which worked well for selling this type of product. Documentum has also moved beyond Xerox's sales force to develop its own channels as well.

Resulting Insights and Relevant Implications

The ultimate role of the business model for an innovation is to ensure that the technological core of the innovation delivers value to the customer. Because discovery-oriented research often produces spillover technologics that lack a clear path to market, discovering a viable business model for these spillovers is a critical and neglected dimension of creating value from technology. By design, in all the six spin-off cases mentioned, the technologies resulted from path-breaking intentions in a research laboratory that had no obvious path to market within the company that funded the research. The situations generally exemplified what is often termed 'technology push'.

All six of the selected ventures were developing promising technology, yet the success of each technology varied. Because both technical and market uncertainty are involved in this translation, the set of all feasible business models is not foreseeable in advance. Heuristic logic is required to discover an appropriate business model, and an established corporation's 'sense-making' task will be constrained by its dominant logic, which is derived from its extant business model. Hence, that filtering process within a successfully established firm is likely to preclude identification of models that differ substantially from the firm's current business model.

In contrast, a start-up company/venture seems likely to be less constrained in the evaluation of alternative models. It seems notable that among the separate spin-off examples we have reviewed here, while some business model was implicit from the start in each, a different model was in place by the time the successful ventures had demonstrated their viability.

The need to span the technical and economic domains, with the attendant complexity and uncertainty, combined with the need to employ heuristic cognitive approaches, cause the business model concept to differ from traditional notions of 'strategy'. The initial business model is more of a proto-strategy, an initial hypothesis for how to deliver value to the customer, that it is a fully elaborated and defined plan of action. It results less from a carefully calculated choice from a diverse menu of well-understood alternatives, and more from a process of sequential adaptation to new information and possibilities. In established companies, this adaptation is also more cognitively bound, as new information is filtered through a heuristic logic that was established from previous success.

If companies that fund research generating spillovers are to develop a better business model to commercialize their spillover technologies, our traditional notions of technology management must be expanded. Creating value from technology is not simply a matter of managing technical uncertainty; there is significant uncertainty in the economic domain as well, and in the many possible ways of mapping between the domains. Identifying and executing a new or different business model is an entrepreneurial act, requiring insight and foresight into both the technology and the market. The discipline enforced by the imperative of reaching a coherent statement of the business model creates a framework for learning about both the technology and its economic environment.

Two of the cases mentioned, Metaphor and LiveWorks, are illustrative failures in this context. Both ventures were built on technologies that seemed to embody attractive potential value propositions. But their failure should not be ascribed to shortcomings in the technologies themselves. The technologies held as much promise as the other PARC technologies that went on to create value. The leaders of these ventures, however, failed to discover appropriate business models that were capable of realizing the value latent in the technologies. In fact, the search process seems to have been very limited in these two cases, in that the business model each venture initially adopted was little modified thereafter.

The Documentum case shows how important, and how subtle, this process of discovery can be. Before the venture was launched, PARC had already developed many of the building blocks of document management software. Documentum was able to utilize Xerox's own sales force for much of its revenue, so even that element of its successful business model was already in place. The missing piece seems to have been the effective pursuit of a powerful value proposition. That process also applied to SynOptics' learning process. Their technological adaptation enabled their product to run on top of already installed IBM PC value network.

It is important here to be careful to avoid circular reasoning. The best measure of the worth of a given business model is the success of the enterprise. But one cannot then simply infer that good business models is what leads to success. Not every Xerox spin-off venture that attempted a new business model went on to success. What emerges from our examples is a conjecture: the process of reshaping an initial business model (which seems to occur in a significant number of cases) creates opportunities to discover new mappings between technical potential and economic value, and these novel mappings may contribute importantly to success. In environments characterized by high technical and market uncertainty where many of such mappings are possible, this learning process may be a critical determinant of creating economic value from a new technology.

This perspective implies that technology managers must regard 'the architecture of the revenues' as a vital and necessary element of capturing value from technology. Technology managers cannot disregard these matters or simply rely on others in the organization to address these questions on their behalf. Instead, technology managers must themselves become conversant in these issues. They need to extend their experiments to include experiments in alternative business models. This is as important as the experiments they conduct to evaluate technical risks inside their labs. This will also require technology managers to create processes to explore the economic domain far more thoroughly, from customers and suppliers in a value chain to third parties and the surrounding elements of the value network. The development of the business model needs to become part of the new dominant logic for managing technology commercialization.

Questions

1. Provide a concise review of the relationships among the concepts of business model, strategy and value network/chain.

2. Why does an organization require a portfolio of business models? And does this differ from the traditional practice of conglomerate organizations with a portfolio of separate businesses (or SBUs)?

3. Contrast the concepts of 'industry' and 'business ecosystem', with the use of several (e.g. at least 3) practical examples.

4. Why is it necessary for organizations to rejuvenate themselves, and what approaches are, or could be used, for this purpose?

5. "Not every Xerox spin-off venture that attempted a new business model went on to success". What were the reasons for this, and should this discourage enterprises to experiment with new business models?

6. The concept of 'organizational poise' should not be confused with the concept of 'organizational balance'. Contrast the differences in the strategic management approaches of 'balancing' in the 1970's, with 'poise' in the early 21st century.

7. With the benefit of hindsight, what should the CEO of Encyclopedia Britannica have done in the early 1990's to avoid its near-demise?

8. "The very best sustaining companies systematically ignore disruptive innovation threats until it is almost too late." Indicate how companies can avoid this by focusing on both 'new-market' disruption and 'original-market' disruption.

9. Should every company strive to be a 'keystone' or 'prime mover' company in its business ecosystem? Why or why not?

References

Chapter 4:
The New Strategic Management Approach for the Innovation Economy: Poised Strategy

[1] Tushman, M.L. and O'Reilly, C.A. (1996), "Ambidextrous Organizations: Managing Evolutionary and Revolutionary Change", *California Management Review*, 38(4), 8-29.

[2] Hamel, G. (2000), *Leading the Revolution*, Boston: Harvard Business School Press.

[3] Timmers, P. (1998), "Business Models for Electronic Commerce", *Electronic Markets*, 8(2), 3-8.

[4] Schmid, B., Alt, R., Zimmermann, H. and Buchet, B. (2001) "Anniversary Edition: Business Models", *Electronic Markets*, 11(1), 3-9.

[5] Viscio, A. and Pasternack, B. (1996), "Towards a New Business Model", *Strategy & Business*, 20, 2nd Quarter.

[6] Hamel, G. (2000), *op.cit.*,

[7] Tucker, R. (2001) "Strategy Innovation Takes Imagination", *Journal of Business Strategy*, 22(3), 23-27.

[8] See e.g., Viscio, A. and Pasternack, B. (1996); Hamel, G. (2000), *op.cit.*; and Tucker (2001), *op.cit.*

[9] Adapted from Evans, P. and Wurster, T. (2000), *Blown to Bits – How the New Economics of Information Transforms Strategy*, Boston: Harvard Business School Press.

[10] See e.g., Sull, D. (1999), "Why Good Companies Go Bad", *Harvard Business Review*, 77(4), 42-52; and Youngblood, M. (2000), "Winning Cultures for the New Economy", *Strategy & Leadership*, 28(6), 4-9.

[11] Adapted from Christensen, C.M. and Raynor, M.E. (2003), *The Innovator's Solution: Creating and Sustaining Successful Growth*, Boston: Harvard Business School Press, 39.

[12] Adapted from Christensen, C.M. and Raynor, M.E. (2003), *op.cit.*, 42.

[13] Adapted from Christensen, C.M. and Raynor, M.E. (2003), *op.cit.*, 41-42.

[14] Leibold, M., Probst, G. and Gibbert, M. (2005). *Strategic Management in the Knowledge Economy*, New York: Wiley, (Second Edition).

[15] Eagle, J.S., Joseph, E.A. and Lempres, E. (2000), "From Products to Ecosystems: Retail 2010", *The McKinsey Quarterly*, 4, 108-115.

[16] Iansiti, M. and Levien, R. (2004), *The Keystone Advantage: What the New Dynamics of Business Ecosystems Mean for Strategy, Innovation and Sustainability*, Boston: Harvard Business School Press.

[17] Moore, J.S. (1993), "Predators and Prey: A New Ecology of Competition", *Harvard Business Review*, 71 (3): 75-86.

[18] Weick, K.E. (2001), *Making Sense of the Organization*, Oxford: Blackwell Publishers Ltd.

[19] Prahalad, C.K. and Bettis, R.A. (1986), "The Dominant Logic: A New Linkage between Diversity and Performance", *Strategic Management Journal*, 7, 485-511.

[20] See Gastle, C.M. (2002), "Innovation and Entropy Within the Global Economy", Submission to Information Technology Association of Canada, Montreal: Government of Canada.

[21] Resulting from shared knowledge and creative interactions, an 'innovation' is a 'meme', a term which was coined by Richard Dawkins as a new form of 'replicator' in an evolutionary system, analogous to the term 'gene' in biology. They are complex ideas that are more or less identifiable as cultural units or imprints, that are propagated when communication with others take place. See Dawkins, R. (1976), *The Selfish Gene*, Oxford: Oxford University Press.

[22] Arthur, B (1994), *Increasing Returns and Path Dependence in the Economy,* East Lansing: University of Michigan Press.

[23] See "Entropy: The Ultimate and Most Pervasive Law of Nature", in Requadt, W.E. (2005), *How Life Really Works*, in point (http://www.rationality.net).

[24] Davenport, T.H. and Beck, J.C. (2001), *The Attention Economy*, Boston: Harvard Business School Press.

Competing with Dual Business Models: A Contingency Approach

[1] See Porter, M. E. 1980. *Competitive strategy.* New York: Free Press; and Porter, M. E. 1996. What is strategy? *Harvard Business Review*, November-December: 61-78.

[2] See Christensen, C. M. 1997. *The innovator's dilemma: When new technologies cause great firms to fail.* Boston: Harvard Business School Press.

[3] See Burgelman, R., & Sayles, L. 1986. *Inside corporate innovation.* New York: The Free Press; and Gilbert, C., & Bower, J. 2002. Disruptive change: When trying harder is part of the problem. *Harvard Business Review*, May: 94-101.

[4] See Porter, M. E. 1996. What is strategy? *Harvard Business Review*, November-December: 77.

[5] See Day, J.D., et al. 2001. The innovative organization: Why new ventures need more than a room of their own. *The McKinsey Quarterly*, No. 2: 21.

[6] See Iansiti, M., McFarlan, F.W., & Westerman, G. 2003. Leveraging the incumbent's advantage. *Sloan Management Review*, Summer, 44 (4): 58.

[7] See Tushman, M. L., & O'Reilly III, C. A. 1996. Ambidextrous organizations: Managing evolutionary and revolutionary change. *California Management Review*, 38 (4): 8-30.

[8] See Lawrence, P., & Lorsch, J. 1967. *Organization and environment.* Boston: Harvard Business School Press.

[9] We offer precise definitions of "conflicts" and "strategic similarity" in the Appendix. Conflicts include tradeoffs at the value-chain level as well as channel and brand conflicts. Strategic similarity captures market relatedness as well as resource similarity.

[10] A similar matrix to help managers determine whether a firm should use a heavyweight (or lightweight) team inside or outside the existing organization to manage a different business model can be found in Clayton Christensen and Michael Overdorf, 2000, Meeting the challenge of disruptive change, *Harvard Business Review*, March-April: 67-76. Our matrix differs from theirs in two important dimensions. First, their model takes into consideration only the

importance of conflicts (in values and processes). By contrast, we argue that the decision regarding what to do is determined not only by conflicts but also by the possibility of exploiting synergies between the two markets that the two business models are serving. In this sense, our model builds on the intellectual tradition started by Lawrence and Lorsch. Second, our model takes time into consideration; we argue that under certain circumstances, it may be better to separate (integrate) the new business model at first, before integrating it into (separating it from) the existing organization.

[11] See Lawrence & Lorsch, op. cit.

[12] See Gulati, R., & Garino, J. 2000. Get the right mix of bricks and clicks. *Harvard Business Review*, May-June: 107-114.

[13] Edward Jones serves individual investors exclusively through an extensive network of more than 4,000 branch offices in all 50 US states.

[14] Kelly, E. 2000. Edward Jones and me. *Fortune*, 12 June 2000: 145

[15] See Dutton, J.E., & Jackson, S.E. 1987. Categorizing strategic issues: Links to organizational action. *Academy of Management Review*, 12 (1): 76-90.

[16] See Gilbert & Bower, op. cit. June, 94-101.

[17] See in particular Markides, C.C., & Williamson, P.W. 1994. Related diversification, core competences, and corporate performance. *Strategic Management Journal*, 15: 149-165; and Verdin, P.J., & Williamson, P.J. 1994. Core competences, competitive advantage, and market analysis: Forging the links. In Hamel, G., & Heene, A. (Eds.), Competence-based competition. New York: John Wiley & Sons Ltd: 77-110.

[18] We also measured relatedness by taking the sum of the absolute differences between the old and new businesses on each of the scales. This did not affect the classification of our sample firms in the figure.

[19] See Dess, G. S., & Robinson, R.B. 1984. Measuring organizational performance in the absence of objective measures. *Strategic Management Journal*, 5: 265-273; and Venkatraman, N., & Ramanujam, V. 1986. Measurement of business performance in strategic research: A comparison of approaches. *Academy of Management Review*, 11 (4): 801-814.

[20] The analysts were also asked to identify other firms (not necessarily sample firms) in the industries that they covered which, in their opinion, responded to the invasion of the new business model in an effective way. Four additional firms were identified for further examination through field research.

V New Strategic Management Processes and Tools

Synopsis

The chapter focuses on the processes and tools required for poised strategic management in the innovation economy – the 'how to' of poised strategic management. Major sections include the presentation of a new strategy-making process, a business model reinvention process, and four categories of business model reinvention tools, consisting of 12 types of tools (incl. new measurement tool PSC). Many (box) examples are provided, including Palm, Hardy, Microsoft, Apple, Starbucks, Holcim, Home Depot, P&G, Ford, Honda, 7-11, and Qualcomm. The case example illustrates innovative business models in the airline industry. Three relevant articles are included.

Chapter 5
Processes and Tools for Poised Strategic Management in the Innovation Economy

The Context of Processes and Tools for Poised Strategic Management

Poised strategic management was defined in the previous chapter as the (ambidextrous) management of multiple business models for sustaining and disruptive value innovation in collaborative business networks (or 'ecosystems'). The initial chapters of the book, especially chapters 1 and 2, made a strong case why traditional strategic management approaches, processes, and tools (with their analytical, goods-centered, and traditional industry focus) are inadequate (although not obsolete) to handle the disruptive, value-innovation requirements of the innovation economy. The obvious questions that now arise are: if the traditional approaches to strategic management are deficient for the innovation economy, what do we put in their place? Furthermore, if the traditional four-step analytical strategy-making process (still displayed by most MBA textbooks) of environmental analysis (external and internal), generation of strategy implementation and change management, are inadequate or deficient, can we devise a process (which is practical and proven) for poised strategy-making, and what are the particular/unique tools to assist in this process?

While the previous chapters provided strong indication of the necessity for particular new approaches, processes, and tools, these were mainly conceptual descriptions of essential requirements, such as business ecosystem sense-making, cultivating new mental space and management attention allocations, new business model formation dynamics, portfolio of multiple business models, and leveraging of innovation capability in collaborative networks (see especially Table 4.2 for an overview and comparison with major eras in the 20th century). This chapter, and its allied company examples and articles, provide specific detail of the 'how-to', i.e. practical processes and tools for poised strategy. These processes and tools are, for purpose of exposition, naturally more generic in nature and require appropriate adaptation for particular companies and their environments. Furthermore, disruptive innovation processes are of course more emergent in nature than deliberate, and some tools are continuously in the process of being shaped and reshaped, i.e. some tools are still in the process of refinement.

The tools for poised strategic management are not discussed separately or in isolation, but in the context of particular required poised strategy processes. This discussion also illustrates the necessity for a holistic approach to processes and tools, beyond an analytical and 'mechanistic' approach. The chapter consists of the following major sections:

- A (new) *holistic process* for poised strategic management, in contrast to the traditional four-step analytical process.
- Contrasting *deliberate processes* for sustaining innovations with *discovery-driven* processes for disruptive innovations.
- The *business model reinvention process.*
- *Sense-making processes and tools* – of business ecosystem dynamics and impacts.
- Categories (four) and types (twelve) of *business model reinvention tools*:
  - Tools to leverage new customer/market space (two major types).
  - Tools to develop new value (product/service) space (four major types).
  - Tools for innovative value chain configurations and leveraging of internal-external knowledge and innovation (three major types).
  - Tools for new valuation (economics, rewards) space and their measurements (three major types).

A (New) Holistic Process for Poised Strategic Management, in Contrast to the Traditional Analytical Process

The holistic strategy process is contrasted with the traditional strategy process in Table 5.1.

Table 5.1 Traditional (analytical) vs. holistic (poised) strategy processes *(continued next page)*

The Traditional Strategy Process	The Holistic Strategy Process
1. Situation Analysis	*1. Sense-Making of Business Ecosystems*
1.1 External Environment	1.1 Dynamics of Existing Business Model
a) Broad External Trends & Forces	1.2 Dynamics of Business Ecosystems
b) Industry Forces: Markets, Competitors, etc.	
1.2 Internal Environment	*2. Business Model Reinvention: Processes & Tools*
a) Resources: Tangible & Intangible	2.1 Existing Business Model Processes
b) Capabilities: Processes & Competencies	2.2 Possible New Business Model(s): Processes & Tools
2. Strategic Analyses and Strategy Pointers	
a) SWOT-Analyses & Strategy Pointers	*3. Business Model & Strategy Options*
b) Key Success Factors	3.1 Deliberate BM & Sustaining Innovations
c) Strategy Options: Generic & Specific	3.2 Discovery-Driven BMs & Disruptive Innovation
d) Balanced Scorecard Indicators	

Table 5.1 Traditional (analytical) vs. holistic (poised) strategy processes *(continued)*

The Traditional Strategy Process	The Holistic Strategy Process
3. Strategy Formulation	*4. Strategy Thrusts*
a) Corporate & Business Vision, Mission, etc.	4.1 Deliberate BM Strategy
b) Corporate Level Strategy	4.2 Discovery-Driven (emergent)
c) Business Level Strategy	BM Strategy
d) Functional Level Strategy	4.3 BM Portfolio & Strategy Integration
4. Strategy Implementation & Change	*5. Enabling Continuous BM & Strategy*
4.1 Strategy Implementation	*Fitness: Capabilities and Methods*
a) Particular Short-Term Objectives	5.1 Networked Innovation Capabilities
b) Programs, Functions, and Tactics	5.2 Poised Strategy Scorecard Indicators
c) Organization: Structures & Networks	5.3 Self-Organizing and Coherence Methods
d) Action Schedules and Processes	5.4 Guiding Internal & External Structures
4.2 Strategy Change	5.5 Enabling Knowledge-Sharing &
a) Contingency Plans	Networking
b) Reengineering & Restructuring Processes	
c) Responsibilities & Review Procedures	
(Note: change is an *add-on* in this *planning* process)	(Note: change is *integrated* in this *dynamic* process)

The holistic strategy process indicated in Table 5.1 is not a hierarchical or mechanistic step-by-step process, but a dynamic and integrated process – as also illustrated later in Figure 5.1. The best way to depict this is by an interactive 'wheel' process, as subsequently outlined with company examples in the *wheel of business model reinvention* process. Change becomes a constant (integrated throughout) in this process, i.e. prevalent in all dimensions, and not an 'add-on' as in traditional strategy processes.

Contrasting Deliberate Processes for Sustaining Innovations with Discovery-Driven Processes for Disruptive Innovations

Christensen and Raynor provide a useful dichotomy (see Table 5.2) of deliberate planning processes for sustaining innovations and discovery-driven planning processes for disruptive innovations.[1]

Executives whose ventures are in a discovery mode need not passively watch what evolves in the emergent strategy process. They can employ a rigorous method called discovery-driven planning to help a viable strategy emerge much more quickly and purposefully than is likely to happen through less-structured trial and error.[2]

Most deliberate strategic planning processes go through four steps, as suggested in Table 5.2. First, innovators make assumptions about the future and about the success that a new business idea will enjoy. These assumptions might be grounded in good predictive theory, but often they are grounded in the way things worked in the past. In the second step, the innovators make financial projections based on those assumptions, and third, senior executives approve the proposal based on the financial projections. Fourth, the team responsible for the new venture goes off to implement the strategy. There is frequently a loop from the second step back to the first in this deliberate process. Because the innovators and middle managers typically know how good the numbers have to look in order for the proposal to get funded, they often will cycle back and revise the assumptions that they are making in order to make the numbers work.

This process is not necessarily a poor one in a world of sustaining improvements and deliberate strategy. But when it is used for decision making in the emergent world of disruption, this process causes poor decisions to be made because the assumptions upon which the projections and decisions are built often prove to be wrong.

Discovery-driven planning is a way to actively manage the emergent strategy process. As depicted in Table 5.2, it involves reordering the four steps. The first step is to make the financial projections – the targeted or required financial performance of the venture. The logic behind this is strong: if everybody knows how good the numbers must look in order to win funding, why go through the cyclical charade of making and revising assumptions in order to make the numbers look good enough? The required income statement and return on investment should just be the standard first slide in every presentation. The second step, where the real work begins, is to compile an assumptions checklist. It answers the question, "We all know how good the numbers need to be. So what assumptions need to prove true in order for us to realistically expect that these numbers will materialize?" The assumptions on this list should be rank-ordered from most to least crucial. The list should include assumptions such as: low-end or new-market disruptions are possible, that the targeted customers will use the new product for the jobs they are trying to get done, that the new venture will lead the company to the point in the value chain where the money will be in the future, and so on.

Table 5.2 A discovery-driven method for managing the emergent strategy process

Sustaining Innovations: Deliberate Planning	Disruptive Innovations: Discovery-Driven Planning
(Note: decisions to initiate these projects can be based on numbers and rules)	(Note: decisions to initiate these projects should be based on pattern recognition)
1. Make assumptions about the future.	1. Make the targeted financial projections.
2. Define a strategy based on those assumptions, and build financial projections based on that strategy.	2. What assumptions must prove true in order for these projections to materialize?
3. Make decisions to invest based on those financial projections.	3. Implement a plan to learn – to test whether the critical assumptions are reasonable.
4. Implement the strategy in order to achieve the project financial results.	4. Invest to implement the strategy.

Managing Deliberate and Discovery-Driven (Emergent) Strategy Processes: Prodigy Communications and Palm

Prodigy Communications, a joint venture between Sears and IBM, was a pioneer in online services in the early 1990s. The managers of Sears and IBM were extraordinarily bold in resource allocation: they invested over a billion dollars in what was a very uncertain, potentially disruptive innovation. But they were not as successful in managing the strategy process – in helping Prodigy define a viable strategy through emergent processes even while the parent companies were managing their mainstream businesses deliberately. Prodigy's original business plan envisioned that consumers would use online services primarily to access information and make online purchases. In 1992, management realized that Prodigy's two million subscribers were spending more time sending e-mail than downloading information or making purchases online. The architecture of Prodigy's computer and communications infrastructure had been designed to optimize transactions processing and information delivery, and Prodigy consequently began charging extra fees to subscribers who sent more than thirty e-mail messages per month. Rather than seeing e-mail as an emergent strategy signal, the company tried to filter it out, because in a deliberate mode, management's job was to implement the original strategy.

America Online (AOL) 'fortunately' entered the market later, after customers had discovered that e-mail was a primary reason for subscribing to an online service. With a technology infrastructure tailored to messaging and its "You've got mail" signature, AOL became much more successful. Prodigy's mistake was not that it entered the market early. Nor was it a mistake that management targeted online information retrieval and shopping as the primary attraction of an online service. Nobody could know at the outset precisely how online services would be used. The executives' mistake was to employ a deliberate strategy process before the strategy's viability could be known. Had Prodigy kept strategic and technological flexibility to respond to emergent strategic evidence, the company could have had a huge lead over AOL and CompuServe (the third major online service provider).

A similar challenge confronted the set of companies that responded in the early 1990s to the widely held view that a large market for handheld personal digital assistants was about to emerge. Many of the leading computer makers – including NCR, Apple, Motorola, IBM, and Hewlett-Packard – targeted this market, along with a few start-up firms such as Palm. All sensed that the market wanted a handheld computing device. Apple was one of the most aggressive innovators in this space. Its Newton cost $350 million to develop because of the technologies, such as handwriting recognition, that were required to build as much functionality into the product as possible. Hewlett-Packard also invested aggressively to design and build its tiny Kittyhawk disk drive for this market.

In the end, the products were just not good enough to be a substitute for notebook computers, and each of the companies scrapped its effort – except Palm. Palm's original strategy was to provide an operating system for these personal digital assistants. When its customers' strategies failed, Palm searched around for another application and came up with the concept of an electronic personal organizer.

What were the strategic mistakes here? The computer companies employed deliberate strategy processes from the beginning to the end. They invested massively to implement their strategies, and then wrote the projects off when the strategies proved wrong. Palm was the only firm that shifted to an emergent strategy process when its original deliberate strategy failed. When a viable strategy emerged, Palm shifted back toward a deliberate process as it migrated up-market.[3]

The third and fourth steps in discovery-driven planning also reverse the order of the deliberate strategy process. The third step is to implement a plan. This is not a deliberate strategic plan, but rather a plan to test the validity of the most important assumptions. This plan needs to generate quickly, and with as little expense as possible, validating or invalidating information about the most critical assumptions. This enables innovators to revise the strategy prior to the fourth step – the decision to implement through significant investment. This can be done after the viability of various assumptions has become more evident. If they are not viable, then the venture or initiative can be tabled (perhaps to be re-examined later), with little money and time expended. Killing unsuccessful projects rapidly, as many pharmaceutical firms have learned in the drug development process, is just as important as ensuring continuation of successful projects.

Innovators who are using the discovery-driven process frequently learn quite early that there just is not a reasonable set of assumptions to support a plan that will achieve the numbers the organization requires. This might imply that the idea simply cannot be shaped into a viable strategy at all. Or it might mean that the idea needs to be placed within a smaller business unit, whose values might not demand that it gets prohibitively big and/or prohibitively fast. At any given point in time, some businesses under a manager's care may need to be managed through aggressive, deliberate strategy processes, while others need emergent processes.

In summary, simply seeking to have the right strategy does not go deep enough. The key is to manage the process by which strategy is developed. Strategic initiatives enter the resource allocation process from two sources – deliberate and emergent.[4] In circumstances of sustaining innovations and certain low-end disruptions, the competitive landscape is clear enough for strategy to be deliberately conceived and implemented. In the nascent stages of a new-market disruption, however, it is almost impossible to get the details of strategy right. Rather than executing a strategy, managers in this situation need to implement a process through which a viable strategy can emerge.

The Business Model Reinvention Process

The continuous processes of business model reinvention, both of existing and new (unique) business model(s), have been shown as fundamental to any company for necessary sustaining and disruptive value innovation, i.e. part of a poised strategy involving the management of multiple business models simultaneously. Table 5.1 indicates business model reinvention processes as one of the key elements of a holistic strategy-making process. Figure 5.1 now illustrates one key part of this process, i.e. the wheel of business model reinvention, with four dimensions – sensing reinvented customer benefits, sensing new customer value propositions, sensing reinvented business system configurations, and sensing new profitability and wider benefits to stakeholders[5] – underpinned by sense-making of business ecosystems and other (integrative) organizational capabilities, e.g. knowledge networking, 'open innovation', and a systemic business model scorecard, which form part of the 'toolbox' for poised strategic management that are subsequently elaborated in this chapter.

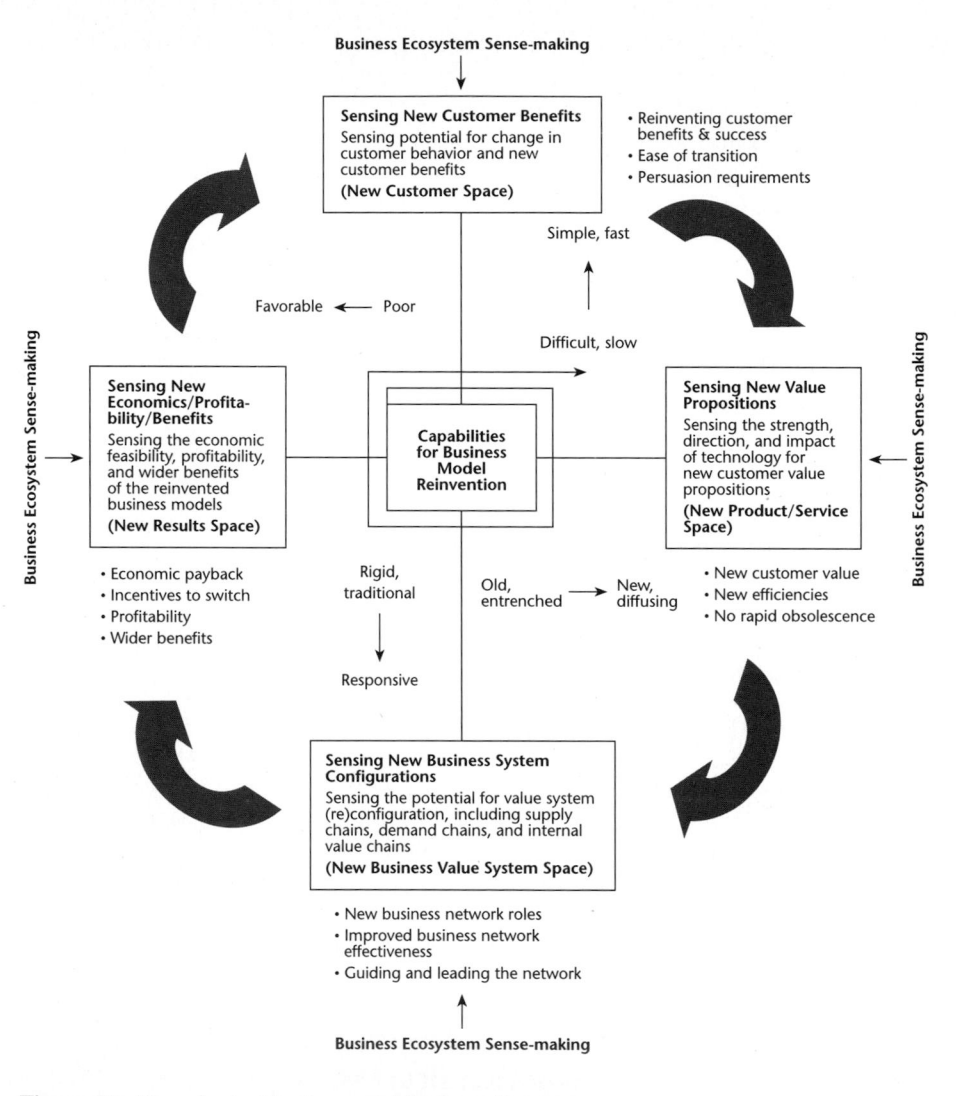

Figure 5.1 The wheel of business model reinvention process

Each of these four major dimensions of business model reinvention is henceforth discussed as a *process*, while the necessary business ecosystem sense-making *tools* and the particular tools for application in the various dimensions of the wheel follow subsequently.

The process depicted in Figure 5.1 could start anywhere in the wheel, as the impulse for business model reinvention could arise in any of its dimensions. Sensing new customer benefits is often a starting point, however, due to its critical viability and importance for any business model – as the well-known adage aptly states 'without a customer you don't have a business'. The four key dimensions depicted in the process influence and shape the development of a potentially new or reinvented business

254

model. These dimensions are: sensing the possibilities of new customer value proposition(s); sensing the impact and proper utilization of technology; sensing the configuration of industry value chains and/or business system infrastructures; and sensing the sustainability of the potential/reinvented business model. The directions of the arrows in the diagram indicate whether a new (or potential) business model is likely to be positively responsive to these four dimensions. For instance, does the proposed business model create a new value proposition that is easily and rapidly accepted and internalized by customers? Does it apply useful existing and new technology? Is the value system network responsive to flexible configurations and reconfigurations? And is the economic feasibility of the business model encouraging or promising? The following describe each of the dimensions:

- *Sensing New Customer Benefits*: Research indicates that the creation of a dramatically new customer value proposition(s) and/or sensing potential breakthrough change in customer behavior, are often the initial driving forces behind sound new business models. Does the value proposition dramatically improve/satisfy customers' needs and wants? Or does it create new customer segments? And if it does, is customers' ease of transition to (or acceptance of) the new value proposition slow and difficult, or fast and swift?

- *Sensing New Value Propositions*: This indicates the relative strength, direction, and impact of technology on new customer value propositions and the business network. Is the available technology still efficient in communicating and delivering new customer value propositions? Or is it becoming obsolete, and perhaps even a new and better technology is being developed (for e.g., the way the Internet has replaced catalogue and mail order)? When a new business model is proposed, does the available or proposed technological infrastructure enable quick organizational reconfiguration? (See the next point about reconfiguration).

- *Sensing New Business System Configurations*: The business environment is a "networked economy" consisting of various business ecosystems, in which a company co-evolves with selected organizations (suppliers, competitors, etc.) and individuals (customers, employees, etc.) in creating/responding to new business models. Is the company (internally) reconfigured and organized in a way that enables it to offer new value propositions? Is the (external) value system configured with the necessary suppliers, customers, even competitors, and other critical stakeholders? Basically, this sense-testing refers to the options for reinvention of business systemic infrastructure (internal and external).

- *Economics/Profitability Sensing:* The proposed new business model(s) should be evaluated as sustainable and relatively inimitable by competitors. They should be economically feasible in due course, if they are to sustain the company and support other business models in the portfolio. Economic payback is also needed to enable the company to experiment with opportunities and innovations without experiencing the shortage of funds. The proposed new model may not seem to be groundbreaking and a particularly lucrative undertaking, and every model may not turn out to be economically feasible in the end, but it is important to have a diverse (robust) range of models to minimize the risk of an unsustainable corporate strategy.

Each of these activities calls for sense-making about a particular aspect of the business model, so a few words on sense-making are appropriate. As might be expected in an emergent strategy world, the term "sense-making" suggests that the analyst is trying – but not always succeeding – to make sense of a variety of information and stimuli. He or she is talking to customers, talking to business partners, trying to glean what competitors are up to, bouncing ideas off other executives, and constantly attempting to clarify and describe the state of the business model (current or future) at any given moment. There is no particular right answer – only the best guess at any point in time. This ambiguity will frustrate many engineering-oriented managers, but the sense-making perspective does not introduce the ambiguity – it was always present in strategy – but only acknowledges it as inevitable.

Looking at the four sense-testing dimensions in conjunction, (i) the higher the acceptance potential of the new value proposition that appeals to a larger customer base, (ii) the higher the acceptance of new value propositions and technological standards, (iii) the higher the increased flexibility in business infrastructure reconstruction, and (iv) the greater the potential sustainability and profitability of the new business model, then the greater the likelihood of a successful new business model. Managers can use these four dimensions in determining which business models from the potential pool of strategies are feasible and possess acceptable success probabilities.

There are numerous companies (mainly start-ups and new market entrants, but also some well known established incumbent companies) that have redefined their businesses or industries in radical ways and successfully transcended traditional industry competitors. These include the well-known "poster children" of today's management thinking: Dell Computer (structuring a "direct sales" value chain of build-to-order manufacturing), Amazon.com (creating virtual stores that offer millions of new, used, and collectable items), Starbucks (America's specialty coffee retailer), Cisco Systems (manufacturing and selling scalable, standards-based networking and communication products), IKEA (a global leader in a wide range of modern home furnishings and accessories), and Nokia (leader in mobile communications). They also include the less-well-known companies Carmax (used-car business model) and BRL Hardy (wine industry business model) – see the boxes below for two cases in point.

Reinventing the Used Car Business Model

Carmax, a subsidiary of Circuit City, is using multimedia and networking technology to radically change the way Americans shop for used cars. The basic concept is to replace the difficult-to-access used car market with an efficient, information-intensive market. Carmax buys used cars at wholesale auctions, and then uses multimedia technology to provide customers with complete and reliable information. The vehicles are resold at accessible Carmax locations. The keys to the success of this new business model are the availability and reliability of its information, the large selection of cars, the convenient locations, the customer-friendly buying process, the effective new business network infrastructure with direct links to wholesalers, and the mutual economic and profitability benefits for Carmax, wholesalers, banks, and other systemic role-players.[6]

BRL Hardy is a major Australian wine company that has reinvented its business model. In retrospect, it is possible to recognize how BRL Hardy reinvented its business model by applying the wheel of business model reinvention tool (see the box below).

How BRL Hardy Reinvented its Business Model from a Wine Exporter to a Global Wine Brand Company

BRL Hardy, the Australian wine company, increased its 1991 international sales of US$31 million to US$178 million in 1998 when it realized the opportunity to build up a global wine brand, something previously unimagined in the highly-fragmented global wine industry. The Old World (European) wine industries of France, Spain, Italy, Germany, and others are so fragmented in producers, cultivars, and brands that it confuses consumers and retailers alike. A large supermarket store in Europe sells hundreds of different types and brands of wine made by a huge variety of producers, from the Old World and New World wine producers. The New World wine producers come from countries such as the USA, Australia, New Zealand, Chile, and South Africa.

In most Old World wine countries, wines are labeled according to region, sub-region, and even village. In addition to that, a vineyard in France can be further categorized according to its historical quality classifications such as the Premier Grand Cru, the (ordinary) Grand Cru, and so on. The world famous wine region Bordeaux alone has over 12,000 producers. Italy has over a million separated wine-growing units in private ownership. In Australia on the other hand, only four companies dominate 80% of the local wine industry, making for a more consolidated industry. It is this power of larger scale that allows New World wine producers to build up brand strength and distribution capability. The major wine importing countries are the United Kingdom and Western European countries such as Germany, Holland, and Sweden, where the range of wine brands have proliferated five-fold in the past ten years.

In the early 1980s, BRL Hardy found itself "trapped" in the shrinking market of the lower quality and price segment of the major wine importing markets, especially the UK. The business model was an "export company" model built on significant quantities of low-margin wine products, with the large supermarket chains in the UK having the power to dictate wine styles, quantities, timing, and prices. In world terms, BRL Hardy was a relatively small and entrepreneurial entity. Steve Millar, the managing director at that time, decided that the only way out would be to "change the rules of the game" and to come up with a new business model. He sensed that wine consumers were frustrated with the proliferation of wine brands and their lack of knowledge of relative wine qualities and service. He further sensed that there was no real global wine brand, while these were commonplace in soft drinks, beer and some high-alcohol spirits. He surmised that a global wine brand would make things easier for suppliers and customers, and could "free" them from the stifling power of large retailers.

A key issue was the eventual realization (or sensing) by BRL Hardy that the major knowledgeable wine customer need, or customer wine value proposition, was made up of three elements: well known global image; consistency of quality and availability; and "value-for-money", including affordability and competitive pricing. Once it was clear that something had to be dramatically changed, it was important to have

257

the necessary prerequisites to engage in disruptive change. In 1991, for example, Christopher Carson, an experienced international wine marketer, was appointed managing director of the company's UK operations. Over the next 18 months, he pruned three-quarters of the items in the fragmented product line, replaced half of his management team, and began building a culture around globalism, creativity and innovation, and global value chain configuration and management. It was realized that dynamic new organizational capabilities were needed, and Hardy embarked on a targeted strategic alliance building with companies in Italy, Spain, and the USA. These alliances added essential expertise, infrastructure, and finance (technological and other resources infrastructure). Several mistakes were made in the process, but nothing survival-critical, and these eventually contributed to the learning experience and overall value-added of the new business model.

The company started to focus on integrated wine production, supplementing their Australian product line by sourcing and supplying wine from around the world. By breaking the tradition of selling only its own wine, Hardy was able to build the scale necessary for creating strong global brands and negotiating on equal basis with large retailers. The advantages of global sense-making to Hardy have been clear and powerful: The company's range of wines – from Australia as well as France, Italy, and Chile – responds to the supermarket companies' need to deal with only a few broad line suppliers. Simultaneously, the scale of operations has supported the brand development that is vital to transforming products from the commodity range.

A radical corporate strategy, as in the case of BRL Hardy, is to introduce new business models that challenge an industry's established rules of competition, or ways of doing business. Results and profitability have been outstanding. In Europe, the volume of Hardy's brands has increased 12-fold in seven years, making it the leading Australian wine brand in the huge UK market, and number two overall to Gallo in the United Kingdom. Hardy has evolved from a mere Australian wine exporter to a truly global wine company, utilizing global scope and scale economies and drawing on knowledge and skills from many parts of the world.[7]

Sense-Making of Business Ecosystem Dynamics: Processes and Tools

The concept of a business ecosystem was described in Chapter 4 as a range of organizations, markets, customers, suppliers, and other stakeholders spanning a variety of (traditional) industries. Such ecosystems form spontaneously and emerge through self-organization by 'agents' (e.g., entrepreneurs) seeking value-innovative cross-industry linkages. The rationale for this is compelling: the quest to break from traditional industry product/service and market boundaries to co-shape new value through the seeking of synergies in many industries and their practices. While such cross-industry innovation-seeking activities cannot be planned and controlled, there are tools to enable and steer the process in a coherent way. The three tools outlined here are:

- Adopting particular *premises and simple rules* to understand and develop business ecosystems.

- Applying an *ecosystem checklist toolkit* to identify and influence the phases of development of a business ecosystem.
- Adhering to particular *organizational capability requirements* to achieve 'fitness' in a business ecosystem.

a) Adopting Particular Premises and Simple Rules

The six core premises for business ecosystem sense-making are listed below, followed by five categories of 'simple' rules. The core premises are:

(i) Influencing and co-shaping of the business ecosystem is achieved by managing initial conditions and the underlying forces ("attractors" or "coherence mechanisms") which organize and guide the system. Attractors, such as mission and vision, create constraints on a firm's activities. Since behavior patterns can emerge without being intended, i.e. in a chaotic way, influence through attractors (or coherence mechanisms) means shaping the basic elements that impose some regularity on a system. Poised strategic management now includes the manipulation of these concurrent and paradoxical elements to create and sustain a healthy, evolving ecosystem.

(ii) Emphasizing the importance of unpredictable, nonlinear, natural consequences. While some strategic consequences are the result of deliberate intent, most are emergent results, i.e. behavior that spontaneously and unexpectedly follows a different set of rules or patterns.

(iii) Understanding that systemic change is a continuous, relentless process. Co-evolution results from interdependent webs or networks experiencing continuous waves of changes – complex systems constantly coalesce, decay, change, and grow.

(iv) Recognizing that individual, unit, or organizational success requires a healthy ecosystem. Task-based, fragmented thinking is discarded in favor of co-evolutionary workflows and process-based activity within and among firms in diverse industries.

(v) Accepting the concept of self-organization that triggers transformation. This means that firms can generate intelligent, effective responses to the need for change without externally imposed direction or plans – they emerge naturally through the implementation of self-organizing principles. In effect, emergent strategies will be more important than intended strategies.

(vi) Recognizing that values and cultural integrity are a basis for establishing relevant boundaries. Ecosystem-based strategy initiatives rely on shared values and common purposes for coherence. Whereas physical systems are shaped by unchanging natural laws, social systems are the result of interventions by individuals and groups, and cultural norms determine the limits on these interventions.

The following box indicates Microsoft's underlying premises to be both adaptive and creative in relevant business ecosystems.

Microsoft's Dynamic Capabilities to Influence Business Ecosystems

In the late 1980s, with the DOS operating system approaching the end of its useful life, Bill Gates focused on moving the industry to another Microsoft product, Windows. Appreciating the uncertainty of this development and its possible acceptance in the business ecosystem, he hedged his bets by also investing in Windows' competitors: Unix, OS/2 and the Apple Macintosh system. In addition, his company developed generic capabilities in object-oriented programming and graphical interface design – skills that would be useful no matter which system won in the ecosystem, even if it were a complete unknown. Gates's approach of pursuing several paths simultaneously was intrinsically complex, and also confusing to both existing customers and employees.

Poised strategy differs from traditional industry and scenario analysis in that it does not presuppose an ability to identify the most or least likely outcomes. Being a poised organization calls for the ability to pursue a range of potentially conflicting strategies at the same time. In the case of Microsoft, it included major *shaping* 'bets' such as Windows, *hedging* 'bets' (support of OS/2), and *no-regrets* dynamic capability moves that are valid regardless of environmental outcome (building object-oriented programming skills). Microsoft operated like a complex adaptive system, i.e. a poised organization, with a range of strategies that covered a spectrum of possibilities, and co-evolved with other organizations in its ecosystem over time. Underlying the thrust of these diverse activities are coherence premises, such as the Microsoft culture and its organizational values.[8]

In coping with the dynamics of evolving business ecosystems, some companies have been adopting coherence rules (or 'simple' rules) that provide general guidelines or generic platforms for behavior, but do not confine, restrict, or limit these in any traditional sense. Companies such as Microsoft, Vodafone, Yahoo!, and Cisco do not plan integrated approaches in any traditional sense – they are unable to do so because their ecosystems are too chaotic. Rather than selecting an ecosystem position or focusing on a particular set of capabilities, they select a few strategically significant options and processes, and craft simple rules in areas such as product innovation, market entry, alliancing, and experimentation. Five categories of simple rules are suggested:[9]

- *Boundary rules*: "rules of thumb", for example in screening opportunities across various business ecosystems.
- *Activity rules*: "how-to" rules that designate a common approach for a company to approach and exploit opportunities in business ecosystems.
- *Priority rules*: rules to determine priorities in resource/capability combination and allocation.
- *Timing rules*: rules for lead and scheduling times in exploratory and experimenting activities.
- *Exit rules*: termination and disengagement rules, subsequent to mutual activities across ecosystems.

These rules provide flexible, adaptive boundaries to each business to enable voluntary innovative collaborations to thrive. For example, Disney's merchandising spin-offs from their movies, such as videos, theme park attractions, stage musicals, and hundreds of merchandise items are not planned by corporate leadership, but emerge through voluntary cooperation across Disney's different divisions and alliance partners, in collaboration with stakeholders in the entertainment, telecommunications, toys, media, and education industries.

b) Applying a Business Ecosystem Checklist

Moore has identified four phases of development of business ecosystems, and proposes a methodology (or checklist) for managers to understand and influence developments in each phase.[10] He incorporates both cooperative and competitive activities relative to the ecosystem. These are illustrated in Table 5.3.

Table 5.3 Checklist to understand and influence phases of a business ecosystem

Stage of Evolution of the Business System	Overall Focus	Managerial Challenges	
		Cooperative Challenges and Action Checklist	Competitive Challenges and Action Checklist
Pioneering (birth of business system)	Value proposition and designing business model	Work with customers and suppliers to develop the seed innovation and define the new value proposition (dramatically more effective than what is available).	Protect ideas from others who might be working toward defining similar offers. Commit critical lead customers, key suppliers, and distribution channels.
Expansion	Critical mass	Bring the new offer to a large market by working with suppliers and partners to increase supply, and to achieve maximum market coverage and critical mass.	Supersede alternative business system implementations of similar ideas; ensure that the new approach is the market standard in its class by dominating key market segments.
Leadership	Lead co-evolution	Provide a compelling vision for the future that encourages suppliers and customers to work together to continue to improve the value proposition and business system. Ensure the business system has a robust community of suppliers.	Maintain strong bargaining power in relation to other players in the business system by controlling key elements of value.
Renewal	Continuous performance improvement	Work with innovators to bring new ideas to the existing business system. Track new trends that may transform the business system.	Maintain high barriers to entry to prevent innovators from building alternative business systems. Maintain high customer switching costs in order to buy time to incorporate new ideas into your own products and services. Ensure robustness of management and other system members.

In a business ecosystem, as indicated in Table 5.3, companies co-evolve capabilities around a new innovation: they work cooperatively and competitively to support new products, satisfy customer needs, and eventually incorporate the next round of innovations. Each of the four phases of business ecosystem development pose their own distinctive challenges. The question arises: how is it that a company can create an entirely new business community – like IBM in personal computers – and then lose control and profitability in that same business? Is there a stable structure of community leadership that matches fast-changing conditions? And how can companies develop leadership that successfully adapts to continual waves of innovation and change? These questions remain unanswered because most managers still frame the problem in the old way: companies go head-to-head in an industry, battling for market share. The following box illustrates how some companies deal with this situation, and why some succeed and others fail in the birth phase of business ecosystems.[11]

c) Adhering to Particular Organizational Capability Requirements

The ecosystems approach as part of poised strategic management processes raises an important question. If everything is connected to everything else, how can we ever hope to understand the complexity of it all, let alone be capable to influence and shape it? The answer: the discovery of approximate knowledge and the principles of complexity theory make this possible. The traditional strategic management approaches are based on the belief of the certainty of scientific knowledge and specific industry and world "views". In the new strategy management mindset, it is recognized that all theories and knowledge are limited and approximate.

In resorting to concepts of self-organization and emergent behavior, we are acknowledging the limits to management as traditionally defined. If the environment of business is complex and unpredictable, we are unable to formulate strategy based on a rational, objective analysis of the firm and its environment, no matter how well trained we are in the art and science of strategic management. This challenge is addressed by complexity theory, evolving from research into complex adaptive systems (CAS). Complexity science is the name commonly used to describe a set of interdisciplinary studies that share the idea that all things tend to self-organize into systems, while complexity theory is based on the observation that in an enormous diversity of systemic patterns there are simple, underlying sets of rules.

Recently, authors such as Roos, Oliver, Eisenhardt, Brown, Sull, Galunic, Martin, Kelly, and Allison have applied the concepts of complexity theory to strategic management in turbulent environments.[12] Their research points to the advantages of business ecosystems that evolve to the "edge of chaos" – an area of business activity where the greatest potential for creativity and innovation resides, with astute management requiring a balance between "no rules" or boundaries (total chaos) and rigid norms and controls (total control). The discipline of ecology resides at a middle point between these two extremes, and hence the concept of "ecosystem" is appropriate to discuss business environments that fall between chaos and control. Such dynamic ecosystems are capable of both adaptations and

The Birth Phase of a Business Ecosystem: Why Some Succeed and Others Fail

Apple Computer is part of an ecosystem that crosses at least four major industries: personal computers, consumer electronics, information, and communications. The Apple ecosystem encompasses an extended web of suppliers that includes Motorola and Sony and a large number of customers in various market segments.

Apple, IBM, Ford, Wal-Mart, and Merck have all been, or still are, the leaders of business ecosystems. While the center may shift over time, the role of the leader is valued by the rest of the community. Such leadership enables all ecosystem members to invest toward a shared future in which they anticipate profiting together.

Yet in any larger business environment, several ecosystems may vie for survival and dominance: the Dell and Apple ecosystems in personal computers, for example, or Wal-Mart and Kmart in discount retailing. In fact, it is competition among business ecosystems, not individual companies, that is largely fueling today's industrial transformation. Managers cannot afford to ignore the birth of new ecosystems or the competition among those that already exist.

Whether that means investing in the right new technology, signing on suppliers to expand a growing business, developing crucial elements of value to maintain leadership, or incorporating new innovations to fend off obsolescence, executives must understand the stages that all business ecosystems pass through – and, more important, how to direct the changes.

Understanding the Birth Phase of Business Ecosystems, and Dealing with its Challenges

Three major challenges arise in the pioneering (birth) phase of a business ecosystem:

– Bet on a seed innovation that can lead to revolutionary products.

– Discover the right customer value proposition.

– Design a business that can serve the potential market.

A business ecosystem, like its biological counterpart, gradually moves from a random collection of elements to a more structured community. During Phase 1 of a business ecosystem, entrepreneurs focus on defining what customers want, that is, the value of a proposed new product or service and the best form for delivering it. Victory at the birth stage, in the short term, often goes to those who best define and implement this customer value proposition. From the leader's standpoint, in particular, business partners help fill out the full package of value for customers. And by attracting important "follower" companies, leaders may stop them from helping other emerging ecosystems.

The rise of the personal computer is a revealing example of ecological business development. In the early 1970s, a new technology – the microprocessor – emerged with the potential to spawn vast new applications and dramatically reduce the cost of computing. Yet this innovation sat dormant for several years. By 1975, hobbyist machines like the Altair and IMSAI had penetrated a narrow market. But these computers were not products that could be used by the average person.

Starting in the late 1970s, Tandy Corporation, Apple, and others introduced early versions of what would eventually become the personal computer. The seed innova-

263

tion they all chose was the microprocessor, but these first designers also recognized that other products and services had to be created to bring the whole package together. These ranged from hardware components to software to services like distribution and customer support.

Apple and Tandy each had a different strategy for creating a full, rich ecosystem. Apple worked with business partners and talked about "evangelizing" to encourage co-evolution. While the company tightly controlled its basic computer design and operating system software, it encouraged independent software developers to write programs for its machine. Apple also cooperated with independent magazines, computer stores, and training institutions – and even seeded a number of school districts with Apple IIs.

Tandy, on the other hand, took a more vertically integrated approach. It attempted to buy and then own its software, ranging from the operating system to programming languages and applications like word processors. The company controlled sales, service, support and training, and market development by selling exclusively through its Radio Shack stores. At the same time, it discouraged independent magazines devoted to its TRS-80 machines. Therefore, Tandy's simpler and more tightly controlled ecosystem did not build the excitement, opportunities, and inner rivalries of Apple's, nor did it harness as much capital and talent through the participation of other companies.

Tandy's approach got the company out front fast: in 1979, it had sales of $95 million compared with Apple's $47.9 million. However, Tandy's over-control of its ecosystem ultimately led to slower growth at a time when establishing market share and a large user base was essential to success. By 1982, Apple's $583.1 million in sales had decisively passed Tandy's $466.4 million.

Meanwhile, a third business ecosystem emerged in the early days of personal computing. It never rivaled Apple's or Tandy's in size, but it did help IBM enter the fray. This third ecosystem centered around two software companies: Digital Research and Micropro. In 1977, Digital Research made its software operating system CP/M available independent of hardware. That separation allowed almost any small manufacturer to assemble components and put out a usable personal computer. Overnight, a variety of small companies entered the business, building on the same Zilog microprocessor used in the early Tandy machines.

In 1979, Micropro brought out a word processor that ran on CP/M-based machines. Wordstar was the first truly powerful word processor, and it took an important group of potential PC customers – writers and editors – by storm. Demand for CP/M machines soared, fueling the growth if not the fortunes of small companies like Morrow and Kaypro.

But during the first stage of any business ecosystem, co-evolving companies must do more than satisfy customers; a leader must also emerge to initiate a process of rapid, ongoing improvement that draws the entire community toward a grander future. In the Apple and Tandy ecosystems, the hardware companies provided such leadership by studying the market, defining new generations of functionality, and orchestrating suppliers and partners to bring improvements to market. In the CP/M ecosystem, however, the hardware companies were bedeviled by rivalry among themselves. Infighting kept down prices and profit margins, and none of the CP/M companies could afford heavy advertising programs.

In phase 1, established companies like IBM are often better off waiting and watching carefully as a new market sorts itself out. The iterative process of trying out innovative ideas and discovering which solutions are attractive to customers is hard to accomplish in a traditional corporate culture. And the diverse experimentation that thrives in an entrepreneurial scene provides more "genetic diversity" from which the market can ultimately select the fittest offering.

reinventions, with capabilities to develop on various knowledge landscapes. Hargadon has also demonstrated that many successful innovations are the product of such ecosystems, and not of individual genius as popular legend would have it.[13]

Knowledge landscapes share several similarities with the concept of fitness landscapes, relevant to evolutionary (Darwinian) science. Species on fitness landscapes take "adaptive walks", thus climbing peaks to improve their chances of survival. Organizations on knowledge landscapes take "knowledge development expeditions", intentionally exploring for and developing new, potential knowledge. Firms, like species, co-evolve with business system members, including competitors, in a seemingly endless "knowledge race". To achieve and maintain "poise" in a knowledge landscape, four requirements have to be developed and sustained:

- *Identity requirements*
  Organizational identity is a reflection of the organization's nature in its knowledge landscape, e.g. its values and culture in a particular industry. Identity can be seen as a purposeful attractor, i.e. a defined range of possible states in which a firm can act in its pursuit of knowledge.

- *Exploration requirements*
  Poised firms climb and explore the dynamics of their landscapes, e.g. through experimentation, socialization, and structural coupling. They are aware of the risk of focusing too much on "climbing", which can lock into path dependency of single or a few peaks. Poised organizations are able to recognize new patterns and distinguish between large and small avalanches of change.

- *Co-evolution requirements*
  Engaging in external relationships, such as strategic alliances, enables an organization to explore different peaks on its knowledge landscapes, and, perhaps, even to discover entirely foreign, but relevant, knowledge landscapes. A poised organization is able to simultaneously explore distant parts of its fitness landscape, while continuing to climb its local peak by allowing itself to reconfigure its network of relationships.

- *Internal coherence requirements*
  The degree of internal coupling of organizational units must be recognized, i.e. the degree of interconnectedness between sub-units of the organization, and between these units and their environments. A high degree of interconnectedness could rigidify an organization's knowledge landscape, while a low degree of coupling could lead to idiosyncratic or selfish behavior, with each unit climbing its own peak. A poised organization resolves this issue of coherence by balancing the degree of coupling as may be necessary.

Co-evolving in various fitness landscapes (or business ecosystems) thus requires particular capabilities, and these should be understood and nurtured (see the earlier example of Microsoft).

Range of Tools for Application in the Process of Business Model Reinvention

In Figure 5.1 the wheel of business model reinvention with its four key dimensions and supporting capabilities was illustrated. Some of the tools applicable in each dimension of the wheel were indicated in Chapter 3 (Figure 3.3), in the context of levers to cultivate new mental space. This section provides a comprehensive outline of the categories and types of tools for application in each of the various key dimensions of the wheel of business model reinvention. Four important points need to be kept in mind when reviewing these tools:

a) The tools are not mutually exclusive to each dimension of the wheel, i.e. some tools such as 'communities of practice' (COPs) and 'open innovation' can be used in various (or all) dimensions.

b) The tools reviewed here are the major categories and types (the more well-known and accepted ones), and therefore do not purport to be exhaustive – in practice there are myriad of tools for value innovation.

c) The necessary organizational leadership 'supports' to enable managers to understand and use these tools effectively, such as appropriate organizational values, culture, structures, style (e.g., self-organization enhancements), facilitation of experimentation (e.g., mixing of 'long jumps' and 'short jumps'), and enabling 'deep smarts'[14] to arise, are the subject of Chapter 6.

d) The various tools are generically available for all types of business model reinvention, i.e. for both sustaining/incremental innovations (reinventing an existing business model), and disruptive innovations (reinventing/creating a new business model).

Table 5.4 provides an overview of the (interrelated) categories and types of tools for application in the process of business model reinvention, and each of the tools is subsequently discussed, with practical illustrations. The arrows in Table 5.4 indicate the interrelationships and multiple applications among the various tools. For this reason the various (12) tools are discussed separately and not in the context of one dimension of business model reinvention only.

1. New Customer/Market Space Tool

This tool provides a methodology to sense new customer benefits by looking not *within* the accepted customer needs and other existing industry boundaries (or norms), but looking systematically *across* them.[15] By doing so, managers find relevant new ecosystems and new needs that represent a real breakthrough in customer value. The methodology is illustrated in Table 5.5.

Table 5.4

Major categories and types of tools for application in the process of business model reinvention

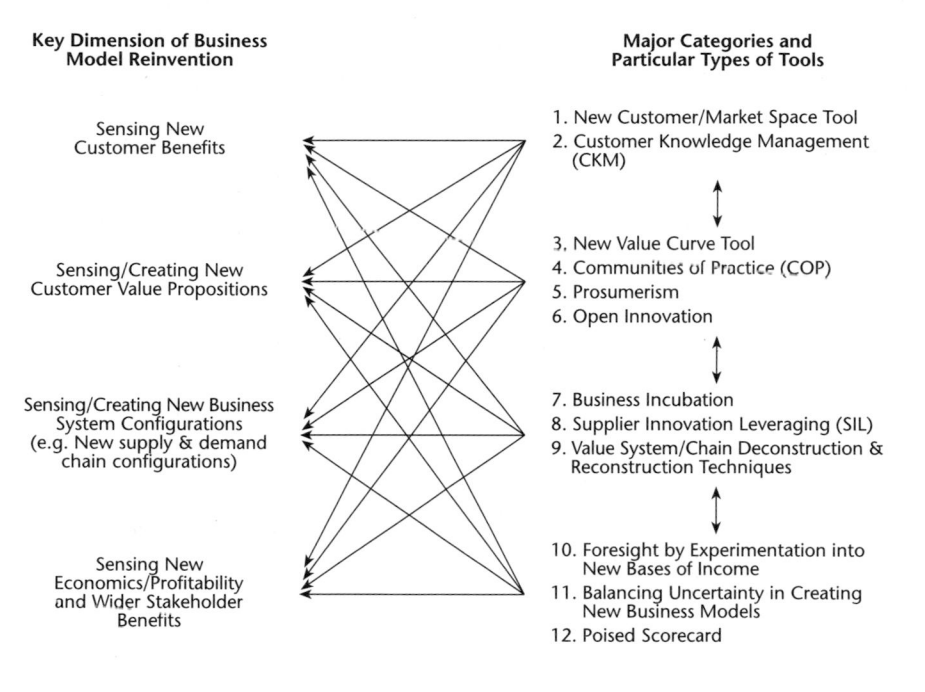

Key Dimension of Business Model Reinvention	Major Categories and Particular Types of Tools
Sensing New Customer Benefits	1. New Customer/Market Space Tool 2. Customer Knowledge Management (CKM)
Sensing/Creating New Customer Value Propositions	3. New Value Curve Tool 4. Communities of Practice (COP) 5. Prosumerism 6. Open Innovation
Sensing/Creating New Business System Configurations (e.g. New supply & demand chain configurations)	7. Business Incubation 8. Supplier Innovation Leveraging (SIL) 9. Value System/Chain Deconstruction & Reconstruction Techniques
Sensing New Economics/Profitability and Wider Stakeholder Benefits	10. Foresight by Experimentation into New Bases of Income 11. Balancing Uncertainty in Creating New Business Models 12. Poised Scorecard

Companies systemically pursue value innovation by looking across the conventionally defined boundaries of markets and competition – across substitute and/or potentially synergistic industries, across strategic groups, across buyer/customer groups, across complementary product and service offerings, across the functional-emotional orientation of the industry, and even across time (from the value delivered today to the co-shaped new value it might deliver tomorrow).

Consider one of these categories – the rethinking of the functional-emotional orientation of the existing industry concerning its markets: Competition in an industry tends to converge not only around an accepted notion of the scope of its products and services but also around one of two possible bases of appeal. Some industries compete principally on price and function based largely on calculations of utility; their appeal is rational. Other industries compete largely on feelings; their appeal is emotional.

Yet the appeal of most products or services is rarely intrinsically 'one or the other'. The phenomenon is a result of the way companies have competed in the past, which has unconsciously educated consumers on what to expect. Companies' behavior affects customers' expectations in a reinforcing cycle. Over time, functionally oriented industries become even more functionally oriented; emotionally oriented industries become even more emotionally oriented. No wonder market research rarely reveals new insights into what customers really want. Industries have trained customers in what to expect. When surveyed, they echo back: more of the same for less.

Table 5.5 Sensing and Creating New Market Space

Conventional Boundaries of Competition	Head-To-Head Competition		Creating New Market Space
Industry	Focuses on rivals within its industry	→	Looks across substitute industries
Strategic group	Focuses on competitive position within strategic group	→	Looks across strategic groups within its industry
Buyer/Customer group	Focuses on better serving the buyer/customer group	→	Redefines the buyer/customer group of the industry
Scope of product and service offerings	Focuses on maximizing the value of product and service offerings within the bounds of its industry	→	Looks across to complementary product and service offerings that go beyond the bounds of its industry
Functional-emotional orientation of an industry	Focuses on improving price-performance in line with the functional-emotional orientation of its industry	→	Rethinks the functional-emotional orientation of its industry
Time	Focuses on adapting to external trends as they occur	→	Participates in shaping external trends over time

Companies often find new market space when they are willing to challenge the functional-emotional orientation of their industry. Two common patterns have been observed: emotionally oriented industries offer many extras that add price without enhancing functionality; stripping those extras away may create a fundamentally simpler, lower-priced, lower-cost business model that customers would welcome. Conversely, functionally oriented industries can often infuse commodity products with new life by adding an ingredient of emotion – and in so doing, can stimulate new demand. Starbucks is a prime example of the transformation of a functional product into an emotional one, as displayed in the following box.

2. Customer Knowledge Management (CKM)

Most companies today consider themselves as market driven, or customer-oriented. Yet only a few companies are actually managing well their, perhaps, most precious resource: the knowledge *of*, i.e. residing in their customers, as opposed to knowledge *about* their customers.[16] By managing the knowledge of their customers, companies are more likely to sense emerging market opportunities before their competitors, to constructively challenge the established wisdom of "doing things around here", and to more rapidly create economic value for the corporation, its shareholders, and last, but not least, its customers. CKM is the strategic process by which cutting edge companies emancipate their customers from pas-

How Starbucks Transformed a Functional Product into an Emotional One

In the late 1980s, General Foods, Nestle, and Procter & Gamble dominated the U.S. coffee market. Consumers drank coffee as part of a daily routine. Coffee was considered a commodity industry, marked by heavy price-cutting and an ongoing battle for market share. The industry had taught customers to shop based on price, discount coupons, and brand names that are expensive for companies to build. The result was paper-thin profit margins and low growth.

Instead of viewing coffee as a functional product, Starbucks set out to make coffee an emotional experience, what customers often refer to as a "caffeine-induced oasis." The big three sold a commodity – coffee by the can; Starbucks sold a retailing concept – the coffee bar. The coffee bars offered a chic gathering place, status, relaxation, conversation, and creative coffee drinks. Starbucks turned coffee into an emotional experience and ordinary people into coffee connoisseurs for whom the steep $3-per-cup price seemed reasonable. With almost no advertising, Starbucks became a national brand with margins roughly five times the industry average. Today, Starbucks is a wireless-connected community meeting place bound together by the image and power of a global brand.

sive recipients of products and services, to empowerment as knowledge partners. CKM is about gaining, sharing, and expanding the knowledge residing in customers, to both customer and corporate benefit. It can be both qualitative and quantitative, relying on customer or salesperson comments or detailed transaction data. It can take the form of prosumerism, mutual innovation, team-based co-learning, communities of practice, and joint intellectual property (IP) management. These have been identified as five styles of CKM, which are distinctively different practices, but not mutually exclusive.[17]

At first glance, CKM may seem just another name for Customer Relationship Management (CRM) or Knowledge Management (KM). But customer knowledge managers require a different mindset along a number of key variables. Customer knowledge managers first and foremost focus on knowledge of the customer (i.e. knowledge residing in customers), rather than focusing on knowledge about the customer, as characteristic of customer relationship management. In other words, smart companies realize that corporate customers are more knowledgeable than one might think, and consequently seek knowledge through direct interaction with customers, in addition to seeking knowledge about customers from their sales representatives. Similarly, conventional knowledge managers typically focus on trying to convert employees from knowledge hoarders into knowledge sharers. This is typically done by intra-net based knowledge sharing platforms, Yellow Page initiatives, and so-called "ShareNets", i.e. platforms and tools that often have sophisticated functions such as urgent requests, or incentive systems that reward both the giver and taker of knowledge using a "miles and more approach".

Consider Amazon.com: The Internet retailer manages customer knowledge successfully through providing book reviews, the customer's own order histories, order history of other customers, and customized suggestions based on prior orders. Effectively, Amazon.com, a commercial enterprise, developed into a platform of book enthusiasts that are keen to exchange knowledge about their favorite topics (intrinsic motivation). Motivating customers to share their knowledge in the Amazon way is a remarkable achievement, particularly if contrasted with the often vain efforts to evangelize employees from egoistic knowledge hoarders to altruistic knowledge sharers by way of rewards systems that are mostly extrinsic. The book retailer's customers not only provide their insights, tips, and tricks in terms of book reviews, they also provide useful pointers for further reading on a given subject, giving a custom-tailored, non-intimidating impetus for other customers to investigate – and possibly buy – these sources. What is more, this customer knowledge can be shared with the authors of new books, giving them ideas for further publications and their market potential. This process bears all the hallmarks of KM: it provides useful information that is used in actions, creates sense, asks for interpretation, and leads to new combinations. Only, the knowledge is not that of the employee, but that of the customer, leading to value creation through innovation and growth, rather than to cost savings as is traditional. Clearly, Internet companies are at a competitive advantage when it comes to engaging in CKM, due to the Internet being a particularly cost-effective locus for such knowledge sharing. But CKM is not limited to successful Internet companies; 'brick and mortar' companies also do it. Indeed, Holcim, an international cement company that produces the very stuff brick and mortars are made of, is a keen customer knowledge management company (see Table 5.6).[18]

Traditionally, market research was used to shed more light on what the customer knew and thought about the product, and how this differed from what the company had to afford the customer, resulting in enormous CRM databases. More recently, firms thought they had found a new approach to access customer knowledge. Drawing on best practices from service companies, such as the big consulting businesses, most large organizations have instituted KM systems. These systems, however, are based on an indirect understanding of what customers want. KM systems are typically geared towards disseminating what their sales force or intermediary has understood from listening to the customers who bought – or did not buy – the company's products.

It is ironic that the conceptual predecessor of KM has surpassed its own offspring. Ten years ago, proponents of the resource-based view to strategy have proclaimed that a company be best conceptualized as a bundle of unique resources, or competencies, rather than as a bundle of product market positions. More recent contributions to the resource-based view question this one-sided thinking about the locus of competence.[19] It has now been claimed that such competence actually moved beyond corporate boundaries, and that it is therefore worthwhile to also look for competence in the heads of customers, rather than only in the heads of employees.

Similarly, CRM has been traditionally popular as a means to tie customers to the company through various loyalty schemes, but left perhaps the greatest source of

Table 5.6 How Holcim Cement applies customer knowledge management

Key area	General description	Benefits
Trouble-shooting	Online solutions to customer-related inquiries (i.e., cement- and concrete-related problems, strengths)	Reduced time to solve problems, savings in labor and materials if rework is prevented, increased satisfaction of concrete manufacturer's customer, enhanced reputation of cement manufacturer
Quality control & product optimization	Collection of test data, document submittal and approvals, mix design	Reduction in usage of cement, optimization of setting times, optimization of raw material resources (co-development of products), reduction of cement customer claims
Inventory/supply management	Automatization of the inventory and supply processes	Elimination of costly plant shut-downs for lack of cement
Purchasing	Enable customer to access HBK purchasing platform	Price reductions in raw materials, trucks, and equipment
Technical library	Comprehensive data warehouse on HBK core products	Easy access to rich sources of information of the cement manufacturer's knowledge base
Engineering consulting	Provide business services and expertise	Educating concrete manufacturers in business management will improve their efficiency
Promotions/ testimonials	Access to tools and information to "grow the pie"	Educating specifiers in concrete lifecycle costs will increase the adoption of concrete vs. other materials
Market information	Consolidation of micro and macro analysis of market information	Exposure of the concrete manufacturer to business opportunities and market tracking information

value under-leveraged: the knowledge residing in customers. While both KM and CRM focused on gaining knowledge about the customer, managing customer knowledge is geared towards gaining knowledge directly from the customer.

3. Creating a New Value Curve

The value curve – a graphic depiction of the way a company or an industry configures its offering to customers – is a powerful tool for creating new market space.[20] It is drawn by plotting the performance of the offering relative to other alternatives along the success factors that define competition in the industry or category.

To identify those alternatives, Intuit, for example, looked within its own industry – software to manage personal finances – and it also looked across substitute products to understand why customers chose one over the other. The dominant

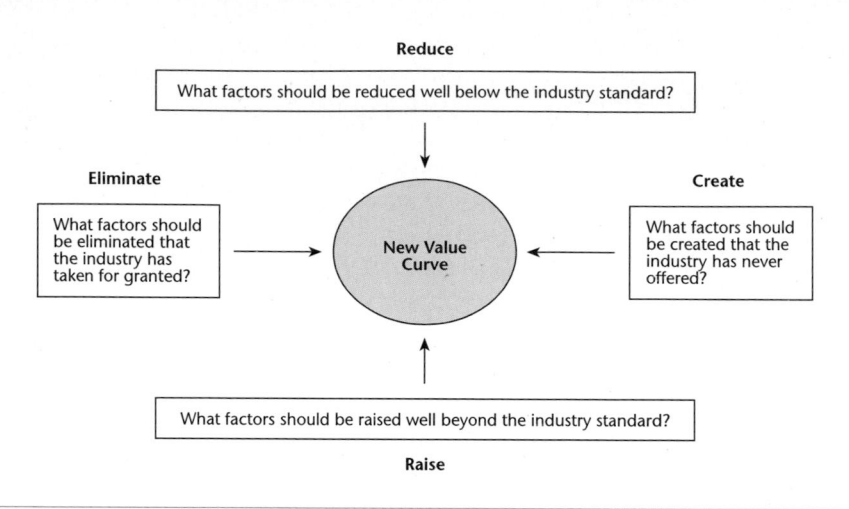

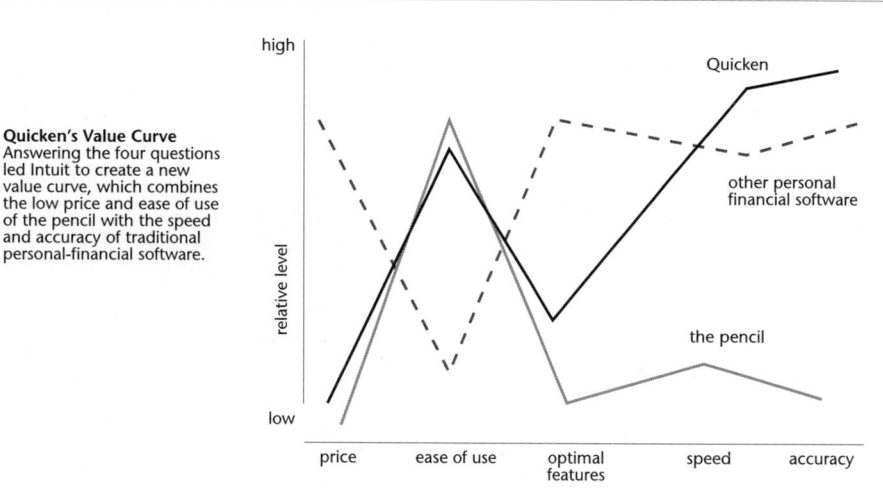

Figure 5.2 Discovering a new value curve

substitute for software was the lowly pencil. The value curves for these two alternatives map out the existing competitive space, as illustrated in Figure 5.2.

The software offered relatively high levels of speed and accuracy. But customers often chose the pencil because of its advantages in price and ease of use, and most customers never used the software's optional features, which added cost and complexity to the product.

Many of the well-known success stories of the past decade have followed this path of looking across substitutes to create new markets. Consider Federal Express and United Parcel Service, which deliver mail at close to the speed of the telephone, and Southwest Airlines, which combines the speed of flying with the convenience of frequent departures and the low cost of driving. Note that Southwest Airlines concentrated on driving as the relevant substitute, not other surface

Creating a New Value Curve: How Home Depot Created New Customer Benefits

In only 20 years, Home Depot has become a $24 billion business, creating over 130,000 new jobs in more than 660 stores. By the end of the year 2000, the company expected to have over 1,100 stores in the Americas. Home Depot did not achieve that level of growth simply by taking market share away from other hardware stores; rather, it has created a new market of 'do-it-yourselfers' out of ordinary home owners. There are many explanations for home Depot's success: its warehouse format, its relatively low-cost store locations, its knowledgeable service, its combination of large stores and low prices generating high volumes and economies of scale. But such explanations miss the more fundamental question: Where did Home Depot get its original insight into how to revolutionize and expand its market?

Home Depot looked at the existing industries serving home improvement needs. It saw that people had two choices: they could hire contractors, or they could buy tools and materials from a hardware store and do the work themselves. The key to Home Depot's original insight was understanding why buyers would choose one substitute over another. Why do people hire a contractor? Surely not because they value having a stranger in their house who will charge them top dollar. Surely not because they enjoy taking time off from work to wait for the contractor to show up. In fact, professional contractors have only one decisive advantage: they have specialized know-how that the home owner lacks.

So executives at Home Depot have made it their mission to bolster the competence and confidence of customers whose expertise in home repair is limited. They recruit sales assistants with significant trade experience, often former carpenters or painters. These assistants are trained to walk customers through any project – installing kitchen cabinets, for example, or building a deck. In addition, Home Depot sponsors in-store clinics that teach customers such skills as electrical wiring, carpentry, and plumbing.

To understand the rest of the Home Depot formula, now consider the flip side: Why do people choose hardware stores over professional contractors? The most common answer would be to save money. Most people can do without the features that add cost to the typical hardware store. They don't need the city locations, the neighborly service, or the nice display shelves. So Home Depot has eliminated those costly features, employing a self-service warehouse format that lowers overhead costs, generates economies of scale in purchasing, and minimizes stock-outs. Essentially, Home Depot offers the expertise of professional home contractors at markedly lower prices than hardware stores. By delivering the decisive advantages of both substitute industries – and eliminating or reducing everything else – Home Depot has transformed enormous latent demand for home improvement into real demand.

transportation such as buses, because only a minority of Americans travels long distances by bus. Another example is Home Depot, who has transformed latent demand for home improvement into real demand by customers whose expertise in home repair is limited (see box).

4. Communities of Practice (COPs)

Communities of practice (COPs) are groups of people informally linked across traditional boundaries by shared expertise, interests, and mutual enterprise passions, either physically (e.g., face-to-face meetings) or virtually (e.g., by email networks).[21] COPs complement existing organizational and network structures, and radically galvanize knowledge sharing, learning, and change across organizational and other boundaries.

COPs differ from other forms of organization in several ways, as illustrated in Table 5.7. From the table, it can be seen that the nature of COPs is informal. They organize themselves, meaning they set their own agendas and establish their own leadership, with membership being self-selected by individual sensing of contributions and benefits. Although COPs are fundamentally informal and self-organizing, they benefit from cultivation. To initiate COPs and cultivate them for ongoing effectiveness, managers should implement three related activities:

- Identify potential COPs that will enhance the organization and its business network's strategic capabilities, e.g.
  - Find commonalities of challenges and problems
  - Define a community's domain, i.e. area of expertise and forms of interest
- Provide the infrastructure that will support such communities, e.g.
  - Designate official sponsors and support teams
  - Invest time and money in support of COPs
  - Cultivate incentives for motivation and reward

Table 5.7 Communities of practice contrasted with other forms of organization

	What is the purpose?	Who belongs?	What holds it together?	How long does it last?
Community of practice	To develop members' capabilities; to build and exchange knowledge	Members who select themselves	Passion, commitment, and identification with the group's expertise	As long as there is interest in maintaining the group
Formal work group	To deliver a product or service	Everyone who reports to the group's manager	Job requirements and common goals	Until the next reorganization
Project team	To accomplish a specified task	Employees assigned by senior management	The project's milestones and goals	Until the project has been completed
Informal network	To collect and pass on business information	Friends and business acquaintances	Mutual needs	As long as people have a reason to connect

- Use non-traditional methods to measure value, e.g.
  - Review members' experience and success through interviews
  - Encourage conversations and mutual agreement on value created

For example, at both the World Bank and American Management Systems (AMS), senior management boards identify and sponsor COPs. Not all COPs at these organizations are successful (the World Bank at one point organized over 150 of them), but many of them have been. Support teams help with COP development and coordinate regular community conferences, knowledge fairs, library services, and technical support. A corporate university is also a method to initiate and coordinate COPs within a larger KM system for an organization or business network.

5. Prosumerism

Alvin Toffler[22] first used the expression "prosumer" to denote that the customer could fill the dual roles of producer and consumer. Such co-production is not new, e.g. Bosch develops engine management systems in co-production with Mercedes-Benz, who conceives and assembles the automobile. What is new is that knowledge co-production with the customer expresses itself in role patterns and codes of interactivity. For example, Quicken enables the customer to learn more about the available resources in financial services, thus creating options and a predisposition within the customer to rapidly tailor-make an offering in the future, also based on creatively suggesting new ideas and benefits.

The way IKEA, the living environment furniture retailer, presents itself to customers is all about co-production, about how benefits and activities have been reallocated between producer and customer. The CKM process in IKEA transforms the customer into a co-value creator, endowing him/her with new competencies and benefaction opportunities. It liberates the customer from the platform of only past, accumulated knowledge by stimulating him with a pattern of open-ended value-creating ideas, thereby effecting co-production and mutual new value-innovation evidenced in IKEA's furniture products and services. The tool involves pre-, concurrent- and post-production integration of customers, with integrated planning, control, and decision supply systems. Today, prosumerism is infiltrating diverse marketplaces, from restaurants where you assemble your own dinner, to medical self-care arenas, where you serve as doctor and patient, to any form of customization where customers have a role in the creation of the product.

6. Open Innovation

Recently there has been a fundamental shift in how companies generate new ideas and innovations and bring them to market. In the old model of closed innovation, firms adhered to the philosophy that successful innovation requires control and strict protection. In the new model of open innovation, firms sense and create innovations by deploying outside (as well as in-house) pathways to the market.[23]

In Chapter 3 (see Table 3.6), the contrasting principles and views of closed and open innovation were listed. These are based primarily on research results and

Industry Examples of a Shifted Locus of Innovation: From Closed to Open Innovation

Many industries – including copiers, computers, disk drives, semiconductors, tele-communications equipment, pharmaceuticals, biotechnology, and even military weapons and communications systems – are currently transitioning from closed to open innovation. For such businesses, a number of critically important innovations have emerged from seemingly unlikely sources. Indeed, the locus of innovation in these industries has migrated beyond the confines of the central R&D laboratories of the largest companies and is now situated among various startups, universities, research consortia, and other outside organizations. This trend goes well beyond high technology – other industries such as automotive, health care, banking, insurance, and consumer packaged goods have also been leaning toward open innovation.

Consider Procter & Gamble, the consumer-product giant with a long and proud tradition of in-house science behind its many leading brands. P&G has recently changed its approach to innovation, extending its internal R&D to the outside world through the slogan "Connect & Develop." The company has created the position of director of external innovation and has set a goal of sourcing 50% of its innovations from outside the company in five years, up from an estimated 10% this year. This approach is a long way from the "not invented here," or NIH, syndrome that afflicts many large, successful industrial organizations. Recently, P&G scored a huge success with SpinBrush, an electric toothbrush that runs on batteries and sells for $5. The idea for the product, which has quickly become the best-selling toothbrush in the United States, came not from P&G's labs but from four entrepreneurs in Cleveland.

P&G also tries to move its own innovations outside. Recently, the company instituted a policy stating that any idea that originates in its labs will be offered to outside firms, even direct competitors, if an internal business does not use the idea within three years. The goal is to prevent promising projects from losing momentum and becoming stuck inside the organization.

At the other extreme, some industries have been open innovators for some time now. Consider Hollywood, which for decades has innovated through a network of partnerships and alliances between production studios, directors, talent agencies, actors, scriptwriters, independent producers, and specialized subcontractors (such as the suppliers of special effects). The mobility of this workforce is legendary: Every waitress is a budding actress; every parking attendant has a screenplay he is working on.[24]

insights (see article at the end of this chapter by Henry Chesbrough). Specifically, the role of R&D needs to extend far beyond the boundaries of the firm, integrating their ideas, expertise and skills with those of others outside the organization.

A slowing of innovation from within large companies does not mean internal R&D should be dismantled; it is not a question of 'make or buy'. However, the open innovation approach poses new management demands. For one thing, companies need to think differently about how the opening of own laboratories to outsiders can create opportunities for technology exchanges that lead to revenue. Internal R&D produces intellectual property that other companies in the web of open innovation may covet. For example, IBM earned $1.9 billion revenue in 2001 from patent licensing and royalties on its software, chips, and systems.

The perspective of internal R&D must also change from depth to breadth and integration. Whereas old-school research labs developed new technologies from basic science to finished product, open innovation labs need to develop technologies that embrace and extend existing intellectual property – even those that are "not invented here." For example, DuPont now partners with biotechnology firms to develop such products as Sonora, a polyesterlike fiber made from corn and a genetically engineered bacterium. Automobile manufacturers do not try to reinvent the wheel; they partner with suppliers and research organizations to stay on top of such new technologies as fuel cells and continuously variable transmissions. Automakers still do internal R&D, but their in-house teams work on how to integrate the technologies they see emerging, using open innovation approaches.

Chesbrough provides a classification of four types of organizations that primarily *generate* innovation: innovation explorers, innovation merchants, innovation architects, and innovation missionaries. Furthermore, he names two types of organizations that are focused on *commercializing* innovation: innovation marketers and one-stop innovation centers. Finally, he suggests two types of organizations focused primarily on *funding* innovation: innovation investors and innovation benefactors. These categories and types are useful, and their application is illustrated in the enclosed article by Chesbrough.

Firms have been focusing their activities into one or more of these three primary areas, based on the principles of open innovation, thereby exploring which external innovation capabilities could synergize with internal innovation capabilities to create and capture new market-feasible value innovation. This involves a business ecosystem orientation, i.e. beyond their traditional industry focus. In order to select among these sources and types of innovation, firms need a sourcing strategy for innovation which identifies the innovation channels on which it is going to focus, and the external relationships it will put energy into maintaining.[25]

7. Business Incubation (Networked Incubators)

The key distinguishing feature of a networked incubator is that it has mechanisms to foster partnerships among start-up teams and other business entities, thus facilitating the flow of knowledge and talent across companies and forging relationships among them.[26] Incubators exploit networking by providing fledgling companies with preferential access to potential partners and advisers. The two critical characteristics are: a) networking is institutionalized, and b) networking leads to preferential access, but not preferential treatment. This is illustrated by Ford's ConsumerConnect networked incubator (see box).

Networked incubators combine the benefits of two diverse worlds – the scale and scope of large established organizations and the entrepreneurial drive of small venture-capital firms, as illustrated in Table 5.8. However, there are also pitfalls: networking may become a slogan rather than a reality, and the incubator may impede the entrepreneurial drive of start-ups by taking too much equity and imposing stringent rules. Entrepreneurs who prefer doing everything themselves might easily become frustrated in an organization that expects networking.

Table 5.8 Benefits of Networked Incubators in Comparison to Established Companies and Venture Capitalists

	Established Companies	Venture Capitalists	Networked Incubators
Scale and Scope *leveraging size and reach in order to lower costs by pooling resources and spreading them across units*	*High* Historically the key advantage of large global companies	*Low* VC-backed start-ups are left alone to obtain services and buy supplies	*Medium* Common services and pooling of resources ensure some benefits, especially time savings
Entrepreneurial Drive *stimulating individuals to pursue risky and disruptive innovations*	*Low* Red tape hinders new ventures; entrepreneurs are not rewarded	*High* Entrepreneurs are free to pursue ventures and own large equity stakes	*High* Entrepreneurs are free of red tape and own equity in ventures
Network Access *forging partnerships, obtaining advice, and recruiting people*	*Medium* Many established companies have some, but not extensive, contacts with Internet companies	*Low* A VC partner may have an excellent personal network, but it doesn't go beyond the individual partner	*High* Organized and active networking among portfolio companies and strategic partners

Ford's ConsumerConnect Networked Incubator in 2001

Business incubators are not just for venture capitalists and Silicon Valley-style entrepreneurs. Ford established an incubator to speed the process of creating and developing Internet businesses. Called ConsumerConnect, the group provides new e-business ventures with basic services, operational and strategic advice, and networking connections with existing Ford businesses. The main purpose of ConsumerConnect is to find new ways to leverage Ford's assets in the new economy, including the company's vast customer base and huge purchasing power.

For example, consider the venture Covisint, an on-line B2B exchange for the auto industry that was formed as a joint venture among Ford, General Motors, Daimler-Chrysler, and Renault/Nissan. By connecting Ford's US$80 billion purchasing volume with Covisint, ConsumerConnect instantly made the start-up a large and viable business.

When setting up ConsumerConnect, Ford executives followed two organizational design principles to ensure that the incubator would work effectively with existing business while promoting entrepreneurial drive. First, they established the group as an independent but powerful entity – ConsumerConnect CEO Brian Kelley has direct access to Ford CEO Jacques Nasser. Second, the incubator was staffed with people from both inside and outside Ford. This mixture combined intimate knowledge of Ford's businesses with a fresh entrepreneurial drive, thus encouraging the creative leveraging of existing assets in new e-business ventures.

Two organizational practices help executives to avoid the potential pitfalls of networked incubators, namely portfolio design and network design.

- Portfolio design: A high-performing networked incubator creates a portfolio of relevant companies and advisors that incubatees can leverage. When enlisting a set of related strategic partners, the difficulties of traditional conglomerates with highly diversified portfolios are avoided.

- Network design: To institutionalize networking, the goal is to establish connections and relationships that are anchored to the incubator rather than to particular individuals. This can be done by the creation of formal links to external experts, bringing outside experts on site, scheduling regular meetings, implementing economic incentives, and hiring specialized deal brokers.

8. Supplier Innovation Leveraging (SIL)

In some respects, the practice of supplier innovation leveraging is a counterpart or complementing tool to customer knowledge management. However, its uniqueness lies in the purposeful acceptance of supplier organizations to co-locate within a principal producing company. The Honda company has been a chief proponent of this innovation tool, as displayed in the following box.

How Honda America Leverages Supplier Innovations

To leverage the capabilities and technology of its suppliers in research and development programs, Honda has developed a process called Design In, which focuses directly on early supplier involvement. Honda will "invite" guest designers – as many as 100 at a time – from its outside supplier organizations to locate within Honda's facilities and work side by side with resident engineers, designers, and technologists in the very early stages of a new project.

Mr. Baker, CEO of Honda America, believes that this process is critical to ensuring that Honda will successfully integrate the best thinking and the latest technology into its new products. He says: "Our focus on building cooperative relationships requires getting the outside designers' input at the very beginning of a project, while we're still in the planning phase for the vehicle. By involving these suppliers early on, we can pick up their latest technology to make sure we're integrating it into our vehicle."

On major strategic systems, where the technology is evolving and the cost implications are large, Honda develops technology road maps and shares them with suppliers. Mr. Baker says: "We use the technology road map to show our critical suppliers the direction we're going in and to ask them to help us. We set high expectations for focused and targeted project management. And, because our development schedule is very compressed, we expect suppliers to make their latest technology available to us and to keep up with us to get the final product to market." Reaffirming Honda's central focus on the customer, Mr. Baker says, "We're very much a product organization, focused on making the product better for the customer. We work best with suppliers who view product development as a strategic process – suppliers who can target and develop technology and apply it in sync with us."[27]

9. Business Value System/Chain Deconstruction and Reconstruction Techniques

Managers dealing with co-evolving coalitions of diverse economic players that do not respect traditional industry boundaries differ sharply from traditional managers in their ability to deconstruct traditional value system configurations (supply and demand chains) and to reconstruct (or reconfigure) new value systems. Over time, a community of innovative value system stakeholders co-evolve their roles and capabilities, and tend to align themselves to leading companies.

The deconstruction of an integrated (traditional) value chain does more than transform the structure of a business or an industry – it alters the sources of competitive advantage. Connectivity and networking in the innovation economy drive this trend – it presents threats to established businesses, but also opportunities to innovators. The framework in Table 5.9 provides examples of types of deconstruction and reconstruction, as part of value system reconfiguration activities.[28]

The new emerging success stories in supply-chain management are companies that have combined new and innovative supply chains with new market approaches. The resulting breakthrough business models have allowed such companies to achieve superior financial results and dominate their industries. Two well-known examples are Dell and IKEA: IKEA offers a compelling counterexample to Dell's direct model. Whereas Dell uses a responsive build-to-order capability with no finished product inventory to dominate competitors who use a build-to-stock policy, IKEA uses a build-to-stock approach with increased product inventory to dominate slow build-to-order competitors.

Often the business breakthrough occurs in the following way: The company and chain initially focus on reducing cost; at some point, however, they discover that there is a bigger opportunity related to addressing a market need. They may conceive of a different way to go to market – to interact with customers – that drives them to implement a new supply chain that, together with the new go-to-market strategy, creates better value for the customer. They also may find that as they improve supply-chain information sharing and coordination, they have new access to information that either has value in the marketplace or can be used to change their business model.

Two major steps are required.[29] First, deconstruction will occur. The companies that function as intermediaries in the supply chain will seek to re-establish their

Table 5.9 Reconfiguring business value systems and intermediaries

	Maintaining Traditional Members	Spawning New Members
Same Network Organization	Traditional Deconstruction	Substitution (e.g. Amazon.com)
Reinvented Network Organization	Innovative Deconstruction (e.g. Auto-by-Tel)	Innovative Reconstruction (e.g. Dell Computers)

roles, business models, and value propositions. Companies, such as contract manufacturers, logistics-service providers, and distributors, will encounter one another as they compete to provide customers with assortment on the basis of product, place, and time. They will increasingly need to balance the leveraging of processes and assets across customers with the creation of differentiated solutions for individual customers.

Second, re-branding and construction will occur. Companies along and across the chain will vie for control of the customer relationship. They will find that when value propositions derive from supply-chain capabilities, new co-branding and co-positioning strategies may be most effective. For example, as IBM co-branded with an Intel or as L.L. Bean co-branded with a FedEx, many supply-chain partners may find co-branding an extremely effective way to present products and services to the customer.

10. Foresight by Experimentation into New Bases of Income

Any new business model must eventually be profitable, i.e. financially viable. Besides that overriding long term requirement, new business models often change the bases (or ways) of obtaining income. Foresight into new bases of income derives mainly from experimentation, i.e. testing of new business models and their new value-innovation income bases in the market place.

How 7-Eleven Innovates Customer Value and New Business Income with Suppliers

Some of 7-Eleven's outsourcing relationships tie suppliers' financial interests to its own. The company took an equity stake in Affiliated Computer Services, for instance, one of its major IT outsourcers. 7-Eleven also agreed to share productivity gains from a services agreement with Hewlett-Packard. In an even deeper collaboration, the company created a joint venture with prepared-foods distributor E.A. Sween: Combined Distribution Centers (CDC) is a direct-store delivery operation that supplies 7-Elevens with sandwiches and other fresh goods. By drawing on the skills and scale of a specialist, 7-Eleven was able to cut its distribution costs from more than 15 percent of revenues to 10 percent and eventually hopes to cut that figure in half again. But cost reduction is only a secondary benefit. The real gains have come in service. When it owned its own distribution network, 7-Eleven delivered fresh goods to its stores only a couple of times a week. CDC now makes deliveries to stores once, and soon twice, a day. More frequent deliveries mean fresher products, which draw more customers into the stores.

By almost any measure, 7-Eleven's sourcing strategy has transformed the company. In narrowing its focus to a small, strategically vital set of capabilities – in store merchandising, pricing, ordering, and customer data analysis – the company has reduced its capital assets and overhead while streamlining its organization. It reduced head count 28 percent from 43,000 in 1991 to 31,000 in 2003 and flattened its organizational structure, cutting managerial levels in half from 12 to six. Importantly, suppliers also benefit financially through productivity and efficiency gains.[30]

The earlier example of Encyclopedia Britannica (see Chapter 4) is relevant here, as companies in the innovation economy often fail to notice that their asset and income base has (or is) shifting from traditional tangible assets and customer value to an intangible asset and customer value base. Before the early 1990s, Encyclopedia Britannica's main assets were its sales force and quality of knowledge in its printed encyclopedias and year books. It did not realize (or foresee) that its traditional assets would become meaningless due to a new business model based on technological innovation and rapid customer acceptance. Furthermore, it was unimaginable to management that their core value (or product) could eventually be given "free" to customers purchasing a portable computer system.

Experimentation with one or more new business models, even forming early alliances with members of other industries (i.e., other business ecosystems), would have gained invaluable insights and foresights for the company. Experimentation often comes after business incubation, when a new business model with new value propositions is tested (with co-evolving partners' involvement) in the market place.

11. Balancing Uncertainty in Creating New Business Models

In the turbulent innovation economy, managers should develop awareness, interpretation and appropriate responses to at least four levels of uncertainty.[31] These responses serve as the filter for responding appropriately to the paradoxical questions of shape or adapt, focus or diversify, acting now or later, and use traditional tools or new systemic tools. The four levels of uncertainty are:

Level 1:   *Clear enough future*: Single view of the future.

Level 2:   *Alternative future*: Limited set of possible future outcomes, one of which will occur.

Level 3:   *Range of futures*: Range of possible future outcomes.

Level 4:   *True ambiguity*: No range of possible future outcomes.

As a rule of thumb, new business shaping activities (disruptive innovation seeking) make the most sense when uncertainty is high, since it can be influenced by an organization's actions. When confronting a future that seems clear enough to predict, strategists have traditionally favored new business adapting activities (sustaining/incremental innovation seeking) geared to the existing industry. Yet even the previously most stable business environments are susceptible to periodic bouts of upheaval. Shaping activities at the lowest level of uncertainty intentionally seeks to create chaos out of order – for example, Federal Express reshaped the sleepy mail-and-package delivery industry. Shaping activities in more uncertain environments attempts to lower the level of uncertainty, thereby creating new order out of chaos.

As executives face their shape-or-adapt choices, they must weigh factors beyond the level of residual uncertainty – factors such as the external market environment and the company's capabilities and aspirations. Shaping activities, for example, makes most sense in markets that offer strong first-mover advantages. One market that they may find challenging is Internet-based commerce, which, by its very nature, invites comparison shopping, thus perhaps undermining one of the most important potential first-mover advantages: brand and customer loyalty.

The following box provides an illustration of how Qualcomm attempts to balance uncertainty and benefits.

How Qualcomm Attempts to Balance Uncertainty and Benefits

Qualcomm has been trying to move the wireless-telephone industry toward its CDMA (Code Division Multiple Access) technology. CDMA, a technical standard that determines how information travels and communicates through a wireless network, is competing with other technologies to become the industry standard for next-generation mobile phones.

Qualcomm realizes that if it wants to shape the industry, it must build a coalition of supporters around the CDMA technology. This approach involves cutting deals with wireless companies to get them on board and convincing consumers that CDMA is superior. To win the standards battle, Qualcomm must be totally committed to the cause or at least look as though it were. If the company tried to hedge its bets by producing chips for a competing technology as well – something such as an adapter might do – it would undoubtedly undermine its shaping efforts. How could Qualcomm convince its potential partners that CDMA was superior if it simultaneously invested in competing standards?

As the story of Qualcomm illustrates, under uncertainty, shaping actions is often at odds with adapting ones. Shape or adapt is therefore a real choice for most companies most of the time. But how, amid rising uncertainty and ever greater risks, can a company nail down the right strategic choice? (See below for pointers).

An essential starting point is to understand the alternatives of shaping and adapting strategies. Shapers generally attempt to get ahead of uncertainty by driving industry to change their way. Some, like Qualcomm, aim to increase the probability that a preferred technology or business process will become an industry standard. Others grapple with uncertainty by introducing fundamental product, service, or business-system innovations intended to redefine the basis of competition in an industry: think of the low-price, point-to-point air travel model of Southwest Airlines, Dell Computer's direct-sales approach, or Netscape Communications' breakthrough Internet browser, Navigator.

Adapters, by contrast, take the existing and future industry structure and conduct as given. When a market is stable, adapters try to define defensible positions within the industry's existing structure. When high uncertainty prevails, they attempt to win through speed and agility in recognizing and capturing new opportunities as the market changes. They might quickly follow a potential shaper's lead, as Compaq Computer did when it bet on Microsoft and Intel with early alliances in the 1980s.

In practice, however, executives facing high uncertainty are often biased in favor of adapting strategies. Part of the problem is a reliance on strategic-planning tools and processes that are ill suited to highly uncertain business environments. Standard tools such as Porter's 'five-forces' industry analysis framework, discounted cash-flow models, and core-competency diagnostics may provide deep insight into untapped strategic opportunities that may arise in rapidly changing ones. Without such foresight, it is not surprising that companies favor adapting strategies; after all, successful shaping strategies require executives to define the future they are trying to create.

This reality implies, paradoxically, that shaping strategies in the most uncertain environments may involve higher returns and lower risk than these strategies do in situations with lower residual uncertainty. If you believe in a new industry standard, for example, and are willing to invest in its development, your creation could well serve as a "touchstone" that others react to. You would, in fact, be bringing some order to a market in chaos: if your company was a credible player in the industry, your commitment might well persuade others to commit themselves as well. Your belief in the new standard may set off a chain of events that creates a self-fulfilling prophecy. The credibility of Netscape's management team, for example, was a key factor in its successful attempt to set new standards for Internet browsers when it first launched Navigator.

12. Poised Strategy Scorecard (PSC)

The well-known balanced scorecard (BSC) popularized by Kaplan and Norton[32] focuses on measuring the performance of an enterprise in financial/profitability terms, with concurrent measuring of the underlying causal factors – customer satisfaction, business process, and learning and growth capabilities. Initially developed as a measuring tool, the BSC has also been refined as a very useful strategic management tool, utilizing an organizational mapping approach of its four key dimensions and their strategic integration. The deficiencies of the BSC as a tool for strategic management in the innovation economy reside in its focus on a single organization, the analytical and hierarchical process implied, the failure of

Table 5.10 A Poised strategy scorecard in comparison to the balanced scorecard

Dimension	Balanced Scorecard Focus	Poised Strategy Scorecard Focus
Financial	Improve organizational shareholder value	Improve network stakeholder value and balance multiple business model profitability
Customer	Improve customer satisfaction and relations for the organization	Improve customer success and customer partnerships in the network
Business processes	Optimize particular internal business processes	Robustness and resilience of business network processes, both competitive and collaborative
Learning and growth	Continuous organizational learning and growth	Systemic knowledge & innovation management

most organizations to relate the different domains of the scorecard to each other,[33] and the implicit assumption of the existing industry parameters.

For poised strategic management, in its focus on sensing new profitability potentials of multiple business models in collaborative business networks, a poised scorecard (PSC) becomes necessary. Table 5.10 compares the BSC with a PSC.

Poised strategy scorecard (PSC) broadens the BSC into a company's business ecosystem, with concurrent measurement of the financial performance and underlying causal dimensions of various business models, as existing or emerging in collaborative business networks. It is systemic in the sense of looking across industries and the corporation's business models, while also viewing the four key dimensions as non-linear and non-hierarchical. Obviously, this tool relates closely to the previous tool of viewing various levels of uncertainty, business model types, and financial and other outcomes.

Conclusion

This chapter illustrated, by way of theory and practical business examples, that a new holistic process of strategic management, based on a poised strategy approach, can be put in place to cope effectively with the demands of the innovation economy. The contrasts between the traditional strategic management process of 'analysis – formulation – implementation – change' and the new process of 'business ecosystem sense-making – business model reinvention – business model and strategy options – strategy thrusts – enabling capabilities' are stark and sobering.

The traditional analytical, mechanistic, and existing industry orientation has to be replaced by a holistic, dynamic, and business ecosystems orientation – and this means business model thinking, multiple business models to cope with various levels of uncertainty, and reinvention (or creation/construction) of business models in new business ecosystems that emerge through co-evolving activities.

The chapter offered a number of *processes* and a range of *tools* for poised strategic management in the innovation economy: the process of sense-making of the ecosystem was discussed in four key phases of ecosystem evolution and their particular process requirements, and three tools to make sense of ecosystem dynamics were presented. Furthermore, the concept of a business model and its reinvention process were outlined as a 'wheel of business model reinvention', with four key dimensions and particular process characteristics. Finally, the major categories and types of tools for application in the business model reinvention process were highlighted, with descriptions and practical business examples. The various approaches, processes, and tools for poised strategic management pose particular challenges for traditional business leadership and management capabilities. These are the subject of Chapter 6.

To end this chapter, it is useful to address two key questions that arise: are the traditional approaches, processes, and tools for strategic management still relevant; and does one have to differentiate between tools for respectively incremental (sustaining) innovation and disruptive innovation?

The answer to the first question is a firm no, even though many companies still use the traditional methods for strategic management and apparently are still successful. However, the contention and evidence provided by this book, especially the fundamental changes due to the innovation economy and their impact on traditional business models – and the consequent necessity for business model reinvention and their organizational diversity – make it critically important to adopt a poised strategy approach, centered on multiple business model co-development and management. The point is that traditional approaches to strategic management most often lead only to sustaining (incremental) innovation and not disruptive innovation, making the use of traditional strategic management approaches and tools inadequate for long term survival. Even if a firm considers itself as a 'follower' in an industry, it still needs to be able to anticipate and co-shape disruptive changes in its industry for survival in the innovation economy.

The answer to the second question is also negative: all of the approaches, processes, and tools discussed as part of poised strategic management are equally applicable to existing (traditional) business model adaptation as they are to new (reinvented, innovative) business models. The world has irrevocably changed from one based on mechanistic mindsets only, to one of holistic mindsets. These issues and questions are further addressed in Chapter 6, when looking at leadership and managerial capabilities that include mindsets, approaches, and skills.

Six Keys to Creating New-Growth Businesses[*]

By Clayton M. Christensen, Michael E. Raynor, and Scott D. Anthony

How better decision making can help address the innovator's dilemma.

Managers today have a problem. They know their companies must grow. But growth is hard, especially given today's economic environment where investment capital is difficult to come by and firms are reluctant to take risks. Managers know innovation is the ticket to successful growth. But they just can't seem to get innovation right.

When companies keep improving their existing products and services to meet their best customers' needs, they eventually run into the "innovator's dilemma." By doing everything right, they create opportunities for new companies to take their markets away. Established companies historically have struggled when trying to create new markets. Success seems fleeting and unpredictable.

Recent research indicates these problems are systemic. Most companies that are started fail. Of those that succeed, most cannot sustain robust growth for more than a few years. Companies need a way to unlock the process of innovation and create innovation-driven growth businesses again and again. How can managers increase the probability that their decisions will lead to success? Now more than ever, managers need robust theories – statements of what causes what, why, and in what situation – to guide their decision making around innovation.

Managers typically grow impatient when we tell them this. "Theory?" they say. "That sounds like *theoretical*. That sounds like *impractical*." But theory is eminently practical. Managers are the world's most voracious consumers of theory. Every plan a manager makes, every action a manager takes, is based on some implicit understanding of what causes what and why.

The problem is, managers all too frequently use a one-size-fits-all theory. But the ground beneath them inevitably shifts. Strategies that worked so wonderfully in the past no longer suffice.

Drawing on the work of a number of thoughtful researchers as well as our own work, we are exploring a set of theories that can help managers respond to the ever-changing circumstances in which they find themselves. Specifically, these six lessons will help managers make the right decisions to successfully build new growth businesses.

---

[*] Taken with permission from *Harvard Management Update* Vol. 8 No. 1, 2003, pp. 3-6

Disruptive Innovations Spur Growth

Companies have two basic options when they seek to build new-growth businesses. They can try to take an existing market from an entrenched competitor with *sustaining* innovations. Or they can try to take on a competitor with *disruptive* innovations that either create new markets or take root among an incumbent's worst customers. Our research overwhelmingly suggests that companies should seek out growth based on disruption.

Sustaining innovations, whether they involve incremental refinements or radical breakthroughs, improve the performance of established products and services along the dimensions that mainstream customers in major markets historically have valued. Examples: a microprocessor that enables personal computers to operate faster and a battery that lets laptop computers operate longer.

Companies march along a performance trajectory by introducing successive sustaining innovations – they must to remain competitive in the short term. But, as noted in *The Innovator's Dilemma: When New Technologies Cause Great Firms to Fail* (Harvard Business School Press, 1997), firms innovate faster than our lives change to adopt those innovations, creating opportunities for disruptive innovations. Although sustaining innovations move firms along the traditional performance trajectory, disruptive ones establish an entirely new performance trajectory.

Disruptive innovations often initially result in worse performance compared with established products and services in mainstream markets. But disruptive innovations have other benefits. They are often cheaper, simpler, smaller, and more convenient to use.

Consider the small off-road motorcycles introduced by Honda in the 1960s, Apple's first personal computer, and Intuit's QuickBooks accounting software. These innovations all initially underperformed the mainstream offerings. But they brought a different value proposition to a new market context that did not need all of the raw performance offered by the incumbent. They all created massive growth; to flip Joseph Schumpeter's famous phrase, *creative destruction*, on its head, this is *creative creation*. After taking root in a simple, undemanding application, disruptive innovations inexorably get better until they change the game, relegating previously dominant firms to the sidelines in often stunning fashion.

Incumbents almost always win battles of sustaining innovations. Their superior resources and well-honed processes are almost insurmountable strengths. Incumbents, however, almost always lose battles where the attacker has a legitimate disruptive innovation. To create a new-growth business, companies – established incumbents and start-ups alike – must be on the right side of the disruptive process by launching their own disruptive attacks.

Disruptive Businesses either Create New Markets or Take the Low End of an Established Market

There are two distinct types of disruptive innovations. The first type creates a new market by targeting nonconsumers, the second competes in the low end of an established market.

In a *new-market* disruption, attackers take root in a new "plane" of competition or a new context of use outside of an existing market. Consumers historically locked out of a market because they lacked the skills or wealth welcome a relatively simple product that allows them to get done what they had always wanted to get done. These markets typically start out small and ill defined. They don't meet the growth needs of large companies. And the incumbent feels no pain at first. Because it creates new consumption, the disruptor's growth doesn't affect the incumbent's core business. But as the innovation improves, it begins to pull customers away from the incumbent. And the incumbent doesn't have the ability to play in this new game.

Transistors were a disruptive innovation. Mainstream suppliers of tabletop radios, which were made with vacuum tubes, couldn't figure out how to use transistors because they couldn't initially handle the power requirements of these components. Then in 1955, Sony introduced the pocket radio. It was a static-laced product with horrible fidelity. But it enabled teenagers to do something that they couldn't before – listen to rock'n'roll out of their parents' earshot. Had Sony targeted consumers in established markets, the pocket radio would have bombed. But for teenagers, the alternative to a Sony pocket radio was no radio at all. By competing against nonconsumption, Sony set a very low technical hurdle for itself: the product just had to be better than nothing in order to find delighted consumers.

The second type of disruptive innovation takes root among an incumbent's worst customers. These *low-end* disruptions do not create new markets, but they can create new growth. The disruption of integrated steel mills by steel minimills demonstrates how low-end disruptors harness what we call asymmetries of motivation.

Minimills first took hold in the steel industry in the mid-1960s. They were very efficient. They had a 20% cost advantage over integrated mills. But the quality of the steel they produced was inferior. The rebar market at the bottom rung of the industry (rebar is small steel bars made from scrap and used to create reinforced concrete) was the only market that would accept the minimills' steel.

The process for identifying and shaping disruptive businesses relies more on pattern recognition than on market-driven analysis.

As the minimills entered the rebar market, the integrated mills were happy to exit it. Their gross margins in the rebar business were a mere 7%, and rebar accounted for only 4% of the industry's tonnage. So the integrated mills decided to focus on higher-profit steel products. The minimills made boatloads of money until they finally drove the last of the integrated mills out of the market – and then the price of rebar dropped 20%, because rebar had essentially become a commodity market. The minimills' reward for victory was that none of them could make money.

To make attractive money again, the minimills had to figure out how to make better-quality steel in larger shapes – not only angle iron but also thicker bars and rods. Profit margins in this market tier were 12%, almost double those of the rebar market; the overall market was also twice as large. So the minimills invested in equipment to make the larger pieces and worked to improve the quality and consistency of their steel. As the minimills began making inroads with better and bigger steel, the integrated mills were happy to exit this market tier to concentrate on more profitable products. When the last integrated mill left the market, the price of angle iron collapsed. Once again, the minimills had to move up to the next tier of the industry in order to survive. And so on.

At each stage of the minimills' climb up-market, an asymmetry of motivation was at work. For the minimills, the need to enter a more profitable market provided the motivation to solve the technological hurdles preventing them from producing higher-quality steel. The integrated mills were happy to leave these markets because the lower tiers in their product mix were always less profitable than products targeting higher-end customers. Eventually, of course, the integrated mills ran out of markets to flee to.

Disruptive Opportunities Require a Separate Business-Planning Process

All innovative ideas start out as halfbaked propositions. They then go through a shaping process as they wind their way through the organization to reach senior management. When firms have a single process for all the various forms of innovation, what comes out the other end of the process looks like what has been approved in the past, and it all looks like sustaining innovations.

Consider IBM's efforts to introduce voice-recognition software. Early iterations of IBM's ViaVoice software package featured IBM's "ideal" customer on the front: an administrative assistant sitting in front of her computer, speaking into a headset. It is easy to see why IBM targeted such customers. They constituted a large, obvious market, well aligned with IBM's needs and capabilities. But think about IBM's value proposition to this woman. She types 80 words a minute and almost never makes a mistake. IBM was telling her, "Why don't you change your behavior and use a system that gives you *lower* accuracy and *slower* speeds. We promise future releases will get better." The only way to attract great typists would be for voice recognition to be faster and more accurate than typing. This is a very high technical hurdle.

Where has voice-recognition technology begun to take off? Kids love the ability to tell their animated toys to "stop" or "go." "Press or say one" menu commands are another obvious application. In these contexts, people are delighted with a crummy voicerecognition product. Another good market for the technology may be all those executives you see standing in airport lines, trying to punch messages into their BlackBerries.

Their fingers are too big to enable accurate typing – they'd be more than happy with a voice-recognition algorithm that's only 80% accurate.

Not surprisingly, disruptive ideas stand a small chance of ever seeing the light of day when they are evaluated with the screens and lenses a company uses to identify and shape sustaining innovations. Companies frustrated by an inability to create new growth shouldn't conclude that they aren't generating enough good ideas. The problem doesn't lie in their creativity; it lies in their processes.

Only by creating a parallel process for developing and shaping disruptive ideas – one that acknowledges their distinctive features – can companies successfully launch disruption after disruption. Such a process relies more on pattern recognition than on datadriven market analysis. After all, markets that do not exist cannot be analyzed. Even when numbers are available, they are never clear.

An intuitive process can still be rigorous if managers use the right tools. For example, discovery-driven planning lets you create a plan to test assumptions; aggregate project planning helps you allocate resources between sustaining and disruptive opportunities; the "schools of experience" theory informs hiring decisions.

Don't Try to Change Your Customers – Help Them

Faulty market segmentation schemes help to explain the stunningly high rate of failure of new-product development. Most companies define markets in terms of product categories and demographics. We just don't live our lives in product categories or in demographics. When companies segment markets this way they often fail to connect with their customers.

Instead of designing products and services that dictate consumers' behavior, let the tasks people are trying to get done inform your design.

How do we live our lives? During the course of the day, problems arise, jobs we need to get done. We look around to hire products to get those jobs done. Products that successfully match the circumstances we find ourselves in end up being the real "killer applications." They make it easier for consumers to do something they were already trying to accomplish.

Some manufacturers pushed digital cameras based on the value proposition that they made it easy to edit out the red eyes from all your images and create an online album of your best photos. Research shows, however, that 98% of all photos get looked at only once. Only the most conscientious of us prioritized editing images or creating albums. Where digital camera makers found success was in marketing their products to consumers who used to order double prints of their photos and mail them to relatives. The digital technology enables consumers to use the Internet to do more easily what they already wanted to do.

A business plan predicated upon asking customers to adopt new priorities and behave differently from how they have in the past is an uphill death march through knee-deep mud. Instead of designing products and services that dictate consumers' behavior, let the tasks people are trying to get done inform your design.

Integrate Across Whatever is not Good Enough

One critical decision firms face when creating an innovation-driven growth business is determining its optimal scope. Specifically, which activities need to be managed internally and which can be safely outsourced?

The answer often is driven by the fad of the day. During the 1960s, everyone thought IBM's integration was an unassailable point of competitive advantage. Because IBM controlled such a wide swath of the industry's value chain, it could make better products than anybody else. So companies copied IBM and tried to integrate. In the 1990s, everyone thought that Cisco's disintegrated business model that made extensive use of outsourcing was an unassailable point of competitive advantage. So companies jumped on this new bandwagon and sought to disintegrate.

The critical question is: What are the circumstances in which my firm should be integrated and what are the circumstances in which my firm can be a specialist? Integration provides advantages whenever a product is not good enough to meet customer needs. Proprietary, interdependent architectures allow companies to run multiple experiments, pushing the frontier of what is possible. Engineers can reconfigure their systems to wring the best performance possible out of the available technology.

Think about the computer industry. In its early days, you simply couldn't exist as a specialist provider. There were too many unpredictable interdependencies across every interface in the first mainframes. The manufacturing process depended on the design of the computer and vice versa. The design of the operating system affected the design of the logic circuitry. IBM had to be integrated across the entire value chain to produce a mainframe that came close to meeting its customers' needs.

By contrast, the modular architectures that characterize disintegration always sacrifice raw performance. Stitching together a system with partner companies reduces the degrees of design freedom engineers have to optimize the entire system. But modular architectures have other benefits. Companies can customize their products by upgrading individual subsystems without having to redesign an entire product. They can mix and match components from best-of-breed suppliers to respond conveniently to individual customers' needs.

But even in a modular architecture, successful companies still are integrated – just in a different place. Consider the computer industry in the 1990s. The computer's basic performance was more than good enough. What did customers want instead? They wanted lower prices and a computer customized for their needs. Because the product's functionality was more than good enough, companies like Dell could outsource the subsystems from which its machines were assembled. What was not good enough? The interface with the customer. By directly interacting with customers, Dell could

292

ensure it delivered what customers wanted – convenience and customization. Value flowed to Dell and to the manufactures of important subsystems that themselves were not good enough, like Microsoft and Intel.

In short, companies must be integrated across whatever interface drives performance along the dimension that customers value. In an industry's early days, integration typically needs to occur across interfaces that drive raw performance – for example, design and assembly. Once a product's basic performance is more than good enough, competition forces firms to compete on convenience or customization. In these situations, specialist firms cmerge and the necessary locus of integration typically shifts to the interface with the customer.

Be Patient for Growth but Impatient for Profitability

Managers inside new-growth businesses often feel tremendous pressure to quickly ramp up sales volume. But disruptive businesses can't get big very fast. The only way to make them grow quickly is to cram them into large, obvious markets. In established markets, customers don't care about the disruptive innovation's strengths. They only care about its weaknesses. This is a recipe for disaster, and one reason why company-backed disruptive ventures can have a leg up. Venture capitalists have become increasingly impatient for businesses to get huge. As long as their core businesses are growing healthily, companies will find it easier to wait for the disruptive businesses to find a foothold market and slowly build commercial mass.

Managers must be patient for growth but impatient for profitability. When you are willing to put up with a lot of losses before a disruptive business turns profitable, that means you are trying to lay the foundation for a huge new business. Insisting on early profitability pushes the new disruptive business to find the markets where its unique capabilities will be uniquely valued. Forced to keep its fixed costs low, the new business can serve small customers who would not meet the needs of a high fixed cost structure.

Managers in large companies who read The *Innovator's* Dilemma may have finished the book thinking they're destined to fail, no matter what they do. We hope to shift their sentiment from despair to hope. If managers understand the theories of innovation, they have the ability to create newgrowth businesses again and again.

Architectural Innovation and Modular Corporate Forms*

By Charles D. Galunic and Kathleen M. Eisenhardt

Based on an intensive and inductive study of a Fortune 100 corporation, this article describes how dynamic capabilities that reconfigure division resources – that is, architectural innovation – may operate within multibusiness firms. We suggest envisaging corporate divisions as combinations of capabilities and product-market areas of responsibility (charters) that may be recombined in various ways, highlighting the interplay of economic and social imperatives that motivate such recombinations. We detail the microsociological patterns by which such recombinations occur and then theorize about an organizational form, termed 'dynamic community,' in which these processes are embedded.

Based on an intensive and inductive study of a Fortune 100 corporation, this article describes how *dynamic capabilities* that reconfigure division resources – that is, architectural innovation – may operate within multibusiness firms. We suggest envisaging corporate divisions as combinations of capabilities and product-market areas of responsibility (charters) that may be recombined in various ways, highlighting the interplay of economic and social imperatives that motivate such recombinations. We detail the microsociological patterns by which such recombinations occur and then theorize about an organizational form, termed "dynamic community," in which these processes are embedded.

A view of corporations that emphasizes innovation and the creation of value within changing markets is emerging (e.g., Bartlett & Ghoshal, 1993; Boisot, 1988; Boisot & Child, 1999; Brown & Eisenhardt, 1998; Guth & Ginsberg, 1990). Although efficiency and control are still important, the spotlight is on flexibility, creativity, and timing. Central to this view is an emphasis on dynamic capabilities (e.g., Amit & Schoemaker, 1993; Conner & Prahalad, 1996; Eisenhardt & Martin, 2000; Henderson, 1994; Henderson & Clark, 1990; Lazonick & O'Sullivan, 1995; Teece, Pisano, & Shuen, 1997; Winter, 1987). Broadly defined, dynamic capabilities are the organizational and strategic processes by which managers manipulate resources into new productive assets in the context of changing markets.

---

* Taken with permission from *Academy of Management Journal* Vol. 44 No. 6, 2001, pp. 1229-1249

A growing number of studies have examined dynamic capabilities; these include studies of knowledge transfer (e.g., Galunic & Rodan, 1998; Leonard-Barton, 1992; Szulanski, 1996; Zander & Kogut, 1995), integrative capabilities (e.g., Brown & Eisenhardt, 1997; Henderson & Cockburn, 1994; Henderson, 1994; Iansiti & Clark, 1994), and product innovation processes (e.g., Dougherty & Hardy, 1996; Eisenhardt & Tabrizi, 1995; Gersick, 1994; Henderson & Clark, 1990). This research is contributing exciting insights into dynamic capabilities, but several issues remain. First, the authors of a good portion of this work assume the existence of dynamic capabilities but do not focus on the specific microprocesses and roles that form these capabilities. Second, an implicit economic logic that optimizes between firm capabilities and market needs is assumed, and so important social imperatives are neglected; readers are led to believe that economic reasoning, without social logic, underpins these phenomena. Finally, little attention is paid to how dynamic capabilities and organizational structures can combine to constitute new organizational forms (Ciborra, 1996; Lewin & Volberda, 1999).

In this work, we explore dynamic capabilities by focusing on the corporate-level processes by which multibusiness firms reconfigure their resources – that is, architectural innovation at the corporate level (cf. Eisenhardt & Brown, 1999; Galunic & Rodan, 1998; Henderson & Clark, 1990; Sanchez & Mahoney, 1996). More broadly, we offer a view of the modern corporation as a *dynamic community*, focusing on the modularity of corporate resources, the processes (particularly the sensibilities or logics) by which these resources are dynamically reconfigured as markets and corporate players (business divisions) coevolve, and the broader organizational form that this may constitute. In particular, we emphasize a view of the corporation as a social community, where dynamic capabilities are based on communal imperatives (such as encouraging the weak, rewarding the loyal, adhering to conceptions of fairness even while tolerating competition and conflict, and rescuing the distressed) rather than on purely economic reasoning (such as optimizing the technical fit between markets and resources to ensure rent maximization) (cf. Goold, Campbell, & Alexander, 1994).

The research setting was a large, multibusiness corporation that competes in a variety of technology-based industries (computing, electronics, and telecommunications) and engages in frequent resource recombinations among its divisions. Specifically, the executives of this corporation routinely transfer product-market domains of responsibility among operating divisions in order to create better matches between these product-market areas and divisional resources. For example, a division that has been responsible for the personal computer business could find this responsibility passed to another division and itself be given responsibility for laptop computing. This process – commonly known in this firm as "charter changes" – frequently realigns the match between divisional resources (the relatively stable skill sets and administrative systems of a division) and evolving product-markets, yielding new combinations of resources and product-market contexts. Critical to this process is the concept of "charter." Our informants defined a charter as the product-market domain in which a division actively participated and for which it was responsible within the corporation; for instance, they referred to the "hand-held computing charter," the "high-end printing charter," and the "video and wideband charter."[*1] One manager said it best:

> A charter is really a time-dependent concept, since it is not something that remains forever with the division. Generally, it is a statement of purpose. It includes the task, market, and the customer the division is concerned with. It also tells you something about how the division is linked to the rest of the company, but these things can change.

As this informant noted, charters were fluid and tradable. Moreover, the result of this frequent realignment of divisions and their charters was the creation of "novel services" from existing divisional resources (Penrose, 1959). By frequently revisiting the corporate architecture as markets and divisions coevolved (that is, by patching divisional resources with charters), this charter change process became an important dynamic capability at Omni, a corporation that has consistently, for over two decades, achieved superior profitability among high-technology firms worldwide.

Our research into this capability conveys a story of a corporation as a dynamic community of businesses. In particular, our data suggest that these processes are shaped by both social and economic logics – corporate actors simultaneously consider these imperatives and weigh their implications for the charter change at hand. Our data also emphasize the inherent tensions that this highly dynamic and adaptive organizational form must balance: modularity and relatedness, competitiveness and cooperation, and order and disorder.

As is typical of inductive research, our account begins with a description of our grounded theory building methodology. We then present our findings for the three patterns. We conclude with a discussion of our findings on charter gains and outline a theory of this organizational form, linking modular structures, corporate culture, dynamic capabilities combining economic and social logics, and managerial roles as constituting what we term a dynamic community.

Methods

The research design is based on multiple cases of the focal event, charter change events, allowing a replication logic whereby we used each case to test emerging theoretical insights (Yin, 1989). This method allows for a close correspondence between theory and data, a process whereby the emergent theory is grounded in the data (Eisenhardt, 1989; Glaser & Strauss, 1967).

This article is the result of an 18-month field study of charter changes in ten divisions, eight domestic and two foreign, of a large corporation based in the United States. Omni Corporation (a pseudonym) is a Fortune 100 high-technology firm whose interests lie across a wide, but related, spectrum. Business areas include electronic instrumentation, computing-information technology (IT), and computer peripherals. The

---

* [1] The notion of a divisional charter resembles the concept of organizational domains (Levine & White, 1961; Thompson, 1967). An organizational domain consists of the goods or services an organization provides and the markets or populations it serves and is similar to the divisional charters we found in Omni. We retain the word "charter" since it was used within the firm.

corporation is divided into several strategic groups, each containing multiple and related divisions. Each division is treated as a profit center and holds global strategic and operational control over its business. Divisions are distinguished according to product dimensions, market dimensions (defined by type of customer, such as commercial or consumer, not by geography), and technological dimensions. Table 5.11 (page 320) lists the divisions studied and describes the case data.

Divisions were selected for study according to the following criteria: (1) They had experienced one or more recent charter changes or else were currently undergoing a charter change. (2) They were from different strategic groups, so that variability in business contexts was increased. And (3) each was matched to at least one other division in its group for comparison.

The unit of analysis was the charter gain experienced by a focal division. A charter gain occurred when a division obtained a product-market area of responsibility that was either new to the corporation or transferred from another division. Data were collected through interviews, questionnaires, observations, and company archives. The main source was semistructured individual interviews. Informants (86 in all) included the corporate vice president responsible for each group to which a studied division belonged, each general manager (one per division), functional managers (multiple managers for each division), and lower-level project managers. Interviews were conducted during site visits to every division. Informants were briefed beforehand regarding the scope of the research, and the vast majority of the interviews were tape-recorded and transcribed. Notes regarding each interview were written within 24 hours of the interview. Interviews typically lasted 90 minutes, although some went on for several hours.

Data analysis used familiar approaches for inductive studies (Eisenhardt, 1989; Glaser & Strauss, 1967; Miles & Huberman, 1984; Yin, 1989). Analysis began with detailed written accounts and schematic representations of each charter gain process. After constructing the case histories, we conducted within-case analyses, which were the basis for developing early constructs surrounding charter gains as experienced by divisions. Cross-case analysis produced our working framework of the charter gain process.

Results

Gaining Charters at Omni Corporation

How do divisions gain new charters at Omni Corporation? We found three distinct patterns of charter gain, each of which made different use of the raw material for recombination – the modular, loosely coupled, yet related, business divisions. In the first pattern, *new charter opportunities*, changes at the industry level created new market, and thus new charter, opportunities. But, rather than apportion charters to the strongest and best-performing divisions, Omni executives used industry changes as an opportunity for the corporate family to encourage and develop weaker divisions. In the second pattern, *charter wars*, gaining divisions attacked other divisions that were weakened by their increasingly poor fit with the business needs of a charter. This pattern highlighted interdivisional competition; rather than simply encouraging a beleaguered division to go through an organizational change process to recover fit, Omni executives allowed other divisions to vie for the troubled charter. Although the process was clearly a competitive one, the gaining divisions had also displayed cooperation and loyalty in the recent past. In other words, superior skills, performance, and fit were important, but so too was good corporate citizenship. In the third pattern, *charter foster homes*, corporate-level actions were highlighted as senior executives rapidly searched for safe havens in which to temporarily store orphaned charters. These moves gave corporate executives more time to consider the eventual fate of these charters while at the same time they recognized the gaining divisions as trustworthy and reliable citizens of the corporate community.[*1] Table 5.11 (page 321) provides an overview of the recombination patterns we observed.

Collectively, our data reveal remarkable attention to social logic in this process. This was surprising, given the popularity of portfolio- and economics-focused perspectives in the treatment of multibusiness firms (Goold et al., 1994; Henderson, 1979). Scholars have treated multibusiness firms as exercises in opportunity maximization whose chief thrust is to best align corporate resources with market opportunities. Roughly, in the context of charter change events, the focus would be on optimally matching business divisions (given their competencies and trajectories) with extant business charters. To be sure, economic reasoning was an important and often visited logic at Omni. After all, gaining divisions had to be able to execute the charters, performing above some standard of fitness, for Omni to survive. However, it was neither the only logic nor the more important. Social logic also was at work, as evidenced by rules for encouraging underprivileged divisions (new charter opportunities), rewards for cooperation and loyalty embedded within rules for conflict and competition (charter wars), and rules for rescuing the distressed and recognizing steady performers (foster homes for charters). Here, divisions needed to be rewarded for helping the corporation and to be given opportunities to refresh their skills in charters where they might more effectively create productive assets. In other words, charter gains always involved economic and social arguments. Sometimes these arguments reinforced one another, better clarifying the decision at hand. But sometimes the arguments suggested different alternatives, and so corporate executives weighed both perspectives to make a judgment. Indeed, the picture that emerged was one of corporate actors simultaneously and continuously juggling these logics, immersed in both an economic, business-minded

---

[*1]In previous research (Galunic & Eisenhardt, 1996), we focused on one aspect of this charter change process by examining how divisions lose charters, focusing on the link between charter losses and the life cycle stage of these businesses. But this work on charter losses explored neither the contrasting side, reconfigurations (charter gains, with their distinct patterns), nor the wider theoretical implications (the social imperatives) and the broader modular form this patching process represents. Nonetheless, there are links between losses and gains. Although they are far from perfect mirror images (our data suggest losses and gains have a life of their own), start-up losses sometimes went with foster home gains (as well as simply being discarded and/or being contested by more openly rivalrous divisions); growth losses sometimes went with new charter opportunity gains (as well as being spun off to form completely new divisions; also some gains were not previously part of other divisions' portfolios; and maturity losses often went with charter wars gains. Together, these works should provide a more complete picture of recombinations.

reality and a communal, familial world. In the long run, both logics are needed to explain the evolution of this corporation. But, in the short run, juggling the two logics, as managers made judgments about how compelling each logic was for the charter change decision at hand, defined the day-to-day reality of the charter changes that we observed.

Finally, each pattern displayed three key forces at work: *industry context* (exogenous competitive environment), *interdivisional dynamics* (business trajectories and capability sets of other divisions), and *corporate influence* (corporate executives). These three forces were useful categories in our understanding of the data and are used in our presentation of the patterns.

New Charter Opportunities: Market-Driven Gains

One pattern of gains occurred when new opportunities for business creation emerged in the marketplace. These gains involved Omni's adding charters to existing divisions in order to attack these novel product-market opportunities. The process was characterized by: (1) industry-level emergence of new strategic opportunities, (2) constrained and modestly performing gaining divisions, (3) other divisions that were equally or sometimes better able to execute the opportunity, but were not chosen, and (4) orchestration of these charter gains by corporate executives. The sample for our study of market-driven gains consisted of these divisions: Mission, Spark, Voyageur, and Quest.

Industry context: Emergent business opportunities. Corporations in dynamic markets inevitably encounter new business opportunities as markets emerge, expand, collide, and diverge. This was the situation surrounding several of Omni's divisions that experienced charter gains.

A good example was Mission. Here a niche emerged in the printing industry, at a lower "price point" than Mission occupied. Mission had been providing a high-end printing product that catered to a very specialized and professional customer base. A fellow division had been providing a low-end offering to the small-business segment. The base technology of these products was much simpler and far less feature-oriented than that of Mission's products. A niche emerged in the middle product range (or the mainstream corporate office printing segment), where less customization than Mission offered was needed, but many more features, greater durability, and better performance than the low-end product offered were required. Mission was given the charter to attack this opportunity emerging in the gap between the two current businesses. As the corporate executive in charge of Mission's business group summarized:

> Sometimes you can work so hard to [to reduce overlaps between divisions] that you leave this gap that a truck can drive through, and in this case that is what happened ... in our attempt to eliminate overlap we end up with a good deal of "underlap" and a big gap for someone, a competitor, to come in and establish a position.

Another example was Voyageur. This division was closely involved in the development of a new imaging technology. The new opportunity was to take this technology and merge it with another to develop a new business. Corporate managers recognized that if Voyageur's technological stream were combined with another technology emerging within Omni (a networking technology), a new business could be developed. Although there was no existing charter for this business opportunity, managers saw market potential for a new business. Voyageur subsequently gained the charter to integrate these two technologies and to create that business.

On the surface, the confluence of new market opportunities and suitable divisions explains these gains. Gaining divisions had market and/or technical competencies that could be effective in realizing these new opportunities. But our data also reveal that this simple explanation is not complete. It does not, for example, explain why Omni executives did not form a new division to handle these new opportunities. Even more surprising, it does not explain why these opportunities were given to these divisions and not to others, some of which were better-performing and better-positioned (from technical and/or market knowledge points of view) candidates. In other words, economic reasoning alone was insufficient to predict how charter changes played out. Although, on the surface, it appeared that the gaining divisions were successful simply because the new charter opportunities matched their skill sets and held promise for rent generation, there were other, more socially informed, selection dynamics at work.

Interdivisional dynamics. In every case, the gaining divisions had a distinct profile in addition to simply having market and/or technical relatedness to the new charter area. These divisions can be labeled "trapped and languishing performers." They (1) were modest to weak performers in their current charter areas, (2) often faced constraints on their existing charters, and (3) were desperate for growth.

First, these divisions were experiencing performance problems, such as falling sales growth and pressure on profit margins, that were typically brought about by shrinking market growth and/or heightened competition. For example, in the cases of Spark and Mission, losses were mounting as these divisions experienced difficulty competing with competitors' lower-priced products. Low morale and agitation for change were typical in these divisions. As two Spark managers noted:

> Performance was pretty crummy really.
>
> Spark was a pit. It was the worst place in the group ... morale was absolutely abysmal on practically every count and a record was set for negative responses [in an employee survey].

Mediocre performance, however, was not simply the result of poor management. Existing charter boundaries often constrained these divisions. In the case of Voyageur, performance problems were exacerbated by limits on charter growth imposed by its position in the firm. The charter was being squeezed by the growth paths of other divisions. In particular, another division had control over a substitute technology that was capturing the low and middle ends of Voyageur's product range, inhibiting its managers from expanding. Moreover, their focal (high-end) marketplace was shrinking, causing managers to feel trapped within their current charter. As one manager grimly noted, "You were with the losing team over here – great market share and "downward" growth!" So, managers welcomed a new charter opportunity as a way of reviving their languishing division.

Managers at Quest, Spark, and Mission were similarly constrained. For example, Mission managers complained that their charter was focused on a "niche market" (professional graphic design). Although initially lucrative and high-growth, this relatively focused market was quickly saturated, and Mission became "a large fish, but in a small pond," as one manager noted.

Finally, the desire of these managers to find somewhere to expand reflected the strongly growth-driven and competitive culture within Omni. As one Quest manager summarized:

> Everybody was encouraged to find growth opportunities. That was the driver.

New charter opportunities, moreover, were doubly enticing for these troubled divisions. They were not only a way to revive growth immediately, but also an impetus to build new competencies that could spur further growth. Such new opportunities were the way to get into the winner's circle at Omni. One corporate executive summarized this sentiment:

> I think the best for Omni was, in a lot of people's mind, to get aggressive and to treat [new charter opportunities] like it was a real start-up operation that tried to make something different happen ... it was a lot of people's shot at making something big happen.

On the whole, therefore, charter gains went to slumping divisions that could use these new businesses to restore performance, revitalize languishing skills, and build new skills that would be relevant for "growing" the new charter. This was their opportunity to get back onto the success track.

In every case of an emergent business opportunity, there were other divisions that could have executed the new charter and, in some cases, were on the way to doing so. They all had relevant technical and/or market capabilities. Sometimes their fit was even better than that of the gaining division. Yet these other divisions were typically running highly successful, fast-growing businesses that limited their managerial "bandwidth." The fact that these divisions were running at full "charter capacity" meant that their managers probably did not have the time to fully focus on and exploit the new opportunities. Moreover, from the corporate point of view, it was crucial that these divisions remain focused on their booming businesses in order to improve their odds of success in these highly attractive markets. Finally, there was a strong shared sense that these divisions were opulent and so could afford to "let some scraps fall from the plate."

For example, both Quest's and Voyageur's charters were originally being developed at Saturn. Saturn was the poster child of the computer peripherals business group; much larger and more successful than Quest and Voyageur, Saturn had widely acknowledged strength in product development and marketing. Reflecting on their recent successes in the marketplace for printing equipment, one Saturn marketing manager stated:

> Nobody was in our league!! We didn't have any competition ... People were totally blown away. Competitors came out with products that were twice if not three times our price, and the retailers who had them literally took them off the

floor the next day. It was an unbelievable time for all of us here. I wish I had written a book because it was really a fascinating time.

On the whole, there was a strong sense that whatever Saturn touched turned to gold – a few respondents referred to Saturn as the Mecca of Omni. One Voyageur manager stated:

> They [Saturn] have so much clout in the industry and within [our group] and within Omni ... You got people on that staff who are "kick butt" kind of people and when they want to go on and do something, they're going to go do it, you know, and "damn the torpedoes, full speed ahead."

However, it was also true that Saturn – a multibillion-dollar business – recognized that its "plate was full."

> We were one big business ... We knew something was going to happen if we overloaded this. (Saturn manager)

> It was an interesting idea for Saturn, but they have lots of opportunities that just fall off the plate – while [this charter] looks like a healthy morsel to us, it is a pittance to them. (Quest manager)

Moreover, Saturn managers, following their successes, adopted a relatively benevolent attitude toward smaller divisions and these charters, providing no real contest for these business areas. Reflecting on why a new business opportunity had left Saturn, their general manager noted:

> We put it alone because it needed more focus. Plus Dale [the future manager] needed a job [laughter]. Very synergistic.

Corporate executives: Entrepreneurs and equalizers. One could imagine that corporate executives would play a relatively late role in efforts to seize emergent market opportunities. Division managers, who are usually close to customers and technologies, would seem more likely to spot new opportunities, jump in, and exploit them. Only later, one might think, would these managers turn to corporate executives for approval. In fact, this was not the case. Instead, corporate executives typically recognized these new product-market opportunities early on and then drove the process to implant them within the corporation; in many cases, these opportunities would have otherwise been lost.

In the case of Quest, for example, the corporate executive was the first manager to spot the new charter opportunity and its growth implications for the firm. His concern for the future of Quest and his perceptiveness regarding the marketplace pushed him to become a key proponent of the ensuing charter gain. As one Quest manager stated:

> [Our corporate executive] was deeply involved all the way through the project ... because it was his baby. It was his idea originally. He drove the dates, he drove just getting the thing out and testing it.

This corporate executive later noted that "what keeps me up at night are new growth areas and new technologies – along with paranoia over changing markets and fear of competitors." His contribution was creative thinking about new business opportunities, not simply control and oversight of divisional ventures and performance. This was crucial because divisions were often simply too busy with their immediate opportunities to fully grasp the significance of new ones.

Similarly, at both Spark and Voyageur, the corporate executive helped envision the new business opportunities and then led the charge to have responses installed. This executive nicely summarized this process:

> The way it develops is a convergence of several things that happen. One, is you look at your range of opportunity – or the fact that you need to pursue another business more effectively than you're doing today – so there's an opportunity that exists. Second, you usually have a situation where a management team or a division is overloaded or lacks focus and therefore that opportunity is not being served. Then, the third issue is that the skills or culture [of the gaining division] match [the new charter opportunity] that needs to exist. So, when those three things kind of occur, you then decide to make a charter change.

Summary: New charter opportunities. In sum, the presence of busy and successful divisions alongside needy and constrained ones, combined with entrepreneurial corporate executives, informed this pattern of charter gains. Surprisingly, although these were Omni's plum opportunities for the future, the gains went to recently unsuccessful divisions, not the high performers. The high performers were often busy, visibly overprivileged, and appropriately focused on their burgeoning empires. As such, they were willing to let their smaller neighbors in on some of the action. Corporate executives encouraged this equalization of opportunities, effectively taking charters that would have made as much or more technical and/or market sense within large, winning, and proven divisions and placing them within the underprivileged and underutilized. As managerial growth theories suggest (e.g., Marris, 1979; Marris & Wood, 1971; Penrose, 1959), fallow managerial resources and skills, along with concentrated penchants for expansion (contained within "quasi firms" [Marris, 1979: 75]), are powerful drivers of growth. Moreover, the symbolic statement behind these charter gains was unequivocal: the weak, underprivileged, and underutilized within Omni should be encouraged and equipped to grow and add value, even if it meant allowing important future growth areas to be managed by historically weaker (although by no means inadequate) divisions. Thus, although economic reasoning was not eschewed – all the divisions considered for these charters met some minimum standards of acceptability and fit – social imperatives provided a powerful impetus to the recombinations, giving a clear sense of direction and meaning to these moves.

Charter Wars: Battle within the Corporate Community

A second pattern of charter gains occurred when rival divisions successfully attacked and captured established charters from other divisions. These gains involved highly competitive processes that were simultaneously fueled by the gaining divisions' desire for more "turf" and the losing divisions' growing misfits with their businesses. Overall, this pattern (labeled "charter wars" by one informant) was characterized by: (1) industry-level shifts in the basis of competition within established markets, (2) the presence of aggressive and better-positioned gaining divisions, which had labored successfully as good corporate citizens, (3) losing divisions that failed to adjust to their shifting markets, and (4) corporate executives playing relatively minor roles at the ends of the processes. Data on these battles came from three divisions: Goliath, Stealth, and Plunder.

Industry context: Shifts in established markets. Over time, the basis of competition within markets often shifts as technologies become standardized, saturation occurs, customer preferences change, price competition emerges, and so forth. Such shifts happened often in Omni's markets.

For example, for Plunder (which produced computers), the proliferation of standardized technologies and related "open system" standards drove down cost structures in the industry. These changes also brought more price-based competition, punctuated by the occasional price war. As prices fell, the various firms within the industry also introduced new distribution channels (from direct sales forces to dealer channels), which again emphasized lower costs. In the other cases (Stealth and Goliath), their markets shifted, respectively, from competition based upon technological innovation to a greater emphasis on superior manufacturing, and from military to commercial buyers. The changing market conditions played to the strengths of Goliath, Stealth, and Plunder.

On the surface, therefore, these charter gains are simply stories of divisions becoming more fit in changing markets and so winning new turf. But again, this simple explanation does not capture the full story. Why did these divisions seek growth by actively "going to war" to capture charters from faltering divisions? Arguably, the aggressive focal divisions could have sought completely new business opportunities. Alternatively, the plundered divisions could have improved, fought back, and won. Or other divisions that were also well-positioned for the charter could have won. So, especially in light of the communal logic that was so apparent in the previous pattern, why did these divisions attack sister divisions, and how did they succeed?

Interdivisional dynamics. Over time, the actions taken by Goliath, Stealth, and Plunder managers played a crucial role in their capture of neighboring charters. These gaining divisions, which we characterize as "fit for battle," had three common characteristics, (1) a capability trajectory that fit the changing market conditions well, (2) successful performance in an existing and often very modest charter that evidenced good corporate citizenship, and (3) an aggressive and effective general manager.

The gaining divisions were all well-suited to take over the evolving business areas. First, there was significant relatedness between the charter areas of the focal divisions and the losing divisions, either horizontal relatedness (complementary products in the same industry, in the case of Goliath) or vertical relatedness (different generations of products within a product-line, in the cases of Stealth and Plunder). This relatedness was an important antecedent to the charter movements because moving well-established charters from their homes required that the gaining divisions be able to effectively manage them and to maintain business momentum. In general, some relatedness in resources and skills (technical competencies, market knowledge, experience with distribution channels) was a prerequisite in any charter change, but it was particularly important in this pattern, where the businesses were well-established and the gaining divisions would have to "hit the road running."

The relatedness of the gaining divisions with the sought-for charters was also increasing. That is, the gaining divisions were becoming better suited to the charters as market conditions shifted. For example, strengths in manufacturing (such as design for manufacturability and throughput speeds) in several of these divisions played into the changing basis of competition in these industries.

Take, for instance, Goliath. In the years preceding the charter change, the markets served by several divisions began to converge, while overall market growth slowed and margins dropped. Moreover, because other divisions (including the losing division) had traditionally built very similar core products, Goliath managers found themselves running into the charters of fellow divisions, as they all tried to expand into the same growth opportunities. One Goliath manager explained the situation:

> When [our industry] was in double-digit growth, in the 70's and 80's, we were making investments and we were making choices within each of our own divisions. And then as the technology evolved, [divisional charters] began to get more redundant because the markets converged on each other and the technology evolved to a place where we started to run into each other more often than we used to ... Also, the growth in the marketplace in general diminished – we were able to get away with [overlaps] in the early 80's because of the amount of government money that was being spent ... I remember suggesting numerous times that we had redundant efforts going on and too many people working on certain pieces of the business.

Unlike the managers of other divisions in its group, however, Goliath's managers decided early on to focus their attention on production systems. As it turned out, this strategy not only provided immediate returns to the division, but also gave it a distinctive manufacturing competence relative to other divisions, placing it in closer harmony with the evolving marketplace and making Goliath an attractive home for manufacturing-oriented charters. As one manager explained:

> We recognized the problem several years earlier than some of the other product lines that we are now taking responsibility for.

The "steals" carried out by Stealth and Plunder revealed a similar process. Over time, their approaches to managing their charters (like Goliath's, a combination of foresight and luck) helped them to develop capabilities that made them better equipped than other divisions for the shifts in the marketplace and, therefore, better suited to managing other charters. That is, there was a reasonable economic rationale for the charter change – corporate resources existed that could earn higher "rents" with existing products.

Economic reasoning, however, was not the whole story. Strong social imperatives were also behind these gains. Specifically, each of these gaining divisions was broadly recognized within Omni as a loyal corporate citizen. Their patient and often long struggles to build relatively unglamorous charter areas demanded communal acknowledgment and reward. For example, the previous corporate charters of Plunder and

Stealth were modest in status. Both divisions manufactured products based on older technologies for low-priced market segments (printers and computers, respectively). These were solid, but not high-potential, businesses within Omni. Importantly, other divisions recognized them as unspectacular charters. Indeed, there was an implicit understanding that these divisions deserved acknowledgment for success in their humble domains. As several managers noted:

> The charter here was to do essentially what the others wouldn't want to do. (Stealth general manager)

> The whole group thought that Stealth wasn't getting proper credit for all the work we would do ... so, we felt a little cheated ... there was definitely this undercurrent which [the group] was all aware of. (Stealth manager)

> In the first six months I was with Plunder, I was really ready to leave – the type of job that we had at the beginning was very very simple. (Plunder manager)

Relatedly, there was also a clear understanding that cooperation in making these charters a success would lead to bigger things. Corporate executives could not ignore a widely felt need to reward good citizenship, and the only currency that truly mattered to division managers was turf expansion. Their success in their modest roles also emboldened these managers to pursue other charters. In the case of Goliath, their improved performance and redirection brought them favorable corporate attention. As one manager related, "Omni knows we deliver, and we've had a great reputation for that. I cannot remember not delivering." The same was true in the cases of Plunder and Stealth:

> I was promised, when I joined Omni, in the interview process, "one or two years from now Plunder will have an [expanded charter]." (Plunder manager)

> Our group VP has been always talking to us in terms of phases. Phase 1 is proof that you know how to manufacture. Phase 2 is proof that you can do enhancements and do well with the simplest responsibilities. Phase 3, you own the [large business] and we have been following pretty much these plans... my perception is that he's very happy how this evolution happened here ... We would have a very good reputation in controlling all expenses and all costs and the quality of the shipment. (Plunder manager)

> Stealth was initially treated like a colony ... I wanted [our smaller divisions] to become whole sites that had whole charters ... In the end we're still working on this evolution, by the way, [but] there won't be sites that aren't whole. (Stealth group VP)

> We were delivering profit to the corporation ... we were managing [our regional market] in such a way that even when we were adding all the costs, allocating all the worldwide costs, we were making profit here. (Stealth manager)

The success, patience, and loyalty of these divisions, therefore, both encouraged them to tackle other areas and gave them implicit rights and leverage in the community in the bargaining process. In essence, they had earned the right to something better.

Omni had other divisions that also had increasingly attractive fits (from technical and/or market perspectives) that would have made them good homes for these charters. For example, one of Plunder's rivals, widely regarded as "the heart of the [corporate group's] program," had successfully doubled revenues in the three years prior to this charter change and enjoyed profit margins well above industry standards. Significantly, this division also had solid manufacturing credentials. Similarly, one of Stealth's neighbors was the originator of a long-standing and very successful product for Omni (calculators), and, in recent years, had been building competencies that brought it closer to Stealth's targeted charter. The corporate executive for the group claimed this rival to Stealth had "the most all round skill sets." Thus, the related competencies and solid performance of these divisions indicated that they were clearly "above the bar" as sites for the contested charters. But, in contrast with the winners, these divisions had not labored for a long time with what were universally regarded as unappealing charters. They already had reasonably good charters.

Finally, in all three cases, the division's general manager played a critical role. Described as "tenacious," "aggressive," and "passionate," these individuals had characteristics that served them well in arguing for greater charter responsibility:

> [Our general manager] was a man for all crises and he fought for what he thought was correct ... he fought a lot for giving a clear charter for Plunder ... I mean he had passion. (Plunder manager)
>
> I think [our general manager] was kind of viewing the [charter options] and saying "Heh! if this is the direction our group is headed in, which division would I rather be general manager of?" And he lobbied effectively there. (Goliath manager)

Arguably, these divisions could have sought completely new business opportunities or helped out the divisions that would lose the charters. But, like Boone-Pickens-style corporate raiders, these divisions found that the product-market areas in question were viable businesses, well-suited to their competencies (and so easier moves than completely new business domains) and were simply floundering under their current managements. The losing divisions were, in essence, easy prey sitting on undervalued charters that could be turned around with new management.

Although the strength, competitive instincts, and good citizenship of the gaining divisions tells part of the story, other divisions were also relevant in these cases. As noted, there were often competent, but less deserving, rival divisions. More important, however, were the losing divisions, who were faltering performers with diminishing fitness. For example, in the charter captured by Goliath, the losing division, Tritan, had strong product design skills. These had been effective when the market was young and growing and customers would pay premiums to have cutting-edge technology. But as the market matured, this division found these competencies were out-of-step with the changing nature of their business:

> We designed this stuff in the heydays of [our industry's] boom. Making all the money we can and spending everything we can. We did not design for manufacturability back then. We had no cost-of-sales pressure ... we got into the classic trap [of our industry], which is "We need one of everything." You need

lots of managers and you need lots of functions. And every product had its own infrastructure. We had no leverage amongst products. We had the world's greatest idea every three years and we redesigned a major new platform and then the next idea came along and we designed the next major new platform. I think we were very "R&D-creative" driven.

As market conditions changed and placed smaller premiums on innovation, Tritan suffered successive periods of negative margins. Not surprisingly, questions arose regarding their ability to manage these charters:

> One of the problems with our division was we always had a very high cost-to-sales percentage, and [our corporate executive] always felt it was because we really hadn't made the hard-nosed decisions to really trim the ship.

These managers were clearly anxious about attacks on their charters – some even labeled these moves "hostile takeovers." However, by even using such terminology and making analogies to accepted practices, they also acknowledged the legitimacy of the attacks. There was a shared understanding that, in the final analysis, no division could retain a charter if there was a growing misfit between competencies and market conditions.

Corporate executives: Judging internal competition. In contrast to the role of executives in the new charter opportunities, executives influence in the charter wars was limited. They clearly could have intervened to stop the wars, but they did not. Rather, in each case they let the divisions compete until uncertainties diminished and a winner emerged – in effect, they let a Darwinian process cull the herd. Only then did corporate executives step in to bring the process to a close. Sometimes corporate fiat was necessary to push things along (replacement of some top divisional managers at a losing division, for instance). But usually the charter wars made the winner reasonably clear to those involved.

Corporate executives also spent considerable time helping losing divisional managers find new charters that better fit their competencies. Although the losing divisions may have fitted the existing demands of the marketplace poorly, they usually possessed skills that could be applied effectively to other business settings. So, while Goliath, Stealth, and Plunder gained established charters, the losing divisions went on to new charters, often ones involving younger, emerging marketplaces and technologies, that could make better use of their skills. There was often significant conflict and emotional anguish in the process, and resignations within the management teams of the losing divisions, but the care taken of these divisions was in line with the communal spirit and concern for the underprivileged displayed in the previous pattern.

Summary: Charter wars. One surprising feature of this pattern was the strong coevolutionary theme that emerged. The developmental paths, divisional objectives, and managerial maneuverings of one division played a key role in determining the fate of another. Although industry-level changes were behind the growing misfits between charters and divisional resources, the alternatives generated by the trajectories of gaining divisions were key in determining what was done with the misfitting charters. Related to this coevolution was the emergence of open competition at Omni. Conflict over charters and stronger divisions' preying on weaker ones was not just tolerated, but expected. To be sure, bitterness and psychological pain were associated with this competition. But there was no real moral indignation; charter wars were part of the culture of the firm and so were legitimate. If divisional resources were available that could better match the business needs of given charters and so generate higher rents, then the charters were fair game. Also related to coevolution was the emergence of two parallel adaptive "motors" operating at different levels of Omni. The first was the coevolution of divisional resources with their changing markets. This motor did often sputter – that is, some divisions adapted, but others did not – but it nonetheless moved Omni along. The second and more powerful motor operated at the corporate level. This was the recombination of divisions with charters. Clearly, at Omni, this was the source of greater change, and indeed it even created change among inertial divisions by recombining their resources with new charters.

A second surprising aspect of this pattern was that although there was clearly competition, even the charter wars involved a weighing of social and economic logics. These rivalries were not only opportunities to rearrange corporate resources into more productive uses, but also opportunities to reward corporate citizenship. As with the previous pattern, we are not suggesting communal logic reversed economic reasoning. Rather, economic and social logics were used together. The strong won, but they had to be good citizens. The weak lost, but they were supported and given another shot. Even in defeat, Omni managers took care of their own.

Foster Homes for Charters: Cooperation in Corporate Communities

Ideally, charters for product-market opportunities can be neatly matched with divisional homes. But, especially in large corporations, this does not always happen. When charters became stranded, Omni corporate executives quickly placed these "orphans" in suitable "foster homes." These charter gains were essentially rapid organizational remedies for problem charters that gave corporate executives breathing room to consider longer-term options. Overall, this pattern was marked by: (1) operational problems or better opportunities arising for losing divisions, thus stranding business areas, (2) the existence of gaining divisions that were stable, well-run performers in steady markets, and (3) active matchmaking by corporate executives. The divisions providing data for this pattern were Fortune, Prosper, and Spark.

Industry context: Charter debris. Unlike the previous two patterns of charter change, this pattern did not occur in a single industry context. Rather, it was driven by organizational predicaments. It was a fact of life that when charters were frequently realigned and markets were constantly changing, charters and divisions did not always perfectly match up with one another. Sometimes divisions wanted to move into new charter areas and, in the process, stranded charters that were too small to stand alone. Sometimes charters were jettisoned from divisions that had too many operational problems. Occasionally, corporate executives found that charter boundaries were too fuzzy and required rationalizing. In other words, neat matches between divisions and charters did not always happen.

For example, a division neighboring Fortune had launched into a very promising business area (information technology). The new area exploded, and this division no longer wanted its older charter (computer storage systems). Given its related experience in computer storage devices, Fortune was asked to quickly adopt the charter in order to free up its neighbor. Similarly, Spark and Prosper were asked to adopt businesses from a neighbor who had taken on too many charter pieces, had lost focus, and needed to consolidate in order to restore financial health. Both gaining divisions had related product-market experience. Of course, as before, other options were possible. Corporate executives could have terminated these charters. Or they could have spent time and resources to either improve their current homes or find new ones. To uncover how these charter gains happened and why the gaining divisions were chosen as the foster homes, we again examine the social dynamics.

Interdivisional dynamics. Beyond having technical and/or market relatedness to the orphaned charter areas, the gaining divisions, or foster homes, had two common characteristics. They were: (1) well-run, with sound financials, and (2) situated in stable (neither growing nor shrinking rapidly) charter areas. That is, although they were not necessarily the optimal long-term solutions for these charters, they were low-risk locations in which to store charters that gave corporate executives time to come up with more permanent solutions for these charters' futures. Of course, the gaining divisions considered the fostered activities to be interesting, if not important, charter opportunities and did not take them on lightly. Moreover, being asked to take on such a charter was a signal throughout Omni that the focal division was a reliable and competent member of the Omni community. However, these charters were neither areas that were aggressively targeted, like the contested prizes in charter wars, nor brand new product-market concepts, like the new charter opportunities.

For example, Prosper had experience with the charter that a distressed neighboring division needed to jettison. Moreover, it had recently undergone internal restructuring and was now showing healthy margins and a renewed market presence. There was a strong sense of accomplishment and confidence in the division, as two Prosper managers reflected: "Prosper had really done a pretty good job" and "Our new condition feels better to everybody." With this accomplishment also came a renewed sense of confidence and expectation of recognition, both on the part of divisional managers and corporate executives searching for homes for orphaned charters. This was important to the process, since a division that had its operations in order would be more trusted than a less orderly peer to handle a fairly rapid and largely unforeseen charter change process and would appear a more legitimate recipient of the recognition and status that naturally came with charter expansion. Note, however, that although Prosper was certainly doing well, it was not a star with a high-growth charter. Rather, it was a steady division with midlevel opportunities. Similarly, Fortune and Spark were also well-run divisions in moderately growing markets.

As noted above, the orphan charters usually came from divisions that needed to unload these charters quickly because they were losing focus and declining, because they needed to turn their attention rapidly to quickly moving new opportunities, or because the charters had become too small to stand alone. So there was no common pattern among the losing divisions.

Looking at this third pattern of recombination in terms of rivalry, we saw few divisions in the running other than the gaining divisions. Partly, this occurred because corporate executives wanted to act quickly and so limited their search. Such limits were particularly reasonable, given that these gains were considered to be temporary. Corporate executives were interested in a particular type of division when charters needed temporary homes. Star divisions that were pursuing Omni's most lucrative charters were not considered to be viable candidates because corporate executives did not want to distract their managers. This exclusion left the well-run performers in steady markets as the likely candidates, a pool that became even smaller when corporate executives factored in the need for some technical and/or market relatedness.

Corporate executives: Housecleaning. This pattern was also marked by intense coordinating activity at the corporate level. Corporate executives had to proactively conceive novel matches (as in pattern 1) and rapidly execute often complex charter transfers (as in pattern 2). These internal organizational predicaments demanded both quick, innovative thinking about corporate structure, and corporate pressure and involvement to effect transfers.

For example, in the gains made by Spark and Prosper, corporate executives had to simultaneously address whether to remove a failing division's charter, where to send the charter and/or its various pieces (that is, to assess the suitability of Spark and Prosper), whether to keep the losing division as a separate entity (to assess effects on span of control and overhead costs), and what the timing and implementation of the change should be. Such issues could not be tackled effectively at the divisional level (as they were in charter wars) but instead required extensive corporate attention. This pattern, therefore, emphasized the matchmaking abilities of corporate executives, who responded to organizational problems with innovative recombinations.

Summary: Charter foster homes. This pattern of charter change serves as a reminder that a neat match between charters and divisions is challenging to achieve as markets and divisions coevolve. In contrast, portfolio perspectives, according to which business divisions are largely mapped with market contexts as reference points (contexts like growth opportunities, market share, and industry attractiveness), often promote naively overlooking this organizational fact of life. Yet, in corporations like Omni, such mismatches occur and sometimes require quick transplanting of charters to maintain the morale and business momentum of the stranded charters.

As before, this pattern also exhibits social sensibilities at work. Charter foster homes perhaps best exemplify the collaborative spirit of Omni, as seen in the willingness of members of the corporate community to help out with organizational predicaments. Of course, the gaining divisions did have some technical and/or market relatedness with their new charters, and these new businesses often offered opportunity. But the gaining divisions were not seeking these charters. Rather, they were helping the corporation by taking them in. To be sure, they did receive recognition within Omni as competent corporate players and trusted stewards. But their actions spoke most loudly about the importance of cooperation within Omni.

Discussion

This paper explores dynamic capabilities by focusing on the dynamic remapping of business charters among divisions of Omni Corporation – on architectural innovation at the corporate level. We found three patterns by which divisions gained new charters. Each pattern exhibited common forces (industry context, interdivisional dynamics, and corporate influence) with variation in their interplay and importance.

Pattern 1, new charter opportunities, emphasized industry context as the driver and the use of emerging new product-market areas to bolster sagging divisions. Surprisingly, top opportunities did not go to the best-performing or best-positioned divisions. Rather, charters were given to weak divisions in order to give them another shot at success. Here, struggling divisions were given the chance to rejuvenate themselves by building on their established strengths and creating new ones in the context of new business opportunities. Executives clearly assumed that positive rents would be generated from these gains, but the social sensibilities behind these moves stood out. To revive the smallest and weakest and to spread the wealth of corporate opportunities amongst the various divisions were motives.

Pattern 2, charter wars, emphasized interdivisional rivalry in established markets that resulted in better matches between divisions and their charters. The surprise here was the coevolutionary process of open competition among businesses within the same corporation. In these established markets, corporate executives let divisions vie for superior match-ups with product-market areas. Aggressive raiders went after more turf by pursuing opportunities that were being managed by faltering divisions. Here, the strong won. However, being strong was defined by more than economic reasoning (that is, by more than fitness). Rather, the strong were also defined by their behavior as communal actors, with victors chosen partly on the basis of their past loyalty and cooperation. The losers were also not forgotten. Instead, they had the chance to play again, with smaller existing charters or with new charter areas that were often better matches for their skills.

Pattern 3, charter foster homes, emphasized the role of corporate executives in rapidly placing orphaned businesses in temporary homes to buy time to consider more permanent moves. Here, we observed that modular organizations that engage in frequent recombinations cannot always perfectly match divisions with charters. Timing and the sheer diversity and scale of the Omni organization made perfect match-ups among all divisions and charters difficult to achieve. When charters became orphans, Omni executives were able to draw upon their diverse set of businesses to provide breathing room while they tackled more pressing problems and took time to figure out more permanent organizational architectures.

Beyond these patterns, our study also offers the broad outline of a theory of the organizational form that enabled these charter change processes. Below, we collect these lessons from our data and present the principal features of the adaptive organizational form that Omni represents. Our discussion highlights the dynamism of modular structures, the simplicity of dynamic capabilities, and the communal sensibilities present in Omni, a view that is underdeveloped in the multibusiness firm literature (Bartlett & Ghoshal, 1993; Galunic & Eisenhardt, 1996).

Architectural Innovation and Modular Corporate Forms:
Dynamics Communities and Dynamic Capabilities

Our findings suggest that charter change (or more broadly, architectural innovation) occurs within an organizational form that we term a *dynamic community.* We define such communities by the following features, elaborated below: (1) a corporate structure that displays modularity (generating vital diversity in the corporate "gene pool"), yet also displays relatedness (facilitating charter recombinations), (2) a corporate culture that combines competitive internal markets for charters with cooperative buffers against the harsher consequences of that competition, (3) dynamic capabilities that are guided by simple rules that embody both economic and social logics, and (4) corporate leaders acting as entrepreneurs and serving as architects of divisional context and guardians of culture.

Modular structures: Independent but related. On the whole, Omni is noted for having autonomous business divisions that are tightly focused on specific product-market domains. In both natural and social systems, such modularity is usually a good thing, contributing novelty and adaptive potential (Buckley, 1968). Within organizational design, modularity implies "subsystems that can be designed independently" with limited consideration of other subsystems (Baldwin & Clark, 1997: 84). In turn, modularity boosts the rate of innovation of subsystems by allowing them to freely adapt, with only limited constraints imposed by other subsystems (Campbell, 1969) and, vis-a-vis architectural innovation, generates recombinant opportunities across the entire system (Henderson & Clark, 1990). Therefore, modularity enhances innovation and adaptation at both the subsystem and system levels.

Modularity within Omni generated diversity among the various divisions. This diversity originated with each division having its own unique product-market domain that demanded different kinds of skills and so encouraged divisions to develop them. A good example is Stealth (see the section on charter wars). This division was initially involved with a charter whose context clearly dictated the importance of price-based competition, and so division managers focused on developing efficient manufacturing capabilities (also see Marris's [1979: 75] concept of divisions as quasi firms). Thus, as divisions like Stealth pursued their different charters in largely independent fashion and evolved with their markets, they replenished Omni's corporate stock of diversity and generated a changing set of recombinant opportunities.

Of course, charters can involve markets with ambiguous or competing signals as to the appropriate developmental paths. In this case, managerial interpretation and strategic choice play a vital role in influencing resource development (Child, 1972). For example, this was the case with Goliath (again, see "Charter Wars"), which participated with its rival divisions in closely related markets and yet chose to focus on developing its manufacturing capabilities as the better bet for the future, while its rivals remained centered on product innovation. Thus, through unique "sense-making" of their business contexts, divisions may also create novel capabilities that are different from those of other divisions (cf. Weick, 1995). The more general point is that with modularity there is gradual reshuffling of the deck of corporate resources that are available for architectural innovation as individual divisions pursue success in the context of their own evolving charters and in counterpoint to the paths of other divisions.

However, the developmental paths undertaken by the divisions were typically slow evolutionary walks when compared with the sudden change of recombinations such as charter gains. In fact, at Omni, a remarkable aspect of charter change was that the divisions themselves did not have to undergo major transformations in their internal resources and capabilities to create significant corporate-level adaptation. Rather, constancy among the divisions was acceptable as charter changes often took advantage of existing resources. So although constancy sometimes posed problems for losing divisions (for instance, recall the struggles of the losing divisions in the charter wars), adaptation at the corporate level nonetheless occurred through recombinations of divisions with charters. Yet this very recombination required some relatedness or standardization among divisions (Sanchez & Mahoney, 1996) in order to facilitate frequent and rapid charter changes between them. That is, the adaptation of modular systems requires standardization, not just quasi-independent entities.

Perhaps the most obvious source of standardization at Omni was the close market and/or technical proximity among the products of Omni divisions. This meant that division managers were often well aware of the competitive situation of their neighboring divisions and even shared competitors. This awareness was enhanced by regular meetings (usually monthly) of the division general managers of related businesses. Although these meetings were targeted at surfacing opportunities for collaboration among neighboring divisions, they also informed the managers of one another's strategic situations in such a way that they understood the major business issues of related charters and how to manage them. In addition, Omni divisions often shared key resources that created further standardization and smoothing of charter changes. For example, it was typical for several divisions to share a sales force, a dealer channel, or a technology platform, such as a microprocessor architecture, which reduced the intradivisional novelty of charters. Omni divisions also shared a strong, distinctive brand; Omni products, from electronics to computers to peripherals, were similarly positioned in the marketplace. So shifts in the location of charters did not require fundamental rethinking of product positioning. Finally, Omni divisions shared a few key processes. There was a common financial system, so that the business results of charters could be readily integrated into those of a gaining division, allowing executives to quickly grasp the business fundamentals. Most significant, Omni had a product development system that was common across much of the corporation. This meant that products under development could be dropped into divisions other than their original ones and meet a high degree of understanding regarding their progress and status. Overall, this standardization greatly facilitated recombinations (which, for our sample, occurred every two to four years for each division) by reducing the considerable transaction costs that would otherwise have been incurred with charter moves. In fact, it was very rare for Omni to need to permanently transfer people and resources (such as laboratories and departments) as part of a charter change. So, though diverse, Omni divisions nonetheless maintained important types of standardization.

Finally, this view of modularity provides an alternative perspective to the Williamson (1975) view of multibusiness corporations. According to Williamson, the main advantage of the traditional M-form is the economy of managerial attention offered by decomposition and specialization. In contrast, the modularity described here emphasizes the recombinant potential of a multibusiness firm. That is, the advantage of having independent business units is not so much their ability to act independently and with narrowed focus. Rather, the advantage lies in the ability to rapidly respond to altered business conditions by recombining diverse divisional resources and product-market domains. Indeed, having more divisions is actually a plus, increasing the set of recombinant opportunities. Finally, corporate headquarters provides value by facilitating the coevolution of dynamic communities in changing markets, not just by solving agency problems and finding scale and scope economies.

Corporate culture: Competition and cooperation. Although our discussion of dynamic communities has so far highlighted their structural features (unique and slowly evolving, but nonetheless related, modules offering recombinant opportunities), it is also important to recognize the role played by corporate culture. We found that capitalizing on related modularity through a freewheeling process of charter change required a corporate culture that emphasized not only the competitive aspects of the organization, but also cooperation and common identity. Kogut and Zander concluded as much when they wrote that "understanding firms as social communities as opposed to efficient communication nets" is the chief advantage of firms over markets (1996: 506; also see Marris's concept of "organic unity" [1971: 317]). Moreover, these elements of culture operated as common rules for behavior that guided the actions of individual managers, creating "agent schemata" – a requirement of self-organizing systems (Anderson, 1999; Brown & Eisenhardt, 1998). We begin to explore this aspect of dynamic communities by considering the corporate culture of Omni.

The Omni culture is rooted in widely shared values about how individuals at Omni should operate and unequivocally supported competition for charters. Foremost, that culture had an emphasis on personal responsibility and initiative, a legacy of the founders of the firm, with whom these traits were strongly associated. In addition, Omni employees prided themselves on respect for individuals and a fundamental belief in their capabilities and good intentions. Collectively, these cultural values supported internal competition and established clear rules of engagement (Kogut, 2000). Competition was tolerated and even encouraged, rather than seen as personal, mean-spirited, or inappropriate. Competition was all part of taking personal initiative, building growing divisions, and ensuring that Omni fielded the best possible lineup of divisions against the competition. Division managers, for example, always felt able to aggressively set their sights on other charters and to position their divisions as alternative hosts to promising product-market opportunities.[1] Indeed, the corporate culture encouraged divisions to go after new opportunities wherever they lay which, in turn, facilitated the charter change process.

We also found, however, that Omni employees held cooperative values that prevented competitive conduct from deteriorating into chaos and hostility. For example, corporate executives took great pains to assist losing divisions (finding new charters for

---

[1] This was particularly salient during one dinner meeting with two general managers from divisions that had recently gone through a charter war (one was the victor, the other the loser). Although the charter battle had been fiercely contested between them, they both acknowledged that this was "the way things worked around here." Moreover, their mutual respect and their confidence in the institution of charter change was not compromised – they still met frequently for discussions. Indeed, the loser in this battle was already contemplating how to best position his division for upcoming market opportunities.

them, helping them to still feel a part of the community). Stable divisions were willing to take stranded charters. Other divisions were willing to accept unexciting ones. Corporate executives were careful to invoke the firm-level advantages of charter changes when justifying moves rather than the advantages winners gained. They were also careful to emphasize the procedural justice of the processes (Kim & Mauborgne, 1998). Charter changes were open processes in which all parties were able to argue their cases. Thus, internal competition was tempered by acts that reinforced the values of unity and collective purpose in the corporate community.

Overall, Omni's culture contrasts with the essentialism implied by economic theories of organization. Agency and transaction cost theories, for example, highlight a narrow and perhaps overly pessimistic view of human nature in which opportunism, shirking, exploitation of asymmetric information, and the focused pursuit of self-interest are the key elements. Individuals dominated by these drivers would be out of step in Omni, where the sensibility is more optimistic and more socially complex, requiring people to, for example, juggle contrasting values such as competition and cooperation.

Dynamic capabilities: Economic and social rules. The Omni case also reveals the intimate relationship between a modular structure and the dynamic capabilities by which executives reconfigure that structure in changing markets. Unlike static conceptions of organizations, adaptive conceptions such as the dynamic community require not only a snapshot of the organizational architecture, but also a moving picture of the processes by which that structure is reconfigured (see Galunic & Weeks, 2001).

These dynamic capabilities at first glance seem complicated. But in fact, they do not match the traditional conception of strategic processes as highly detailed routines, but rather consist of a few simple, often competing, rules that enable highly adaptive behaviour (e.g., Eisenhardt & Martin, 2000; Kogut, 2000). Managers use a few rules to construct the most promising line of reasoning for dealing with the situation at hand (Boisot & Child, 1999; Child, 1972) without slipping into the rigidity of too many rules or the chaos of too few (Eisenhardt & Bhatia, 2001). In particular, the following rules inform the selection of charter-division pairings: (1) Ensure that the gaining division has the relevant R&D, marketing, and manufacturing skills needed to manage the charter at issue (that is, has acceptable fitness). (2) Give new charter opportunities to constrained divisions. (3) Reward loyal, up-and-coming divisions with charters in strong, established markets. (4) Help losers regain stability and new vision. And (5) store charter orphans in midperforming divisions. Omni corporate executives orchestrated charter changes, adjusting in real time to the most promising charter match-ups while following these rules.

Most significant, as we have argued throughout, the content of these rules shaping architectural innovation is both economic and social. At Omni, for example, economic reasoning was evident in the widespread desire to optimally match successful and related (given their capabilities and trajectories) divisions and charters. Our data suggest that this was an often-visited logic; so, a minimum level of economic fitness was always a prerequisite for charter gain. After all, Omni had to field divisions that were competitive within the marketplace to succeed. But if only an economic logic were used, the diversity of the divisional gene pool might diminish and cooperative behavior disappear. Moreover, the motivational value of these rules should not be overlooked – people in this setting valued, and were inspired by, these social sensibilities, outcomes that may have had important repercussions on their loyalty and commitment. Therefore, a social logic was at work that simultaneously encouraged helping the corporation and finding opportunities to help lagging divisions to revive their competencies and build new ones. But if the only logic were social, Omni might lose its competitive edge in its markets, have its values of personal initiative and responsibility undermined, and become a set of also-ran divisions. In other words, both logics operated, and the two balanced each other.

More subtly, neither logic always gave a definitive solution to a recombination opportunity – both were blunted by measurement problems. For example, deciding which division should receive a charter depended upon a corporate comparison of divisional capabilities. But measures of capabilities can be (1) inexact (consider the large amounts of tacit knowledge that each division holds and cannot perfectly convey) or (2) too time consuming to gather (requiring lengthy investigations that sometimes span the globe, while the market rapidly moves on). Similarly, applying a social logic may also bring measurement problems (for instance, figuring out which division has the less spectacular charter and so better deserves a new one). Using both logics facilitates the charter change process, helping managers to parse the alternatives more quickly.

In sum, dynamic capabilities are the means by which modular structures are reconfigured to produce new productive assets. Simple rules, informed by contrasting economic and social logics, shape those capabilities. The picture that emerges is one of corporate actors simultaneously and continuously juggling these logics – weighing the various rules, interpreting what proportions are the most compelling for the charter situation at hand, and using their judgment to direct corporate recombinations. This view emphasizes the counter-intuitive insight that adaptive organizational configurations emanate from simple rules (Eisenhardt & Martin, 2000; Galunic & Weeks, 2001). Finally, although social and economic logics are weighed against one another in the short run, this diversity of rules and logics ensures the viability of dynamic communities in the long run.

Leaders as architects, entrepreneurs, and cultural guardians. Finally, our conception of dynamic communities suggests a reshaping of managerial roles within multibusiness corporations. In particular, corporate executives played roles that went beyond the traditional ones of managing corporate boundaries and overseeing performance. Perhaps their most important role within the dynamic community lay in the process of architectural innovation by which divisions were frequently recombined with charters (Brown & Eisenhardt, 1998; Galunic & Eisenhardt, 1996). As we observed at Omni, executive influence included the entrepreneurial spotting of opportunities for recombination (best exemplified by new charter opportunities and foster homes, as described above). In fact, executives were much more entrepreneurial in spotting opportunities at the division level than is traditionally recognized (cf. Chandler, 1962; Williamson, 1975). Their influence also included the implementation of already developed ideas for recombination (see "Charter Wars"). In this way, executives were key in recrafting the corporate architecture, taking advantage of the diverse resource stocks present in Omni, even while helping to generate them. Moreover, because executives are more likely than others to have broad architectural knowledge of their firm and are arguably the only ones with the formal power and clout to effect such changes, their involvement is key. Finally, their influence included reinforcing the corporate culture throughout – that is, emphasizing the competitive values of rewarding individual initiative as well as the cooperative values of helping out losers. In short, corporate executives were entrepreneurs, corporate architects, and guardians of the culture. In contrast, division managers were tightly focused on growing their charters and had great freedom in their approaches to doing so. Thus, we see corporate executives as shaping the architectural and social context in which divisions created and drove the competitive strategy of Omni as they pursued their charters in accordance with the cultural values of Omni.

Conclusion

Taken together, these four features suggest the outline of a theory of the adaptive organizational form we have termed "dynamic community." Corporations with this form are *dynamic* in that they involve diverse and quasi-independent divisions whose charters and capabilities are frequently recombined to create new productive assets within the context of changing markets and coevolving divisions. They are *communities* in that their underlying culture is deeply informed by shared identity and values and in that their dynamic capabilities are guided by social as well as economic rules. Although corporate executives strongly influence the architecture of the dynamic community, divisions' actions do not display central design or control, but rather, decentralized and self-organized behavior.

Our work relates to several fields of research in strategy and organization. First, it links to classic managerial theories of the firm and of growth (Marris & Wood, 1971; Penrose, 1959; Schumpeter, 1934). These theories introduced the importance of seeking innovative uses for existing corporate resources and so provided the earliest versions of architectural innovation, an increasingly recognized motor of innovation (e.g., Brown & Eisenhardt, 1998; Galunic & Rodan, 1998; Henderson & Clark, 1990; Henderson & Cockburn, 1994; Kogut & Zander, 1992; Tushman & O'Reilly, 1997). In our view, their authors (Schumpeter, Penrose, and Marris), some of the most visible economists of the 20th century, ironically provided managerial theorists with powerful sociological insights into large-firm dynamics, themes contemporary research often neglects. From the Penrosian (1959) emphasis on managerial talent and process as the real limits to firm growth, to the Schumpeterian (1934) focus on the "bursting" influence of entrepreneurship on different institutional forms, to Marris's (1971) eye for sociological context and "organic unity" in corporate growth, these authors' ideas implied that understanding the social and communal nature of large corporations, together with their innovative dynamics and concern for growth, was pivotal. What we have attempted to do is to extend their legacy to the contemporary literature by describing in more empirical detail how these social, innovative, and growth-oriented imperatives unfold as dynamic capabilities in the context of the modern corporation.

In contrast, our work differs in emphasis from much of the extant contemporary research on multidivisional organizing. For example, portfolio theorists (e.g., Henderson, 1979) provide analytical devices for examining how divisions fit their environments and how much investment they should receive. Others (Chandler, 1962; Williamson, 1975) strongly justify multibusiness firms in terms of bounded rationality, fit, and contingency, but not in terms of dynamism and innovation. To be sure, useful theories of corporate entrepreneurship exist (e.g., Burgelman, 1983; Guth & Ginsberg, 1990; Jelinek & Schoonhoven, 1990), but these are theories about entrepreneurship *within* corporations (that is, being entrepreneurial in large firms), not entrepreneurship *through* dynamic corporate form. This research, therefore, does not really address how large corporations find advantage through the dynamics of their multibusiness structures per se. Moreover, little work has considered the social constitution of multibusiness firms. For example, Goold, Campbell, and Alexander (1994) provided a coherent account of how corporate parents should interact with divisions, but their thinking is embedded in economics (an exception is Bartlett and Ghoshal [1993]).

Second, our work addresses recent writing on novel organizational forms. Although inquiry into new organizational forms is still embryonic (Lewin & Volberda, 1999), this research can be roughly divided into two parts. First, there are studies that focus on holistic accounts of unusual organizational structures, such as the "shamrock" organization (Handy, 1995), the "virtual" corporation (Davidow & Malone, 1992), and the "hypertext" organization (Nonaka & Takeuchi, 1995). These are usually long works that contribute divergent and futuristic perspectives on how modern firms should organize. Second, there are more convergent studies (e.g., Anderson, 1999; Baldwin & Clark, 1997; Bartlett & Ghoshal, 1993; Brown & Eisenhardt, 1998; Ciborra, 1996; Henderson, 1994; Iansiti & Clark, 1994; Lewin, Long, & Carroll, 1999; Sanchez & Mahoney, 1996) describing organizational structures and processes that some believe are contributing to a "new underlying managerial logic" (Lewin & Volberda, 1999: 530). The common themes are adaptability, modularity, coevolution, and recently, self-organization. Our work is in line with this latter stream.

We extend this research stream in several ways. First, we attempt to expose the tensions that highly adaptive organizations balance: modularity and relatedness, competitiveness and cooperation, and order and disorder. We believe that the simultaneous presence of competing tensions is an important motor of firm adaptation. More pointedly, we describe the links among modular structures, dynamic capabilities, culture, and managerial roles that constitute the outline of a theory of an adaptive organizational form, the dynamic community. Obviously, we cannot base normative claims on one corporation, but we can reveal that Omni has been a star performer, achieving excellent profitability among high-technology corporations worldwide for over two decades. Most important, we emphasize the social dynamics of adaptive, evolving organizations. It is perhaps an early failing of this stream that accounts of self-organizing, modular, and complex adaptive systems are often short on sociocultural understanding and too easily rest on abstract and, for social scientists, distancing terminology (such as "rugged landscapes" and "dissipative structures"). The result, we fear, is that this literature will not fully connect the "hard" rules of complex systems and the natural sciences to the "soft" underbelly that underpins social phenomena – that is, scholars' accumulated understanding of sociocultural entities. So, although we

319

believe that complex, adaptive behavior is evident in firms as a consequence of the interplay of simple rules, these rules per se are a social construction whose qualities are usefully examined through such disciplines as psychology and sociology. The literature on novel organizational forms, we believe, must continue to detail this underbelly, even as it introduces provocative and useful new metaphors and mechanisms.

Table 5.11 Description of case data

Division	Number of Interviews	Business Group's Products	Strategic Profile[a]	Capability Profile[a]	Pattern of Charter Gain[b]
Quest	13	Computer peripherals	Small ($50); young (4 years). Innovation/growth focus. Modest-to-weak performance.	R&D and marketing focus; innovative, nimble, and aggressive division, desperate for a "home run" charter.	New charter opportunity
Voyageur	9	Computer peripherals	Small ($75); young (3 years). Innovation/growth focus. profitable; weak growth.	R&D and marketing focus; good manufacturing; resentful of being cast as a cash cow, eager to expand charter.	New charter opportunity
Mission	5	Computer peripherals	Medium ($250); old (22 years). Growth refocus. Profitable; weak growth.	Solid product development; good manufacturing; after years of successfully growing a niche market product, managers wanted to refocus on their new product development talents.	New charter opportunity
Spark[c]	6	Computing/information technology	Medium ($175); old (18 years). Innovation/growth refocus. Weak profits; weak growth.	R&D focus; after years of nearly ruinous performance in a commodity industry, division wished to return to its core competence – R&D and market development.	New charter opportunity and charter foster homes
Fortune	9[d]	Computing/information technology	Medium ($330); old (15 years). Stable growth focus. Strong profits; adequate growth.	Manufacturing focus; good R&D; solid, all-around division.	Charter foster homes
Prosper			Large ($500); old (17 years). Stable growth focus. Strong profits; strong growth.	Manufacturing focus; good R&D; solid all-around division.	Charter foster homes
Stealth	5	Computing/information technology	Medium ($400); old (20 years). Profitable growth focus. Strong performance.	Manufacturing focus; good marketing; excellent in cost control.	Charter wars

Table 5.11 Description of case data *(continued)*

Division	Number of Interviews	Business Group's Products	Strategic Profile[a]	Capability Profile[a]	Pattern of Charter Gain[b]
Plunder	5	Computer peripherals	Medium (approx. $300); young (6 years). Profitable growth focus. Strong performance.	Manufacturing focus; good product development; excellent in operations and cost control; a strong desire to gain a significant charter.	Charter wars
Goliath	11	Instruments	Medium ($240); young (7 years). Profitability focus. Strong performance.	Manufacturing focus; good product development; excellent in cost control.	Charter wars
Triton	12	Instruments	Medium ($150); old (11 years). Growth focus. Weak performance.	Good product development; weak in operations and cost control.	
Saturn	11	Computer peripherals	Large ($2B+); old (19 years). Profitable growth focus. Excellent performance.	Solid in most areas; launched a new product line that was a huge success; excellent all-around competencies.	

[a] Profiles are for the period prior to the gains examined here. Figures in parentheses (in millions of dollars for all divisions except Saturn) are averaged net over the two years prior to the charter gain.

[b] All divisions experienced at least one charter gain, except for Saturn and Triton, which experienced only losses – Saturn lost to Quest and Voyageur, and Triton lost to Goliath.

[c] Two gains occurring at different times and involving different product-market areas were separately documented.

[d] Interviews were carried out at one corporate site, but this division had been two divisions, each with charter changes that we documented. We therefore name and profile both.

Table 5.11 Summary of recombination patterns *(continued on next page)*
(Italics indicate particularly important forces within each pattern.)

Influence on Pattern	New Charter Opportunities	Charter Wars	Charter Foster Homes
Sample	Quest, Voyageur, Spark, Mission	Goliath, Stealth, Plunder	Fortune, Prosper, Spark
Industry-level forces	*New markets emerge with attractive opportunities that demand attention.*	Basis of competition shifts in existing markets.	Various, no single condition.
Interdivisional dynamics	Gaining divisions: Weak-to-modest performers with underutilized resources and constrained charter positions get a boost.	*Gaining divisions: Up-and-coming divisions with strong desire for growth, well-suited capabilities, and aggressive general managers. Also loyal corporate citizens that had succeeded with low-status charters and expected progress.*	Gaining divisions: Steady and well-run divisions in stable markets, willing to accept new charters. Other divisions: Divisions with recently failed charters, or with more attractive growth opportunities that need greater attention, or with insufficient scale.

Table 5.11 Summary of Recombination Patterns
(Italics indicate particularly important forces within each pattern) *(continued)*

Influence on Pattern	New Charter Opportunities	Charter Wars	Charter Foster Homes
	Other divisions: Some potential rivals for charter exist, some with superior resources, but often these are busy and overprivileged	*Other divisions: Sluggish performers increasingly poorly fitting a new market-place. Other, economically viable divisions exist, but with less sense of social imperative.*	Other related divisions exist but are busy running star charters or dealing with their own problems.
Corporate executives	Involved early as corporate entrepreneur, helping to find and launch new domains.	Involved late, helping to declare the winner, imple-ment the charter gain, and reposition the loser.	*Involved throughout the process, both in initiating and implementing the gain.*
Economic logic	Match divisions and char-ters to ensure a minimum standard of rent-generation potential.		
Social logic	Encourage the small and needy. Spread the wealth – don't feed the overprivileged.	Reward the loyal corporate citizen. Do not humiliate losers.	Rescue the distressed. Help your neighbor.

The Innovation Meme: Managing Innovation Replicators for Organizational Fitness[*]

Sven C. Voelpel, Marius Leibold & Christoph K. Streb†

Recent academic and business evidence indicate that innovation is the key factor for companies' success and sustained fitness in a rapidly evolving, knowledge-networked economy. Companies that are able to embed and leverage an innovation culture in their organizations and stakeholders are likely to achieve superior performance.
The innovation meme (a unit of cultural transmission or imitation that carries information responsible for innovations) is proposed as a key construct in identifying and leveraging the replicators of an organizational innovation culture. The article further suggests that the organizational fitness profiling process (OFP) is an appropriate tool for identifying the status of a company's innovation culture, and that a process of innovation meme management which focuses on various types of innovation replicators should include innovation meme tracking, shaping, and creation.

Introduction: Towards the Innovation Economy

During the past two decades the world has changed dramatically towards a more complex and networked, but also more unstable and chaotic environment (Hamel, 1998; Beinhocker, 1999; Leibold, Probst and Gibbert, 2002; Voelpel, 2003). In the 1990s knowledge became the predominant source of competitive advantage and economic wealth (Drucker, 1964; Nonaka and Takeuchi, 1995; Davenport and Prusak, 1997; Davenport and Voelpel, 2001; Gibbert, Leibold and Probst, 2003; Voelpel and Davenport, 2004; Voelpel, Dous and Davenport, 2005). This was called the 'knowledge economy'. Practically the same forces that had given birth to the knowledge economy have resulted in the development of what can be called the innovation economy in which competitiveness for organizational survival and advancement is mainly achieved through innovative excellence (uniqueness, relevance, speed etc).

Recent research done by Senge and Carstedt (2001), Govindarajan and Gupta (2001), Von Hippel and Katz (2002), Christensen, Raynor and Anthony (2003) and others

---

[*] Taken with permission from *Journal of Change Management* Vol. 5 No. 1, March 2005, pp. 57-69

illustrate the rising relevance and impact of innovation on organizational behavior and performance. Currently it is estimated that innovative products will account for 80% of companies' future revenues (PwC, 1999; Voelpel, 2003). The 3M-business case (see below) demonstrates the importance of innovation for today's companies that are striving to find new ways of creating value and ensuring long-term survival.

Getting Innovative at 3M

Few companies in the world are more famous for their exceptional product ideas and innovations than 3M. Founded in 1902, the company first focused on sandpaper products. In the 1920s the company invented the world's first waterproof sandpaper, which reduced airborne dusts in automobile manufacturing. The next major break-through occurred in 1925 when a young lab assistant came up with the idea for masking tape. This soon led to more diversification of the products and became the first of a variety of Scotch Tapes. During the next decades the company's history was marked by milestones of innovation in various industries such as pharmaceuticals, radiology, and energy control. Today everybody knows and uses Post-it, one of the company's most simple, but best-known products.

For this company it is an everyday challenge to come up with new innovative ideas and to turn them into a commercial success. In today's economy, growth and innova-tive breakthroughs often determine the survival of the company itself. In the 1990s 3M already realized that product developers didn't know how to make big, profitable innovations and breakthroughs part of their daily routine. There was no system that they could utilize to become innovative, – therefore breakthroughs were a matter of coincidence. This was dangerous for a company whose reputation and survival largely depended on successful innovations. Management 'managed' the product developers, who were largely working independently, by keeping out of their way. The developers, on the other hand, worked according to the aphorism: 'It's better to seek forgiveness than ask for permission'.

3M became aware that too much of the company's growth was the result of incremen-tal changes to existing products. In fact, new innovations were few and far between. This was not what the top managers at 3M expected of their company, so they came up with a very challenging objective: in future, 30% of sales would have to come from products that had not existed four years earlier.

This had an effect on the way many employees, especially the product developers and scientists, perceived their role in innovation. The answer to that challenge: They introduced the lead user process to become more innovative and make big break-throughs. Research had namely found that many breakthroughs were initially not made by manufactures, but by lead users. They can be companies, organizations, or individuals with needs advanced beyond those of the average user and beyond the scope of ordinary product solutions – needs that often led them to search for solutions themselves. Using this insight, the lead user process refines those ideas into commer-cially useful and marketable innovations and products.

A product development team in 3M's medical market division became one of the first groups in the company to test the lead user process. The results tell their own tale:

Approximately one year after the introduction of the process, the team had not only come up with a proposal for three major new product lines, but also for a new strategy that would revolutionize the treating of infection.

Since then 3M has successfully tested the lead user process in many other divisions. While it is clear that this tool is not always successful, it can lead to new ways and approaches to deal with a problem as well as help those who are looking for new ways of becoming innovative. At 3M the innovation continues. (Case adapted from Von Hippel, Thomke and Sonnak; 1999).

In view of the changing demands of the innovation economy, research efforts have started to provide an understanding of organizations as complex evolutionary systems, obeying the same laws and rules as equivalent systems in nature (Moore, 1993). These systems possess remarkable flexibility, robustness, and dynamics when it comes to survival in unstable, constantly changing environments, where there is high interaction with other systems. This can be equated to the situation in business today, where there is a similar 'struggle for survival of the fittest'. Beinhocker (1999) argues that the same tools that help biologists to understand strategies in nature can be applied to the business world. Increasing systemic interactions can be the basis for producing new stakeholder value, since customers and consumers are now being included in the socio-cultural business system when it comes to the generation of new ideas and organizational innovations (Von Hippel et al., 1999).

The innovation economy and the perception of organizations as complex adaptive systems, require the development of new approaches that will allow organizations to build the necessary capabilities, especially innovation culture replication capabilities, for continuous value creation. Meme, or memetics, is a concept that originates from biology and the theory of the evolution of living organisms. In innovation it is a cultural element that is passed on from one individual to the next by imitation. It offers a potentially promising field through which to explore the opportunities to skillfully manage replicators (innovation meme) in an organizational culture in order to improve innovation capability.

This article describes organizational fitness profiling (OFP) as a process with which to identify and manage the innovation meme. First, an introduction to the organizational meme concept is provided, which forms the basis for understanding the innovation meme. Thereafter, a brief illustration of the process of organizational fitness profiling follows. This tool is then adapted to identify the innovation meme. The proposed management of the innovation meme, i.e., the tracking, shaping, and deliberate creation of the innovation meme replicator(s) is designed to assist organizations in unfolding their innovative capabilities. Finally, a continuous managerial process for the identification and management of the innovation meme is proposed.

The Concept of Organizational Meme

An extensive analysis of the latest interdisciplinary research reveals the potential for the application of the organizational meme concept to the field of business management. For example, Vos and Kelleher (2001) attempt to explain the phenomenon of mergers and acquisitions using the concept of meme. Williams (2000) takes a closer look at the prospects for memetic approaches in marketing and management, while Lord and Price (2001) study meme's potential for organizational science, Frank (1999) attempts to apply memetics to financial markets, and Lissack (2003) explains why research on memetics seems to have reached a critical phase in its development towards a real theory. Considering the scope of interest and progress in the application of memetics to management, it seems opportune to take a detailed and focused view of the concept in its application to organizational innovation. For expositionary purposes, it is necessary to first trace the historical roots of the concept of meme.

In 1976 Richard Dawkins introduced the idea of meme in his book The Selfish Gene. According to him (Dawkins, 1976, p. 192), meme (a term derived from the linguistic consonance to gene) was defined as 'a unit of cultural imitation [...] leaping from brain to brain'. He attributed similar qualities – in terms of dispersion and, especially, replication – that genes have in the physical world to meme in world of organizational culture. It is a replicator, i.e. a self-replicating and self-propagating entity whose survival to a large extent depends on its success and advantage in relation to other competing meme.

The acceptance of the analogy between human culture and organizational culture is an important prerequisite for further research into the domain of organizational meme. Starting from there, meme in organizations can be provisionally identified. If there is indeed something like organizational meme, it can be logically concluded that one must be able to find it in the realms of organizational culture. This would be the parallel to Dawkins' well-accepted theory of meme in human culture. Schreyögg et al. (1995, p. 168) point out that the term culture originates from anthropology and defines organizational culture as 'the transmitted patterns of values, beliefs and expectations shared by people, including the system of symbols which imparts them to members of the group'. For example, employees can simultaneously be both carriers and creators of culture. The keyword is carrier, which is again analogous to Dawkins' understanding of meme, in which meme is a unit of imitation transferred from one of its carrier's brain to the next. Utilizing a synthesis of the general meme definitions (see Table 5.12), organizational meme can, for the purposes of this article, be defined as a unit of transmission or imitation in organizational culture:

Definition of 'organizational meme': Any of the core elements of organizational culture, like basic assumptions, norms, standards, and symbolic systems that can be transferred by imitation from one human mind to the next.

Organizational meme could be inspiring examples, unofficial dress codes, ways of organizing the work place, rites and rituals within the company, as well as stories and legends etc. More specific replicators (or bases of replication activity) of organizational meme are, e.g. the restaurant where some employees use to meet during lunchtime or after work, the motto a founder of a firm always quotes, self-organizing teams, or internal nicknames for departments. Thus an employee walking through the office hall whistling a melody that is whistled by many others the next day has simply spread a meme. Such a meme might happen incidentally, or could be cultivated on purpose.

Table 5.12 Established definitions of 'meme'

Dawkins	Gelb	Blackmore	The New Oxford American Dictionary
'... a unit of cultural transmission, or a unit of imitation [...] leaping from brain to brain ...' (1976, p. 192)	'... self-replicating ideas that move through time and space without further effort from the source ...' (1997, p. 57)	'... whatever is passed on by imitation ...' (1999, p. 43)	'... an element of a culture or system of behavior that may be considered to be passed from one individual to another by nongenetic means, esp. imitation ...' [Jewell & Abate (Eds), 2001, p. 1066]

Since meme is a concept derived from Dawkins' physiological and evolutionary studies, it makes intuitive sense to adopt this approach to environmental and organizational conditions which are, more than ever, characterized by analogies to biological and evolutionary organizational models. In these models, such as business ecosystems, organizational fitness is a logical analogy to 'survival of the fittest'. Flowing logically from this, this article will later demonstrate that the concept of organizational fitness profiling (OFP) provides a way with which to identify an innovation meme within the organization, and with which management could deliberately influence and manage meme.

Towards an Understanding of Innovation Meme

The results of the analysis of the organizational meme can now be utilized to achieve a focused understanding of the innovation meme concept as a subset of the organizational meme. Cultural evolution, including the evolution of innovation, can be viewed as applying the same basic principles of variation and selection that underlie biological evolution. Variation, replication, and selection on the basis of meme fitness, and innovation meme fitness creating and sustaining organizational fitness, are determined by complex dynamic factors.

As is the case with genes, it is not necessary to know the exact coding or even the exact size or boundaries of a meme in order to discuss its relevance and fitness, and thus make predictions about its further spread, survival, or extinction. For example, a memetic hypothesis might state that 'simpler' meme will spread more quickly. Eisenhardt and Sull (2001) have suggested a number of 'simple rules' to manage replications of desired innovative organizational meme in a more self-organizing and dynamic way. What is important, however, is that when organizations are managed and controlled by humans who behave with strictly bounded rationality, their actions and deliberations are guided by already existing lineages of organizational meme (often referred to as 'path dependency'), thus stifling innovation. In our knowledge-networked, fast-moving world it is therefore crucial that the innovation meme in the organization are skillfully managed, i.e. identified, tracked, shaped (enabled), and created (creatively intervened) by way of, e.g. a new 'appropriate attractor' of innovative behavior.

Organizational fitness profiling, as discussed in the next section, offers an appropriate starting point for the identification of innovation meme, and this subsequently leads to the proposed overall approach to managing the innovation meme.

Organizational Fitness Profiling as a Starting Point to Identify the Innovation Meme

The term organizational fitness refers to organizational relevance and adaptability in fast-changing and turbulent business environments (Beer and Eisenstat, 2000; Beer, 2003; Voelpel et al., 2004). In order not only to adapt, but also to co-shape their business ecosystem, companies should strive to make sense of socio-cultural trends and to provide context to internal and external stakeholders (Leibold et al., 2005; Voelpel et al., 2004).

According to Beer (2003), competitive environments influence results in a process of continuous redesign of the six organizational layers: leadership team, work system, management process, human resource system, principles and culture, and corporate context (see Figure 5.3). This results in the development of the 'seven Cs' of organizational capabilities, namely co-ordination, competence, commitment, communication, conflict management, creativity, and capacity management, that are compatible with the environment (Beer, 2003).

In addition, Beer and Eisenstat (2000) identify six key barriers to organizational fitness, termed 'silent killers': First there is top-down or laissez fair senior management style. This is a crucial barrier, because if this barrier is not transformed into a capability, none of the other six barriers can be transformed either. If top management is not willing or able to lead, strategy implementation and organizational development will never be successful. Conflicting priorities and poor coordination are interrelated. If the organizational forces are not aligned, resources will necessarily be wasted and unity is lacking. If the top senior management is not willing to open up and to cooperate, this can be described as the third silent killer. Poor communication is the fourth barrier, and inadequate down-the-line leadership skills and development the last barrier to successful strategy implementation and organizational learning.

Organizational fitness profiling (OFP) is a proven and useful organization-wide assessment process of the enablers of and barriers to organizational success. It is a procedure developed to support management to create honest and open communication within the organization in order to overcome the six 'silent killers' and to enable the organizational capabilities to become effective (Beer and Eisenstat, 2000).

According to Beer and Eisenstat (2000), the OFP procedure can be described in the following steps: First the senior management has to create a statement about the future strategy. This should happen in alignment with the overall environmental challenges and the organizations goals. This strategy should thereafter be communicated across

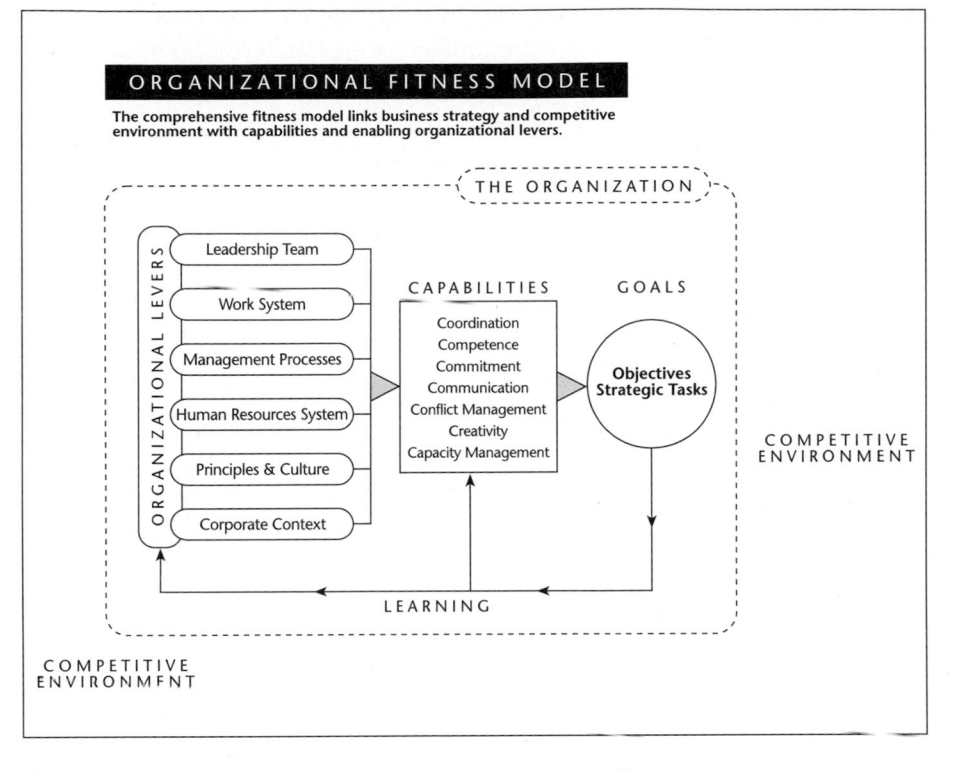

Figure 5.3 Organizational fitness profiling. Source: Beer (2003)

the organization. In a second step, a task force, designed as a cross-functional team of managers who are one or two levels below the top senior management team, should be deployed. They should conduct interviews inside and outside the organization in order to collect data on barriers to and enablers of the announced strategy. Once this has been achieved, the senior management should use the data to determine a vision for redesigning the organization. Then the proposed plan for change should be refined and reviewed with the employee task force. Finally, this plan should be implemented. The process of OFP thus provides an important procedure for embedding cultural meme in the organization.

Utilizing the OFP to Enable Management of the Innovation Meme

Organizational fitness profiling aims at improving the entire organization in order to build co-ordination and co-operation between different functions or departments, and to enable the creation of organizational capabilities. The process of organizational interviews, implemented to collect data, provides a good basis for the identification of organizational innovation meme within the company. Skillful interviewing should allow the innovation meme to be tracked, and its power of self-replication to be utilized to generate a culture of innovation within the organization. This would form a promising basis for sustained organizational fitness.

The profiling process itself only needs to be slightly changed and adapted over time. Even so, just adding 'innovative organizational culture' as one of the strategic goals, among others, in a general OFP will not be enough. When top management defines the organization's goals, they should keep the meaning and importance of innovation in today's fast-changing economy in mind. In fact, the underlying basis of any company's strategy has to be innovation. The following is an example of the key questions in the OFP 'questionnaire' with which to track down the innovation meme:

1. What have been successful innovations affecting the company? During the past years, what have been the most unique and influential innovations in general? This must not only focus on the own industry or market: brilliant innovations are made everywhere.

2. How were they developed? Where do they come from? Behind every important innovation there is a story of how it was developed, or how the innovator got the idea. It is important to look for the origin of the creativity.

3. Who are the innovative 'masters' (originators or drivers)? The creative minds behind the innovations should be identified.

4. What are they doing differently? What makes the approach the innovator used different from others? Very often exceptional circumstances have caused/nurtured the discovery of innovations. It is important to know the story behind the innovation.

5. Is what has been found in the answers to the above questions a cultural unit that can be transferred by imitation? Only if it has particular meme characteristics can it be called an innovation meme.

3M might have used a similar system without even explicitly noticing it. When looking for ideas on how to become more innovative, they came across the lead user process. Management can do the same intentionally by using a structured process. The first four questions are examples of how to track the innovative process and the elements behind the innovation itself. They can be adapted and refined arbitrarily. The last question is the most important one since this will identify whether what has been found is really a meme. Should this question be answered positively, it can be termed an innovation meme. Thus the innovation meme can be defined as:

Definition of 'innovation meme': A unit of cultural transmission or imitation that carries information responsible for innovations, and that can be transferred to other carriers, e.g., employees, departments, organizations etc.

When trying to find an innovation meme, the task force should not limit itself to the inward perspective. Innovation meme can exist beyond the boundaries of the own organization, for example, in other organizations or in other industries (Voelpel et al., 2004). Broadening one's perspective in this respect is a necessary condition for dramatic (disruptive) improvement and for not only becoming better than others, but making competitors irrelevant by forming a new basis for competition.

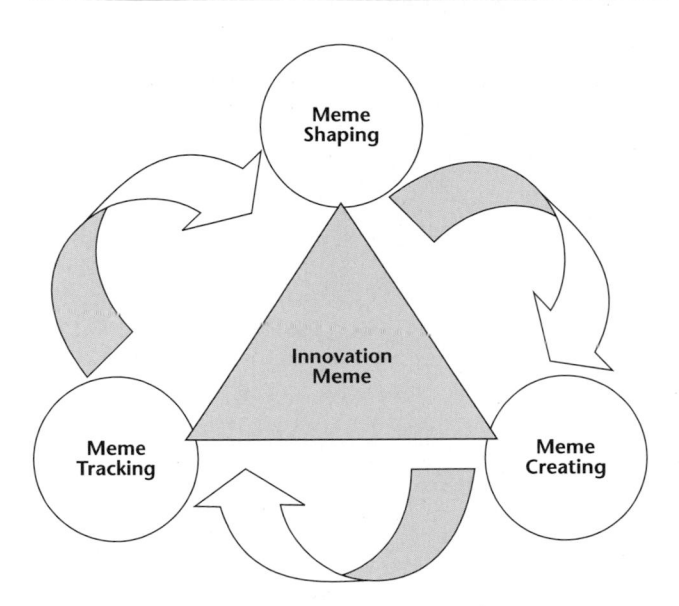

Figure 5.4 A conceptual approach to managing the innovation meme

Similar to what occurs in the OFP as described above, once the innovation meme is identified, the organizational top team and task force should decide how to proceed with what they have discovered. Organizational meme, and especially the innovation meme, seems to be a vital part of an evolutionary emergent process resulting from the interaction of the organizational members within the socio-cultural system. This kind of self-organizing, or self-emergent, socio-cultural system does not provide much space for planned intervention through traditional managerial approaches. To the extent management is able to influence, guide, and shape its own organizational culture in a self-organizing, continuous, and action-learning way, it should be capable of influencing and shaping innovation meme in general. This process can be called meme management (see Figure 5.4).

In general one can differentiate three major approaches to meme engineering, which might be appropriate and suitable under different conditions, namely:

Meme tracking is important to monitor the development and the mutations of the meme as well as the appearance of new innovation meme, no matter where they may originate. Meme is an evolving concept, dynamic and always changing within its environment, the organizational culture. It is important to track whether the innovation meme (and the information it is carrying) is always in alignment with the ultimate goal of the organization. If this is not the case, management has to intervene and to adapt by using one or both of the other elements of meme engineering: meme shaping and meme creating.

Meme shaping refers to an existing meme within the organization that has to be reconfigured, because it does not fit with the existing strategy. Slight modifications by management could create a mutation that destroys or replaces the old meme and has a better fit with the company's goals.

Meme creation simply means the total new design of a meme that should be implemented within the organization, because management aims to increase competitiveness and strategic alignment.

If applied in a meaningful order, all three elements together have a procedural character. Meme tracking should always be important in order to monitor the effect of the meme in the company. If deviations from organizational goals become apparent, meme shaping (as a less interventionist approach) can be followed by meme creating. Effective replicators of the innovation meme, prevalent in each of the three categories of meme management, are key to organizational fitness and survival. The careful adoption of this process seems to be the basis for enabling the organization to do so continuously.

The 3M-business case provides a good example of how the innovation meme could be managed. The concept of the lead user process would be the innovation meme that could be transferred through imitation from one employee, department or division to the other. While in this case the concept was propagated by top management, the lead user process as an innovation meme would propagate itself in the organization once it is successful and there is an opportunity for it to become widely spread through imitation. This could happen by providing the opportunity for cross-functional, casual meetings of interdisciplinary staff and divisions in order to foster the sharing of experiences and ideas. Successful meme will always spread spontaneously due to their positive, demonstrable effects, and soon a working idea might spread across the whole organization. In the context of the 3M-business case, meme tracking would mean the continuous monitoring of the success of the lead user process as a meme. Slight modifications in its adaptation to the organization could be called meme shaping,

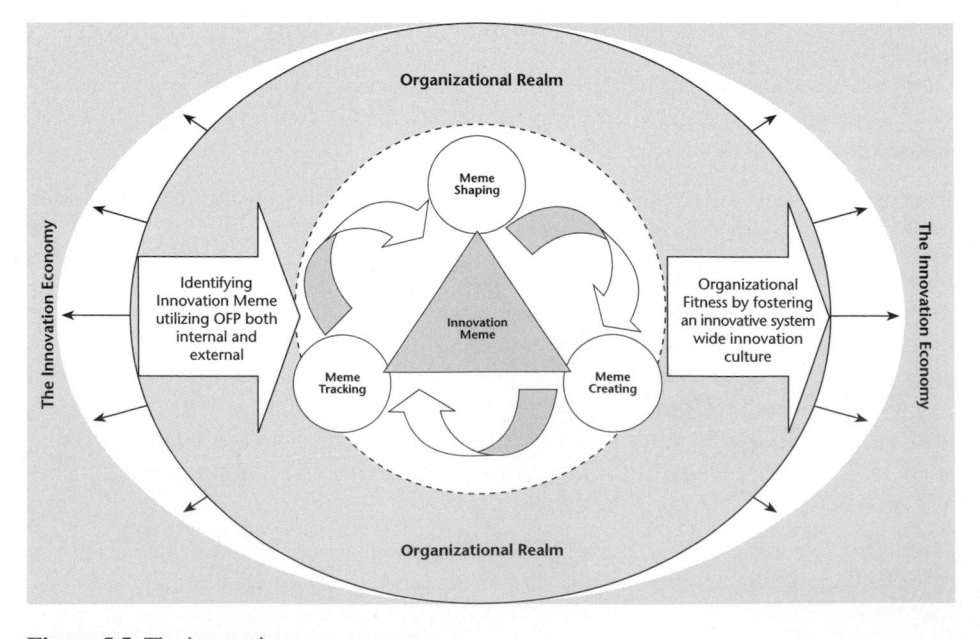

Figure 5.5 The innovation meme process

while the totally new introduction and propagation of the process in an organization is meme creation.

It is important to keep the general characteristics of meme, as mentioned before, in mind – especially those that it seems to have in common with genes. If successful, the innovation meme will propagate itself throughout the system. If not, the meme will become extinct like a weaker genetic mutation in nature that is not able to gain a competitive advantage over others in the environment. The benefit for management and organizational development is obvious. Nevertheless, the organization should continuously repeat this process in order to ensure the success of meme engineering and of the overall cultural change towards a more (and continuously) innovative culture. Figure 5.5 illustrates this process.

Managerial Implications

The innovation economy requires today's management to make a mental shift towards a different and advanced appreciation of innovation, and requires them to become organizationally innovative. Just improving what is already on the market will not be sufficient for survival and advancement in the long run. At the same time, the opportunities for innovative breakthroughs have never been better. Keeping in mind the specific traits and characteristics of meme, management and executives can improve their ability to become more innovative by utilizing the organizational fitness profiling process. They can thereby identify and break down barriers to change, and improve the organizational abilities of self-organization and action learning, thus releasing the company's creativity, innovation, adaptability, and survival power. Organizational fitness profiling provides a well-proven and established basis for utilizing the concept of innovation meme. As long as innovation is the basis for strategy, management can easily adapt the organizational fitness profiling process to manage the innovation meme through the necessary research questions and subsequent managerial levers. It is important to stress the fact that the acceptance and understanding of the innovation meme is a necessary prerequisite for an organization to deal successfully with the challenge of developing a continuously innovative organization.

When it comes to generating organizational innovation, everybody inside and outside the organization is a potential innovator, or impetus for innovation. Management can use this knowledge to allow the innovation meme to spread itself across the whole organization and business ecosystem, thereby creating an overall culture of innovation.

Conclusion

The organization is embedded in what can be called the innovation economy with its dynamic competitive challenges and the need for innovative value creation. The organizational fitness profiling process (OFP) can be adapted and used to identify and manage the innovation meme within the organization and in its relevant business ecosystem. Meme management can be used to guide and influence, i.e. to track, shape, and to create the innovation meme. Once it is known what the company's innovation meme is, it enables management to support its spread over the organization in order to exploit its benefits as widely as possible, and to achieve sustained organizational fitness through an overall culture of innovation.

While this article has provided a description of the innovation meme and a broad approach to its management, its scope prevents an analysis of particular techniques and methods to enable organizational culture replicators to be disseminated and embedded in the organization. This is the subject of further research by the authors. What has been suggested should be understood as the basis for further refinement, development, and testing of the concept and application of innovation meme under real business conditions, and as the starting point for further scholarly debate and investigations.

An Opportunity-Based Strategy Process for Innovation*

by D. Quinn Mills

The Strategy Process Challenge in the Innovation Economy

To be successful a modern corporation in the age of the innovation economy must be fast on its feet. Firms must migrate key elements of business strategy and planning out of the corporate office and into decentralized business units. Top executives must liberate planning from budgeting. The following pages suggest a simple, three-step process that combines business strategy and execution at the business unit level in a fast, iterative process in order to take advantages of the opportunities created by innovation.

Three Crucial Steps

With structural barriers to competition fast disappearing as a consequence of electronic connectivity, market deregulation and improving technologies of many sorts, how well and quickly a company reacts to change are all that protect its positions. The effective executive recognizes that fast adaptability is the latest stage in the evolution of business strategy. Initially, companies were urged to procure market share, the data seeming to correlate it with profitability. Then strategists dissected industry structure and urged companies to seek strategic position, either by being low cost producers or by differentiating their products in such a way that a price premium could be obtained. This was followed by exhortations to define core competencies and strategic intent – this was strategy as stretch. In today's fast moving and unpredictable marketplace, emphasis has shifted to speed.

But not to chaos. Those who heed the gurus who insist that chaos is a necessary accompaniment to speed are prey to confusion. In the absence of clear and logical direction a business is subject to disastrous mistakes. Chaos not only engenders confusion, it is not the right solution because it is subject to disastrous mistakes. What is needed is a disciplined process by which speed can be achieved quickly.

An effective executive helps his firm to abandon the archaic separation of strategy and execution, of planning and implementation, and instead seeks to have it intertwine

---

* Adapted from: Mills, D.Q. (2001), *e-Leadership*, New York: Prentice-Hall Press, Chapters 9 and 10.

planning and execution in time as if in a double helix. The requisite process for accomplishing this can be built around three steps: seeking; shaping; and securing. Generally, seeking is about discovering global opportunity, shaping about locking in the opportunity, and securing about seizing its value.

Seeking involves knowing where to look for, shaping understanding how to extract value from global opportunities. Securing is the dynamic process of realizing that value. A firm that moves too fast will be consumed by innovation from which it will not derive full payoff; a firm that moves too slowly will be left behind. The dynamic process of seeking, shaping, and securing must appropriately be paced and executed in the correct sequence.

Although each firm's strategic journey will be unique, the preferred sequence of steps will be common to all. A firm chooses a place to participate in the economic landscape, organizes if it can how the game is played, then seizes all the value it can.

Implicit in the new strategy of speed, as in so many innovations, is the discarding of current habits. Many companies' approach to business continues to reflect the ancient military paradigm that treats strategy and its execution as separate activities, a legacy of a brief period during which large companies that commanded dominant market shares enjoyed the luxury of sufficient time and excess resources to invest in this artificial distinction. In strategy formulation according to the military paradigm – a rigidly-formal and hierarchical process – executives are the generals who plan, mangers the majors who assign, and employees the soldiers who execute. Strategy is thus dictated on high, communicated down the ranks, and implemented at the bottom. Because it so fully defines roles and responsibilities, it is a comfortable system for executives, management, and staff alike. But it is slow, rigid, often poorly informed, and crippling in today's fast-moving world. Firms plan things they can't execute and execute what they haven't planned.

What is needed is a system that can unite strategy formulation and execution, in a manner that is iterative and inclusive, that is to say, that is continuous – not undertaken once to yield results that will be adjusted only at distant and discrete intervals – and bring the company's full experience base, not just the thinking of a few top executives, to bear.

What has evolved to satisfy this need is the three-step strategy of speed: seeking opportunities; shaping capabilities; and securing the potential. Employed as a process, this strategy ensures that the changing potential of global business is explored and opportunities identified, assessed, and the most valuable targeted for action and resource allocation (seeking), that organizational capabilities are developed and strategic positions established (shaping), and value realized (securing). Seeking is a process of exploration, shaping of configuration, and securing of realization.

STEP 1: SEEKING

The world economy today is not only more complex, challenging, and risky than it has been, but likely to become more so. Not widely understood today, this is why exploring different directions of global development is so important.

The seeking step involves:

- anticipating the geographical, industrial, and competitive "high grounds" that will enable an enterprise to capture value as the global landscape shifts;
- exploring trends in a changing world for value creation opportunities;
- selecting the opportunities with the greatest potential for building value

Seeking is thus about anticipating the demands of 21st century business. The companies that have made the most money in recent years are those that have anticipated the future and positioned themselves to take advantage of resulting opportunities. Anticipating the future also means assessing non-traditional opportunities created by economic growth and restructuring.

STEP 2: SHAPING

To win big a company must shape its chosen markets to suit its competitive strengths, in part, by tapping the potential of interconnectivity. This is done by creating self-serving boundaries around business opportunities. Historically, methods of creating boundaries – including ownership, lawsuits, patents, government regulation, and location – are fast disappearing as a consequence of market deregulation, variation in legal standards among nations, electronic interchanges, and technological advances in a growing number of industries.

Many newer methods of creating boundaries remain unfamiliar to today's executives. Consulting, for example, is an industry that lives within other industries in symbiotic relationships that are themselves barriers to competitors. Alternatively, alliances – especially with government and local institutions – afford companies access to value that would not otherwise be available to them. Competitors can also be kept at bay by tying up key suppliers or customers as alliance partners and by mounting one-to-one marketing initiatives that exploit information technology to support highly targeted sales and promotion efforts paired with customer retention and loyalty programs.

Successful barriers to new entrants and existing competitors are erected by leveraging key intangible assets – knowledge and brands – far more effectively than has likely been done in the past. Throughout the centuries value has largely been created by controlling and exploiting physical assets, for example, finding, mining, and marketing the world's minerals. In today's over-exploited world companies that are able to assemble, support, and maximize the effectiveness of global terms are better able to anticipate and react to changes in the ever more volatile international arena.

The primary strategic challenge to management in the 21st century will no longer be how to maximize the finite life-spans of given technologies or innovations, but rather to learn to ride the waves of innovation that continually wash over and through the market space. Companies that do not learn to surf the continuous changes in technology will not survive long enough to need coherent strategies.

The new barriers to entry will be metaphysical, not physical, barriers in the mind rather than statutory barriers such as preferred access to resources or state-sponsored protections, which will be auctioned off to the highest bidder and thereby become no barriers at all. The new barriers to entry will be attributes to flexibility, opportunity seeking, and speed of execution. Strategy will become a hunt for ideas, not niches, as transaction costs continue to fall and the sizes and shapes of companies shift in response. Most strategists want the actors on the business stage to try to change the script; few see that today the other actors and the stage itself can also be managed.

STEP 3: SECURING

How is a company that has expended time, energy, and resources shaping an industry or a market to ensure that it will not lose the value generated by its investment to a competitor? There is nothing automatic about realizing value. It does not simply fall into an innovator's hands. The last step of the strategy for speed, securing, involves extracting value for as long as possible without undermining the future. Balancing value extraction and new innovation in a continuously changing world is as difficult as it is essential. Too many companies stop short of the final step of ensuring that all potential value is realized.

A Unified Strategy Model

What if the convenient and familiar separation of business processes into strategy formulation and execution should prove impossible to abandon? Can the new model be adopted by a firm that retains the bureaucratic process of strategy formulation? Upon the answer to this question depends whether many executives in traditional firms can ever become effective. Fortunately, the answer is yes, at least to a degree – the new model can be applied, albeit imperfectly, in the old setting.

Having refocused from industries and competencies to opportunities and potentialities, the effective executive proceeds to construct processes that apply the new thinking. Only if they remain applicable in specific circumstances should old approaches be retained, appropriately supplemented and cast in a broader framework. The latter is achieved by means of a new, unified model of strategy formulation.

A unified strategic model (USM) integrates existing shareholder value and strategic change models with new front-end elements and contemporary management initiatives such as reengineering and value chain analysis. It clarifies where what has been done conventionally fits into an overall strategic scheme and what has been left out or done only imperfectly. Value chain, organizational change, and shareholder value are treated as modules in the larger model, each a fully articulated sub-model of the USM.

Underlying the model and driving its application is the new way of thinking that emphasizes opportunity and potentiality. Strategy today is, or should be, concerned with identifying and selecting among opportunities, changing the organization so as to be able to seize these opportunities, and optimizing the financial aspects of the new initiatives that result. Each of these four activities involves a separate and complex process that has a strategic orientation. In fact, various commentators and consultants have identified each as the core strategy to the exclusion of the others.

The USM consists of the following elements in this order:

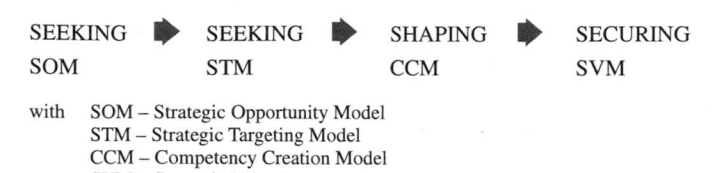

SEEKING   SEEKING   SHAPING   SECURING
SOM   STM   CCM   SVM

with   SOM – Strategic Opportunity Model
       STM – Strategic Targeting Model
       CCM – Competency Creation Model
       SVM – Strategic Value Model

The Strategic Opportunity Model

Largely missing from recent strategy discussions and poorly spelled-out even when recognized, the strategic opportunity model (SOM) is the front-end of the strategy model. It is surprising that the front-end should be so little developed, because identifying opportunity has become crucial to strategy. Many winning companies are creating rather than simply serving markets. Value-chain approaches, because they treat as more mature firms that cease to create markets, drive strategy towards serving existing markets. This is because growth generates shareholder value and market creation generates growth – providing a powerful alternative strategy for growth, albeit less viable today than before. (The export promotion strategy of the Japanese and their imitators involves serving existing markets, especially in the United States, and periodically sacrificing profitability for market share. The Japanese capital market was prepared to pay for growth without regard to profitability. Today's world capital market is not.)

Today's other big winning strategy revolves around market restructuring – displacing existing providers with a dramatically different approach to the market. The best examples are the great retail chains, franchises and category killers, that displace existing firms. Thus, MacDonald's by and large supplanted diners, Wal-Mart, small town department stores, Home Depot, downtown hardware stores, and CVS, corner drug stores. Opportunity consists of recognizing when an industry is ripe for restructuring.

Top executives instigate the search for opportunities by soliciting information and support within the organization and committing enthusiasm and resources. They thereby set in motion three simultaneous processes: a market review in conjunction with outsiders; idea gathering within the firm; and a technological application review. The first is analytic, the second happenstance (involving whomever has some notion), the third selective and collective (brainstorming among individuals with particular expertise). These inputs feed a broader process of opportunity identification.

If an opportunity is in a business related to what a firm does, one track is followed; if it is in an unrelated business, a different track is taken. For opportunities in related businesses it is generally presumed that a firm possesses key competencies (if it does not, their absence must be addressed separately and directly). An assessment of the organization's ability to seize the new opportunity will attempt to answer questions such as: "Can it do so successfully?" "If not, what is needed?" These questions should instigate a process of competence enhancement in which the applicability of new information technology, because it is the basis for creating or enabling strategic opportunities in many businesses today, is likely to play a large part. The amount of investment needed to capture the opportunity must then be determined, at which point the firm is positioned to pursue it through a process of managed change.

For opportunities in unrelated businesses the process is only somewhat different. A careful analysis must be made of the new customers' needs and behaviors and elements of the new business that will have to be supplied identified. The output of these stages suggests the new competencies the firm must develop if it is to be able to exploit the opportunity. These competencies must be secured one way or another, whether through purchase or acquisition, internal development, or partnering. If through the latter, potential partners must be identified. Finally, the level of investment must be determined and a process of managed strategic change inaugurated.

At the identification stage it is useful to think in terms of an opportunity spectrum. Strategy involves identifying high potential points on the opportunity spectrum.

There are two types of customers in the world, individuals and organizations. In general, customer demand is driven by personal lifestyle mix (PLM), which creates opportunities by virtue of changing over time. PLM has been quite different in different countries, but is believed to be converging on that of the developed countries. Strategists examining PLM ask:

- Where can a new product or service be introduced?
- Can an existing industry (i.e., a component of consumer spending)
  be revolutionized?

In general, organizational demand is driven by corporate input mix (CIM). "Corporate" is here understood to refer to government and not-for-profit entities as well. Opportunities are created in this realm as the proportion of spending shifts over time among elements of the mix. Because corporate is a derived, not final, demand, CIM should be considered in a context that involves its customers and its suppliers.

The first element of this context is the personal expenditure distribution, which is derived from the PLM, the second the value chain in which the corporation participates, and the third is the CIM itself. That is, each element of the PLM defines an industry that has a value chain that comprises corporations with associated spending mixes for the inputs they need to operate. For example, each of the companies that comprise the value chain for the housing industry that exists to satisfy customers' need has an input spending pattern. Opportunities are created for sales to corporations both by changes in the personal expenditure mix (i.e., the change in corporate demand derived from changes in consumer demand) and by shifts among firms along the value chain.

The essence of strategy for a firm seeking to sell to individuals is to anticipate shifts in their lifestyle mix and, therefore, spending patterns, the essence of strategy for a firm seeking to sell to organizations to anticipate changes in their customers' spending patterns or in the positioning of firms on the value chain, and reposition so as to be able to seize opportunities created thereby.

Strategy can be reactive or proactive. Reactive strategies seek to capitalize on expected shifts in the PLM or CIM, proactive strategies to create markets via new products or services that then become part of the PLM or CIM.

The most successful businesses are proactive strategists. They introduce new products or services and capitalize on the new markets they define (e.g., the railway, the electric light, the telephone, the television, the personal computer). But a new product or service is not a sure thing. Some firms invent a product only to have others capitalize on it (e.g., Microsoft Apple's innovation); others invent products and services for which there is no demand.

An adjunct to the opportunity spectrum, the opportunity profit spectrum identifies relative profitability of business opportunities, as indicated in the following box.

Opportunity Profit Spectrum			
Most Profitable			*Least Profitable*
Market creation (new products)	Market seizure (better value or lower cost)	Sales diffusion (expanded markets)	Sales penetration (gaining market share)

The Strategic Targeting Model

The strategic targeting model (STM) is a three way matrix that relates goals to methods to contribution. Opportunities derived from the STM are analyzed for fit with a firm's goals and ability to execute (methods) and for their potential contribution to its financial performance. Goals are often multiple and imposed on an executive or a firm (although firms sometimes set goals as well); methods involve both options and alternatives. Alternatives are necessary in order that the selection decision can be decoupled for the positioning decision (driven by the value chain). Because the associated analytic process threatens to become expensive and lengthy, executives tend to be inclined to minimize the search for alternatives. Indeed, most strategy represents a leap to a particular course of action sans examination of alternatives, a short-cut often characterized as intuition. There is always an advantage to trying to generate alternatives and it can be done efficiently; it is not necessary to fully analyze all alternatives, only those that show promise. Potential contributions are measured by means of financial analyses of the various alternatives. Contributions must be risk-weighed (e.g., globalization opportunities often incur added risk). The contribution should be maximized subject to constraints on a firm's ability to undertake new strategic initiatives.

The Competency Creation Model

Efforts of behavioral scientists and organizational consultants to define the process whereby a company's organization and culture can be redirected to facilitate the pursuit of specific strategic business goals yielded the competency creation model (CCM). The model posits that a company's culture is not static, changing only in response to change initiatives, but evolves continuously and, hence, should be managed with strategic intent. This adds a second dimension to the STM, which usually focuses only on initiated change.

The direction of organizational change (in people, structure, culture, morale, and so forth) is driven by the results of the strategic targeting activity. This direction must be imposed on, introduced as a new element in, the evolution of the organization. Trying to direct evolutionary change might be perceived to be defensive, trying to direct the organization towards some new desired state an offensive act.

If evolutionary change is in the desired direction, it can be reinforced in a variety of ways, if not, it must be challenged. Redirecting evolution involves establishing incentives that promote behavior that is consistent with the desired change, allaying employees' fears about risks that appear to be associated with the change, promoting voluntary acceptance of, and establishing disincentives for failure to accept, the proposed changes, incentives and evaluating the consistency of the measures that are adopted. Inconsistencies must be rectified and the resulting incentives, penalties, and attitudinal interventions imposed to direct both evolutionary and desired changes.

The purpose of this module is to turn a business in the desired direction or, if it is on the desired path, ensure that it remains so.

The Strategic Value Model

Having identified and targeted specific opportunities, developed competencies, and entered selected, potentially high profit businesses, it is time to turn attention to deriving full value from the effort what has been made. The strategic value model (SVM), although originated as a business valuation model, can be used to direct strategic thinking to the maximization of shareholder wealth as well as to value a company. The model's seen elements are described briefly below, and listed in a subsequent table.

1. When appropriate, systemic value chain analysis could be used to position a business unit correctly in its industry. This is possible for businesses in existing industries, extremely difficult or impossible for businesses that are Internet-based or in other ways novel.

2. Bottom-line contribution from the business must be maximized by rationalizing or reengineering its components to minimize cost.

3. Value creation is maximized by creating virtual barriers to entry such as staying ahead by running ahead, engaging in alliances to forestall competitors, and gaining first mover advantage.

4. Opportunities for expanding the existing business are defined, analyzed, and selected on a contribution analysis basis, whereby net present value is the standard of selection among competing investment opportunities. The traditional cash-cow/star matrix is applicable here. Some businesses merit further investment; some do not.

5. Opportunities for financial restructuring, increasing leverage, and improving cash management are explored and financial engineering exploited to add to the return from the business.

6. Consideration is given to augmenting the business via acquisitions, mergers, partnerships, or divestitures.

7. All elements of existing businesses are assessed as if they were part of a financial portfolio, and a determination whether to hold or sell each made on the basis of its financial contribution, strategic relevance and risk profiles.

Elements of a Strategic Value Model		
STAGE 1	Repositioning, if appropriate	*e.g. Systemic Value Chain Analysis; Business Ecosystem Sense-making*
STAGE 2	Rationalization: creating efficiency	*e.g. Business Process Reengineering; TQM, BSC*
STAGE 3	Creating barriers to competition, virtual and actual	*e.g. Competitive Analysis; New Industry Parameters*
STAGE 4	Optimization and expansion	*e.g. Present Value Analysis*
STAGE 5	Financial restructuring	*e.g. Leverage and Cash Analysis*
STAGE 6	Augmentation; mergers and acquisitions	*e.g. Contribution Analysis*
STAGE 7	Portfolio Analysis: what to keep; what to sell; what to acquire/start	*e.g. Shareholder Value Analysis; Risk Options Analysis*

Conclusion

The effective executive recognizes that:

- Existing strategic models require a broader framework and new front-end because (1) core competency analysis is too backward looking (for example, how does one introduce new and needed competencies?), and (2) value-chain analysis is too myopic.
- The needed new framework is realized by casting existing models in a broader strategic process of opportunity identification (selection stage), value-chain/competency assessment (analysis stage), change direction or redirection (implementation stage), and value maximization with an underlying theme of strategy as execution.
- This new framework, termed the unified strategic model (USM), incorporates systematic approaches to opportunity identification; opportunity targeting; competency creation; and full value realization.
- Companies can use the USM to capture the full potential of opportunities in the innovation economy.

Case Example
Innovative Business Models in the Airline Industry*

Deluded Optimists

Network passenger airlines everywhere face the same challenge. They were designed for an age of regulation and state ownership that is passing. Competition from budget airlines is the biggest manifestation of this change, while creeping international deregulation and new planes, big and small, that can fly longer distances direct are undermining the dominance of the traditional hub-and-spoke network in many regions.

The traditional network carriers are not just grappling with a cyclical slump aggravated by the external shocks of the past three years. Some observers take the view that the basic business model of the network carriers is broken, and that they will have to reinvent themselves or go out of business, despite the stream of subsidies emanating from the federal government.

Budget airlines such as Southwest, AirTran and JetBlue enjoy about a 30% cost advantage. If the comparison is adjusted for the fact that budget airlines do shorter (i.e., proportionately more costly to operate) routes, some think the budget carriers' costs, measured on a comparable basis, would be as low as half those of traditional airlines. Nor is a non-unionized workforce the budget airlines' only advantage. In a recent study of American and European airlines, Booz Allen Hamilton pointed out that about two-thirds of their cost advantage comes from having superior, more economical business processes such as selling seats over the internet or flying their aircraft more hours each day.

Budget Carriers and Mainstream Airlines

While the full-service carriers are struggling to get back to the traffic levels they enjoyed in 2000, the budget airlines are growing by more than 10% a year and little is

* Adapted from Dann, J. (2003), "Disruption: Flying the Not-So-Friendly Skies", *Harvard Business School Working Knowledge,* October 20, 1-6; and "Airlines Under Siege: Silver Linings, Darkening Clouds", *The Economist*, Special Report, March 27 – April 2, 2004, 67-82.

getting in their way. The biggest difference between budget carriers and mainstream airlines is their radically different way of working. Traditional airlines run networks, based around hubs, while low-cost airlines offer simple point-to-point services, with no provision for transfers and no frills such as lounges and free food and drink.

The value of hubs (whether the big domestic ones in America or international ones such as London's Heathrow, Paris's Charles de Gaulle or Singapore's Changi) is that they minimize the risk to an airline's revenue. They do this by sucking in passengers from a variety of cities (including many small ones, in America) to fill up a given flight, by offering a wide range of destinations via the hub. But to make this work, airlines tend to have their planes sitting around on the ground for a long time to make the connections. The same thing goes for flight crews, and there are extra ground staff hanging around as well.

Budget airlines running point-to-point services fill their planes by making the ticket so cheap it expands demand, even for a new destination, while their simple route model means that aircraft fly more hours each day. The no-frills service makes it possible to clean up and turn round a plane in about 25 minutes, compared with the hour-and-a-half or more it takes to turn round a jumbo jet.

Flattery by Imitation

Network carriers have already learned some tricks from budget rivals, such as selling flights over the internet and doing away with printed tickets. They have also copied with some success the variable pricing used so brilliantly by budget airlines to fill seats at times of low demand. American carriers have also altered their schedules, going for rolling waves of connecting flights rather than holding planes on the ground in anticipation of any particular connection. The aim is to get more flying hours out of each plane and its crew.

Apart from lowering costs and fares, budget airlines have unbundled the old air-travel experience: now, if you want food and drink, you pay, and the airline pockets a healthy profit for every such transaction.

A consensus seems to be emerging that it is time for airlines to learn lessons from other mature sectors, such as cars. In particular, airlines seem to be ripe for the lean techniques exemplified by Toyota's legendary production system.

A recent McKinsey study urging airlines to adopt lean techniques starts with a paradox. Each day airlines achieve the remarkable by safely moving 5m people some 40m air miles around the world. Yet they often fail to deliver ordinary things such as prompt arrival according to the published schedule. Too often a plane lands only to hang around for a ground crew to unload it, or for an earlier flight to move away from a gate. Routine maintenance work causes continual delays.

Not Only Connect

Scheduling flights to make easier connections leads to the low aircraft-utilization that American carriers are trying to improve by "de-peaking" their hubs. Booz Allen suggests that American carriers should be combing through their flight operations and schedules with the aim of having a new business model that makes connections a by-product rather than a key objective. With this would go rapid turn-arounds and a 30% increase in plane and crew utilization, as well as a doubling of productivity by ground crews.

Airlines that try to get lean should, however, note that few carmakers have learned to be lean winners. Several have been swallowed by rivals and others face extinction. The same would already be true of lots of big airlines, were it not for their indulgent governments. Even with help, big carriers will struggle to survive their industry's rapid transition towards a new business model.

Disruptive Innovation by Southwest Airlines

Southwest Airlines was the primary instigator during the mid-1980s of a low-end disruption in the air travel market. Low-end disruptions target the least-demanding customers in an existing marketplace with lower-priced products that are good enough to get the job done, but no better.

Rather than trying to beat the majors at their own game, Southwest rejected the hub-and-spoke system. Instead, it created an economical network of point-to-point short-haul flights while using less-expensive gate slots at secondary airports whenever possible. Southwest offered no assigned seating and minimal food service, allowing rapid airplane turnaround and increased capacity utilization.

At the same time Southwest created this low-end disruption, it simultaneously instigated a new-market disruption by targeting segments of the potential marketplace where people were not flying or not flying often. Southwest and other discounters have grown sales by getting travelers out of cars and trains and enticing underserved customers in many smaller cities to make that extra bargain trip.

Comparing a Start-up (JetBlue Airways) and an Incumbent (Delta's Song Airlines)

JetBlue Airways is an innovative but vulnerable newcomer potentially trapped between a well-entrenched Southwest and a horde of large carriers motivated to come back and fight for the lower tiers of the air travel marketplace. However, over the last few years, JetBlue has gained renown as a smart, nimble upstart that has created what appears – right now, at least – to be a winning formula.

"Starting with a blank slate, we had an opportunity to simply 'build a better mouse-trap,' which gave us a tremendous advantage in our markets," says CEO Neeleman. "Larger airlines might have fine operations people and fine planning people, but if your product – from a service, delivery, and cost level – does not work, you're in trouble." Actually, Neeleman acknowledges, JetBlue's slate was not completely blank – Southwest's operational practices were an early source of inspiration.

Neeleman first earned his wings at a start-up airline, then joined Southwest after the discount airline bought out Neeleman and his partners. Neeleman soon parted ways with Southwest, but when his noncompete expired, he formed JetBlue Airways, which launched in early 2000. By spring of 2003, JetBlue served twenty U.S. cities with more than forty aircraft.

Delta's Song: Building on a Legacy

Song is not Delta's first foray into the discount air travel game. The new subsidiary is replacing Delta Express, which will be phased out gradually. Delta's experience to date with the "airline within an airline" concept has been similar to that of other major U.S. carriers; US Airways, Continental, and United have all started and then shuttered in-house low-frills operations.

To its credit, Delta seems to be establishing a stronger underpinning for Song than it did for its previous effort. "This is an evolution of the Delta Express product, but founded on a much more solid basis. Delta Express was created with a temporarily lowered pilot pay scale and a temporarily deferred maintenance cost program," says Stacy Geagan, Song's general manager for corporate communications. "Those were transitory cost benefits, and not the best basis to start a business for the long term."

Early on, Delta faced two questions that many large firms must address when they attempt to launch a business around a disruptive innovation: How should we position the new unit within the corporate structure? What capabilities should we transfer over from the parent and which should we develop from scratch? Delta chose a model that, though granting a great delta of autonomy in the areas of marketing, branding, and in-cabin operations, keeps Song very dependent on the parent's resources and processes. "Delta considers itself the 'operation' – we consider ourselves the 'marketing engine,'" says Geagan.

Different Organizations, Different Choices

In many ways, Song's and JetBlue's service offering are similar. Both use nontraditional brand and marketing approaches to attract customers. Both build much of their in-flight customer experiences around advanced seat-back entertainment systems. Both boast novel cleaning and turnaround processes that get their planes back in the air much faster than most competitors are able to. (Song's jets will be in the air on average 1.2 hours more per day than Delta's, generating significant cost savings.)

But Song's heavy reliance on the resources of its parent could prevent it from reshaping key elements of its operations, a limitation not facing JetBlue. JetBlue may yet avoid being trapped between an entrenched Southwest and struggling but motivated incumbents. In early June, JetBlue announced its intention to purchase 100 regional jets from Brazil's Embraer. JetBlue has the potential to establish the kind of disruptive business that regional airlines – so deeply enmeshed with major carriers – have thus far not rolled out.

Ultimately, a business unit like Song may not represent the type of incumbent repositioning that will cause the likes of JetBlue to falter. While it has created and borrowed many operational elements that may make it an interesting player in the discount travel market. Song may very well face limitations due to its tight operational linkages to Delta, and it is questionable, if an entity like Song will have the strategic and operational freedom to pursue truly disruptive strategies.

Whether they turn to regional jets, fully autonomous business units, or some other as-yet-untried innovations, America's large carriers will need entirely new competitive tools to survive in this complex and hypercompetitive sector.

Questions

1. Why have some traditional large airline passenger companies not been successful in creating and implementing an additional discount, low-cost business model?

2. Provide an insightful and concise comparison (e.g. similarities, differences) between the traditional strategy creation process (analysis-formulation-implementation-change), and the holistic (poised) strategy process (sense-making-reinvention-options&thrusts-capabilities).

3. Select any company, and apply the wheel of business model reinvention process to (hypothetically) reinvent its business model. Indicate where & how you start the process, and why.

4. Sense-making of business ecosystem trends and their underlying influences is important for business model reinvention. What sense-making capabilities should an organization such as Shell have, and what range of tools would you recommend it to use?

5. Starbucks 'discovered' new market space opportunities and transformed a functional product into an emotional one. Could the same be achieved for other 'commodity' products such as tea, milk, and even some categories of soft drinks? Apply the market space tool in your investigation.

6. What capabilities are required to create a 'new value curve', and thereby a new customer value proposition, as Home Depot did?

7. Are some industries, and their companies, more amenable to open innovation practices than others? Substantiate your response by comparing a number of industries and prominent companies.

8. Development of new business models inherently involves additional costs and risks. What tool(s) are available for balancing (and reducing) such risks?

9. Develop particular measurements (evaluation criteria/norms) for each of the four dimensions of the poised strategy scorecard (PSC), and explain how they differ from the measurements of the balanced scorecard (BSC).

References

Chapter 5:
Processes and Tools for Poised Strategic Management in the Innovation Economy

[1] This subsection is primarily based on Christensen, C.M. and Raynor, M.E. (2003), *The Innovator's Solution: Creating and Sustaining Successful Growth*, Boston: Harvard Business School Press, pp. 226-231.

[2] McGrath, R.G. and MacMillan, I.C. (1995), "Discovery-Driven Planning", *Harvard Business Review*, 73(4), 44-56.

[3] Christensen, C.M. and Raynor, M.E. (2003), *op.cit.*, 222-224.

[4] The co-existence of the two different strategy processes – deliberate and emergent – was also postulated by a number of other prominent authors, e.g. Mintzberg, H. and Waters, J. (1985), "Of Strategies, Deliberate and Emergent", *Strategic Management Journal*, 6, 257; and Burgelman, R. (2002), "Strategy as Vector and the Inertia of Co-evolutionary Lock-in", *Administrative Science Quarterly*, 47, 325-357.

[5] These four key dimensions have originally been suggested, in different ways, by a number of authors. See Voelpel, S., Leibold, M., Tekie, E. and von Krogh, G. (2005): "Escaping the Red Queen Effect in Competitive Strategy: How Managers Can Change Industry Rules by Sense-Testing their Business Models", *European Management Journal*, Vol. 23, No. 1, 37-49.

[6] Adapted from Bradley, S.P.(1998), "Capturing Value in the Network Era", in Bradley, S.P. and Nolan, R.L. (1998), *Sense and Respond*, Boston: Harvard Business School Press.

[7] Adapted from Bartlett, C.A. and Ghoshal, S. (2000), "Going Global – Lessons from Late Movers", *Harvard Business Review*, 78(2), 132-142.

[8] Adapted from Beinhocker, E.D. (1997), "Strategy at the Edge of Chaos", *McKinsey Quarterly*, 1, 34.

[9] See e.g., Eisenhardt, K.M. and Sull, D. (2001), "Strategy as Simple Rules", *Harvard Business Review*, 79(1), 107-116.

[10] Adapted from Moore, J.F. (1996), *The Death of Competition*, New York: Harper Business.

[11] Adapted from Moore, J.F., *op.cit.*

[12] See: Roos, J. and Oliver, D. (1999), "The Poised Organization: Navigating Effectively on Knowledge", http://www.imd.ch./fac/roos.paper_po.html, November 2, 1-21; Brown, S.L. and Eisenhardt, K.M. (1998), *Competing on the Edge: Strategy as Structured Chaos*, Boston: Harvard Business School Press; Eisenhardt, K.M. and Sull, D. (2001), "Strategy as Simple Rules", *Harvard Business Review*, 79(1), 107-116; Eisenhardt, K.M. and Galunic, D.C. (2000), "Co-evolving: At Last, a Way to Make Synergies Work", *Harvard Business Review*, 78(1), 91-101; Eisenhardt, K.M. and Martin, J.A. (2000), "Dynamic Capabilities: What are They?", *Strategic Management Journal*, 21, 1105-21; Kelly, S. and Allison, M.A. (1999), *The Complexity Advantage*, New York: Business Week Books.

[13] Hargadon, A (2003). *How Breakthroughs Happen*, Boston: Harvard Business School Press.

[14] See Leonard, D. and Swap, W., "Deep Smarts", *Harvard Business Review*, 82 (9), 88-97 (2004).

[15] This tool (and sub-section) is based predominantly on the work of Kim, W.C. and Mauborgne, R. (1999), "Creating New Market Space", *Harvard Business Review*, 77(1), 83-93; and (2005) "Blue Ocean Strategy: From Theory to Practice", *California Management Review*, Vol. 47, No. 3, 105-121.

[16] Davenport, T.H., Harris, J.G., and Kohli, A.K.,(2001) "How Do They Know Their Customers So Well?" *MIT Sloan Management Review*, 2(42), 63-73.

[17] See: Gibbert, M., Leibold, M. and Probst, G. (2002), "Five Styles of Customer Knowledge Management, and How Smart Companies Use Them to Create Value", *European Management Journal,* 20(5), 459-469.

[18] Davenport, T.H. and Probst, G.J.B (2002), *Knowledge Management Case Book: Siemens Best Practices*, Second edition, Erlangen: Publicis.

[19] See: Prahalad, C. and Ramaswamy, V. (2000), "Co-opting Customer Competence", *Harvard Business Review*; 78(1), 79-87; and Inkpen, A.C. (1996), "Creating Knowledge through Collaboration", *California Management Review,* 39(1), 123-139.

[20] The tool 'Creating a New Value Curve', and examples used in this section, are predominantly based on Kim, W.C. and Mauborgne, R. (1999), *op.cit.*, and (2005), *op. cit.*

[21] This subsection is predominantly based on Wenger, E.C. and Snyder, W.M. (2000), "Communities of Practice: the Organizational Frontier", *Harvard Business Review*, 78(1), 145.

[22] Toffler, A. (1980), *The Third Wave*, New York: Morrow.

[23] Chesbrough, H.W. (2003), "The Era of Open Innovation", *MIT Sloan Management Review*, 44(3), 35-41.

[24] Chesbrough, H.W. (2003), *op.cit*, 37-38.

[25] Linder, J., Jarvenpaa, S., and Davenport, T.H., (2003) "Toward an Innovation Sourcing Strategy," *MIT Sloan Management Review*, Summer, 43-49.

[26] This section is primarily based on Hansen, M.T., Chesbrough, H.W., Nohria, N., and Sull, D.N. (2000), "Networked Incubators: Hothouses of the New Economy", *Harvard Business Review*, September-October, 76-79.

[27] See: Laseter, T.M. (1998), "Balanced Sourcing the Honda Way", *Strategy & Business*, Fourth Quarter, 4.

[28] Table adapted from Jallat, F. and Capek, M.J. (2001), "Disintermediation in Question: New Economy, New Networks, New Middlemen", *Business Horizons*, 44(2), 57.

[29] See Kopczak, L.R. and Johnson, M.E. (2003), "The Supply-Chain Management Effect", *MIT Sloan Management Review*, 44(3), 27-34.

[30] Gottfredson, M., Puryear, R. and Phillips, S. (2005), *HBS Working Knowledge*, March 28, 3.

[31] This section is adapted from Courtney, H., (2001), *20/20 Foresight: Crafting Strategy in an Uncertain World*, Boston: Harvard Business School Press.

[32] See various publications by Kaplan and Norton, e.g. Kaplan, R.S. and Norton, D.P. (2003), *Strategy Maps*, Boston: Harvard Business School Press.

[33] Larcker, D. and Ittner, C. (2003), "Coming Up Short on Nonfinancial Measurement," *Harvard Business Review,* November, 88-95; Voelpel, S.C., Leibold, M., Eckhof, R. and Davenport, T.H. (2005), "The Tyranny of the Balanced Scorecard", *Journal of Intellectual Capital,* December, in print.

Architectural Innovation and Modular Corporate Forms

Amit, R., & Schoemaker, P. J. H. 1993. Strategic assets and organizational rent. *Strategic Management Journal*, 14: 33-46.

Anderson, P. 1999. Complexity theory and organization science. *Organization Science*, 10: 216-232.

Baldwin, C. Y., & Clark, K. B. 1997. Managing in an age of modularity. *Harvard Business Review*, 75(5): 84-93.

Bartlett, C. A., & Ghoshal, S. 1993. Beyond the M-form: Toward a managerial theory of the firm. *Strategic Management Journal* 14 (special issue): 23-46.

Boisot, M. H. 1998. *Knowledge assets: Securing competitive advantage in the information economy.* Oxford, England: Oxford University Press.

Boisot, M., & Child, J. 1999. Organizations as adaptive systems in complex environments: The case of China. *Organization Science*, 10: 237-252.

Brown, S. L. & Eisenhardt, K. M. 1997. The art of continuous change: Linking complexity theory and time-paced evolution in relentlessly shifting organizations. *Administrative Science Quarterly*, 42: 1-34.

Brown, S. L., & Eisenhardt, K. M. 1998. *Competing on the edge: Strategy as structured chaos*, Boston: Harvard Business School Press.

Buckley, W. 1968. Society as a complex adaptive system. In W. Buckley (Ed.), *Modern systems research for the behavioral scientist*: 490-513. Chicago: Aldine.

Burgelman, R. A. 1983. A process model of internal corporate venturing in the diversified firm. *Administrative Science Quarterly*, 28: 223-244.

Campbell, D. 1969. Variation and selective retention in socio-cultural evolution. *General Systems*, 14: 69-85.

Chandler, A. D. J. 1962. *Strategy and structure: Chapters in the history of the American industrial enterprise*. Cambridge, MA: MIT Press.

Child, J. 1972. Organizational structure, environment and performance: The role of strategic choice. *Sociology*, 6:1-22.

Ciborra, C. 1996. The platform organization: Recombining strategies, structures, and surprises. *Organization Science*, 7: 103-118.

Conner, K. R., & Prahalad, C. K. 1996. A resource-based theory of the firm: Knowledge versus opportunism. *Organization Science*, 7: 477-501.

Davidow, W. H. & Malone, M. S. 1992. *The virtual corporation: Structuring and revitalizing the corporation for the 21st century.* New York: Harper Business.

Dougherty, D., & Hardy, C. 1996. Sustained product innovation in large, mature organizations: Overcoming innovation-to-organization problems. *Academy of Management Journal*, 39: 1120-1153.

Eisenhardt, K. M. 1989. Building theories from case study research. *Academy of Management Review*, 14: 488-511.

Eisenhardt, K. M., & Bhatia, M. 2001. Organizational complexity and computation. In J. A. C. Baum (Ed.), *Companion to organizations*: 442-466. London: Blackwell.

Eisenhardt, K. M., & Brown, S. L. 1999. *Patching: Restitching business portfolios in dynamic markets*. Harvard Business Review, 77(3): 71-82.

Eisenhardt, K. M., & Martin, J. A. 2000. Dynamic capabilities: What are they? *Strategic Management Journal*, 21: 1105-1121.

Eisenhardt, K. M., & Tabrizi, B. N. 1995. Accelerating adaptive processes: Product innovation in the global computer industry. *Administrative Science Quarterly*, 40: 84-110.

Galunic, D. C., & Eisenhardt, K. M. 1996. The evolution of intracorporate domains: Divisional charter losses in high-technology, multidivisional corporations. *Organization Science*, 7: 255-282.

Galunic, D. C., & Rodan, S. 1998. Resource recombinations in the firm: Knowledge structures and the potential for Schumpeterian innovation. *Strategic Management Journal*, 19: 1193-1201.

Galunic, D. C., & Weeks, J. R. 2001. Intraorganizational ecology. In J. A. C. Baum (Ed.), *Companion to organizations*: 75-97. Oxford, England: Blackwell.

Gersick, C. J. G. 1994. Pacing strategic change: The case of a new venture. *Academy of Management Journal*, 37: 9-45.

Glaser, B., & Strauss, A. 1967. *The discovery of grounded theory: Strategies for qualitative research*. London: Wiedenfeld & Nicholson.

Goold, M., Campbell, A., & Alexander, M. 1994. *Corporate-level strategy: Creating value in the multibusiness firm*. New York: Wiley.

Guth, W. D., & Ginsberg, A. 1990. Corporate entrepreneurship. *Strategic Management Journal*, 11: 5-15.

Handy, C. 1995. *The age of unreason*. London: Arrow Business Books.

Henderson, B. D. 1979. *Henderson on corporate strategy*. Cambridge, MA: ABT Books.

Henderson, R. M. 1994. The evolution of integrative capability: Innovation in cardiovascular drug discovery. *Industrial and Corporate Change*, 3: 607-630.

Henderson, R., & Clark, K. 1990. Architectural innovation: The reconfiguration of existing product technologies and the failure of established firms. *Administrative Science Quarterly*, 35: 9-30.

Henderson, R., & Cockburn, I. 1994. Measuring competence? Exploring firm effects in pharmaceutical research. *Strategic Management Journal*, 15: 63-84.

Iansiti, M., & Clark, K. 1994. Integration and dynamic capability: Evidence from product development in automobiles and mainframe computers. *Industrial and Corporate Change*, 3: 557-606.

Jelinek, M., & Schoonhoven, C. B. 1990. *Innovation marathon: Lessons from high technology firms*. Oxford, England: Blackwell.

Kim, W. C., & Mauborgne, R. 1998. Procedural justice, strategic decision making, and the knowledge economy. *Strategic Management Journal*, 19: 323-338.

Kogut, B. 2000. The network as knowledge: Generative rules and the emergence of structure. *Strategic Management Journal*, 21: 405-425.

Kogut, B., & Zander, U. 1992. Knowledge of the firm, combinative capabilities, and the replication of technology. *Organization Science*, 3: 383-397.

Kogut, B., & Zander, U. 1996. What firms do? Coordination, identity, and learning. *Organization Science*, 7: 502-518.

Lazonick, W., & O'Sullivan, M. 1995. Organization, finance and international competition. *Industrial and Corporate Change*, 5: 1-49.

Leonard-Barton, D. 1992. Core capabilities and core rigidities: A paradox in managing new product development. *Strategic Management Journal*, 13: 111-125.

Levine, S., & White, P. E. 1961. Exchange as a conceptual framework for the study of interorganizational relationships. *Administrative Science Quarterly*, 6: 583-601.

Lewin, A. Y., Long, C. P., & Carroll, T. N. 1999. The coevolution of new organizational forms. *Organization Science*, 10: 535-550.

Lewin, A. Y., & Volberda, H. W. 1999. Prolegomena on coevolution: A framework for research on strategy and new organizational forms. *Organization Science*, 10: 519-534.

Marris, R. 1979. *The theory and future of the corporate economy and society.* Amsterdam: North-Holland.

Marris, R., & Wood, A. 1971. *The corporate economy.* Cambridge, MA: Harvard University Press.

Miles, M. B., & Huberman, A. M. 1984. *Qualitative data analysis.* Beverly Hills, CA: Sage.

Nonaka, I., & Takeuchi, H. 1995. *The knowledge-creating company.* New York: Oxford University Press.

Penrose, E. G. 1959. *The theory of the growth of the firm.* New York: Wiley.

Sanchez, R., & Mahoney, J. T. 1996. Modularity, flexibility, and knowledge management in product and organizational design. *Strategic Management Journal*, 17 (winter special issue): 63-76.

Schumpeter, J. A. 1934. *The theory of economic development: An inquiry into profits, capital, credit, interest, and the business cycle.* Cambridge, MA: Harvard University Press.

Szulanski, G. 1996. Exploring internal stickiness: Impediments to the transfer of best practice within the firm. *Strategic Management Journal*, 17 (winter special issue): 27-44.

Teece, D. J., Pisano, G., & Shuen, A. 1997. Dynamic capabilities and strategic management. *Strategic Management Journal*, 18: 509-533.

Thompson, J. D. 1967. *Organizations in action.* New York: McGraw-Hill.

Tushman, M., & O'Reilly, C. 1997. *Winning through innovation.* Boston: Harvard Business School.

Weick, K. E. 1995. *Sensemaking in organizations.* Thousand Oaks, CA: Sage.

Williamson, O. E. 1975. *Markets and hierarchies: Analysis and antitrust implications.* New York: Free Press.

Winter, S. G. 1987. Knowledge and competence as strategic assets. In D. J. Teece (Ed.), *The competitive challenge: Strategies for industrial innovation and renewal*: 159-184. Cambridge, MA: Ballinger.

Yin, R. K. 1989. *Case study research: Design and methods*. Newbury Park, CA: Sage.

Zander, U., & Kogut, B. 1995. Knowledge and the speed of the transfer and imitation of organizational capabilities: An empirical test. *Organization Science*, 6: 76-92.

The Innovation Meme: Managing Innovation Replicators for Organizational Fitness

Beer, M. (2003) Building organizational fitness, in S. Chowdhry (Ed) *Organizations 21C* (Upper Saddle Ridge, NJ: Financial Times-Prentice Hall).

Beer, M. and Eisenstat, R. (2000) The silent killers of strategy implementation and learning, *Sloan Management Review*, 41(4), pp. 29-41.

Beinhocker, E. (1999) Robust adaptive strategies, *Sloan Management Review*, 40(3), pp. 95-106.

Blackmore, S. (1999) *The Meme Machine* (Oxford/New York: Oxford University Press).

Christensen, C., Raynor, M. and Anthony, S. (2003) Six keys to creating new-growth businesses, *Harvard Management Update*, 8(1), pp. 3-6.

Davenport, T. and Prusak, L. (1997) *Working Knowledge: How Organizations Manage What They Know* (Boston: Harvard Business School Press).

Davenport, T. and Voelpel, S. (2001) The rise of knowledge towards attention management, *Journal of Knowledge Management*, 5(3), pp. 212-21.

Dawkins, R. (1976) *The Selfish Gene* (Oxford/New York: Oxford University Press).

Drucker, P. (1964) *Managing for Results* (New York: Harper and Row Publishers).

Eisenhardt, K. and Sull, D. (2001) Strategy as simple rules, *Harvard Business Review*, 79(1), pp. 106-116.

Frank, J. (1999) Applying memetics to financial markets: Do markets evolve towards efficiency?, *Journal of Memetics – Evolutionary Models of Information Transmission*, 3(2), pp. 1-14.

Gelb, B. (1997) Creating 'memes' while creating advertising, *Journal of Advertising Research*, 37(6), pp. 57-59.

Gibbert, M., Leibold, M. and Probst G. (2003) Five styles of customer knowledge management, and how smart companies use them to create value, *European Management Journal*, 20(5), pp. 459-469.

Govindarajan, V. and Gupta, A. (2001) Strategy innovation: A conceptual road map, *Business Horizons*, 44(4), pp. 3-12.

Hamel, G. (1998) The challenge today: Changing the rules of the game, *Business Strategy Review*, 9(2), pp. 19-27.

Jewell, E. and Abate, F. (Eds) (2001) *The New Oxford American Dictionary* (Oxford/New York: Oxford University Press.

Leibold, M., Probst, G. and Gibbert, M. (2005) *Strategic Management in the Knowledge Economy – New Approaches and Business Applications*, Second Edition (Erlangen: Publicis).

Lissack, M. (2003) The redefinition of memes: Ascribing meaning to an empty cliche', *Emergence*, 5(3), pp. 48-65.

Lord, A. and Price, I. (2001) Reconstruction of organizational phylogeny from memetic similarity analysis: Proof of feasibility, *Journal of Memetics – Evolutionary Models of Information Transmission*, 5(2), pp. 1-51.

Moore, J. (1993) Predators and prey: A new ecology of competition, *Harvard Business Review*, 71(3), pp. 75-86; Nonaka, I. and Takeuchi, H. (1995) *The Knowledge Creating Company* (Oxford/New York: Oxford University Press).

PwC (1999) *Innovation and growth: A global perspective*. Research report at Pricewaterhouse-Coopers.

Schreyögg, G., Oechsler, W. and Wächter, H. (1995) *Managing in a European Context: Human Resources, Corporate Culture, Industrial Relations* (Wiesbaden: Gabler).

Senge, P. and Carstedt, G. (2001) Innovating our way to the next industrial revolution, *Sloan Management Review*, 42(2), pp. 24-38.

Voelpel, S. (2003) *The Mobile Company. An Advanced Organizational Model for Mobilizing Knowledge, Innovation and Value Creation* (St. Gallen: IFPM).

Voelpel, S. and Davenport, T. (2004) Siemens takes four steps – Establishing of a global knowledge-sharing system, *Harvard Business Review* (China), 3(9), pp. 128-137.

Voelpel, S., Dous, M. and Davenport, T. (2004) Five steps to creating a global knowledge-sharing system: Siemens share-net, *Academy of Management Executive*, 19(2).

Voelpel, S., Leibold, M. and Habtay, S. (2004) The three-phased approach for developing dynamic organizational fitness in fast-changing business environments, *Management Dynamics*, 13(3), pp. 40-51.

Voelpel, S., Leibold, M. and Mahmoud, K. (2004) The organizational fitness navigator: enabling and measuring organizational fitness for rapid change, *Journal of Change Management*, 4(2), pp. 123-140.

Voelpel, S., Leibold, M. and Tekie, E. (2004) The wheel of business model reinvention: How to reshape your business model to leapfrog competitors, *Journal of Change Management*, 4(3), pp. 259-276.

Von Hippel, E. and Katz, R. (2002) Shifting innovation to users via toolkits, *Management Science*, 48(7), pp. 821-833.

Vos, E. and Kelleher, B. (2001) Mergers and takeovers: A memetic approach, *Journal of Memetics – Evolutionary Models of Information Transmission*, 5(2), pp. 10-23.

Von Hippel, E., Thomke, S. and Sonnak, M. (1999) Creating breakthroughs at 3M, *Harvard Business Review*, 43(4), pp. 47-57.

Williams, R. (2000) The business of memes: Memetic possibilities for marketing and management, *Management Decision*, 38(4), pp. 272-279.

VI Strategy Leadership and Management in the Innovation Economy

Synopsis

A framework is presented and motivated for Poised Strategic Management in the innovation economy, consisting of leadership, managerial and frontline requirements; and organizational structure and capability issues. The new business dynamics formula for survival in the innovation economy, $E_b^n = MI^2$, is now finally explicated in its full and applied context, and the entrepreneurial, synergizing and energizing roles of management are outlined (with reference also to 'organizational meme'). Major 'box' examples are Shell, IBM, Walt Disney, Novartis, P&G, Outsourcing (various firms); major case example is GE (Immelt); and three relevant articles are included.

Chapter 6
Leadership and Managerial Requirements for Poised Strategy in the Innovation Economy

New Organizational Capability Challenges for Leadership and Management

The poised strategy approach in the innovation economy requires substantially different ways in which corporations are led, businesses are managed, and organizational capabilities and structures are developed and utilized. Managing multiple business models, with different approaches for sustaining and disruptive business models, and shifting the focus to business ecosystem collaboration and not just company and industry value chain effectiveness, raise a number of challenges concerning ambidextrous capabilities and innovation-enabling organizational structures. The previous chapters indicated, with partial scope, the significant leadership and managerial requirements for Poised Strategic Management; this chapter provides a coherent overview of, and particular guidelines for these requirements.

Poised strategy involves the capability of an enterprise to continually rejuvenate (renew and re-energize) itself with value innovation arising from multiple business models in business ecosystems. The formula used in Chapter 1 and expanded in Chapter 4 becomes critically important concerning leadership and management:

$$E_b^n = MI^2$$

where

Organizational Energy (from a portfolio of business models)	=	Leading and Managing Value-Innovation Activities in Collaborative Business Networks, with Dynamic Capabilities and Increasing Speed-to-Market

Organizational energy, in the sense of positive and continuous dynamics (or impetus) to be able to rejuvenate organizational value, is the result of managing a portfolio of business models for desired value-innovation activities in business ecosystems. This is effected through dynamic innovation capabilities with focus on a relevant range of speed-to-market value-innovation configurations.

Tables 4.1 and 4.2 (see Chapter 4) encapsulated the leadership and managerial requirements for successful poised strategy: these provided frameworks for Poised Strategic Management context, content, and process, and listed the principal capabilities, tools, and structural issues to be managed. This chapter is structured around these core issues as follows:

- *Key Leadership Roles for Poised Strategy*: sensing corporate domain and providing context, through particular leadership guiding, cohering, energizing, and cultivating capabilities. The role of leadership is especially at corporate level, through ambidextrous management of a portfolio of business models, and making sense of, and utilizing business ecosystem opportunities and challenges.

- *Key managerial capabilities for poised strategy*: managing particular business models within overall corporate poised strategy, each with their own particular business model strategy requirements, through business model reinvention, self-organization, guided experimentation, and systemic performance measurements.

- *Key frontline "community" and "specialist" capabilities*: at lower level and/or specialized activities of an organization, this involves creating and pursuing opportunities, and experimenting as well as embedding efficiencies in functions and networks.

- *Organizational structures and capabilities for Poised Strategic Management*: Structural decisions about the designing, developing, testing, and guiding of different types of business models, some inside the company (e.g., divisions or units) and some outside (e.g., separate companies/subsidiaries), and their implications for corporate capabilities.

The above categorization is made only for discussion purposes, but in reality the leadership, managerial, frontline, and structural issues are of course intertwined, non-hierarchical and not mutually exclusive. Figure 6.1 provides an overview of the roles of leadership, management, and frontline groups and individuals in a three-dimensional process of entrepreneuring, synergizing, and energizing.[1]

From Figure 6.1, it can be seen that each of the three key role-players have entrepreneurial, synergizing, and energizing roles to fulfill, and these link and flow in a non-linear way. Each of the three role-players is henceforth discussed.

Key Leadership Roles for Poised Strategy

The key leadership roles, and their required capabilities, are discussed in three categories below:[2]

Providing Context and Clarifying Domain

Leadership in socio-cultural business networks is contingent on having a clear identity – a context for action and landscape domains. Identity in networks and organizations is established through shared vision, culture and beliefs, mutual sense-making and understanding, and member alignment:

The Energizing Process		
• Sustaining Personal & Team Energy and Commitment	• Building & Maintaining Organizational Flexibility • Mentoring, Incentivizing	• Inspiring and Motivating • Guiding the Tension between Short Term and Long Term Objectives and Performance • Destabilizing as Necessary
The Synergizing Process		
• Driving Operational Linkages inside & outside the company • Managing Systemic Efficiencies	• Guiding, Self-Organizing BM Skills Knowledge & Resources, inside & outside the company • Managing external & internal value chains	• Configuring in Business Ecosystems • Cultivating Portfolio of BMs • Nurturing Relationships • Facilitating Incubation and Experimentation
The Entrepreneurial Process		
• Creating and Pursuing Opportunities	• Reviewing & Supporting BM Initiatives in the Business Ecosystem	• Providing Context & Sense • Clarifying Domain
Frontline "Communities & Specialists" [Focus: Renewal & Efficiency] ⟷	**Business Model "Managers"** [Focus: Business Model] ⟷	**Corporate "Leaders"** [Focus: Corporate BM Portfolio]

Figure 6.1 Overview of Leadership, Managerial and Frontline Roles for Poised Enterprise Strategy in the Innovation Economy

- *Clarifying shared vision*
  The leaders bring into focus the shared vision of the network and its organizations. They provide the initial impetus of the shared vision, which is co-shaped by the members of the network, and then they act as the main agent for its clarification and focus.

- *Enriching the culture and beliefs*
  Members are able to operate with the guidance of only a few rules and still create self-directed, productive, purposeful results through the organizing power of a strong culture. The culture is the network's collective mindset – its intentions, memories, and beliefs. The leaders actively nurture and expand the network's culture, which involves changing traditional mindsets and overcoming inertia.

- *Mutual understanding*
  The leaders assist the network in sense-making and meaning-making – understanding and interpreting information and events, clarifying contradictory "noise", and gaining mutual meaning and a sense of why the network arose, exists, and benefits from collaboration and competition. This has always been a function of a leader, but it is even more critical and difficult in a diffuse network than in a cohesive organization.

- *Member alignment*
  A highly aligned network of members and activities is focused and purposeful, yet made up of independent, self-organizing organizations. The leaders use their overall perspective of socio-cultural systems and align the network around a shared vision, purpose, and core beliefs.

Configuring and Cultivating Business Ecosystems and Developing a Portfolio of Business Models

Leadership plays a critical role in configuring and cultivating business networks and business models by way of promoting self-organization mechanisms, enabling ownership, shaping business models and systems, while nurturing relationships and nourishing learning and the human spirit:

- *Promoting self-organizing mechanisms*
  Leadership should initiate and promote self-organizing mechanisms such as communities of practice and networked incubators, and also provide incentives for specifically identified agents to consider membership in a network.

- *Enabling ownership*
  Leadership enables members to experience ownership of their work, their organization, and the business network. They communicate the importance of commitment and self-reliance, and of belonging to a co-owned and co-beneficial group of dynamic, value-creating entities.

- *Shaping the portfolio of business models and nurturing relationships*
  Leaders reinforce the vital importance of the long-term health of relationships, actively promoting collaboration, cooperation, and mutual enrichment. In the web-like structures of socio-cultural business networks, strong relationships are essential for individual and group effectiveness. They have to adapt to or shape each phase of the business socio-cultural system, e.g. the pioneering, growth, leadership, and renewal phases (see Chapter 5).

- *Nourishing learning and the human spirit*
  People need inspiration, hope, meaning, and satisfaction in achievements. Given the right environment and atmosphere by leaders, people will self-organize to create a dynamic, thriving, vital organization through their commitment and positive energy. Instead of repressing emotions, leaders should seek to channel them into positive and productive directions by nourishing these emotions. Learning is a process of expanding people's self-awareness and broadening their worldview, and leaders diffuse learning and knowledge in the business network for further knowledge creation, personal meaning, and satisfaction. The learning process includes tolerance of failures and mistakes as an essential part of learning through trial and error.

Destabilizing, Energizing, and Guiding the Business System

Leaders need to create an environment that elicits, supports, and nurtures creativity by deliberately upsetting the status quo, escalating some changes while dampening others, and seeking states of disequilibrium. Such instability can be created by compelling goals and slogans, enabling supportive information flows to members, promoting diversity of opinion, and maintaining a state of tension (see box: Destabilizing the Equilibrium at Shell):[3]

Destabilizing the Equilibrium at Shell

In 1996, Shell found itself captive to its hundred-year-old history. The numbing effects of tradition – a staggering US $130 billion in annual revenues, 105,000 predominantly long-tenured employees, and global operations – left Shell vulnerable.

Steve Miller was appointed group managing director of Shell's worldwide oil products business (known as "Downstream"), which in 1996 accounted for $40 billion of revenues within the Shell group. During the previous two years the company had been engaged in a program to "transform" the organization. Yet the regimen of massive reorganization, traumatic downsizing, and senior management workshops accomplished little. Shell's earnings, while solid, were disappointing to financial analysts who expected more from the industry's largest competitor. There was widespread resignation and cynicism among employees.

For Steve Miller, Shell's impenetrable culture was worrisome. The Downstream business accounted for 37 percent of Shell's assets. Of the businesses in the Shell Group's portfolio, Downstream faced the gravest competitive threats. New competitors, global customers, and shrewder national oil companies were demanding a radically different approach to the marketplace. In addition to Downstream's 61,000 full-time employees, Shell's 47,000 filling stations employed hundreds of thousands of, mostly part-time, attendants and catered to more than 10 million customers every day. In the language of complexity, Miller believed it necessary to tap the emergent properties of Shell's enormous distribution system and to shift the locus of strategic initiative to the front lines. The alternative wasn't centralization – it was a radical change in the responsiveness of the Downstream business to the dynamics of the market place. This change had to occur from top to bottom, so that people could come together in appropriate groups, solve problems, and operate in a manner which transcended the old headquarters versus field schism. What initially seemed like a huge conflict has gradually melted away, because leadership stopped treating the Downstream business like a machine to be driven and began to regard it as a living system that needed to evolve.

Miller's solution was to cut through the organization's layers and barriers, put senior management in direct contact with the people at the grassroots level, foster strategic initiatives, create a new sense of urgency, and overwhelm the older order. The first wave of initiatives spawned other initiatives. In Malaysia, for example, Miller's pilot efforts with four initiative teams (called "action labs") have proliferated to forty. "It worked," he states, "because the people at the coal face usually know what's going on. They see the competitive threats and our inadequate response every day. Once you give them the context, they can do a better job of spotting opportunities and stepping up to decisions. In less than two years, we've seen astonishing progress in our retail business in some twenty-five countries. This represents around 85 percent of our retail sales volume, and we have now begun to use this approach in our service organizations and lubricant business". Results? Overall, Shell gained in brand-share preference throughout Europe and ranked first in share among other major oil companies. By the close of 1998, approximately 10,000 Downstream employees had been involved in this effort with audited results (directly attributed to the program), exceeding a $300 million contribution to Shell's bottom line.

- *Compelling goals and slogans*
  Large, audacious, and contentious (even alarming) goals and slogans can destabilize and energize a business network and individuals. Jack Welch's slogan of
  "managing yourself out of a job within a year", and Motorola's "six-sigma quality
  goals" are good examples. Such goals have the features of being a) inspiring, b)
  audacious, and c) unifying in common – they inflame the imagination, stretch
  credibility, and lead to collaboration among members.

- *Enabling supportive information flows*
  Leaders are essential in enabling members to obtain relevant and accurate information and feedback from the socio-cultural business network. Leaders especially
  help members to see important information that is being ignored, denied, or dis-
  torted.

- *Promoting diversity of opinion*
  Systems thrive on diversity, which leads to change and growth. The issue is to
  develop networks and members that value different viewpoints, instead of fearing
  them. Conflict, a natural outcome of diversity, is an opportunity for catalyzing
  novel ideas and approaches.

- *Maintaining a state of tension*
  Change and disturbance create anxiety in people, and the leadership challenge is to
  maintain this anxiety and still function positively – as energizing "sparks" for
  creative action – without exceeding people's ability to handle the stress engendered. Another way is to seek disconfirmation of beliefs by e.g. using humor and
  satire to hold conventional thinking up to ridicule and self-deprecation, thus testing
  ideas and rewarding tough questions and contrary views.

The following box illustrates how some business leaders create an innovative environment in their companies, while the case example (see at the end of this Chapter) of
General Electric's CEO Jeffrey Immelt illustrates how a corporate culture is turned
around and a portfolio of business models are managed for increasing innovation.[4]

How some Leaders Create an Innovative Environment in their Companies

"Ask WHAT IF?"

*Mark Dean is an IBM fellow and the vice president of systems of IBM Research
in Yorktown Heights, New York. An engineer and inventor, he has more than 30
patents or patents pending, including three of IBM's nine original PC patents:*

Since December 1999, IBM has been working on a project called Blue Gene,
which is a computer designed to model the protein-folding process in genetics.
That work will require a huge advance in computing power, and we're using a
radical approach to allow a very small machine to perform more than one
quadrillion operations per second (a petaflop). Moore's law – that the amount of
information able to be stored on a transistor will double every 18 months –
predicts that it will take us 15 years to produce those calculations, but we're on
course to deliver them in five.

We can aim for this kind of breakthrough at IBM because the company places very few constraints on its researchers. We are continually encouraged to spend time exploring new ideas and asking "what if?" questions, and we're allowed to pursue the ones we think have the most promise. For instance, the PC/AT that IBM launched in 1984 – which featured an enhanced way to make peripherals work efficiently with a PC or PC compatible – was developed from something I'd been doing in my spare time. I have to say the only constraint I've ever felt deeply is the number of hours in the day.

I try to create that same unconstrained environment in the project teams I oversee. I do, of course, try to provide focus, set reasonable goals, and map out timelines. I also stress the importance of getting something out there, even if the product isn't 100% of what we envisioned. Researchers always want to go for that last 2% of performance, but I have to remind them that it's better to get a sufficient solution out fast and then continue to enhance it. My main role, though, is not to draw the boundaries but to encourage people to keep reaching. People have a lot of great ideas, if you give them space to do their thing and create an environment that is collaborative, not competitive – if you never say "that's silly" when they're thinking out of the box.

"Experiment like crazy"

Betty Cohen is a corporate executive for the Youth Segment at the Turner Broadcasting System. She is also the founder and former president of Cartoon Network Worldwide. Both organizations are headquartered in Atlanta.

My favorite way to encourage innovation is to take an experimental approach to R&D. A couple of years ago, the cable world was abuzz with talk of convergence, but nobody really knew what that meant. Since it was a brave new world, we recognized that we had to experiment with a variety of experiences for Cartoon Network fans that brought together on-air and on-line participation with the channel. I encouraged my TV and online creative leaders to plot three different approaches to the future, and I also set an expectation of learning, knowing that some ideas would play better than others but that we'd end up with insight about why each played like it did. And then we tested everything – from simulcasting Web and TV versions of the same cartoon character premier to a live on-line viewer request weekend to a more interactive on-line action and adventure show.

What prevents innovation? The dangerous brew of fear and complacency – staying where you are out of fear of failing, of blowing too much money, or a placing the wrong bets.

Key Managerial Capabilities for Poised Strategy

As depicted in Figure 6.1, the managerial capabilities for entrepreneurial, synergistic, and energizing process requirements, focusing on various business models, are:

Managing Paradox for Both Reinvention and Efficiency

The self-organizing principles of co-shaping networks might lead one to conclude that managers are superfluous. On the contrary, they have a critical role in providing the balance between the need for order and the imperative to change. This paradox, which is really a constellation of paradoxes consisting of stability and instability, simplicity and complexity, predictability and unpredictability, and effectiveness and innovation, calls for tremendous agility. This can be achieved through separate teams, shadow organizations, self-reinforcing groups, and resilience techniques:

- *Separate teams*
  Separate teams, e.g. a present business team (focused on today) and a future business team (focused on tomorrow), can be guided by management and cohered on overall network levels.

- *Shadow organizations*
  Besides the "normal", traditional business organization and network, managers can initiate a "shadow" organization and network – a form of experimentation and self-development which falls outside the normal structures and activities.

- *Self-reinforcing groups*
  Managers could avoid the potential difficulties of organizational politics and dissensions arising from separate teams and shadow organizations by integrating order and disorder into the same group of people or business entities. Such groups are self-reinforcing, i.e. they reinforce each other by enriching both efficiency and innovation objectives. A strong, shared vision and culture particularly contribute to the success of such a practice.

- *Building resilience*
  People, organizations, and networks become resilient if they are able to adapt to and to enact in a responsive and appropriate manner to environmental turbulence. Managers should always have either a number of shadow organizations, separate teams, or self-reinforcing groups simultaneously active to enable resilient responses to environmental impacts of whatever magnitude. This requires various strategic options for distinct levels of uncertainty, as subsequently described.

Guiding Self-Organizing Activities for Business Model Synergies

Anderson proposes seven qualities (or "levers") for guiding the self-organizing enterprise. These are environment selection, performance definition, managing meaning, choosing people, reconfiguring the network, developing indirect selection systems, and energizing the system.[5] To understand what managers do in self-organizing enterprises, it is useful to ask why management exists at all. Self-organization does not mean "no management necessary", but rather "no central controller necessary". Managers provide context influence and governance, not control.

- *Environment selection*
  Self-organizing systems structure themselves to fit their environment. Managers decide what environments (or landscapes) to occupy, and this provides the external "scaffolding" that allows members to focus on a few controllable parameters. The managerial quality is to define the environments to occupy, thereby channeling the rate and direction of evolution.

- *Defining performance*
  Business systems adapt by changing their behavior to move upwards on particular peaks in a knowledge landscape. Given particular performance indicators, they move towards higher fitness levels without a central controller. Managers must be able to provide the relevant performance indicators, in both financial and non-financial terms.

- *Managing meaning*
  Managers help guide the evolution of a self-organizing system by managing meaning, which is accomplished more through the managing of symbols (e.g., "stretch" goals and slogans) than by the managing of things. They have to propagate mores, values, and culture through tools such as stories, myths, and play-making rituals. In a sense, management consists in part of asking agents "what do you think you are doing?", i.e. tagging and retagging flows through the network to increase the general understanding.

- *Choosing people*
  Managers have to select the members of a network. Attracting the most capable agents is only one part of the task. The requirements of sufficient diversity, to avoid constraining homogeneity, and positive connective behavior and association have to be adhered to.

- *Reconfiguring the network*
  In business networks, managers alter the node structure when they add or delete roles. When managers establish strategic alliances, create programs to attract value-added resellers and complementary asset providers, build user communities, or join R&D associations, they create new sources of variation that can alter the network's evolutionary path. Managers may also reshape network flows by making or breaking connections between nodes, e.g. by linking internal communities of practice with external communities of customers through the Internet, or by placing people together, cross-functional teams, thereby altering interaction patterns.

- *Develop indirect selection systems*
  Managers should be able to develop and implement indirect selection systems for choosing among various options, e.g. various business models. Such indirect (or "vicarious") selection systems predict outcomes and detect possible failures of various strategic options. Managers should be careful that indirect selection systems do not become institutionalized and prone to manipulation.

- *Energizing the system*
  Managers should have the ability to provide inspiration and challenges to network members. By setting aggressive goals, managers create a perceived mismatch between present performance and required performance. Often a business network becomes "stuck" on a local peak in a fitness landscape, and managers have to drive its behavior beyond the normal comfort zone.

Self-Organization at Shell

Building on the principles of self-organization and utilizing "action labs", Steve Miller and his colleagues at Shell channeled the potential of co-evolving networks. He says: "Shell has always been a wholesaler. Yet the forecourt of every service station is an artery for commerce that any retailer would envy. Our task was to tap the potential of that real estate, and we needed both the insight and the initiatives of our front-line troops to pull it off. For a company as large as Shell, leadership can't drive these answers down from the top. We needed to tap into ideas that were out there in the ranks – latent but ready to bear fruit if given encouragement."

Miller began bringing six- to eight-person teams from six operating companies from around the world into "retailing boot camps". The first five-day workshop introduced tools for identifying and exploiting market opportunities. The participants returned home ready to apply the tools to achieve breakthroughs, such as doubling the net income of filling stations on the major north-south highways of Malaysia, or tripling the market share of bottled gas in South Africa. They were then replaced by six other teams.

During the next sixty days, the first group of teams used the analytical tools to sample customers, identify segments, and develop a value proposition. The group would then return to the workshop for a "peer challenge" – tough give-and-take exchanges with other teams. Thereafter they would return home for another sixty days to perfect a business plan. At the close of the third workshop, each action lab spent three hours in the "fishbowl" with Miller and several of his direct reports, reviewing business plans, while the other teams observed the proceedings. At the close of each session, plans were approved, rejected, amended. Financial commitments were made in exchange for promised results. Then the teams went back to the field for another sixty days to put their ideas into action and returned for a follow-up session for a total of four workshops.

"Week after week, team after team", says Miller, "my six direct reportees and I and our internal coaches reached out and worked directly with a diverse cross-section of customers, dealers, shop stewards, and young and mid-level professionals. And it worked. Operating company CEOs, historically leery of any "help" from headquarters, saw their people return energized and armed with solid plans to beat the competition. The grassroots employees who participated in the program got to touch and feel the new Shell – a far more informal, give-and-take culture. The conversation down in the ranks of the organization began to change. "Guerrilla" leaders, historically resigned to Shell's conventional way of doing things, stepped forward to champion ingenious marketplace innovations (such as the Coca-Cola Challenge in Malaysia – a free Coke to any service-station customer who is not offered the full menu of forecourt services. It sounds trivial, but it increased volume by 15 percent). Many, if not most, of the ideas came from the lower ranks of our company who are in direct contact with the customer. Best of all, we learned together. I can't overstate how infections the optimism and energy of these committed employees was for the many managers above them".

Miller pioneered a very different model from that which had always prevailed at Shell. His "design for emergence" generated hundreds of informal connections between headquarters and the field, resembling the parallel networks of the nervous system to the brain. It contrasted with the historical model of mechanical linkages analogous to those that transfer the energy from the engine in a car through a drive train to the tires that perform the "work."

The box 'Self-Organization at Shell' illustrates how a 'design for emergence' has been accomplished in business practice.[6]

The managerial capability of managing both for stability and efficiency on the one hand, and instability and renewal on the other hand, is often called 'managing at the edge of chaos', i.e. managing to avoid chaos but at the same time to maximize the potential for creativity and innovation by avoiding stifling policies, norms, rules and regulations. Walt Disney is an example, as depicted in the box below.[7]

The Walt Disney Company: Managing at the Edge of Chaos

The Walt Disney Company is a firm that prospers at the edge of chaos. Its theme parks and other businesses are run in a deeply conservative fashion. A strong culture supports Disney's mission of providing family entertainment. In operations, no detail is too small, right down to the personal grooming of the parking-lot attendants. This culture is ingrained in the organization and constantly reinforced through management processes.

In many organizations, such a conservative culture and such tightly controlled operations would snuff out creativity. Yet Disney manages to be one of the most innovative companies in the world. It pioneered animated films and destination theme parks, built EPCOT, linked media and retail with its Disney Stores, and took an early lead in cable television. Disney manages the tension between conservatism and innovation by maintaining an almost cult-like attention to detail and discipline, while simultaneously forgiving honest mistakes made in the pursuit of innovation.

Disney's core value of wholesome family entertainment, its dedication to putting smiles on customers' faces, and its strict operating discipline are the spinal cord around which it has innovated. Simultaneously conservative and radical, it has forged its success at the edge of chaos, becoming a poised organization.

Managing Organizational Flexibility and Coherence

In complex, adaptive business networks, between the extremes of stasis and chaos, lies a region where fitness is maximized – the "edge of chaos". At the edge of chaos, one is simultaneously conservative and radical. Evolution is adept at keeping existing things work well, while at the same time making bold experiments.

A poised organization and business network that are being managed at the edge of chaos, are provided with just enough structure and discipline to allow them to capture the best opportunities. Besides strong vision, values and culture that act as coherence mechanisms for diverse actions, they also make use of simple rules to focus on key processes and routines – i.e., disciplined flexibility. Examples of simple rules are provided by Eisenhardt and Sull, as summarized in Table 6.1.[8]

Managers should encourage improvisation among business network members, but also ensure that they know how to do it according to embedded simple rules.

Table 6.1 Simple rules

Type	Purpose	Example
"How to" rules	They spell out key features of how a process is executed – "What makes our process unique?"	Akamai's rules for the customer service process: staff must consist of technical gurus, every question must be answered on the first call or email, and R&D staff must rotate through customer service.
Boundary rules	They help focus managers on the opportunities that can be pursued and help to determine those that are not feasible.	Cisco's early acquisitions rule: companies to be acquired must have no more than 75 employees, 75% of whom are engineers.
Priority rules	They help managers rank the accepted opportunities.	Intel's rule for allocating manufacturing capacity: allocation is based on a product's gross margin.
Timing rules	They synchronize managers with the pace of emerging opportunities and other parts of the company.	Nortel's rules for product development: project teams must know when a product has to be delivered to the leading customer to win, and product development time must be less than 18 months.
Exit rules	They help managers decide when to pull out of yesterday's opportunities.	Oticon's rule for pulling the plug on projects in development: if a key team member – manager or not – chooses to leave the project for another within the company, the project is killed.

Key Frontline "Community" and "Specialist" Capabilities

Frontline communities and specialists include teams and individuals that create and pursue opportunities, drive operational linkages and value configurations (both existing and new), and sustain personal and team energy and commitment. These teams and individuals are from across corporate and industry boundaries, and from across traditional functions and hierarchies. In other words, the individuals are not necessarily functional specialists, and the various teams can consist of leaders, managers and individuals at all levels of the enterprise. They exhibit entrepreneurial, synergizing and energizing capabilities, as subsequently explained.

Frontline Entrepreneurial Capabilities

Operating in the format of communities of practice (COP), business incubators, and project teams (see Chapter 5), the orientation is towards creating and pursuing opportunities in business ecosystems. This does not involve only idea-generation and opportunity investigation, but the development of conceptual new business models – requiring an understanding of the corporation's domain, values and existing business models (see box).[9]

Further Examples of How Some Leaders are Attempting to Creating an Innovative Environment in their Companies

"Make it meaningful"

Daniel Vasella trained as a physician and is now the chairman and chief executive officer of Novartis, a pharmaceutical company based in Basel, Switzerland.

One way we try to foster innovation – both the technological innovation that leads to new drugs and the organizational innovation that improves the way we do business – is to align our business objectives with our ideals. Doing so reaches people's intrinsic motivation. Certainly, extrinsic motivation is important; we offer stock options to our scientists and sponsor company research awards that enhance a researcher's visibility both within and outside Novartis. But I believe that people also do a better job when they believe in what they do and in how the company behaves, when they see that their work does more than enrich shareholders.

In the past few years, we have complemented our goal of economic value creation with another goal: good worldwide corporate citizenship. So while we're developing what we hope will be blockbuster drugs for the developed world, we've agreed, for example, to donate our leprosy multidrug therapy to the World Health Organization until the disease is eradicated.

We also recognize that many ailments pervading the poorest countries are neglected diseases, with few R&D resources dedicated to finding treatments. With this in mind, we founded a research center in Singapore that focuses on developing drugs to treat diseases such as dengue hemorrhagic fever and tuberculosis; in all likelihood, such drugs will be barely profitable at best.

These activities have deep meaning for our employees and unleash their energy and enthusiasm. With regard to our breakthrough cancer drug Glivec (called Gleevec in the United States), for instance, our researchers overcame every obstacle to develop the drug, and our production teams worked around the clock to produce enough supply for clinical trials. The alignment of objectives, ideals, and values contributes greatly to the motivation and thereby the energy that employees at all levels, myself included, devote to their work.

"Abandon the crowd"

Larry Keeley is the president of Doblin, an innovation strategy firm with offices in Chicago and San Francisco.

A nearly universal misconception about innovation is that the ideal goal is to create the next hot product. That's why most companies focus their R&D dollars there. But because it's increasingly easy for other companies to copy any new product, you rarely get a return on those investments. So the principal thing we've done to encourage innovation is to help people see that there are actually many types of innovation – product innovation is one type, but so is innovation in customer service, in business models, in networking, and so on.

Consider the Chrysler minivan. Chrysler developed it at a time when the company was on the verge of bankruptcy. It created the van as a platform and depended on a network of suppliers to develop family-oriented advances that could be plugged into the platform – video games, removable seats, integral baby seats that fold down so beleaguered parents don't have to wrestle with them. The suppliers had to bear the cost of the R&D. That's an example not of product innovation but of networking innovation.

Companies miss out on all sorts of opportunities for innovation because they focus so closely on their competitors. If you map out the different types of innovation activity in a given industry, you'll almost always find that most organizations are concentrating on the same types – they're all investing in the same things, just to keep up. There may be lot of activity in customer service innovation, for example, but nothing's happening in networking.

Mapping innovation activity gives you a sense of the terrain – the peaks and valleys in investments and actions. There's an old saying that "there's gold in them thar hills." Well, there may be even more gold in them thar valleys. You can actually spend less and make more money in innovation if you pay attention to the valleys, those places your competitors have overlooked.

Frontline Synergizing Capabilities

Frontline communities and specialists drive the operational linkages inside and outside the enterprise, shaping and embedding new business ecosystem configurations and new business model operational requirements. This is both a reinventing and an efficiency orientation, requiring ambidextrous capabilities. GE's success appears to be rooted in the 'boundaryless' movement of ideas and knowledge inside and across diverse corporations, as reflected in the box below.[10]

GE's Pursuit of Boundarylessness and Synergies

Under the legendary Jack Welch, GE has been one of the fastest-growing, most profitable and highly rated conglomerates in the world, with a market capitalization in the range of US$250 billion. GE has constantly outperformed its rivals and has consistently topped the polls as the world's most admired company.

At a time when many firms have focused on only a few core businesses, GE is highly diverse. Between 1981 and 1997, GE made 509 acquisitions worth US$21 billion. Its businesses are as varied as light bulbs, home appliances, jet engines and financial services. GE has also successfully managed multiple brands simultaneously and chosen to maintain separate identities for their acquired brands, such as Hotpoint, NBC and RCA.

Many commentators have tried to explain the success of GE. Most agree that major factors are the management style of Jack Welch, and the importance of the mission and principles which guide the businesses and the managers. These principles are few:

- Be number one or two in the market in every business. GE is no. 1, not just in market share, but in expanding the scope of its markets. (GE later relaxed this principle).

- Share and adopt successful new ideas across businesses; the pursuit of 'boundary-lessness'. A business CEO is expected to try out ideas successful in other GE businesses and to promote the sharing of successful ideas from his/her own business. Groups of employees from all levels regularly meet to propose means of improving efficiency and solving problems. And pay and promotion are tied to boundaryless behavior via the sharing of ideas and transfer of knowledge. GE's success appears to be rooted in Welch's movement of ideas and also management talent around a diverse corporation.

- Challenge and question the status quo. Welch regularly meets with his managers and insists that they challenge him about his policies and initiatives; this is filtered down the corporation by sessions of lower-level employees questioning their managers face-to-face.

These principles provide challenging, even ambiguous, demands on management. A business CEO may naturally wish to focus on that business rather than spending time and effort sharing ideas across businesses, experimenting with the ideas of other businesses, or being challenged about bases of success. However, it is not enough for the CEO to point to high business performance; sharing is seen as equally important even if potentially time consuming. Nor can managers claim that the requirement for sharing is an excuse for poor performance of their business; Welch's management control systems required high levels of performance in terms of market share, financial targets and shareholder value.

Frontline Energizing Capabilities

Personal and team energies should be self-sustaining, feeding on close identification with the purpose and values of the corporation, and its culture of innovation and providing new value in society. The fundamental shift from functional efficiency (only), to a wider enterprise-strategic value-creating orientation and activity is personally enriching and satisfying, releasing proactive energies. Coupled with monetary and non-monetary incentives and feedback mechanisms, these are powerful methods to ensure personal commitment and satisfaction. This means that frontline role-players should be supported by visibility, recognition, clout and rewards, and that innovative energies should become generally accepted (the norm) in an enterprise (see box).[11]

Further Examples of How Some Leaders Create an Innovative Environment in Their Companies

"Make it the norm"

Craig Wynett is the general manager of future growth initiatives at Procter & Gamble in Cincinnati.

What we've done to encourage innovation is make it ordinary. By that I mean we don't separate it from the rest of our business. Many companies make innovation front-page news, and all that special attention has a paradoxical effect. By serving it up as something exotic, you isolate it from what's normal. Companies don't trumpet their quality assurance processes or their packaging as special practices because they're part of the fiber of what they do – they're ordinary business. The same has to be true of innovation. Too many times we've seen corporate innovation programs that are the business equivalent of football's Hail Mary pass – they start with all kinds of hope and excitement, but in the end they rarely produce results. And why would they? For innovation to be reliable, it needs to be addressed systematically, like any business issue in which you define the problem and then solve it: What do we want to accomplish, and how? What resources will we need? Who will be on the team? How do we motivate and reward them? And how will we measure success?

Today's most sought-after business talent is the ability to originate. But the perception of the creative process is still based on self-limiting assumptions about eureka light-bulbs flashing over the head of some inspired genius rather than the well-managed diligence of ordinary people. At P&G, we think of creativity not as a mysterious gift of the talented few but as the everyday task of making non-obvious connections – bringing together things that don't normally go together.

One way to do that is to look at contradictions in the marketplace. For example, we developed a product called ThermaCare, a disposable heating pad that provides regulated low-level heat for at least eight hours. How'd we come up with it? Lots of aging baby boomers out there have all kinds of creaks and muscle twinges. Drugs can treat the pain, but they can also create other problems, like stomach ailments. So you have a contradiction: People don't want to live with pain, but they don't want to take painkillers. We saw that contradiction in the market and viewed it as an invitation to create a breakthrough product, one that resolves a paradox without requiring any trade-offs. You can see how opportunities like this can come up in just about any industry. In the telecommunications business, before call waiting, for example, you could either talk on the phone or receive phone calls but not both.

A final word of caution. Isolating innovation from mainstream business can produce a dangerous cultural side effect: Creativity and leadership can be perceived as opposites. This artificial disconnect means that innovators often lack the visibility and clout to compete for the resources necessary for success. Only when innovators operate with the credibility of leaders will innovation become a productive part of everyday business.

Organizational Structures and Capabilities for Poised Strategic Management

Poised strategic management raises significant questions about organizational structures for various types of business models (e.g., inside or outside the main organization, or combination?), whether innovation activities should be outsourced or insourced (or both), and how to evaluate an organization's innovation capabilities.

Organizational Structures for Poised Strategic Management

Traditional strategic management approaches lead to organizational inertia in business models and networks. It is human nature to prefer, to seek out, and even to expect certainty. The innovation economy with its paradoxes threatens that world view. Even in the face of overwhelming evidence for change, managers often fall into competence and path dependency 'traps'. Shifting to a Poised Strategic Management paradigm means that many organizations should forcefully jettison many elements embedded in their traditional strategy mindset, and unlearn crucial assumptions and lenses that comprise traditional business models and strategies.

Firms attempting a shift to Poised Strategic Management face four types of inertia:[12]

- *Structural inertia* – established structural linkages of internal and external relationships, i.e. institutionalized patterns of culture, norms and ideologies, are often difficult to change.

- *Competitive inertia* – the focus on preserving an established competitive advantage, and on avoiding cannibalization of existing market shares and product lines, are powerful inertia factors.

- *Momentum inertia* – organizational momentum causes organization members to act in ways consistent with previous experience. Learning to act in ways that contradict experienced responses that have led to prior success is necessary to overcome this inertia.

- *Strategic architecture inertia* – inertia residing in different mental models (schemas) on which patterns of strategic responses are based, especially between various organizations in a business network.

These types of inertia cause particular managerial and leadership challenges, which often demand new organizing structures to enable co-shaping and co-evolving organizational capabilities and behavior to develop. This presents strategic management with a paradox, which cannot be resolved as simple trade-offs: having business models and strategies that are both focused and robust; operating both conservatively and innovating radically; being efficient today while also adapting for tomorrow; maintaining diversity while establishing standards and routines; optimizing both the scale of a large organization, and the entrepreneurial flexibility and flair of an innovative start-up. The central strategic management challenge in a complex adaptive business ecosystem is to be both an efficient and an innovative evolver, and this also includes the implementation of structures that drive efficiencies but are also conducive to innovation. For example:

- Disney manages the tension between conservation and innovation by maintaining focused attention to detail and discipline, but simultaneously allowing experimentation and mistakes in the pursuit of innovation. (see box earlier in the chapter)

- General Motors started its Saturn division in a "green-fields" organization to free itself from the constraints of corporate bureaucracy of its established organization.

- AT&T split itself into three companies to create smaller organizations and reduce strategic conflict between established practices and entrepreneurial ventures.

The effects of the above strategy paradoxes present huge management challenges. General Motors, for example, was successful in creating customer service innovations within its Saturn business unit, but found it very difficult to transfer those into the larger corporation. We witness how many big (incumbent) organizations, despite their resources, are unable to respond to smaller, entrepreneurial competitors; likewise, many traditional small enterprises go out of business due to their inability to adapt to industry innovations. The fact is that traditional strategic management approaches and tools prepare companies well to be competitors, but not evolvers. Grant proposes a new strategy mindset in the design of organizations to a) develop and deploy multiple organizational capabilities; and b) permit rapid adaptability.[13]

a) Multiple structures for development and deployment of organizational capabilities

One solution to the strategic management paradoxes in turbulent environments is to simultaneously deploy different structures for different purposes and tasks. The principles of knowledge management provide one approach to understand how different capabilities require different types of structure. Knowledge management distinguishes between building the organization's stock of knowledge ("exploration") and deploying the existing stock of knowledge ("exploitation"). Separate (or parallel) structures for pursuing both exploratory activities, e.g. for experimenting with new business models, and exploiting activities and optimizing existing value chain configurations, are necessary.

Examples of separate structures include:

- GE's "Work-Out" program is a classic example of a separate structure effecting change within the formal organization structure.

- Chevron's "Breakthrough Teams" were formed from multiple levels and functions in the company.

- Texaco's "Star Quality" program created a multiplicity of quality management groups in different organizational structures.

- 3M's innovative new products emerge from separate informal organization structures, which may ultimately form the basis for new business units within the formal structure.

The move towards team-based, project-based and process-based structures indicates that the building of dynamic capabilities may be better undertaken by teams that self-organize, rather than relying on management direction. For example, processes that co-opt customers embrace the entirety of an organization's interaction with its customers, enabling co-shaping of innovations and new customer value propositions.

b) Organizational design for rapid adaptability

To successfully manage gradual evolutionary change with occasional revolutionary leaps requires an ambidextrous strategic management mindset – one rooted in "loosening" the formal organizational structure for rapid adaptability. Welch's approach to management while CEO at GE involved a minimalist approach to formal control systems – GE's elaborate strategic planning system was simplified to focus on a few issues with a minimal degree of direction and control. Slogans such as "boundaryless", "destroy-your-company-dot-com", "six-sigma" and "work-out" directly influenced the culture of GE and permitted more complex patterns of collaboration with resilience for rapid adaptability and innovation in the GE ecosystem.

In order to create an organization that can resolve the paradoxes between efficiency and creativity, management should be more concerned with developing and maintaining an enterprise system guided by coherence mechanisms such as purpose, values and behavioral norms, rather than rigid conformity-based mechanisms. Four concepts are useful in formulating coherence mechanisms: identity, knowledge, modularity and networks.

- *Identity*: An organization's purpose must reside in the heads and hearts of its members – a shared concept of what the organization fundamentally is.
- *Knowledge*: Information provides the medium through which an organization relates to its environment, but knowledge enables individuals within the organization to know how to react to external changes, and how to influence and shape the environment.
- *Modularity*: Structures based on loosely-coupled, semi-autonomous modules possess considerable adaptation advantages over more tightly integrated structures. Modular structures are particularly useful in reconciling the need for close collaboration at the small group level with the benefits of critical mass at divisional or organizational levels.
- *Networks*: Responsiveness to a wide range of external circumstances necessitates every individual to have a wide range of connections to other individuals, with the potential for unplanned connections. For example, the use of intranets and extranets to link together the different parts of the organization and outside companies, as well as customers, has the effect of blurring the boundaries between internal units and external companies. The flexibility of these linkages enables the capabilities resident within inter-firm networks to be reconfigured in order to adapt quickly to external change.

The concepts indicated above are especially relevant when considering the outsourcing of innovation and its management.

Outsourcing or Insourcing Innovation?

The innovation economy is causing a rethink of the status of innovation activities and capabilities for the modern enterprise. Specifically, the question is asked "what has to be done in-house any more?" Most leading Western companies are turning toward an outsourced model of innovation, one that utilizes a global network of partners and outside capabilities (see box: Outsourced Innovation: Implications for Companies and Countries).

How does a company manage outsourced innovation? The best analogy is surfing.[14] With many waves of change occurring at once, innovation surfers cannot be sure of riding the right one. So they position themselves where experience or intuition tells them many waves will be forming. They prepare themselves with the best equipment and training, including hundreds of hours of studying waves and other surfers. They learn to discern a likely surfing opportunity from the sea's random motion, seeking waves that build on the energy of previous waves until they can tell that a really big one is forming. They may test a few. When a truly attractive wave starts to form, they speed into the curl and try to adapt quickly to each shift of a long, fast (profitable) ride. Finally – and just as importantly – they recognize when the wave is fading and get off before it hits the beach. Using the same equipment and skills, they reposition and look for the new wave, as illustrated in the box below.[15]

Outsourcing Innovation: Implications for Companies and Countries

When Western corporations began selling their factories and farming out manufacturing in the 80's and 90's to boost efficiency and focus their energies, most insisted all the important research and development would remain in-house.

But that pledge is now passé. Today, the likes of Dell, Motorola, and Philips are buying complete designs of some digital devices from Asian developers, tweaking them to their own specifications, and slapping on their own brand names. It's not just cell phones. Asian contract manufacturers and independent design houses have become forces in nearly every tech device, from laptops and high-definition TVs to MP3 music players and digital cameras.

While the electronics sector is furthest down this road, the search for offshore help with innovation is spreading to nearly every corner of the economy. On February 8, 2005 Boeing Co. said it is working with India's HCL Technologies to co-develop software for everything from the navigation systems and landing gear to the cockpit controls for its upcoming 7E7 Dreamliner jet. Pharmaceutical giants such as Glaxo-SmithKline and Eli Lilly are teaming up with Asian biotech research companies in a bid to cut the average $500 million cost of bringing a new drug to market. And Procter & Gamble Co. says it wants half of its new product ideas to be generated from outside by 2010, compared with 20% now.

Underlying this trend is a growing consensus that more innovation is vital – but that current R&D spending isn't yielding enough bang for the buck. After spending years squeezing costs out of the factory floor, back office, and warehouse, CEOs are asking tough questions about their once-cloistered R&D operations: Why are so few hit

---

products making it out of the labs into the market? How many of those pricey engineers are really creating game-changing products or technology breakthroughs? "R&D is the biggest single remaining controllable expense to work on," says Allen J. Delattre, head of Accenture Ltd.'s high-tech consulting practice. "Companies either will have to cut costs or increase R&D productivity."

The result is a rethinking of the structure of the modern corporation. What, specifically, has to be done in-house anymore? At a minimum, most leading Western companies are turning toward a new model of innovation, one that employs global networks of partners. These can include U.S. chipmakers, Taiwanese engineers, Indian software developers, and Chinese factories. IBM is even offering the smarts of its famed research labs and a new global team of 1,200 engineers to help customers develop future products using next-generation technologies. When the whole chain works in sync, there can be a dramatic leap in the speed and efficiency of product development.

The downside of getting the balance wrong, however, can be steep. Start with the danger of fostering new competitors. Motorola hired Taiwan's BenQ Corp. to design and manufacture millions of mobile phones. But then BenQ began selling phones last year in the prized China market under its own brand. That prompted Motorola to pull its contract. Another risk is that brand-name companies will lose the incentive to keep investing in new technology. "It is a slippery slope," says Boston Consulting Group Senior Vice-President Jim Andrew. "If the innovation starts residing in the suppliers, you could incrementalize yourself to the point where there isn't much left."

Such perceptions are a big reason even companies that outsource heavily refuse to discuss what hardware designs they buy from whom and impose strict confidentiality on suppliers. "It is still taboo to talk openly about outsourced design," says Forrester Research Inc. consultant Navi Radjou, an expert on corporate innovation.

The concerns also explain why different companies are adopting widely varying approaches to this new paradigm. Dell, for example, does little of its own design for notebook PCs, digital TVs, or other products. Hewlett-Packard Co. says it contributes key technology and at least some design input to all its products but relies on outside partners to co-develop everything from servers to printers. Motorola buys complete designs for its cheapest phones but controls all of the development of high-end handsets like its hot-selling Razr. The key, execs say, is to guard some sustainable competitive advantage, whether it's control over the latest technologies, the look and feel of new products, or the customer relationship. "You have to draw a line," says Motorola CEO Edward J. Zander. At Motorola, "core intellectual property is above it, and commodity technology is below."

Wherever companies draw the line, there's no question that the demarcation between mission-critical R&D and commodity work is sliding year by year. The implications for the global economy are immense. Countries such as India and China, where wages remain low and new engineering graduates are abundant, likely will continue to be the biggest gainers in tech employment and become increasingly important suppliers of intellectual property. Some analysts even see a new global division of labor emerging: The rich West will focus on the highest levels of product creation, and all the jobs of turning concepts into actual products or services can be shipped out. Consultant Daniel H. Pink, author of the new book *A Whole New Mind*, argues that the "left brain" intellectual tasks that "are routine, computer-like, and can be boiled down to a spec sheet are migrating to where it is cheaper, thanks to

Asia's rising economies and the miracle of cyberspace." The U.S. will remain strong in "right brain" work that entails "artistry, creativity, and empathy with the customer that requires being physically close to the market."

Hewlett-Packard, a company with such a proud history of innovation that its advertising tag line is simply "invent," also works with design partners on all the hardware it outsources. "Our strategy is now to work with global networks to leverage the best technologies on the planet," says Dick Conrad, HP's senior vice-president for global operations.

Who will ultimately profit most from the outsourcing of innovation is not clear. The early evidence suggests that today's Western titans can remain leaders by orchestrating global innovation networks. Yet if they lose their technology edge and their touch with customers, they could be tomorrow's great shrinking conglomerates. What is clear is that an army of in-house engineers no longer means a company can control its fate. Instead, the winners will be those most adept at marshaling the creativity and skills of workers around the world.

In today's world, attempting to build permanent marketing, innovation, R&D or production dominance is futile. But building up skill sets, platforms and sensing capabilities can produce successive benefits. Companies should drop outmoded core competencies, learn from each 'ride' and develop a genuine sense-making capability for future opportunities. In contemporary stormy markets, high-level technical, market-scanning, sensing and responsiveness skills – and a well-designed platform for continual innovation – are essential for survival.

Furthermore, to attract innovative cooperation, a company must have some capabilities to access desired markets that supplier-inventors cannot duplicate. That means developing best-in-world performance in a grouping of services, skills or systems important to customers. It also means focusing on those genuine core competencies – and a few other essential competencies – that protect the core or are demanded by customers. Those central activities define the way the company creates value for customers. They also provide essential bargaining leverage with suppliers and serve as a strategic block against suppliers or competitors wishing to bypass the company and move into its markets.

Consider the example of Nintendo.[16] Exploiting its powerful marketing, mass production, brand and distribution capabilities, Nintendo offers outside game designers a low-investment opportunity to roll out their innovations worldwide. The company's complex presentation technologies and patents (as well as its massive marketing capabilities) prevent independents from attacking its markets directly. Although it creates some games itself, Nintendo focuses its resources on those core activities – and lets many outsiders create the games that have made more Japanese game designers into millionaires than any other company.

Every outsourcing opportunity offers possibilities to improve innovation. Leading professional outsourcers – real estate, human relations, software systems or financial firms – are just as likely to come up with major innovations as specialized technical-

Table 6.2 Identifying the Primary Source for Innovation

	Incremental	**Breakthrough**
Product	Internal scientists	Small biotech firms
Process/service	Customer focus groups	Quality council
Management	First-line managers	University faculty
Business model	Business unit managers	Consulting firms

research or product-design houses are. That is how they maintain their own margins, satisfy customers' needs and leverage their own intellectual resources.

Given that there are many types of innovation, executives should develop a sourcing strategy that identifies a particular "channel" for each type. They may also want to differentiate the sourcing strategy by another factor – whether the innovation needed is incremental or radical. This yields the model in Table 6.2, which has some hypothetical innovation channels identified for each type of innovation in a typical company.

Structural Options to Create New Innovation Capabilities

Managers who seek to create new innovation capabilities for their enterprise are faced with three major options through which to create new capabilities:[17]

a) Acquire a different organization whose processes and values are a close match with the new task.

b) Try to change the processes and values of the current organization.

c) Separate out an independent organization and develop within it the new processes and values required to solve the new problem.

a) Creating Capabilities by way of acquisitions

Managers often sense that acquiring rather than developing a set of capabilities makes competitive and financial sense. Unfortunately, companies' track records in developing new capabilities through acquisition are indifferent.

If the acquired company's processes and values are the real drivers of its success, then the last thing the acquiring manager wants to do is to integrate the company into the new parent organization. Integration will vaporize many of the processes and values of the acquired firm as its managers are required to adopt the buyer's way of doing business and have their proposals for innovation evaluated according to the decision criteria of the acquiring company. If the acquiree's processes and values were the reason for its historical success, a better strategy is to let the business stand alone, and for the parent to infuse its resources into the acquired firm's processes and values. This strategy, in essence, truly constitutes the acquisition of new capabilities.

If, on the other hand, the company's resources were the primary rationale for the acquisition, then integrating the firm into the parent can make a lot of sense – essentially plugging the acquired people, products, technology, and customers into the parent's processes as a way of leveraging the parent's existing capabilities.

b) Creating new capabilities internally

Companies that have tried to develop new capabilities within established organizational units also have a mixed track record. Assembling a beefed-up set of resources as a means of changing what an existing organization can do is relatively straightforward. People with new skills can be hired, technology can be licensed, capital can be raised, and product lines, brands, and information can be acquired. Too often, however, resources such as these are then plugged into fundamentally unchanged processes – and little change results. Unfortunately, processes are very hard to change. Organizational boundaries are often drawn to facilitate the operation of present processes. Those boundaries can impede the creation of new processes that cut across those boundaries. When new challenges require people or groups to interact differently than they habitually have done – addressing different challenges with different timing than historically required – managers need to pull the relevant people out of the existing organization and draw a new boundary around a new group. New team boundaries enable or facilitate new patterns of working together that ultimately can coalesce as new processes – new capabilities for transforming inputs into outputs.

c) Creating capabilities through a spin-out organization

The third mechanism for creating new capabilities – spawning them within spin-out ventures – is in vogue among many managers as they wrestle with how to address innovation economy. When are spin-outs a crucial step in building new capabilities to exploit change, and what are the guidelines by which they should be managed? A separate organization is required when the mainstream business model would render it incapable of focusing resources on the innovation project. Large organizations cannot be expected to freely allocate the critical financial and human resources needed to build a strong position in small, emerging markets. And it is very difficult for a company whose cost structure is tailored to compete in high-end markets to be profitable in low-end markets as well. When a threatening disruptive technology requires a different cost structure to be profitable and competitive, or when the current size of the opportunity is insignificant relative to the growth needs of the mainstream organization, then spin-out organization is a required part of the solution.

A Concluding View on Poised Strategic Management: Managing Multiple Business Models with Ambidexterity to Increase Organizational Energy, Innovative Capability and Business Performance

When coping with more complex internal and external environments in the innovation economy, managers should be able to develop robust business models and adaptive strategies, i.e. strategies that provide general direction and guidance but without confirming activities and behavior. Qualities required for this are awareness and interpretation of various environmental uncertainty levels, and the ability to develop and sustain a family (or range) of robust business models and their respective strategies. The overall corporate strategy is now one of poise, i.e. a robust family of business models and their individual strategies.

Beinhocker contends that strategic managers should develop and sustain a family (or population) of strategies that cover a range of uncertainties and options.[18] He states that the "best corporate strategy" for searching a fitness landscape and building sustainable strategies is a mixture of an adaptive walk (adaptation) and the occasional medium and long (reinvention) "jumps".

Thus, in creating a population of strategies, it is essential that the population contains a balanced mixture of initiatives, ranging from short-jump incremental extensions of the current business, to long-jump initiatives, which have longer time frames, are higher in risk and farther afield, but have the potential to build capability and create opportunities in other businesses.

In general, successful corporate leaders would manage a portfolio of strategic business model initiatives across three horizons:

Horizon 1 initiatives are efforts to extend and defend existing businesses (adaptive walks).

Horizon 2 initiatives seek to build on existing capabilities to create new businesses (medium jumps).

Horizon 3 initiatives plant the seeds for future businesses that do not as yet exist (long jumps).

For example, Bombardier, the Canadian aerospace, transportation, and recreational vehicles company, has achieved more than 20 percent annual revenue and earnings growth for ten years by constantly creating and harvesting strategic initiatives that cover all three horizons. Current initiatives include a new class of ultra long-range business jets (Horizon 1), military aircraft maintenance services (Horizon 2), and electric vehicles for neighborhood transportation (Horizon 3).

Shifting managers to a mindset of robust business models and strategies is not easy. Often the organizational processes, measurement metrics, and incentives are geared toward a linear view of strategy and this must change to support a new mindset. Beinhocker proposes six actions that can reinforce the robust adaptive mindset, namely investing in a diversity of people, valuing potential strategies as real options, mapping "jumps" on the landscape, testing the population of strategies (e.g., systems dynamics modeling, and game theory), bringing financiers such as venture capitalists on board at an early stage, and using differential performance metrics for each type of strategy initiative.[19]

Enabling a Shift in Managerial Mindsets

A shift in managerial mindsets for Poised Strategic Management has to occur in two categories: a change in the nature of perceived reality of organizational life, and a

Table 6.3 A poised model as conceptual base of strategic management

Perception of Reality / Nature of Inquiry (Means of Knowing)	Machine Model Mindless System	Biological Model Uni-minded System	Poised Model Multi-minded System
Analytical Approach *Independent Variables*	Division or Partition of Parts and Labor	Diversity & Growth	Participative, Holistic Management
	Henry Ford's Mass Production System	Alfred Sloan's Divisional Structure	Participative Teams and Individuals
Systems Approach *Interdependent Variables*	Joint Optimization	Flexibility & Emergence	Co-creative Network Management
	Operations Research	Cybernetics Model	Systemic Redesign Model

change in the method of inquiry about organizational renewal – as indicated in Table 6.3.[20]

We are now facing the challenge of a dual shift in the innovation economy of the 21st century. Not only has there been a shift of paradigm in our understanding of the conception of an organization from machine to organism to poised co-shaper, but there has also been a profound shift in our assumptions regarding the means of knowing (or method of inquiry) from analytical thinking, i.e. the science of dealing with independent sets of variables, to holistic thinking, i.e. the art and science of handling interdependent sets of variables.

The resolution of the organizational paradoxes described previously requires a dual shift in the strategic management mindset. The first shift will result in the ability to see the organization as a multi-minded, poised system, consisting of a voluntary association of purposeful members who come together to serve themselves by serving a need in the environment. The second shift enables management to comprehend chaos and complexity, and to learn to deal with an interdependent set of variables. The nature of this dual shift is briefly reviewed:

- *The first paradigm shift: From a mechanistic view to a multi-minded poised view*
  The mechanistic view maintains that the universe is a machine, and an organization consists of discrete parts, each performing only a simple task of horizontal, vertical and circular motions. The essence of the machine mode is that an organization is a mindless system – it has no purpose of its own. It is used by its owner/s as a tool to make profit, and is based on performance criteria of reliability and efficiency. The biological view, or living organism paradigm, is also simple and elegant: an organization is considered a uni-minded living system, just like a human being, with a purpose of its own. The purpose is survival, and to survive in unstable structures of open systems, it has to grow, with profit being the means to achieve this. In contrast to mechanistic views, in which profit is an end in itself, in the biological mode it is only a means to an end. Although uni-minded systems

have a choice, their parts do not – the organization is seen as being under the control of an executive function, and its parts have no choice – if parts should display choice, conflict would arise and the organization as a system would experience major difficulties.

The poised view considers the organization as a voluntary association of purposeful members who manifest themselves as a choice of both ends and means. The critical variable is purpose – it is a purposeful system, and organizations are part of a larger purposeful whole, the society. Simultaneously, it has purposeful individuals and units as its own members. The fulfillment of a purposeful part's desires depends on fulfillment of the larger system's requirements, and vice versa. While the elements of mechanical systems are energy-bonded, those of biological systems are information and coordination bonded, and those of poised organizational systems are knowledge and interaction/sharing bonded. The members of the poised organization are held together by coherence mechanisms, such as common objectives and sharing of values embedded in their culture. The culture is the "glue" that integrates the parts into a cohesive whole.

• *The second paradigm shift: From analytical thinking to systemic thinking*
Analytical thinking and systemic thinking are very distinct. Analysis is a three-step process of firstly taking apart, then observing and attempting to explain the behavior of the parts separately, and finally trying to understand the parts as an explanation of the whole. Systemic thinking uses a completely different process: it puts the system in the context of the larger environment of which it is part, and studies the role it plays (or should/could play) in the larger whole.

While the analytical approach has remained intact for the past four hundred years or more, systemic thinking has already progressed through three distinct generations of change, namely:

– First generation systems thinking: *operations research* (interdependency in the context of mechanistic systems)

– Second generation systems thinking: *cybernetics and open systems* (interdependency and self-organization in the context of biological systems)

– Third generation systemic thinking: *systemic redesign* (the triple challenge of interdependency, self-organization, and choice and design in business ecosystems)

Biological systems primarily self-organize through genetic codes, while poised systems primarily self-organize through cultural codes (or 'memes' – see Chapter 4). In addition to being a living system, poised organizations are also purposeful and capable of innovatively co-shaping (or co-designing) their value propositions and other activities.

The DNA of poised systems is their culture, and third generation systems thinking has to deal with both the existing cultural "prints" (or 'memes', analogous to genes in biological metaphor), which are reproducing traditional value propositions, while also co-shaping innovative, new cultural "prints" necessary in a turbulent environment. Purposeful poised systems are capable of recreating their future, and they do so by redesigning themselves – members of an organization, unlike the parts of a biological being, do not react passively to the information and knowledge they receive or engender.

In reality, a large part of organizational life in the world today is still caught in the analytical and mechanistic mindsets of the 20th century. The analytical thinking cannot deal with the issues of trust, knowledge, belonging, care, nurturing, empowerment and co-shaping required in a world of increasing collaboration (e.g., strategic alliances), choice and personal fulfillment. Members increasingly behave knowledgeably and independently, and frustration associated with excessive levels of conflict often reinforces the organizational inability to change. Shifting the conceptual base of strategic management to a poised strategy model is a prerequisite to handling the challenges of the networked innovation economy of the 21st century.

Conclusion

Organizational leadership and strategic managers require particular qualities and capabilities in the innovation economy. Leadership should have the mindset and ability to provide context and meaning to the organization and its networks, to destabilize (or "disturb") and guide the system and its evolution, and to configure appropriate new business models and their respective strategies. Strategic managers should be able to "manage at the edge of chaos" by developing and implementing appropriate coherence mechanisms, and handling the challenges of paradox by developing robust adaptive strategies.

These invaluable agents of future change seek neither stability nor predictability, thereby developing a comfort level that tolerates disequilibrium. They know that "messiness" and ambiguity are part of the process of self-organization and self-emergence and that, rather than attempting to manage it through command-and-control, their role is to support it by the enabling of resources and the design of an appropriate culture. They recognize the futility of attempting to draw a map of the future in advance, appreciating the fact that when the waters are uncharted, their destination can only be discovered through the actual process in real time; that the map can only get drawn as they go along. Being a successful manager in the 21st century innovation economy calls for a new mental model – a manager suited to a world of turbulence and seeming chaos.

Leadership and the Networked Economy[*]

By Albert A. Vicere

"The times," once sang Bob Dylan, "they are a changing."
No better anthem exists to describe the dawn of the 21st Century.
We are surrounded by change, continuously challenged to rethink
our values, our careers, our lifestyles. It is no different for
organizations. Today's volatile economic environment demands
that organizations rethink their strategies, processes, and cultures.
And that places a powerful premium on leadership capabilities.
This article discusses the fundamental "waves of change" that have
affected the economic environment over the past two decades and
how those changes have redefined the nature of organizational and
leadership effectiveness. Suggestions are made regarding how
organizations can enhance their approaches to leadership
development in this exciting but demanding era of change
and opportunity.

The Shifting Economic Landscape

Despite the economic chaos of the past two years, the term "new economy" still exists as a popular descriptor of our evolving economic environment. But keep in mind that this "new" economy has little to do with the rapid growth and equally rapid demise of the dot.com sector. Rather, it involves major philosophical and infrastructure shifts that have challenged and fundamentally changed traditional assumptions surrounding leadership and organizational effectiveness.

A better description of today's business environment may be the "networked economy," and two major inflection points have driven its emergence: globalization and the information technology explosion. Globalization has brought us flatter, faster-paced organizations with global reach. Information technology has enabled us to work in partnerships linked by powerful information networks. Together these forces have triggered the ongoing reconfiguration and restructuring of both industries and organizations worldwide.

[*] Taken with permission from *Human Resource Planning* Vol. 25 No. 2, 2002, pp. 26-33

The First Wave

"Old" economy views of organizational effectiveness were built on notions of control. People were controlled through structure and hierarchy, and resources were controlled through vertical and horizontal integration – in today's terminology, control of the major elements of an industry's supply chain. In the old economy, the most successful companies often were those that mastered tight controls and established supply chain dominance to gain supremacy over their respective industries. Companies like U.S. Steel, Xerox, Polaroid, and Eastman Kodak are prime examples. Those companies helped to create their industries and ruled them for decades. Today, all of them are struggling.

Part of the problem is that those companies grew up in a primarily domestic marketplace. They may have sold products outside their home country and even manufactured products overseas, but the real heart of their business was a robust and growing domestic marketplace where, as dominant players, they set the standards and effectively controlled the pace of change in their respective industries.

Globalization changed all of that. Take the steel industry. When competitors from Japan entered the North American steel market in the 1960s and 1970s, U.S. Steel's dominance of the domestic marketplace did not matter to them. They had their own sources of materials and capital and were able to develop new channels of distribution. Whether they were subsidized or not is irrelevant. What was most important was that they forever changed the rules of the business game. In rapid succession, industry after industry was attacked by offshore competitors, all of them equally unencumbered and unafraid of dominant U.S. market leaders. They went after machine tools, consumer electronics, automobiles, and so on. Eventually, established U.S. companies had no choice but to respond.

During the 1980s and 1990s, in response to this global competitive challenge, established companies aggressively pursued a new organizational model that was faster, more efficient, closer to the customer, and above all, flatter. The resulting de-layered organizational form was a natural response to global competition. Speed, efficiency, and customer focus were the competitive advantages used by offshore competitors to combat incumbent market leaders. Flatter organizations seemed far more likely to spawn those critical competitive characteristics. Yet, although downsized companies often saw short-term improvements in business conditions, they frequently found themselves back in trouble a few quarters down the road. This led many companies to engage in a cycle of continuous downsizing that not only failed to pay off in business performance improvement, but also triggered a permanent shift in traditional employee values toward loyalty and commitment in the workplace. Many companies find themselves caught up in this death spiral even today.

The Second Wave

Why don't reductions in headcount, in and of themselves, produce sustainable performance improvements for organizations? When an organization simply has fewer people trying to do all the things they did in its pre-downsized form, the end result is likely to be confusion and burnout – not performance improvement. A breakthrough in addressing this challenge was proposed by C.K. Prahalad and Gary Hamel in a series of *Harvard Business Review* articles that culminated in their 1994 landmark book, *Competing for the Future*. They noted that high-performance companies tended to organize around "core competencies," the things the organization did or wanted to do better than anyone else. We learned in the 1990s that downsizing, coupled with a focus on core competencies, could enable an organization to flatten, focus, and move ahead with exceptional intensity.

But there was a catch. The flat, focused organization did a few things exceptionally well, but it needed help. That help came in the form of tactical partnerships such as outsourcing arrangements that enabled the organization to handle efficiently operational tasks that were not core competencies. It also came in the form of strategic partnerships that helped the organization to grow revenue through joint ventures, alliances, or partnerships. We learned in the later half of the 1990s that flat, focused organizations that operated in webs of partnerships were far more likely to succeed than those that stayed committed to tall, monolithic bureaucracies.

The Current Wave

The lessons of the past two decades have immense implications, especially for long-established companies – organizations that for the most part were used to control, hierarchy, and going it alone. That is because old economy management processes were based primarily on *control* while networked economy management processes are based primarily on *relationships*. Without question, there is a fundamental difference between the two perspectives.

Clearly, no business can maintain performance without effective control over its operations. But in the old economy, companies ensured control by operating in tightly defined hierarchies and doing everything themselves. That is not the case in the networked economy, where partnerships – strategic and tactical, customer and supplier, personal and organizational – are essential to competitive effectiveness. And an organization's ability to manage, coordinate, and control such webs of relationships is directly related to the second inflection point in the evolution of the networked economy: the information technology revolution.

The technology transformation taking place today has spawned the development of computer and telecommunications networks, e-commerce systems, enterprise software, and other forms of connectivity that link networks of business partners together in a new business infrastructure, one built upon webs of information linkages. These linkages enable organizations to control and streamline their businesses in ways never before imagined. They enable both individuals and organizations to work in tightly linked partnerships. In effect, they have redefined requirements for organizational effectiveness in today's business environment and redefined the essence of effective business infrastructure. The impact of integrated information sharing software like SAP, Oracle, Baan, Siebel Systems, and PeopleSoft is undisputed. The rapid expansion of electronic market exchanges and e-commerce business platforms is unprecedented. The dominance of the information superhighway as the foundation for a new wave of economic development is nearly unquestioned. The technology revolution is changing the face of nearly everything around us, especially processes for managing organizations. And the demise of the dot.com sector is only helping us to get it right. The soul of the e-revolution is not just buying and selling via the Internet; another consideration is the fundamental reconfiguration of business infrastructure. Michael Porter referred to this in his recent *Harvard Business Review* article, *Strategy and the Internet*. From massive gains in productivity, to operational flexibility, to the gathering of insightful customer intelligence, to the opening of new markets and the creation of new channels of distribution, to real-time learning platforms, the Internet has an effect on all aspects of the value chain and influences new approaches to organizational effectiveness and leadership development.

The Next Wave

In the aftermath of these waves of economic, technological, and organizational change, one of the most challenging questions facing the CEOs of major corporations today may be: How do we create globally competitive, networked organizations that are capable of sustained effective performance in an environment of economic and technological transition? That is a mouthful and a tough question indeed. To answer the question, it is necessary to rethink the essence of leadership. Broadly speaking, leadership may be defined as the art and science of enabling an organization to get results while building stakeholder commitment to its values and ideals. The evolving economic order necessitates that we put these requirements into a new context.

Organizational effectiveness in the networked economy involves the ability to get results and at the same time build commitment and enthusiasm among networks of highly mobile knowledge workers, independent business partners, performance-minded investors, and service-demanding customers. It requires an ability to inspire these diverse constituents to function in teams, work in partnerships, share information, and operate in networks. To accomplish this task, organizations need leaders that can create what Doug Ready of the International Consortium for Executive Development Research calls "collective ambition," a common sense of focus and purpose that drives cooperation and performance. Developing collective ambition in our era of change requires us to rethink the essence of leadership and leadership development in our evolving economic environment.

Two dimensions of organizational effectiveness frame this challenge: *value and uniqueness*. Value may be defined as the essence of an organization's identity – why stakeholders (customers, employees, investors, suppliers, partners, etc.) choose to do business with that organization. Uniqueness refers to the inimitable aspects of the organization that incite stakeholders to stay loyal to the organization over time, in effect, the things that make the organization special. The most critical challenge facing 21st Century leaders may well be the need to ensure a relevant sense of value and uniqueness for their organization. And relevance in a world of change means helping the organization to develop both "roots" and "wings.".

An organization's "roots" constitute its sense of identity, what it stands for in the marketplace. Jim Collins and Jerry Porras referred to the notion of roots in their landmark book, *Built to Last*. In it they show how organizations with a strong sense of identity and a clearly defined set of enduring values tend to prosper and evolve over time. At the heart of organizational longevity are healthy roots, a lasting, value-based culture that elicits a competitive energy that sparks organizational members to strive for success. Collins follows up on that notion in his new book, *Good to Great*. He again shows that greatness in an organization – that is, sustained toplevel performance – is directly related to a clear, compelling sense of purpose that enables an organization to carve out a positive identity with customers, investors, employees, and other stakeholders.

"Wings" refers to an organization's ability to change and evolve in advance of the perceived need to change. Clayton Christensen, in his book, *The Innovator's Dilemma*, profiles this challenge quite effectively. He notes that "roots" also frequently reflect a commitment to an established business model. If an organization has strong roots, it also has a tendency to overlook what he calls "disruptive technologies." These are new technologies and developments that challenge existing business models and, should they catch on, have the potential to undermine and destroy the essence of the firmly rooted organization's value and uniqueness in the marketplace. Missing a disruptive technology can cause an organization to lose relevance in the eyes of stakeholders at all levels. "Wings" are the cultural characteristics and organizational capabilities that enable an organization to change and innovate – to build on the past but also to advance beyond history to maintain relevance in a changing world.

Leaders face a real dilemma as we shift from the industrial-based, domestically focused business models that were the norm at the outset of the first wave of change to the information/knowledge-based, globally focused business models of the future. That is, how do we retain relevance to our existing stakeholders – customers, investors, employees, etc. – all of whom have become committed to our organization's current capabilities and values, and at the same time evolve what we stand for to establish relevance and uniqueness in a world of change? Either extreme, hanging on to old world views and models at the expense of new, or throwing out the wisdom of experience in favor of only the new, will result in disaster. On the other hand, a compromise without careful thought is likely to breed mediocrity and the loss of uniqueness. True resolution requires a leader to take the best of the old and the potential of the new and blend them together into a new organizational order, one that not only attracts and maintains customers, investors, employees, partners, and other stakeholder relationships, but also inspires commitment and transfers responsibility for success across the entire stakeholder network.

Rethinking the Essence of Leadership

What does all of this mean for leadership in the networked economy? Consider the following three propositions. First, core competencies, by definition, are knowledge sets and technical skill sets. It stands to reason, then, that until companies master the science of creating knowledge management systems, core competencies will continue to reside in the minds of the people who are within an organization's network of stakeholders. Second, relationships are owned by people within organizations and not by the organizations themselves. People make the difference with regard to establishing and maintaining relationships. Third, the ability to initiate organizational change requires respect for the past (roots) and enthusiasm for the future (wings). These three propositions suggest why effective leadership is so crucial in today's relationship-driven world. Leaders must be able to attract stakeholders (customers, employees, investors, partners, etc.), motivate them, keep them networked and connected, keep them engaged in the organization's progress, all while helping the organization to evolve in an effort to stay relevant in a changing world. And that brings leadership development to the forefront of business strategy as a key element of an organization's ability to compete in a relationship world.

Nearly 30 years ago, Henry Mintzberg outlined the roles of an effective leader in his landmark book *The Nature of Managerial Work.* He noted that effective leaders play three sets of roles: interpersonal roles that include serving as an internal leader and external liaison; informational roles that include the collection and dissemination of information both within the organization and with external constituencies; and decisional roles that include the identification and pursuit of opportunities and resources, the handling of disturbances, and the allocation of resources. Mintzberg's work has remained remarkably relevant over this period of economic transition. Yet, the shift to the network economy has put these roles into a new context. Leaders today do indeed have interpersonal and informational responsibilities, though it may be argued that the informational responsibilities have moved to a position of primacy. And leaders indeed retain decisional responsibilities, but those responsibilities increasingly are shared with various stakeholders and network partners. The nature of leadership, as defined by Mintzberg's work, may be similar today, but the networked economy places new demands on leaders at all levels. And that requires us to consider, perhaps, a different set of roles.

Unquestionably, most leaders today are aware of the basic essence of their job: *To get results and to build stakeholder commitment to the organization's culture and values.* There is also little doubt that today's leaders face an incredibly complex challenge. Not only are they charged with ensuring the performance of the organization and building on its cultural legacy, they also are charged with helping the organization transition to the new economic order. Based on discussions with dozens of leaders and first-hand observation of them dealing with leadership challenges, leaders in the networked economy have four key roles. These roles can be broken down into 13 key dimensions, described later. The framework is not intended to serve as a competency model, but rather as a delineation of the perspectives essential for effective leadership in today's business environment.

Boundaryless Thinker

Leaders in the networked economy need to think outside of the box and help their organization to do the same. They cannot be bogged down in traditional orthodoxies, but must be open to new ideas. They must help their organization and the people within it to know themselves – their strengths, competencies, and limitations. And they must help them to recognize both the value of new ideas and the strengths and capabilities of potential partners, whether internal or external to the firm, who can be sources of unique synergies and differentiated competitive advantage. Three skill sets seem essential to developing this broad-based mindset:

1. *Big picture perspective* – the ability to rise above details and activities to see a situation in terms of correlations, patterns, and potential. This includes boundary-less views of markets, products, services, organizational forms, business models, and the myriad potential opportunities that face a leader at any given point in time.

2. *Openness to ideas* – the ability to appreciate and integrate new ideas and different ways of thinking across the organization at all levels and across all functions and processes.

3. *Willingness to look beyond oneself for capabilities and resources* – the under-standing that no one individual or organization can possess all the capabilities and resources necessary for success in today's environment and that partnerships and linkages, both internal and external to the firm, are essential to the future. This includes a perspective in which customer relationships are seen as partnerships that involve the sharing of resources, information, and capabilities.

Network Builder

Leaders who think in a boundaryless manner are more likely to have a relationship mindset, one focused on helping the people around them to share ideas, information, knowledge, resources, and capabilities. Organizational effectiveness in the networked economy is rooted in relationships and networking on both a personal and technologi-cal level. Complementary partners must be identified and linked together in a knowl-edge-sharing culture in focused pursuit of organizational success. Four skill sets are essential to developing a network-oriented mindset:

1. *Relationship mindset* – an openness to finding and linking with complementary partners across the value chain, including viewing customers as partners in the execution of a business proposition. Knowledge of own uniqueness – the ability to identify and clearly articulate the core competencies and capabilities of oneself and one's organization.

2. *Ability to recognize others' uniqueness* – the ability to recognize, identify, and appreciate the core competencies, capabilities, and capacities of potential part-ners.

3. *Searching for synergies* – the ability to recognize and articulate how one's own competencies, capabilities, and capacities, when combined with those of a pro-spective partner, can create potential that extends well beyond the potential that exists for the stand alone entities.

Diplomat

To develop and maintain the effectiveness of networks, today's leaders must be able not only to bring constituencies together, but also to help them work together and

Networked economy leadership roles	
Boundaryless Thinker Thinking beyond the status quo	1. Big picture perspective 2. Openness to ideas 3. Willingness to look beyond oneself for capabilities
Network Builder Finding and linking with complementary partners	1. Relationship to mindset 2. Knowledge of personal value and uniqueness 3. Ability to recognize others' value and uniqueness 4. Searching for synergy
Diplomat Developing the skills to manage networks	1. Ability to relate 2. Ability to communicate 3. Ability to negotiate
Interpreter Helping partners see the benefits of working together	1. Solid knowledge of business 2. Broad knowledge of marketplace 3. Ability to influence others

appreciate that by working together they can achieve more than they could on their own. Three critical skill sets comprise this dimension:

1. *Ability to relate* – the ability to identify and connect with others, to be seen as credible and trustworthy.

2. *Ability to communicate* – the ability to communicate and interact effectively with others, both on an interpersonal basis and via information networks.

3. *Ability to negotiate* – the ability to create connections and commitments among potential partners, both internal and external to the firm and including customer networks. This particular dimension requires a little more reflection. In the traditional "tall pyramid" organization of the Industrial Age, the most senior leaders had the luxury of "outsourcing" the preceding requirements to professional functionaries (the public relations department, the human resource management department, the legal department, the IT department, etc.). Often, the specialists did all the heavy lifting around these skill sets with the leader as the advisor. In the networked economy, these requirements have emerged as hands-on, roll-up-the-sleeves, and get-in-there-and-do-it imperatives for leaders. They are absolutely essential leadership skills in the networked economy.

Interpreter

To complement their skills of diplomacy, leaders must have the ability to interpret the nature of business opportunities to the network, the perspective to help partners understand each other, and the skills to coach, facilitate, and provide feedback to an organization that is no longer a collection of lines and boxes, but a living, growing, expanding ecosystem. Three skill sets seem essential to this role:

1. *Solid knowledge of the organization* – the ability to explain and articulate the value and uniqueness of the network and delineate its capabilities and cultural characteristics across stakeholder groups.

2. *Broad knowledge of the marketplace* – an awareness of market trends and developments, knowledge of competitors and their capabilities, and knowledge of the needs and capabilities of potential partners and customers.

3. *Ability to influence others* – the ability to inspire, communicate, and connect with others, to convince stakeholder groups and constituents to work together to address challenges and capitalize on opportunities.

Leadership Development in the Networked Economy

This list of capabilities makes it easy to conclude that developing effective 21st Century leaders is a daunting task for any organization and a considerable challenge for any individual. Not because the perspectives outlined are new; individually they are not. Not because they have heretofore been disassociated with effective leadership; they have not. In the networked economy, leadership will be the telling factor. Boundaryless thinking, network building, diplomacy, and interpretation are critical skill sets that need to be cultivated, practiced, and developed among leaders at all levels. And they are skill sets that require both organizations and individuals to understand the evolving essence of leadership in our ever-changing world. All of that suggests that leadership development initiatives must be reconsidered from a new perspective, one that reflects the critical role they play in helping organizations to transition to the networked economy. Some reflections to consider:

- *Make leadership development a strategic priority.* Developing leaders who are able to get results and be boundaryless thinkers, network builders, diplomats, and interpreters is no easy task. It cannot be left to chance, nor can it be left to consultants. Rather, it must become a strategic priority, championed and driven by an organization's senior leaders who must be the spokespersons, teachers, mentors, and sponsors for the process. Now is the time for leaders to address the dilemma of the networked organization and take on the real responsibility of leadership – generating results today while developing leaders for the next generation.

- *Get leaders to lead.* In the old economy, leaders were often auditors. They watched over things, approved things, and kept things running smoothly. Today, that is not enough. Today's leaders must facilitate, interpret, coach, teach, mentor, and develop both people and relationships. They cannot do those things unless they have the right skills and mindsets, and they will not develop those capabilities until they are educated in them and held accountable for demonstrating them. Leadership development, in this sense, becomes a strategic imperative for all organizations. Leaders must be helped to master the shift from the old control-oriented management philosophies of the industrial age to the new relationship philosophies of the information age. No company will continue to grow and succeed until it addresses this challenge, until it ensures that its leaders can not only get short-term results, but that they can do so while demonstrating the ability to be boundaryless thinkers, network builders, diplomats, and interpreters.

- *Expand the definition of diversity.* In the networked economy, diversity takes on a whole new meaning and becomes even more critical. Diversity is no longer an individual or personal issue, it is a strategic issue that requires a new view of people, structures, and strategies. The relationship imperative of the networked economy demands that leaders be able to appreciate, respect, and synergize differences. They must recognize value in unique perspectives and capabilities across both individuals and organizations. They must appreciate the best of what is along with the potential of what can be. They must cultivate roots and at the same time develop wings across their partner networks. Understanding and embracing diversity in this broader context is the order of the day and a critical strategic imperative.

- *Facilitate networks.* A networked-economy organization is made up of talented people who work together, share resources and information, and are committed to both personal and organizational success. By seeking out the best minds in the organization regardless of where they reside, putting those minds to work on challenging opportunities, and creating mechanisms to share the knowledge they possess across the organization, resources are generated that can be allocated to pursue even more opportunities. The networked-economy organization must keep people challenged and connected, help them to learn from and with each other, and support their continued growth and development.

- *Never doubt the power of purpose.* What is the difference between a job and a calling? It is a sense of purpose, a feeling of making a contribution, making a difference. Human beings long for a sense of purpose and identity. They want to be part of something bigger than they are. For further information, read Jim Collins' *Good to Great* or, better yet, Viktor Frankl's *Man's Search for Meaning.* The only way to create a network of committed, enthusiastic stakeholders is to create an organization with a purpose, a cause, a sense of passion. That cannot be done by analysts. It must be done by leaders.

- *Champion learning.* Critical to an organization's ability to make the transition to the networked economy is its ability continuously to seek out sources of information and ideas, and to learn from them. Real-time, just-in-time enterprise learning platforms through which organizations can catalog and disseminate the wisdom gained through experience as well as the ideas gained through futuristic, long-range, lateral thinking are the next big challenge. Knowledge management is not a fad, but rather an essential capability. Organizations that lead the way in the effort to unlock the secrets of effective knowledge management systems development will be the leaders in the early 21st Century business environment.

- *Make leadership development hands-on, real-time.* Ongoing, relevant opportunities for leadership development are essential in the networked economy. These experiences should be less classroom-oriented, and more linked to real-time learning from hands-on experiences. Action learning, leader-led development, and just-in-time education are the watchwords of the day for strategic leadership development in the networked economy. Dare to be creative when structuring the work environment. Use project and task force assignments to keep the workplace enriched and vibrant, but make sure project team members get the coaching and feedback they desire and the development plans they need to move ahead.

Conclusion

The networked economy requires that companies rethink and refocus their leadership development practices to accommodate the shift to new, relationship-oriented business models. To make that shift, organizations must redefine requirements for leadership effectiveness, refine practices and policies for leadership development, and hold leaders accountable for real leadership in the networked economy. Perhaps most importantly in this era of transition, leaders themselves must understand that their real legacy will not be the past performance of their organization, but its sustainable success. Helping leaders learn how to get results by being boundaryless thinkers, network builders, diplomats, and interpreters is a first step in meeting this challenge. Holding them accountable for getting results today and developing next-generation leaders for tomorrow is the quantum leap.

Unleashing Organizational Energy[*]

By Heike Bruch and Sumantra Ghoshal

Four types of organizational energy can either stimulate or handicap competitiveness. Companies are learning to identify and focus the kind best suited to their culture and goals.

For 50 years, management theory and practice have adopted a technical, analytical approach in which the role of the so-called soft factors like emotions and feelings has largely been denied. That trend is now being reversed, with both academics and managers recognizing the powerful role that emotions play in shaping corporate behavior. The real challenge, however, is to link emotions to performance goals and objectives. The leadership task is not just to make people happy in the hope that happy people will do the right things. The central leadership responsibility is to ensure that the company's vision and strategy capture people's emotional excitement, engage their intellectual capacities, and produce a sense of urgency for taking action. In essence, it is a task of unleashing organizational energy and marshaling it in support of key strategic goals.

Four Energy Zones

Research suggests that the best leaders first mobilize organizational energy, then focus it.[1] But how to define a force like the wind, both invisible and powerful? Organizational energy is seen only in its effect: the force with which a company functions. Just as burnout is said to have three dimensions (emotional, cognitive and physical), so is organizational energy considered the interplay among a company's emotional, cognitive and physical states.[2] Though difficult to directly observe or measure, organizational energy is palpable when put to use – driving the intensity, pace and endurance of a company's work, change and innovation processes.[3]

Organizational energy is related but not identical to the sum of the energy of individuals. Individual energy, especially of leaders, influences organizational energy, and the energy state of the organization affects the energy of individuals. Long recognized by managers, the distinction between individual and organizational energy is now receiving more attention in academic circles.[4]

---

[*] Taken with permission from *MIT Sloan Management Review* Vol. 45 No. 1, Fall 2003, pp. 45-51

The Four Energy Zones

Companies are more likely to be successful in the aggression zone (responding to a threat) or the passion zone (responding to an exciting goal), both of which feature high levels of energy. Companies in the comfort zone are coasting dangerously on past success, and those in the resignation zone have nearly given up.

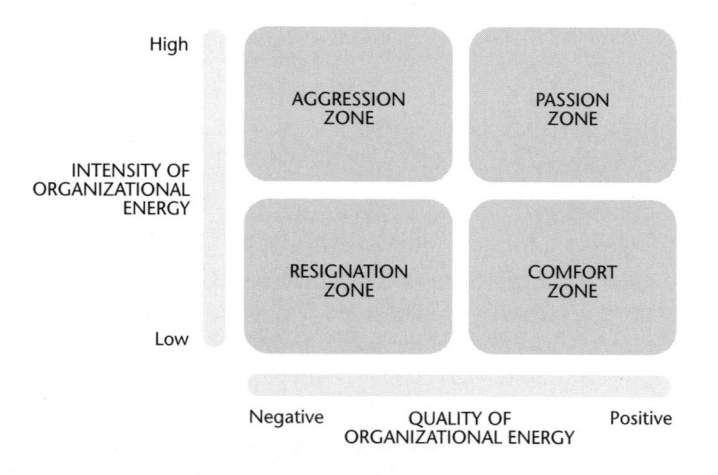

Companies differ in both *intensity* and *quality* of energy. Intensity refers to the strength of organizational energy as seen in the level of activity, the amount of interaction, the extent of alertness and the extent of emotional excitement. Symptoms of low energy are often obvious: apathy and inertia, tiredness, inflexibility and cynicism.[5] Qualitatively, organizational energy can be characterized as positive energy (for example, enthusiasm, joy and satisfaction) or negative energy (fear, frustration or sorrow). In fact, it is the intersection of intensity and quality that determines an organization's energy state, which usually falls into one of four categories. (See "The Four Energy Zones.")

Although different parts of an organization can be mapped to different energy zones, most organizations are characterized by one particular zone at any given point. The exception would be a highly diverse and decentralized company, in which the business unit may be the most appropriate level for analyzing and managing energy. Sometimes diverse energy states within one company suggest the need for greater intraorganizational integration.

Comfort Zone. Companies in the comfort zone have low animation and a relatively high level of satisfaction.[6] With weak but positive emotions such as calm and contentedness, they lack the vitality, alertness and emotional tension necessary for initiating bold new strategic thrusts or significant change.

For a long period before its listing in the London Stock Exchange, Old Mutual Plc – South Africa's dominant insurance company – exemplified this energy state. Populated with decent, educated people – almost entirely white – and widely considered upright and responsible, Old Mutual was South Africa's "Ma Bell." Managers strongly identified with OM, were proud to belong and happy with the status quo. They spoke politely, avoided contentious issues and worked at a steady pace. The financial results, although not spectacular, were average, and the company was well-liked.

Post-apartheid, Old Mutual began to experience aggressive competition in financial services, along with new opportunities, such as international expansion. OM's new leadership recognized the need for drastic action: changing the legal structure, establishing a corporate center in London and launching a massive transformation program.

Resignation Zone. Companies in this energy state demonstrate weak, negative emotions – frustration, disappointment, sorrow. People suffer from lethargy and feel emotionally distant from company goals. They lack excitement or hope.

Aktiebolegat SKF – the Swedish company that invented the bearing business – was in the resignation zone for most of the last two decades. It was only modestly profitable despite outstanding technology, brand strength and global footprint. Market share inched down, and there was constant incremental restructuring and rationalization. The share price slid lower in relative terms.

An engineer's company, SKF was always attractive to technically qualified, mild-mannered people who disliked open competitiveness. Until Sune Carlsson (CEO from September 1998 to April 2003) jolted SKF into action, SKF managers operated in a state of mild frustration.

Aggression Zone. Companies in the aggression zone experience internal tension founded on strong, negative emotions. Tension drives their intensely competitive spirit, which manifests itself in high levels of activity and alertness – and focused efforts to achieve company goals.

Oracle Corp. – the California-based, No. 2 software company – operates in the aggression zone. Employees live by the mantra: "It's never good enough to win; all others must lose." Oracle's comparative advertising reinforces this intensely aggressive culture. Driven by individual-level financial incentives and CEO Larry Ellison's personal embodiment of aggressiveness, Oracle has attracted employees who love to fight and win.

Directing that aggressiveness toward competitors has led to outstanding results for Oracle. Salespeople earn double commission whenever Oracle products or services supplant those of its main competitors. At each stage of its evolution, Oracle has surpassed competitors: "Remember Ashton-Tate?" asked Ellison, two years before his 2003 unsolicited bid to acquire PeopleSoft Inc. "Similarly, Siebel will disappear and so will PeopleSoft."

Passion Zone. In the passion zone, companies thrive on strong, positive emotions – joy and pride in the work. Employees' enthusiasm and excitement mean that attention is directed toward shared organizational priorities. Consider Alain Dominique Perrin, the legendary CEO of Cartier SA. Perrin stimulated organizational exuberance for 20 years and moved the French luxury products company from $50 million to $1.2 billion in revenues.

Although the Perrin-led Cartier engaged in intense competition with Rolex, Chanel and Christian Dior, competitors were never its focus – creativity was. Well-established Cartier norms strengthened that passion for creativity, including one requiring that all new products bridge the old and the new. Designers were to capture the zeitgeist of an early Cartier piece and combine it with inspiration from the finest contemporary art.

Weak emotions, positive or negative, do not spur people to action. Companies in the comfort zone or the resignation zone operate at low levels of attention, emotion and activity. Companies in the aggression zone or the passion zone display higher levels of focused emotional tension, collective excitement and action taking.

High-energy companies display an urgency that makes them more productive.[7] Being constantly alert allows them to process information and mobilize resources quickly. They strive for larger-than-life goals. Low-energy companies prefer standardization and institutionalization. They try to avoid the surprises, exceptions and risks on which high-energy companies thrive.

High energy helps align employees' perceptions, emotions and activities. Low-energy organizations suffer from conflicting priorities and lack of cooperation; high-energy companies bundle and channel their forces for shared goals, creating a foundation for organizational cohesion.

Energy Traps

Energy is not an unmixed blessing, however, and unless managed wisely, it can degenerate into one of three main pathologies or energy traps.

Acceleration Trap. Some CEOs drive an organization beyond its capabilities. Relentless efforts to accelerate can lead to organizational burnout. Companies that keep adopting major change initiatives without making time for regeneration are susceptible to the acceleration trap. Most change-management programs assume that the change is an exceptional episode. In reality, most employees contend with ongoing change, which tends to dilute the credibility of management demands to "give one's all." [8]

Consider ABB Ltd. Between 1988 and 1995, the European engineering giant responded magnificently to CEO Percy Barnevik's radical restructuring. Costs were reduced, acquisitions integrated and new markets entered. Revenues grew from $17.8 billion to $36.2 billion.

But ABB was continuously under pressure, and the strains began to show. For example, according to numerous media reports and our interviews and research, internal conflicts in the power-generation sector mushroomed. What had formerly been a healthy level of tension in ABB's organizational energy degenerated into intense rivalries.

In September 1998, new CEO Goran Lindahl added one more initiative to the already tired company: a drastic reorganization. Once again, people had to forgo established relationships orchestrated by mature geographical managers and start working for young, ambitious and aggressive business-area executives.

Classic organizational exhaustion resulted, bringing with it fragmented managerial attention and increased difficulty with prioritizing.[9] Pressured field managers ended up spinning their wheels. The exhaustion caused Lindahl and his successor, Jürgen Centerman, to exert even more pressure, and the acceleration trap finally took complete hold of the company by 2002, with little reserve energy left to revitalize this nearly burned-out organization. (Today, under CEO Jürgen Dormann, there are positive signs, but he nevertheless has a tough fight ahead to ensure the company's survival.)

Managers must resist the temptation to drive organizations to their limits. Energy is first built as a capacity – a potential for intense action – and then that capacity must be used in phases. Successful application of organizational energy is self-reinforcing, expanding the energy potential. To manage the process of creating and deploying energy, managers must adopt a rhythm of highly intense and less intense phases.[10]

Inertia Trap. Weakening a company's ability to leverage resources is the inertia trap. This trap ensnares victims after too long a stretch of either success or poor performance.

Long success in a stable environment may convince companies (say, Old Mutual) that they have found the ideal system. As long as the environment does not change too radically, the company's tight alignment of strategy, organizational structures and culture improves performance. But inevitably the environment does change. The alignment becomes a handicap as companies find they can't muster the energy to overcome its rigidity.[11] Similarly, with too long a stretch of operating below capacity, companies lose elasticity (like SKF). Mediocrity makes them lose confidence; they become either reactive or passive.

Old Mutual escaped inertia by initiating a listing on the London Stock Exchange. The complete change in OM's operating context and its new, forceful leadership jolted managers out of complacency. In SKF's case, Carlsson and, later, Tom Johnstone openly broke with company norms to focus on productivity and profitability.

Corrosion Trap. When a company faces external threats (or opportunities) at the same time as it confronts internal discord, it may fall into the corrosion trap. Instead of working together to meet external challenges, people channel their energy into internal fights. We have observed that often the behavior of senior managers is responsible. Leaders who act in a patently self-interested way or demonstrate little personal involvement with the external challenges erode people's passion for business, their optimism and their readiness to collaborate.

Consider one large, Europe-based corporation that suffered a crisis in 2002. Senior managers successfully created a sense of urgency that employees could identify with, and workers manifested their commitment by accepting a modest 3% raise. That is, until they learned that board members had given themselves a 14% raise. The sense of betrayal was corrosive, leading to massive strikes and the frostiest labor relations in company history. In the end, top management was obliged to leave.

Corrosive energy leads to self-reinforcing negativity. Because people unconsciously respond to one another's emotional displays by imitating or exaggerating them, even relatively minor events evolve into negative emotions that spiral out of control.[12]

When Paul Lego was at Westinghouse Electric Corp. (between 1990 and 1993), his arrogance and isolation within a coterie of favorites led to a breakdown of trust and self-confidence among managers. Divisional heads focused anger on colleagues rather than on outside competitors. Eventually, the corrosive forces of internal rivalry destroyed the company.

Unleashing Organizational Energy

Companies that succeed at radical change generally adopt one of two approaches for unleashing and channeling organizational energy: the "slaying the dragon" strategy (moving into the aggression zone by focusing people's attention, emotions and effort on a threat), or the "winning the princess" strategy (moving into the passion zone by building enthusiasm for an exciting vision).[13] On the rare occasions when a company can combine the strong positive and negative emotions of both zones, the results are spectacular. Companies with neither strategy fall victim to an energy trap and decline to mediocrity or to crisis.

Slaying the Dragon. This strategy involves a clear articulation of an imminent threat, the release of strong, negative emotions and the channeling of those emotions toward overcoming the threat. Threats such as bankruptcy, a dangerous competitor or a dis-

Strategies for Unleashing Organizational Energy

Companies may move from the unproductive resignation or comfort zones by increasing the intensity of organizational energy. The suitability of an aggressive "slay the dragon" strategy over an enthusiastic "win the princess" strategy depends in part on company culture and leader proclivities.

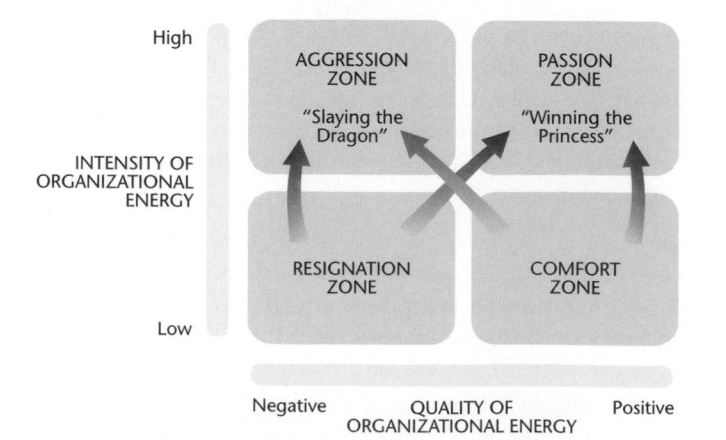

ruptive technology require moving employees from the comfort or resignation zone to the aggression zone. (See "Strategies for Unleashing Organizational Energy.")

In July 1990, when Dutch giant Philips Electronics shocked the financial world with a huge loss, the semiconductor division was the primary culprit. But within three years' time, the division achieved radically improved performance. The new division CEO, Heinz Hagmeister, moved employees from the comfort zone (people in the profitable passive-components business) and others from the resignation zone (those in unprofitable integrated circuits) to the aggression zone.

Jan Timmer, the new corporate CEO, started the ball rolling. In a senior-team meeting that came to be called Centurion I, he presented a dummy newspaper postdated by seven months with the headline "Philips Declares Bankruptcy." As participants studied Timmer's financial figures, stunned disbelief turned to anger and fear. Only drastic cost cutting would avert bankruptcy.

Hagmeister used the same shock therapy within his division. Detailed benchmarking vis-á-vis Motorola Inc. revealed dramatic gaps not only in inventory levels, sales expenses and overall costs, but also in customer delivery and in the time it took to develop new products. Given the crisis in the overall company, divesting (or even closing) the semiconductor division was a real possibility. The dragon was defined.

Having aroused strong negative feelings, Hagmeister channeled them into dragon slaying. He created projects for reducing head count, cutting sales cost, improving delivery time, pruning the product portfolio and integrating the U.S. arm of the business into the divisional structure. For each project, managers specified accountability, milestones, measurements and deadlines. In some instances, the majority of team members had no other operational responsibility. By means of a regular review, called Centurion II, executives monitored the progress of each project in detail, backed by new norms. (For example, managers offering excuses were asked to leave the meeting and were allowed to return only after devising a new plan consistent with the agreed-on goals).

Hagmeister had to be tough to lead his division into the aggression zone. He stayed engaged, never avoiding or delegating a necessary task because it was unpleasant. Numbers had to be exact or get redone. "There are no unimportant numbers," he insisted, "and no approximations. This is a fight; not a game." [14]

So first, the dragon must be made visible. People must experience the threat personally in order for collective emotions to be unleashed.[15] Second, a highly disciplined process must channel the emotions. Third, leaders must continuously guide, monitor and control the process. Their visible involvement and personal commitment are essential.

Because anger, fear, hate or shame are such powerful emotions, slaying the dragon can effectively shock people into action. However, the strategy has its downside. Sometimes it leads to organizational myopia, with people overly focused on one well-defined threat. Also, companies with the slay-the-dragon strategy rarely create major innovations or succeed in building new growth trajectories. And once the dragon is slain, there may be a rush for the comfort zone.

Winning the Princess. This strategy relies on strong, positive emotions (excitement, enthusiasm) to move people into the passion zone. To engage people's dreams and openness to heroic effort, leaders have to create an object of desire – the princess – and invoke passion so strong that people will overcome passivity and satisfaction with the status quo.[16] An excellent example occurred at Sony Corp.

As the new century dawned, few companies were changing as fundamentally as Sony. Historically a producer of analog-technology-based stand-alone audio and video products, Sony was confronting a transformation of its business. The IT, media and consumer electronics industries were converging toward a digital, Internet-based home entertainment business. Sony CEO Nobuyuki Idei articulated a new vision to enlist the organization in an adventure: "Young and old alike are truly mesmerized by digital technology," he said. "These people, the digital dream kids, are our future customers. We must also become dream kids at all levels of Sony to create something new, something that will meet our future customers' expectations."

To make the princess real, Idei created VAIO World, a way for Sony's employees to visualize how linking Sony's diverse offerings could help the company excel at meeting the new world's entertainment requirements.[17]

Although it's too early to judge whether Sony will be successful with its winning-the-princess strategy, Idei's vision has dispelled the self-doubt that many within the company were voicing and has created an energy spurt resulting in new VAIO computers.

Thus, slaying the dragon requires high-energy, brave and commanding leadership; winning the princess needs calm, gentle, inspiring and empathic leaders. Because the former strategy channels aggressive energy into disciplined execution, it requires top-down instructions and meticulous plans. A strategy that unleashes passion, however, needs leaders who create an environment of curiosity, excitement and ownership.

Hagmeister was the disciplinarian; Idei the source of inspiration. Idei does not exercise hierarchical authority. When his first call for a new personal computer found no volunteers, he did not force anyone to develop one. Instead, he and Kunitake Ando, who later assumed the role of Sony's chief operating officer, created the VAIO Center, a virtual organization intended to help employees from all product divisions fall in love with the concept. Those who finally enlisted did so voluntarily.[18]

Making people see, believe in and commit to an opportunity is inherently more difficult than getting them to acknowledge a threat. The first and most difficult task in pursuing the winning-the-princess strategy is to define, describe and substantiate the intangible. Leaders fail when the vision remains too abstract. It must be simple, clear, convincing and moving. Second, leaders must embody that vision. Their personal credibility and symbolic actions are key in attracting and retaining people's commitment, suppressing the noise of day-to-day activities and creating space and excitement for what is initially a fragile aspiration. Third, leaders have to balance the often playful activities involved in seeking an intangible future with the comparatively unexciting protection of the ongoing business.

Slaying the Dragon To Win the Princess. The ideal would be to combine the aggression zone's immediacy, discipline and decisiveness with the passion zone's enthusiasm, joy and pride. But it's a major challenge to blend top-down, planned change that is focused on survival with the experimentation, creativity and playfulness of pursuing a long-term vision. One risk is that the contradictions and ambiguities inherent in integrating the strategies might lead to the worst of all worlds in which neither works.

The only way to combine the two strategies is to create a path to the princess that automatically involves slaying the dragon – that is, to envision a future that can only be realized if current problems and threats are overcome, as Larry Ellison is attempting to do in his dramatic makeover of Oracle.

The princess (the vision) is to see Oracle transform the IT industry into a utility, with hardware, data and applications residing in a central location and customers gaining access to them over the Internet. In such a world, Oracle would evolve from a database company into a provider of integrated services, covering a full range of mutually compatible applications. In addition to buying database products from Oracle, customers would rely on Oracle for all applications – a fully integrated product and service offering.

To Oracle employees, the princess is clear – if they succeed in making Ellison's vision a reality, they would be part of the world's dominant software company. To any software engineer, the idea of people everywhere in the world being able to access the full power of IT using only a PC and a Web browser has enormous intellectual and emotional appeal and thus is likely to spur involvement.

But the dragon is built into the strategy. In order to make the vision credible to customers, Oracle had to become its own test site. "Eat your own dog food," Ellison said, when he announced a target of saving $1 billion by adopting the approach internally. Between 2000 and 2001, the company succeeded in moving its operating margin from 14% to 37%. This strategy is also in keeping with Oracle's hotly competitive spirit. For if the vision were to be realized, key competitors would suffer: IBM would lose its main source of revenue – systems integration – and Microsoft would cease to control business customers' IT access.

Leaders at some companies do not have a choice of strategy for creating energy. If the company faces a visible threat, it has to create a dragon: Princesses mean little to people worried about survival. Similarly, when there really is no imminent threat, no leader can make a dragon credible. In most cases, however, the situation is neither black nor white, and managers have a choice.

A sound strategy choice is rarely founded on external factors such as competition or market climate. Internal organizational factors are more significant, in particular these three: top-management style, the company's existing energy state and its organizational heritage.

First is senior managers' behavior or style. When managers try to behave at cross-purposes to their true nature, they create cynicism, not energy. Most CEOs are inherently better leaders of one or the other strategy, and their companies are more likely to succeed when the strategy meshes with the leaders' natural style.

A second criterion for strategy choice is the existing energy state of the company. Slaying the dragon is easier to implement and more effective for unleashing energy in companies caught in the comfort zone. Given a state of relative satisfaction, it is difficult to create excitement and sustainable energy in these companies by calling for a better future. Companies trapped in the resignation zone, in contrast, already perceive a discrepancy between the reality and the ideal. Winning the princess is best here because it can more easily transform latent desire into productive energy. Companies experiencing low, negative energy have a harder time trying to slay dragons, because they risk sinking into deeper despair and passivity, even paralysis.

Third, company history matters. Sony has never been good at aggression. It's a lover not a fighter and prefers to spend its energy on creating new products that customers could not have imagined. Winning the princess comes more naturally to a company that began with the express purpose of allowing engineers to have fun at work by playing with new technologies. Oracle's history, in contrast, is more like the history of the samurai warriors that Ellison is known to admire.

In short, organizational energy creates the necessary combination of cognitive, emotional and action-taking capabilities and aligns the resulting force to achieve business goals. That is why, without a high level of energy, a company cannot achieve radical productivity improvements, cannot grow fast and cannot create major innovations. It is time that corporate leaders acknowledge this simple reality and begin to pay explicit attention to how they can unleash the energy their organizations need if they are going to achieve the kind of performance they seek.

How to Pick Managers for Disruptive Growth*

By Clayton Christensen and Michael Raynor

We suspect that the mistakes happen when firms choose managers at any level – from CEO to business unit head to project manager – based on what we call "right stuff" thinking, borrowing the term from Tom Wolfe's famous book and the 1983 movie of the same name. Many search committees and hiring executives classify candidates by right-stuff attributes. They assume that successful managers can be identified using phrases such as "good communicator," "results oriented," "decisive," and "good people skills." They often look for an uninterrupted string of past successes to predict that more successes are in store. The theory in use is that if you find someone with a track record and with the right-stuff attributes, then he or she can successfully manage the new business venture. But in the parlance of this book, right-stuff thinking gets the categories wrong.

An alternative, circumstance-based theory articulated by Professor Morgan McCall can, in our view, serve as a much more reliable guide for executives who are attempting to get the right people in the right positions at the right time. McCall asserts that the management skills and intuition that enable people to succeed in new assignments were shaped through their experiences in previous assignments in their careers. A business unit therefore

One problem with predicting future success from past success is that managers can succeed for reasons not of their own making.

can be thought of as a school, and the problems that managers have confronted within it constitute the "curriculum" that was offered in that school. The skills that managers can be expected to have and lack, therefore, depend heavily upon which "courses" they did and did not take as they attended various schools of experience.

Managers who have successfully worked their way up the ladder of a stable business unit – for example, a division that manufactures standard high-volume electric motors for the appliance industry – are likely to have acquired the skills that were necessary to succeed in that context. The "graduates" of this school would have finely honed operational skills in managing quality programs, process improvement teams, and cost-control efforts. Even the most senior manufacturing executives from such a school would likely be weak, however, in starting up a new plant, because one encounters very different problems in starting up a new plant than in running a well-tuned one.

---

* Taken with permission from *Harvard Business School Working Knowledge* October 2003, pp. 1-4

When a slowly growing firm's leaders decide they need to launch a new-growth business to restore their company's vitality, who should they tap to head the venture? A talented manager from the core business who has demonstrated a record of success? An outsider who has started and grown a successful company? The school-of-experience view suggests that both of these managers might be risky hires. The internal candidate would have learned how to meet budgeted numbers, negotiate major supply contracts, and improve operational efficiency and quality, but might not have attended any "courses" on starting a new business in his or her prior career assignments. An outside entrepreneur might have learned a lot about building new fast-moving organizations, but would have little experience competing for resources and bucking inappropriate processes within a stable, efficiency-oriented operating culture.

In order to be confident that managers have developed the skills required to succeed at a new assignment, one should examine the sorts of problems they have wrestled with in the past. It is not as important that managers have succeeded with the problem as it is for them to have wrestled with it and developed the skills and intuition for how to meet the challenge successfully the next time around. One problem with predicting future success from past success is that managers can succeed for reasons not of their own making – and we often learn far more from our failures than our successes. Failure and bouncing back from failure can be critical courses in the school of experience. As long as they are willing and able to learn, doing things wrong and recovering from mistakes can give managers an instinct for better navigating through the minefield the next time around.

To illustrate how powerfully managers' prior experiences can shape the skills that they bring to a new assignment, let us continue the discussion of Pandesic, the high-profile joint venture between Intel and SAP that was launched in 1997 to create a new-market disruption selling enterprise resource planning (ERP) software to small businesses. Intel and SAP hand-picked some of their most successful, tried-and-true executives to lead the venture.

Pandesic ramped to 100 employees in eight months, and quickly established offices in Europe and Asia. Within a year it had announced forty strategic partnerships with companies such as Compaq, Hewlett-Packard, and Citibank. Pandesic executives boldly announced their first product in advance of launch to warn would-be competitors to stay away from the small business marketspace. The company inked distribution and implementation agreements with the same IT consulting firms that had served as such capable channel partners for SAP's large-company systems. The product, initially intended to be simple ERP software delivered to small businesses via the Internet, evolved into a completely automated end-to-end solution. Pandesic was a spectacular failure. It sold very few systems and shut its doors in February 2001 after having spent more than $100 million.

It is tempting to use 20/20 hindsight to explain this failure. Pandesic's channel partners weren't motivated to sell the product because it was disruptive to their economic model. The company quickly ramped up expenses to establish a global presence, hoping to build a steeper ramp to volume. But this increased dramatically the volume required to break even. The product evolved into a complex solution instead of the simple small business software that originally was envisioned. Its features got specified and locked in before a single paying customer had used the product.

The Pandesic team did a lot of things wrong, certainly. But the truly interesting question isn't what they did wrong. It is how such capable, experienced, and respected managers – among the best that Intel and SAP had to offer – could have made these mistakes.

To see how managers with great track records could steer a venture so wrong, let's look at their qualifications for the task from the schools-of-experience point of view. This can be done in three steps. First, imagine yourself at Pandesic on day one, when the executives were agreeing to start this disruptive venture. With only foresight and no hindsight allowed, what challenges or problems could you predict with perfect certainty that this venture would encounter? Here are a few of the problems that we could know we would face:

- We know for sure that we aren't sure if our strategy is right – and yet we have to figure out the right strategy, develop consensus, and build a business around it.
- We don't know how this market ought to be segmented. "Small business" probably isn't right, and "industry vertical" probably isn't right. We have to figure out what jobs the customers are trying to get done, and then design products and services that do the job.
- We need to find or create a distribution channel that will be energized by the opportunity to sell this product.
- Our corporate parents will bequeath gifts upon us such as overhead, planning requirements, and budgeting cycles. We will need to accept some and fend off others.
- We need to become profitable, and we must manage perceptions and expectations so that our corporate parents will willingly continue to make the investments required to fuel our profitable growth.

Now, as the second step, let's apply McCall's theory. List the courses that we would want members of Pandesic's management team to have taken in earlier career assignments in the school of experience – experiences through which they would have developed the intuition and skill to understand and manage this set of foreseeable problems. This listing of experiences should constitute a "hiring specification" for the senior management team. Rather than specifying a set of right-stuff attributes, the first step specifies the circumstances in which the new team will be asked to manage. The second step matches those circumstances against the challenges with which the managers of the new venture need already to have wrestled.

Finding managers who have been appropriately schooled is a critical first step in assembling the capabilities required to succeed.

We would, in Pandesic's instance, want a CEO who in the past had launched a venture thinking he or she had the right strategy, realized it wasn't working, and then iterated toward a strategy that did work. We'd want a marketing executive who had insightfully figured out how a just-emerging market was structured, had helped to shape a new product and service package that did an important job well for customers who had been nonconsumers, and so on.

With that list complete, our third step would be to compare that set of needed experiences and perspectives with the experiences on the resumes of the managers who led Pandesic. Despite their extraordinary track records in managing the global operations of very successful companies, none of the executives who were tapped to run this venture had faced any of these kinds of problems before. The schools of experience that they had attended taught them how to manage huge, complex, global organizations that served established markets with well-defined product lines. None of them had ever wrestled with establishing an initial market foothold with a disruptive product.

One of the most vexing dilemmas that stable corporations face when they seek to rekindle growth by launching new businesses is that their internal schools of experience have offered precious few courses in which managers could have learned how to launch new disruptive businesses. In many ways, the managers that corporate executives have come to trust the most because they have consistently delivered the needed results in the core businesses cannot be trusted to shepherd the creation of new growth. Human resources executives in this situation need to shoulder a major burden. They need to monitor where in the corporation's schools of experience the needed courses might be created, and ensure that promising managers have the opportunity to be appropriately schooled before they are asked to take the helm of a new-growth business. When managers with the requisite education cannot be found internally, they need to ensure that the management team, as a balanced composite, has within it the requisite perspectives from the right schools of experience. We will return to this challenge later in this chapter.

Finding managers who have been appropriately schooled is a critical first step in assembling the capabilities required to succeed. But it is only the first step, because the capabilities of organizations are a function of resources other than people, and of elements beyond just resources, namely, processes and values.

Managerial Challenges for Organizational Rejuvenation

by Charles Baden-Fuller

Who are the Rejuvenators in the Organization?

Rejuvenation is not the work of just a few top managers; building a strategic staircase (or step-wise renewal path) requires effort and creativity from all who are involved in a business. The task is not impossible, because most mature and poorly performing organizations do have spirited entrepreneurial and innovative individuals. The difficulty lies in innovative behavior being individualistic and unconnected and having little overall effect. Rejuvenation is not a final goal; many firms aspire to attain industry leadership, while others strive for sustainability or survival. That also requires innovative behavior which is more extensive, more deeply embedded, and connected across the whole enterprise and its value system, including customers, suppliers and distributors. The fact that industry leaders engage in similar activities, but on a larger scale, to firms which rejuvenate lends further support to the notion that rejuvenation has to be built in stages, and with balance between knowledge exploitation and knowledge exploration, and that transformation of seriously troubled firms cannot happen overnight.

The problem faced by many mature organizations is that renewal and change appear very risky, much more risky than the status quo. This perception has to be altered. The real risks of rejuvenation, especially if it is undertaken in stages, are less than imagined. Clever rejuvenators manage their risks most carefully. They all understand that when one is far behind, only innovative plays will succeed in radically altering their positions. Just as in a sailing race or sports event where the distant follower can catch the leader only if he or she tries a new tactic, so too in industry. The challenge in the real world of business is to make creative plays with low risk and with limited resources, something only entrepreneurial organizations can do.

At the start, constrained by their history and their resource limitations, mature organizations look for creative plays that do not expose them unduly. They also encourage many small investments, each of which could fail without causing serious damage, but each of which, if it succeeded, would further progress. These initiatives are especially aimed to encourage individual and small-team entrepreneurial behavior. Based on research evidence, one therefore depict the first phases or rejuvenation – galvanizing and taking many new initiatives – as of low risk.[1]

As each organization makes progress on its strategic staircase (see the figure below), it becomes imperative to create new competitive advantages and to take the steps required to secure the renewal. These initiatives are aimed at connecting functions and teams to form a more business-driven entrepreneurial activity. Usually involving much larger moves than those of the first stage, the risks, although greater, are acceptable because the organization has a more secure foundation and is better resourced. These frame-breaking investments could not be successfully undertaken earlier; they require a level of skills and capabilities coupled with aspirations and beliefs not previously in evidence.

The few rejuvenators that succeed in attaining and maintaining industry leadership face the biggest risk. To get in front, they have to find new patterns of activity that required the whole organization to work together. To stay in front required fending off competitors and, from time to time, undertaking radical reshaping. Teamwork on an organizational scale is risky as well as rewarding. Successful industry leaders have the resources and capabilities to bear these risks, but they too can fail.

The figure is a diagrammatic illustration to capture these differential risks and spheres of activities and emphasize the staircase of progress from renewal to industry leadership. At the start, many small initiatives (small circles) are undertaken by individuals and small groups throughout the organization, each of which generally involves only small resources. In renewal, the entrepreneurship becomes more prevalent, the smaller initiatives more numerous and supplemented by bigger collective projects (medium-size circles) that cross functional divides. At the third stage, major projects are required which involve all parts of the organization working together entrepreneur-

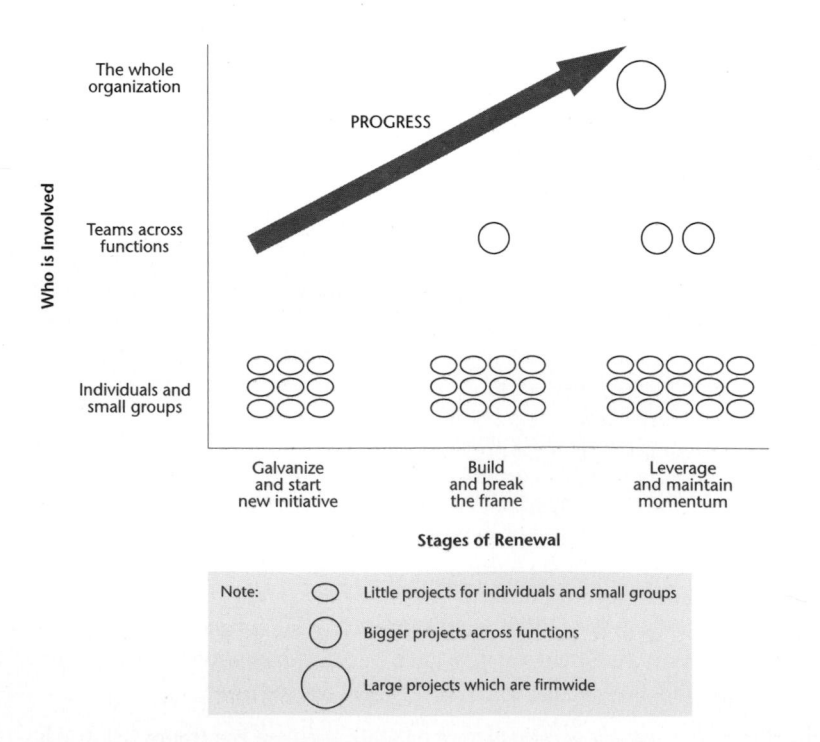

Figure 1: The locus of activity in different stages of rejuvenation

412

ially, hence the large circles. These projects supplement other, more numerous individual initiatives and, collectively, permit the business to master its industry.

In our research evidence, those who take risks and succeed know that they have to appreciate the role of fortune, and all our rejuvenators claimed, "We were lucky." For example, Hotpoint was lucky that its rivals ignored it and that the chain stores eventually fell into line. The Edwards company was lucky that just as it launched a new pump, designed originally for the chemical industry, the U.S. semiconductor market boomed and created new demand for which this pump was best suited. The Richardson company was lucky with its remarkable owner who set the challenge of the Laser knife. But luck is exploited best by those who are well prepared. As Arnold Palmer once said of his putting performance, "The more I practice, the luckier I become." Or, as Louis Pasteur, the world-famous French scientist, observed more than a century ago, "Chance favors the prepared mind." So Danny Rozenkranz at Edwards made the luck possible by 'sensing' the boom early and recognizing the potential of the new pump.

Balancing Knowledge Exploitation and Knowledge Exploration

It is often argued that as a firm matures, exploitation of current organizational knowledge drives out exploration of new ideas, and that this increases rigidity and the likelihood of organizational failure. Our research documents the initial decline of Celltech (one of Europe's oldest biotechnology firms), its rejuvenation from near bankruptcy, and its subsequent ability to prosper to become one of the largest biotech firms in the EU[2]. In its early life, Celltech had two businesses: pure R&D of novel therapeutic drugs, and a much bigger business undertaking specialized contract manufacturing (biologics division). In this latter area, it developed a leading edge technological capability centered on recombinant DNA and hybridoma technologies. In the early 1990s it hit a crisis and unusually shifted its emphasis, diminishing contract manufacturing and greatly expanding and altering its strategic focus towards drug discovery and development in a higher technological space.

This was unusual in that it defied the theoretical convention that exploitation of current knowledge tends, over time, to dominate over exploration for new knowledge. Despite the fact that the R&D investment for this change had yet to yield a drug approved for marketing by drug regulatory authorities, the strategic shift resulted in the firm becoming more, rather than less, successful financially by the mid-1990s. The essence of this success was in the breadth and quality of Celltech's new collaborators in the USA and EU, and moving to a new business model. It enabled Celltech to exploit its knowledge base before going to the end market, via cash milestone payments from collaborators, but without selling a full interest in the downstream property rights. Celltech had in six years converted itself into a firm solely focused on the R&D of innovative drugs to the exclusion of contract manufacturing and research – the renewal occurred not by intensifying the firm's focus on the exploitation of organizational knowledge, but by refocusing on exploration. There were three aspects of exploration within therapeutics: discovery of new drugs; phase one clinical trials; and development of a capability in collaborating with large firms.

How did Celltech engineer the changes? In particular, how did it reverse the decline of exploration versus exploitation and created the more balanced, higher value therapeutic division? Five developments were revealed as especially important:

* The occurrence of a series of crises in 1990;
* Appointment of a new CEO and new top management;
* Redundancies in the (profitable) biologics division and the hiring of 30 medicinal chemists, injecting a new knowledge base into the (loss-making) therapeutics division;
* The reforming of teams from a functional organization of technically oriented teams to multi-functional project-oriented teams; and
* The development of a shared culture and 'language' across the firm.

Celltech moved to exploration not just in terms of new scientific capabilities, but also in terms of new managerial capabilities. This is a key lesson of Celltech's rejuvenation, with renewal requiring the coordinating of changes in both managerial and technical capabilities. Other lessons include managerial capabilities in handling crises, galvanizing the commitment of key organizational actors, managing new collaboration activities, linking results of exploration activities to efforts, and stimulating knowledge creation through an injection of both external and internal diversity.

Managerial Challenges for Continuous Rejuvenation

Success provokes new challenges and new questions. One pressing question is whether leaders must repeat the full cycle of the staircase model to maintain their vitality. Is it possible to learn from the experience of the first full "loop" of progress and put in place actions that preserve momentum and remove the need for wholesale galvanization, simplification, and rebuilding? We believe that this new challenge can be mastered, even though we heard some who were more pessimistic.

To explain our optimism, we must recap the territory we have covered. By the time firms have reached the last stage of rejuvenation, most of the managers and even many in the work force are clear that changes in the "rules" of competition are a fact of life. They know that they cannot forecast with any confidence the form of future shifts and have prepared themselves to adapt as need or opportunity arises. They know that they must continue to invest in building capabilities and go on improving their ability to innovate through greater variety, higher quality, and the like, all at lower cost. They know that they face a stream of choices about where to concentrate their strategic market focus. Their growing sense of "winning" can create greater confidence in their ability to escape the trap of believing that industry economics determines their future.

Their progress, it would seem, has come from an ability to combine four factors: a collective sense of shared purpose and "stretching" goals; knowledge and the perception of possibilities; willingness to go on innovating and experimenting; and meticulous attention to the details of the stream of hard strategy choices. These virtues may seem a far cry from those of rational strategy beloved of many textbooks, but our evidence convinces us that they are the basis of effective and adaptive strategic management.

Based on our research, it was clear to the managers of successful firms that the detailed elements of strategy had changed over time. What worked at one stage may not have worked at another. Thus it was that action at the beginning or rejuvenation was quite different from that required later on. As time passed, it became a more subtle art to determine where and how to compete. The ability to find ever more sources of organizational leverage, to husband scarce resources and still meet stretching goals, sorted out the winners from the losers.

Case Example
Jeffrey Immelt: How GE's Chief is Turning Corporate Culture Around and Managing a Portfolio of Businesses for Increased Innovation*

Jeffrey Immelt, 49, is clearly pushing for a cultural revolution. For the past 3 $\frac{1}{2}$ years, the GE chairman and CEO has been on a mission to transform the hard-driving, process-oriented company into one steeped in creativity and wired for growth. He wants to move GE's average organic growth rate – the increase in revenue that comes from existing operations, rather than deals and currency fluctuations – to at least 8% from about 5% over the past decade. Under his former boss, the renowned Jack Welch, the skills GE prized above all others were cost-cutting, efficiency, and deal-making. What mattered was the continual improvement of operations, and that mind-set helped make the $152 billion industrial and finance behemoth a marvel of earnings consistency. Immelt hasn't turned his back on the old ways. But in his GE, the new imperatives are risk-taking, sophisticated marketing, and above all, innovation.

This is change borne of necessity. The Welch era reached its zenith in the booming, anything-goes economy of the late 1990s. Back then, GE always seemed to beat the consensus forecasts by a penny a share – and investors felt no burning need to figure out exactly how they did it. Immelt has no such luxury. With a slower-growing domestic economy, less tolerance among investors for buying your way to growth, and more global competitors, Immelt, like many of his peers, has been forced to shift the emphasis from deals and cost-cutting to new products, services, and markets. Any other course risks a slow descent into irrelevance. "It's a different era," says Immelt, a natural salesman who still happily recounts the days when he drove around his territory in a Ford Taurus while at GE Plastics. He knows the world looks to GE as a harbinger of future trends, says Ogilvy & Mather Worldwide Chief Executive Rochelle B. Lazarus, who sits on the GE board. "He really feels GE has a responsibility to get out in front and play a leadership role."

So how, exactly, do you make a culture as ingrained as GE's sizzle with bold thinking and creative energy? Most of all, Immelt has made the need to generate blockbuster ideas more than an abstract concept. In true GE fashion, he has engineered a quantifi-

---

* Adapted from "The Immelt Revolution," *Business Week*, March 28, 2005, 52-56

able and scalable process for coming up with money-making "eureka!" moments. While Welch was best known for the annual Session C meetings during which he personally evaluated the performance of GE's top several hundred managers, Immelt's highest-profile new gathering is the Commercial Council. Immelt leads the group of roughly a dozen top sales and marketing executives, including some unit heads such as GE Consumer Finance CEO David R. Nissen. The members hold phone meetings every month and meet each quarter to discuss growth strategies, think up ways to reach customers, and evaluate ideas from the senior ranks that aim to take GE out on a limb. "Jeff has launched us on a journey to become one of the best sales and marketing companies in the world," says Nissen, who describes the meetings as collegial and more experimental than other GE gatherings.

This is no free-for-all, however. Business leaders must submit at least three "Imagination Breakthrough" proposals per year that ultimately go before the council for review and discussion. The projects, which will receive billions in funding in the coming years, have to take GE incremental growth of at least $100 million.

Such change can be scary stuff for folks steeped in Six Sigma, who were led to believe that if you made your numbers and were prepared to uproot your family every year or two, you had a shot at the top rungs. Now they're being asked to develop real prowess in areas such as creativity, strategy, and customer service that are harder to measure. They are being told to embrace risky ventures, many of which may fail. Immelt's GE can be seen as a grand experiment, still in its early days, to determine whether bold innovation can thrive in a productivity-driven company.

To inspire the fresh thinking he's looking for, Immelt is wielding the one thing that speaks loud and clear: money. The GE chief is tying executives' compensation to their ability to come up with ideas, show improved customer service, generate cash growth, and boost sales instead of simply meeting bottom-line targets. As Immelt puts it, "you're not going to stick around this place and not take bets." More concretely, 20% of 2005 bonuses will come from meeting pre-established measures of how well a business is improving its ability to meet customer needs. And while he hasn't exactly repudiated Welch's insistence that managers cull the bottom 10% of their staff, insiders say there's more flexibility, more subjectivity to the process. Risking failure is a badge of honor at GE these days.

To lay the groundwork for an organization that grows through innovation, Immelt took steps early on to rejigger the GE portfolio. He committed to sell $15 billion of less profitable businesses such as insurance, while shelling out more than $60 billion in acquisitions to dive into hot areas such as bioscience, cable and film entertainment, security, and wind power that have better growth prospects. In doing so, he pared the low-margin, slow-growth businesses like appliances or lighting, which he diplomatically calls "cash generators" instead of "losers," down to 10% of the portfolio, from 33% in 2000. Nicole M. Parent of Credit Suisse First Boston is impressed with "the way they have been able to evolve the portfolio in such a short time" and with so little disruption. "This is a company where managers will do anything to achieve their goals."

Good thing, as their back-slapping chief is now looking for "those things that grow the boundaries of this company." He's confident that the new business mix and growth incentives are already paying off. At GE's annual gathering of its top 650 executives in Boca Raton, Fla., in January, he insisted that "there's never been a better place to be [at GE]!" Strong words in a company that stretches back 127 years to founder Thomas Edison. After an 18% jump in revenues and earnings in the fourth quarter, to $43.7 billion and $5.4 billion, respectively, Immelt predicts up to 17% earnings growth and 10% sales gains for all of 2005, with double-digit returns through 2006. While economists scratch their heads over the next quarter, Immelt is promising two years of explosive growth. No wonder Sharon Garavel, a quality leader at GE Commercial Finance says that, at Boca, "everyone was talking about a $60 stock price," or about $24 more than its current price.

That in itself may be a stretch of the imagination for now, but Immelt is trying to recast the company for decades to come. He's spending big bucks to create the kind of infrastructure that can equip and foster an army of dreamers. That means beefing up GE's research facilities, creating something akin to a global brain trust that GE can tap to spur innovation. He has sunk $100 million into overhauling the company's research center in Niskayuna, N.Y., and forked out for cutting-edge centers in Bangalore, Shanghai, and Munich.

Globalizing research has allowed GE to get closer to overseas customers. The simple fact is that most of GE's growth will come from outside the U.S. Immelt predicts that developing countries will account for 60% of the company's growth in the next 10 years, vs. about 20% for the past decade. But he is also spreading new practices to lethargic economies such as Germany. After a 2002 meeting with German Chancellor Gerhard Schröder reinforced his notion that GE could be doing more in that country, Immelt decided to open the Munich center. As Immelt explains, "there's no place in GE where you feel more like a loser than in Germany. You have Siemens and Philips, and we haven't been that good." By July, 2004, a new center was up, and the results were immediate. According to Nani Beccalli-Falco, CEO of GE International, the company saw a 21.5% growth in German-speaking markets last year from 2003.

Now that Immelt has repositioned the portfolio and added resources, his main objective is to get more immediate growth out of the businesses he already has. That's where the Imagination Breakthroughs come in. Over the past 18 months, Immelt has agreed to invest $5 billion in 80 projects that range from creating microjet engines to overhauling the brand image of 3,000 consumer-finance locations. The hope is that the first lot will generate $25 billion in revenue by 2007 – cheap, if it works, when you consider what it would cost to acquire something from the outside with that level of sales. In the next year or two, Immelt expects to have 200 such projects under way.

The pressure to produce could not be more intense. Many of the company's 607,000 workers weren't exactly hired to be part of a diverse, creative, fleet-footed army of visionaries who are acutely sensitive to customers' needs. "These guys just aren't dreamer types," says one consultant who has worked with the company. "It almost seems painful to them, like a waste of time." Even insiders who are openly euphoric about the changes under Chairman Jeff admit to feeling some fear in the depth of their guts.

"This is a big fundamental structural change, and that can be tough," says Paul T. Bossidy, CEO of GE Commercial Equipment Financing, who is reorganizing his sales force so that each person represents all of GE to particular customers. Susan P. Peters, GE's vice-president for executive development, even talks about the need for employees to "reconceptualize" themselves. "What you have been to date isn't good enough for tomorrow," she says.

But there's a limit to how much Immelt can transform his own people. A key strategy – and one that amounts to a gut punch to the culture – involves bringing in more outsiders. In sales and marketing alone, GE has hired more than 1,700 new employees in the past few years, including hundreds of seasoned veterans such as David J. Slump, a former ABB Group executive who is the chief marketing officer of GE Energy. "I just didn't think outsiders would do well here," says Slump, who was surprised at the unit's openness to changing its ways, though one of the senior executives did warn him about coming off as "too intense." That said, he was also amazed at the lack of attention to marketing when he arrived – with no marketers among the senior ranks and no real sense of strategy beyond the occasional ad or product push. Slump felt needed.

Immelt is also looking for more leaders who are intensely passionate about their businesses and are experts in the details. "I want to see our people become part of their industries," he says. Investors are still waiting to see whether GE's evangelizing chairman can truly make his company grow faster than the world around it. Even some of his fans think that GE's new momentum has more to do with the overall economy than with idea generation. Says Steve Roukis of Matrix Asset Advisors, which owns 2 million GE shares: "If you have a revolutionary decade of growth around the world, who's going to be there to capture it? GE."

Capture it? Jeff Immelt wants to shape it, drive it, make it his own. For him, reinventing GE is the only way to make his company dominate this century, much as it led the one before.

Questions

1. What are the major approaches/methods used by Jeffrey Immelt to turn GE's corporate culture around to one focused on innovation, without sacrificing process-oriented excellence?

2. Leaders, managers and frontline specialists all have prominent roles in enabling poised strategy, and thus organizational survival through innovation. Discuss these roles in terms of their scope, boundaries, interactions and 'specifications'.

3. Can the methods used by Steve Miller at Shell, to destabilize organizational equilibrium, be applied in any organizational context? Why or why not?

4. Effective self-organization activities imply 'managing at the edge of chaos'. Compare Walt Disney Company with Shell in managing the paradox of simultaneous efficiency and renewal.

5. Some companies pursue the practice of 'boundarylessness'. Does this imply that boundaries – be they organizational, geographical, functional, etc. – are necessarily obsolete or 'bad'? Can boundary concepts still be used to generate disruptive innovation, and if so how?

6. Inertia, rigidities and 'path dependencies' are well-known phenomena for any large organization. How can these be overcome?

7. Is it not extremely dangerous for any organization to outsource innovation activities? If anything can be outsourced, what remains of distinctive competencies in the organization, or are these not necessary for sustainability any more?

8. Contrast the biological metaphor of the organization as a uni-minded adaptive organism with the poised model of a multi-minded, purposeful and co-creative system.

References

Chapter 6: Leadership and Managerial Requirements for Poised Strategy in the Innovation Economy

[1] Figure adapted from Bartlett, C.A, Ghoshal, S. and Birkinshaw, J. (2003), *Transnational Management*: *Text, Cases and Readings in Cross-Border Management*, 3rd Edition, Boston: McGraw-Hill.

[2] Adapted from various authors, especially Youngblood, M.D. (1997), "Leadership at the Edge of Chaos", *Strategy and Leadership*, 25(5), 8-14; and Tetenbaum, T.J. (1998), "Shifting Paradigms: From Newton to Chaos", *Organizational Dynamics*, 26(4), 21-32.

[3] Adapted from Pascale, R.T. (1999), "Surfing at the Edge of Chaos", *Sloan Management Review*, 40(3), 83-94.

[4] Voices (2002), "Inspiring Innovation: The Innovative Enterprise," *Harvard Business Review*, 80(8), 46-47.

[5] Anderson, P. (1999), "Seven Levers for Guiding the Evolving Enterprise", in Clippinger, J.H. (Editor), *The Biology of Business*, San Francisco: Jossey-Bass Publishers, 113-152.

[6] Adapted from Pascale, R.T. (1999), *op.cit.*, 37.

[7] Beinhocker, E.D. (1997), "Strategy at the Edge of Chaos", *McKinsey Quarterly*, 1, 36.

[8] Eisenhardt, K.M. and Sull, D.N. (2001), "Strategy as Simple Rules", *Harvard Business Review*, 79(1), 111.

[9] Voices (2002), *op.cit.*

[10] Adapted from Slater, R. (1999), *Jack Welch and the GE Way*, New York: McGraw-Hill Professional Books.

[11] Voices (2002), *op.cit.*, 40.

[12] Lengnick-Hall, C.A. and Wolff, J.A. (1999), "Similarities and Contradictions in the Core of Three Strategy Research Streams", *Strategic Management Journal*, 20(12), 1109-1132.

[13] Grant, R.M. (2002), *Contemporary Strategy Analysis,* 4th Edition, Oxford: Blackwell Publishers.

[14] See Quinn, J.B. (2000), "Outsourcing Innovation: The New Engine for Growth," *Sloan Management Review*, 41(4), 18-19.

[15] Engardio, P., Einhorn, B., Kripalani, M., Reinhardt, A., Nussbaum, B. and Burrows, P. (2005), "Outsourcing Innovation", Special Report, *Business Week*, European Edition, March 21, 46-53.

[16] See Quinn, J.B. (2000), *op.cit*, 19.

[17] This section is adapted from Christensen, C.M. (2001), "Assessing Your Organization's Innovation Capabilities", *Leader to Leader*, 21, 27-37.

[18] Beinhocker, *op.cit*. 10.

[19] Beinhocker, *op.cit*. 10.

[20] Table adapted from Gharajedaghi, J. (1999), *Systems Thinking: Managing Chaos and Complexity*, Boston: Butterworth-Heinemann.

Leadership and the Networked Economy

G. Hamel and C. K. Prahalad, *Competing for the Future*, Boston: HBS Press, 1994.

Michael Porter, *Strategy and the Internet*, Harvard Business Review, March 2001, pp. 63-78. (reprinted in M. Leibold et al., *Strategic Management in the Knowledge Economy*, Publicis Corporate Publishing and Wiley, Erlangen 2002/2005).

D. Ready, *Mobilizing Collective Ambition – How Effective Top Teams Lead Enterprise-Wide Change*, Lexington, MA: The International Consortium for Executive Development Research (ICEDR), 2000.

J. Collins and J. Porras, *Built to Last*, New York: Harper Business, 1994, and: J. Collins, *Good to Great*, New York: Harper Business, 2001.

C. Christensen, *The Innovator's Dilemma*, Boston: HBS Press, 1997.

Henry Mintzberg, *The Nature of Managerial Work*, New York: Harper and Row, 1973.

Viktor Frankl, *Man's Search for Meaning*, published in numerous English editions since 1959.

Unleashing Organizational Energy

[1] See M. Tushman and C.A. O'Reilly III, "The Ambidextrous Organization: Managing Evolutionary and Revolutionary Change," California Management Review 38 (summer 1996): 8-30.

[2] See A. Pines and E. Aronson, "Career Burnout: Causes and Cures" (New York: Free Press, 1988).

[3] For a description of the consequences of collective energy, see A. Etzioni, "The Active Society: A Theory of Societal and Political Processes" (New York: Free Press, 1975).

[4] For both a review and an important contribution, see Q.N. Huy, "Emotional Balancing of Organizational Continuity and Radical Change: The Contribution of Middle Managers," Administrative Science Quarterly 47 (2002): 31-69.

[5] For a description of the causes and consequences of the low-energy state, see J.W. Dean Jr., P. Brandes and R. Dharwadkar, "Organizational Cynicism," Academy of Management Review 23, no. 2 (1998): 341-352.

[6] The term "comfort zone" was introduced by J.P. Kotter, "Leading Change: Why Transformation Efforts Fail," Harvard Business Review 73 (1995): 59-67.

[7] For a description of the links between organizational energy and company performance, see R. Cross, W. Baker and A. Parker, "What Creates Energy in Organizations?" MIT Sloan Management Review 44 (summer 2003): 51-56.

[8] On the strains of change, see A. Pettigrew and R. Whipp, "Managing Change for Competitive Success" (Oxford and Cambridge: Blackwell, 1991).

[9] See T.H. Davenport and J.C. Beck, "Getting the Attention You Need," Harvard Business Review 78 (2000): 118-126.

[10] Q.N. Huy and H. Mintzberg, "The Rhythm of Change," MIT Sloan Management Review 44 (summer 2003): 79-84.

[11] For a rich description and analysis of the pathology experienced by companies trapped in the comfort zone, see D.H. Sull, "Why Good Companies Go Bad," Harvard Business Review 76 (1999): 42-52.

[12] Negative emotional spirals can be attributed to reasons such as emotional contagion, feeling affect vicariously and behavioral entrainment; see J.R. Kelly and S.G. Barsade, "Moods and Emotions in Small Groups and Work Teams," Organizational Behavior and Human Decision Processes 86, no. 1 (2001): 99-130. The dynamic of collective emotion derives from imitating and exaggerating the emotions of others; see B. Parkinson, "Emotions Are Social," British Journal of Psychology 87 (November 1996): 663-684. For a review, see D.C. Hambrick and R.A. D'Aveni, "Large Corporate Failures as Downward Spirals," Administrative Science Quarterly 33, no. 1 (1988): 1-22.

[13] The distinction between these two strategies for unleashing organizational energy mirrors the distinction between theories E and O of change. See M. Beer and N. Nohria, eds., "Breaking the Code of Change" (Boston: Harvard Business School Press, 2000). Consider also the distinction between top-down, programmatic change and emergent change: M. Beer, R.A. Eisenstat and B.A. Spector, "The Critical Path to Corporate Renewal" (Boston: Harvard Business School Press, 1990).

[14] In his article "Effective Change Begins at the Top" in Beer and Nohria's "Breaking the Code of Change," J. Conger uses the metaphor of the CEO as a general, which mirrors the role of leaders in executing the slaying-the-dragon strategy.

[15] A key challenge for top management is that a profound trauma must take place in the company before it becomes aware of the threat and is willing to change. This idea goes back to the process model of unfreezing-refreezing introduced in K. Lewin, "Frontiers in Group Dynamics," Human Relations 1 (1947): 5-41. For a more recent description of this approach, see M. Tushman and C.A. O'Reilly III, "The Ambidextrous Organization: Managing Evolutionary and Revolutionary Change," California Management Review 38, no. 4 (1996): 8-30.

[16] See A. Wrzesniewski and J.E. Dutton, "Crafting a Job: Revisioning Employees as Active Crafters of Their Work," Academy of Management Review 26, no. 2 (2001): 179-201.

[17] VAIO stands for "Video Audio Integrated Operations" to represent the challenge of integrating all of Sony's different product and service offerings. It also symbolizes the need for combining analog (the wave of VA) and digital (IO) technologies.

[18] In Beer and Nohria's "Breaking the Code of Change," this model of leadership is recommended by both W. Bennis in the chapter titled "Leadership of Change" and by K. Weick in his chapter, "Emergent Change as a Universal in Organizations." Reprint 45111.

Managerial Challenges for Organizational Rejuvenation

[1] See Baden-Fuller, C. and Stopford, J.M. (1999), *Rejuvenating the Mature Business: The Competitive Challenge*, Second Edition, London: International Thomson Business Press.

[2] McNamara, P. and Baden-Fuller, C. (1999), "Lessons from the Celltech Case: Balancing Knowledge Exploration and Exploitation in Organizational Renewal", *British Journal of Management*, Vol.10, 291-307.

Glossary of Major Terms

Ambidextrous Management: A coupling of the word 'ambivalent' (contrary properties) and 'dexterous' (mentally deft), the term 'ambidextrous' refers to the managerial ability to handle paradox and contrariness in mentally adroit ways.

Business Ecosystem: Also termed 'biocorporate system', it refers to an organization as a living organism within a larger system of business ecology, i.e. crossing a variety of industries and diversity of stakeholders that are variable and co-shaping organizations and their environments.

Business Model: This refers to the particular business concept, or 'way of doing business', of an organization. It includes the customer value proposition (product or service at the right place, price and time), the organization's choice of internal value chain (how it conceives and builds up the value proposition), and its particular external socio-cultural system linkages (e.g. supply chain, delivery chain) to provide customer value proposition(s).

Business Socio-Cultural System: A purposeful, voluntary group of organizations and their stakeholders within large societal networks, held together ('cohered') by common objectives, values and culture. While a business ecosystem focuses on information and coordination (genetic codes), a business socio-cultural system is knowledge and relationship bonded (cultural codes or 'memes').

Co-Creation: Customers are increasingly becoming involved with organizations in the value production/creation process. This is also known as prosumption where the distinction between production and consumption is progressively getting blurred.

Co-Evolution: Evolution is the study of how species (humans, animals, organizations) adapt, survive and expire over time. In organizational context, each organization changes over time due to internal and external adaptation, in close relationships with other organizations and individuals. It does not evolve by itself, but co-evolves with others (stakeholders, communities, individuals) that co-shape its role, characteristics and behavior.

Coherence: Coherence means to 'stick together', remain united, or to be well-knit and consistent. *Organizational coherence* points to application of techniques such as organizational values, purpose and culture to enable diverse organizational or network members to 'stick together', without central direction, coordination and control. Coherence mechanisms enable unity to emerge from diversity.

Communities of Practice (COPs): Groups of people informally bound together across traditional organizational or industry boundaries, by e.g. shared expertise, interests and passions (e.g. by e-mail networks).

Complexity Management: A body of managerial techniques, including application of 'simple rules', to guide and cohere seemingly chaotic, diverse and complex activities in organizations and business networks. It is based on complexity science, a body of knowledge focusing on purposeful co-evolution of systems via the influencing of underlying patterns of self-organizing behavior. A synonymous term is 'chaos management', i.e. managing chaos by focusing on underlying pattern similarities.

Constructing/Deconstructing/Reconstructing Value Chains: Organizations and industries can be constructed, deconstructed and reconstructed according to the range and sequencing of value-adding activities. For example, traditional organizational structures are increasingly being deconstructed by removing bureaucratic layers of middle management, while many traditional industries are being reconstructed through technology (e.g. service call centers displacing branch offices in the insurance industry).

Convergent/Divergent Thinking: As competition becomes more intense in an industry (or market), organizations struggle to remain competitive and resort to copying or imitating successful strategies. This convergent thinking (and business models) only drains away existing competitive advantages and generally, one way to break away from this vicious cycle is to encourage divergent thinking that would enhance creativity and innovation in providing new customer value propositions.

Customer Competence: The competences (i.e. knowledge, skills, capabilities) residing in customers, regarding products and services, and their utilization.

Customer Knowledge Management (CKM): Managerial activities to develop and utilize the knowledge residing in customers for purpose of enhancing the performance of socio-cultural business networks and their constituent organizations and individuals.

Cybernetics Research: The field of study focusing on the optimization of relationships between machines and living systems – regarded as second-generation systems thinking (e.g. interdependency and self-organizing methods in living systems).

Deliberate and Emergent Strategies: It is misleading to try to cleanly separate strategy into strategy formulation and strategy implementation. The best strategies can simply emerge in response to changing circumstances, and not necessarily from a rigorous strategy planning process. In these times of increasing changes in the environment, it becomes more significant than ever to identify emerging strategies and integrate them into the formal strategy.

Disequilibrium: As organizations, indeed any living system, achieve equilibrium and harmony, they become trapped in their existing realms that ultimately hinder their ability to cope with changing circumstances and they eventually cease to exist. Conversely, an internal or external disequilibrium promotes creative solution or response from the organization (or organism) to survive. To ensure success then, organizations can deliberately generate disequilibrium as people are at their most creativeness when faced with disruption (see also related concepts of 'Complexity Management' and 'Managing at the Edge of Chaos').

Dominant Logic: Organizational members have implicit assumptions about their organization, the environment and competition, among other things. These are embedded in the culture and procedures that guide members in how they act and think. It is the lens through which the organization sees opportunities and threats in the environment, how it deals with the competition and how it creates value (see also related concept of 'Mental Space').

Dynamic Capabilities: An organization's abilities residing especially in its resources and processes, to configure and reconfigure internal and external competencies to appropriately address rapidly changing environments.

Enterprise Resource Management (ERM): A logical extension of the concept of Enterprise Resource Planning (ERP) – while ERP focuses on the resources supply chain of an organization, ERM includes the management of all possible resources, including customers as potential sources of knowledge and co-developers of new value propositions.

Entropy: It is an idea born from classical thermodynamics and represents the tendency towards disorder within a closed system, as potential energy gets "spent" and the inevitable and steady deterioration of a system.

Fitness Landscape: The particular business landscape (e.g., an industry) in which an organization has chosen to play a role and evolve in, and consequently in which it has to remain a 'fit' player for continued success and survival. (See also the related concepts of 'Knowledge Landscape' and 'Organizational Fitness').

Intermediation/Disintermediation/Reintermediation of Industry Role-players: The types and numbers of industry role-players (or intermediaries) in industry value systems can emerge or be deleted, adjusted or redefined, depending on feasibility in changing conditions. For example, the Internet is causing the emergence of new role-players in many industries, ranging from travel and tourism to grocery retailing and financial services.

Knowledge Landscape: A particular business landscape (e.g. industry) in which an organization is not necessarily involved at present, (but may) decide to become involved in, characterized by specific knowledge and capability requirements. New knowledge landscapes continually arise, and pose new knowledge challenges and organizational fitness challenges. Being involved in various knowledge landscapes, with various fitness dimensions, displays an organization's robust strategic management capabilities.

Managing at the 'Edge of Chaos': The 'edge of chaos' is a concept describing an area between order and chaos – just enough order and not too much chaos: if there is too much order, creativity is stifled; if there is too much chaos, there is self-destruction. Managing at the 'edge of chaos' indicates the appropriate utilization of complexity management techniques for optimization of innovation.

Mental Space/Model: Organizations, as living systems that operate and strive to survive and succeed in a competitive environment, have certain beliefs, views and principles of how they regard themselves and their environment. Mental space is the core assumptions that reside within the organization and its constituents, and that facilitates the interpretation of the environment.

Networked Incubators: The guided cultivation of innovative business start-ups through mechanisms that foster partnerships and other forms of linkages among a range of (potential) stakeholders.

Open Innovation: Different businesses can be located on a continuum from essentially closed to completely open, but the distinguishing characteristic of open innovation is that the several approaches to innovation rely on a continued supply of useful ideas and technologies from outside the ("boundaries" of the) organization. Such innovation strengthens an organization's knowledge and experience base that is needed in creating new and innovative customer value.

Operations Research: The field of study focusing on interdependency in the context of mechanistic systems (machine model of thinking, e.g. joint optimization of various production systems – regarded as 'first-generation systems thinking').

Organizational Energy: Positive energy (e.g., satisfaction, happiness) and negative energy (e.g. frustration, anxiety) can represent the "energy state" of an organization and its individuals. Channeling positive organizational energy of excitement and ownership enhances an organization's ability for self-renewal and rejuvenation.

Organizational Fitness: Organizational fitness is a concept that transcends traditional profitability measures, by including an organization's dynamic capabilities to be innovative for continuous organizational survival and prosperity. Organizational fitness can be measured in two ways:

- First, looking *within* the organization, by its *ability to self-organize* internally quickly and effectively in the face of change. This ability ranges from (1) ineffective self-organization that freezes a business in place, through (2) an ability to keep pace with today's rapid rate of change but not to lead this change, and culminates in (3) an ability to reorganize much faster than others.

- Second, looking *externally,* by the *adaptation* an entity exhibits within its *changing context.* The type and level of adaptation determines the success and, therefore, continued life of the organization. Status in this area ranges from (1) being endangered due to total adaptation for a context that no longer exists through (2) being

427

well suited to today's environment to (3) shaping the environment by creating major shifts in the business landscape.

Paradoxical Management/Leadership: A concept indicating the provision of managerial provision of direction without being directive; being authoritative without being dominating; being strong while being open to influence and persuasion; enabling individuals and groups to develop and grow, without being manipulative; incentivizing and measuring performance without being controlling; sharing knowledge while also reserving key intellectual capital; and creating 'new' knowledge while destroying/unlearning 'old' knowledge.

Poised Organization: An organization that continuously and successfully changes on its knowledge landscape – a particular chosen arena of business activity – by simultaneously balancing survival (effectiveness) and advancement (renewal) activities. It essentially means an ability to effectively rejuvenate itself.

Poised Scorecard (PSC): The PSC is a systemic scorecard that builds on the Balanced Scorecard (BSC) by extending its four key dimensions to include collaborative business networks as well as the various business models that embody an ambidextrous organization.

Robust Strategy: Strategy that provides organizational purpose, values and general direction, but without rigid policies, objectives, programs and control practices. Robustness indicates the ability to respond in several different modes (or strategic options), and the ability to be both proactive (first-mover; shaping) and reactive (late-mover; following), depending on the situation(s).

Self-organization: Collaboration and mutual activities that arise spontaneously through the interrelationships of a system's parts, without central control or direction, is termed 'self-organization'. A good example is the Internet, which evolves spontaneously over time without being centrally directed, coordinated or controlled.

Serious Play: Imaginative techniques to enable 'as-if' or 'make believe' thinking among organizational and business network members. The purposeful 'playing-around' with new ideas, concepts and applications engender innovative strategies.

Shadow Organization: An experimental business entity, separate from the conventional organization or business enterprise, that is utilized for development and testing of a new business model.

Systemic Scorecard (SCC): Derived from the well-known Balanced Scorecard (BSC), it refers to a measurement technique for overall fitness of a socio-cultural business system.

Systemic Strategic Management: The managerial activity of co-shaping viable customer value propositions through dynamic organizational and network capabilities in socio-cultural business systems, to enable organizational fitness.

Systematic Thinking: Logical, analytical, step-by-step thinking – often characterized by the approach to reduce large entities into smaller units for easier analysis and understanding.

Systemic Thinking: Connective, holistic and patternistic thinking – often characterized by the approach that 'the whole is more than the sum of the parts'.

Tipping Point: The concept originated in the field of epidemiology to describe when a critical point in an evolving situation leads to a new and irreversible development. The tipping point is the threshold or boiling point where small changes (or the unexpected) have far-reaching, uncontrollable effect.

Written by

Authors and Contributors

Authors and Editors

Thomas H. Davenport

is the President's Distinguished Professor of Information Technology and Management at Babson College, Director of Research at Babson Executive Education, and an Accenture Fellow. He has a Ph.D. from Harvard University in organizational behavior. His most recent book is *Thinking for a Living: How to Get Better Performance and Results from Knowledge Workers* (Harvard Business School Press 2005).
He can be contacted at: tdavenport@babson.edu

Marius Leibold

is Professor in Strategy at Stellenbosch University and at the Netherlands Business School. His research focuses on new business models and innovation for global competitiveness, incorporating strategic fitness, systemic innovation and paradoxical management approaches applied in various industries and companies. He has authored a number of articles and books in strategic management, and is a Director of the WISE program, a collaborative research program between academic and business organizations in the USA, Europe, Africa and Asia.
He can be contacted at: ml@leibold.cc

Sven C. Voelpel

is Director of the research group WISE (for Wisdom - Innovation - Strategy - Energy) and Professor of Business Administration at the Jacobs Center for Lifelong Learning and Institutional Development, International University Bremen (IUB), Germany. Apart from various professorships around the world he is also a Visiting Fellow at Harvard Business School and the Graduate School of Arts and Sciences at Harvard University since 2001.
He can be contacted at: svoelpel@post.harvard.edu

Article Authors

Charles Baden-Fuller

is the Centenary Professor of Strategy at City University Business School and Editor-in-Chief of *LRP: Long Range Planning*.

Scott D. Anthony

is a partner at Innosight LLC, a management consulting and education company based in Watertown, Massachusetts, and also serves as the editor of *Strategy & Innovation*.

Heike Bruch

is a professor of Strategic Leadership and Director of the Institute for Leadership and Human Resource Management (IFPM) at the University of St Gallen.

Goran Carstedt

is the former head of IKEA Retail Europe and member of the IKEA Group Management Board, and former president of Volvo Svenska Bil AB, the Swedish Volvo sales organization.

Constantinos Charitou

is the CEO of N.P. Lanitis Ltd. The company has trading operations in Cyprus and Greece in products such as timber, steel, gas and fertilizers.

Henry W. Chesbrough

is an assistant professor of Business Administration, and the Class of 1961 Fellow at Harvard Business School. He holds a joint appointment in the Technology and Operations Management and Entrepreneurial Management areas at the Harvard Business School.

Clayton M. Christensen

is the Robert and Jane Cizik Professor of Business Administration at Harvard Business School, with a joint appointment in the Technology and Operations Management and General Management faculty groups.

Kathleen M. Eisenhardt

is professor of Strategy and Organization at Stanford University, and a fellow of the Academy of Management and president of the OMT Division of the Academy.

D. Charles Galunic

is the Cora Chaired Professor of Retailing and Management and professor of Organisational Behaviour at INSEAD. He is on the editorial boards of *Organization Science* and the *Strategic Management Journal*, as well as a departmental editor for the *Journal of International Business Studies*.

Sumantra Ghoshal

was the Robert P. Bauman Chair in Strategic Leadership at the London Business School and a Fellow of the Advanced Institute of Management Research in the U.K. He passed away in March 2004.

Mark Gottfredson

is a partner at Bain & Company and co-head of the Capability Sourcing Practice in Dallas.

Brian Huffman

is assistant professor of Business Administration at University of Wisconsin - River Falls.

Vijay Govindarajan

is the Earl C. Daum 1924 Professor of International Business and Director of the William F. Achtmeyer Center for Global Leadership at the Tuck School of Business at Dartmouth College.

Marco Iansiti

is the David Sarnoff Professor of Business Administration at Harvard Business School, and is a faculty member in the Technology and Operations Management Unit. He is a member of the board of directors of Keystone Strategy Inc., a consulting firm he co-founded.

Roy Levien

is an inventor at Intellectual Ventures, an intellectual property fund, and the manager and principal of Keystone Advantage LLC, a technology consultancy in Lexington, Massachusetts.

Constantinos Markides

is Professor of Strategic and International Management at London Business School.

D. Quinn Mills

is the Alfred J. Weatherhead Jr. Professor of Business Administration at the Harvard Business School.

Charles A. O'Reilly III

is the Frank E. Buck Professor of Human Resources Management and Organizational Behavior at Stanford Graduate School of Business.

Stephen Phillips

is a Bain & Company partner responsible for the IT practice in London.

Rudy Puryear

is a Bain & Company partner and director of IT practice in Chicago.

Michael E. Raynor

is a Director in Deloitte, the global professional services firm, and part of Deloitte Research, the thought leadership arm of Deloitte. He is also a professor at the Richard Ivey School of business.

Johan Roos

is a former professor of Strategy and General Management at the International Institute for Management Development (IMD) and is the founding director of Imagination Lab Foundation in Lausanne, Switzerland.

Peter Senge

is a senior lecturer at the Massachusetts Institute of Technology. He is also founding chair of the Society for Organizational Learning (SoL), a global community of corporations, researchers, and consultants.

Christoph K. Streb

is a Ph.D. candidate at International University Bremen (IUB) and a Research Assistant in the WISE research group.

Chris Trimble

is on the faculty at the Tuck School of Business at Dartmouth College, with expertise in strategic innovation. He is also the Executive Director of the William F. Achtmeyer Center for Global Leadership at Tuck.

Michael L. Tushman

is the Paul R. Lawrence MBA Class of 1942 Professor of Business Administration at Harvard Business School.

Albert A. Vicere

is Executive Education Professor of Strategic Leadership for the Smeal College of Business at Pennsylvania State University and president of Vicere Associates Inc., a consulting firm with clients spanning the globe.

Index

Thomas H. Davenport, Gilbert J.B. Probst (Editors)

Knowledge Management Case Book

Siemens Best Practises
With a Foreword by Dr. Heinrich von Pierer

2nd revised and enlarged edition, 2002
336 pages, 79 illustrations, 4 tables
17.3 cm x 25 cm, hardcover
ISBN 3-89578-181-9, € 39.90 / sFr 64.00

This book provides a perspective on knowledge management at Siemens – according to an international benchmarking (MAKE) one of the "top ten KM companies worldwide" – by presenting the reader with the best of the corporation's practical applications and experiences. Davenport and Probst bring together instructive case studies from different areas that reflect the rich insights gained from years of experience in practising knowledge management.

Presenting applications from very different areas, this practice-orientated book is really outstanding in the broad field of KM literature.

"Perhaps the most revealing – and interesting – part of the cases in this book is not the analysis of the various knowledge management tools and processes, but the description of their development, of how they come about, of how commitment was gained, of how implementation was led."

Yves Doz, The Timken Chaired Professor of Global Technology and Innovation at INSEAD, Fontainebleau

"This case book brings insights how our most valuable resource makes those tools happen. I found this book exciting reading, because it is, to my knowledge, the only book where a single company with a wide variety of knowledge management approaches accumulates years of experiences and lessons learned. Edited by two of the leading thinkers in the field of knowledge management, this book will show the way you practise knowledge management in your company."

Heinz Fischer, Global Head of HR, Deutsche Bank AG

"This book is a rare and valuable description of a single company's knowledge management journey. Siemens has made impressive advances in becoming a knowledge-driven firm, and this volume details many of its directions and waystations."

Laurence Prusak, Executive Director, IBM Institute for Knowledge Management

Kai Lucks (Editor)

Transatlantic Mergers and Acquisitions

Opportunities and Pitfalls in German-American Partnerships

November 2005
approx. 480 pages, hardcover
ISBN 3-89578-262-9
€ 88.00 / sFr 141.00

This book is intended to show ways to successful cooperation. Going beyond M&A, it demonstrates how economical ties and personal behaviour can positively influence our international relations. The value to M&A professionals will be generated through better understanding the views from the other side of the Atlantic, through new M&A insights from other industries and from experts working in consulting and finance. Thus, it is also of high value to all those working on partnerships between the USA or Germany and any other country.

The book deals with many different aspects, starting from overall strategies, and ending up with lessons learnt from the special cases. Reflecting behavioural, economic or legal aspects, there are articles showing one side only to work out country or industry specifics and others comparing the nationally different systems and surroundings.

The authors of the book are executives with specific experiences in M&A, high-level professionals in the M&A area, experienced international M&A managers and top consultants in different areas of M&A – each from both sides of the Atlantic.

Contents

Introductions and topic overviews

Markets and structures: M&A in Germany· Success factors in Transatlantic M&A · Markets and Trends from German and US perspectives.

Experiences from different industries: Automotive · Banking & Finance · Chemical, Pharmaceutical & Healthcare · Consumer · Food · Power Generation & Electronics · Information & Communication · Logistics & Transportation · Materials · Media · Private Equity Investments in various Industries.

Professional & Functional Contributions: Communications in Transatlantic M&A · Leadership, Strategy and Structure · Corporate Governance · Legal & Tax Conditions · Antitrust Control · Financial & Accounting · Patents & Technology · Culture, Communications & Personnel.

Marius Leibold, Gilbert J.B. Probst, Michael Gibbert

Strategic Management in the Knowledge Economy

New Approaches and Business Applications

2nd updated edition, 2005
355 pages, 17.3 cm × 25 cm, hardcover
ISBN 3-89578-257-2
€ 49.90 / sFr 80.00

Due to the dramatic shifts in the knowledge economy, this book provides a significant departure from traditional strategic management concepts and practice. Designed for both advanced students and business managers, it presents a unique combination of new strategic management theory, carefully selected strategic management articles by prominent scholars such as Gary Hamel, Michael Porter, Peter Senge, and real-world case studies.

On top of this, the authors link powerful new benchmarks in strategic management thinking, including the concepts of Socio-Cultural Network Dynamics, Systemic Scorecards, and Customer Knowledge Management with practical business challenges and solutions of blue-chip companies with a superior performance (Lafite-Rothschild, Who's Who, Holcim, BRL Hardy, Kuoni BTI, Deutsche Bank, Unisys, Novartis).

Contents

Fundamental impacts of the global knowledge economy on strategic management · Traditional strategic management approaches, and their deficencies · New mindset: systemic strategic management · Frameworks for systemic strategic management · Strategic management tools for the knowledge economy · Managing the new strategic leadership challenges.